Afro-American Folk Culture

Part I—North America

Publications of the American Folklore Society

Bibliographical and Special Series

Volume 31

General Editors:

Dan Ben-Amos and Kenneth S. Goldstein

Afro-American Folk Culture *An Annotated Bibliography of Materials from North, Central and South America and the West Indies*

Part I—North America

John F. Szwed *and* **Roger D. Abrahams**

with Robert Baron, Linda Rabben, Richard Raichelson, Beverly Robinson, Robert Ulle and Richard Wright

A Publication of the
Institute for the Study of Human Issues
Philadelphia

Manufactured in the United States of America

Library of Congress Cataloging in Publication Data:

Szwed, John F. 1936-
    Afro-American folk culture.

    (Publications of the American Folklore Society, Bibliographical and special series; v. 31-32)
    CONTENTS: pt. 1. North America.—pt. 2. The West Indies, Central and South America.
    Includes indexes.
    1. Folk-lore, Black—America—Bibliography. 2. Blacks—America—Bibliography. I. Abrahams, Roger D., joint author. II. Title. III. Series: American Folklore Society. Bibliographical and special series; v. 31-32.
Z5984.A44S95 [GR103]   016.909′04′96   77-16567
ISBN 0-915980-80-0 (two-volume set)
ISBN 0-915980-69-X (pt. I)
ISBN 0-915980-70-3 (pt. II)

For information, write:

Director of Publications
ISHI
3401 Science Center
Philadelphia, Pennsylvania 19104
U.S.A.

CONTENTS

LIST OF ABBREVIATIONS

AA	*American Anthropologist*
AS	*American Speech*
BBE	*Bulletin du Bureau d'Ethnologie*
BLAM	*Boletín Latino-Americano de Música*
BPM	*Black Perspective in Music*
BTLV	*Bijdragen tot de Taal-, Land- en Volkenkunde van Nederlandsch-Indië*
BU	*Blues Unlimited*
CQ	*Caribbean Quarterly*
CRAL	*Comptes Rendus of the Athénée Louisianais (New Orleans)*
CS	*Caribbean Studies*
EM	*Ethnomusicology*
EM Newsletter	*Ethnomusicology Newsletter*
FLJ	*Folk-Lore Journal (London)*
FSSNE	*Bulletin of the Folk Song Society of the Northeast*
GHQ	*Georgia Historical Quarterly*
HF	*Hoosier Folklore*
HFB	*Hoosier Folklore Bulletin*
IJAL	*International Journal of Anthropological Linguistics*
JAF	*Journal of American Folklore*
JEMFQ	*John Edwards Memorial Foundation Quarterly*
JFI	*Journal of the Folklore Institute*
JIFMC	*Journal of the International Folk Music Council*
JJ	*Jazz Journal*
JM	*Jazz Monthly*
JNE	*Journal of Negro Education*
JNH	*Journal of Negro History*
JRAI	*Journal of the Royal Anthropological Institute*
KFQ	*Keystone Folklore Quarterly*

KFR	Kentucky Folklore Record
LFM	Louisiana Folklore Miscellany
MF	Midwest Folklore
MFR	Mississippi Folklore Register
MQ	Musical Quarterly
NCF	North Carolina Folklore
NHB	Negro History Bulletin
NYFQ	New York Folklore Quarterly
PMLA	Publications of the Modern Language Association
PTFS	Publications of the Texas Folklore Society
RAMSP	Revue do Arquivo Municipal de São Paulo
RBF	Revista Brasileira de Folclore
RC	Record Changer
RR	Record Research
SFQ	Southern Folklore Quarterly
SO	Sing Out
SW	Southern Workman
SWJA	Southwestern Journal of Anthropology
TFSB	Bulletin of the Tennessee Folklore Society
WF	Western Folklore
WIG	De West-Indische Gids

INTRODUCTION

This is a bibliography with a thesis, assembled not through a desire to spend years in libraries making up cards and shuffling them about, but because of our frustrations arising from the unwillingness of both the academic community and the general public to recognize that a huge body of material exists on Afro-American traditions and cultural expressions.

Or again, this bibliography might be understood as an attempt to offer thousands of footnotes to a single sentence: *Afro-American cultures exist, cultures which are neither entirely African nor Euro-American in origin, but which contain elements of both, plus the inevitable developments attendant upon enslavement, the plantation experience, Native American contact, poverty and racism, as well as the vigor and creativity of human beings.*

I

Rediscovering the Past

Afro-Americans, historian Eugene Genovese has noted, have had to reinvent their past every generation. For the last century or so, Afro-Americans have had to recreate their identities without having access to the insights and research in the preceding generation.* And often enough, it was the same materials and processes which were discovered--or rediscovered. This situation exists because researches either are not published or appear in inaccessible forms and places.

*A quick look at Melville J. Herskovits, ed., *The Interdisciplinary Aspects of Negro Studies* (American Council of Learned Societies Bulletin No. 32, September, 1941) is enough to show how much knowledge of black life has been *lost* in the past thirty years.

Too many of the items included here are hard to find for even the most ardent bibliographer. The more casual researcher or the interested layman hardly knows where to begin.

But, more important, most of those concerned with Africans and people of African descent in the New World have been operating on the assumption that they are a deculturated people, culturally stripped by the slavery experience and its aftermath. It has been assumed that if expressions of culture found uniquely among Afro-American groups are shared from one black community to another, from one New World country to another, it must be--so the argument goes--because of the common experience of enslavement and continuing economic and social marginality. Even the specific variations in these experiences are ruled unimportant in light of the overall deculturating process. This bibliography provides the means for shattering such myths of the Negro past through cross-cultural comparison.

An example or two might be useful here, to show what kinds of comparisons this bibliography can lead to. Take graffiti in the United States. Graffiti have been called vandalism, a sign of the times, pop art and the outlet of untrained artists too poor to buy canvas, but the entries in the bibliography suggest the need for more historical depth and cultural breadth. Start with, say, entry numbers NA 1157, NA 1759, NA 1760 and NA 1986. These lead us to consider the general use of outdoor areas for written declarations and personal proclamations, as well as the use of African day-names and naming practices in all of the countries of the Americas. Consider the similarity of nicknames in early twentieth-century New Orleans to those which appear in contemporary graffiti (NA 145 and NA 146). And notice African day-names in Jamaica (EWI 242) and Nova Scotia (NA 783) as well as a wide range of African names in the U.S. (NA 646, NA 1603, NA 2918, NA 2920, NA 3074, to mention a few herein). Indeed, the flexibility of black naming practices has apparently long been a source of wonder and confusion for whites in North America (NA 295, NA 1086, NA 1465 and NA 1907), especially since there is some evidence that black naming has influenced white names (NA 504).

On the question of personal inscriptions in public we find truck inscriptions in Brazil (BR 314 and BR 375), Ecuador (EC 1) and elsewhere (GEN 63 and GEN 66); boat names in the French-speaking West Indies (FWI 97); proverbs, slogans and rhymes in store names in Puerto Rico (PR 18), the nineteenth-century United States (NA 191), the contemporary U.S. (NA 2713) and elsewhere (GEN 63); and the use of license plate numbers as names in the English-speaking West Indies (EWI 452). Much the same course could be followed by considering church names (NA 782, NA 948 and NA 2229). Finally, there are bibliographical entries that begin to integrate the naming practices in all of the black areas of the Americas (FGS 143 and EWI 713) with those of West Africa (GEN 63 and GEN 66).

Yet another example. For those convinced that drums were completely forbidden under slavery in North America with the result that African drums and drumming were irretrievably lost, there is the counter-testimony of NA 248, NA 456, NA 651, NA 841, NA 1551, NA 1793, NA 1999, NA 2078 and NA 2958 for a beginning. From Congo Square in New Orleans to upstate New York, from backwoods Louisiana to coastal Georgia, drums have been heard and remarked upon from the 1700's to the present. During Juneteenth celebrations--Emancipation Day--drums and drum dances are still important (NA 3199) and local oral history traces the custom to slavery times. And the bibliography offers the basis for smashing other myths: the disappearance of African languages under slavery, the lack of influence of African religions and social structure on American blacks, the disappearance of African clothing, gestures, manners and so on.

One of the saddest features of the need to reinvent Afro-American history and culture is that it has permitted the same arguments and rationalizations to be explored and exploded by each group of investigators. On the other hand, in spite of the continuing terms of debate, changes in fashion have arisen to alter the perspectives used by those who have bothered to describe and analyze Afro-American traditions. One of the benefits of gathering these bibliographic materials is that some of these patterns have asserted themselves, and one can see that what is true of scholarship in one language and culture area in each generation is in most cases also true in the other areas--in spite of the overwhelming evidence that these investigators seldom read each other's writings.

Four Phases of the Literature

If we look at the writings on black culture in all of the Americas some striking similarities appear. Beginning in the mid-1600's there is an abundance of writing in travel accounts and slavers' journals. At first, these early writers dealt with the question of whether or not slaves were humans, and therefore justifiably enslaved. Did their actions constitute genuine human behavior? The question of whether the slaves were capable of becoming "civilized"--that is, capable of altering their attitudes and behaviors-- was also discussed. But at the same time questions were raised as to whether or not the Europeans themselves might become savages through their contact with Africans in the already feared tropical and semi-tropical areas of the New World. Certainly, these writings show an awe of African cultural patterns: the slaves' particular beliefs in the supernatural, their religious ceremonies often held outdoors at night, their music and dance, their talk. This concern led to the writing of guidebooks for potential planters and European emigrants, books that in their own way were ethnographic accounts.

A second phase of writing began in the early 1800's when abolitionists and missionaries (often the same people) concerned themselves with what would have to be contended with in converting slaves to Christianity, and whether or not emancipation could be successful in a multi-racial, multi-cultural setting. Again, there was a concern with the exoticism of "native" ways, but now, instead of slaves being seen as savages, they were more often than not treated as innocent children, capable of learning. So, for example, American abolitionists and missionaries wrote enthusiastically of spirituals and various expressions of otherworldly faith, often completely ignoring mundane, day-to-day life.

In a third phase, that which followed the abolition of slavery, there were several divergent types of writing. One, by ex-slaveholders and their children, was an expression of sentiment for the "old types" who were passing, the people who were said to be happier and healthier under slavery. Here "native ways" were recalled and described as a reminder of why blacks could survive only under the domination of the plantocracy. But in the British West Indies, where ex-slaves were in the vast majority, or in the case of Haiti, which had successfully abolished slavery by revolution, the "native" middle class recognized the same cultural features that the ex-slaveholders and missionaries noted, but with some argument that these represented creative cultural accomplishments. This latter tradition of writing continues today, often in the form of locally printed pamphlets, leading most recently to a call among the local literati for a folk-based literature and national culture: e.g., writings by Jean Price-Mars on Haitian folktales and religion, or works about the former British West Indies by Olive Lewin, Olive Walke, Louise Bennett, Rex Nettleford and others, in defense of calypso, creole speech, carnival, folktales and the like.

The situation in the United States was quite different, however. With a preponderance of whites in economic and social control, and the imposition of severe Jim Crow laws in the late nineteenth century, blacks and the whites who defended them were inclined, like the abolitionists of an earlier period, to deny the existence of black cultural patterns, to ignore blacks' musical and choreographic abilities, their unique religious rituals, anything which distinguished them culturally from whites.

Starting in the 1930's and reaching a peak in the 1950's, a fourth phase developed, applying the research methods then in vogue in criminology, social work and psychiatry. Now black cultural patterns were seen as manifestations of pathology, a deviance from American "mainstream" standards resulting from the various manifestations of injustice and racism. In the British West Indies, this was the position associated with Madeline Kerr and Edith Clarke; in the United States, it was the view of Abram Kardiner and Lionel Ovesey, Gunnar Myrdal, E. Franklin Frazier, William H. Grier, Price M. Cobbs and many others.

Three very powerful exceptions must be noted here. In the United States, Melville J. Herskovits applied the comparative method of anthropology to what appeared to be on the surface a strictly American phenomenon, and found many overriding similarities of culture shared by the black peoples of West Africa and those of most of the countries of the New World. In Cuba, Fernando Ortiz, a lawyer and criminologist, had initially been interested in the pathological aspects of black life, but abandoned that position to become Cuba's chief scholar of Afro-Cuban culture. Similarly, in Brazil, Arthur Ramos, a psychiatrist, had first seen Afro-Brazilian culture as a mere manifestation of primitive mind, but later came to be the chief advocate and scholar of African cultural retentions in that country.

II

A few words about what this bibliography includes and excludes. First, there is no pretense here of completeness. Bibliographies are nearly always incomplete, even under the best of circumstances. But in this instance, where all libraries are inadequate, where more than six languages are involved, and where more than a dozen countries are covered, the problems are exceptionally great.

Take the case of Cuba: United States library holdings on Cuba were slim to begin with, and when political conflicts prevent full access to and exchange of scholarly and popular materials, a claim to completeness would be absurd. Further, since a number of countries do not officially encourage or even recognize research on the black contribution to their societies, bibliographies developed at a distance from the resources are discouraging. One need only compare our listings for Haiti with those for the neighboring Dominican Republic to appreciate the contrast. As a result, we have required the aid of a variety of scholars for different areas; but for some countries our listings are still distressingly sparse. Particularly problematic for us were Central America and the former Danish West Indies.

We have set as our limits the *published* works on Afro-American folk culture, thus excluding dissertations, manuscripts and the like. But we have taken account of a number of marginal items such as pamphlets and phonograph record notes, especially where important material might exist in these forms. Similarly, we have tended to include literary materials (novels, drama, poetry, etc.) when we felt they were especially useful in covering topics not thoroughly treated elsewhere. Our definition of "folk culture" is a deliberately loose one. Some might want to argue that we have included too much under this rubric, that we ought to have omitted, say, early jazz, Creole French poetry in nineteenth-century New Orleans, or folk cultural forms no longer produced by blacks but continued by whites. But this is a risk we are happy to run.

Even so, we have by no means included everything available on black folk culture, especially at the points at which it shades over into the larger culture of the countries in which it is found. Much of the literature in journals on the blues is not here; nor are all of the technical writings on speech and dialect; nor are contemporary song books. Material on contemporary jazz and literary culture is treated only where we felt that not to do so would distort the total work.

What we are most interested in here are the expressive and symbolic aspects of the lives of ordinary people. Unlike most historians, we are not so interested in the institutional as in the social history; not so much concerned with the lives of the exceptional as with ordinary individuals. Yet much here will be quite exceptional, for in the cultural means which black people have developed in the Americas there is much that will or should strike awe in the observer. And while we are more concerned here with values, symbols, language, "small" behaviors and the like than we are with the conditions under which Afro-Americans have had to exist, it would be hard not to see the shadow of those conditions over the arts and manners we have documented. It is our intention that this bibliography be used in conjunction with those other bibliographies which are more concerned with the history, economics and social organization of black people, and we have listed a few of these in the first section, "Bibliographies."

The initial cutoff date for the addition of materials to the bibliography was December 31, 1973, though a few items postdate this, and a few important journals had not issued all of their numbers for 1973 by that date. We hope that a means may be found to update this list periodically, as well as to fill in additional older references as they are discovered.

Citations

A word about citations: Sometimes the information provided for a particular book comes not from the first edition but from a later one. This occurred in some instances because the later edition was the fuller or the more accurate, but in many cases we have never seen the earlier editions. With materials as difficult as many of these are to come by, edition problems are not so important as they might be in other kinds of bibliographies. We have not listed reissues or paperback editions except where we felt such information to be essential. Nor have we included libraries where the materials may be found, for the (hopefully forgivable) reason that we began our researches in our own and in friends' libraries and built up the bulk of our listings in this way.

We have occasionally listed a work for which we lack complete information (pages, date, etc.) when we felt that it was important and when we had enough information to offer at least a chance for locating it later.

Titles in languages other than English are written according to the rules of capitalization of English.

Annotation Method

Annotations present a special problem. It is difficult to maintain consistency in style and comprehensiveness with a corps of workers. And it is always a problem to know what to include or exclude from the annotations. We have tried not to be judgmental about the quality of the materials, even those of severely uneven quality and those whose patronizing or racist tone cries out for comment. Since it is impossible to know what a user may be seeking in a particular source, it is difficult to know how and where judgments can be of use. To take a single case, the history of the study of Black English amply shows that if scholars had ignored the sources which gave racist *interpretations* of black speech, we might have lost nearly all of the unique *data* that many such accounts paradoxically contain. Suffice it to say, let readers beware and judge for themselves.

In some instances we received our information from a secondary source and were unable ourselves to verify the item's existence; these entries, of course, are not annotated. For titles in a language other than English, we have attempted translations only where we have not been able to annotate.

*Organi-
zation*

      The rationale for the organization of this material emerges from the complex history that underlies the presence of Afro-Americans in the New World. In order not to distort this history and the traditions which sustain the peoples, we have attempted to stay close to the commonsense, everyday classifications of peoples and places. Thus, some of the divisions are linguistic or political (the English-speaking West Indies, for example, also includes Guyana, which is located on the mainland of South America); others are merely practical (areas such as Cuba, Haiti and Puerto Rico have such substantial or distinctive bodies of literature that separate treatment seems justified). Mexico is considered as part of Central America although geographically, of course, it is not. Clearly, there might be better ways to group these entries. As a case in point, the southeastern coastal areas of the United States might better be seen in relation-ship to the English-speaking West Indies; or the Black Caribs--who are here spread through the English- and French-speaking West Indies and Belize--might better form a separate bibliographical category. But we have attempted to make these divisions less troublesome by including in the index substantial cross-references for peoples, genres and subjects. Most of the sections also begin with a list of cross-references.

      Included in Part I, besides the material on North America, are two sections whose references concern more than one people, nation or culture area: "General" and "Bibliographies." Part II contains entries on the Caribbean, Central America and South America.

Indexes

      Indexing this work has not been easy, especially since we have attempted to document continuities in Afro-American cultures through-out the Americas. Many difficulties arise in attempting to relate genres in different language and geographical areas. Also, the quality and usefulness of an index ultimately depends upon the detail of the annotations--and all of the annotations in this volume, as we have said, are not equally detailed. For example, if one looks up Brer Rabbit in the General Index, one is referred to animal tales and Uncle Remus tales, but this does not mean that Brer Rabbit is not also to be found under the general heading of "tales and tale tell-ing," and possibly under still other headings where the sources have not been so closely annotated. Generic classification, a knotty problem in an undertaking of this kind, as it is in contemporary folklore theory, was especially tricky throughout the indexing of tales, songs and categories relating to religion and belief, domains highly elaborated throughout Afro-America. Suffice it to say, then, that the indexes included here are far from exhaustive, and some initiative on the part of the user is necessary. To make their use as mechanically simple as possible, we have reproduced them in full in both Part I and Part II.

III

      We are not professional bibliographers, sad to say, and though we paid dues in the form of five years' effort, there is much we missed and much we fear may be awry in what we have caught. We accept the blame for the errors and shortcomings of this bibliography, and we have nothing but praise for the generous help we received from a small band of scholars, enthusiasts and fanatics.

First, we wish to recognize Bruce Jackson, whose bibliographical efforts for his book *The Negro and His Folklore in Nineteenth Century Periodicals* gave us the inspiration to begin the whole project. Secondly, this work literally could not have been completed without the help of Kenneth and Rochelle Goldstein, who supplied us with an unsurpassed personal library to work with, who gave us scholarly and practical counsel and the kindness and generosity which only those who know these gracious people can appreciate and understand. Two individuals, William A. Stewart and Robert Farris Thompson, both larger than life, also fed us with bibliography, annotations and translations so numerous that it embarrasses us to recall. Then there were those whose own bibliographies or expertise allowed us to undertake geographical areas and subjects which we would have otherwise never attempted: Joan Baratz, William R. Bascom, Roger Bastide, Ben Blount, Erika Bourguignon, Roy S. Bryce-Laporte, Lydia Cabrera, Lambros Comitas, Lee Cooper, Daniel J. Crowley, William R. Ferris, Jr., Jerome J. Handler, Charles Haywood, Bette Landman, Sidney W. Mintz, Peter Neumann, Pedro Pedraza, Charles L. Perdue, Jr., Angelina Pollak-Eltz, Richard and Sally Price, Karl Reisman, Douglas Shaffer, Reina Torres de Arauz, Hazel Weidman and Norman E. Whitten, Jr.

Those who sweated through the unrewarding and painful tasks of library work, typing and reworking include Karen Alvarez, Kathy Baily, Mary Ann Castle, Alan Goldberg, Gloria Goode, Cheryl Gregory, Edward Hirsch, Stephen Holt, T. R. Polhemus, Diana Stewart Raichelson, Marylin Sandlin, Jennifer Disbrow Scott, Amy Shuman, Anna Cara Walker, Drexel Woodson and Sally M. Yerkovich. Considerable editorial work was done by the staff of ISHI, and much of what is readable here is a result of the efforts of Douglas Gordon.

A special and deeply felt recognition is due Stephen S. Baratz, whose friendship and support transcend acknowledgment.

Though the research for this bibliography led us through the libraries of several countries and many small towns and counties, special attention and thanks need to be given to the reference and circulation staffs of the libraries of Yale University, the City of Charleston, South Carolina, the University of Miami, the British Museum, the University of Texas at Austin, the University of Pennsylvania, the Pan American Union, the Jamaica Institute, the University of the West Indies at Mona, Jamaica, and especially to Margarita Anderson Imbert of Widener Library, Harvard University, and Joseph C. Hickerson of the Archive of Folksong, Library of Congress. Some booksellers of uncommon knowledge and generosity are also acknowledged with thanks: William Crawford of the New World Bookstore of Philadelphia; John Chilton of the Bloomsbury Bookstore of London, England; and the staffs of Pennsylvania Book Center, Philadelphia, and the University Place Bookstore, New York City.

Finally, it is with pleasure that we acknowledge the sources which made this bibliography financially possible: the National Institute of Mental Health, for Public Health Grant No. MH-17216, which established and sustained the Center for Urban Ethnography at the University of Pennsylvania; the American Philosophical Society, which provided travel and research funds; and the African and Afro-American Research Institute of the University of Texas at Austin.

BIBLIOGRAPHIES

BIB
1
Abonnence, E., *et al. Bibliographie de la Guyane Française* (Bibliography of French Guiana), Vol. 1. Paris: Editions Larose, 1957.

BIB
2
Acosta Saignes, Miguel. "Introducción al Estudio de los Repositorios Documentales sobre los Africanos y sus Descendientes en América," in *América Indígena,* 29 (1969), 727-786.
Lists and evaluates archives and libraries, public and private, throughout Latin America containing materials pertinent to Afro-America studies; includes a bibliography of major works on the subject.

BIB
3
Andrade, Mario de. "Folclore," in *Manual Bibliográfico de Estudos Brasileiros*. Rio de Janeiro: Gráfica Editôra Souza, 1949, 285-317.
Bibliography of Brazilian folklore with annotations.

BIB
4
Baa, Enid. *Theses on Caribbean Topics, 1778-1968*. San Juan: Institute of Caribbean Studies, University of Puerto Rico, 1970.

BIB
5
Baldus, Herbert. *Bibliografia Crítica da Ethnologia Brasileira*. Sao Paulo: n.p., 1954; Hannover: Komissionsverlag Munstermann-Druck, 1968.

BIB
6
Bibliografía de Centroamérica y del Caribe, 1956-1959 (Title varies). Madrid and Havana: Dirección General de Archivos y Bibliotecas de España, 1958-1961.

BIB
7
Bibliography of Latin American Folk Music. Washington, D.C.: Library of Congress, Division of Music, 1942.

BIB 8   Bissainthe, Max. *Dictionnaire de Bibliographie Haitienne* (Dictionary of
           Haitian Bibliography). Washington, D.C.: Scarecrow Press, 1951.

BIB 9   Boggs, Ralph S. *Bibliography of Latin American Folklore*. Washington, D.C.
           Inter-American Bibliographical and Library Association, 1940.
           General bibliography arranged by folklore topics, listing countries
           together with works for each topic.

BIB 10   Brasch, Ila Wales and Brasch, Walter M. *A Comprehensive Annotated Bibli-
           ography of American Black English*. Baton Rouge: Louisiana State
           University Press, 1974.

BIB 11   Burr, Nelson R. *A Critical Bibliography of Religion in America*. Vol. 4.
           Princeton: Princeton University Press, 1961.
           Contains section of black churches and music.

BIB 12   Carneiro, Edison. *O Folclore Nacional*. Rio de Janeiro: Editora Souza,
           1954.
           An annotated bibliography of articles and books on Brazilian folklore
           published between 1943-1953. Contains several annotations of works
           dealing with Afro-Brazilians.

BIB 13   Carvalho-Neto, Paulo de. "Bibliografía Afro-Ecuatoriana," *Boletín Ecua-
           toriano de Antropología* (Quito), 1963, 5-19.
           Bibliography of works containing data on the Negro in Ecuador. These
           works deal with topics other than the black population and make refer-
           ences to Negro life and history in passing.

BIB 14   Carvalho-Neto, Paulo de. "Bibliografía del Folklore Uruguayo," *Boletín
           Bibliográfico de Antropología Americana* (México), 21-22, (1958-1959),
           Part I, 162-180.

BIB 15   *Checklist of Recorded Songs in the English Language in the Archive
           of American Folksong to July, 1940*. Washington, D.C.: Music Division,
           Library of Congress, 1942.

BIB 16   Chicago Public Library WPA Omnibus Project. *Subject Index to Literature
           on Negro Art*. Chicago: n.p., 1941.
           Covers a broad range on Negro arts, crafts, etc.

BIB 17   Comitas, Lambros. *Caribbeana 1900-65: A Topical Bibliography*. Seattle:
           University of Washington Press, 1968.

Costas Arguedas, José Felipe. *Diccionario del Folklore Boliviano*, Vols. 1 and 2. See No. BO 1.

Damon, S. Foster. "The Negro in Early American Songsters." See No. NA 710.

BIB
18
Dillard, J.L. "Toward A Bibliography of Works Dealing with the Creole Languages of the Caribbean Area, Louisiana, and the Guianas," *CS,* 3, No. 1 (1963), 84-95.
Corrections and numerous additions to No. BIB 56. Also includes Gullah entries.

BIB
19
Duran, Gustavo. *Recordings of Latin American Songs and Dances: An Annotated Selected List of Popular and Folk Music*. Washington, D.C.: Pan American Union, 1942.
Includes descriptions of Negro dances and accompanying music.

BIB
20
Epstein, Dena J. "The Search for Black Music's African Roots," *The University of Chicago Magazine*, 66, No. 1 (1973), 18-24.
Account of a bibliographer's problems in tracing early sources on black music.

Epstein, Dena J. "Slave Music in the United States before 1860: A Survey of Sources." See No. NA 915.

BIB
21
Ernst, Robert T. *The Geographical Literature of Black America, 1949-1972: A Selected Bibliography of Journal Articles, Serial Publications, Theses and Dissertations*. Exchange Bibliography No. 492. Monticello, Ill.: Council of Planning Librarians, 1973.

BIB
22
Ferris, William R., Jr. "A Discography of Mississippi Negro Folk Music," *Mississippi Folklore Register*, 2, No. 2 (1968), 51-54.

BIB
23
Ferris, William R., Jr. *Mississippi Black Folklore: A Research Bibliography and Discography*. Hattiesburg, Miss.: University and College Press of Mississippi, 1971.

BIB
24
Folk Music: A Catalog of Folk Songs, Ballads, Dances, Instrumental Pieces, and Folk Tales of the United States and Latin America on Phonography Records. Washington, D.C.: Music Division, Library of Congress, 1964.

BIB 25 Gaidoz, Henri and Paul Sebillot. *Bibliographie des Traditions et de la Littérature Populaire des Frances d'Outre-Mer*. Paris: Maisonneuve and Leclerc, 1886.

BIB 26 Gaskin, L.J.P. *A Selected Bibliography of Music in Africa*. London: International African Institute, Africa Bibliography Series B, 1965.

BIB 27 Gazin, Jacques. *Eléments de Bibliographie Méthodique et Historique de la Martinique* (Elements of a Methodical and Historical Bibliography of Martinique). Fort-de-France: Impr. Antillaise, 1926.

BIB 28 Giese, Wilhelm. *Los Pueblos Románicos y su Cultura Popular: Guía Etnográfica-Folklórica*. Bogotá: Instituto Caro y Cuervo, 1962.
Includes some material on black folklore.

BIB 29 Gillis, Frank and Merriam, Alan P. *Ethnomusicology and Folk Music: An International Bibliography of Dissertations and Theses*. Middletown, Conn.: Wesleyan University Press (for the Society of Ethnomusicology), 1966.

BIB 30 Gorham, Rex. *The Folkways of Brazil: A Bibliography*, Karl Brown, ed. New York: New York Public Library, 1944. (Also published in *Bulletin of the New York Public Library*, April and July, 1943; April and May, 1944.) A 53-page bibliography of works concerned with various aspects of Brazilian folklife and lore. Concerning blacks, see especially the sections "Music and Poetry" and "The Negro in Brazil." Contains a glossary of African and other non-Portuguese terms.

BIB 31 Griffin, A.P.C. *A List of Books on the Danish West Indies*. Washington, D.C.: United States Government Printing Office, 1901.

BIB 32 *Handbook of Latin American Studies*. Cambridge, Mass.: Harvard University Press, 1936-.

BIB 33 Handler, Jerome S. *A Guide to Source Materials for the Study of Barbados History, 1627-1834*. Carbondale, Ill.: Southern Illinois University Press, 1972.

BIB 34 Hayes, Floyd W., III. "The African Presence in America Before Columbus: A Bibliographical Essay," *Black World*, 22, No. 9 (1973), 4-22.

BIB
35
Haywood, Charles. *A Bibliography of North American Folklore and Folksong*, 2 vols. New York: Dover, 1961.

BIB
36
Henry, Mellinger Edward. *A Bibliography for the Study of American Folksongs with Many Titles of Folksongs (and Titles that Have to Do with Folksongs from Other Lands)*. London: The Mitre Press, 1937.

BIB
37
Hollyman, K.J. "Bibliographie des Créoles et Dialectes Regionaux Français d'Outre-Mer Modernes," *Le Français Moderne*, 33 (1965), 117-132. Bibliography of French Creole dialects spoken in the Antilles.

BIB
38
Horn, David. *The Literature of American Music*. Exeter, U.K.: American Arts Documentation Centre and the Exeter University Library, 1972.

BIB
39
Index to Latin American Periodicals: Humanities and Social Sciences. Boston: G.K. Hall, 1961-.

BIB
40
Jahn, Janheinz. *A Bibliography of Neo-African Literature from Africa, America and the Caribbean*. London: Deutsch, 1965.

BIB
41
Jandel, Jean Pierre, Maurice Nicolas, and Charles Relouzat. *Bibliographie de la Martinique*. Fort-de-France: Centre d'Études Régionales Antilles-Guyane, 1969.

BIB
42
King, James F. "The Negro in Continental South America: A Select Bibliography," *Hispanic American Historical Review*, 24 (1944), 547-559. 62 works, with an introductory essay.

BIB
43
Laws, G. Malcolm. *Native American Balladry: A Descriptive Study and a Bibliographic Syllabus*, revised edition. Philadelphia: Publications of the American Folklore Society, Bibliographical and Special Series, Vol. 1, 1964.

BIB
44
Leffall, Dolores C. *The Black Church: An Annotated Bibliography*. Washington, D.C.: Minority Research Center, 1973.

BIB
45
Luper, A.T. *The Music of Brazil*. Washington, D.C.: Pan-American Union, 1943.

BIB   McCarthy, Albert, *et al. Jazz on Record: A Critical Guide to the First 50*
46   *Years, 1917-1967*. London: Hanover, 1968.
            An annotated discography, arranged alphabetically by musician and by
            style; includes folk music.

BIB   McPherson, James M., Lawrence B. Holland, *et al. Blacks in America: Bibli-*
47   *ographical Essays*. Garden City, N.Y.: Doubleday, 1971.
            Includes bibliographical essays on African background, slavery, African
            cultural survivals, literature, art, drama, music, urban life and
            folklore, religion, etc.

        Magalhaes, Basilio de. See No. BR 318.

        Meléndez, Carlos and Quince Duncan, eds. *El Negro en Costa Rica*. See No.
            CR 5.

BIB   Merriam, Alan P. "An Annotated Bibliography of African and African-Derived
48   Music since 1936," *Africa*, 21 (1951), 319-329.
            An extension of Douglas H. Varley's *African Native Music: An Annotated*
            Bibliography.

BIB   Merriam, Alan P. and Robert J. Benford. *A Bibliography of Jazz*. Publications
49   of the American Folklore Society, Bibliographical Series, Vol. 4. Phil-
            adelphia: American Folklore Society, 1954.

BIB   Miller, Elizabeth W. *The Negro in America: A Bibliography*. Cambridge, Mass.:
50   Harvard University Press, 1966.

BIB   Mintz, Sidney W. and Vern Carrol, "A Selective Social Science Bibliography
51   of the Republic of Haiti," *Revista Interamericana de Ciencias Sociales*,
            Ser. 2, Vol. 2, No. 3 (1963), 405-419.

BIB   O'Leary, Timothy. *Ethnographic Bibliography of South America*. New Haven:
52   Human Relations Area Files, 1963.

BIB   Pereira Salas, Eugenio. *Guía Bibliográfica para el Estudio del Folklore*
53   *Chileno*. Santiago de Chile: Instituto de Investigaciones Musicales,
            Universidad de Chile, 1952.
            Bibliography of Chilean folklore, cites works which deal with black
            folklore in other Latin American countries.

BIB
54
Pollak-Eltz, Angelina. "Afro-American Studies," *Review of Ethnology*
(Vienna), No. 8 (April, 1969), 1-8; No. 9 (April, 1969), 1-4.
Annotated bibliography of Afro-American studies.

BIB
55
Robaina, Tomás F. *Bibliografía sobre Estudios Afro-Americanos (Bibliography of Afro-American Studies)*. Havana: Nacional José Martí, 1968.

BIB
56
Rubin, Joan. "A Bibliography of Caribbean Languages," *CS*, 2, No. 4, (1963);
51-61.
See No. BIB 18 for corrections and additions.

BIB
57
Salles, Vincente. "Bibliografia Crítica do Folclore Brasileiro: Capoeira,"
RBF, 8 (1969), 79-103.
Annotated bibliography of Afro-Brazilian folk music, focusing on the
capoeira.

BIB
58
Salles, Vincente and Sênia Sampaio. "Bibliografia Crítica do Folclore
Brasileiro: Bumba-Meu-Boi," *RBF*, 8 (1968), 93-99; 209-226; 325-340.
Annotated bibliography of Afro-Brazilian dramatic dances, especially
bumba-meu-boi.

BIB
59
Standifer, James and Barbara Reeder. *Source Book of African and Afro-
American Materials for Music Education*. Washington, D.C.: Contemporary
Music Project, Music Educators' National Conference, 1972.
A listing of books, articles (some annotated) and artists, exercise
for training the ear to hear jazz rhythms, etc.

BIB
60
Thieme, Darius L. *African Music: A Briefly Annotated Bibliography*. Washington, D.C.: Library of Congress, Music Division, 1964.

BIB
61
Thieme, Darius L. "Negro Folksong Scholarship in the United States," *African Music*, 2, No. 3 (1960), 67-72.
Review of bibliographical tools, publications, archives, and discography
for the study of the Negro folksong.

BIB
62
Tinker, Edward Larocque. *Les Écrits de Langue Française en Louisiane aux
XIXe Siècle* (Writers of the French Language in 19th Century Louisiana).
Paris: Librairie Ancienne Honoré Champion, 1932.

BIB
63
Valdman, Albert. *Créole et Francais aux Antilles: Bibliographie Créole
Succincte* (Creole and French in the Antilles: Succinct Creole Bibliography). Les Documents du GERAG, No. 3, 1970.

BIB   Valle, Rafael Heliodoro. "Para la Bibliografía Afroamericana," in
64   *Misceláneá de Estudios Dedicados a Fernando Ortiz*. Havana:
            Sociedad Económica de Amigos del País, 1955-1957, 1427-1465.
            Bibliography of publications on Afro-Americans, largely in Spanish.

BIB   Varley, Douglas H. *African Native Music, An Annotated Bibliography*. Lon-
65   don: The Royal Empire Society, 1936.

BIB   Welding, Pete. "The Best of Blues and Roots," in *Down Beat's Music '68*,
66   Dan Morgenstern, ed. Chicago: Maher Publications, 1968, 56-59, 86,
            88-93.
            An annotated discography of gospel, blues, r 'n' b and ragtime records.

BIB   Williams, Daniel T. and Carolyn L. Redden. *The Black Muslims in the United
67   States: A Selected Bibliography*. Tuskegee, Alabama: Hollis Burke Fris-
            sell Library, Tuskegee Institute, 1964.

BIB   Williams, Ethel L. and Clifton L. Brown. *Afro-American Religious Studies:
68   A Comprehensive Bibliography with Locations in American Libraries*.
            Metuchen, N.J.: Scarecrow Press, 1972.

BIB   Wolfe, Richard J. *Secular Music in America, 1801-1825: A Bibliography*, 3
69   vols. New York: The New York Public Library, 1964.
            Gives tune titles, publisher and date with an annotation and listing
            of first lines. Includes a small number of Negro or Negro-derived
            songs.

BIB   Work, Monroe N. *A Bibliography of the Negro in Africa and America*. New
70   York: H.W. Wilson, 1928.

GENERAL

GEN
1
Abadia M., Geullermo and David Lewiston. "In Praise of Oxala and Other
Gods: Black Music of South America, Recorded in Colombia, Ecuador,
and Brazil by David Lewiston," record notes to Nonesuch LP record
H-72036.
Texts and discussion of 11 songs.

GEN
2
Les Afro-Américains. Mémoir 27, Institut Français d'Afrique Noire
(Dakar), 1953.
Collection of anthropological papers on various aspects of Afro-
American life.

GEN
3
Aguirre Beltrán, Gonzalo. "African Influences in the Development of Regional Cultures in the New World," in *Plantation Systems of the New
World*. Washington, D.C.: Pan American Union, 1959, 64-70. (Also published as "Influencias Africanas en el Desarrollo de las Culturas
Regionales del Nuevo Mundo," *Revista Geográfica* (Brazil), 24, No. 50
(1959), 43-52.)

Aletti, Vince. "Music: Some Like It Hot." See No. NA 41.

GEN
4
Alleyne, Mervyn C. "Acculturation and the Cultural Matrix of Creolization,"
in *Pidginization and Creolization of Languages*, Dell Hymes, ed. Cambridge, U.K.: Cambridge University Press, 1971, 169-186.
Overview of the processes of cultural and linguistic change among Afro-
Americans.

GEN
5
Alleyne, Mervyn C. "Panorama de la Lingüística y Enseñanza de Idiomas
en el Caribe" (Panorama of the Linguistics and Teaching of Idioms in

9

Carib), *CS*, 12 (1973), 5-14.

GEN   Almeida, Renato. *Dances Africaines en Amérique Latine*. Rio de Janeiro:
6   Ministerio da Educacao e Cultura, 1969.
        Afro-American dances in Latin America--*merengue, calenda, samba,
        tango, bossa nova*--and their roots in Africa, Afro-American cults,
        etc.; review of Afro-American dance scholarship.

GEN   Apel, Paul Hermann. *Music of the Americas, North and South*. New York:
7   Vantage, 1958.
        Includes descriptions of dances, some of which are black, in North,
        Central and South America.

GEN   Arciniegas, Germán. *Latin America: A Cultural History*. New York: Knopf,
8   1966. (Originally published as *El Continente de Siete Colores*. Buenos
        Aires: Editorial Sudamericana Anonima, 1965.)
        Includes the African contribution to the societies and cultures of
        various Caribbean, Central and South American countries. Chapter 21
        ("Appointment with Necromancy") deals with the contributions of Euro-
        peans, Africans, and Indians to Latin American witchcraft and magic.

GEN   Arróm, José Juan. "Certidumbre de América; Estudios de Letras, Folklore
9   y Cultura," *Anuario Bibliográfico Cubano*. Havana, 1959.
        Chapter 5 has materials on black folklore in the New World.

GEN   Arróm, José Juan. "El Negro en la Poesía Folklórica Americana," in
10   *Miscelánea de Estudios Dedicados a Fernando Ortiz*, Vol. 1. Havana:
        Sociedad Económica de Amigos del País, 1955, 81-106.
        The influence of Negroes on the poetry of Argentina, Venezuela, Colom-
        bia, Ecuador, Cuba.

GEN   Assuncão, Fernando. "Aportaciones para un Estudio Sobre los Orígenes de
11   la Zamacuecca (Baile Popular Hispanoamericano de las Regiones
        Costeras del Pacífico)," *Folklore Americano* (Lima), 17-18, No. 16
        (1969-70), 5-39.
        Survey of African influences in the New World with emphasis on the
        Zamacueca dance on the Pacific Coast of South America; texts and
        music; illus.

GEN   Ballesteros-Gaibrois, Manuel. "Negros en la Nueva Granada," in
12   *Miscelánea de Estudios Dedicados a Fernando Ortiz*, Vol. 1. Havana:
        Sociedad Económica de Amigos del País, 1955, 107-123.
        Brief article on the religious practices of blacks in the New World
        during the 17th century.

GEN
13
Barrera y Domingo, Francisco. *Reflexiones*. Havana: Ediciones C.R.,
1953.
Includes discussion of medical lore and practices, eating habits,
clothing, diseases and remedies of New World Negros.

GEN
14
Barrett, Leonard E. *Soul-Force: African Heritage in Afro-American
Religions*. Garden City: N.Y.: Anchor-Doubleday, 1974.

GEN
15
Bastide, Roger. *African Civilizations in the New World*. New York:
Harper and Row, 1972. (Originally published as *Les Amériques Noires*.
Paris: Payot, 1967.)
A summary of scholarship on Africans in the Americas: chapters on
communities of escaped slaves; the relations between Indians and
Negroes; the nature of Afro-American religions; varieties of Afro-
American folklore; types of communities; *négritude* and the spread of
Afro-American culture among whites; bibliography in chapter references.

GEN
16
Bastide, Roger. "Amérique du Sud," *Présence Africaine*, No. 8-9 (1950),
383-391.
Overview of African-Christian acculturation in Latin America.

GEN
17
Bastide, Roger. "Les Apports Culturels des Africains en Amerique
Latine: Essai de Synthese" (The Cultural Contributions of Africans
in Latin America: Synthesizing Essay), *Cahiers d'Histoire Mondiale*,
13, No. 2 (1971), 333-352.

GEN
18
Bastide, Roger. "La Divination chez les Afro-Américains" (Divination
among Afro-Americans), in *La Divination*, A. Caquot and M. Leibovici,
eds. Paris: Presses Universitaires de France, 1968, 393-427.

GEN
19
Bastide, Roger. "Dusky Venus, Black Apollo," *Race*, 3 (1961), 10-18.
The aesthetics of cross-racial sexual relations in Brazil and France.

GEN
20
Bastide, Roger. "État Actuel et Perspectives d'Avenir des Recherches
Afro-Américaines," *Journal de la Société des Américanistes*, 58 (1968),
7-29.
Review of Afro-American studies--subjects, scholars, etc.--with sug-
gested programs for further research.

GEN
21
Bastide, Roger. "Immigration et Métamorphose d'un Dieu," *Cahiers Inter-
nationaux de Sociologie*, N.S. 20, No. 3 (1956), 45-60.
Comparative analysis of African-based religious concepts in Cuba,
Brazil and Haiti.

GEN
22
Bastide, Roger. "Le Syncretisme en Amérique Latine," *Bulletin St.
Jean-Baptiste* (Paris), 5 (1965), 166-171.
Develops and redefines the notions of syncretism and culture change
using examples drawn from Afro-American religion and magic.

GEN
23
Bastide, Roger. "La Théorie de la Réincarnation chez les Afro-Américains,"
in *Réincarnation et Vie Mystique en Afrique Noire*, R. Bastide and D.
Zahan, eds. Paris: Presses Universitaires de France, 1965, 9-29.
Discusses the African beliefs of reincarnation among various Afro-
American peoples.

GEN
24
Bastien, Remy. "Procesos de Aculturación en las Antillas" (Processes of
Acculturation in the Antilles), *La Revista de Indias* (Madrid), Nos.
95-96 (1964), 177-196.

GEN
25
Bayard, Frank. "The Black Latin American Impact on Western Culture," in
The Negro Impact on Western Civilization, Joseph S. Roucek and Thomas
Kiernan, eds. New York: Philosophical Library, 1970, 287-335.
Includes comments on Latin American black music.

GEN
26
Becco, Horacio Jorge. *Lexicografía Religiosa de los Afroamericanos* (Religious Lexicography of the Afro-Americans). Buenos Aires: Coni, 1952.
(Also published in *Boletín de la Academia Argentina de Letras*, 20
(1952).)

GEN
27
Becco, Horacio Jorge. *El Tema del Negro en Cantos*. Buenos Aires: Editorial
Ollantay, 1951.
Miscellany of songs and poetry on blacks from Spain and the New World
from the 16th and 17th centuries.

GEN
28
Ben-Jochannan, Yosef. *African Origins of the Major "Western Religions."*
New York: Alkebu-Lan Books, 1970.
A critique of Western scholarship on African and Afro-American religions which argues for the influence of African religions on Western
religious thought and practices; information on U.S. storefront
churches, Father Divine's and Daddy Grace's churches, Black Jews,
charms, the religious content of jazz, blues and spirituals, Afro-
American religious groups in various countries of the Americas,
Africanisms in Western religions, etc.

GEN
29
Blanco, Guillermo. "El Rostro Negro en la Conquista de América."
Finis Terrae, (Chile), No. 23 (1959), 35-46.
Historical discussion of the role of blacks in the conquest of
America.

GEN 30   Blasis, Charles. *Traité Elémentaire, Théorique et Pratique de l'Art de la Danse*. Milan, 1820.
Includes a chapter on Negro dancing in North and South America.

GEN 31   Bourguignon, Erika E. "Afro-American Religions: Traditions and Transformations," in *Black America*, John F. Szwed, ed. New York: Basic Books, 1970, 190-202.
Review of Afro-American religions in Brazil, Cuba, Haiti, Trinidad and the U.S.

GEN 32   Bourguignon, Erika E. "Ritual Dissociation and Possession Belief in Caribbean Negro Religion," in *Afro-American Anthropology: Contemporary Perspectives*, Norman E. Whitten, Jr. and John F. Szwed, eds. New York: Free Press, 1970, 87-101.
Patterns of dissociation and possession and their African background.

GEN 33   Bourguignon, Erika E. "Trance Dance," *Dance Perspectives*, 35 (Autumn, 1968), 1-61.
Discusses visionary dancing (Trinidad's Spiritual Baptists and St. Vincent's Shakers) and possessional dancing (Haiti's *Vodû* and Brazil's *umbanda*) in the New World and their African sources or counterparts; illus.

GEN 34   Brathwaite, Edward Kamau. "The African Presence in Caribbean Literature," in "Slavery, Colonialism, and Racism," Special issue of *Daedalus*, Spring, 1974, 73-109.

GEN 35   Brunelli, Elsa. *Los Negros en América* (The Negroes in America). Buenos Aires: Editorial Atlántida, 1941.

GEN 36   Bryan, Patrick. "African Affinities--The Blacks of Latin America," *CQ*, 17, Nos. 3-4 (1971), 45-52.
Notes on African cultural survivals, primarily in Brazil and Cuba.

GEN 37   Cartey, Wilfred. *The West Indies: Islands in the Sun*. Camden, N.J.: Thomas Nelson, 1967.
Overview of a number of Caribbean countries; includes notes on cuisine, music, religion, carnival, etc.

GEN 38   Carvalho-Neto, Paulo de. *Folklore and Psychoanalysis*. Miami: University of Miami Press, 1972. (Originally published as *Folklore y Psicoanálisis*. México: Mortiz, 1968.)
A psychoanalytic study of folklore which includes translated portions of texts and descriptions from studies of Afro-American folklore in

Brazil, Paraguay, Ecuador, and elsewhere.

GEN
39
Carvalho-Neto, Paulo de. *History of Ibero-American Folklore: Mestizo Cultures*. Oosterhout: Anthropological Publications, 1969.

GEN
40
Chase, Gilbert. *The Music of Spain*. New York: Dover, 1959. (2nd Revised Edition)
Chapter 17, "Hispanic Music in the Americas," concerns the *tango* and *habanera*, Creole songs and dances, and Brazilian music.

GEN
41
Chauvet, Stephan. *Musique Nègre*. Paris: Societe d'Editions Géographiques, Maritimes et Coloniales, 1929.
General discussion of black African music; includes descriptions of several instruments; transcriptions; illus.

GEN
42
Colomban Rosario, José and Justina Carrión. "El Negro," *Boletín de la Universidad de Puerto Rico*, 10, No. 2, (1940).
An examination of the status and history of the Negro in Puerto Rico, Haiti, and the U.S., with special emphasis on cultural adaptations.

GEN
43
Coluccio, Felix. *Antología Ibérica y Americana del Folklore*. Buenos Aires: Guillermo Kraft, 1953.
Includes some folklore material from blacks in Brazil and Cuba.

GEN
44
Coombs, Orde, ed. *Is Massa Day Dead? Black Moods in the Caribbean*. Garden City, New York: Anchor Books/Doubleday, 1974.
Essays on politics and culture.

GEN
45
Coulthard, G.R. "Negritude--Reality and Mystification," *CS*, 10, No. 1 (1970), 42-51.
Discussion of the *Négritude* movement in the West Indies.

GEN
46
Coulthard, G.R. "Parallelisms and Divergencies between 'Negritude' and 'Indigenismo,'" *CS*, 8, No. 1 (1968), 31-55.
Comparison of cultural nationalism movements in Mexico (Indian) and the West Indies (Afro-American).

GEN
47
Coulthard, G.R. *Race and Colour in Caribbean Literature*. London and New York: Oxford University Press, 1962.
Survey of Afro-American literature in the Caribbean and its folk background: special attention to the themes of Africa, anti-slavery, *négritude*, women, and the rejection of European culture; the folkloristic work of F. Ortiz, L. Denis, J. Price-Mars, *et al*.

GEN
48
Courlander, Harold. "African and Afro-American Drums," booklet included with Folkways LP record 4502.
Notes on drumming in Puerto Rico, Cuba, Haiti, Brazil, the Bahamas, and the U.S., with African parallels.

GEN
49
Courlander, Harold. "Caribbean Folk Music," booklet included with Folkways LP record 4533.
Notes and texts to music from various parts of the West Indies, Puerto Rico, Cuba, etc.

GEN
50
Courlander, Harold. *Tales of Yoruba Gods and Heroes*. New York: Crown, 1973.
Includes appendices with a list of Yoruba gods in the Americas; 6 Cuban tales; and 5 Yoruba-based songs from Brazil, Cuba and Haiti.

GEN
51
Courlander, Harold and Prempeh Albert Kafi. *The Hat-Shaking Dance and Other Tales from the Gold Coast*. New York: Harcourt, Brace, 1957.
Collection of African folktales for children contains notes which compare African and New World spider tales.

GEN
52
Courlander, Harold and Richard A. Waterman. "Negro Folk Music of Africa and America," booklet included with Folkways LP record FE-4500.
Notes on musical selections from Colombia, Brazil, Haiti, Puerto Rico, Trinidad, Cuba, the United States and Africa.

GEN
53
Crowley, Daniel J. "African Folktales in Afro-America," in *Black America,* John F. Szwed, ed. New York: Basic Books, 1970, 179-189.
The African, European-derived and new elements of folktales of Afro-Americans.

GEN
54
Crowley, Daniel J. "Art in the West Indies," *Trinidad Guardian, Special Federation Supplement* (April 22, 1958), 55, 59.
Newspaper article on painting, sculpture and crafts.

GEN
55
Crowley, Daniel J. "The Emergence of a West Indian Culture," *Trinidad Guardian, Special Federation Supplement* (April 22, 1958), 52, 61.
Newspaper article foretelling the development of new forms of arts and crafts, theater and dance, literature, etc.

GEN
56
Cunard, Nancy, ed. *Negro Anthology*. London: Wishart & Co., 1934.
Articles on all aspects of Negro life on several continents.

GEN   Curtin, Philip D., ed. *Africa Remembered: Narratives by West Africans*
57   *from the Era of the Slave Trade*. Madison, Wisc.: University of Wis-
           consin Press, 1968.
           Includes narratives by Africans sold into slavery in Maryland, Vir-
           ginia, Georgia, Brazil, Jamaica, and Barbados; with notes and com-
           mentary.

GEN   Curtin, Philip D. *The Atlantic Slave Trade: A Census*. Madison, Wisc.:
58   University of Wisconsin Press, 1969.
           A compilation and reassessment of statistics on the Atlantic slave
           trade; sources and destinations of slaves, etc.

GEN   Dalby, David. *Black through White: Patterns of Communication.* Bloomington,
59   Ind.: African Studies Program, Indiana University, 1970.
           The mechanisms of development of Creole languages in Africa and Afro-
           America. The continuity of African elements in English and other
           European languages; African vocabulary in the U.S.

GEN   Daniels, Cora Linn and C.M. Stevans, eds. *Encyclopedia of Superstitions,*
60   *Folklore, and the Occult Sciences of the World*, 3 vols. Chicago:
           J.H. Yewdale, 1903.
           Contains entries on *hoodoo, voodoo, obeah, roots, jumbies*, etc., from
           the U.S. and the West Indies.

       Dauer, Alfons M. *Der Jazz. Seine Ursprunge und Seine Entwicklung*. See
           No. NA 721.

GEN   De Onis, Harriet, ed. *The Golden Land*. New York: Knopf, 1948.
61   An anthology of Latin American folklore in literature. Includes Eng-
           lish translations from José Lins do Rego's novels (Brazil) and Carmen
           Lyra's folktales (Costa Rica).

GEN   Diderot, Denis. *Encyclopedie, ou Dictionnaire Raisonne des Sciences, des*
62   *Arts et des Metiers*. N.p., n.p., 1751.
           See entries on "*Negres*," "*Calinda*," and "*Tamboula*."

GEN   Dillard, J.L. *Afro-American Vehicle and Other Names*. Institute of Carib-
63   bean Studies, Special Studies (Río Piedras, Puerto Rico), No. 1, 1965.
           Vehicle, personal and store names from Puerto Rico, Haiti, Dominica,
           Nassau, Virgin Islands, Guadeloupe, Jamaica, and West Africa.

GEN   Dillard, J.L. "Creole Portuguese and Creole English: The Early Records,"
64   *Center for African and African-American Studies Papers in Linguistics*
           (Atlanta), No. 3, 1971.
           A review of materials on the connection between English and Portuguese
           Creoles.

GEN
65

Dillard, J.L. "How Not to Classify the Folk Tales of the Antilles," *CS*, 3, No. 4 (1964), 30-34.
Argues for the origin of certain tale variants within the Antilles as due to Negro influence.

GEN
66

Dillard, J.L. "Names or Slogans: Some Problems from the Cameroun, the Caribbean, Burundi, and the United States," *CS*, 9, No. 4 (1970), 104-110.
The similarities between names and slogans as used on buses, shops, etc., by Africans and Afro-Americans.

GEN
67

Dillard, J.L. "The Writings of Herskovits and the Study of the Language of the Negro in the New World." *CS*, 4, No. 2 (1964), 35-41.
Herskovits' work on Creole languages, in the context of a review of writings on Afro-American speech.

Dorson, Richard. "Introduction," in *Folklore of Chile*. See Pino-Saavedra, Yolando, No. CH 1.

GEN
68

Drake, St. Clair. *The Redemption of Africa and Black Religion*. Chicago: Third World Press; and Atlanta: Institute of the Black World, 1970.

GEN
69

Duryea, D. "Notes on the Cha-Cha, the Mambo, and the Merengue," *Dance Magazine*, 30 (March, 1956), 42-44.

GEN
70

Ekwueme, Lazarus E.N. "African-Music Retentions in the New World," *BPM*, 2 (1974), 128-144.

GEN
71

Ekwueme, Lazarus E.N. "African Sources in New World Black Music," *Black Images* (Toronto), 1, Nos. 3-4, (1972), 3-12.
Overview of African sources of West Indian and United States Afro-American music; includes 8 transcribed songs.

Emery, Lynne Fauley. *Black Dance in the United States from 1619 to 1970*. See No. NA 902.

GEN
72

Equiano, Olaudah. *The Interesting Narrative of the Life of Olaudah Equiano*. London, 1789.
Autobiography of a Beni, sold into slavery in Barbados and Virginia; gives accounts of black culture in Benin, the United States, Montserrat and Jamaica; describes African-Afro-American continuities for Jamaica in burial practices, dress and dance; describes an early form of the "nation" dance.

GEN 73   Fanon, Frantz. *Black Skin, White Masks: The Experiences of a Black Man in a White World*. New York: Grove Press, 1967. (Originally published as *Peau Noire, Masques Blancs*. Paris: Editions de Seuil, 1952.) Chapter 1, "The Negro and Language," treats the matter of Creole seen as a defective language by whites. Elsewhere Afro-American folklore is discussed in the context of colonialism and psychopathology.

GEN 74   *Folk Songs and Stories of the Americas,* Vol. 1. Washington, D.C.: Organization of American States, 1968.
1 animal tale from Costa Rica, and 1 from Haiti, both translated into English.

GEN 75   Franco, Jean. *The Modern Culture of Latin America: Society and the Artist*. London: Pall Mall Press, 1967.
A general work on the rise of intellectual and artistic culture in Latin America. Black consciousness among intellectuals, writers and artists, especially in Puerto Rico, Cuba and Brazil. Several examples of black folk verses and ritual songs.

GEN 76   Franco, José Luciano. "La Presencia Negra en el Nuevo Mundo" (The Negro Presence in the New World), *Casa de las Americas,* 7 (1968), 7-135.

GEN 77   Freyre, Gilberto. *The Racial Factor in Contemporary Politics*. Occasional Papers of Research Unit for the Study of Multi-Racial Societies, University of Sussex (U.K.), No. 1, 1966.
Discusses the influence of Afro-American political and cultural styles on other countries.

GEN 78   Friedenthal, Albert. *Musik, Tanz, und Dichtung bei den Kreolen Amerikas*. Berlin: H. Schnippel, 1913.
An early attempt to see the music, song and dance of Negroes of various parts of the New World as a unified whole. Discusses the mutual influence of European and African music, the development of the *tango*, the *habenera,* the *meringue*, etc.

GEN 79   Gilbert, Will G. *Rumbamuziek: Volksmuziek van de Midden-Amerikaansche Negers* (The Rumba: Folk Music of Central American Negroes). The Hague: J.P. Kruseman, n.d.

GEN 80   Gleason, Judith. *Orisha: The Gods of Yorubaland*. New York: Atheneum, 1971.
Retellings of myths of Yoruba gods, drawn from Nigeria, Brazil, Cuba, Puerto Rico, and New York City.

GEN 81   Goeje, C.H. de. "Verwanten van de Curaçaose Wiri" (Relatives of the Curaçao Wiri-Wiri), *WIG*, 31 (1950), 180.

GEN
82
    Goines, Leonard. "The African in the Americas," *Allegro*, June, 1971,
       4, 29.
       African musical survivals throughout the New World, with emphasis on
       rhythmic elements and drums and idiophones, especially in reli-
       gious musical practices.

GEN
83
    Goines, Leonard. "Afro-American Music," *Allegro*, April, 1971. 14, 19.
       Sub-Saharan African backgrounds of Afro-American artistic expression,
       including discussion of magic, religion, and social structure.

GEN
84
    Goines, Leonard. "Afro-American Music: A Definition and the Problem,"
       Allegro, March, 1971, 15.
       General introduction to Afro-American music in the New World.

GEN
85
    Goines, Leonard. "Latin American and Caribbean Music IV: Black Music of
       the French Speaking Islands," *Allegro*, December, 1972, 4, 24.
       Surveys music in Haitian life, especially in *Vodû*, in work groups,
       and in Mardi Gras; as well as the *calenda belain,* and *beguine* from
       Martinique and Guadaloupe.

GEN
86
    Goines, Leonard. "Latin American and Caribbean Music VI: Black Music
       of the Coastal Areas," *Allegro*, February, 1973, 6, 16.
       Brief survey of Afro-American song and dance forms from Mexico
       (*huapango*), Honduras (*John Canoe*), Panama (*tambourito*), Colombia
       (*cumbia*), Ecuador, Peru, Uruguay and Venezuela.

GEN
87
    Goines, Leonard. "Latin American and Caribbean Music VII: Jamaica,
       Carnival and the Dutch Possessions," *Allegro*, March, 1973, 14.
       Survey of Jamaican music, song and dance forms from Trinidad Carnival,
       and material from Surinam and the Dutch West Indies.

GEN
88
    Goines, Leonard. "Latin and Caribbean Music: Racial and Cultural Influ-
       ences," *Allegro*, September, 1972, 19.
       Historical and cultural backgrounds leading to the creation of Afro-
       America.

GEN
89
    Goines, Leonard. "Latin and Caribbean Music III: Black Music of the Spanish-
       Speaking Islands," *Allegro*, November, 1972, 7.
       Surveys Afro-American songs and dances from Puerto Rico, Cuba, and the
       Dominican Republic.

GEN
90
    Goldstein, Rhoda L., ed. *Black Life and Culture in the United States.*
       New York: Thomas Crowell, 1971.
       Includes articles on speech, folktales, art, music, dance, slavery,
       drama, etc., in the New World.

GEN
91
González-Wippler, Migene. *Santería: African Magic in Latin America*. New
    York: Julian Press, 1973.

GEN
92
Goodman, Felicitas. *Speaking in Tongues: A Cross-Cultural Study of
    Glossolalia*. Chicago: University of Chicago Press, 1972.
    A study of the kinesics, linguistics, and conversion experiences of
    members of churches in Trinidad, St. Vincent, Brazil, Indiana, etc.

GEN
93
Goodman, Morris F. *A Comparative Study of Creole French Dialects*. The
    Hague: Mouton, 1964.
    Historical study of various French Creoles.

GEN
94
Gottschalk, Louis Moreau. *Notes of a Pianist*. Philadelphia: J.B. Lippin-
    cott, 1881.
    Includes the 19th century composer's comments on Negro folk Music in
    the U.S., Cuba and the West Indies.

GEN
95
Gray, Daniel. "La Música Africana," *Revista Musical Chilena* (Santiago de
    Chile), 43 (1952), 34-40.
    General essay on African music and its diffusion throughout the world.

GEN
96
Green, Helen Bagenstose. "Temporal Attitudes in Four Negro Subcultures,"
    Stadium Generale (Berlin), 23 (1970), 571-586.
    The sources of similar attitudes towards time among West Africans and
    Afro-Americans in Brazil, the Caribbean, and the United States are
    African cosmology, ideas of child-training and community, as well as
    colonial subjugation and slavery.

GEN
97
Guillot, Carlos Federico. "Los Negros Cimarrones," *Nosotros*, Vol. 11-12
    (1939-40), 261-267.
    Article on the fugitive slave societies of the colonial era in the
    New World. Discusses attempts of blacks to reestablish tribal organi-
    zation, religion, etc.

GEN
98
Guillot, Carlos Federico. *Negros Rebeldes y Negros Cimarrones*. Buenos
    Aires: Fariña Editores, 1961.
    Mainly a historical work on Negro revolts during the 16th century and
    attempts of fugitive slaves to establish independent, self-sufficient
    black communities.

GEN
99
Hammond, Peter B. "Afro-American Indians and Afro-Asians: Cultural Con-
    tacts between Africa and the Peoples of Asia and Aboriginal America,"
    in *Expanding Horizons in African Studies*, Gwendolen M. Carter and Ann
    Paden, eds. Evanston, Ill.: Northwestern University Press, 1969, 275-290.
    Poses a number of questions on cultural and racial contacts.

GEN
100
Hancock, Ian F. "A Provisional Comparison of the English-Based Atlantic
Creoles," in *Pidginization and Creolization of Languages*, Dell
Hymes, ed. Cambridge, U.K.: Cambridge University Press, 1971, 287-291.

GEN
101
Hancock, Ian F. "A Survey of the Pidgins and Creoles of the New World,"
in *Pidginization and Creolization of Languages*, Dell Hymes, ed. Cambridge, U.K.: Cambridge University Press, 1971, 509-523.
List (with map) which includes the Afro-American Creoles.

GEN
102
Hansen, Terrence. *The Types of the Folk Tale in Cuba, Puerto Rico, the
Dominican Republic, and Spanish South America*. Berkeley and Los Angeles:
University of California Press, 1957.

GEN
103
Harman, Carter, and the Editors of *Life*. *The West Indies*. New York: Time,
1963.
Illustrated survey of the West Indies includes photos and descriptions
of carnival, music, dance, art and religion in a variety of countries;
French and African influences.

GEN
104
Haskins, James. *Witchcraft, Mysticism and Magic in the Black World*. New
York: Doubleday, 1974.
A popular review of African and Afro-American practices.

GEN
105
Hawley, E.H. "Distribution of the Notched Rattle," *AA*, 11 (1898), 344-
346.
Rattles of Africa and the West Indies.

GEN
106
Hayes, Floyd W., III. "The African Presence in America," *Black World,* 22
(July, 1973), 4-22.

Hearn, Lafcadio. "The Scientific Value of Creole." See No. NA 1385.

GEN
107
Herskovits, Melville J. "African Ethnology and the New World Negro,"
Man, 38 (1938), 9-10.
Argues for anthropological research on the Negro in the "natural labor-
atory" of all of the countries of the New World.

GEN
108
Herskovits, Melville J. "African Gods and Catholic Saints in New World
Negro Belief," *AA*, 39 (1937), 635-643.
The interaction of Catholic and African beliefs and rituals in Brazil,
Cuba and Haiti.

GEN 109 Herskovits, Melville J. "African Literature (Negro Folklore)," *Encyclopedia of Literature*, Joseph T. Shipley, ed. New York: Philosophical Library, 1946, 3-15.
The genres of African and Afro-American folklore; collections and typologies; trickster tales; proverbs, riddles, tales, and their social functions; diffusion from Old World to New; bibliography.

GEN 110 Herskovits, Melville J. "Afro-American Art," *Encyclopedia of World Art*, Vol. 1. New York: McGraw-Hill, 1959, 150-158.
A general survey of Afro-American art. African retentions, etc. Illus.

GEN 111 Herskovits, Melville J. "Afro-American Art," *Studies in Latin American Art*, Elizabeth Wilder, ed. Washington, D.C.: American Council of Learned Societies, 1949, 58-64.
Discusses African retentions in "Bush Negro" and Bahian (Brazil) art, and the reasons for their absence elsewhere in the Americas.

GEN 112 Herskovits, Melville J. "El Estudio de la Música Negra en el Hemisferio Occidental," *Boletín Latino-Americano de Música* (Montevideo, Uruguay), 5 (1941), 133-142.
Stresses the importance of African survivals in New World Negro music.

GEN 113 Herskovits, Melville J. "Freudian Mechanisms in Negro Psychology," in *Essays Presented to C.G. Seligman*, E.E. Evans-Pritchard, R. Firth, *et al.*, eds. London: Kegan, Paul, Trench, Trubner, 1934, 75-84. (Reprinted in No. GEN 120.)
Cultural data from Haiti, Surinam, and Dahomey used to show the applicability of Freudian theory to Afro-Americans.

GEN 114 Herskovits, Melville J. "The Historical Approach to Afroamerican Studies: A Critique," *AA*, 62 (1960), 559-568. (Reprinted in No. GEN 120.)
The limitations of synchronic research in anthropology; the study of Afro-Americans is used as the illustrative case.

GEN 115 Herskovits, Melville J., ed. *The Interdisciplinary Aspects of Negro Studies*. American Council of Learned Societies Bulletin No. 32, 1941.
Essays (with transcribed discussions) on bibliography, linguistic studies, history, blacks in Latin America, etc. Participants include Melville J. Herskovits, Herbert Aptheker, William Bascom, Sterling Brown, Ralph J. Bunche, E. Franklin Frazier, Charles S. Johnson, Alain Locke, N.N. Puckett, George Simpson, Lorenzo Turner, Eric Williams, *et al.*

GEN 116 Herskovits, Melville J. "Introduction" to *Acculturation in the Americas*. Proceedings and Selected Papers of the 29th International Congress of

Americanists, Vol. 2, Sol Tax, ed. Chicago: University of Chicago
Press, 1952, 48-63.
Discussion of culture change in the Americas; includes Afro-Americans.

GEN
117
Herskovits, Melville J. *Man and His Works: The Science of Cultural Anthropology*. New York: Knopf, 1948.
Includes examples of Afro-American folkloristic elements as illustrations of principles of cultural processes.

GEN
118
Herskovits, Melville J. "O Negro do Novo Mundo" (The Negro in the New World), in *Vida Intelectual vos Estados Unidos*. Sao Paulo: Editora Universitaria, 1942, 205-226.

GEN
119
Herskovits, Melville J. "The Negro in the New World: The Statement of a Problem," *AA*, 32 (1930), 145-155. (Reprinted in No. GEN 120.)
The range of cultural adaptations of Afro-Americans in various places is seen as useful data for ascertaining the interrelationship of culture and physical form.

GEN
120
Herskovits, Melville J. *The New World Negro*, Frances S. Herskovits, ed. Bloomington, Ind.: Indiana University Press, 1966.
Papers on aspects of various Afro-American cultures and societies.

GEN
121
Herskovits, Melville J. "The New World Negro as an Anthropological Problem," *Man*, 31 (1931), 68-69.
Argues for treating Negroes as part of a culture area covering 2 continents.

GEN
122
Herskovits, Melville J. "On Some Modes of Ethnographic Comparison," *BTLV*, 112 (1956), 128-148. (Reprinted in No. GEN 120).
Argues for the rejection of the concept of area research in favor of the study of historically related peoples; Afro-American peoples and cultures are the example.

GEN
123
Herskovits, Melville J. "On the Provenience of New World Negroes," *Social Forces*, 12 (1933), 247-262.
Overview of the African sources of Negroes throughout the Americas; includes cultural parallels.

GEN
124
Herskovits, Melville J. "Patterns of Negro Music," *Transactions of the Illinois State Academy of Science*, 34, No. 1 (1941), 19-23.
Comparisons of African, Brazilian, Haitian, Trinidadian and U.S. black music: their common stylistic features.

GEN
125

Herskovits, Melville J. "The Present Status and Needs of Afro-American Research," *JNH*, 36 (1951), 123-147. (Reprinted in No. GEN 120.)
A survey of research among Afro-Americans in the New World with proposals for further work.

GEN
126

Herskovits, Melville J. "Problem, Method and Theory in Afro-American Studies," *Afroamérica* (México), 1 (1945), 5-24. (Reprinted in GEN 120.)
A definition of Afro-American studies with an attempt to show the range of culture change among Negroes in the New World.

GEN
127

Herskovits, Melville J. "Social History of the Negro," in *Handbook of Social Psychology*, Carl Murchison, ed. Worcester, Mass.: Clark University Press, 207-267.
The unity and dissimilarities of New World Negro cultures; customs, practices, etc.

GEN
128

Herskovits, Melville J. "Some Next Steps in the Study of Negro Folklore," *JAF*, 56 (1943), 1-7.
A survey of the state of Afro-American folklore scholarship.

GEN
129

Herskovits, Melville J. "Some Psychological Implications of Afro-American Studies," in *Acculturation in the Americas*. Proceedings of the 29th International Congress of Americanists, Vol 2. Sol Tax, ed. Chicago: University of Chicago Press, 1952, 152-160. (Reprinted in No. GEN 120.)
The interplay of individual psychology and culture illustrated by examples from West Africa and Afro-America.

GEN
130

Herskovits, Melville J. "Wari in the New World," *Journal of the Royal Anthropological Institute*, 62 (1932), 23-38.
An African game found in Surinam, British Guiana, St. Kitts, Barbados, St. Lucia, Grenada, Dominica, Antigua, Martinique, Haiti, and Louisiana; illustrated.

Herskovits, Melville J. See Simpson, George E., No. GEN 239.

Herskovits, Melville J. and Frances S. Herskovits. *Suriname Folklore*. See No. FGS 62.

GEN
131

Higginson, Thomas Wentworth. *Travellers and Outlaws: Episodes in American History*. Boston: 1889. (Abridged version printed as *Black Rebellion*. New York: Arno, 1969.)
Essays on U.S. slave revolts and the Maroons of Surinam and Jamaica.

GEN Howard, Joseph H. *Drums in the Americas*. New York: Oak, 1967.
132   Extensive material on Afro-American drumming--construction, uses,
          rhythms, and social setting; bibliography, illustrated.

GEN Howes, Barbara, ed. *From the Green Antilles: Writings of the Caribbean*.
133   New York: Macmillan, 1966.
          Includes English translations of a short story by Phillippe Thoby-
          Marcelin (Haiti) with folkloric content, and 2 Afro-Cuban folktales
          from Lydia Cabrera's *Cuentos Negros de Cuba*.

GEN Hudson, Randall O. "The Status of the Negro in Northern South America,
134   1820-1860," *JNH*, 49 (1964), 225-239.
          Reference to Negro-Indian restrictions during this period.

GEN Hymes, Dell, ed. *Pidginization and Creolization of Languages*. Cambridge,
135   U.K.: Cambridge University Press, 1971.
          Collection of articles which includes some on Afro-American Creoles.

GEN *Introducción a la Cultura Africana en América Latina*. Paris: UNESCO, 1970.
136   A survey of scholars, libraries, and research institutes concerned with
          blacks in South America and the West Indies; includes an essay on Latin
          American slavery; bibliography.

GEN Jahn, Janheinz. *Muntu: An Outline of the New African Culture*. New York:
137   Grove Press, 1961.
          Traces the spread of African philosophy and aesthetics in Afro-Ameri-
          can areas and their continuity in West Africa. Includes discussion of
          spirituals, blues, dance, *Vodû*, etc., in all the Americas. Bibliography.

GEN Jahn, Janheinz. *Neo-African Literature: A History of Black Writing*. New
138   York: Grove Press, 1968.
          An attempt to relate Afro-American folklore and literature to African
          traditions; discussions on blues, spirituals, calypso, *Vodû*, minstrelsy,
          etc.; bibliography.

GEN Johnston, Harry H. *The Negro in the New World*. London: Methuen, 1910.
139   Early survey of the life and customs of Afro-Americans throughout the
          Americas; illustrated.

GEN King, Bruce. "Introducing the High-Life," *JM,* 12, No. 5 (1966), 3-8.
140   The influence of Afro-American music on West Africa.

GEN Knight, Franklin W., ed. *The African Dimension in Latin American Societies*.
141   New York: Macmillan, 1974.

GEN   Kurath, Gertrude P. "Stylistic Blends of Afro-American Dance Cults of
142   Catholic Origins," *Papers of the Michigan Academy of Science, Arts,
            and Letters*, 48 (1963), 577-584.
            Outline of dance forms in Latin America and the West Indies.

GEN   Landeck, Beatrice. *Echoes of Africa in Folksongs of the Americas*. New
143   York: David McKay, 1961.
            Arrangements of songs from Africa (19), Haiti (8), Louisiana Creole
            (7), Cuba (8), Puerto Rico (4), Mexico (2), Brazil (13), Venezuela
            (2), Panama (3); plus 2 street songs, 7 spirituals and shouts, 6
            worksongs, 9 blues, and 5 minstrel songs from the U.S. and 6 calypsos
            from Trinidad and Jamaica; all largely from printed or recorded sources;
            discography and bibliography.

GEN   Leach, Maria, ed. *Funk and Wagnall's Standard Dictionary of Folklore,
144   Mythology, and Legend*, 2 vols. New York: Funk and Wagnall, 1949, 1950.
            Entries on all aspects of Afro-American expressive culture (including
            names of deities, type of folktales, etc.) for all New World areas.
            Entries were virtually all written by Melville J. Herskovits.

GEN   Leaf, Earl. *Isles of Rhythm*. New York: A.S. Barnes, 1948.
145   A travel-survey of Caribbean dance; illustrated.

GEN   Lekis, Lisa. "Caribbean Festival," record notes to Puerto Rico Visitors
146   Bureau LP record.
            Notes to music from Haiti, Trinidad, Guadeloupe, Antigua, Puerto
            Rico, Surinam, Martinique, and Dutch West Indies; includes an "Anansi"
            song in "*talkie-talkie*."

GEN   Lekis, Lisa. "The Dance as an Expression of Caribbean Folklore," in *The
147   Caribbean: Its Culture*, A. Curtis Wilgus, ed. Gainesville, Fla.: Uni-
            versity of Florida Press, 1955, 43-73.

GEN   Lekis, Lisa. *Dancing Gods*. New York: Scarecrow Press, 1960.
148   Description and setting of the social and religious dances of the Carib-
            bean (British and French).

GEN   Lekis, Lisa. *Folk Dances of Latin America*. New York: Scarecrow Press, 1958.
149   Includes discussion of African-derived dances, by country; bibliography.

GEN   Lekis, Lisa and Walter Lekis. "Caribbean Dances," booklet included with
150   Folkways LP record 840.
            Notes to dances from the Virgin Islands, Dutch Antilles, Martinique,
            Trinidad, Antigua and Guadeloupe.

GEN
151
Leon, Argeliers. "Música Popular de Origen Africano en América Latina," *América Indígena*, 24 (1969), 627-664.
Discusses the songs, music, instruments and dances of African origin in Latin America and the sources of differences in acculturation.

GEN
152
LePage, R.B., ed. *Proceedings of the Conference on Creole Language Studies*. London: Macmillan, 1961.
Includes papers on various aspects of the languages and dialects of the Caribbean area.

GEN
153
Lewis, I.M. *Ecstatic Religion: An Anthropological Study of Spirit Possession and Shamanism*. Harmondsworth, U.K.: Penguin, 1971.
Cross-cultural study with discussion of possessional behavior in Brazil, Haiti and British Guiana.

GEN
154
Lichtveld, Lou. "Enerlei Creools" (Similar Kinds of Creoles), *WIG*, 35 (1954), 59-71.

GEN
155
Lichtveld, Lou. "Op Zoek naar de Spin," *WIG*, 12 (1930), 209-230; 305-324.
Study of the African origins of the tales of the spider.

GEN
156
Little, Kenneth. "The Significance of the West African Creole for the Africanist and Afro-American Studies," *African Affairs*, 49 (1950), 308-319.

GEN
157
Lomax, Alan. *Folk Song Style and Culture*. Washington, D.C.: American Association for the Advancement of Science, 1968.
The correlation of musical and dance styles to cultural and social characteristics. Includes material on Africans and Afro-Americans.

GEN
158
Lomax, Alan. "The Homogeneity of African-Afro-American Musical Style," in *Afro-American Anthropology: Contemporary Perspectives*, Norman E. Whitten, Jr. and John F. Szwed, eds. New York: Free Press, 1970, 165-185.
The close relationship of African and Afro-American music established by an analysis of their characteristics.

GEN
159
Longstreet, Stephen and Alfons M. Dauer. *Knaurs Jazzlexikon*. Munich and Zurich: Knaur, 1957. (Also published as *Encyclopédie du Jazz*. Paris: Somogy-Grundt, 1958.)
Encyclopedia of jazz which includes entries on "Minstrels," "Calypso," etc.

GEN
160
Lord, Priscilla and Daniel J. Foley. *Easter the World Over*. Philadelphia:
Chilton, 1971.
Brief description of carnival in the West Indies and South America;
illustrated, bibliography.

GEN
161
McHardy, Cecile. "The Other America: Some Critical Opinions on the Interpretation of the African Past," *Présence Africaine*, 63 (1967), 187-201.
A general critique of Western approaches to the study of Afro-American
culture; argues for the study of the political functions of religious
and secret societies in Latin America.

GEN
162
McKay, Claude. *Banjo*. New York: Harper, 1929.
Novel of West Indians in France, with folkloric content.

GEN
163
MacLean y Estenas, Roberto. *Negros en el Mundo Nuevo*. Lima: Editorial
PTCM, 1948.
Discusses the slave trade, colonization, and the eventual abolition of
slavery in the New World; songs, poetry, dances, and music of blacks.

GEN
164
McNamara, Rosalind. "Music in the Caribbean," *Caribbean*, 14, No. 3 (1960),
45-50; 14, No. 4 (1960), 69-70, 84-85, 100.
Analysis of the combination of surviving African musical traditions and
outside influences in organizing a specific and distinct folk song
and dance style in each of the Caribbean islands; includes texts;
illustrations.

GEN
165
Made of Iron. Houston, Texas: University of St. Thomas Art Department,
1966.
Includes Virginian, Haitian, and Brazilian art and implements; illustrations.

GEN
166
Maran, R. "Contribution to the Black Race of European Art," *Phylon*, 10
(1949), 240-241.
Discussion of the "vitality" which the Negro brings to European popular
music.

GEN
167
Mathews, J.F. "African Footprints in Hispanic-American Literature," *JNH*,
23 (1938), 265-289.
Includes examples of prose and poetry.

GEN
168
Maynard, Olga. "Apparitions in Dance," *Dance Magazine*, 37 (Oct. 1963),
32-35, 58-59.
The possessional dances of Trinidad, Bahia (Brazil) and those of
Indians in the Amazon Valley are compared and shown to be derived from
common Yoruba (Africa) sources.

GEN   Menkman, W.R. "Nog eens het Eiland der Reuzen" (Once Again in the
169   Island of the Giants), *WIG*, 19 (1937), 85-86.

GEN   Merriam, Alan P. "African Music," in *Continuity and Change in African
170   Cultures*, William R. Bascom and Melville J. Herskovits, eds. Chicago:
            University of Chicago Press, 1959, 49-86.
            Primarily a survey of African music and its characteristics which
            includes cross-references to Afro-American music: hymns in Africa,
            jazz, and Afro-American dances in Africa, etc.

GEN   Milne, Jean. *Fiesta Time in Latin America*. Los Angeles: Ward Ritchie
171   Press, 1965.
            A general work chronologically summarizing the various festivals and
            traditional celebrations of Latin America. Includes some Afro-Ameri-
            can festivals.

GEN   Mintz, Sidney W. "The Caribbean Region," in "Slavery, Colonialism, and
172   Racism," special issue of *Daedalus*, Spring, 1974, 45-71.

GEN   Mintz, Sidney W. "Creating Culture in the Americas," *Columbia Forum* (New
173   York), 13 (1970), 4-11.
            Processes of development of Afro-American cultures; Afro-American
            Studies as an academic discipline.

GEN   Mintz, Sidney W. "The House and the Yard among Three Caribbean Peasan-
174   tries," in *Actes du VIe Congrès International des Sciences Anthropo-
            logiques et Ethnologiques*, Vol. 2, Part 1. Paris: Musée de l'Homme,
            1963, 591-596.
            Domestic, kinship, economic and ritual uses of space in Puerto Rico,
            Haitian and Jamaican homes.

GEN   Mintz, Sidney W. "Melville J. Herskovits and Caribbean Studies: A Retro-
175   spective Tribute," *CS*, 4, No. 2 (1964), 42-51.
            A review of Herskovits' work in developing Afro-American culture studies
            for the Caribbean area.

GEN   Mintz, Sidney W. "Slavery and the Afro-American World," in *Black America*,
176   John F. Szwed, ed. New York: Basic Books, 1970, 29-44.
            Review of the issues in the history of Afro-American slavery in the
            Western world.

GEN   Mintz, Sidney W. "Toward an Afro-American History," *Cahiers d'Histoire
177   Mondiale*, 13 (1971), 317-332.
            Three problems of slaves--resistance, communication and economic self-
            defense--are examined.

Mintz, Sidney W. See Whitten and Szwed, No. GEN 294.

GEN
178
Morse, Jim. *Folk Songs of the Caribbean*. New York: Bantam, 1958.
    Songs in Spanish, French, Creole, etc., with English translations.

GEN
179
Morton, Julia F. "The Calabash (Crescentia cuijete) in Folk Medicine,"
    Economic Botany, 22 (1968), 273-280.
    Afro-American uses of the calabash in the West Indies, Cuba, Brazil,
    Costa Rica, Panama and Florida; names for the calabash in these areas.

GEN
180
Muller, Julius. "Among Caribbean Devils and Duppies," *Century*, 88 (1914),
    446-454.
    Retention of African "*juju*" and "*obi*" mysteries in West Indian culture
    and traditions; the silk-cotton tree as home of *duppies* (devil); tales
    of *loogaroo* (werewolf).

GEN
181
Naipaul, V.S. *The Middle Passage*. London: André Deutsch, 1962.
    Travels in Trinidad, Surinam, British Guiana, Martinique, and Jamaica,
    with emphasis on the social and cultural heritage from slavery and
    colonialism.

GEN
182
Nettl, Bruno. *Folk and Traditional Music of the Western Continents*. Engle-
    wood Cliffs, N.J.: Prentice-Hall, 1965.
    Chapter 9 includes origins of New World Negro styles and instruments
    and discussion of Negro music in Latin America and the U.S.

GEN
183
Nettl, Bruno. *Music in Primitive Culture*. Cambridge, Mass.: Harvard Uni-
    versity Press, 1956.
    A chapter entitled "African and New World Negro Music" is included.

GEN
184
"New Directions in Jazz Research," *Record Changer*, July-August, 1953, 8-22,
    48, 50.
    The minutes of 2 meetings of the Institute of Jazz Studies; suggested
    research on black music in the Americas and Africa; miscellaneous in-
    formation on blues, Haitian music, work songs, etc. Participants in-
    cluded B.A. Botkin, Stanley Diamond, Marshall Stearns, Alan Merriam,
    Lorenzo Turner, Richard Waterman, Monroe Berger, Harold Courlander,
    Curt Sachs, *et al*.

GEN
185
Nketia, J.H. "The Contribution of African Culture to Christian Worship,"
    International Review of Missions, 47 (1958), 265-278.
    Argues for an African interpretation of Christianity in ritual, cere-
    monial, architectural, and musical respects.

GEN
186
Nketia, J.H. "The Study of African and Afro-American Music," *BPM*, 1 (1973), 7-15.
Review and programmatic paper on comparative studies of African and Afro-American music.

GEN
187
Orrego Salas, Juan. "Perceptiva de la Música Africana," *Revista Musical Chilena* (Santiago de Chile), 43 (1952), 7.
Review of the early scholars and published works on African music in the New World.

GEN
188
Ortiz, Fernando. "Los Afrocubanos Dientimellados," *Archivos del Folklore Cubano*, 4, No. 1 (1929), 16-29.
Comparative study of tooth mutilation among Afro-Cubans, Africans, Brazilians, Guianese, etc.

GEN
189
Ortiz, Fernando. "La Habilidad Musical del Negro," *Estudios Afro-cubanos*, 5 (1940-1946), 110-112.
Musical talents shown by blacks in the New World.

GEN
190
Ortiz, Fernando. "Los Negros y la Trasculturación" (Negroes and Transculturation), *Khana, Revista Municipal de Arte y Letras* (Bolivia), March, 1955, 115-118.

GEN
191
Ortiz, Fernando. "La Transculturación de los Tambours de los Negros," *Archivos Venezolanos de Folklore*, 1 (1952), 235-265.
Discussion of drumming and drums in Africa and its diffusion. A few pages on Afro-Cuban drumming.

GEN
192
Oserjeman, Ofuntola. *Orisha: A First Glimpse of the African Religion of Brazil, Cuba, Haiti, Trinidad, and Now USA*. New York: Great Benin Books, n.d.
Booklet with a brief description of the influence of Yoruba religion on the New World; discussion of 11 Orisha and their myths; designed for use in U.S. groups; illustrations.

GEN
193
Palau Marti, Montserrat. "Africa en América a Través de sus Dioses," *Proceedings of the 36th International Congress of Americanists, 1964*, Vol. 3. Seville: 1966, 627-632.
A review of the African sources of a number of Afro-American religions.

GEN
194
Palau Marti, Montserrat. "Noirs d'Amérique et Dieux d'Afrique" (Blacks of America and Gods of Africa), *Revue de l'Histoire des Religions* (Paris), 156 (1959), 189-201.

GEN   Parsons, Elsie Clews. *Folk-Lore of the Antilles, French and English*, 3 vols.
195   Memoirs of the American Folk-Lore Society, 26 (1933, 1936, 1943).
            Vol. 1 includes tale texts from Trinidad, the Grenadines, St. Vincent
            and St. Lucia (in French Creole and English); and, in French Creole
            only, from Martinique and Dominica; Vol. 2 includes tale texts in
            French Creole from Guadeloupe, Les Saints, and Marie Galante; Vol 3
            contains bibliography, summaries of the tales, proverbs, beliefs, rid-
            dles, verse, linguistic notes, and a glossary.

GEN   Parsons, Elsie Clews. "The Provenience of Certain Negro Folk Tales, I,"
196   *Folk-Lore*, 28 (1917), 409-414.
            Discussion of variants of the "Playing Dead Twice in the Road" tale in
            the U.S., the West Indies, Brazil, and Europe; includes 2 texts.

GEN   Parsons, Elsie Clews. "The Provenience of Certain Negro Folk Tales, II,"
197   *Folk-Lore*, 29 (1918), 206-218.
            Discusses variants of the "Pass-word" tale in the U.S., Cape Verde (in
            New England), Africa and the West Indies; includes 3 texts.

GEN   Parsons, Elsie Clews. "The Provenience of Certain Negro Folk Tales, III,"
198   *Folk-Lore*, 30 (1919), 227-234.
            Discussion of variants of the "Tar Baby" tale in the West Indies, the
            U.S., Cape Verde (in New England); includes 3 texts.

GEN   Parsons, Elsie Clews. "The Provenience of Certain Negro Folk Tales, IV,"
199   *Folk-Lore*, 32 (1921), 194-201.
            Discussion of Cape Verdean (in New England), South Carolinian, and West
            Indian variants of the "Missing Tongues" tale; includes 2 texts and
            several fragments.

GEN   Pattee, Richard. "La América Latina Presta Atención al Negro" (Latin America
200   Pays Attention to the Negro), *Revista Bimestre Cubana* (Havana), 38 (1936),
            17-23.

GEN   Pearse, Andrew. "Caribbean Folk Culture," *Caribbean*, 9 (1955), 62-65.
201   Review of the variety of folk cultures in the West Indies.

GEN   Pearse, Andrew. "Ethnography and the Lay Scholar in the Caribbean," *WIG*,
202   36 (1956), 133-146.

GEN   Pereda Valdés, Ildefonso. *Línea de Color*. Santiago de Chile: Ercilla, 1938.
203   A series of essays on black traditions and culture in the U.S. and Latin
            America; includes articles on black music and dance, songs, verse, festi-
            vals, and musical instruments. Includes material on Uruguay and Brazil.

GEN
204
Pereda Valdés, Ildefonso. "La Madre Negra," *Afroamérica* (México), 1 (1945), 63-65.
Discusses the part played by the Negro mother in South America, showing her great influence in maintaining cultural tradition in beliefs, customs, cradle songs and other folklore.

GEN
205
Pereda Valdés, Ildefonso. "El Negro en la Literatura Ibero-américana," *Cuadernos*, July-August, 1956, 104-110.
Analysis of African elements of onomatopoeia and rhyme present in New World black poetry.

GEN
206
Pereda Valdés, Ildefonso. *El Rancho y Otros Temas de Etnografía y Folklore*. Montevideo: Livraria Anticuaria Américana, 1957.
Ethnographic and folkloric essay on various aspects of folklife, especially Indian and African elements in the New World. The section entitled "Temas Afro-Américanos" contains a discussion of Afro-American cuisine mainly in Brazil and Cuba. Also discusses Negro music in the U.S.

GEN
207
Pérez de la Riva, Juan. "El Negro, Elemento Esencial en la Navegación Atlántica en los Siglos XVII y XVIII" (The Negro, Essential Element in Atlantic Navigation in the 17th and 18th Centuries), *Ultra*, 14, No. 89 (1944), 50-52.

GEN
208
Pollak-Eltz, Angelina. *Afro-Amerikaanse Godsdiensten en Culten*. Roermond, Holland: J.J. Romen, 1970. (Also published as *Cultos Afroaméricanos*. Caracas: Universidad Católica "Andrés Bello," Facultad de Humanidades y Educación, Instituto de Investigaciones Históricas, 1972.)
Includes a discussion of Shango in Trinidad; Afro-American religions in Brazil, Trinidad, Grenada, Jamaica, St. Vincent, Haiti, Cuba, Venezuela, Surinam, and North America: *Candomblé, Xango, Umbanda, Shango,* Shouter Baptists, *Myalism, obeah, convince, Vodû, Santería, Maria-Lionza,* etc.; religions in West Africa.

GEN
209
Pollak-Eltz, Angelina. *El Concepto de Múltiples Almas y Algunos Ritos Fúnebres entre los Negros Américanos*. Caracas: Universidad Católica "Andrés Bello," Instituto de Investigaciones Históricas, 1974.

GEN
210
Pollak-Eltz, Angelina. "El Culto de los Gemelos en Africa Occidental y en las Américas," *América Latina*, 12, No. 2 (1969), 66-78.
A review of reports of West African cults of twins and associated rituals from Haiti, Brazil, the U.S., Cuba, Trinidad and Venezuela.

GEN
211
Pollak-Eltz, Angelina. "Las Culturas Negras en las Américas," *Eco*, 15 (1967), 430-452.
Aspects of African influences and acculturative processes in the Americas.

GEN   Pollak-Eltz, Angelina. "Kulturwandel bei Negern der Neuen Welt," *Umschau*
212   *in Wissenschaft und Technik* (Frankfurt), No. 19 (1967), 623-626.
            Review of acculturation among Afro-Americans throughout the New
            World.

GEN   Pollak-Eltz, Angelina. "Panorama de Estudios Afroamericanos," *Montalbán*
213   (Caracas), No. 1 (1972), 259-317.
            An overview of Afro-American studies, with emphasis on Latin America;
            bibliography.

GEN   Pollak-Eltz, Angelina. "Religiones Africanas en las Américas," *Boletín*
214   *de la Asociación Cultural Humboldt*, No. 4 (1968), 51-65.
            A review of African influences on New World Negro religious groups;
            illustrations.

GEN   Pollak-Eltz, Angelina. "Woher Stammen die Neger Südamerikas?" *Umschau in*
215   *Wissenschaft und Technik* (Frankfurt), No. 8 (1967), 244-249.
            The African sources of South American Negroes; illustrations.

GEN   Pollak-Eltz, Angelina. "Zwillingskulte in Westafrika und in Amerika"
216   (Twin Cultures in West Africa and in America), *Mitteilungen der*
            Anthropologischen Gesellschaft in Wien, 99 (1969), 101-110.

GEN   Price, Richard, ed. *Maroon Societies*. Garden City, N.Y.: Doubleday, 1973.
217   Essays on escaped slave communities throughout the New World.

GEN   Price-Mars, Jean. "Survivances Africaines et Dynamisme de la Culture
218   Noire Outre-Atlantique," *Présence Africaine*, No. 8, 9, 10 (1956),
            272-280.
            Linguistic, religious and other forms of African cultural survivals
            in the countries of the Americas.

        Quirino dos Santos, Benedicta. "Haiti Sings." See No. HA 305.

GEN   Ramos, Arthur. *As Culturas Negras no Novo Mundo*. Rio de Janeiro:
219   Civilização Brasileira, 1937.
            General work on African cultures in the New World, but with emphasis
            on Brazil and the Antilles; illustrations.

GEN   Rhodes, Willard. "La Musique Noire dans le Nouveau Monde?" *La Musique dans*
220   *la Vie* (Paris), 2 (1969), 24-41.
            An overview of black music in the Americas, its influences, styles
            and developments.

GEN
221
Rickford, John. "The Insights of the Mesolect," in *Pidgins and Creoles: Current Trends and Prospects*. David DeCamp and Ian F. Hancock, eds. Washington, D.C.: Georgetown University Press, 1974, pp. 92-117.

GEN
222
Roberts, John Storm. *Black Music of Two Worlds*. New York: Praeger, 1972.
A survey of black music and dance forms in the New World; mumming and mime; African influences and Afro-America; Afro-American influence on African music. Illustrations, bibliography, discography.

GEN
223
Robeson, Paul. "The Culture of the Negro," *Spectator*, 152 (June 15, 1934), 916-917.
Argues for the cultural (linguistic, musical and religious) unity of Africans and Afro-Americans in North and South America.

GEN
224
Rodney, Walter and Earl Augustus. "The Negro Slave," *CQ*, 10, No. 2 (1964), 40-47.
Criticism of historical writing on slaves and their culture.

GEN
225
Rogers, J.A. *Nature Knows No Color-Line: Research into the Negro Ancestry in the White Race*. New York: Helga M. Rogers, 1952.
Includes West Indian and North American Negro folk artists, performers, etc. in Europe.

GEN
226
Romero, Fernando. "El Negro en Tierra Firme en el Siglo 16," *Lotería* (Panamá), February, 1956, 47-68.
Historical and sociological description of blacks and their contribution to the New World of the 16th century.

GEN
227
Rosa-Nieves, Cesáreo. *Diapasón Negro* (Negro Musicality). Barcelona: Impreso Rumbos, 1961.

GEN
228
Rosenblatt, Angel. "Un Presunto Africanismo: Macandá, Brujería," in *Miscelánea de Estudios Dedicados a Fernando Ortiz*, Vol. 2. Havana: Sociedad Económica de Amigos del País, 1956, 1289-1296.
Traces the African sources of the Latin American word *macandá*.

GEN
229
Rubin, Vera, ed. "Social and Cultural Pluralism in the Caribbean," *Annals of the New York Academy of Sciences*, 83 (1960), 761-916.
Essays on cultural pluralism and metropolitan influence in the Caribbean.

GEN
230
Sachs, Curt. *World History of the Dance*. New York: Norton, 1937.
Historical treatment of dancing.

GEN   Saco, José Antonio. *Historia de la Esclavitud de la Raza Africana en*
231   *el Nuevo Mundo y en Especial es los Páises Américo-Hispánicos*, 4 vols.
           Havana: Cultural, S.A., 1938.
           Historical work on black slavery in the Spanish-speaking republics of
           the New World; some references to African cultural survivals.

GEN   Sanz y Diaz, José. *Lira Negra (Selecciones Españolas y Afroamericanas)*
232   (Negro Song (Spanish and Afro-American Selections)). Madrid: M.
           Aguilar, 1945.

GEN   Sargent, William. "Witch Doctoring, Zen and Voodoo: Their Relation to
233   Modern Psychiatric Treatments," *Proceedings of the Royal Society of*
           Medicine, 60 (1967), 1055-1060.
           The psychiatric benefits of "voodoo" in Haiti and Brazil.

GEN   Schaeffner, André. "Notes sur la Musique des Afro-Américains," *Menestral*
234   (Paris), 88 (1926), 285-287, 297-300, 309-312, 321-323, 337-339,
           345-347.
           Review of the data on the relation between the music of West Africans
           and that of the Negroes of the Americas.

GEN   Schuler, Monica. "Ethnic Slave Rebellions in the Caribbean and the
235   Guianas," *Journal of Social History*, 3 (1970), 374-385.

GEN   Schurz, William Lytle. *This New World: The Civilization of Latin America*.
236   New York: Dutton, 1954.
           Chapter 5, "The Negro," discusses the influence of Negro culture and
           society in Haiti, Brazil, and elsewhere in Latin America; bibliography.

GEN   Simpson, George E. "Afro-American Religions and Religious Behavior," *CS*,
237   12, No. 2 (1972), 5-30.
           Cultural, sociological and psychological viewpoints on the subject;
           data from several Caribbean and South American countries, West Africa,
           and the U.S.

GEN   Simpson, George E. *Caribbean Papers*. Cuernavaca, México: Centro Inter-
238   cultural de Documentación, 1970.
           Essays on Caribbean religion, folklore, medicine, etc.

GEN   Simpson, George E. *Melville J. Herskovits*. New York: Columbia University
239   Press, 1973.
           Biography includes a review of Herskovits' writings on Negro cultures
           in a variety of countries and settings.

GEN
240
Simpson, George E. *Religious Cults of the Caribbean: Trinidad, Jamaica, and Haiti*. Río Piedras, Puerto Rico: Institute of Caribbean Studies, 1970. (Revised and enlarged version of *The Shango Cult in Trinidad*. Rio Piedras, Puerto Rico: Institute of Caribbean Studies, 1965.) Essays on Caribbean cults plus papers on Yoruba rituals in Nigeria and on the relationship of Haitian *Vodû* to Christianity. Illustrations, bibliography.

GEN
241
Simpson, George E. and Peter B. Hammond. "Discussion of M.G. Smith's 'The African Heritage in the Caribbean,'" in *Caribbean Studies: A Symposium*, Vera Rubin, ed. Seattle: University of Washington Press, 1957, 46-53.
Argues for the "Africanisms" or survivals approach to Afro-American culture; forcuses on spirit possession. See M.G. Smith, No. GEN 244.

GEN
242
Slonimsky, Nicolas. *Music of Latin America*. New York: Thomas Crowell, 1945.
Includes a discussion of African elements in the music of Brazil, Colombia, Cuba, Dominican Republic, Haiti, Panama, Uruguay and Venezuela.

GEN
243
Smith, Edna M. "Popular Music in West Africa," *African Music*, 3, No. 1 (1962), 11-17.
Description of the high-life dance, calypso, West African jazz--forms influenced by New World Negro music and dance.

GEN
244
Smith, M.G. "The African Heritage in the Caribbean," in *Caribbean Studies: A Symposium*, Vera Rubin, ed. Seattle: University of Washington Press, 1957, 34-46.
A critique of the "Africanisms" approach in the study of Afro-American culture. (For a response, see Simpson and Hammond, No. GEN 241.)

GEN
245
Smith, M.G. "A Framework for Caribbean Studies," in *The Plural Society in the British West Indies*. Berkeley and Los Angeles: University of California Press, 1965, 18-74.
In the context of a criticism of the work of Melville J. Herskovits and others, Smith makes suggestions for means of understanding Afro-American culture.

GEN
246
Stevenson, Robert. "The Afro-American Musical Legacy to 1800," *MQ*, 54 (1968), 475-502.
Evidence for the presence and variety of Afro-American music in North and South America before 1800.

GEN
247
Stevenson, Robert, "The Negro in Latin American Music to 1800," *Noticiero*, No. 3 (June, 1968), 2-3.

GEN Stewart, T.D. and John R. Groome. "The African Custom of Tooth Mutila-
248   tion in America," *American Journal of Physical Anthropology*, 28
         (1969), 31-42.
         Discussion of the African sources of tooth mutilation in America;
         indicates the lack of study of New World practices; an example
         from Grenada, West Indies is discussed.

GEN Stewart, William A. "Creole Languages in the Caribbean," in *Study of
249   the Role of Second Languages in Asia, Africa and Latin America*,
         Frank A. Rice, ed. Washington, D.C.: Center for Applied Linguistics,
         1962, 34-53.

     Szwed, John F. "Discovering Afro-America." See No. NA 2933.

     Szwed, John F. "Musical Adaptation among Afro-Americans." See No. NA 2934.

GEN Talbot, George A. "Pictorial Essay," in *Afro-American Anthropology: Con-
250   temporary Perspectives*, Norman E. Whitten, Jr. and John F. Szwed, eds.
         New York: Free Press, 1970, 22ff.
         32 pages of photographs of Afro-Americans illustrating music, rituals,
         dance, etc., in most of the countries of the New World.

GEN Tannenbaum, Frank. *Slave and Citizen*. New York: Knopf, 1946.
251   An historical account of the treatment of slaves throughout the
         Americas.

GEN Taylor, Douglas, "Carib, Caliban, Cannibal," *IJAL*, 24 (1958), 156-157.
252

GEN Taylor, Douglas, "Certain Carib Morphological Influences on Creole,"
253   *IJAL*, 11 (1945), 140-155.

GEN Taylor, Douglas. "Language Contact in the West Indies: On the Classifica-
254   tion of Creolized Languages," *Word*, 12 (1956), 407-414.
         Includes a comparison of West Indian and West African languages.

GEN Taylor, Douglas. "New Language from Old in the West Indies," *Comparative
255   Studies in Society and History*, 3 (1961), 277-288.
         Discusses the development of pidgins and creoles in the Caribbean.

GEN
256

Taylor, Douglas. "On Function vs. Form in 'Non-Traditional' Languages," *Word*, 15 (1959), 485-488.

GEN
257

Taylor, Douglas. "The Origin of West Indian Creole Languages: Evidence from Grammatical Categories," *AA*, 65 (1963), 800-814.
West Indian Creoles as derived from African languages.

GEN
258

Taylor, Douglas. "Phonemes of Caribbean Creole," *Word*, 3 (1947), 173-179.

GEN
259

Taylor, Douglas. "Review of Marius Valkhoff, *Studies in Portuguese and Creole*," *Language*, 44 (1966), 3, 654-658.

GEN
260

Taylor, Douglas. "Structural Outline of Caribbean Creole," *Word*, 7, No. 1 (1951), 43-59.
A discussion of the syntax of Creoles.

GEN
261

Taylor, Douglas. "Use and Disuse of Languages in the West Indies," *CQ*, 5, No. 2 (1958), 67-77.
Overview of the variety of Creoles in the West Indies.

GEN
262

Thompson, Donald. "Poor Man's Bass Fiddle," *Caribbean Review* (San Juan), 3, No. 1 (1971), 11-12.
The *marímbula* (plucked idiophone) in the music of various Caribbean peoples.

GEN
263

Thompson, Robert Farris. "An Aesthetic of the Cool," *African Arts* (Los Angeles), 7, No. 1 (1973), 40-43, 64-67, 84-91.
An elaborated version of No. GEN 264 with additional historical material on African sources.

GEN
264

Thompson, Robert Farris. "An Aesthetic of the Cool: West African Dance," *African Forum*, 2, No. 2 (1966), 85-102.
The aesthetics of balance and symmetry in West African and West African-derived dance in Cuba, Puerto Rico and the U.S. (tap dance, *mambo*, *rhumba*, etc.).

GEN
265

Thompson, Robert Farris. *African Art in Motion: The Catherine White Collection of African Sculpture*. Los Angeles: U.C.L.A. Art Gallery, 1974.
Norms of dance performance and their interrelationship with music and the plastic arts in a variety of African and Afro-American settings; illustrations, bibliography.

GEN   Thompson, Robert Farris. "African Dancers at the Fair," *Saturday Review*,
266   July 25, 1964, 37-39.
            The characteristics of African dance; includes discussion of dancing
            in Haiti, Brazil and New York City; illustrations.

GEN   Thompson, Robert Farris. *Black Gods and Kings: Yoruba Art at U.C.L.A.*
267   Occasional Papers of the Museum and Laboratories of Ethnic Arts and
            Technology, University of California, Los Angeles, No. 2, 1971.
            Includes discussion of Yoruba-derived art, dress, and material cul-
            ture in Cuba, Brazil, and New York City; illustrations.

GEN   Thompson, Robert Farris. "From Africa," *Yale Alumni Magazine*, 34 (Novem-
268   ber, 1970), 16-21.
            African influences on the art of Brazil, Cuba and South Carolina.

GEN   Thompson, Robert Farris. "Highlife in Nigeria," *Saturday Review*, 44, No.
269   34 (August 26, 1961), 34-35.
            Music in modern Nigeria in which Western jazz influences are common.

        Thompson, Robert Farris. "Palladium Mambo-1, Ballroom U.S.A." See No.
            NA 2986.

GEN   Thompson, Robert Farris. "The Sign of the Divine King: An Essay on Yoruba
270   Bead-Embroidered Crowns with Veil and Bird Decorations," *African Arts*
            (Los Angeles), 3, No. 3 (1970), 8-17, 74-80.
            Includes discussion of signs of kingship among Yoruba descendants in
            Cuba and Brazil.

GEN   Thompson, Robert Wallace. "Creoles and Pidgins, East and West," *New World
271   Quarterly*, 2, No. 4 (1966), 11-16.
            Overview of Afro-American languages, contrasting the process of their
            development with those of other parts of the world.

GEN   Thompson, Robert Wallace. "Duckanoo--A Word and a Thing," *Caribbean*, 9
272   (1956), 218-219, 229.
            Distribution of a West African-derived word for an item of food in the
            West Indies; names for cooperative work groups.

GEN   Thompson, Robert Wallace. "The Mushroom and the Parasol: A West Indian
273   Riddle," *WIG*, 35-36 (1955), 162-164.

GEN
274
Thompson, Robert Wallace. "Mushrooms, Umbrellas, and Black Magic: A West
Indian Linguistic Problem," *AS*, 33 (1958), 170-175.
The names for mushrooms in all of the islands of the West Indies con-
nect them to umbrellas and the supernatural, and seem to be African
in origin.

GEN
275
Turner, Lorenzo D. "African Survivals in the New World with Special Emphasis on the Arts," in *Africa Seen by American Negroes*, John A. Davis,
ed. Paris: *Présence Africaine*, 1958, 101-116.
Review of "Africanisms" found in the languages, folk literature, religion, art, music, names and dances of Afro-Americans in various
countries.

GEN
276
Turner, Lorenzo D. "Linguistic Research and African Survivals," in *The
Interdisciplinary Aspects of Negro Studies*, Melville J. Herskovits,
ed. American Council of Learned Societies Bulletin No. 32, 1941,
68-89.
A review of studies of Negro dialects in various New World countries;
problems of studying their African sources and parallels.

GEN
277
Twining, Mary A. "Shared Images in Yoruba and Afro-American Folklore; An
Open Question for Further Research," *Folklore Forum*, Bibliographic and
Special Series, No. 4, 1973, 53-62.
Common motifs in African and Afro-American folktales and drama.

GEN
278
Utley, Francis Lee. "The Migration of Folktales: Four Channels to the
Americas," *Current Anthropology* (Chicago), 15, No. 1 (1974), 5-27.
Includes discussion of African influences on North and South American
folktales.

GEN
279
Uya, Okon E. "The Culture of Slavery: Black Experience through a White
Filter," *Black Lines* (Pittsburgh), 1, No. 2 (1970), 27-33.
Critical survey of the scholarship on slave life in the Americas.

GEN
280
Vajro, Massimiliano. "La Musica Negro e gli studii di Afroamericanista,"
Revista de Etnografia (Naples), 3 (1949), 88-95.
Survey of research on Afro-American music.

GEN
281
Valldejuli, Carmen Aboy. *The Art of Caribbean Cookery*. Garden City, N.Y.:
Doubleday, 1963.

GEN
282
Van Dam, Theodore. "The Influences of the West African Songs of Derision in
the New World," *Record Changer*, April, 1954, 7, 21; May, 1954, 4, 16.
(Reprinted in *African Music* 1954, 53-56.)
Musical influence in the calypso of Trinidad, Jamaica and Barbados;

songs of the Virgin Islands, Antigua, Haiti and Puerto Rico. The
spread and influence of calypso; discography.

GEN
283

Vansertima, Ivan. "African Linguistic and Mythological Structures in
the New World," in *Black Life and Culture in the United States*, Rhoda
L. Goldstein, ed. New York: Thomas Crowell, 1971, 12-35.
A survey of black speech and folktales in the Americas.

GEN
284

"Vaudoux and Voodoo," *Saturday Review* (London), 59 (March 28, 1885),
408-409.
Accounts of "voodoo" practice from blacks in Philadelphia, New York,
South Carolina, Haiti, Guiana and Guinea. Emphasis on African sources,
language survivals.

GEN
285

Verger, Pierre. "Oral Tradition in the Cult of the Orishas and Its Connection with the History of the Yoruba," *Journal of the Historical
Society of Nigeria*, 1, No. 1 (1956), 61-63.

GEN
286

Wagner, Max Leopold. *Lingua e Dialetti dell'America Spagnola* (Language
and Dialect in Spanish America). Florence: G.B. Vica, 1949.

GEN
287

Walker, Sheila S. *Ceremonial Spirit Possession in Africa and Afro-America*.
New York: Humanities Press, 1972.

GEN
288

Waterman, Richard A. "African Influence on the Music of the Americas," in
Acculturation in the Americas. Proceedings and Selected Papers of the
29th International Congress of Americanists, Vol. 2, Sol Tax, ed. Chicago: University of Chicago Press, 1952, 207-218.
African musical elements--percussion, polymeter, overlapping, off-beat
phrasing--and their distribution in Protestant and Catholic areas of
the Americas.

GEN
289

Waterman, Richard A. "'Hot' Rhythm in Negro Music," *Journal of the American
Musicological Society*, 1 (1948), 24-37.
Characterizes African rhythmic style (polyrhythm) and its spread to the
New World; includes songs from Trinidad.

GEN
290

Waterman, Richard A. "On Flogging a Dead Horse: Lessons Learned from the
Africanisms Controversy," *EM*, 7 (1963), 83-87.
Waterman suggests that in order to understand the derivation of Afro-
American music, scholars must get relevant facts, discard unexamined
assumptions, and must deal with music with reference to the dynamics
of culture in general.

GEN
291
Waterman, Richard A. and William R. Bascom. "African and New World Negro Folklore," *Funk and Wagnall's Standard Dictionary of Folklore, Mythology, and Legend*, Vol. 2, Maria Leach, ed. New York: Funk and Wagnall, 1949, 18-24.
Survey of proverbs, riddles, verbal formulae, praise names, songs, folktales, trickster figures, and explanatory elements in African and Afro-American cultures.

GEN
292
Webb, Julie Yvonne. *Love Charms--Worldwide*. New Orleans: Hope, 1973.
Includes charms and recipes from New Orleans practitioners, as well as those reprinted from a variety of other New World sources.

GEN
293
Wesley, Charles H. *The Negro in the Americas*. Washington, D.C.: Howard University, 1940.

GEN
294
Whitten, Norman E., Jr. and John F. Szwed, eds. *Afro-American Anthropology: Contemporary Perspectives*. New York: Free Press, 1970.
Collection of papers on Afro-American cultures and societies; "Foreword" (by Sidney W. Mintz) and "Introduction" (by Whitten and Szwed) review the history of Afro-American anthropology, folklore and linguistics. Illustrations, bibliography.

GEN
295
Whitten, Norman E., Jr. and John F. Szwed. "Anthropologists Look at Afro-Americans," *Trans-action*, 5, No. 8 (1968), 49-56.
A survey of anthropological contributions to Afro-American studies. (An abbreviated version of the Introduction to No. GEN 294.)

GEN
296
Wiener, Leo. *Africa and the Discovery of America*, 3 vols. Philadelphia: Innes, 1920-1922.
Volume 1 includes discussion of African influences on Amer-Indian languages, etc.; Vol. 3 discusses the Caribs, Mandingo elements in Mexico, etc.

Willeford, Mary Jo. "Negro New World Religions and Witchcraft." See No. EWI 721.

GEN
297
Wolfe, Linda and the Editors of Time-Life Books. *The Cooking of the Caribbean Islands*. New York: Time-Life Books, 1970.
Travel-cookbook contains accounts of Caribbean crops, fishing techniques, foods and the "Creolization" of Amer-indian, African, East Indian and European cuisine; recipes, illustrations of foods and buildings; glossary.

GEN   Woodbridge, Hensley C. "Glossary of Names Used in Colonial Latin America
298   for Crosses among Indians, Negroes, and Whites," *Journal of the Wash-*
             ington Academy of Sciences (Washington, D.C.), March, 1948, 353-362.

GEN   Wuthenau, Alexander von. *The Art of Terracotta Pottery in Pre-Colombian*
299   *Central and South America*. New York: Crown, 1970.
             Contains material on African influences in Pre-Colombian pottery.

GEN   Zelinsky, Wilbur. "The Historical Geography of the Negro Population of
300   Latin America," *JNH*, 34, No. 2 (1949), 153-221.
             An attempt to map the distribution of the black population of Latin
             America at various historical points.

NORTH AMERICA

[See also GEN 31, 40, 42, 48, 52, 59,
60, 80, 90, 91, 92, 93, 94, 96, 115,
124, 130, 137, 138, 139, 143, 159, 165,
179, 184, 192, 197, 198, 199, 203, 206,
208, 237, 264, 266, 267, 268, 269, 275,
276, 284.]

NA
1
Abbot, Ernest H. "Religious Tendencies of the Negro," *Outlook*, 69 (1901),
1070-1076.
Discussion includes short accounts of religious services.

NA
2
Abbot, Francis H. *Eight Negro Songs from Bedford County*. Alfred J. Swan,
ed. New York: Enoch, 1924.
8 dialect songs.

Abrahams, Roger D. "Black Culture in the Classroom." See Gay, Geneva,
No. NA 1102.

NA
3
Abrahams, Roger D. "The 'Catch' in Negro Philadelphia," *KFQ*, 8 (1963),
107-111.
Children's verbal tricks, with texts of "catch" routines.

NA
4
Abrahams, Roger D. "The Changing Concept of the Negro Hero," *PTFS*, No. 31
(1962), 119-134.
Discussion of the shift of emphasis in Negro folklore from the trickster (who gives psychological satisfaction by outwitting) to the "badman hero" (who is admired because of his will, strength and ability to
defeat his rivals); includes texts, largely from South Philadelphia.

NA
5
Abrahams, Roger D. *Deep Down in the Jungle; Negro Narrative Folklore from
the Streets of Philadelphia*. Hatboro, Pa.: Folklore Associates, 1964.
(Revised edition, Chicago: Aldine, 1970.)

NA
6

Abrahams, Roger D. "Folk Beliefs in Southern Joke Books," *WF*, 23 (1964), 259-261.
  44 items.

Abrahams, Roger D. "Foreword," in *The Negro and His Songs*. See Odum, Howard W. and Guy B. Johnson, No. NA 2253.

Abrahams, Roger D. "Foreword," in *On the Trail of Negro Folksong*. See Scarborough, Dorothy, No. NA 2655.

Abrahams, Roger D. "Joking: The Training of the Man of Words in Talking Broad." See No. EWI 8.

Abrahams, Roger D. *Jump Rope Rhymes: A Dictionary*. See No. EWI 9.

NA
7

Abrahams, Roger D. "The Negro Stereotype, Negro Folklore and the Riots," *JAF*, 83 (1970), 228-249.
  Essay on the possible performative relationships between black badman stories and participants in the riots of the 1960's; explores the importance of the white stereotype of blacks on the development of the badman tradition.

NA
8

Abrahams, Roger D. "Playing the Dozens," *JAF*, 75 (1962), 209-219.
  Descriptive analysis of a verbal argument game and texts of 30 rhymes and 12 replies.

NA
9

Abrahams, Roger D. "Rapping and Capping: Black Talk as Art," in *Black America*, John F. Szwed, ed. New York: Basic Books, 1970, 132-142.
  Black speaking style and vocabulary in the U.S.

NA
10

Abrahams, Roger D. "Some Jump-Rope Rhymes from South Philadelphia," *KFQ*, 8 (1963), 3-15.
  25 jump-rope rhymes from Negro children with a description of the game types.

Abrahams, Roger D. "Some Plantation Remedies and Recipes." See Gracy, David B., No. NA 1176.

NA
11

Abrahams, Roger D. "Some Riddles from the Negro of Philadelphia," *KFQ*, 7, No. 4 (1962), 10-17.
  58 texts.

NA
12
Abrahams, Roger D. "Some Varieties of Heroes in America," *JFI*, 3 (1967), 341-362.
Includes a survey of Negro trickster and badman hero types.

NA
13
Abrahams, Roger D. "There's a Black Girl in the Ring," in *Two Penny Ballads and Four Dollar Whiskey,* Kenneth S. Goldstein and Robert H. Byington, eds. Hatboro, Pa.: Folklore Associates, 1966, 121-135.
Singing games in Philadelphia; includes music, words, and descriptions of 8 games.

NA
14
Abrahams, Roger D. "The Toast," in *Folklore in Action, Essays for Discussion in Honor of MacEdward Leach*, Horace P. Beck, ed. Hatboro, Pa.: Folklore Associates, 1962.
A description of a short epic form of rhymed narrative. Examples given from South Philadelphia performers.

NA
15
Abrahams, Roger D. "Toward a Black Rhetoric: Being a Survey of Afro-American Communication Styles and Role Relationships," *Texas Working Papers in Sociolinguistics*, No. 15, Austin, Texas, 1973.
Surveys the popular literature and folklore; studies the range of speaking relationships and their associated lore and language.

NA
16
Abrahams, Roger D. "Trickster, the Outrageous Hero," in *Our Living Traditions*, Tristram P. Coffin, ed. New York: Basic Books, 1968, 170-178.
Includes a section on black heroes.

Abrahams, Roger D. See Mintz, Sidney W. No. NA 2076.

NA
17
Abrahams, Roger D. and Geneva Gay. "Talking Black in the Classroom," in *Language and Cultural Diversity in American Education*, Roger D. Abrahams and Rudolphe C. Troike, eds. Englewood Cliffs: Prentice-Hall, 1972, 200-207.
Black speech genres and their importance in education.

NA
18
Abrahams, Roger D. and John F. Szwed, eds. *Discovering Afro-America.* Leiden: E.J. Brill, 1975.
Essays on various aspects of black culture and society.

NA
19
Achille, Louis T. "Chanter avec Dieu, Danser avec Lui," *Présence Africaine* (Paris), 54 (1965), 127-136.
A commentary on spirituals.

NA
20
Achille, Louis T. "Les Negro Spirituals," *Le Monde Réligieux*, 28 (1960-1961), 526-532.

NA
21
Achille, Louis T. "Die 'Negro Spirituals' als Geistliche Volkmusik," *Musik und Altar*, 2, No. 2 (1958), 64-70.

NA
22
Achille, Louis T. "Les Negro-spirituals et l'Expansion de la Culture Noire," *Présence Africaine*. No. 8, 9, 10 (1956), 227-237.
The endurance and spread of the spiritual in the United States, Europe, and Africa.

NA
23
Adams, Charles G. "Some Aspects of Black Worship," *Andover-Newton Quarterly*, 11 (1971), 124-138.

NA
24
Adams, Edward C.L. "Carolina Folklore; Spirituals in the Making," *Charleston Museum Quarterly*, 1, No. 2 (1925), 18-24.
Article in drama form with spiritual fragments.

NA
25
Adams, Edward, C.L. *Congaree Sketches. Scenes from Negro Life in the Swamps of the Congaree and Tales by Tad and Scip of Heaven and Hell with Other Miscellany*. Chapel Hill: The University of North Carolina Press, 1927.
54 tales of life in the Congaree area of South Carolina, including religious tales, ghost tales, animal tales, sermons, etc.

NA
26
Adams, Edward, C.L. *Nigger to Nigger*. New York: Scribner's, 1928.
Includes 27 South Carolina Negro conversations, 7 tales of the swamps, 18 of white folks, 5 of ghosts and angels, 12 of Brer Rabbit, 9 of preachers, 5 of slavery, and 10 of funerals. Most are written as dialogues; glossary.

NA
27
Adams, Edward, C.L. "A South Carolina Folksong," *SW*, 54 (1925), 568.
Song fragment from a funeral sermon by a plantation slave.

NA
28
Adams, George C.S. "Rattlesnake Eye," *SFQ*, 2 (1938), 37-38.
1 tale from South Carolina.

NA
29
Adams, Nehemiah. *A Southside View of Slavery: or, Three Months at the South, in 1854*. Boston: T. R. Marvin, 1854.
Accounts of slave religion, sermons, recreation, dress, music, etc.

NA
30
Adams, Samuel C., Jr. "The Acculturation of the Delta Negro," *Social Forces*, 26 (1947), 202-205. (Reprinted in Dundes, No. NA 854.)
Changes in traditional music and religion; includes texts.

NA
31
Adams, Samuel Hopkins. "Dr. Bug, Dr. Buzzard and the U.S.A.," *True*, July, 1949, 33, 69-71.
Beaufort, South Carolina hoodoo doctors' attempts to aid patients to escape the military draft.

NA
32
Adins, George. "Sleepy John Estes," *JJ*, 16, No. 8 (1963), 8-11.
The life and recordings of a Tennessee blues singer.

NA
33
Adler, Thomas. "The Physical Development of the Banjo," *NYFQ*, 28 (1972), 187-208.
The evolution of banjo-making.

NA
34
Agar, Michael H. "Folklore of the Heroin Addict: Two Examples," *JAF*, 84 (1971), 175-185.
Toasts as recited and interpreted by black and white addicts in a federal clinic; includes 2 texts.

NA
35
Agar, Michael H. *Ripping and Running: A Formal Ethnography of Urban Heroin Addicts*. New York: Seminar Press, 1973.
Includes a glossary and an analysis of slang terms.

NA
36
Agee, G.W. *Alabama--A Guide to the Deep South*. New York: Alabama Writers' Program, 1941.
Includes a review of Negro folk culture in Alabama.

NA
37
Aimes, Hubert H.S. "African Institutions in America," *JAF*, 18 (1905), 15-32.
The author discusses the customs, holidays, elections of "governor," and the election parade and ball which were practiced by slaves brought from Africa.

NA
38
"Alabama Folklore," *SW*, 32 (1904), 49-52.
3 Brer Rabbit tales, signs and proverbs from Calhoun, Alabama.

NA
39
Albertson, Chris. *Bessie*. New York: Stein and Day, 1972.
Biography of a blues singer, Bessie Smith, which contradicts some earlier biographies; illustrations.

NA
40
Alderham, Joseph. "Story of an Old-Timer," *Dance Magazine*, 36 (September, 1962), 5-52.
Influence of black minstrel dance on the development of eccentric dance and vaudeville.

NA
41
Aletti, Vince. "Music: Some Like It Hot," *New York*, 5, No. 32 (1972), 37, 40.
Brief history of Cuban and Puerto Rican music in New York City; the chief musical figures in the 1970's.

NA
42
Alexander, Hartley Burr. "North American," in *The Mythology of All Races*, Vol. 10, Louis Herbert Gray, ed. New York: Cooper Square, 1964, 67-69.
Reference to J.C. Harris' Brer Rabbit stories, giving origin of the cycle as Cherokee.

NA
43
Alexander, John Breward. *Reminiscences of the Past 60 Years*. Charlotte, N.C.: Ray Printing Company, 1908.
Descriptions of life and customs in the plantation era, including descriptions of black singing and attendance at church, slave marriages, travelling circuses, barbecues, sewing frolics, Christmas, 4th of July, etc.

NA
44
Allain, Helene d'Aguin. *Souvenirs d'Amérique et de France par une Créole*. Paris, 1883.
Description of Congo Square dancing in New Orleans (pp. 171-172) compared with Moreau de Saint-Mery's Haitian accounts.

NA
45
Alland, Alexander. "'Possession' in a Revivalistic Negro Church," *Journal for the Scientific Study of Religion*, 1 (1962), 204-213.
Discusses socio-cultural and individual physiological and psychological states causing trances: salvation is attained upon realizing a Holy Ghost manifestation in a trance state in Wareham United House of Prayer Church near New Bedford, Mass.

NA
46
Alland, Alexander. "The Semantics of a Revivalism," in *America as a Mass Society: Changing Community and Identity*, Philip Olson, ed. New York: Free Press, 1963, 347-352.
Description of ritual in Daddy Grace's United House of Prayer for All People; possessional experiences.

NA
47
Allan-Olney, Mary. *The New Virginians*. 2 vols. Edinburgh: Blackwood, 1880.
Includes descriptions of black dress, domestic customs, religion, hymns, especially with contrast to poor whites' practices.

NA 48   Allen, Cleveland G. "The Negro and His Songs," *Musical Courier*, 103 (Oct. 3, 1931), 7.
Characteristics of Negro folksongs, with a discussion of the Jubilee Singers.

NA 49   Allen, Cleveland G. "The Negro's Contribution to American Music," *Current History*, 26 (1927), 245-249.
Includes discussion of the Fisk singers and secular and sacred categories of song.

NA 50   Allen, Richard C. "The Colored Population of Frankford," in *Papers Read before the Historical Society of Frankford* (Pa.), 1, No. 1 (1906), pp. 8-14.
A general discription of black inhabitants and occupations, with accounts of several unusual persons--a boy preacher, a woman who talked to animals, a stutterer, *et al.* (Reprinted from the *Frankford Gazette*.)

NA 51   Allen, William Francis, Charles Pickard Ware and Lucy McKim Garrison. *Slave Songs of the United States.* New York: A. Simpson & Co., 1867.
Includes texts and music of 136 spirituals and a discussion of religious services, black speech, music, etc.

NA 52   Allsopp, Fred W. *Folklore of Romantic Arkansas*, Vol. 2. Kansas City: The Grolier Society, 1931.
Chapter 5, "Negro Folklore," includes spirituals and folksongs, ghost tales, description of panpipes, beliefs, and stories about Negro characters; Christmas description (pp. 96-97).

NA 53   Alterman, Loraine. "It's Here--Reggae Rock," *New York Times*, February 4, 1973, Section D, 28.
A brief account of Jamaican popular music and dance ("ska," "rock steady," "reggae") in New York, London and Jamaica from 1950 to the 1970's.

NA 54   Amalric, J. "Les Noirs Americains et l'Afrique," in *Mois en Afrique* (Dakar), March, 1966, 42-52.
Survey of the history of African and Afro-American ties.

NA 55   "American Jazz Is Not African," *New York Times*, September 19, 1926, Section 20, 8. (Reprinted in *Metronome*, 42 (October 1, 1926), 21.)
African musicologist Ballanta-Taylor argues that the spirituals, but not jazz, are closely related to African music.

NA
56
    American Slavery as It Is: Testimony of A Thousand Witnesses. New York: American Anti-Slavery Society, 1839.
        Descriptions of conditions of life, maiming and mistreatment, work, views of slaves, clothing, food, and shelter; some songs given.

NA
57
    Ames, David W. "Black Nationalism and the Afro-American's Search for Identity," in *Proceedings of the 35th International Congress of Americanists, 1962*. Mexico, 1963. 3-14.
        Analysis of 2 black nationalist groups ("Black Muslims" and the Afro-American Association) and their response to Afro-American culture.

NA
58
    Ames, Russell. "Art in Negro Folksong," *JAF*, 56 (1943), 241-254.
        Describes the aesthetic qualities found in folksongs; includes fragments of Negro songs.

NA
59
    Ames, Russell. "Implications of Negro Folk Song," *Science and Society*, 15 (1951), 163-173.
        The case for traditional black songs as art, with portions of texts.

NA
60
    Ames, Russell. "Protest and Irony in Negro Folksongs," *Science and Society*, 14 (1950), 193-213.
        Resistance to slavery and oppression through the use of songs in the South. Dwells on the ambiguity between freedom and death.

NA
61
    Ames, Russell. *The Story of American Folk Song*. New York: Grosset and Dunlap, 1960.
        Sections on spirituals, worksongs, blues, etc.

NA
62
    Anderson, Alston. *All God's Children*. Indianapolis: Bobbs-Merrill, 1965.
        Novel, set in slavery, with folkloric content.

NA
63
    Anderson, Alston. *Lover Man*. Garden City: N.Y.: Doubleday, 1959.
        Short stories with folkloric content: includes the dozens, signifying, toasts, hipsters' jargon, the play-mother relationship, *et al*.

NA
64
    Anderson, Floyd J. and Norman C. Meier. "The Rationality and Control-Strength of Superstitious Beliefs Among Negroes," *Social Forces*, 15 (1936), 91-96.

NA
65
    Anderson, John Q. "The New Orleans Voodoo Ritual Dance and its Twentieth-Century Survivals," *SFQ*, 24 (1960), 135-143.
        Examines the ritual dance of the voodoo cult as a source of contemporary social dance.

NA 66 Anderson, John Q. "Old John and the Master," *SFQ*, 25 (1961), 195-197.
5 "Master and John" stories (as told by whites) in Northeast Texas.

NA 67 Anderson, John Q. *Texas Folk Medicine: 1,333 Cures, Remedies, Preventives, and Health Practices*. Austin, Texas: Encino Press, 1970.
Includes Negro material.

NA 68 Anderson, W.T. "Jack and the King," *SW*, 28 (1899), 232.
1 tale.

NA 69 Anderson, W.F. *Look Away: 50 Negro Folk Songs*. Delaware, Ohio: Cooperative Recreation Service, Inc., n.d.
50 hymns, with music; no notes or details.

NA 70 Andreu, Enrique. "Los 'Spiritual Negro Songs' y su Accion Etnico-social," *Estudios Afrocubanos*, 1, No. 1 (1937), 76-91.
Relationship of jazz and blues music to the spirituals; the origin, development and functions of the spiritual.

NA 71 Andrews, Sidney. *The South Since the War*. Boston: Ticknor and Fields, 1866.
Description and analysis of Sea Island speech and grammar.

NA 72 Andrews, W.D. "Negro Folk Games," *Playground*, 21 (June, 1923), 132-134.

NA 73 "The Appeal of the Primitive Jazz," *Literary Digest*, 55, No. 8 (1917), 28-29.
Argues that jazz emerged from rhythmic sources in Africa and the West Indies.

NA 74 Arditi, Claude. "Qui Sont 'Les Black Muslims'?" *Partisans* (Paris), 11 (1963), 71-82.

NA 75 Arkansas Writers' Program. *Survey of Negroes in Little Rock and North Little Rock*. Little Rock: Urban League, 1941.

NA 76 Armistead, S.G. "Two Brer Rabbit Stories from the Eastern Shore of Maryland," *JAF*, 84 (1971), 442-444.
2 texts with discussion.

NA
77
Armstrong, Louis. *Satchmo: My Life in New Orleans*. Englewood Cliffs:
Prentice-Hall, 1954.
Jazz musician Armstrong's memoirs of early New Orleans: food, cures,
parades, music, funerals, etc.

NA
78
Armstrong, Mrs. Mary Frances. *Hampton and Its Students*. New York: Putnam's,
1874.
Includes 50 songs, with music.

NA
79
Armstrong, Orland Kay. *Old Massa's People. The Old Slaves Tell Their
Story*. Indianapolis: Bobbs-Merrill, 1931.
Slaves' accounts of escape, music and dance, courtship, material culture, work practices, sermons, conjure, charms, memories of Africa,
kinship, naming, child-care, medicine, food, clothing, "play" kinship,
games, holidays; includes song texts.

NA
80
Arnez, Nancy Levi and Clara B. Anthony. "Contemporary Negro Humor as Social
Satire," *Phylon*, 29 (1968), 339-346.
Humor as an indicator of black attitudes.

NA
81
Arnold, Byron. *Folksongs of Alabama*. University, Alabama: University of
Alabama Press, 1950.
Several Negro folksongs; texts and music.

NA
82
Arnold, Byron. "Some Historical Folk Songs from Alabama," *JIFMC*, 6 (1954),
45-47.
Collection of folk songs from Alabama with a few recordings of religious
services.

NA
83
Arntzenius, L.M.G. *Amerikaansche Kunstindrukhen*. Amsterdam: A. de Lange,
1927.
Includes a discussion of Negro music and jazz.

NA
84
Arrowood, Charles F. "Well Done, Liar," *PTFS*, No. 18 (1943), 78-88.
1 tale of a hound dog used for hunting quail.

NA
85
Arrowood, Mary and Thomas Hamilton. "Nine Negro Spirituals," *JAF*, 41 (1928),
579-584.
9 spirituals from lower South Carolina with music.

NA
86
"Art from the Cabin Door," *Outlook*, 141 (October 21, 1925), 268-269.
Efforts of Negro schools (Tuskegee, Hampton, Fisk *et al*.) to preserve
Negro Spirituals.

NA
87
Arvey, Verna. "Negro Dance and Its Influence on Negro Music," in *Black Music in Our Culture: Curricular Ideas on the Subjects, Materials and Problems*, Dominique-Réné de Lerma, ed. Kent, Ohio: Kent State University Press, 1970, 79-92.
Discussion of Negro dance from Africa to North and South America with dance descriptions.

NA
88
Asbell, Bernard. "A Man Ain't Nothin' But a Man," *American Heritage*, 14 (June, 1963), 34-37.
Historical evidence for the existence of John Henry.

NA
89
Asch, Moses and Alan Lomax, eds. *The Leadbelly Songbook*. New York: Oak, 1962.
74 texts with music; essays on Leadbelly.

NA
90
Ashbury, Samuel E. and Henry E. Meyer. "Old-Time White Camp-Meeting Spiritual," *PTFS*, No. 10 (1932), 169-185.
Discussion of relation of "old-time" white camp-meeting spirituals to Negro spirituals; argues that Negro spirituals are derived melodically and harmonically, but not rhythmically, from white spirituals.

NA
91
Ashton, J. *The Devil in Britain and America*. London, 1896.

NA
92
Aswell, James R., Julia Willhoit, *et al. God Bless the Devil: Liars' Bench Tales*. Chapel Hill: The University of North Carolina Press, 1940.
Part 2 includes 7 Negro tall tales collected in Tennessee.

NA
93
Aubert, Alvin. "Black American Poetry, Language, and The Folk Tradition," *Black Academy Review*, 2 (1971), 71-80.
The use of dialect and folklore by black American poets.

NA
94
Autobiography of a Female Slave. New York: Redfield, 1857.
Anecdotes of slaves' feelings about their masters, religion, and slavery; examples of dialect.

NA
95
"Autobiography of Omar ibn Said, Slave in North Carolina, 1831," *American History Review*, 30 (1924), 787-795.

NA
96
Avary, Myrta Lockett. *Dixie After the War*. New York: Doubleday, 1906.
Chapter 17, entitled "Back to Voodooism," quotes a slave informant concerning activities at a trance meeting (p. 204); custom of groom giving minister at a marriage an iced cake (p. 203); reminiscences, etc.

NA
97

Avirett, James Battle. *The Old Plantation* . . . New York: F. Tennyson
     Neely, 1901.
     Descriptions of a slave wedding, Christmas, a corn-shucking, cloth-
     ing, food, slave quarters, a funeral, a coon hunt, a black musician
     at a white dance, etc.

NA
98

Ayoub, Millicent and Stephen A. Barnett. "Ritualized Verbal Insult in
     White High School Culture," *JAF*, 78 (1965), 337-344.
     The existence of "sounding" and the "dozens" among white as well as
     black youth in a Midwestern small town. (See Bruce Jackson, No. NA
     1578 for a response.)

NA
99

Babcock, C. Merton. "A Word-List from Zora Neale Hurston," *Publications
     of the American Dialect Society*, No. 40 (November, 1963), 1-11.
     A list of idiomatic expressions used in Hurston's fiction.

NA
100

Babcock, William H. "Carols and Child-Lore at the Capital," *Lippincott's
     Magazine*, 38 (1886), 320-342.
     Includes 1 black rhyme.

NA
101

Babcock, William H. "Folklore Jottings from Rockhaven, D.C.," *JAF*, 4
     (1891), 171-173.
     Contains an owl dialogue and an account of two ghosts.

NA
102

Babcock, William H. "Games of Washington Children," *AA*, 1 (1888), 243-284.
     Includes 1 Negro chant, collected from white children.

NA
103

Backus, Emma M. "Animal Tales from North Carolina," *JAF*, 11 (1898), 284-
     292.
     Texts of 7 animal tales with notes on dialect.

NA
104

Backus, Emma M. "Cradle-Songs of Negroes in North Carolina," *JAF*, 7 (1894),
     310.
     Texts of 2 songs in dialect.

NA
105

Backus, Emma M. "Folk-Tales from Georgia," *JAF*, 13 (1900), 19-32.
     Contains 10 tales in dialect.

NA
106

Backus, Emma M. "Negro Ghost Stories," *JAF*, 9 (1896), 228-230.
     3 short ghost tales.

NA
107
Backus, Emma M. "Negro Hymns from Georgia," *JAF*, 10 (1897), 116, 202, 264; 11 (1898), 22; 12 (1899), 272.
6 hymn texts.

NA
108
Backus, Emma M. "Negro Song from Georgia," *JAF*, 10 (1897), 216.
1 song.

NA
109
Backus, Emma M. "Negro Song from North Carolina," *JAF*, 11 (1898), 60.
1 song.

NA
110
Backus, Emma M. "Tales of the Rabbit from Georgia Negroes," *JAF*, 12 (1899), 108-115.
6 Brer Rabbit tales.

NA
111
Backus, Emma M. and Ethel H. Leitner. "Negro Tales from Georgia," *JAF*, 25 (1912), 125-136.
9 tales.

NA
112
Bacon, Alice Mabel. "Conjuring and Conjure-Doctors in the Southern United States," *SW*, 24 (1895), 193-194, 209-211. (Reprinted in *JAF*, 9 (1896), 143-147, 224-226, and in No. NA 1568.)
A discussion of poisons, charms, and the role of the conjure doctor.

NA
113
Bacon, Alice Mabel. "Proposal for Folk-Lore Research at Hampton, Virginia," *JAF*, 6 (1893), 305-309.
Brief note stresses need for recording Negro folklore so future historians can trace Negro history. Gives examples of customs, African words, superstitions, proverbs, and oral genealogies of African ancestry.

NA
114
Bacon, Alice Mabel. "Silhouettes," *SW*, 17 (1888), 5.
A white teacher's account of classroom interaction, confusion over black naming practices.

NA
115
Bacon, Alice Mabel. "Work and Methods of the Hampton Folk-Lore Society," *JAF*, 11 (1898), 17-21.
Discusses the possibility that folklore peculiar to the Negro may be lost because of the reluctance of many Negroes to reveal something they think of as "all bad."

NA
116
Bacon, Alice Mabel and Elsie Clews Parsons. "Folk-Lore from Elizabeth City County, Virginia," *JAF*, 35 (1922), 250-327.
114 tales and 136 riddles.

NA   Bacon, Eugenia J. *Lyddy: A Tale of the Old South*. New York: Continental
117   Publishing, 1898.
            Includes beliefs, dialect, interracial deference patterns, etc.

NA   Bacon, Lenice Ingram. "Banjo's Ringin', Darkies Singin'," *Christian Science
118   Monitor Magazine*, January 24, 1942, 4.

NA   Bacote, C. "Some Aspects of Negro Life in Georgia, 1880-1908," *JNH*, 43
119   (1958), 186-213.
            Black collective spirit and its significance in the social, economic
            and cultural life of the Georgia Negro.

NA   Badeaux, Ed. "Please Don't Tell What Train I'm On," *SO*, 14, No. 4 (1964),
120   6-13.
            The life and style of Elizabeth Cotton, singer, guitarist and composer;
            includes 1 song.

NA   Bagley, Julian E. "I'm Gwine ter Trust in de Lord," *SW*, 51 (1922), 324.
121   1 spiritual.

NA   Bailey, Beryl Loftman. "Toward a New Perspective in Negro English Dia-
122   lectology," *AS*, 40 (1965), 171-177.

NA   Bailey, Thomas Pearce. *Race Orthodoxy in the South, and Other Aspects of
123   the Negro Question*. New York: Neale Publishing Co., 1914.
            Includes accounts of black schools, children's behavior, etc.

NA   Baker, David N. "A Periodization of Black Music History," in *Reflections
124   on Afro-American Music*, Dominique-René de Lerma, ed. Kent, Ohio: Kent
            State University Press, 1973, 113-160.
            An overview of Afro-American music and its African background.

NA   Baker, Houston A., Jr. "Completely Well: One View of Black American Cul-
125   ture," in *Key Issues in the Afro-American Experience*, Vol. 1, Nathan E.
            Huggins, Martin Kilson and Daniel M. Fox, eds. New York: Harcourt,
            Brace, Jovanovich, 1971, 20-33.
            Considers the importance of certain kinds of folk heroes in the con-
            ceptualizing of a black American culture by blacks.

NA   Baker, Houston A., Jr. *Long Black Song: Essays in Black Literature and
126   Culture*. Charlottesville, Va.: University Press of Virginia, 1972.
            Essays on black folklore, music and speech, and their relation to lit-
            erature, history and education.

NA
127
Baldwin, James. *Go Tell It on the Mountain*. New York: Dial, 1953.
Novel set in a Harlem storefront church.

NA
128
Bales, Mary V. "Some Negro Folk Songs of Texas," *PTFS*, No 7 (1928), 85-112.
A discussion of 9 spirituals and 23 love songs, work songs, etc., including musical notation.

NA
129
Bales, Mary V. "Some Texas Spirituals," *PTFS*, No. 26 (1954), 167-174.
9 spirituals with discussion.

NA
130
Ballanta-Taylor, N.G.J. *St. Helena Island Spirituals*. New York: G. Schirmer,
1925.
114 South Carolina song texts with musical transcriptions and introductory explanation of rhythmical and melodic patterns.

NA
131
Ballanta-Taylor, N.G.J. See "Traces Negro Spirituals," No. NA 3020.

NA
132
Ballard, Lou Ellen. "Some Tales of Local Color from Southeast Alabama,"
SFQ, 24 (1960), 147-156.
11 tales.

NA
133
Balliett, Whitney, "It's Detestable When You Live It: Profile of Ray
Charles," *New Yorker*, 46 (March 28, 1970), 44-76.
The career of blues singer Ray Charles; the gospel, jazz and hill-
billy influences of his singing.

NA
134
Balliett, Whitney. *Such Sweet Thunder*. Indianapolis: Bobbs-Merrill, 1966.
Includes essays on tap dancing (pp. 131-135) and New Orleans music
and funeral parades (pp. 298-334).

NA
135
Ballowe, Hewitt L. *Creole Folk Tales*. Baton Rouge: Louisiana State University Press, 1948.
19 "literary" tales of folklife from the Louisiana marsh country.

NA
136
Ballowe, Hewitt L. *The Lawd Sayin' the Same: Negro Folk Tales of the
Creole Country*. Baton Rouge: Louisiana State University Press, 1947.
24 tales, a few of them traditional but retold, from the Mississippi
River country below New Orleans (more folklife descriptions than
folklore texts).

NA   Banks, Frank D. "Oldtime Courtship," *SW*, 24 (1895), 14-15.
137   Courting riddles from Calhoun, Alabama, collected by Portia Smiley.

NA   Banks, Frank D. "Plantation Courtship," *JAF*, 7 (1894), 147-149.
138   A slave courtship; includes a sample conversation.

NA   Banks, Mary Ross. *Bright Days in the Old Plantation Times*. Boston: Lea
139   and Shephard; New York: Charles T. Dillingham, 1882.
            Includes anecdotes on slave names, Brer Rabbit stories, dialect ex-
            pressions, and anecdotes showing the influence of slaves on a young
            white girl's life.

NA   Banks, Ruth. "Idioms of the Present-Day American Negro," *AS*, 13 (1938),
140   313-314.
            List of expressions of urban Negroes.

NA   Banting, John. "The Dancing of Harlem," in *Negro Anthology*, Nancy Cunard,
141   ed. London: Wishart, 1934.
            Description of a dance in a Harlem club.

        Baraka, Imamu Amiri. "Blues, Jazz and the Negro." See Jones, LeRoi, No.
            NA 1670.

        Baraka, Imamu Amiri. *Blues People*. See Jones, LeRoi, No. NA 1671.

        Baraka, Imamu Amiri. *Home: Social Essays*. See Jones, LeRoi, No. NA 1672.

        Baraka, Imamu Amiri (LeRoi Jones). *Raise Race Rays Raze: Essays Since
            1965*. See Jones, LeRoi, No. NA 1673.

        Baraka, Imamu Amiri. *Tales*. See Jones, LeRoi, No. NA 1674.

NA   Baratz, Joan and Stephen Baratz. "Black Culture on Black Terms: A Rejec-
142   tion of the Social Pathology Model," in *Rappin' and Stylin' Out*, Thomas
            Kochmam, ed. Urbana, Ill.: University of Illinois Press, 1972, 3-16.
            An account of the ways in which black culture is treated as "patho-
            logical" by social scientists.

NA
143
Barber, John W. *A History of the Amistad Captives*. New Haven: E.L. & J.W. Barber, 1846.
    Pictures and biographical sketches of each of the captives and the African territories from which they were taken.

NA
144
Baring-Gould, S. *A Book of Nursery Songs and Rhymes*. London, 1895.

NA
145
Barker, Danny. "A Memory of King Bolden," *Evergreen Review*, No. 37 (September, 1965), 66–74.
    Memoirs of turn-of-the-century New Orleans street life: music, names, the dozens, dress, etc.

NA
146
Barker, Danny. "Way Down Yonder in New Orleans," in *Hear Me Talkin' to Ya*, Nat Shapiro and Nat Hentoff, eds. New York: Rinehart, 1955, 3, 4, 5, 10–11, 14–16, 18, 20–21, 26, 34, 38–39, 49–53, 66–68.
    Memoirs of New Orleans life and musicians in the early 1900's: slang, nicknames, dress, funerals, minstrel shows, etc.

NA
147
Barker, Howard F. "Family Names of American Negroes," *AS*, 14 (1939), 163–174.
    History of the acquisition of surnames; geographical, cultural, and situational influences.

NA
148
Barker, Mrs. L.J. *Influence of Slavery upon the White Population*. New York: American Anti-Slavery Society, 1855.
    The slaves' influence on American language and pronunciation, etc.

NA
149
Barnes, Daniel R. "The Bosom Serpent: A Legend in American Literature and Culture," *JAF*, 85 (1972), 11–122.
    Analysis of oral and literary variants of the "swallowed snake" motif.

NA
150
Barnes, Ruth A. *I Hear America Singing*. Chicago: Winston, 1937.
    Includes texts of black songs.

NA
151
Barnette, V.G. and C.H. Herbert, "'Why the Dog Cannot Talk' and 'Why the Rabbit Has a Short Tail,'" *SW*, 27 (1898), 36–37.
    2 tales.

NA
152
Barnie, John. "Standards in Blues Criticism: A Change of Emphasis," *JJ*, 17, No. 7 (1964), 6–7.
    Essay on the Mississippi Delta blues arguing that blues should be evaluated as folk poetry.

NA
153
  Barrett, Harris. *Negro Folk Songs*. Hampton, Va.: Hampton Institute, 1912.
    (Reprinted from *SW*, 41 (1912), 238-245).
    Classifies Negro folk songs into spirituals, cradle songs, labor songs,
    game and dance songs, and freedom songs; explains and illustrates each
    classification.

NA
154
  Barrett, W.A. "Negro Hymnology," *Musical Times* (London), 15 (1871-73),
    559-561.
    Discussion of manner of singing, content, and nature of spirituals;
    includes 4 songs with music.

NA
155
  Barrois, Julie. "Herb Cures in an Isolated Black Community in the Florida
    Parishes," *LFM*, 3, No. 1 (1970), 25-27.
    Herbal lore from a Louisiana community, with texts.

NA
156
  Barron, Elwyn A. "Shadowy Memories of Negro-Lore," *The Folklorist* (Chica-
    go), 1 (1892), 46-53.
    Reminiscence of "superstitions" and cures, etc., used by blacks during
    the Civil War.

NA
157
  Barrow, David C. "A Georgia Corn-Shucking," *Century Magazine*, n.s. 2
    (1882), 873-878. (Reprinted in No. NA 1568.)
    Description of corn-shucking gathering with text and music of corn-
    songs.

NA
158
  Barrow, David C. "My Grandmother's Key Basket," *Bulletin of the University
    of Georgia*, 17, No. 1 (1916), 1-16.
    Gives weaving songs, cider beating songs, Negro expressions in dialect,
    and names given to slaves (and whites).

NA
159
  Barry, Phillips. "Negro Folk Songs from Maine," *Bulletin of the Folk Song
    Society of the North East*, 8 (1934), 13-16; 9 (1935), 10-14; 10 (1935),
    21-24.
    Songs among Negroes who lived in Brownville, Maine between 1866-1880;
    argues that Afro-American music is derived from white sources.

NA
160
  Barth, Ernest A.T. "The Language Behavior of Negroes and Whites," *Pacific
    Sociological Review*, 4 (1961), 69-72.

NA
161
  Bartlett, Napier. *Stories of the Crescent City*. New Orleans, 1869.
    An account of New Orleans voodoo, pp. 100-102.

NA
162
Barton, William E. "Hymns of the Slave and the Freedman," *New England Magazine*, 19 (1899), 609-624. (Reprinted in No. NA 1698.)
An annotated collection of sacred and secular folksongs with musical examples.

NA
163
Barton, William E. "Old Plantation Hymns," *New England Magazine*, 19 (1898), 443-465. (Reprinted in No. NA 1698.)
A collection of 29 religious songs with musical examples and source material on each song.

NA
164
Barton, William E. *Old Plantation Hymns: A Collection of Hitherto Unpublished Melodies of the Slave and the Freedman, with Historical and Descriptive Notes.* Boston: Lamson, Wolffe, 1899.
70 songs of slaves and freedman with comments. (Songs first published by Barton in *New England Magazine*.)

NA
165
Barton, William E. "Recent Negro Melodies," *New England Magazine*, 19 (1899), 707-719. (Reprinted in Nos. NA 1568 and NA 1698.)
A collection of 13 railroad songs and hymns with background and narration; attempt at classification.

NA
166
Bascom, William R. "Acculturation among the Gullah Negroes," *AA*, 42 (1941), 43-50. (Reprinted in *The Making of Black America*, August Meier and Elliot Rudwick, eds. New York: Atheneum, 1969, Vol. 1, 34-41.)
Review of the African background of the Gullah people of South Carolina and Georgia, and a description of their cooperative work and social groups, agricultural practices, music, beliefs, speech, and family rituals.

NA
167
Baskin, Joseph. "Good-by, Mr. Bones," *New York Times Magazine*, May 1, 1966, 31, 84, 86, 88, 90, 92.
Negro humor as a socializing agent used for group identity.

NA
168
Bass, Robert Duncan. "Negro Songs from the Pedee Country," *JAF*, 44 (1931), 418-436.
64 song texts from South Carolina with music for 6 songs.

NA
169
Bass, Ruth. "Fern Seed--For Peace," *Folk-Say*, 2 (1930), 145-156.
Account of a Negro "cure-woman."

NA
170
Bass, Ruth. "The Little Man," *Scribner's*, 97 (1935), 120-123. (Reprinted in Dundes, No. NA 854.)
Description of conjure and death signs in Mississippi.

NA   Bass, Ruth. "Mojo," *Scribner's*, 87 (1930), 83-90. (Reprinted in Dundes,
171   No. NA 854.)
            Description of conjuring in Mississippi.

NA   Bass, Ruth. "Ole Miss," *Folk-Say*, 3 (1931), 48-69.
172   Short story with folkloric content set among Catholic Negroes along
            the Mississippi River; beliefs, etc.

NA   Bassett, A.L. "Going to Housekeeping in North Carolina," *Lippincott's
173   Magazine*, 28 (1881), 205-208.
            Manners and customs with an explanation of the cakewalk.

NA   Bassett, John Spencer. *Slavery in the State of North Carolina*. Baltimore,
174   1899.
            Contains a description of slaves marching into the sea, towards Africa,
            during "evening singin's" (pp. 92-93).

NA   Basshe, Emanuel. *Earth*. New York: Macauley, 1927.
175   Drama with folkloric content.

NA   Bastin, Bruce. "The Devil's Goin' to Get You," *NCF*, 21 (1973), 189-194.
176   4 tales told by a family of country musicians; with notes.

NA   Bastin, Bruce. *Crying for the Carolines*. London: Studio Vista, 1971.
177   A study of the blues as sung and played in Virginia, Georgia and
            North and South Carolina; bibliography, discography; illustrations.

NA   Batchelder, Ruth. "Beaufort, of the Real South," *Travel*, 28 (February,
178   1917), 28-31.
            Includes a South Carolina work song, a street cry and a "superstition."

NA   Bauer, Raymond A. and Alice H. Bauer. "Day to Day Resistance to Slavery,"
179   *JNH*, 27 (1942), 388-419.
            Examples of black domestic opposition to slavery; development of the
            slave "personality."

NA   Baxter, Robert. *Baxter's Finger-Picking Blues and Ragtime Manual*. New
180   York: Amaco Music, 1969.

NA   Beadle, Samuel Alfred. *Adam Shuffler*. Jackson, Miss.: Harmon Publishing
181   Co., 1901.
            13 dialect stories of Negro life in the South by a black author; titles

include "Molasses Smoked Ham," "The Voodoo's Jack," "Home Missions vs. a Cock Fight"; some folk rhymes and songs given.

NA
182
Bean, Lura. *He Called Them by the Lightning: A Teacher's Odyssey in the Negro South, 1908-1919.* Indianapolis: Bobbs-Merrill, 1967.
Memoirs with description of funerals, spirituals, sermons, dialects, etc.

NA
183
Beard, James Melville. *K.K.K. Sketches, Humorous and Didactic.* Philadelphia: Claxtom, Remsen and Heffelfinger, 1877.
Chapter 6 describes voodooism and beliefs of Negroes, story-telling, "ghost palaces" where ghost stories were told, their influence on white children.

NA
184
Beaufort County, South Carolina. Its Shrines and Early History. Augusta, Ga.: N.L. Willett, n.d.
Accounts of slavery; Gullah attitudes, music, language and food.

NA
185
Bechet, Sidney. *Treat It Gentle.* New York: Hill and Wang, 1960.
Autobiography of a New Orleans jazz musician; New Orleans music, parades, social functions, etc. in the early 1900's.

NA
186
Beckman, Albert Sidney. "The Psychology of Negro Spirituals," *SW,* 60 (1931), 391-394.
Contends that most spirituals are appeals to the emotions and that they describe fundamental passions, desires, hopes and experiences.

NA
187
Bedford, Rev. "Another Tribute to the Negro Melodies," *SW,* 23 (1894), 45.

NA
188
Beja, Morris. "Negroes in Contemporary American Fiction," *Antioch Review,* 24 (1964), 323-336.
Examples, in dialect, from novels of black writers depicting reasons for the emergence of the "Noble Savage"; ambivalence of the black identity quest coupled with "violent primitivism."

NA
189
"Beliefs and Customs Connected with Death and Burial," *SW,* 26 (1897), 18-19.
An account of Southern death superstitions and burial practices; wake, funeral service, grave digging, and burial in Gloucester County, Virginia.

NA   "Beliefs of Southern Negroes Concerning Hags," *JAF*, 7 (1894), 66-67.
190   Two methods of securing protection against being hag-ridden. (Re-
             printed from *SW*, March, 1894.)

NA   Bell, Andrew. *Men and Things in America; Being the Experience of a*
191   *Year's Residence in the U.S.* London: William Smith, 1838.
             Letter 12 (pp. 177-196, "Colored People of the United States") dis-
             cusses songs of Philadelphia chimney sweepers, names of black busi-
             nesses, and rhymes posted over business doors.

NA   Bell, Bernard W. *The Folk Roots of Contemporary Afro-American Poetry.*
192   Broadside Critics Series No. 3. Detroit: Broadside Press, 1974.
             The use of folk dialect, music, belief and ideology in black poetry
             between 1962 and 1972.

NA   Bell, H.S. "Plantation Life of the Negro in the Lower Mississippi Valley,"
193   *SW*, 28 (1899), 313-314.
             The life of Arkansas and Mississippi cotton plantation slaves; argues
             that their condition is wretched because of ignorance and superstition.

NA   Bellamann, Henry. *The Gray Man Walks.* New York: Doubleday, Doran, 1936.
194

NA   Benardete, Dolores. "Eloise," *AS*, 7 (1932), 349-364.
195   Memoirs recounting a slave girl's language, customs, and background;
             analysis of pronunciation, with examples.

NA   Benedict, Helen Dymond. *Belair Plantation Melodies.* Cincinnati, Ohio:
196   Willis, 1924.
             8 arranged songs collected in Louisiana.

NA   Bennett, John. "Charleston Folk-Tales," *Negro Digest*, 1 (September, 1943),
197   33-36.
             Discusses Negro folktales and tellers; 1 text.

NA   Bennett, John. *The Doctor to the Dead.* New York: Rinehart, 1946.
198   Includes Negro folktales in Charleston, S.C.

NA   Bennett, John. "Gullah: A Negro Patois," *South Atlantic Quarterly*, 7
199   (1908), 332-347; and 8 (1909), 39-52.
             Detailed discussion of Gullah with numerous examples. Finds British
             as well as African survivals in Gullah.

NA
200   Bennett, John. *Madame Margot*. New York: The Century Co., 1921.
            A Gullah legend of Charleston, S.C., retold.

NA
201   Bennett, John. "Note on Gullah," *South Carolina History Magazine*, 50
            (1949), 56-57.

NA
202   Bennett, John. "Revival Sermon at Little St. John's," *Atlantic Monthly*,
            98 (August, 1906), 256-268.
            Music, prayer and ritual in a church in South Carolina.

NA
203   Bennett, John. "South Carolina Folk Tales," *The News and Courier* (Charles-
            ton, S.C.)
            A newspaper column which included Brer Rabbit tales in the following
            issues: August 9, 14, 17, September 7, 10, November 8, 1951.

NA
204   Bennett, Lerone, Jr. *The Negro Mood and Other Essays*. Chicago: Johnson,
            1964. (Reprinted as *The Black Mood*. New York: Barnes and Noble, 1970.)
            Includes essays on black aesthetics, spirituals, blues, jazz, religion,
            etc.

NA
205   Bennett, Lerone, Jr. "The World of the Slave," *Ebony*, 26, No. 4 (1971),
            44-56.
            A review of the development of slave culture, ethos, folklore, etc.

NA
206   Bennett, Lerone, Jr., *et al. William Styron's Nat Turner: Ten Black Writers
            Respond*. Boston: Beacon, 1968.
            Critical studies of Styron's novel *The Confessions of Nat Turner*, many
            of which draw upon Afro-American folklore.

NA
207   Bentley, John. "Origin of the Blues," *Music Memories* (Birmingham, Ala.),
            3, No. 4 (1963), 4-5.
            Argues the blues originated by secular lyrics being substituted for
            spiritual lyrics by field laborers.

NA
208   Benton, Thomas Hart. *An Artist in America*. New York: Robert M. McBride,
            1937.
            Chapter on the South has description of black folklife, including
            chain-gang singing, deference behavior, and a camp meeting.

NA
209   Berdie, Ralph F. "Playing the Dozens," *Journal of Abnormal and Social
            Psychology*, 42 (1947), 120-121.
            Analysis of the dozens (verbal duelling) as a formalized expression
            of Negro aggression.

NA
210
Berendt, Joachim Ernst, ed. *Blues: Ein Essay*. Munich: Nymphenburger, 1957.
Discusses the form of blues and the social conditions under which they emerged; includes tunes and texts; discography.

NA
211
Berendt, Joachim Ernst. *Schwarzer Gesang II: Blues*. Munich: Nymphenburger, 1962.
67 blues, in English and German.

NA
212
Berendt, Joachim Ernst and Paridam von dem Knesebeck. *Spirituals: Geistliche Lieder der Neger Amerikas*. Munich: Nymphenburger, 1955.

NA
213
Bergen, Fanny D. *Animal and Plant Lore*. Memoirs of the American Folk-Lore Society, Vol. 7. New York: American Folk-Lore Society, 1899.
Includes Negro and white charms, omens and weather signs.

NA
214
Bergen, Fanny D. *Current Superstitions*. Memoirs of the American Folk-Lore Society, Vol. 4. New York: American Folk-Lore Society, 1896.
Includes Negro and white material.

NA
215
Bergen, Fanny D. "Louisiana Ghost Story," *JAF*, 12 (1899), 146-147.
1 ghost tale which deals with the art of trying to "lay" a ghost.

NA
216
Bergen, Fanny D. "On the Eastern Shore," *JAF*, 2 (1889), 295-300.
A sample of "superstitions," spirituals, tales and lore, collected in the Chesapeake Bay area.

NA
217
Bergen, Fanny D. "Some Bits of Plant Lore," *JAF*, 5 (1892), 20-21.
Collection of remedies.

NA
218
Bergen, Fanny D. "Two Negro Witch Stories," *JAF*, 12 (1899), 145-146.
Stories summarized by the author as heard from an individual from Salisbury, Md.

NA
219
Bergen, Fanny D. "Two Witch Stories," *JAF*, 12 (1899), 68-69.
2 stories.

NA
220
Bergen, Fanny D. "Uncle Remus and Folklore," *Outlook*, 48 (1893), 427-428.

NA
221
Berger, Monroe. "Jazz: Resistance to the Diffusion of a Culture Pattern," *JNH*, 32 (1947), 461-494.
Examination of the diffusion of jazz as dependent on the social status of the Negro, and white rejection of black culture; the meaning of the acceptance of the spiritual versus the rejection of jazz.

NA
222
Berquin-Duvallon. *Travels in Louisiana and the Floridas in the Year 1802.* New York: I. Riley, 1806.
Describes a New Orleans carnival, with blacks in the band; the special characteristics of Guinea slaves, activities of slaves in their spare time, food, clothing, and shelter, patois and standard French spoken by blacks, etc.

NA
223
Berry, Brewton. *Almost White*. New York: Collier-Macmillan, 1963.
The "mixed blood" groups of the United States: "Red-bones," "Brass Ankles," etc.; bibliography, illustrations.

NA
224
Berry, Brewton. *You and Your Superstitions*. Columbia, Mo.: Lucas Brothers, 1940.

NA
225
Berry, Pike. *Birthed into Glory*. Boston: Christopher, 1966.
Chapter 14 is on beliefs, conjure practice and folk medicine of a South Carolina woman.

NA
226
Berry, R.E. "Home of the Blues," *New York Times Magazine*, May 5, 1940, 21.
George Washington Lee talks of the significance of the "Beale Street Blues," by W.C. Handy.

NA
227
Beynon, Erdmann Doane. "The Voodoo Cult among Negro Migrants in Detroit," *American Journal of Sociology*, 43 (1938), 894-907.
The history and organization of the Nation of Islam sect.

NA
228
"Beyond the Ears of the Greys." *Time*, 82 (August 2, 1963), 14.
Discussion of the derivation and use of slang terms.

NA
229
Bilheimer, R.S. "Race Relations and the American Church: A People Different from My Own," *Religion in Life*, 26 (1957), 368-374.
Conversion experiences of black congregations in New York City as recounted by a white minister.

NA
230
Billups, Edgar P. "Some Practices for the Representation of Negro Dialect in Fiction," *Texas Review*, 8 (1923), 99-123.
Suggestions for conventionalizing dialect forms.

NA   Bird, Archibald Brian. *Skiffle: The Story of Folk-Song with a Jazz Beat.*
231   London: Robert Hale, 1958.
            Includes a chapter on Negro folk music.

NA   "Birmingham Blues--The Story of Robert McCoy," *Music Memories* (Birmingham,
232   Ala.), 3, No. 2 (1963), 13-14.
            Story of an Alabama blues pianist.

NA   Bivins, S. Thomas. *The Southern Cookbook.* Hampton, Va.: Hampton Institute
233   Press, 1912.

NA   Black, Elizabeth. "A Show at the Quarter," *Theater Arts Monthly*, 16 (June,
234   1932), 493-500.
            A reminiscence of plantation entertainment by Negroes: guitar playing,
            singing, dancing, caricaturing of ballroom dancers, story telling,
            whistling, etc.

        Black Girls at Play: Folkloric Perspectives on Child Development. See
            Brady, Margaret K., No. NA 329 and Eckhardt, Rosalind, No. NA 871.

NA   "The Black Mammy of the South," *Literary Digest*, 76, (March 31, 1923),
235   56.
            Discussion of the historical and cultural significance of the Southern
            "mammy."

NA   "Black Voices," *Nation*, 119 (1924), 278.
236   Discusses the content and meaning of spirituals.

NA   Blackburn, Mary Johnson. *Folk Lore from Mammy Days.* Boston: Walter H. Baker,
237   1924.
            Includes 14 songs with music.

NA   Blacknall, O.W. "The New Departure in Negro Life," *Atlantic Monthly*, 52
238   (1883), 680-685.
            Discusses the Negro and his religion including attitudes toward musi-
            cal instruments and importance of the preacher in the community.

NA   Blades, William C. *Negro Poems, Melodies, Plantation Pieces, Camp Meeting
239   Songs, etc.* Boston: R.G. Badger, 1921.
            Songs, without music.

NA   Blair, Walter, ed. *Native American Humor*. New York: American Book Co.,
240   1937.
            "Uncle Remus" stories and others of the Old Southwest (1830-1867) of
            uncertain source.

NA   Blanchet, Catherine. "Louisiana Cajun Music, Vol. 1: First Recordings,
241   the 1920's," Record notes to Old-Timey LP record 108.
            Notes on the first black "cajun" recording, and on the influence of
            black French on whites.

NA   Blanton, Joshua E. "I Sho Ben Lub Dat Buckra," *SW*, 37 (1908), 242-246.
242   Reminiscences of the death of a planter in the dialect of the Sea
            Islanders of South Carolina.

NA   Blassingame, John W. *Black New Orleans, 1860-1880*. Chicago: University
243   of Chicago Press, 1973.
            Historical account includes material on social clubs, religion, music,
            dance, Mardi Gras, etc.; bibliography of black newspapers of the
            period; illustrations.

NA   Blau, George. "W.C. Handy," *Music Memories* (Birmingham, Ala.), 3, No. 2
244   (1963), 16-18.
            Anecdotes about Handy from letters written by him to the author;
            discography.

NA   Blauner, Robert. "Black Culture: Myth or Reality?" in *Afro-American Anthro-
245   pology: Contemporary Perspectives*, Norman E. Whitten, Jr. and John F.
            Szwed, eds. New York: Free Press, 1970, 347-366. (Reprinted in abridged
            form as "The Question of Black Culture," in *Black America*, John F.
            Szwed, ed. New York: Basic Books, 1970, 110-120.)
            The nature of Afro-American culture in North America, its roots and
            components.

NA   Blaustein, Richard. "More in Slave Fiddling," *Devil's Box* (Madison, Ala.),
246   16, (February 15, 1972), 11-15. (Reprinted in the *University of Mich-
            igan Folklore Society Calendar and Newsletter* (Ann Arbor, Mich.), 1,
            No. 3 (1972), 5-8.)

NA   Blesh, Rudi. *O Susanna. A Sampler of the Riches of American Folk Music*.
247   New York: Grove Press, 1960.

NA   Blesh, Rudi. *Shining Trumpets: A History of Jazz*. New York: Knopf, 1946.
248   (2nd edition, 1958.)
            The history of jazz; African sources and American folk music and pre-

jazz. Appendix contains a set of musical transcriptions referred to in the text; bibliography, discography.

NA
249   "Blind Tom," *Dwight's Journal of Music*, 22 (1862), 250–252.
         Background and career of a pianist.

NA
250   Blok, H.P. "Annotations to Mr. Turner's Africanisms in the Gullah Dialect,"
         Lingua, 8 (1959), 306–321.
         Detailed analysis and criticism of the work.

NA
251   Bluestein, Gene. "Blues as a Literary Theme," *Massachusetts Review*, 8
         (1967), 593–617. (Reprinted in *Black and White in American Culture*,
         Jules Chametzky and Sidney Kaplan, eds. Amherst, Mass.: University of
         Massachusetts Press, 1969, 229–255.)
         Examines the literary works of F. Scott Fitzgerald, Ralph Ellison
         and others and discusses the importance of their references to jazz
         and blues themes.

NA
252   Bluestein, Gene. *The Voice of the Folk: Folklore and American Literary*
         Theory. Amherst, Mass.: University of Massachusetts Press, 1972.
         Discusses the writings of Constance Rourke and John and Alan Lomax
         on Negro Folklore; essays on the blues as a literary theme and on
         the development of the banjo in the U.S.

NA
253   Boag, Mrs. E.T. "De Secon' Flood: Story of a Negro Nurse," *JAF*, 11 (1898),
         237–238.
         Account of a flood (in dialect).

NA
254   Boas, Franz. "Romance Folk-Lore among American Indians," *The Romantic*
         Review, 16 (1925), 199–207. (Reprinted in Franz Boas, *Race, Language*
         and Culture. New York: Macmillan, 1940, 517–524.)
         On the spread of Negro folktales among American Indians.

NA
255   Boas, Franziska. "Negro and the Dance as an Art," *Phylon*, 10 (1949),
         38–42.
         The history of Negro dancing; black attitudes toward dancing.

NA
256   Boatner, Edward and Willa A. Townsend. *Spirituals Triumphant, Old and*
         New. Nashville, Tennessee: Sunday School Publishing Board, National
         Baptist Convention, 1927.
         86 arranged spirituals.

NA
257
Bocock, Mike, Chuck Berry, Paul Roberton, and Mike Leadbitter. "Chuck Berry and Bo Diddley," *BU*, Collectors Classic Booklet, No. 3 (April, 1964).
    Short biographical sketches of two blues men; discography.

NA
258
Bogaert, Karel. *Blues Lexicon: Blues, Cajun, Boogie Woogie, Gospel*. Antwerp: Standaard Uitgeverij, 1971.

NA
259
Boggs, Ralph. "Spanish Folklore from Tampa, Florida," *SFQ*, 1 (1937), 1-12.
    Discussion of the Spanish-speaking community of Tampa; includes a collection of riddles which may be Afro-Cuban in source.

NA
260
Boggs, Ralph S. "Spanish Folklore from Tampa, Florida: *Una Ledi de Naso*," *SFQ*, 1 (1937), 9-13.
    A street song (possibly Afro-Cuban).

NA
261
Bolden, T.J. "Brer Rabbit's Box," *SW*, 28 (1899), 25-26.
    1 tale.

NA
262
Bolick, Julian Stevenson. *Georgetown Ghosts*. Clinton, S.C.: Jacobs, 1956.
    Includes several Negro ghost legends from the South Carolina coast.

NA
263
Bollaert, William. *William Bollaert's Texas*. Norman, Oklahoma: University of Oklahoma Press, 1956.
    Includes accounts of slaves' recreation, hymn parodies, work, etc.

NA
264
Bolton, Dorothy G. and Harry T. Burleigh. *Old Songs Hymnal*. New York: Century, 1929.
    Words and melodies of Negro spirituals from Georgia.

NA
265
Bolton, H. Carrington. "Decoration of Graves of Negroes in South Carolina," *JAF*, 4 (1891), 214.
    Origin and significance of grave decoration.

NA
266
Bontemps, Arna. "Rock, Church, Rock!" *Common Ground*, 3 (Autumn, 1942), 75-80.
    Biographical sketch of Thomas A. Dorsey (Georgia Tom), singer-composer of blues and gospel music.

Bontemps, Arna. See Weil, Dorothy, No. NA 3139.

NA   Bontemps, Arna and Jack Conroy. *They Seek a City*. Garden City: Doubleday,
267   1945. (Revised edition retitled *Anyplace but Here*. New York: Hill and
            Wang, 1966.)
            Account of the Negro migration to the North includes folkloric mater-
            ials, information on early jazz, etc.

NA   Booth, Stanley. "Furry's Blues," *Playboy*, 17, No. 4 (1970), 100-102, 104,
268   114, 193-194.
            Profile of bluesman Furry Lewis.

NA   Borneman, Ernest. "The Blues--A Study in Ambiguity," in *Just Jazz, 3*,
269   Sinclair Traill and Gerald Lascelles, eds. London: Four Square Books,
            1959, 75-91.
            The African elements of the blues; blues as adaptations to slavery;
            themes and imagery.

NA   Borneman, Ernest. "Boogie Woogie," in *Just Jazz*, Sinclair Traill and
270   Gerald Lascelles, eds. London: Peter Davies, 1957, 13-40.
            The origins of boogie woogie, its musical elements, etc.

NA   Borneman, Ernest. "Creole Echoes," *The Jazz Review*, 2, No. 8 (1959),
271   13-15; 2, No. 10 (1959), 26-27.
            A programmatic discussion of the African, French and Spanish musical
            background of New Orleans jazz.

NA   Borneman, Ernest. *A Critic Looks at Jazz*. London: Jazz Music Books, 1946.
272   (Originally published as "The Anthropologist Looks at Jazz," and under
            other titles, in *RC*, April, 1944, 5-9, 53; May, 1944, 5, 36-39; June,
            1944, 5-6, 37, 39-43; July, 1944, 5, 38-40; August, 8-10; September,
            9-11, 47; October, 6-8; December, 5-6, 51; January, 1945, 3, 5, 7-8,
            11; February, 1945, 6-10.)
            A study of the folk roots, social setting and history of jazz. Chapters
            discuss African music, work songs, blues, spirituals, ring shouts,
            minstrelsy, ragtime, dances, etc.; West Indian parallels to early
            jazz.

NA   Borneman, Ernest, "Jazz and the Creole Tradition," *Jazzforschung* (Graz),
273   1 (1969), 99-112.

NA   Borneman, Ernest. "Les Racines de la Musique Américaine Noire," *Présence
274   Africaine*, 4 (1948), 576-589.
            West African music and its appearance in the United States.

NA
275

Borneman, Ernest. "The Roots of Jazz," in *Jazz*, Nat Hentoff and Albert J. McCarthy, eds. New York: Rinehart, 1959, 1-20, 345-351.
Survey of the African and Afro-American folk music background of the development of jazz; discography.

NA
276

Borris, Siegfried. "Jazz--Wesen und Werden," *Musik im Unterrecht*, 58, No. 4 (1967), 113-116, 118-119.
Discusses the origins of jazz in blues, ragtime, and "open-air wind music."

NA
277

Boskin, Joseph. "Sambo: The National Jester in the Popular Culture," in *The Great Fear: Race in the Mind of America*, Gary B. Nash and Richard Weiss, eds. New York: Holt, Rinehart and Winston, 1970, 165-185.
Argues that the interaction of culture and prejudice produced the "Sambo" stereotype--the slow-witted, comical, happy black figure--on stage, radio, and films.

NA
278

"The Boston Songs," *Crisis*, 9 (1915), 128.

NA
279

Boswell, George W. "Traditional Verse and Music Influence in Faulkner," *Notes on Mississippi Writers*, 1, No. 1 (1968), 23-31.
William Faulkner's use of spirituals, hymns and blues in his fiction.

NA
280

Botkin, B.A., ed. *The American People in Their Stories, Legends, Tall Tales, Traditions, Ballads and Songs*. London: Pilot Press, 1946.
Includes 8 animal tales and nursery tales, 8 tales of witches, devils and ghosts.

NA
281

Botkin, B.A., ed. *A Civil War Treasury*. New York: Random House, 1960.
12 folktales in Chapter 4, "Run, Slave, Run" and Chapter 18, "Free at Last."

NA
282

Botkin, B.A. "Folk and Folklore," in *Culture in the South*, W.T. Couch, ed. Chapel Hill: University of North Carolina Press, 1934, 570-593.
Argues that the source of black culture is European; hoodoo and conjuration discussed.

NA
283

Botkin, B.A., ed. *Lay My Burden Down. A Folk History of Slavery*. Chicago: University of Chicago Press, 1945.
15 slave autobiographies, 100 recollections of slavery and remembrances of the aftermath of the war, 100 "Marster and John" stories, animal tales, religious tales and anecdotes. All material from interviews collected for the Federal Writers' Project in 1938.

NA   Botkin, B.A. "Negro Religious Songs and Services," booklet included with
284   Library of Congress LP record AAFS L10.
            Notes on 15 religious songs and sermons from Virginia, Mississippi,
            Alabama, and Texas.

NA   Botkin, B.A. "Negro Work Songs and Calls," booklet included with Library
285   of Congress LP record AAFS L8.
            Notes to 18 songs, calls and hollers from the Deep South; includes one
            launching song from the Bahamas.

NA   Botkin, B.A. "Play and Dance Songs and Tunes," booklet included with
286   Library of Congress LP record AAFS L9.
            Notes on 8 game songs from Mississippi.

NA   Botkin, B.A. "Self-Portraiture and Social Criticism in Negro Folksong,"
287   *Opportunity*, 5 (February, 1927), 38-42.

NA   Botkin, B.A., ed. *Sidewalks of America*. Indianapolis: Bobbs-Merrill,
288   1954.
            Miscellaneous folk material reprinted from other sources.

NA   Botkin, B.A. "The Slave as His Own Interpreter," *Library of Congress*
289   *Quarterly Journal of Current Acquisitions*, 2 (1944), 37-63.
            Background of the WPA interviews with ex-slaves; includes some ex-
            cerpts from the interviews.

NA   Botkin, B.A., ed. *A Treasury of American Folklore. Stories, Ballads and*
290   *Traditions of the People*. New York: Crown, 1944.
            Mostly white material, but includes some black animal tales, jests,
            nursery tales, ballads, etc.

NA   Botkin, B.A., ed. *A Treasury of Mississippi River Folklore*. New York:
291   Crown, 1955.
            Miscellaneous folk material--songs, tales, hollers, etc.--reprinted
            from other sources.

NA   Botkin, B.A., ed. *A Treasury of Southern Folklore: Stories, Ballads,*
292   *Traditions, and Folkways of the People of the South*. New York: Crown,
            1949.
            Part 2 includes fables and myths, place legends, animal and nursery
            tales; ghost, witch, and devil tales.

NA 293 — Botkin, B.A. and Alvin F. Harlow. *A Treasury of Railroad Folklore*. New York: Crown, 1953.
Includes words and music for 3 Negro gang work songs and words for 3 more.

NA 294 — Botsford, Florence Hudson. *Botsford Collection of Folk Songs*. 2 Vols. New York: Women's Press, 1921-22.
Vol. 1 has 10 Negro and Creole folksongs (pp. 32-54).

NA 295 — Botume, Elizabeth Hyde. *First Days Amongst the Contrabands*. Boston: Lee and Shephard, 1893.
Memoirs of life and lore of the Gullah of the Carolina coast; music, speech, naming, clothing, etc.

NA 296 — Boucher, Jonathan. *Boucher's Glossary of Archaic and Provincial Words. A Supplement to the Dictionaries of the English Language*. London: Black, Young & Young, 1832.
Contains an entry on the musical instrument the *bandore*, among Virginia and Maryland slaves.

NA 297 — Boulware, Marcus H. *Jive and Slang of Students in Negro Colleges*. Hampton, Va.: Boulware, n.d.

NA 298 — Bourgare, Darrell. "Cauchemar and Fen Follet," *LFM*, 2, No. 4 (1968), 69-84.
Accounts of 2 Afro-Catholic spirits in Louisiana and beliefs associated with them.

NA 299 — Bowen, Elbert R. "Negro Minstrels in Early Rural Missouri," *Missouri Historical Review*, 47 (1953), 103-109.
A history of early minstrelsy considering its beginnings and activities in Missouri during the mid-1800's.

NA 300 — Bowers, Lessie. *Plantation Recipes*. New York: R. Speller, 1959.

NA 301 — Bowman, James Cloyd. *John Henry, The Rambling Black Ulysses*. Chicago: Albert Whitman, 1942.
Sketches of slave life, travel and celebrations. Includes 43 song texts with music throughout the text; gives sources.

NA 302 — Boyd, Joe Dan. "Ballad of the Black Sharecropper," *Farm Journal*, January, 1969, 39.
Brief history of the boll weevil ballad.

NA
303

Boyd, Joe Dan. "Judge Jackson: Black Giant of White Spirituals," *JAF*, 83 (1970), 446-451.
> Discusses the work of the compiler of *The Colored Sacred Harp*, a 1934 collection of Negro songs in shape notation.

NA
304

Boyd, Joe Dan. "Negro Sacred Harp Songsters in Mississippi," *MFR*, 5 (1971), 60-83.

NA
305

Boyd, Minnie Claire. *Alabama in the Fifties*. New York: Columbia University Press, 1931.
> Discusses folklife in general: Negro hunting games, etc.

NA
306

Boyer, Horace C. "Gospel Music Comes of Age," *Black World*, November, 1973, 42-48.
> Relates gospel songs to traditional styles and discusses their influence on other musics.

NA
307

Boyle, Virginia F. "Asmodeus in the Quarters," *Harper's*, 100 (1900), 217-222.
> Short story from Louisiana with folkloric content.

NA
308

Boyle, Virginia F. "Dark er de Moon," *Harper's*, 100 (1899), 58-68.
> Short story set in Louisiana with folkloric content.

NA
309

Boyle, Virginia F. *Devil Tales*. New York and London: Harper, 1900.
> 10 dialect tales told by "Mammy" to Negro and white children about the Devil and "the good hoodoo who must beat the devil at his own game."

NA
310

Boyle, Virginia F. "The Devil's Little Fly," *Harper's*, 101 (1900), 597-602.
> Short story from Louisiana with folkloric content.

NA
311

Boyle, Virginia F. "Old Cinder Cat," *Harper's*, 101 (1900), 416-422.
> Short story from Louisiana with folkloric content.

NA
312

Brackett, Jeffrey Richardson. "Colored People of Maryland Since the War," *Johns Hopkins Studies in Historical and Political Science*, 8 (1890), 347-442.
> Includes discussion of changing attitudes in the church towards the "shout" and emotionalism due to urbanization; social life of Baltimore: urban and rural types, social club promenades, drum-corps matches.

NA
313
Bradford, Alex. "Gospel Music," *JJ*, 16, No. 7 (1963), 13-14, 22.
Defines blues, gospel, spiritual.

NA
314
Bradford, Perry. *Born With the Blues*. New York: Oak, 1965.
Autobiography of a blues promoter and entrepreneur. Discussion of musicians and singers during early 1900's.

NA
315
Bradford, Roark. *John Henry*. New York: The Literary Guild, 1931.
Retelling of the life story of this legendary figure. Depicts many aspects of Negro life and work, including descriptions of "Coonjine" (cotton rolling), cotton picking, railroading, "superstitions," and other folkloric materials.

NA
316
Bradford, Roark. *John Henry: A Play*. New York: Harper, 1939.
Play with folkloric content.

NA
317
Bradford, Roark. *Kingdom Coming*. New York and London: Harper, 1933.
Novel of Louisiana plantation life with folkloric content.

NA
318
Bradford, Roark. *Let the Band Play Dixie, and Other Stories*. New York: Harper, 1934.
Short stories with folkloric content.

NA
319
Bradford, Roark. *Ol' King David an' The Philistine Boys*. New York and London: Harper, 1930.
The author retells 25 Bible stories in dialect.

NA
320
Bradford, Roark. *Ol' Man Adam an' His Chillun*. New York: Harper, 1928.
The author retells 32 Bible stories in dialect.

NA
321
Bradford, Roark. "Swing Low, Sweet Chariot," *Collier's*, 96 (September 21, 1935), 16-17, 69-70, 72.
Discussion of the Southern church with comments and sermons by preachers and an account of money collection in the church.

NA
322
Bradford, Roark. *This Side of Jordan*. New York and London: Harper, 1929.
A novel of Negro life in the Bayou which contains examples of folklife and folkways as well as much dialect.

NA
323
Bradford, S. Sidney. "The Negro Ironworker in Ante-Bellum Virginia," *Journal of Southern History*, 25 (1959), 194-206.

NA   Bradley, A.G. "A Peep at the Southern Negro," *Macmillan's Magazine*, 39
324   (1878), 61-68.
            Comments on Southern Negro houses, tenants, workers, entertainments.

NA   Bradley, A.G. "Some Plantation Memories," *Blackwood's Magazine*, 161
325   (1897), 331-341.
            Reminiscence of life on a Virginia plantation with reference to slave
            superstitions, names, and songs.

NA   Bradley, F.W. "The Bo' Dollar," *SFQ*, 25 (1961), 198-199.
326   An explanation of the meaning and origin of the term "Bo' Dollar."

NA   Bradley, F.W. "South Carolina Folklore," *The News and Courier* (Charleston,
327   South Carolina).
            A newspaper column which ran for a number of years carrying readers'
            contributions. Columns which contain Negro folklore include the fol-
            lowing: November 20. 1949 (notes on *nyam* and *geechie* and African pro-
            totypes); December 4, 18, 1949 (Gullah words and sayings); August 8,
            1954 (sayings); February 13, 20, 1955 (spiritual and secular song
            texts); February 27, 1955 (game song texts, counting out rhymes);
            March 13, 1955 (song texts and a description of the Buzzard Lope dance);
            March 20, 1955 (juba song texts); July 4, 11, 1955 (secular song texts);
            August 8 (description of a death watch, beliefs); August 15 (railroad
            workers' chants); October 9 (railroad song texts); October 17 (text of
            "Run, Nigger, Run"); October 24 (song texts); November 14 (work song
            texts); December 18 (railroad song texts, spirituals, etc.); January 16,
            1956 (song texts, swamp haunts).

NA   Brady, Margaret K. "'Gonna Shimmy 'til the Sun Goes Down:' Aspects of Ver-
328   bal and Nonverbal Socialization in the Play of Black Girls," in *Folk-
            lore Annual of the University Folklore Association*, No. 6, Austin:
            The University of Texas, 1974, 1-16.
            Communicative elements in play activities and their role in the social-
            ization of children.

NA   Brady, Margaret K. "'This Little Lady's Gonna Boogaloo': Elements of
329   Socialization in the Play of Black Girls," in *Black Girls at Play:
            Folkloric Perspectives on Child Development*. Austin, Texas: Southwest
            Educational Development Laboratory, 1975, pp. 1-51.
            Various folklore and play forms of girls five to nine are explored for
            their implications for socialization patterns; includes ring games,
            hand claps, jump rope rhymes and other games; texts.

NA   Brandon, Elizabeth. "Superstitions in Vermilion Parish," *PTFS*, No. 31
330   (1962), 108-118.
            Superstition in Vermilion Parish, the author concludes, is a mixture

of Negro and European (primarily French) influences. Discussion of charms, conjurations, ghosts, etc.

NA
331
Branner, John C. *How and Why Stories*. New York: Henry Holt, 1921.
22 explanatory tales recorded by the author from childhood memories.

NA
332
Brannon, P.A. "Central Alabama Negro Superstitions," *Birmingham (Alabama) News*. January 18, 1925, 15.

NA
333
Brawley, Benjamin. "Singing of Spirituals," *SW*, 63 (1934), 209-213.
Argues that black spirituals serve as degrading reminders of past slavery days.

NA
334
Bray, J.C. "More Mammy Stories," *New England Magazine*, n.s. 45 (February, 1912), 594-606.

NA
335
Brearly, H.C. "Ba-ad Nigger," *South Atlantic Quarterly*, 38 (1939), 75-81.
The badman among Southern Afro-Americans. (See No. NA 1427 for comments by Melville J. Herskovits.)

NA
336
Breman, Paul. *Blues: En Andere Wereldlijke Volksmusiek van de Noordameri- kaanse Neger*. The Hague: Servire-Wassenaar, 1961.
The blues as folk song; the subjects of the blues; the music; relations to ballads, hollers, worksongs, etc.; includes 35 blues texts with music and discussion; bibliography and discography.

NA
337
Breman, Paul. *Spirituals: Noordamerikaanse Geestelijke Volksliederen*. The Hague: Servire-Wassenaar, 1958.

NA
338
Bremer, Fredrika. *The Homes of the New World; Impressions of America*, 2 vols. New York: Harper, 1853.
Descriptions of church music and activities, a boat song, etc., in the South.

NA
339
"Brer Rabbit Outdone," *SW*, 25 (1896), 61.
1 tale.

NA
340
Brewer, John Mason. "Afro-American Folklore," *JAF*, 60 (1947), 371-382.
A discussion of research potential in Afro-American folklore.

NA 341   Brewer, John Mason. "American Negro Folklore," *Phylon*, 6 (1945), 354-361.
  Points out the primary forms of Negro folklore current in the present era; contains excerpts from 3 social songs, rhymes, and folk tales.

NA 342   Brewer, John Mason. *American Negro Folklore*. Chicago: Quadrangle Books, 1968.
  80 tales concerning animals, "how come" and "why;" folk figures, ghosts, ranch life, "Aunt Dicy," and the North and South; 11 tales concerning religion; 6 sermons; 3 prayers; 17 spirituals; 6 folk blues; 10 slave secular and work songs; 8 ballads, 6 other songs; 28 personal experiences of slavery time, Reconstruction, religious conversion, wartime experiences, etc.; 17 superstitions; 350 proverbs; 19 rhymes; 40 riddles; and collections of names and children's rhymes and pastimes; primarily from previously published or manuscript sources.

NA 343   Brewer, John Mason. *Aunt Dicey Tales: Snuff-Dipping Tales of the Texas Negro*. Austin, Texas: n.p., 1956.
  14 tales from Lee County, Texas; illustrations.

NA 344   Brewer, John Mason. *Dog Ghosts and Other Texas Negro Folk Tales*. Austin, Texas: University of Texas Press, 1958.
  9 tales of slavery and its legacy, 12 tales of animals and ranch life, 9 religious tales, 18 dog ghost tales, and other collected in the Red River bottoms and elsewhere in Texas. Presented as told but with dialect regularized. Informants listed.

NA 345   Brewer, John Mason. "Hidden Language: Ghetto Children Know What They're Talking About," *New York Times Magazine*, December 25, 1966, 32-35. (Reprinted in Dundes, No. NA 854.)
  Examples of urban children's slang and verbal art, and a teacher's use of them.

NA 346   Brewer, John Mason, ed. *Humorous Folk Tales of the South Carolina Negro*. Orangeburg, South Carolina: South Carolina Negro Folklore Guild, Publication No. 1 (1945).
  5 tales of master and slave; 4 concerning the farm; 6 school tales, 8 church tales, 5 railroad tales, and others.

NA 347   Brewer, John Mason. "John Tales," *PTFS*, No. 21 (1946), 81-104.
  22 "John" tales from South Carolina.

NA 348   Brewer, John Mason. "Juneteenth," *PTFS*, No. 10 (1932), 9-54.
  39 tales.

NA
349

Brewer, John Mason. *Negrito: Negro Dialect Poems of the Southwest*. San Antonio, Texas: Naylor, 1933.

NA
350

Brewer, John Mason. "North Carolina Negro Oral Narratives," *NCF*, 9 (1961), 21-33.
Mentions the popular "migrant son" theme, and notes the conspicuous absence of animal tales. Includes 7 religious anecdotes, 9 secular tales and anecdotes, 2 Negro individual experiences, 5 traditional Negro tales about whites.

NA
351

Brewer, John Mason. "Old-Time Negro Proverbs," *PTFS*, No. 11 (1933), 101-105.
A collection of proverbs "taken from the speech of ex-slaves and elderly Negroes living in Central Texas."

NA
352

Brewer, John Mason. *The Word on the Brazos. Negro Preacher Tales from the Brazos Bottoms of Texas*. Austin, Texas: University of Texas Press, 1953.
56 tales collected by the author and included in five main topics: "Bad Religion"; "Baptizings, Conversions, and Church Meetings"; "Good Religion"; "Heaven and Hell"; "Preachers and Little Boys."

NA
353

Brewer, John Mason. *Worser Days and Better Times. The Folklore of the North Carolina Negro*. Chicago: Quadrangle Books, 1965.
19 tales about religion, church and ministers; 11 puns and comic misunderstandings; 10 tales of the wise and foolish; 4 animal tales; 4 tales concerning marriage; 6 about mountain whites; 3 ghost stories; 5 tall tales; 16 tales about race.

NA
354

Brinton, Daniel G. "On Certain Supposed Nanticoke Words, Shown to be of African Origin," *American Antiquarian*, 9, No. 6 (1887), 350-354.
Notes on the language of Mandingo (African) slaves living among Nanticoke Indians of Maryland.

NA
355

Broddy, Haldeen. "The Spook of Sulphur Springs, Texas," *JAF*, 59 (1946), 317-319.
Legend of a haunting in 1945.

NA
356

Bronsard, James F. *Louisiana Creole Dialect*. Baton Rouge, Louisiana: Louisiana State University Press, 1942.
Includes proverbs, magical formulas, "superstitions," poetry, and tales of the French-speaking Negroes of Southern Louisiana.

NA
357

Brookes, Stella Brewer. *Joel Chandler Harris--Folklorist*. Athens, Georgia:
The University of Georgia Press, 1950.
Includes summaries of 22 "myths" and 3 moral tales all from Harris's
writings. Synopses of a few trickster tales. Summaries of 2 ghost
stories, 3 tales of conjure, a few devil tales. (Only short paragraphs
of narratives are included.)

NA
358

Brookins, Melvin S. "Aspiration," in *Rappin' and Stylin' Out*, Thomas
Kochman, ed. Urbana, Ill.: University of Illinois Press, 1972, 381-
385. (Reprinted from *Liberator*, Dec., 1967.)
Short story includes description of the style and verbal idioms of
a "hustler."

NA
359

Brooks, Cleanth. *The Relation of the Alabama-Georgia Dialect to the
Provincial Dialects of Great Britain*. Baton Rouge, Louisiana: Louisi-
ana State University Press, 1935.
Southern Black English seen as a dialect exclusively derived from
British dialects.

NA
360

Broonzy, Big Bill. *Big Bill Blues: William Broonzy's Story (As Told to
Yannick Bruynoghe)*. London: Cassel, 1955 (New edition, New York:
Oak, 1964, has a new introduction by Charles Edward Smith.)
Autobiography of a Mississippi blues singer; discography; texts of
blues.

NA
361

Brotz, Howard. *The Black Jews of Harlem*. New York: Free Press, 1964.
Account of the origin and structure of a sect.

NA
362

Broun, Lawrence. *Spirituals*. London: Schott, 1923.
5 songs.

NA
363

Broven, John J. "Chester 'Howlin Wolf' Barnett," *BU*, Collectors Classics
No. 4 (December, 1964).
Biography of a Mississippi bluesman; discography.

NA
364

Brown, C.C. *Uncle Dan'l and his Friends*. Greenville, South Carolina: Keys
and Thomas, n.d.
Includes beliefs and descriptions of sermons, religious services, wakes,
and religious experiences among High Country South Carolina Negroes.

NA
365

Brown, Cecil. "James Brown, Hoodoo and Black Culture," in *Black Review*,
No. 1, Mel Watkins, ed. New York: William Morrow, 1971, 180-185.
Pop singer Brown as creator of folk poetry.

NA
366

Brown, Cecil. *The Life and Loves of Mr. Jiveass Nigger.* Greenwich,
Conn.: Fawcett, 1971.
A novel, with traditional joke texts interspersed.

NA
367

Brown, Claude. "The Language of Soul," *Esquire*, 69 (April, 1968),
88, 160, 162.
"Hip" vocabulary list.

NA
368

The Frank C. Brown Collection of North Carolina Folklore, 7 vols.,
Newman Ivey White, ed. Durham, N.C.: Duke University Press, 1952-1964.
Vol. 1 includes Negro games, rhymes, beliefs, customs, riddles, proverbs,
speech tales and legends; Vol. 2 includes ballads, Vol. 3 songs (spirituals), Vol. 4 music of the ballads, Vol. 5 music of the songs, Vols.
6-7 beliefs and "superstitions."

NA
369

Brown, H. Rap. *Die Nigger Die!* New York: Dial, 1969.
Includes discussion and examples of the dozens, signifying and toasts.

NA
370

Brown, Hugh S. "Voodooism in Northwest Louisiana," *LFM*, 2, No. 2 (1965),
74-86.
Accounts of voodoo practice.

NA
371

Brown, John Mason. "Songs of the Slave," *Lippincott's Magazine,* 9 (1868),
617-623. (Reprinted in Nos. NA 1568 and NA 1698.)
A collection of varied songs--spirituals, steamboat, farm, leisure
songs and ballads--with musical examples.

NA
372

Brown, Marcie. "Notes on Classical and Renaissance Analogues of Mississippi
Negro Folklore," *MFR*, 2 (1968), 37-41.
Medical folklore with comparisons in literature.

NA
373

Brown, Marion. "Improvisation and the Aural Tradition in Afro-American
Music," *Black World*, November, 1973, 14-19.
The importance of oral-aural culture in Afro-American life and values,
with an emphasis on improvisation as an aural technique. Discusses
jazz and jazzmen as exemplars of the tradition.

NA
374

Brown, Sterling A. "Background of Folklore in Negro Literature," *Jackson
College Bulletin,* 2, No. 1 (1953), 26-30. (Reprinted in Dundes, No. NA 854.)

NA
375

Brown, Sterling A. "The Blues," *Phylon*, 13 (1952), 286-292.
A general discussion of blues which includes some historical data, text
explanations and remarks about the influence of blues on white singers
and modern singers.

NA
376
Brown, Sterling A. "The Blues as Folk Poetry," in *Folk-Say*, 2 (1930), 324-339.
Blues as an introduction to folklife; blues containing "superstitions," proverbs, actual events, love; imagery, rhymes, hyperbole, poetic transcriptions of folk expressions.

NA
377
Brown, Sterling A. "Blues, Ballads, and Social Songs," in *75 Years of Freedom. Commemoration of the 75th Anniversary of the Proclamation of the 13th Amendment to the Constitution of the U.S.* Washington, D.C.: Library of Congress, 1943, 17-25.
A discussion of the subject matter of the blues.

NA
378
Brown, Sterling A. "The Devil and the Black Man," *Folk-Say*, 4 (1932), 246-256.
Poems with folkloric content.

NA
379
Brown, Sterling A. "Lonesome Valley," *Folk-Say*, 3 (1931), 112-123.
Poems with folkloric content.

NA
380
Brown, Sterling A. "The Muted South," *Phylon*, 6 (1945), 22-34.
5 sketches of Negro life in the South; the sketch entitled "Po' Wanderin' Pildom, Miserus Chile," contains excerpts from 4 spriituals.

NA
381
Brown, Sterling A. "Negro Folk Expression," *Phylon*, 11 (1950), 318-327.
Overview of Negro folk tales.

NA
382
Brown, Sterling A. "Negro Folk Expression: Spirituals, Seculars, Ballads and Work Songs," *Phylon*, 14 (1953), 45-61.
Uses texts of songs to demonstrate special meaning in Negro spirituals; hero, anti-religious, and slavery themes in Ballads; social protest in work songs; also discusses the relationship of Negro and white spirituals and trends in Negro folk culture.

NA
383
Brown, Sterling A. *The Negro in American Fiction.* Washington, D.C.: Associates in Negro Folk Education, 1937.
Chapter 8, "Realism and the Folk," critically reviews the writings of A. Gonzales, D. Heyward, J. Peterkin, H. Odum, R. Bradford, *et al.*

NA
384
Brown, Sterling A. *Negro Poetry and Drama.* Washington, D.C.: Associates in Negro Folk Education, 1937.
Chapter 2, "Negro Folk Poetry," is a review of folk song and verse forms.

NA
385

Brown, Sterling A., Arthur P. Davis and Ulysses Lee, eds. *Negro Caravan*.
New York: Dryden Press, 1942.
Section 4 ("Folk Literature") has a 22 page introduction; 19 spiritual
texts of songs; 8 secular song texts; 7 ballad texts; 6 work and
social songs; 5 social protest songs; 11 blues; 6 folktales and 1
folk sermon.

NA
386

Brown, W. Norman. "Hindu Stories in American Negro Folklore," *Asia*, 21
(1921), 703-707. (Reprinted in *Literary Digest*, 70 (August 6, 1921),
28.)
Argues for the Hindu ancestry of "Uncle Remus" Tales (especially "Br'er
Rabbit and the Gizzard Eater").

NA
387

Brown, W. Norman. "The Tar-Baby at Home," *Scientific Monthly*, 15 (September, 1922), 228-234.
The tar-baby motif examined: argues that it occurred in India 2000
years earlier than elsewhere, but rejects it as a source for the
Afro-American motif.

NA
388

Brown, William Wells. *Clotel, or the President's Daughter*. London: Partridge
and Oakey, 1853.
Novel by an ex-slave, with folkloric content: slaves' reaction to
white religion, African customs among slaves, speech, etc.

NA
389

Brown, William Wells. *My Southern Home: or, The South and its People*. Boston: A.G. Brown and Co., 1880.
Descriptions by an ex-slave, of slave life, dress, religion, rituals,
voodoo, crafts, tribal names, music, burial societies, etc. (pp. 167-
170, 172-176).

NA
390

Browne, B.W. "The Buzzard in the Folklore of Western Kentucky," *KFR*, 4
(1958), 11-12.
Reference to the buzzard in sayings, games, etc.

NA
391

Browne, Ray B. "The Alabama 'Holler' and Street Cries," *JAF*, 70 (1957),
363.
2 texts from literary sources.

NA
392

Browne, Ray B. "Negro Folktales from Alabama," *SFQ*, 18 (1954), 129-134.
12 preacher-parables.

NA
393

Browne, Ray B. *Popular Beliefs and Practices From Alabama*. Berkeley:
University of California Press, 1958.
"A fourth of the collection is 'Negro,'" though only 6 of the author's
informants were black.

NA
394
Browne, Ray B. "Shakespeare in American Vaudeville and Negro Minstrelsy," *American Quarterly*, 12 (1960), 374-391.
Lyrics from 12 Negro minstrel songs with references to Shakespeare; detailed description of nineteenth century vaudeville and the Shakespearian influence; excerpts of texts; bibliography.

NA
395
Browne, Ray. B. "Some Notes on the Southern 'Holler'," *JAF*, 67 (1954), 73-77.
Examines the use of the "holler" among Alabama whites and discusses its origin and relationship to the Negro "holler."

NA
396
Browne, Theodore. *Natural Man*. n.p., 1936.

NA
397
Browning, Elizabeth Jones. "Don't Yet Fetch It!" *TFSB*, 25 (1959), 79.

NA
398
Browning, James Blackwell. "The Free Negro in Ante-Bellum North Carolina," *North Carolina Historical Review*, 15, No. 1 (1938), 23-33.
Describes free Negro occupations, blacks at markets, a West Indian black arbitrating a dispute between the North Carolina governor and a senator in 1808.

NA
399
Broyard, Anatole. "Keep Cool, Man. The Negro Reflection of Jazz," *Commentary*, 11 (April, 1951), 359-362.
Development of new vocabulary and grammar among black Harlem musicians; "coolness" as the "congealing of the Negro's unfulfilled wishes."

NA
400
Broyard, Anatole. "A Portrait of the Hipster," *Partisan Review*, 15 (June, 1948), 721-727. (Reprinted in *The Scene Before You: A New Approach to American Culture*, Chandler Brossard, ed. New York: Rinehart, 1955, 113-119.)
Describes the lifestyle of some urban black "street" figures of the 1940's.

NA
401
Broyard, Anatole. "Portrait of the Inauthentic Negro," *Commentary*, 10 (July, 1950), 56-64.
Explores a variety of avenues of "escape from the self": "tomming," "being bad," etc.; discusses issues of speech, style, and role.

NA
402
Bruce, Dickson D., Jr. "Religion, Society and Culture in the Old South: A Comparative View," *American Quarterly*, 26 (1974), 399-416.

NA
403
Brunner, Theodore B. "Thirteen Tales from Houston County," *PTFS*, No. 31 (1962), 8-22.
Collection of folk tales gathered from an agricultural-lumbering region in the Piney Woods of East Texas.

NA
404
Bryant, Margaret M. "Folklore from Edgefield County, South Carolina," *SFQ*, 12 (1948), 197-209; 279-291; 13 (1949), 136-148.
8 tales; 91 riddles, 118 beliefs and practices; 239 "superstitions," cures, etc.

NA
405
Bryant, William Cullen. *Letters of a Traveller; or Notes of Things Seen in Europe and America*. New York: Putnam, 1850.
Includes an account of black tobacco rollers singing psalms (p. 74), corn-shucking (p. 84), stump-speech (p. 85), tombstone script (p. 95).

NA
406
Bryant, Winifred. "Negro Services," *American Missionary*, 46 (1892), 301-302.

NA
407
Brymer, D. "The Jamaica Maroons: How They Came to Nova Scotia--How They Left It," *Transactions of the Royal Society of Canada* (2nd series), 1, No. 2 (1895), 81-90.

NA
408
Buckingham, James Silk. *The Slave States of America*. Vol. 1. London: 1842.
Accounts of Negro dress, food, beliefs, Free Negro businesses, etc.

NA
409
Buckley, Bruce R. "Uncle Ira Cephas--A Negro Folk Singer in Ohio," *MF*, 3 (1953), 5-18.
Narrative work songs, old blues, "little ditties," hymns, and spirituals.

NA
410
Buehler, Richard E. "Stacker Lee: A Partial Investigation into the Historicity of a Negro Murder Ballad," *KFQ*, 12 (1967), 187-191.
Offers some tentative facts about Stacker Lee, who seems to have been the historical personage whose name became associated with the hero of a Negro murder ballad, "Stacker-lee."

NA
411
Buel, J.W. *Mysteries and Miseries of America's Great Cities*. San Francisco: A.L. Bancroft, 1883.
Sections on New Orleans deal with voodoo extensively: texts, comparisons with Africa, etc.; includes a sermon text, description of dances; illustrations.

NA
412
Buerkle, Jack V. and Danny Barker. *Bourbon Street Black: The New Orleans Black Jazzman*. New York: Oxford University Press, 1973.
Includes accounts of the lifestyle of early jazz musicians.

NA
413
Bullen, Frank R. and W.F. Arnold. *Songs of Sea Labour*. London: Swan, 1914.
Texts and music of chanties, a number of them of Negro origin, with annotation and a discussion of Negro chanty music.

NA
414
Bullock, Mrs. Waller R. "The Collection of Maryland Folklore," *JAF*, 11 (1898), 7-16.
Sayings and tales, collected from compositions from students of various schools.

NA
415
Burch, Charles E. "Negro Character in the Novels of William Gilmore Simms," *SW*, 52 (1923), 192-195.
Examines the life-style of slaves through the character portrayals in William Simms' novels.

NA
416
Burch, Charles E. "The Plantation Negro in Dunbar's Poetry," *SW*, 50 (1921), 227-229.
Examines the poetry of Dunbar with emphasis on black character portrayals and documented accounts of Southern plantation life and customs.

NA
417
Burchard, Hank. "In Quest of the Historical John Henry," *The Washington Post and Times-Herald* (Potomac Section) (August 24, 1969), 12-16, 22-24.
Evidence that John Henry could have indeed beaten a Burleigh steam drill on the Big Bend Tunnel.

NA
418
Burleigh, Henry Thacker. *Album of Negro Spirituals*. New York: Ricardi, 1917-1924.
43 songs.

NA
419
Burleigh, Henry Thacker. *Negro Folk Songs*, 4 vols. New York: Ricardi, 1921.

NA
420
Burleigh, Henry Thacker. "On Spirituals," *Challenge*, 1, No. 1 (1934), 26-27.
Argues against the "desecration" of spirituals by dance musicians. (See reply by Walter Everette Hawkins in *Challenge*, 1, No. 2 (1934), 13-14.)

NA
421
    Burleigh, Henry Thacker. *Plantation Melodies: Old and New*. New York:
        Schirmer, 1901.

NA
422
    Burley, Dan. *Dan Burley's Original Handbook of Harlem Jive*. New York:
        Published by the Author, 1944.

NA
423
    Burley, Dan. *Diggeth Thou?* Chicago: Burley, Cross, 1959.

    Burley, Dan. See Simmons, Gloria M., No. NA 2729.

NA
424
    Burlin, Natalie Curtis. "Again the Negro," *Poetry*, 11 (1917), 147-151.
        4 folksongs from St. Helena Island, analyzed as poetry.

NA
425
    Burlin, Natalie Curtis. *Hampton Series Negro Folk-Songs*. 4 vols. New
        York: Schirmer, 1918-1919.
        Hampton Series: Vols. 1-2, 8 spirituals; Vols. 2-4, 11 work and play
        songs. (Notation of what was sung by the Hampton Quartet.)

NA
426
    Burlin, Natalie Curtis. "How Negro Folk-Songs are Born," *Current Opinion*,
        66 (March, 1919), 165-166.
        Black "intuitive" song and music: accounts of African influenced revi-
        val-spirituals.

NA
427
    Burlin, Natalie Curtis. "Negro Music at Birth," *MQ*, 5 (1919), 86-89.
        Description of collective spontaneity of Negro musicians.

NA
428
    Burlin, Natalie Curtis. "The Negro's Contribution to the Music of Ameri-
        ca," *Craftsman*, 23 (1913), 660-669.

NA
429
    Burlin, Natalie Curtis. *Two Old Negro Christmas Songs*. New York: Huntzinger
        and Dilworth, 1919.

    Burlin, Natalie Curtis. See also Curtis, Natalie.

NA
430
    Burma, John H. "Humor As a Technique in Race Conflict," *American Sociolog-
        ical Review*, 2 (1946), 710-715.
        Discussion of Negro and white jokes which utilize racial stereotypes
        and their role. Examples.

NA   Burman, Ben Lucien. "Mississippi Roustabout," *Harper's Magazine*, 180
431   (1940), 635-643.
              Memoirs and description of hoodoo doctors on the Mississippi River;
              accounts of roustabouts and their rhythmic chants, with lyrics.

NA   Burman, Ben Lucien. "Music on the Mississippi," *Saturday Review*, 38
432   (December 3, 1955), 15-16, 36-38.
              The author discusses his experiences with folk music, including some
              black material, and how it was incorporated into his novels.

NA   Burns, Jim. "The Hipster," *JJ*, 21, No. 7 (1968), 2-4.
433   Review of literature of an urban figure located in black music circles
              in the late 1940's and '50's.

NA   Burns, Jim. "What's Your Song King Kong?" *Jazz and Blues* (London), 1
434   (August-September, 1971), 12-13.
              A review of Clarence Major's *Dictionary of Afro-American Slang* with
              further comments on black slang and the problems of studying it.

NA   Burrison, John A. *"The Golden Arm": The Folk Tale and Its Literary Use by
435   Mark Twain and Joel C. Harris*. Atlanta: School of Arts and Sciences,
              Georgia State College, Research Paper No. 19, 1968.
              The study of a folktale used by Twain and Harris; includes several Afro-
              American variants.

NA   Burroughs, Margaret Taylor. *Did You Feed My Cow? Street Games, Chants and
436   Rhymes Collected in Chicago's South Side*. New York: Crowell, 1956.
              (Revised edition, Chicago: Follett, 1969.)

NA   Burroughs, Margaret Taylor. *Whip Me Whop Me Pudding and Other Stories of
437   Riley Rabbit and His Fabulous Friends*. Chicago: printed for the author,
              1966.
              29 retold Brer Rabbit tales, some reprinted from folklore journals,
              others collected from adults.

NA   Burt, Olive Wooley. *American Murder Ballads and Their Stories*. New York:
438   Oxford University Press, 1958.
              Includes Negro and white ballad material with discussion.

NA   Burt, Mrs. W.C. "The Baptist Ox," *JAF*, 34 (1921), 397-398.
439   1 tale in dialect from South Carolina.

NA
440
Burwell, Letitia M. *A Girl's Life in Virginia Before the War*. New York: Stokes, 1895.
Account of a dance around the deathbed of a slave (p. 163).

NA
441
Butcher, Margaret Just. *The Negro in American Culture*. New York: Knopf, 1956.
Includes chapters reviewing Negro folklore, music, dance and poetry, and an account of their recognition in the United States; division of Negro folk music into 6 regions.

NA
442
Butler, Melvin Arthur. "African Linguistic Remnants in the Speech of Black Louisianians," *Bulletin of the Southern University and A & M College*, 55 (June, 1969), 45-52.

NA
443
Butterfield, Stephen. *Black Autobiography in America*. Amherst: University of Massachusetts Press, 1974.
Includes an analysis of slave and ex-slave autobiographies, their use of language and the influence of white writers.

NA
444
Butterworth, Hezekiah. *A Zigzag Journey in the Sunny South*. Boston: Estes and Lauriat, 1887.
Includes tale texts, song texts, an illustration of an elevated burial place, accounts of collecting folk songs, etc.

NA
445
Buttitta, Anthony J. "Negro Folklore in North Carolina," in *Negro Anthology*, Nancy Cunard, ed. London: Wishart, 1934, 62-66.
Concerned with "superstitions"--voodoo, medical lore, bad luck and omens--but there is a paragraph on songs.

NA
446
Byers, James F. "Voodoo: Tropical Pharmacology or Psychosomatic Psychology?" *NYFQ*, 26 (1970), 305-312.
Argues that voodoo practices depend more on toxicology than on psychology.

NA
447
Byers, Paul and Hoppie Byers. "Nonverbal Communication and the Education of Children," in *Functions of Language in the Classroom*, Courtney B. Cazden, Vera P. John, and Dell Hymes, eds. New York: Teachers College Press, 1972, 3-31.
Discusses black non-verbal communication.

NA
448
Byrd, James W. "Current Jazz Lingo," *TFSB*, 22 (1956), 21-25.
A discussion with examples of words and phrases.

NA
449

Byrd, James W. *J. Mason Brewer: Negro Folklorist*. Austin, Texas: Steck-Vaughn, 1968.
Brief sketch of Brewer's life and works; reprints selections from his books.

NA
450

Byrd, James W. "Zora Neale Hurston: A Novel Folklorist," *TFSB*, 21 (1955), 37-41.
Hurston's capacity for appropriating Negro folklore to the purposes of fiction; with excerpts.

NA
451

Byrd, Mabel. "Plantation Proverbs of 'Uncle Remus,'" *Crisis*, 27 (January, 1924), 118-119.
Discussion of Uncle Remus' proverbs as typical of those of the ante-bellum Negro.

NA
452

C.H.F. "Negro Worship and Music," *New York Times*, February 25, 1877, p. 5.
Description of a Negro church service in Alabama.

NA
453

C.W.D. "Contraband Singing," *Dwight's Journal of Music*, 19 (September 7, 1861), 182. (Reprinted in No. NA 1568.)

NA
454

Cable, George W. "Creole Slave Songs," *Century Magazine*, 31 (1886), 807-828 (Reprinted in No. NA 1568.)
Texts and music of 7 love songs, "dirges," work songs, "voodoo" rituals, etc.

NA
455

Cable, George W. *Creoles and Cajuns; Stories of Old Louisiana*, Arlin Turner, ed. New York: Doubleday, 1959.
13 stories, text and music for 6 different dances and 5 types of songs.

NA
456

Cable, George W. "The Dance in Place Congo," *Century Magazine*, New Series 2 (1886), 517-532. (Reprinted in Nos. NA 1568 and NA 1698.)
A discussion of the background of Congo Square--its people and its function. Also a treatment of individual slave dances and instruments with musical examples.

NA
457

Cable, George W. *The Grandissimes*. New York: Scribners, 1880.
Novel of Louisiana Creole life with folkloric content.

NA
458

Cable, George W. "A Negro Folksong," *The Folklorist* (Chicago), 1 (1892), 54.
Game rhyme with music and annotation.

Cable, George W. See *Historical Sketch Book and Guide to New Orleans*, No. NA 1449.

Cable, George W. See Pugh, Griffith T., No. NA 2504.

Cable, George W. See Smith, Hugh, No. NA 2770.

Cable, George W. See Tinker, Edward L., No. NA 2998.

Cable, George W. See Turner, Arlin, No. NA 3034.

NA
459
Cade, John B. "Out of the Mouth of Ex-Slaves," *JNH*, 20 (1935), 294-337.
Selections from 82 interviews with ex-slaves, including food, clothing, and family life, etc.

NA
460
Cadwallader, D.E. and J.F. Wilson. "Folklore Medicine among Georgia's Piedmont Negroes after the Civil War," *GHQ*, 49 (1965), 217-226.
Plant cures from unpublished WPA Georgia Writers Project manuscripts.

NA
461
"Cakewalk King; 81 Year Old Charles E. Johnson Still Dreams of New Comeback with Dance Step of Gay 90's," *Ebony*, February, 1953, 99-102.

NA
462
Cajun, Andre. *Louisiana Voodoo*. New Orleans: Harmanson, n.d.

NA
463
Caldwell, Joan. "Christmas in Old Natchez," *Journal of Mississippi History*, 21 (1959), 257-270.

NA
464
Caldwell, Lewis A.H. *The Policy King*. Chicago: New Vistas, 1945.
Novel of black life, gambling in Chicago.

NA
465
Calloway, Al and Claude Brown. "An Introduction to Soul," *Esquire*, 69, (April, 1968), 79-87.
Illustrated essay on black style, food, etc.

NA   Calloway, Cab. *Cab Calloway's Cat-ologue*. New York: Mills Artists, 1938.
467   Definition of 150 "jive" terms, most of them connected with music.

NA   Calloway, Cab. *The New Cab Calloway's Hepsters Dictionary*. New York:
468   C. Calloway, 1944.
            15 page "hip" slang dictionary.

NA   Cameron, Ian. "Negro Songs," *Musical Times*, (London), 68 (1922), 431-432.
469   Discussion of content and expression in Negro secular and religious
            songs, with 9 texts.

NA   Cameron, Rebecca. "Christmas at Buchoi, a North Carolina Rice Plantation,"
470   *The North Carolina Booklet*, 13 (July, 1913), 3, 8-10. (Originally pub-
            lished in the *Ladies Home Journal* in 1891.)
            Description of "John Coonah" festivities in North Carolina.

NA   Cameron, William Bruce. "Is Jazz a Folk-Art?" *NYFQ*, 12 (1956), 263-271.
471   Argues that jazz is a folk-art by comparing it to such folk elements
            as group intimacy, isolation, loyalty, jargon, and improvisation.

NA   Campbell, E. Simms. "Blues are the Negroes' Lament," *Esquire*, 7 (Decem-
472   ber, 1939), 100, 276-280. (Reprinted as "Blues," in *Jazzmen*, Frederic
            Ramsey, Jr. and Charles Edward Smith, eds. New York: Harcourt, Brace,
            1939, 101-117.)
            The nature and meaning of the blues.

NA   Campbell, E. Simms. "Early Jam," in *The Negro Caravan*, Sterling A. Brown,
473   Arthur P. Davis, and Ulysses Lee, eds. New York: Dryden, 1941, 983-990.
            (Reprinted from "Jam in the Nineties," *Esquire*, 10 (December, 1938).)
            Overview of urban night-life music and dance from 1880-1930.

NA   Campbell, James Edwin. *Driftings and Gleanings*. Charleston, West Virginia,
474   1887.

NA   Campbell, James Edwin. *Echoes from the Cabin and Elsewhere*. Chicago: Dona-
475   hue and Henneberry, 1895.
            Includes a black poet's fables in poem form; poetry on everyday rural
            life--hunting, cooking, work, dance, religion, etc.; in dialect.

NA   Campbell, Killis. "Poe's Treatment of the Negro and Negro Dialect," *Uni-
476   versity of Texas Studies in English*, 16 (1936), 107-114.

NA 477 Campbell, Marie. "Folk Remedies From South Georgia," *TFSB*, 19 (1953), 1-4.
Folk remedies in practice among the Gullah of the South Georgia coastal area.

NA 478 Campbell, Marie. *Folks Do Get Born*. New York: Rinehart, 1946.
Birth and childrearing lore from Georgia midwives; Anancy beliefs recorded.

NA 479 "A Camp-Meeting in Tennessee," *Harper's*, 26, No. 151 (1862), 97-101.
Account of a camp-meeting in 1856 with text of a sermon and description of the camp.

NA 480 Candler, Myrtie Long. "Reminiscences of Life in Georgia during the 1850's and 1860's," *GHQ*, 33 (1949), 36-49, 110-124, 218-228, 303-314; 34 (1950), 10-19.
A white woman's account of black influences on her belief in ghosts (p. 39); house servants' dress, housing, etc., in town (p. 110); plantation slaves' games and belief in spirits (p. 120); cooking (p. 224).

NA 481 Canfield, Ruth. "The Tale of the Six Toed Negro," *KFQ*, 6, No. 2 (1961), 29-31.
1 ghost tale.

NA 482 "Canning Negro Melodies," *Literary Digest*, 52 (1916), 1556, 1558-1559.
Plantation songs and melodies of South Carolina Negroes; 1 work song, 1 cotton chant, 1 ditcher's cry, 1 dance song.

NA 483 Cannon, Elizabeth Perry and Catherine J. Duncan. "Leaves From A Rural Journal," *Phylon*, 1 (1940), 57-68.
Details of life in rural Georgia--names, dialect, diet, etc.

NA 484 Cantril, Hadley and Muzafer Sherif. "The Kingdom of Father Divine," *Journal of Abnormal Psychology*, 33 (April, 1938), 147-167.
Songs and testimonial practices of a Harlem religious group.

NA 485 Canziani, Willy. "Negro Spirituals," *Jazz Podium*, 6, No. 12 (1957), 12-13.

NA 486 Carawan, Guy. "The Living Heritage of the Sea Islands," *SO*, 14, No. 2 (1964), 29-32.
A description of folk singing, worship, festivals, etc., of the inhabitants of the South Carolina and Georgia Sea Islands. Includes songs with text and music.

NA   Carawan, Guy. "Spiritual Singing in the South Carolina Sea Islands,"
487   *Caravan*, No. 20 (1960), 20-25.
          Description of singing with a transcription of a song.

NA   Carawan, Guy and Candie Carawan. *Freedom is a Constant Struggle: Songs*
488   *of the Freedom Movement*. New York: Oak, 1968.
          Adaptations of traditional songs from: Alabama (4), Florida (3),
          Georgia (1), Mississippi (1), and South Carolina (4).

NA   Carawan, Guy and Candie Carawan. "John's Island," *SO*, 16, No. 1 (1966),
489   25-30.
          A look at a South Carolina island, isolated for many years from the
          mainland, finds many songs and customs preserved from slavery and
          Africa.

NA   Carawan, Guy and Candie Carawan. *We Shall Overcome!* New York: Oak, 1963.
490   A songbook of the Freedom Movement with photographs of the central
          figures involved.

NA   Carawan, Guy and Alan Lomax. "Sea Island Folk Festival," booklet included
491   with Folkways LP record 3841.
          Notes and texts for 12 songs.

NA   Carawan, Guy, Candie Carawan and Robert Yellin. *Ain't You Got a Right to*
492   *the Tree of Life? The People of Johns Island, South Carolina--Their*
          Faces, Their Words and Their Songs. New York: Simon and Schuster,
          1966.
          21 remembrances of past life, 11 accounts of contemporary life, 10
          descriptions of religious services and several shouts, prayers, and
          sermons; 10 stories and other comments as well as 21 songs, spirituals
          and photographs.

NA   Carew, Roy J. "New Orleans Recollection," *RC*, April, 1943, 8-9; May, 10-
493   11; June, 2-3; July, 3-4; September, 3-4; October, 3-4; November,
          3; December, 14-15; January, 1944, 3.
          Reminiscences of New Orleans at the turn of the century including
          social life, musicians, etc.

NA   Carew, Roy J. "Of This and That and Jelly Roll," *JJ*, 10, No. 12 (1957),
494   10-12.
          Reminiscences of pianist Jelly Roll Morton and popular and jazz music
          of the early 1900's.

NA
495
Carew, Roy J. "Reminiscing in Ragtime," *JJ*, 17, No. 11 (1964), 8-9.
Discussion of the origins of ragtime piano in the Midwest and New
Orleans.

Carew, Roy J. See Kay, George W., No. NA 1700.

NA
496
Carew, Roy J. and Don E. Fowler. "Scott Joplin: Overlooked Genius," *RC*,
September, 1944, 12-14, 59; October, 1944, 10-12, 65; December, 1944,
10-11, 48.
Life and music of an early ragtime composer.

NA
497
Carleton, George. *The Suppressed Book about Slavery*. New York, 1864.
Accounts of slave life; interviews with slaves; "blanket marriages,"
songs and rhymes, etc.

NA
498
Carlisle, Natalie Taylor. "Old Time Darky Plantation Melodies," *PTFS*,
No. 5 (1926), 137-143.
Texts and music of songs from Texas with discussions of their musical
characteristics.

NA
499
Carlson, A.D. "Negro Spirituals at our own Firesides," *Better Homes and
Gardens*, 10 (July, 1932), 16.

NA
500
Carlton, Robert (Hall, Baynard Rush). *The New Purchase*. New York: D. Appleton; Philadelphia: G.S. Appleton, 1843.
Includes Rev. Mizraim Ham's Discourse, a sermon by a Negro preacher
in Indiana.

NA
501
Carmer, Carl. *Stars Fell on Alabama*. New York: Doubleday, 1934.
2 black "rituals" from the Tuscaloosa area, 6 conjuring stories, 5
Brer Rabbit tales, sketches of black and white life.

NA
502
Carnes, Frederick G. *Kentucky Jubilee Singers' Schottische*. San Francisco:
L. Budd Rosenberg Music Publishing House, 1889.
3 Kentucky spirituals.

NA
503
Carpenter, Esther Bernon. *South County Neighbors*. Boston: Roberts, 1887.
Includes samples of Rhode Island black dialogue in dialect.

NA 504   Carradine, B. *Mississippi Stories*. Chicago: Christian Witness Co., 1904.
    Plantocracy memoirs showing cultural influence of blacks on whites in
    Mississippi: whites named by blacks, etc.

NA 505   Carrol, F.J. "Mysticism Among the Negroes," *New York Medical Journal*, 71
    (1900), 594-596.

NA 506   Carrothers, James David. *The Black Cat Club: Negro Humor and Folklore*.
    New York: Funk and Wagnalls, 1902.
    Sketches of black life in dialect with folkloric content--voodoo, con-
    juration, beliefs, rapping, etc.

NA 507   Carter, Wilmoth A. "Nicknames and Minority Groups," *Phylon*, 5 (1944),
    241-245.
    Many of the nicknames of minority groups seem to use food, economic
    factors, physical attributes, behavioral patterns, and accomodation
    and adjustment as their basis.

NA 508   Carter, Wilmoth A. *The Urban Negro in the South*. New York: Vantage, 1962
    (reprinted, New York: Russell and Russell, 1973).
    A sociological study of the black business section of Raleigh, North
    Carolina; discusses lifestyle, food, recreation, symbolism, etc.

NA 509   Castellanos, Henry C. *New Orleans as It Was*. New Orleans: L. Graham, 1895.
    Description of Congo Square dancing and music; voodoo.

NA 510   Castledon, Louise Decatur. *Otha*. Washington, D.C.: published by the author,
    1962.
    Brief biography of a Virginia handyman-musician-acrobat; largely an ac-
    count of his conversion experience.

NA 511   Castro, Janet. "Untapped Verbal Fluency of Black Schoolchildren," in *The
    Culture of Poverty: A Critique*, Eleanor Burke Leacock, ed. New York:
    Simon and Schuster, 1971, 81-108.
    Children's games and verbal art in a Brooklyn school; includes the
    text of a play written by children, based on traditional material.

NA 512   Cather, Pat. "Birmingham Blues," in *Back Woods Blues*. Oxford: Blues Un-
    limited Publication, 1968, 5-7.
    Biography of bluesman Jaybird Coleman.

NA
513
Caulfield, Mina Davis. "Slavery and the Origins of Black Culture: Elkins Revisited," in *Americans from Africa: Slavery and Its Aftermath*, Peter I. Rose, ed. New York: Atherton, 1970, 171-193.
    The development of a black social structure under slavery as the basis of a black culture and identity.

NA
514
Caulkins, Francis M. *History of Norwich, Connecticut*. Norwich, 1845.
    Includes material on the election of slave governors.

NA
515
Cayou, Dolores Kirton. "The Origins of Modern Jazz Dance," *The Black Scholar*, 1, No. 8 (1970), 26-31.
    Brief review of dance from Africa and the U.S. in the 1930's.

Cecil, C.H. "The Maroons in Canada." See No. EWI 159.

NA
516
"The Ceremony of the 'Foot Wash' in Virginia," *SW*, 25 (1896), 82.
    An account of the annual Virginia foot-washing ceremony, a religious ritual held at Covenant Meetings; includes short description of Bible reading, singing, supper serving, benediction, and a "Christian shout."

NA
517
"Certain Beliefs and Superstitions of the Negro," *Atlantic Monthly*, (August, 1891), 286-288. (Reprinted in No. NA 1568.)
    Negro cosmological beliefs, conversion experiences, and origin legends.

NA
518
Chamberlain, Alexander F. "African and American: The Contact of Negro and Indian," *Science*, 17, No. 419 (February 13, 1891), 85-90.
    A survey of Negro-Indian contacts in the U.S. and Canada, using folkloric and linguistic evidence.

NA
519
Chamberlain, Alexander F. "Goober, a Negro Word for Peanuts," *American Notes and Queries*, 2 (January 5, 1889), 120.

NA
520
Chamberlain, Alexander F. "Negro and Indian," in *Handbook of American Indians North of Mexico*, Vol. 2, Frederick Webb Hodge, ed. Bureau of American Ethnology Bulletin 30. Washington, D.C.: Smithsonian Institute, 1912, 51-53.
    A bibliographical entry with notes on folklore and language shared by Negroes and Indians in North America.

NA
521
Chamberlain, Alexander F. "Negro Creation Legend," *JAF*, 3 (1890), 302.
    Tale explaining the creation of "a man of each nation."

NA
522   Chamberlain, Alexander F. "Negro Dialect," *Science*, 12 (1888), 23-24.
　　　　Seeks the origins of the words "buccra" (white man) and "goober."

NA
523   Chamberlain, Alexander F. "Race-Character and Local Color in Proverbs,"
　　　　JAF, 17 (1904), 28-31.
　　　　A list of proverbs taken from a dictionary published by the Smithsonian
　　　　Institution in 1858, including Yoruba and Negro-English proverbs.

NA
524   Chambers, Herbert Arthur, ed. *The Treasury of Negro Spirituals*. New
　　　　York: Emerson Books, 1963. (First published in London: Blandford,
　　　　1959.)
　　　　Arrangements of 42 spirituals.

NA
525   Chametzky, Jules and Sidney Kaplan, eds. *Black and White in American Cul-
　　　　ture*. Amherst, Mass.: University of Massachusetts Press, 1969.
　　　　Includes articles on jazz, blues, and black folk culture reprinted
　　　　from *The Massachusetts Review*.

NA
526   Champion, Selwyn Gurney. *Racial Proverbs*. London: George Routledge, 1938.
　　　　Includes U.S. Negro proverbs.

NA
527   "Chanteys in the Age of Sail," *New York Times* (Oct., 30, 1938), Section
　　　　10, p. 6.
　　　　Chanteymen picked up and used Negro gang-work songs as part of their
　　　　chantey tunes.

NA
528   Chapin, Kate. *Bayou Folk*. Boston: Houghton, Mifflin, 1894.
　　　　Short stories about Creoles with folkloric content.

NA
529   Chappell, Louis W. "John Hardy," *Philological Quarterly*, 9 (1930), 260-
　　　　272.
　　　　By discussing the current literature, the author attempts to show that
　　　　John Hardy and John Henry were different persons; bibliography.

NA
530   Chappell, Louis W. *John Henry--A Folklore Study*. Jena: Biedermann, 1933.
　　　　A study of the historical and folkloristic elements of the John Henry
　　　　song-legend. Review of scholarship on the subject; contains 5 hammer
　　　　songs, 300 John Henry songs, and 15 John Hardy songs collected by the
　　　　author in West Virginia, Pennsylvania, Kentucky, Virginia and North
　　　　Carolina.

NA
531   Chappel, Naomi C. "Negro Names," *AS*, 4 (1929), 272-275.
　　　　Names of Negroes and their origin.

NA 532   Charters, Ann. "Negro Folk Elements in Classic Ragtime," *EM*, 5 (1961), 174-183.
         The folk musical structure of rags.

NA 533   Charters, Ann. *Nobody: The Story of Bert Williams*. New York: Macmillan, 1970.
         Includes material on medicine shows, minstrelsy, dancing, etc.

NA 534   Charters, Ann, ed. *The Ragtime Songbook*. New York: Oak, 1965.
         Ragtime songs, with music and historical discussion.

NA 535   Charters, Ann. "Treemonisha--The First Negro Folk Opera," *JM*, 8, No. 6 (1962), 6-11.
         Folklore, music and dance found in the rag opera; includes excerpts of the opera's text.

NA 536   Charters, Samuel B. "American Skiffle Bands," booklet included with Folkways LP record FA-2610.

NA 537   Charters, Samuel B. "Blind Willie Johnson: Documentary," booklet included with Folkways LP record FG 3585.

NA 538   Charters, Samuel B. *The Bluesmen*. New York: Oak, 1967.
         Characteristics of regional country blues styles and blues artists representative of Mississippi, Alabama and Texas.

NA 539   Charters, Samuel B. *The Country Blues*. New York: Rinehart, 1959.
         A study of blues, historically focused; biographical accounts of blues singers as well as interviews concerning record producers; discography. (See Smith, Charles Edward, No. NA 2753.)

NA 540   Charters, Samuel B. "An Introduction to Gospel Song," booklet included with RBF LP record RF 5.
         Survey of the history of black sacred music in the United States.

NA 541   Charters, Samuel B. *Jazz: New Orleans; An Index to the Negro Musicians of New Orleans, 1885-1963*. Revised edition. New York: Oak, 1963. (Previous edition published Stanhope, N.J.: Walter C. Allen, 1958.)
         Biographies of New Orleans musicians; discography, photos and maps.

NA
542
Charters, Samuel B. "Pink Anderson, Vol. 2: Medicine Show Man," record
notes to Prestige Bluesville LP record 1051.
Notes on the music of travelling medicine shows.

NA
543
Charters, Samuel B. *Poetry of the Blues*. New York: Oak, 1963.
Social comment on the background of the blues and its content; the
poetic conventions of the blues.

NA
544
Charters, Samuel B. *Robert Johnson*. New York: Oak, 1973.
Biography of a Mississippi bluesman; discography; bibliography, illustrations; texts.

NA
545
Charters, Samuel B. "The Rural Blues: A Study of the Vocal and Instrumental Resources," booklet included with RBF LP record RF 202.
The varieties of styles and techniques of blues singing; illustrations.

NA
546
Charters, Samuel B. and Walter C. Allen. "The Jug Bands of Memphis," *JM*,
4, No. 12 (1959), 2-5, 31.
A review of bands and their styles; discography, illustration.

NA
547
Charters, Samuel B. and L. Kunstadt. *Jazz, A History of the New York Scene*.
Garden City, New York: Doubleday, 1962.
Utilizes material from interviews, newspapers, etc.; white and black
jazz; New Orleans background; minstrelsy to modern jazz.

NA
548
Chase, Gilbert, ed. *The American Composer Speaks: A Historical Anthology,
1770-1965*. Baton Rouge: Louisiana State University Press, 1966.
Includes chapters on L.M. Gottschalk, Stephen Foster, Jelly Roll
Morton, and G. Gershwin.

NA
549
Chase, Gilbert. *America's Music from the Pilgrims to the Present*. New
York: McGraw Hill, 1955.
Devotes chapter-length studies to spirituals, blues, jazz; includes
popular dances.

NA
550
Chase, Gilbert. "A Note on Negro Spirituals," *Civil War History*, 4, No.
3 (1958), 261-267.
Gives eye-witness accounts of the shout, boatman's songs, spiritual
singing, and inquiries made of the origin of spirituals from letters
and articles of the 1860's.

NA
551

Chase, Judith Wragg. *Afro-American Art and Craft*. New York: Van Nostrand, 1971.
Chapters on African arts and crafts, Afro-American ironwork, basketry, sewing, furniture making, quilting, etc.; illustrations, bibliography.

NA
552

Chase, Kathleen. "Syncopated Dirges, Ragtime Parades," *Americas*, 16, No. 3 (1964), 16-20.
Describes funeral and Sunday parading of brass bands in modern New Orleans.

NA
553

Chesnutt, Charles W. *Conjure Tales*. New York: Dutton, 1973.
Retellings (by Ray Anthony Shepard) of Chesnutt's fictional renderings of folktales and beliefs; intended primarily for children.

NA
554

Chesnutt, Charles W. *The Conjure Woman*. Boston: Houghton and Mifflin, 1899.
Short stories with folkloric content.

NA
555

Chesnutt, Charles W. "Post-Bellum--Pre-Harlem," *Crisis*, 38 (1931), 193-194.

NA
556

Chesnutt, Charles W. "Superstitions and Folklore of the South," *Modern Culture*, 13 (1901), 231-235. (Reprinted in Dundes, No. NA 854.)
Description of conjure and folk-curing in North Carolina.

Chesnutt, Charles W. See Jaskoski, Helen, No. NA 1601.

Chesnutt, Charles W. See Smith, Robert, No. NA 2781.

Chesnutt, Charles W. See Winkleman, Donald M., No. NA 3251.

NA
557

Child, David Lee. *The Despotism of Freedom*. Boston: Young Men's Anti-Slavery Society, 1833.
Mentions slave burials and graveyards; marriages and family ties.

NA
558

Chirgwin, A.M. "Vogue of the Negro Spiritual," *Edinburgh Review*, 247 (January, 1928), 57-74.

NA   Choppin, Jules. "La Chasse Chaoue," *CRAL*, 15 (March, 1898), 257.
559   Account of a hunting trip told in Louisiana Creole verse.

NA   Choppin, Jules. "La Cigale et la Fourmi," *CRAL*, 13 (May, 1896), 479.
560   1 tale in the Creole dialects of Louisiana, Martinique, and Reunion.

NA   Choppin, Jules. "Entretien sur les 12 Mois de l'Année par un Vieux Nègre
561   St. Jacquois Nommé 'Pa Guitin,'" *CRAL*, 14 (January, 1897), 17-20;
            March, 1897, 57-61.
            An account (in Louisiana Creole dialect verse) of an old man's activi-
            ties through a full year.

NA   Choppin, Jules. "Les Singes et le Leopard," *CRAL*, 17 (July, 1900), 114.
562   An animal tale written in French and translated into Creole.

NA   Chotzinoff, Samuel. "Jazz: A Brief History," *Vanity Fair*, 20 (June, 1923),
563   69, 104, 106.
            Discusses the background of music in the U.S. and Negro music as the
            prototype of American music.

NA   Christensen, Mrs. Abigal M. *Afro-American Folk Lore Told Round Cabin Fires
564   on the Sea Islands of South Carolina*. Boston: J.G. Cupples, 1892.
            Includes 17 tales, 12 of which concern rabbit (which represents the
            Negro, according to the author). Some data on informants.

NA   Christensen, Mrs. Abigal M. "Spirituals and 'Shouts' of Southern Negroes,"
565   *JAF*, 7 (1894), 154-155.
            A description of a ritual dance.

NA   Cimino, Miriam Pope. "Muscadines for Pink Dorsets," *Scribner's Magazine*,
566   91 (1932), 361-365.
            Dress, customs, etc. among Georgia black women.

NA   *City Cries: Or, A Peep at Scenes in Town*. Philadelphia: George A. Apple-
567   ton, 1851.
            Includes cries by chimney sweeps, whitewash men, crab, hot corn, fish,
            hominy, firewood and pepper-pot sellers. Illustrations.

NA   Claerbaut, David. *Black Jargon in White America*. Grand Rapids, Mich.:
568   Eerdmans, 1972.
            A slang listing of terms of uncertain provenience; includes an intro-
            duction on the author's experience in teaching black children.

NA
569

Claiborne, John Francis Hamtramck. "A Trip through the Piney Woods," *Publications of the Mississippi Historical Society*, 9, Franklin L. Riley, ed. Oxford, Miss.: Mississippi Historical Society, 1906, 487-538.

NA
570

Clar, Mimi. "Folk Beliefs and Custom in the Blues," *WF*, 19 (1960), 173-189. (Reprinted from *The Second Line*, 11, Nos. 9-10 (1961), 1-8; 11, Nos. 11-12 (1961), 17-21; Nos. 1-2 (1962), 23-30.)
Negro beliefs from blues texts, especially regarding sorcery, death and luck.

NA
571

Clar, Mimi. "Negro Beliefs," *WF*, 18 (1959), 332-334.
33 beliefs from Los Angeles (learned from a woman who was originally from Virginia).

NA
572

Clar, Mimi. "The Negro Church: Its Influence on Modern Jazz," *The Jazz Review*, 1, No. 1 (1958), 16-18; No. 2 (1958), 21-23; 2, No. 1 (1959), 22-24; No. 2 (1959), 28-29.
Parallels and influences between gospel music and jazz; discography and transcriptions of musical examples.

Clar, Mimi. Also see Melnick, Mimi Clar, No. NA 2031.

NA
573

Clark, A. Grayson. "Last Journey of a Jazzman: The Funeral of Lester Santiago," record notes to Nobility Recording Co., Vol. 1, 2.
Notes on a New Orleans funeral.

NA
574

Clark, Edgar R. *Copper Sun: A Collection of Negro Folk Songs*. Bryn Mawr: Theodore Presser, 1957.

NA
575

Clark, Edgar R. "Negro Folk Music in America," *JAF*, 64 (1951), 281-287.
A discussion of the origin, development, and social and economic conditions which inspired Negro folk music.

NA
576

Clark, Edgar R. "What Is Negro Folklore?" *NHB*, 27 (November, 1963), 40-41.
A definition of Negro folklore which includes tales, music, and graphic arts.

NA
577

Clark, Elmer T. *The Small Sects in America*. New York: Abingdon Press, 1953. (Rev. ed. 1955.)
Brief description of the beliefs, organization, and membership of the black Methodist sects, the "charismatic sects," Churches of God, Churches of the Living God, "Hard-Shell" Baptist sects, American Baptists, Church of God and Saints of Chirst ("Black Jews"), *et al*.

NA
578
Clark, Joseph D. "North Carolina Popular Beliefs and Superstitions," *NCF*, 18, No. 1 (1970), 1-68.
1,683 beliefs of uncertain provenience.

NA
579
Clark, Joseph D. "Proverbs and Sayings in North Carolina," *NCF*, 16 (1968), 38-43.
Collection from several Negro colleges from 1955 and later.

NA
580
Clark, W.A. "Sanctification in Negro Religion," *Social Forces*, 15 (May, 1937), 544-551.
Evolution of black doctrines of sanctification since 1865; religion as an escape from difficulties.

NA
581
Clarke, John Henrick, ed. *Harlem: A Community in Transition*. New York: Citadel, 1964.
Essays on politics and culture in Harlem.

NA
582
Clarke, Kenneth. "Folklore of Negro Children in Greater Louisville Reflecting Attitudes Toward Race," *KFR*, 10 (1964), 1-11.
Discussion of rhymes containing themes of racial awareness.

NA
583
Clarke, Lewis Garrard. *Narratives of the Sufferings of Lewis and Milton Clarke . . . during a Captivity of More than Twenty Years among the Slave-holders of Kentucky, One of the So-called Christian States of North America*. Boston: B. Marsh, 1846.
Anecdotes giving slave opinions, treatment of slaves; religious observances and beliefs of slaves; marriage and family relations, etc.

NA
584
Clarke, Mary Olmsted. "Song Games of Negro Children in Virginia," *JAF*, 3 (1890), 288-290.
9 examples of song-games played by children of the District of Columbia.

NA
585
Claudel, Calvin. "Creole Folk Tales," *Southern Literary Messenger*, 4 (1942), 7-13.
French and African characteristics joined in Louisiana Creole folk tales; includes examples.

NA
586
Claudel, Calvin. "Four Tales From The French Folklore of Louisiana," *SFQ*, 9 (1945), 191-208.
The fourth tale is a version of "Gamblin' Bill and Gamblin' Jack," collected from the English-speaking Negroes around Avery Island, Louisiana.

NA Claudel, Calvin. "Golden Hair," *SFQ*, 5 (1941), 257-263.
587   A tale which contains the golden ball and the lice motif.

NA Claudel, Calvin. "Louisiana Tales of Jean Sot and Boqui and Lapin," *SFQ*,
588   8 (1944), 287-299.
         Contains 6 Boqui and Lapin type tales.

NA Claudel, Calvin. "The Negro's Contribution to the World of Entertainment,"
589   in *The Negro Impact on Western Civilization*, Joseph S. Roucek and Thomas
         Kiernan, eds. New York: Philosophical Library, 1970, 231-249.
         Brief comments on the variety of Afro-American music.

NA Claudel, Calvin. "Some Creole Folktales," *Iconograph* (New Orleans), No. 2
590   (March, 1941).
         2 tales from Louisiana.

NA Claudel, Calvin and J.M. Carriere. "Three Tales from the French Folklore of
591   Louisiana," *JAF*, 56 (1943), 38-44.
         A short discussion of the origin of the word *bougie* and texts of 3 tales.

NA Clinkscales, John George. *On the Old Plantation: Reminiscences of his Child-*
592   *hood*. Spartanburg, S.C.: Bond and White, 1916.
         Describes religious services, slave escapes, fiddlers, etc.

NA Clive, R.I. "The Tar-Baby Story," *American Literature*, 2 (1930), 72-78.
593

NA Clothier, Agnes E. "Two Negro Spirituals from Georgia," *JAF*, 55 (1942), 98.
594   2 texts.

NA Cobb, Lucy M. and Mary A. Hicks. *Animal Tales from the Old North State*.
595   New York: E.P. Dutton, 1938.
         48 tales from 7 storytellers of North Carolina on characters such as
         found in Joel Chandler Harris' works.

NA Cobb, Lucy M. and Mary A. Hicks. "Negro Folktales," *PTFS*, No. 17 (1941),
596   108-112.
         3 tales.

NA
597
Cobb, Lucy M. and Mary A. Hicks. "Why Brer Buzzard Vomits and Why Brer
Possum Faints," *SFQ*, 2 (1938), 203-204.
2 tales from Wake County, North Carolina.

NA
598
Cobbs, Hamner. "Give Me the Black Belt," *Alabama Review*, 17 (1964), 163-
180.
Discussion of Negro humor under 4 categories: 1) the Negro who "refuses
to accept white standards of life"; 2) the Negro who has an "innate
desire to be well-mannered"; 3) the humor that comes from the "practiced
ear of the Negro"; and 4) the humor that comes from the illiterate.

NA
599
Cobbs, Hamner. "Negro Colloquialisms in the Black Belt," *Alabama Review*,
5 (1952), 203-212.
Traditional expressions and usages.

NA
600
Cobbs, Hamner. "Superstitions of the Black Belt," *Alabama Review*, 11
(1958), 55-65.
Discussion of "voodoo-magical" and other beliefs; description of the
use of a "mojo hand."

NA
601
Cocke, Ed. "Voodoo," *New Orleans Magazine*, 4 (January, 1970), 50-53.

NA
602
Cocke, Sarah Johnson. *By Paths in Dixie; Folk Tales of the South*. New
York: E.P. Dutton, 1911.
"Uncle-Remus"-like tales, possibly from Georgia.

NA
603
Cocke, Sarah Johnson. *Old Mammy Tales from Dixie Land*. New York: E.P. Dutton, 1926.
17 animal tales, explanatory tales and others reproduced as told by an
African nurse in a white family. Illustrations.

NA
604
Coeuroy, André. *Panorama de la Musique Contemporaine* . . . Paris: Kra,
1928.
A chapter on folksong and jazz is included.

NA
605
Coeuroy, André and André Schaeffer. *La Musique Moderne II: Le Jazz*. Paris:
Aveline, 1926.
Evolution of jazz from African music.

NA
606
Cohen, B. Bernard and Irvin Ehrenpreis. "Tales from Indiana University Students," *HF*, 6 (1947), 57-65.
1 ghost story (pp. 60-61).

NA
607
Cohen, Hennig. "Burial of the Drowned Among the Gullah Negroes," *SFQ*, 22 (1958), 93-97.
A comment on a burial custom, taken from local popular printed sources and American folklore publications.

NA
608
Cohen, Hennig. "Caroline Gilman and Negro Boatmen's Songs," *SFQ*, 20 (1956), 116-117.
Discovery of a rare text of a Negro boatman's songs from Caroline Gilman's *Recollections of a Southern Matron*, New York: Harper & Bros., 1838.

NA
609
Cohen, Hennig. "A Negro 'Folk Game' in Colonial South Carolina," *SFQ*, 16 (1952), 183-185.
Discusses the reaction of whites to social gatherings of slaves in Charleston.

NA
610
Cohen, Hennig. "Slave Names in Colonial South Carolina," *AS*, 27 (1952), 102-107.
The use of African and other names in 18th Century South Carolina.

NA
611
Cohen, Inez Topez, ed. *Our Darktown Press*. New York: O. Appleton, 1932.
600 "humorous" stories taken "verbatim" from representative Negro newspapers.

NA
612
Cohen, John. "The Folk Music Interchange; Negro and White," *SO*, 14, No. 6 (1964), 42-49.
Discussion of the mutual musical influences between whites and blacks in country music.

NA
613
Cohen, John. "I Got a Witness," *The Jazz Review*, 2, No. 4 (1959), 19-24.
Photos of services in a Harlem storefront church.

NA
614
Cohen, Lily Young. *Lost Spirituals*. New York: Walter Neale, 1928.
41 spirituals, text and music with running commentary from Charleston, S.C. Negroes. Recognition of Gullah as African in source; includes several Charleston dialects.

NA
615
Cohen, Norman. "'Casey Jones': At the Crossroads of Two Ballad Traditions," *WF*, 32 (1973), 77-103.

NA
616
Cohen, Norman. "Railroad Folk-Songs on Record--A Survey," *NYFQ*, 26 (1970), 91-113.
    Includes discography and discussion of "Railroad Bill."

NA
617
Cohn, David. *Where I Was Born and Raised*. South Bend, Ind.: University of Notre Dame, 1967. (This edition includes David Cohn's *God Shakes Creation*. New York: Harper, 1935.)
    Memoirs of the Mississippi Delta; includes section on burial rites, religion, dozens, voodoo, music, etc.

NA
618
Cohn, Lawrence. "Leadbelly: The Library of Congress Recordings," booklet included with Elektra LP record set EKL 301/2.
    Notes on the life of songster Leadbelly and the texts of 43 work songs, blues, ballads, etc.; includes transcriptions of interviews.

NA
619
Cohn, Lawrence. "Son House," *Sounds & Fury* (Utica, N.Y.), No. 3 (1965), 18-19, 21.
    Biography of a Mississippi blues singer.

NA
620
Cohn, Michael. "Collectors' Notes: No Dovecot," *Antiques*, 98, No. 2 (1970), 270.
    Description and photo of an African brick building on a Virginia plantation; rammed-earth buildings in Virginia.

NA
621
Colcock, Erroll Hay and Patti Lee Hay Colcock. *Dusky Land: Gullah Poems and Sketches of Coastal South Carolina*. Clinton, South Carolina: Jacobs, 1942.
    Poems and prose sketches in Gullah dialect, by whites, includes beliefs, animal tales, etc.

NA
622
Colcord, Joanna. *Songs of American Sailorman*. New York: 1938.
    Discusses worksongs from the Mississippi cotton trade (p. 59).

NA
623
Cole, Helen Rosemary. "Why is Mistletoe," *JAF*, 59 (1946), 528-529.
    Legend of the origin of mistletoe from Texas.

NA
624
Cole, Johnnetta B. "Culture: Negro, Black and Nigger," *The Black Scholar*, 1, No. 8 (1970), 40-44.
    The components of the black subculture: "soul" and lifestyle. Describes "street", "down home" and "militant" styles.

NA
625
Coleman, J. Winston. *Slave Times in Kentucky*. Chapel Hill, N.C.: University of North Carolina Press, 1940.
Chapter on slave life, including placement and set-up of quarters, passages of day and year, marriage and family life, clothing, "superstitions," funerals, Christmas, corn shuckings, songs, and dances.

NA
626
Coleman, Richard. *Don't You Weep, Don't You Moan*. New York: Macmillan, 1935.
Novel of South Carolina life with folkloric content.

NA
627
Coleman, Z.A. *The Jubilee Singers, A Collection of Plantation Melodies*. Cincinnati: John Church & Co., 1883.

NA
628
Coleridge-Taylor, Samuel. *Twenty-Four Negro Melodies*. Boston: Ditson, 1905.
Piano transcriptions of songs from the United States, the West Indies, and Africa. Notes by Booker T. Washington.

NA
629
Collier, Eugenia. "James Weldon Johnson: Mirror of Change," *Phylon*, 21 (1960), 351-359.
James Weldon Johnson's writing is seen to reflect the change in the handling of folk material in poetry by Negro writers from traditional dialect to an imitation of the idiom; contains 7 poems by Johnson and 1 by Dunbar.

NA
630
Collins, Herbert. "Store Front Churches," *Negro American Literary Forum*, 4 (1970), 64-68.
The development of the ideology of small urban sects.

NA
631
"The Colored Fair at Raleigh, N.C.," *Frank Leslie's Illustrated Newspaper*, 49 (December 6, 1879), 240-243.
Description of a Negro fair, including a song text, speech, food; illustrations.

NA
632
A Concise Historical Account of All the British Colonies in North-America. Dublin: C. Jenkins, 1776.
Describes jig-dancing among whites in Virginia, "a practice originally borrowed . . . from the Negroes" (pp. 212-213). The same passage is reprinted in James Franklin, *The Philosophical and Political History of the Thirteen United States of America*. London, 1784, p. 91.

NA   Cone, James H. *The Spiritual and the Blues: An Interpretation*. New York:
633   Seabury, 1972.
            A theological and political interpretation.

NA   "Conjuring in Arkansas," *JAF*, 1 (1888), 83.
634   Conjuring in Arkansas among blacks, from the *Boston Herald*, May 29,
            1887.

NA   Conley, D.L. "Origin of the Negro Spiritual," *NHB*, 25 (1962), 179-180.
635

NA   Conrad, Earl. "The Philology of Negro Dialect," *JNE*, 13 (1944), 150-154.
636

NA   Conrad, Georgia Bryan. "Reminiscences of a Southern Woman," *SW*, 30 (1901),
637   77-80, 167-171, 252-257, 357-359, 409-411. (Also appears in Georgia
            Bryan Conrad, *Reminiscences of a Southern Woman*. Hampton, Va.: Hampton
            Institute Press, n.d.)
            Descriptions of life in the "Old South"; anecdotes about slaves on a
            Georgia rice plantation: boat races, Islamic slaves in the U.S.,
            African folktales, parades, dress, etc.

NA   Conroy, Pat. *The Water Is Wide*. Boston: Houghton Mifflin, 1972.
638   A teacher's experiences on a South Carolina Sea Island; includes des-
            criptions of a funeral, ghost accounts, taunts, etc.

NA   Cons, C. Lynn. "The Jargon of Jazz," *American Mercury*, 38, No. 149 (1936),
639   10.
            A glossary of slang terms used by musicians.

NA   Cook, Bruce. *Listen to the Blues*. New York: Scribners, 1973.
640   A history of the blues in popular form; black influence on ballads and
            bluegrass.

NA   Cook, Will Marion. "Clorindy, the Origin of the Cakewalk," *Theatre Arts*,
641   31, September, 1947, 61-65.

NA   Cooke, Benjamin G. "Nonverbal Communication among Afro-Americans: An Initial
642   Classification," in *Rappin' and Stylin' Out*, Thomas Kochman, ed. Urbana,
            Ill.: University of Illinois Press, 1972, 32-64.
            Hand gestures, walking and posture styles, clothing, hair styles in ur-
            ban areas; illustrations.

NA 643   Cooke, Elizabeth Johnston.   "English Folktales in America," *JAF*, 12 (1899),
126-130.
Tale text from a Martinique Negro living in Louisiana.

NA 644   Cooley, Rossa Belle. "Aunt Jane and Her People: The Real Negroes of the
Sea Island," *Outlook*, 90 (1908), 424-432.
Folkloric traditions of Negroes on the South Carolina Sea Islands;
descriptions of spirituals, work customs and chants; illustrations.

NA 645   Cooley, Rossa Belle.   *Homes of the Freed*. New York: New Republic, 1926.
Discussion of housing, hoodoo, baskets, manners, diet, cuisine, etc.

NA 646   Cooley, Rossa Belle. *School Acres: An Adventure in Rural Education*. New
Haven: Yale University Press, 1930.
Accounts of work songs, shouts, baptism, beliefs, speech, naming, etc.
(pp. 50-55, 68-71).

NA 647   Coolidge, Richard A. "The Blues in Theory," *NAJE Educator*, 3, No. 3 (1971),
13-16.

NA 648   Coomaraswamy, Ananda K. "A Note on the Stickfast Motif," *JAF*, 57 (1944),
128-132.
Argues that the "stickfast" motif, with or without tar baby, may have
originated in India.

NA 649   "Coonjining," *AS*, 8 (1933), 77-78.
The source of a Negro word.

NA 650   Cooper, Clarence. *The Scene*. New York: Crown, 1960.
Novel on black drug addiction; contains a slang glossary.

NA 651   Cooper, James Fenimore. *Satanstoe*, 2 vols. New York: Burgess, Stringer
& Co., 1845.
Vol. 1 contains descriptions of Pinkster (Pentecost) day celebrations
in New York State: music, drums, dances, etc.

NA 652   Cothran, Tilman C. "Negro Conceptions of White People," *American Journal
of Sociology*, 56 (1951), 458-467.
Descriptions of black "stereotyped conceptions" about white people in
Arkansas.

NA
653
Cotten, Sallie S. *Negro Folk Lore Stories*. Charlotte, N.C.: Charlotte
    Federation of Women's Clubs, 1923.

NA
654
Cotter, Joseph Seaman, Sr. *Negroes and Others at Work and Play*. New York:
    Paebar, 1947.
    Includes poems, tales, sayings, songs, etc., by a black poet-collector.

NA
655
Cotter, Joseph Seaman, Sr. *Negro Tales*. New York: Cosmopolitan Press, 1912.

NA
656
Cotter, Joseph Seaman, Sr. *Twenty-Fifth Anniversary of the Founding of
    Colored Parkland or "Little Africa," Louisville, Ky., 1891-1916*.
    Louisville: I. Willis Cole, 1934.

NA
657
Coulter, E. Merton. "Cudjo Fye's Insurrection," *GHQ*, 38 (1954), 213-226.
    Account of an insurrection discusses the formation of Negro "Union
    Clubs": semi-secret societies for rights, protection, etc.

NA
658
Councill, William Hooper. *Synopsis of Three Addresses: 1. Building the
    South, 2. The Children of the South, 3. Negro Religion and Character:
    No Apology*. Normal, Alabama: n.p., 1900.
    Reconstruction education and religion; religious attitudes of slaves;
    descriptions of a conjure woman in 1862; singing and artistic worth of
    Negroes.

NA
659
Courlander, Harold. *The African*. New York: Crown, 1967.
    Novel with folkloric content on slaves from Dahomey sold to Georgia
    slaveholders.

NA
660
Courlander, Harold. *The Big Old World of Richard Crebs*. Philadelphia, Pa.:
    Chilton, 1962.
    Novel with folkloric material concerning a blues singer in his wander-
    ings: manners, customs, conjure doctors, entertainment, etc.

NA
661
Courlander, Harold. "Negro Folk Music of Alabama, Vols. 1-6," booklet in-
    cluded with Folkways LP records 417, 418, 471, 472, 473, 474.
    Notes and texts of blues, train songs, ring and line games, lullabies,
    work songs, spirituals, prayers, sermons, gospel songs, field ballads,
    playparty songs, riddles, Brer Rabbit tales, and legends from central
    and western Alabama; description of African, Haitian and United States
    earth bows and washtub basses; illustrations.

NA 662
Courlander, Harold. *Negro Folk Music U.S.A.* New York: Columbia University Press, 1963.
History, social significance and aesthetic characteristics of Negro folk music.

NA 663
Courlander, Harold. "Ring Games," booklet included with Folkways LP record FC 7004.
Directions for playing games played by Alabama children; with texts and illustrations.

NA 664
Courlander, Harold. *Terrapin's Pot of Sense*. New York: Henry Holt, 1957.
31 retold tales with notes collected in Alabama, New Jersey, and Michigan.

Courlander, Harold. See Smith, Charles Edward, No. NA 2756.

NA 665
Courlander, Harold and John Benson Brooks. *Negro Songs from Alabama*. New York: Oak, 1960.
A collection of transcriptions of field recordings made in and around Livingston, Alabama in 1950. 84 song texts, 45 with music transcribed.

NA 666
"Courtship Formulas of Southern Negroes," *JAF*, 8 (1895), 155-156.
Contains several courtship formulas taken from the *Southern Workman*, January, 1895.

NA 667
Cousins, Paul M. *Joel Chandler Harris: A Biography*. Baton Rouge: Louisiana State University, 1968.

NA 668
Covarrubias, Miguel. *Negro Drawings*. New York: Knopf, 1927.
Drawings by a Mexican artist of Negro customs, dance, musical activities, rituals, etc.

NA 669
Covington, Ben. "Blues in the Archway Road," *Anarchy*, 5, No. 5, (1965), 129-133.

NA 670
Cox, E. "Rustic Imagery in Mississippi Proverbs," *SFQ*, 9 (1947), 263-267.
Includes a few Negro proverbs and terms.

NA 671
Cox, John Harrington. *Folk Songs of the South*. Boston: Harvard University Press, 1925. (Reprinted with a new forward by Arthur Kyle Davis. Hatboro, Pennsylvania: Folklore Associates, 1963.)
Includes variants of "John Hardy" and "John Henry" ballads, with notes.

NA   Cox, John Harrington. "John Hardy," *JAF*, 32 (1919), 505-520.
672   Discussion of the origin of the song "John Hardy" with 5 versions of
              the song included.

NA   Cox, John Harrington. "Negro Tales from West Virginia," *JAF*, 47 (1934),
673   341-357.
              8 tales.

NA   Cox, John Harrington. "The Yew Pine Mountains," *AS*, 2 (1927), 226-227.
674   Relationship of John Hardy and John Henry ballads.

NA   Craig, Alberta Ratliffe. "Old Wentworth Sketches," *North Carolina Histori-*
675   *cal Review*, 11, No. 3 (1934), 185-204.
              Describes a Negro corn-shucking party with songs; the section on "Some
              Old Wentworth Negroes" describes a Negro band, quotes sayings of an
              old woman, discusses the use of "Uncle" and "Aunt" as titles, describes
              the "holy dance" and its accompanying song.

NA   Craig, William. "Recreational Activity Patterns in a Small Negro Urban
676   Community: The Role of the Cultural Base," *Economic Geography*, 48
              (1972), 107-115.
              Historical changes in recreational activities among a Louisiana Negro
              population.

NA   Crane, Maurice A. "Vox Bop," *AS*, 33 (1958), 223-226.
677   Examples of jazz slang with commentary.

NA   Crane, T.F. "Plantation Folklore," *Popular Science Monthly*, 18 (1881),
678   824-833. (Reprinted in No. NA 1578.)
              The first scholarly commentary on the Joel Chandler Harris "Uncle
              Remus" material.

NA   Crawford, Portia Naomi. "A Study of Negro Folksongs from Greensboro, North
679   Carolina and Surrounding Towns," *NCF*, 16 (1968), 69-139.
              25 songs with musicological analysis.

NA   Cray, Ed. "An Acculturative Continuum for Negro Folk Song in the United
680   States," *EM*, 5 (1961), 10-15.
              Negro music in terms of Charles Seeger's concept of levels of an accul-
              turative continuum of folk, popular and art. The black relationship to
              the white continuum and the possibility of an eventual assimilation
              into a common musical tradition; illustrations.

NA 681   Creighton, Helen. "Folk Music from Nova Scotia," booklet included with Folkways LP record P 1006.
Includes 1 jubilee with text and notes.

NA 682   Creighton, Helen and Doreen H. Senior. *Traditional Songs from Nova Scotia.* Toronto: Ryerson, 1950.
Includes Negro material.

NA 683   "Creole Proverbs," *SW*, 25 (1896), 206.
Collection of Louisiana proverbs.

NA 684   Crichton, Kyle. "Thar's Gold in Them Hill-Billies," *Colliers*, 101 (April 30, 1938), 24, 27.
Beginnings of commercial race and hillbilly recordings in the 1920's.

NA 685   Crimmons, Martin L. "Mr. 'Possum and Mr. Coon." *PTFS*, No. 9 (1931), 165-166.
1 tale.

NA 686   Cromwell, J.W. "First Negro Churches in the District of Columbia," *JNH*, 7 (January, 1922), 64-106.
Account of Negro religious customs and practices, African survivals in New World worship practices, sermons, etc.

NA 687   Cromwell, S.C. "Corn-Shucking Song," *Harper's*, 69 (1884), 807.
1 song text.

NA 688   Cross, Paulette. "Jokes and Black Consciousness," *Folklore Forum* (Bloomington, Ind.), 2, No. 6 (1969), 140-161.
Texts of 7 jokes stressing the racial consciousness of black Americans; interviews with two informants and some observations on the texts of the jokes.

NA 689   Cross, Tom Peete. "Folklore from the Southern States," *JAF*, 22 (1909), 251-255.
Superstitions about witches and preventative measures against them; collected in Southeastern Virginia.

NA 690   Cross, Tom Peete. "Witchcraft in North Carolina," *Studies in Philology*, 16 (1919), 217-287.
Documentation of beliefs and practices in witchcraft among blacks, whites, and Indians in North Carolina.

Crowley, Daniel J. "American Credit Institutions of Yoruba Type."
See No. EWI 196.

NA
691

Crowley, Daniel J. "Negro Folklore, An Africanist's View," *Texas Quarterly*,
5 (1962), 65-71.

NA
692

Crum, Mason. *Gullah: Negro Life in the Carolina Sea Islands*. Durham, North
Carolina: Duke University Press, 1940.
A social history containing descriptions of dialect, songs, customs,
food, and various other aspects of folklore interest.

NA
693

Culbertson, Anne Virginia. *At the Big House Where Aunt Nancey and Aunt
Phrony Held Forth on the Animal Folk*. Indianapolis: Bobbs-Merrill,
1904.
"Edited" folk tales from "persons well on in years."

NA
694

Culbertson, Anne Virginia. *Banjo Talks*. Indianapolis: Bobbs-Merrill, 1905.

NA
695

Culin, Stewart. "Concerning Negro Sorcery in the United States," *JAF*, 3
(1890), 281-287.
Newspaper items on voodoo, enchanted girls, conjure bags, and an invisible white doctor who steals blood, charms, and clairvoyants.

NA
696

Culin, Stewart. "Reports Concerning Voodooism," *JAF*, 2 (1889), 232-233.
3 accounts of voodoo from Haiti, San Domingo, Georgia and Philadelphia.

NA
697

Cullen, Countee. *One Way to Heaven*. New York: Harper, 1932.
Novel with folkloric content.

NA
698

Cunard, Nancy. "Some Negro Slang," in *Negro Anthology*, Nancy Cunard, ed.
London: Wishart, 1934, 75-78.
A short glossary of slang terms.

NA
699

"Cures by Conjure Doctors," *JAF*, 12 (1899), 288-289.
Contains information concerning the methods of conjure doctors and the
effects of their treatment. (From *SW*, August, 1889.)

NA
700

Curtis, Natalie. "Folk Music of America: Four Types of Folk-Songs in the
United States Alone," *The Craftsman*, 21 No. 4 (1912), 414-420.
Includes discussion of the harmony of Negro songs.

NA
701
Curtis, Natalie. "The Negro's Contribution to the Music of America: The Larger Opportunity of the Colored Man of Today," *The Craftsman*, 23, No 6 (1913), 660-669.
The sources of ragtime seen in plantation music.

Curtis, Natalie. See also Burlin, Natalie Curtis.

NA
702
Cussler, Margaret and Mary L. DeGive. *'Twixt the Cup and the Lip: Psychological and Socio-Cultural Factors Affecting Food Habits*. New York: Twayne, 1952.

NA
703
Cuthbert, J.H. *Life of Richard Fuller, D.D.* New York, 1878.
Reprints an article from the *Cincinnati Gazette* (n.d.) describing the songs and reception on the return of a South Carolina Sea Island slave master to his plantation.

NA
704
Dabbs, Edith M. *Face of an Island: Leigh Richmond Miner's Photographs of Saint Helena Island*. New York: Grossman, 1971.
Photographs taken on a South Carolina Sea Island between 1900 and 1925; includes "tabby" construction, ex-slave cabins, baskets and basket-weaving, work activities, dress, iron work, etc.

NA
705
"Daddy Grace," *Life*, 19 (October, 1945), 51-56.
Sermons of Bishop ("Daddy") Charles Manuel Grace, leader of the Church on the Rock of the Apostolic Faith, a cult with 100 Prayerhouses, 500,000 members and "saints"; illustrations.

NA
706
Daingerfield, Henrietta G. *Our Mammy and Other Stories*. Lexington, Ky.: Hampton Institute Press, 1906.
Collection of 10 stories which give a picture of life on a Southern plantation around the turn of the century.

NA
707
Dalby, David. "The African Element in American English," in *Rappin' and Stylin' Out*, Thomas Kochman, ed. Urbana, Ill.: University of Illinois Press, 1972, 170-186.
Unrecognized African words in American speech and the reasons for their survival.

NA
708
Dalby, David. "Americanisms that May Once Have Been Africanisms," London *Times*, July 19, 1969, 9. (Reprinted in *New York Times*, November 10, 1970, 47, as "Jazz, Jitter, and Jam.")
The influence of Wolof (West Africa) language on Afro-American vocabulary and, through jazz, etc., on standard American English as well.

NA
709

Dalby, David. "O.K., A.O.K. and O Ke," *New York Times*, January 8, 1971, 31. (Reprinted in the London *Times* as "The Etymology of O.K." January 14, 1971.)

Dalby, David. *Black through White: Patterns of Communication*. See No. GEN 59.

NA
710

Damon, S. Foster. "The Negro in Early American Songsters," *Papers of the Bibliographical Society of America*, 28 (1934), 132-163.
A historical-bibliographical account of Negro songs, sacred and secular, from the late 18th century to the early 20th century; comments on dialect, melody, syncopation, etc. A bibliography of songsters in the Harris Collection of American Poetry and Plays and other sources is included.

NA
711

Dana, Katherine Floyd. *Our Phil and Other Stories*. Boston: Houghton Mifflin, 1889. (Reprinted from articles published in the *Atlantic Monthly*.)
Accounts of plantation life, interaction, importance of names, a wedding, with songs, poems, and "city" and "country" dancing.

NA
712

Danberg, A.R. "The American Minstrel Theatre on Phonograph Records, 1894-1929," *RR*, No. 22 (1959), 3-5; 24 (1959), 7-9; 25 (1959), 11; 27 (1960), 9; 30 (1960), 10; 32 (1961), 11, 20; 33 (1961), 11, 24; 34 (1961), 24.
History and biographies of minstrelsy with an extensive discography.

NA
713

Dane, Barbara. "Lone Cat Jesse Fuller," *SO*, 16, No. 1 (1966), 5-11.
A biographical sketch through interview of a one-man band; discography.

NA
714

Dangerfield, Nettie G. "Aunt Lucy," *SW*, 34 (1905), 279-285.
1 tale.

NA
715

Daniel, Vattel Elbert. "Negro Classes and Life in Church," *JNE*, 13 (1944), 19-29.
Ritualization of church life according to class status in the Negro community.

NA
716

Daniel, Vattel Elbert. "Ritual and Stratification in Chicago Negro Churches," *American Sociological Review*, 7 (1942), 352-361.
Description of behavior in "ecstatic" cults.

NA
717
Danker, Frederick E. "Towards an Intrinsic Study of the Blues Ballads: 'Casey Jones' and 'Louis Collins'," *SFQ*, 34 (1970), 90-103.
Argues for more structured studies of ballads with a discussion of 2 ballads.

NA
718
Dann, Hollis Ellsworth. *Fifty-Eight Spirituals For Choral Use*. Boston: C.C. Birchard, 1924.
58 arranged songs.

NA
719
Darby, Loraine. "Ring-Games From Georgia," *JAF*, 30 (1917), 218-221.
6 ring games, 2 with music.

NA
720
Darch, Robert R. "Blind Boone," *The Ragtimer*, 6, No. 5/6 (1967), 9-13.
Biography of an early composer of rags.

NA
721
Dauer, Alfons M. *Der Jazz. Seine Ursprünge und seine Entwicklung*. Kassel and Eisenach: Röth, 1958.
Two chapters on the music of West Africa and the music of Afro-Americans in South America and the West Indies; one chapter on Afro-American music in the United States; includes 70 musical transcriptions.

NA
722
Dauner, Louise. "Myth and Humor in the Uncle Remus Tales," *American Literature*, 20 (1948), 129-143.
The psychological sources of humor in the tales; their "mythic" properties.

NA
723
Dauson, William L. "Interpretation of Religious Folk Song of the American Negro," *Etude*, 73 (1955), 11, 58, 61.
Negro religion and song as expressions of a difficult social situation; discusses rhythm in spirituals.

NA
724
Davenport, Frederick Morgan. *Primitive Traits in Religious Revivals: A Study in Mental and Social Evolution*. New York: Macmillan, 1905.
Chapter 5, "The Religion of the American Negro," treats music, possession, etc., as manifestations of a "child race."

NA
725
Davenport, Frederick Morgan. "The Religions of the American Negro," *Contemporary Review*, 88 (September, 1905), 369-375.
"Experience meetin'" of blacks in Tennessee; Negro preacher and his link with African medicine-men, among hard-shell Baptists, Friends, and early Methodists.

NA   Davenport, Gertrude C. "Folk Cures from Kansas," *JAF*, 11 (1898), 129-132.
726   A list of cures.

NA   Davidoff, Henry. *A World Treasury of Proverbs*. New York: Random, 1946.
727   Includes Negro proverbs.

NA   Davies, John R.T. "Eubie Blake: His Life and Times," *Storyville*, 1, No. 6
728   (1966), 19-20; 2, No. 7 (1966), 12-13, 27.
            Story of a ragtime pianist and composer from his early years up to 1930.

NA   Davin, Tom. "Conversations with James P. Johnson," *The Jazz Review*, 2, No.
729   5 (1959), 14-17; No. 6 (1959), 10-13; No. 7 (1959), 13-15; No. 8 (1959),
            26-27.
            Memoirs of music and musicians in New York City in the early 1900's by
            an early jazz pianist; comments on style, dress, kinesics, marching,
            dances (Catwalk, Charleston, Square).

NA   Davis, Arthur Kyle, Jr. *Folk-Songs of Virginia*. Durham, N.C.: Duke Univer-
730   sity Press, 1949.
            21 traditional folksongs from Virginia.

NA   Davis, Arthur P. "Dark Laughter," *Negro Digest*, (April, 1943), 13-14.
731   Several jokes and examples of "shucking and jiving."

NA   Davis, Arthur P. "When I Was in Knee Pants," *Common Ground*, 4 (1944), 50.
732

NA   Davis, Daniel Webster. "Conjuration," *SW*, 27 (1898), 251-252.
733   Description of reliance on the conjure doctor to exorcise spells and
            cure diseases; argues that the conjurer succeeds, not by trickery, but
            by his knowledge of medicinal herbs, and by the confidence his people
            place in him.

NA   Davis, Daniel Webster. "Echoes from a Plantation Party," *SW*, 28 (1899),
734   54-59.
            8 ring-play texts; description of slave parties, tale telling, riddles,
            songs, etc.

NA   Davis, Daniel Webster. *The Industrial History of the Negro Race in the
735   United States*. Richmond, Virginia: Virginia Press, 1908.
            Includes a black author's discussion of white and black dialect in the
            various states of the South.

NA
736

Davis, Daniel Webster. *'Weh Down Souf*. Cleveland, Ohio: Helman-Taylor, 1897.
Dialect poetry by an ex-slave contains material on plantation life;
discusses dialect in the introduction; glossary.

NA
737

Davis, Edwin Adams. *Plantation Life in the Florida Parishes of Louisiana,
1836-1846 as Reflected in the Diary of Bennet H. Barrow*. New York:
Columbia University Press, 1945.
Includes comments on slave conditions, life, amusements, housing,
religion, etc.

NA
738

Davis, Gerald L. "Meet Sonny Diggs, A Baltimore Arabber," *1972 Festival
of American Folklife*. Washington, D.C.: Smithsonian Institution, 1972,
24-25.
The verse and cries of street merchants; their history; includes 2
texts.

NA
739

Davis, Henry C. "Negro Folk-Lore in South Carolina," *JAF*, 27 (1914), 241-
254.
Tales, sayings, superstitions, religious and dance songs from South
Carolina, with discussion.

NA
740

Davis, John. *Travels of Four Years and a Half in the United States of
America*. London, 1803.
Contains a slave narrative with mention of music and dress.

NA
741

Davis, John A. "The Influence of Africans on American Culture," in *Africa
in the United States*, Vernon McKay, ed. New York: Macfadden-Bartell,
1967, 89-109.
Review of African cultural influences on Afro-American dance, music,
art, etc.

NA
742

Davis, M.E.N. "The Cotton-Wood Tree: Louisiana Superstition" and "De
Witch-'ooman an' De Spinin'-Wheel," *JAF*, 18 (1905), 251-252.
2 tales from Louisiana.

NA
743

Davis, Rebecca Harding. "Here and There in the South," *Harper's*, 75 (1887),
431-443.
Description of black life and customs in Mobile, Alabama, with beliefs
and "superstitions."

NA
744

Davis, Reuben. *Butcher Bird*. Boston: Little, Brown, 1936.

NA
745
Davis, Sidney Fant. *Mississippi Negro Lore*. Jackson, Tenn.: McCowat-Mercer, 1914.

NA
746
Dawson, Warrington. "Le Caractère Spécial de la Musique Nègre en Amérique," *Journal de la Société des Américanistes* (Paris), n.s., 24 (1932), 273-286.
History and description of slave music in South Carolina.

NA
747
Day, Charles H. *Fun in Black; or, Sketches of Minstrel Life, with the Origins of Minstrelsy, by Colonel T. Allston Brown*. New York: Robert M. De Witt, 1874. (Portions are reprinted as "Black Musicians and Early Ethniopian Minstrelsy," *BPM*, 3 (1975), 77-83.)

NA
748
De Corse, Helen Camp. *Charlottesville: A Study of Negro Life and Personality*. Publications of the University of Virginia Phelps-Stokes Fellowship Papers, No. 11, Charlottesville, Va., 1933.
Chapter 3 ("Social Activities") includes a brief description of revival services and sermons; Chapter 4 ("Superstitions and the Negro") briefly discusses conjuration and charms.

NA
749
De Coy, Robert H. *The Nigger Bible*. Los Angeles: Holloway House, 1967.
Includes a glossary of slang terms, (some of which are apparently idiosyncratic) and a discussion of the meaning of Mardi Gras to Negroes in New Orleans.

NA
750
Deedes, Henry. *Sketches of the South and West*. Edinburgh: William Blackwood, 1869.
Negro oratorical style (pp. 83-86) described; an argument (pp. 143-146), a Christmas prayer meeting (p. 157), etc.

NA
751
Dégh, Linda. "The Negro in the Concrete," *Indiana Folklore* (Bloomington), 1 (1968), 61-67.
A legend of a Negro bridge builder in Indiana.

NA
752
Dehn, Mura. "'Be for Real.' An Interview with James Berry," *Dance Magazine*, 35 (September, 1961), 48-49, 70, 71, 73.
An interview with an early jazz tap dancer.

NA
753
Dehn, Mura. "Jazz Dance," *Sound and Fury* (Utica, N.Y.), 2, No. 3 (1966), 14-17.
Traces the advent of popular dance and its advocates from the Charleston of the mid-1920's to Rock and Roll of the 1960's.

NA
754

Dehn, Mura. "Night Life in Georgia," *JM*, 6, No. 9 (1960), 11-12.
Brief account of dance performances in a black nightclub.

NA
755

DeKnight, Freda. *A Date with a Dish: A Cook Book of American Negro Recipes*.
New York: Hermitage, 1948.

NA
756

DeKnight, Freda. *The Ebony Cookbook*. Chicago: Johnson, 1962.

NA
757

Delehant, Jim. "The Fall of the Singing Group Era," *Hit Parade*, 26, No. 35
(1967), 32-34.
The black rhythm and blues singing groups of the 1950's.

NA
758

Delehant, Jim. "The Panorama of Negro Music," *Rhythm and Blues*, 3, No. 61
(1963), 18-19.
The author discusses the origins of black music and its far-reaching
influences on all phases of contemporary popular music.

NA
759

De Lerma, Dominique-Réné, ed. *Reflections on Afro-American Music*. Kent,
Ohio: Kent State University Press, 1973.
A collection of essays, includes material on early black classical
musicians and composers (pp. 161-179); brief comments on soul music
(pp. 180-188) and on similarities between African and Afro-American
music (pp. 208-221), etc.

NA
760

Deming, Clarence. *Byways of Nature and Life*. New York: G.P. Putnam, 1884.
9 legends from Mississippi, recorded in spirituals.

NA
761

Dennison, Tim. *The American Negro and His Amazing Music*. New York: Vantage,
1963.
Short account of the blues, spirituals, jazz, and popular music and
their influences.

NA
762

"Depicts Negro Life in Carolina Island Retreat," *Art Digest*, 10 (December,
1935), 17.
Report of an exhibition of drawings depicting life on the South Carolina
Sea Islands by Henry Botkin, George Gershwin's cousin. Includes 1 print.

NA
763

"Desecration of 'Spirituals,'" *SW*, 51 (1922), 501-503.
Editorial which argues that spirituals should not be commercialized in
theatres.

NA   DeStefano, Johanna S., ed. *Language, Society, and Education: A Profile of*
764   *Black English*. Worthington, Ohio: Charles A. Jones, 1973.
          Reprints a number of papers on Black English by Labov, Abrahams, Stewart,
          et al.

NA   Dett, R. Nathaniel. *The Dett Collections of Negro Spirituals*, 4 vols.
765   Chicago: Hall and McCreary, 1936.
          74 choral arrangements.

NA   Dett, R. Nathaniel. *Negro Spirituals*, 3 vols. Cincinnati: John Church,
766   1919.

NA   Dett, R. Nathaniel. *Religious Folk Songs of the Negro as Sung at Hampton*
767   *Institute*. Hampton, Va.: Hampton Institute, 1927.
          165 choral arrangements.

NA   Devereux, Margaret. *Plantation Sketches*. Cambridge, Mass.: Riverside Press,
768   1906.
          Stories set in Halifax and Pertie Counties, North Carolina; the activi-
          ties of "trick," "goomer" or "hoodie" Negroes; notes on language (pp. 32-
          34).

NA   Devoe, Thomas F. *The Market Book, Containing a Historical Account of the*
769   *Public Markets in the Cities of New York, Boston, Philadelphia and*
          Brooklyn, etc., Vol. 1. New York, 1862.
          Accounts of dancing, festivities, and slave street gangs in New York
          City in the 1700's (pp. 264-265, 344-345).

NA   Diamond, Stanley. "The Great Black Hope," in *Black America*, John F. Szwed,
770   ed. New York: Basic Books, 1970, 171-178. (Reprinted in revised form
          from *Dissent*, 12 (1965), 474-478.
          Race relations in the U.S. as farce; black style in music, folklore,
          and sports; the Cassius Clay-Sonny Liston fight as cultural drama.

NA   Diamond, Stanley. "Malcolm X: The Apostate Muslim," *Dissent*, 12 (1965),
771   193-197. (Reprinted in *The Radical Imagination*, Irving Howe, ed. New
          York: The New American Library, 1967, 219-224.)
          The murder of Malcolm X seen in light of the history and ideology of
          Negro religion in the United States.

NA   Dickins, Dorothy and Robert N. Ford. "Geophagy (Dirt-Eating) among Missis-
772   sippi Negro School Children," *American Sociological Review*, 7 (1942),
          59-65.
          Dirt-eating as a cultural trait.

NA 773
"A Difficult Courtship," *SW*, 25 (1896), 226.
Short play involving courting customs and practices on a Southern plantation.

NA 774
Dill, Stephen and Donald Bebeau, eds. *Current Slang*, cumulation Vols. 3 and 4. Vermillion, S.D.: University of South Dakota, n.d.
A dictionary of black slang, drawn from Watts, California, New Mexico, and elsewhere.

NA 775
Dillard, J.L. "Black English in New York," *The English Record*, 21 (1971), 114-120.
A comprehensive account of grammar and usage, in a historical framework; educational applications; bibliography.

NA 776
Dillard, J.L. *Black English: Its History and Use in the United States*. New York: Random House, 1972.

NA 777
Dillard, J.L. "Creole, Cajuns, and Cable with Some Heart and a Few Assorted Babies: Review of Lafcadio Hearn, *Gombo Zhèbes*, and George Washington Cable, *Creoles and Cajuns; The Negro Question*," *Caribbean Studies*, 3 (1963), 84-89.
Considers the popular confusion of Creole languages with "baby talk" and the implications of this confusion.

NA 778
Dillard, J.L. "Creole Studies and American Dialectology," *CS*, 12 (1973), 76-91.
A critique of dialectologists' treatment of Black English; examples of American words of African origin; the maritime connection between Creole, Cockney and Newfoundland dialects.

NA 779
Dillard, J.L. "The Creolist and the Study of Negro Non-Standard Dialects in the Continental United States," in *Pidginization and Creolization of Languages*, Dell Hymes, ed. Cambridge, U.K.: Cambridge University Press, 1971, 393-408.
U.S. Negro dialect as part of a continuum of New World Creoles; includes examples.

NA 780
Dillard, J.L. "Negro Children's Dialect in the Inner City," *The Florida FL Reporter*, 5, No. 3 (1967), 7-10.
Age-graded black dialect.

NA   Dillard, J.L. "Non-Standard Negro Dialects: Convergence or Divergence?" in
781   *Afro-American Anthropology, Contemporary Perspectives*, Norman E. Whit-
            ten, Jr. and John F. Szwed, eds. New York: Free Press, 1970, 119-127.
            Black English in the United States as part of a larger continuum of
            black Creole languages in the New World.

NA   Dillard, J.L. "On the Grammar of Afro-American Naming Practices," *Names*,
782   16 (1968), 230-237.
            A structural study of ghetto storefront church names from the Washing-
            ton, D.C. area compared with names taken from traditional churches
            from the Washington metropolitan and surrounding areas where the congre-
            gations are middle class and mostly white.

NA   Dillard, J.L. "The West African Day-Names in Nova-Scotia," *Names*, 19
783   (1971), 257-261.
            Evidence of day-name practices.

NA   *Dimensions of Black*. La Jolla, California: La Jolla Museum of Art, 1970.
784   Catalog of an exhibition of African and Afro-American art includes
            chapters on "Slavery," "Slave Art," "*Vodoun*, (Haiti)," "Religion,"
            "Reconstruction," and later periods of Afro-American art, architecture,
            and religion; illustrations.

NA   "Discobolus." "The Jargon of Jazz," *Lingua* (Cape Town, South Africa), 1,
785   No. 6 (August, 1949), 48-50.
            A listing of Harlem slang terms; includes an example of Cape Town "hip"
            talk.

NA   *A Discourse by Cudjo, December 25, 1847, to the Male and Female Bredren
786   of Alabama*. Lancaster, Pa.: Pearsall and Geist, n.d.
            Sermon ascribed to a slave includes scripture interpretation, songs,
            etc.

NA   Diton, Carl. *Thirty-Six South Carolina Spirituals*. New York: G. Schirmer,
787   1928.
            Texts and four-part musical arrangements.

NA   "'Divination with the Sifter' and 'Crossing the Back'," *JAF*, 5 (1892),
788   63-64.
            First article deals with Negro "superstitions" (printed in *Lippincott's
            Monthly Magazine*, December, 1891). The second article contains "childish
            superstitions" and a few examples not peculiar to blacks.

NA 789   Dixon, Christa. *Wesen und Wandel Geistlicher Volkslieder: Negro Spirituals*, (Change and Substance in Spiritual Folksongs: Negro Spirituals). Wupertal: Jugenddienst-Verlag, 1967.

NA 790   Dixon, Robert Malcolm Ward and William John Godrich. *Recording the Blues*. New York: Stein and Day, 1970.
An account of the early recording companies and their activities; discography; illustrations.

NA 791   Dixwell, John. "Mourning Customs of Negroes," *JAF*, 21 (1908), 365.
Seeks the origin of the custom among Negroes whereby male mourners wear hats at a funeral indoors.

NA 792   Doar, David. "Negro Proverbs," *Charleston Museum Quarterly*, 2 (1932), 23-24.

NA 793   Dobie, Bertha McKee. "The Death Bell of the Brazos," *PTFS*, No. 3 (1924), 141-142.
Legend of a death bell ringing for 300 slaves on the Brazos.

NA 794   Dobie, Bertha McKee. "The Ghost of Lake Jackson," *PTFS*, No. 7 (1928), 135-136.
1 tale.

NA 795   Dobie, J. Frank. "How Dollars Turned into Bumble Bees and Other Legends," *PTFS*, No. 3 (1924), 52-56.
4 tales.

NA 796   Dodds, Baby. *The Baby Dodds Story* (as told to Larry Gara). Los Angeles: Contemporary Press, 1959.
The autobiography of a New Orleans jazz drummer; New Orleans parades and social functions; drum construction and playing techniques ("right hand was 'mammy' and the left, 'daddy'"), etc.

NA 797   Dodge, N.S. "Negro Patois and Its Humor," *Appleton's Journal of Popular Literature, Science and Art*, 3, No. 45 (1870), 161-162.
Gives several illustrations of what the author considers to be the inherently humorous nature of Negro dialect.

NA 798   Dodge, Roger Pryor. "Jazz Dance/Mambo Dance," *The Jazz Review*, 2, No. 10 (1959), 59-63; 3, No. 1 (1960), 39-41.
A discussion of the similarities and differences between music and dance, with examples of Afro-American dances.

NA
799
Doerflinger, William M. *Songs of the Sailor and Lumberman*. New York: Macmillan, 1972, revised edition. (Originally published as *Shantymen
and Shantyboys: Songs of the Sailor and Lumbermen*. New York: Macmillan,
1951.)
Includes several Negro sea shanties and brief discussion of the relation between minstrelsy and work songs.

NA
800
Dollard, John. *Caste and Class in a Southern Town*. New Haven: Yale University Press, 1937.
The social psychology of race relations in a town in Mississippi. Includes descriptions of church services, etiquette, verbal aggression,
etc.

NA
801
Dollard, John. "The Dozens: The Dialect of Insult," *American Imago*, 1
(1939), 3-24.
The dozens game among adolescents and adults of several different
groups. Expurgated examples.

NA
802
Donald, Henderson Hamilton. *The Negro Freedman*. New York: Schuman, 1952.
Pp. 149-151 discuss the naming of freed slaves.

NA
803
"Done All I Kin Do," *SW*, 36 (1907), 144.
A spiritual with music.

NA
804
Donnan, Elizabeth. *Documents Illustrative of the History of the Slave
Trade to America*. 4 vols. Washington, D.C.: Carnegie Institution,
1930-1935.
Basic documents and statistics on the Atlantic slave trade to the
United States.

NA
805
"'Don't' Superstitions" and "Birds of Ill Omen," *SW*, 28 (1899), 449-
450.
Includes several Tidewater, Virginia superstitions and Louisiana folk-
legends regarding "Devil's Birds" (the blue heron, the yellow hammer,
the purple grackle, magpies, starlings, and black martins).

NA
806
Dorsey, Thomas A. "Gospel Music," in *Reflections on Afro-American Music*,
Dominique-Réné de Lerma, ed. Kent, Ohio: Kent State University Press,
1973, 189-195.
An interview with a gospel song composer, stressing the sources of
his music.

NA
807
Dorson, Richard M. *American Folklore*. Chicago: University of Chicago Press, 1959.
    Chapter on "The Negro" traces the history of Negro narrative and song, including the chief bibliographical references.

NA
808
Dorson, Richard M. *American Negro Folktales*. Greenwich, Conn.: Fawcett, 1967.
    Tales drawn from 2 previous books, *Negro Folktales in Michigan*, 1956 (almost all tales reprinted) and *Negro Tales from Pine Bluff, Arkansas and Calvin, Michigan*, 1958 (about half of the tales reproduced). Also tales taken from 4 articles and 4 previously unpublished tales. Some reorganization and references to work published since previous books.

NA
809
Dorson, Richard M. "The Astonishing Repertoire of James Douglas Suggs, a Michigan Negro Storyteller," *Michigan History*, 40 (1956), 152-166.
    Mississippi-born man told the author 175 assorted "yarns," chiefly tales, which the author here surveys, with Suggs' biography and comments on his style.

NA
810
Dorson, Richard M. *Buying the Wind*. Chicago: University of Chicago Press, 1964.
    Section 4, "Louisiana Cajuns," contains black and black-influenced folktales, cures, conjure, etc.; folk definitions of "conjure," "voodoo," and "gris-gris."

NA
811
Dorson, Richard M. "The Career of John Henry," *WF*, 24 (1965), 155-163. (Reprinted in condensed form as "The Ballad of John Henry c. 1872," in *An American Primer*, Daniel J. Boorstin, ed. Chicago: University of Chicago Press, 1966, 437-445.)
    A general view of the literature concerning John Henry.

NA
812
Dorson, Richard M. "Ethnology and Ethnic Folklore," *Ethnohistory*, 8 (1961), 12-30.
    Black protest lore discussed in the context of the folk history of American ethnic groups.

NA
813
Dorson, Richard M. "A Fresh Look at Negro Storytelling," *Arkansas Folklore*, 4, No. 1 (1953), 2-3.
    Summary of a lecture: a thematic means of classifying Negro folktales.

NA
814
Dorson, Richard M. "Is There a Folk in the City?," *JAF*, 83 (1970), 185-216.
    Seeks to provide an answer to the question of what business has a folklorist in the city. Includes a section on the Negro.

NA   Dorson, Richard M. "King Beast of the Forest Meets Man," *SFQ*, 18 (1954),
815   118-128.
           Contains 16 folk narratives of one tale type (No. 157) from Michigan.

NA   Dorson, Richard M., ed. *Negro Folktales in Michigan*. Cambridge, Mass.:
816   Harvard University Press, 1956.
           19 animal tales, 24 tales of "Old Marster and John," 8 on "Colored
           Man," 13 on horrors, 16 on hoodoos and two-heads, 13 on spirits and
           "hants," 16 on witches and wonders, 15 on the "Lord and the Devil,"
           12 on preachers, 14 on liars and Irishmen, 15 fairy tales. Introduc-
           tion on the communities, the storytellers and the art of Negro story-
           telling. List of tales, bibliography and notes, index of informants,
           index of motifs and tale types.

NA   Dorson, Richard M. "A Negro Storytelling Session on Tape," *MF*, 3 (1953),
817   201-212.
           Tales from a storytelling group; includes a version of "Jesse James."

NA   Dorson, Richard M. "Negro Tales," *WF*, 13 (1954), 77-97, 160-169, 256-259.
818   27 texts collected from John Blackamore, a Southern-born Negro now
           living in Benton Harbor, Michigan.

NA   Dorson, Richard M. "Negro Tales from Bolivar County, Mississippi," *SFQ*,
819   19 (1955), 104-116.
           20 black tales as told by residents of the all-Negro town of Mound
           Bayou.

NA   Dorson, Richard M. *Negro Tales from Pine Bluff, Arkansas and Calvin, Michi-
820   gan*. Bloomington: Indiana University Press, 1958.
           Transcriptions of field recordings from Pine Bluff (17 animal, 14 "Old
           Marster and John" stories, 8 spirit tales, 18 jocular tales, and 23
           protest tales); and from Calvin (10 animal stories, 10 race stories,
           20 concerning the supernatural and hoodoos, 8 cures and signs, 11 "true
           wonders," 9 protest tales, 6 scriptural tales, 8 tall tales, 5 tales
           about Irishmen, 4 about preachers, 6 "noodles," 12 jocular tales, 12
           riddles and endings).

NA   Dorson, Richard M. "Negro Tales of Mary Richardson," *MF*, 6 (1956), 1-26.
821   29 tale texts. Gives details of the life of the informant, tale types,
           motifs and references.

NA   Dorson, Richard M. "Negro Witch Stories on Tape," *MF*, 2 (1952), 229-241.
822   Reminiscences of Mississippi days about hoodoo experience, comparisons
           of hoodoo and witch narratives; transcribed from tape recordings.

NA
823
Dorson, Richard M. "Oral Styles of American Folk Narrators," in *Style in Language*, Thomas A. Sebeok, ed. Cambridge, Mass.: Massachusetts Institute of Technology, 1960, 27-51.
Includes discussion of 2 Negro folktale narrators and their storytelling styles.

NA
824
Dorson, Richard M. "Southern Negro Storytellers in Michigan," *Michigan History*, 37 (1953), 197-204.
Report on field trips to communities of Michigan Negroes (mostly migrated from Southern states) during 1952, when over 500 texts were obtained.

NA
825
Dorson, Richard M., George List, and Neil Rosenberg. "Negro Folksongs in Michigan from the Repertoire of J.D. Suggs," *The Folklore and Folk Music Archivist* (Bloomington, Ind.), 9 (1966), 3-41.
22 songs with annotations and musical transcriptions.

NA
826
Douglas, Byrd. *Steamboatin' on the Cumberland*. Nashville, Tenn.: Book Co., 1961.

NA
827
Douglas, S.W. "Difficulties and Superstitions Encountered in Practice among Negroes," *Southern Medical Journal*, 19 (1926), 957-959.

NA
828
Douglass, Frederick. *Life and Times of Frederick Douglass*. Hartford, Conn.: Park, 1881.
Ex-slave's account of slave life, music, etc.

Douglass, Frederick. See Jaskoski, Helen, No. NA 1601.

NA
829
Douglass, Joseph H. "The Funeral of Sister President," *Journal of Abnormal Psychology*, 39 (1944), 217-223.

NA
830
Dove, Adrian. "Soul Story," *New York Times Magazine*, November 8, 1969, 82, 84, 86, 88, 90, 92, 94, 96.
The cultural bias in white, middle-class achievement tests; glossary of Afro-American slang.

NA
831
Dowd, Jerome. "Art in Negro Homes," *SW*, 30 (1901), 90-95.
A survey of housing types, musical instruments, material culture, photographs, prints, paints, books, etc., in Hayti (near Durham), North Carolina.

NA
832
Dowd, Jerome. "Rev. Moses Hester: Sketch of a Quaint Negro Preacher in North Carolina," *Trinity Archives*, 9 (February, 1896), 283-296.

NA
833
Dowd, Jerome. "Sermon of an Ante-Bellum Negro Preacher," *SW*, 30 (1901), 655-658.
Reverend Moses Hester's ("Uncle Mose") Christmas sermon to the congregation in Durham, North Carolina.

NA
834
Downey, James C. "Revivalism, the Gospel Songs and Social Reforms," *EM*, 9 (1965), 115-125.
A treatment of music used in the Dwight Moody and Billy Sunday revival services (1875-1930) and establishment of the relationship between the forces of social reform and gospel songs. Includes 4 musical examples.

NA
835
Doyle, Bertram W. *The Etiquette of Race Relations in the South*. Chicago: The University of Chicago Press, 1937.
A study of interracial behavior with references to pre- and post-Civil War Negro religion, entertainment, etc.; bibliography.

NA
836
Doyle, Bertram W. "The Etiquette of Race Relations--Past, Present and Future," *JNH*, 5 (1936), 191-208.
Ante-bellum Negro-white relationships and resulting Negro folkways.

NA
837
Drake, St. Clair and Horace R. Cayton. *Black Metropolis: A Study of Negro Life in a Northern City*. New York: Harcourt, Brace, 1945.
A sociological study of urban Afro-Americans discusses street life, religion, behavior, etc.

NA
838
Drake, Samuel G. *The Witchcraft Delusion in New England*. Roxbury, Mass., 1866.
Contains the confession (in partial dialect) of Tituba, a Barbadian slave, to her role in the Salem witch trials of the 17th century.

NA
839
Dresser, Norine. "The Metamorphosis of the Humor of the Black Man," *NYFQ*, 26 (1970), 226-228.
The changing self-image of black Americans as revealed in jokes.

NA
840
Driggs, Franklin S. "Kansas City and the Southwest," in *Jazz*, Nat Hentoff and Albert J. McCarthy, eds. New York: Rinehart, 1959, 191-230, 365-366.
The development of jazz in the southwestern United States; discography.

NA
841
Drums and Shadows: Survival Studies among the Georgia Coastal Negroes.
Georgia Writers Project. Athens: University of Georgia Press, 1940.
Transcription of dialect in recorded interviews with Georgia coastal
Negroes on belief in sorcery, spirits and workings of fate. Narrative
materials from 20 locations, including descriptions of locations and
informants; art, sculpture and crafts; domestic practices; African
genealogies and royalty; burial practices; typology of roots for curing and magic; musical instruments; appendix, glossary, 31 photos,
bibliography.

NA
842
Drysdale, Isabel. *Scenes in Georgia*. Philadelphia: American Sunday School
Union, 1827.
The second story concerns an aged slave, with filed teeth and tatooed
face, being taught about Christ by her 9-year-old charge.

NA
843
DuBois, W.E.B. *The Gift of Black Folk: The Negroes in the Making of America*. Boston: Strafford, 1924.
Includes chapters reviewing Afro-American music, art, literature, and
religion.

NA
844
DuBois, W.E.B., ed. *The Negro Church*. Atlanta, Ga.: Atlanta University
Press, 1903.
Discusses African background, obeah, religion and slavery, religion
and slave revolts, early church history, etc.

NA
845
DuBois, W.E.B. *The Souls of Black Folk*. Chicago: A.C. McClurg, 1938.
A description of the spiritual world of the American Negro, including
discussions of Emancipation, leadership, the practice of black religions,
and the "sorrow songs."

NA
846
Duganne, A.J.H. *Camps and Prisons: 20 Months in the Department of the Gulf.*
New York: J.P. Robens, 1865.
Interviews with blacks; descriptions of army occupation, houses, farming activities, etc. Includes examples of plantation song (p. 74), long
passage on a Negro church service, quoting sermon, responses, etc.
(pp. 79-83).

NA
847
Duke, Basil W. *Reminiscences of Basil W. Duke*. New York: Doubleday Page,
1911.
Notes on white-black relations on plantations (p. 228), hog killing
and Christmas (p. 230), Negro humor (pp. 232-236), witchcraft, voodoo,
and ghosts (pp. 237-238), the Ku Klux Klan and Negro superstitions.

NA
848
Dunbar, Paul Laurence. *The Best Stories of Paul Laurence Dunbar*. New
York: Dodd, Mead, 1938.

NA   Dunbar, Paul Laurence. *The Complete Poems of Paul Laurence Dunbar*. New
849   York: Dodd, Mead, 1913.

NA   Duncan, Eula G. *Big Road Walker*. New York: Fred A. Stokes, 1940.
850   17 retold South Carolina tales of a black "Paul Bunyan" type.

NA   Duncan, John. "Negro Spirituals--Once More," *NHB*, 10 (1947), 80-82, 95.
851   A brief account of the history and elements of the spirituals.

NA   Duncan, Mary L. *America as I Found It*. London: James Nisbet, 1852.
852   Includes a New York song (p. 73), black and white interaction at a
            Brooklyn wedding (p. 139), a black funeral (p. 205), black musical
            abilities and attitudes towards white minstrelsy (p. 219), a Negro
            woman's prayer meeting, attended by whites and blacks (p. 221-222),
            religious possession (pp. 222-223).

NA   Dundes, Alan. "African Tales Among the North American Indians," *SFQ*, 29
853   (1965), 207-219.
            Evidence that American Indians borrowed a considerable number of
            African tale types.

NA   Dundes, Alan. *Mother Wit from the Laughing Barrel: Readings in the Inter-
854   pretation of Afro-American Folklore*. Englewood Cliffs, New Jersey:
            Prentice-Hall, 1973.
            Reprints articles and excerpts on the origins and meanings of Afro-
            American speech, narrative, humor, music, belief, and verbal arts;
            contains editor's notes and bibliography.

NA   Dunham, Katherine. "Ethnic Dancing," *Dance Magazine*, 20 (September, 1946),
855   22, 34-35.

NA   Dunham, Katherine. "The Negro Dances," in *The Negro Caravan*, Sterling A.
856   Brown, Arthur P. Davis, and Ulysses Lee, eds. New York: Dryden, 1941,
            991-1000.
            Overview of Afro-American dancing.

NA   Dunlap, A.R. and C.A. Weslager. "Trends in the Naming of Tri-Racial
857   Mixed-Blood Groups in the Eastern United States," *AS*, 22 (1947),
            81-87.
            Includes names of Negro mixed groups.

NA 858   Dunn, Caroline. "Safety Pins for Peeling Onions," *HF*, 6 (1947), 112.
     A note on cooking practice.

NA 859   Dunson, Josh. "Blues on the South Side," *SO*, 15, No. 5 (1965), 16-20.
     The sociological background of music on Chicago's South Side; the blues people and their place in the contemporary world.

NA 860   Dunson, Josh. *Freedom in the Air: Song Movements of the 60's*. New York: International Publishers, 1965.
     Includes background and development of songs of the Negro freedom movement in the U.S. South.

NA 861   Durham, Frank M. *DuBose Heyward's Use of Folklore in His Negro Fiction*. Citadel Monograph Series, No. 2; Charleston, S.C.: The Citadel Military College of South Carolina, 1961.

NA 862   Durham, Phillip. "Negro Cowboy," *American Quarterly*, 7 (Fall, 1955), 291-301.
     Excerpts from a number of books concerning the Negro cowboy.

NA 863   Durham, Phillip and Everett L. Jones. *The Negro Cowboys*. New York: Dodd, Mead, 1965.
     History of the black cowboy, badmen, jockeys, black cowboy songs, etc.

NA 864   Duval, Margaret L. "Legends of Wilkinson County and the Surrounding Area," *LFM*, 3, No. 4 ("1975 for 1973"), 47-64.
     Includes white accounts of blacks and hoodoo.

NA 865   Dvorak, Antonin. "Music in America," *Harper's*, 90 (1895), 428-434. (Reprinted in No. NA 1698.)
     Argues that Negro and Indian music should be the basis for American art music.

NA 866   Earle, Alice Morse. *Customs and Fashions in Old New England*. New York: Scribner's, 1896.
     Discusses slaves' games ("pow-wow"), election of a black governor, the burial rituals performed by a suicide.

NA 867   Earle, Alice Morse. *In Old Narragansett: Romances and Realities*. New York: Scribners, 1898.
     Includes accounts of a black governor and a conjure woman in Rhode Island.

NA   Earle, Alice Morse. "Pinkster Day," *Outlook*, 46 (1894), 743-744.
868   Pinkster (Pentacost) Day celebrations in New York State in the
           18th and 19th centuries.

NA   Eaton, Walter P. "Dramatic Evolution and the Popular Theatre," *The*
869   *American Scholar*, 4, No. 1 (1935), 148-159.
           A short history of minstrelsy including an examination of its reper-
           toire.

NA   Eby, C.D., Jr. "Classical Names among Southern Negro Slave," *AS*, 36
870   (1961), 140-141.
           Appearance of Caesar, Cato, Juniper, etc. in slave records before 1800
           attributed to English "gentlemen" settling in America and transferring
           the practice of naming animals after classical personages to slaves.

NA   Eckhardt, Rosalind. "From Handclap to Line Play," in *Black Girls at Play:*
871   *Folkloric Perspectives on Child Development*. Austin, Texas: Southwest
           Educational Development Laboratory, 1975, pp. 57-99.
           An analysis of the proxemics of handclaps, ring plays and line plays,
           their sequence in play and in social development; illustrations.

NA   Eddington, Neil A. "Genital Superiority in Oakland Negro Folklore: A Theme,"
872   *The Kroeber Anthropological Society Papers*, 33 (1965), 99-105.
           5 folktales with analysis in terms of their sexual content.

NA   Eddins, A.W. "Brazos Bottom Philosophy," *PTFS*, No. 2 (1923), 50-51.
873   2 fables.

NA   Eddins, A.W. "Brazos Bottom Philosophy," *PTFS*, No. 9 (1931), 153-164.
874   10 anecdotes.

NA   Eddins, A.W. "From the Brazos Bottom," *PTFS*, No. 26 (1954), 50-55.
875   4 joking tales.

NA   Eddins, A.W. "'How Sandy Got His Meat'--A Negro Tale from the Brazos Bot-
876   tom," *PTFS*, No. 1 (1916), 47-49.
           1 Brer Rabbit tale.

NA   Eddins, A.W. "The State Industrial School Boy's Slang," *PTFS*, No. 1 (1916),
877   44-46.
           Nicknames and a reference to the dozens.

NA
878
Eddy, Norman. "Store-Front Religion," *Religion in Life*, 29 (1959-1960), 68-85.
  The needs and worship practices of city dwellers.

NA
879
Edmonds, Emma E. *Nurse and Spy in the Union Army*. Hartford: W. Simms & Co., 1865.
  Describes contrabands, giving several songs.

NA
880
Edmonds, Randolph. *Six Plays For a Negro Theatre*. Boston: W.H. Baker, 1934.
  One-act plays with folkloric content.

NA
881
Edmonson, Munro S. "Carnival in New Orleans," *CQ*, 4 (1956), 233-245.
  Descriptions of Mardi Gras events, black and white.

NA
882
Edwards, Harry Stillwell. *The Two Runaways and Other Stories*. New York: Century, 1889.
  Short stories with folkloric content: preaching (pp. 176-178, 232-239), description of music and dance--fiddler and fiddlesticks (pp. 162-167) --with song texts, hymn singing (pp. 35-37), an African slave's conjure and carving of turtle shells and bird beaks (pp. 202-203, 205), an "African" accounting system (p. 204), etc.

NA
883
Egg, Bernhard. *Jazz-Fremdwörterbuch*. Leipzig: W. Ehrler, 1927.
  A dictionary of jazz talk.

NA
884
Egypt, Uphelia Settle, J. Masuoka, and Charles S. Johnson, eds. *Unwritten History of Slavery*. Social Science Source Documents, No. 1. Nashville: Fisk University, 1945. (For reprinted edition, see Rawick, George, *The American Slave*, No. NA 2547.)
  38 ex-slave autobiographies collected in Tennessee and Kentucky between 1929 and 1930.

NA
885
Elam, William Cecil. "Lingo in Literature," *Lippincott's Magazine*, 55 (1895), 286-288.
  Argues that Negro dialect is a mispronunciation and misuse of words and not a dialect form; examples with explanations.

NA
886
Eliason, Norman E. "Some Negro Slang," *AS*, 13 (1938), 151-152.
  Slang terms used among Negro students, with definitions and observations.

NA
887
Eliason, Norman E. "Some Negro Terms," *AS*, 13 (1938), 151-152.
  Slang terms used among Negro students, with definitions and observations.

NA 888   Eliason, Norman E. *Tarheel Talk: An Historical Study of the English Language in North Carolina to 1860*. Chapel Hill: University of North Carolina, 1956.

NA 889   Elkins, Stanley M. *Slavery: A Problem in American Institutional and Intellectual Life*. Chicago: University of Chicago Press, 1959.
The nature of slavery in North America; the development of the slave ("Sambo") personality.

NA 890   Elliot, Gilbert, Jr. "Our Musical Kinship With the Spaniards," *MQ*, 8, (1922), 413-418.
Influence of Spanish music on jazz.

NA 891   Ellis, A.B. "Evolution in Folklore: Some West African Prototypes of the Uncle Remus Stories," *Popular Science*, 48 (November, 1895), 93-104.
African analogues to Afro-American folktales.

NA 892   Ellis, A.B. "On Vôdu Worship," *Popular Science*, 38 (March, 1891), 651-663.
Vôdu in Haiti and Louisiana: the oracle's role.

NA 893   Ellis, Herbert C., and Stanley M. Newman. "'Gowster,' 'Ivy Leaguer,' 'Hustler," 'Conservative,' 'Mackman,' and 'Continental': A Functional Analysis of Six Ghetto Roles," in *The Culture of Poverty: A Critique*, Eleanor Burke Leacock, ed. New York: Simon and Schuster, 1971, 229-314.
A typology of Chicago young men's street roles: dress, slang, kinesics, etc.

NA 894   Ellis, Herbert C. and Stanley M. Newman. "The Greaser Is a 'Bad Ass'; the Gowster Is a 'Muthah': An Analysis of Two Urban Youth Roles," in *Rappin' and Stylin' Out*, Thomas Kochman, ed. Urbana, Ill.: University of Illinois Press, 1972, 369-380.
The style, dress and values of parallel white and black street youths' roles.

NA 895   Ellison, J. Malcus. "A Negro Church in Rural Virginia," *SW*, 60 (1931), 67-73, 176-179, 201-210, 307-314.
Examines problems of a black congregation in rural Virginia in terms of participation, leadership, and lack of interested youth; contains the description of a revival meeting (pp. 201-210).

NA 896   Ellison, Ralph. *Invisible Man*. New York: Random, 1947.
Novel with folkloric content.

NA
897
Ellison, Ralph. *Shadow and Act*. New York: Random House, 1964.
    Essays on the Afro-American contribution to U.S. culture: folklore,
    jazz, the blues, style, myth, etc.

Ellison, Ralph. See Kent, George, No. NA 1726.

Ellison, Ralph. See Neal, Larry, No. NA 2161.

NA
898
Ellison, Ralph and James Alan McPherson. "Indivisible Man," *Atlantic*,
    226, No. 6 (1970), 45-60.
    A dialogue on the role of the black man and Afro-American culture in
    shaping American culture.

NA
899
Elton, William. "Playing the Dozens," *AS*, 25 (1950), 148-149, 230-233.
    Origins and uses of the dozens.

NA
900
Embree, Edwin R. *Brown America*. New York: Viking, 1931.
    The chapter entitled "Soil and Soul" includes words of 4 Negro spirituals,
    2 work songs, 1 blues songs and part of 1 sermon in verse.

NA
901
Emerson, William C. *Stories and Spirituals of the Negro Slaves*. Boston:
    Gorham, 1930.
    11 slave narratives; 14 song texts with music; illustrations.

NA
902
Emery, Lynne Fauley. *Black Dance in the United States from 1619 to 1970*.
    Palo Alto, Calif.: National Press, 1972.
    History of black dance forms, their connection to religion, other arts;
    includes Caribbean dances; bibliography, illustrations.

NA
903
Emmons, Martha. "Confidences from Old Nacogdoches," *PTFS*, No. 7 (1928),
    119-134.
    Material on omens, ghosts, etc.

NA
904
Emmons, Martha. *Deep Like the Rivers. Stories of My Negro Friends*. Austin,
    Texas: Encino, 1969.
    Includes 40 tales and stories of ghosts, death, revelations, and folk
    wisdom collected from Texas. (No indication as to whether or not mater-
    ial is traditional.)

NA
905
Emmons, Martha. "Dyin' Easy," *PTFS*, No. 10 (1932), 55-61.
    "Superstitions," prophecies and signs of approaching death.

NA   Emmons, Martha. "Walk Around My Bedside," *PTFS*, No. 13 (1937), 130-136.
906   Spiritual visitations at time of death.

NA   Emrich, Duncan. "Animal Tales Told in the Gullah Dialect by Albert H.
907   Stoddard of Savannah, Georgia," booklet included with Library of Con-
            gress LP records AAFS L44, L45.
            Texts of 16 tales, with glossary.

NA   Ende, A. von. "Die Musik der Amerikanischen Neger," *Die Musik* (Berlin),
908   5 (1906), 368-375.
            Analysis of the ethnic and musical characteristics of American Negro
            music.

NA   Engel, Carl. *An Introduction to the Study of National Music.* London:
909   Longmans, Green, Reader and Dyer, 1866.
            Includes a discussion of African music with reference to the American
            Negro.

NA   Engel, Carl. "Views and Reviews," *MQ*, 12 (1926), 306-314.
910   Comments on J. Rosamond Johnson's *The Book of American Negro Spirituals*,
            R. Emmet Kennedy's *Mellows* and others.

NA   Engel, Carl. "Views and Reviews," *MQ*, 23 (1937), 388-395.
911   Critical review of Alan Lomax's *Negro Folk Songs as Sung by Leadbelly*.

NA   "The Enlisted Soldier," *SW*, 46 (1917), 479.
912   1 spiritual text from a black regiment in Maryland.

NA   Epstein, Dena J. "African Music in British and French America," *MQ*, 59
913   (1973), 61-91.
            A survey of early sources in print and manuscript.

NA   Epstein, Dena J. "The Folk Banjo: A Documentary History," *EM*, 19 (1975),
914   347-371.

NA   Epstein, Dena J. "Slave Music in the United States before 1860: A Survey
915   of Sources," *Music Library Association Notes*, 20 (1963), 195-212, 377-
            390.
            Annotated bibliography of early materials, with quotes; includes sources
            for spirituals, style of singing, secular music, corn songs, boat songs,
            juba, instruments, restrictions on singing, ring shouts, and Congo
            Square in New Orleans.

NA
916
Espinosa, Aurelio M. "European Version of Tar-Baby Story," *Folk-lore*, 40 (1929), 217-227.
Discussion of the origin of the Tar-Baby story with 2 texts.

NA
917
Espinosa, Aurelio M. "More Notes on the Origin and History of the Tar-Baby Story," *Folklore*, 49 (1938), 168-181.
Argues for the East Indian origin of the story.

NA
918
Espinosa, Aurelio M. "A New Classification of the Fundamental Elements of the Tar-Baby Story on the Basis of Two Hundred and Sixty-Seven Versions," *JAF*, 56 (1943), 31-37.
Affirms belief in the Hindu origin of the tale on the basis of a number of versions, some of which are Hispanic.

NA
919
Espinosa, Aurelio M. "Notes on the Origin and History of the Tar-Baby Story," *JAF*, 42 (1930), 129-209.
Relates tale to Lithuanian sources rather than African origins: agrees with Joseph Jacobs on Hindu origin. Collection of 200 versions, with a study of the versions according to distribution.

NA
920
Espinosa, Aurelio M. "A Third European Version of the Tar-Baby Story," *JAF*, 43 (1930), 329-331.
1 text.

NA
921
Espinosa, Aurelio M. "Three More Peninsular Spanish Folktales that Contain the Tar-Baby Story," *Folklore*, 50 (1939), 366-377.
English and Spanish transcriptions.

NA
922
Essien-Udom, E.U. *Black Nationalism: A Search for an Identity in America*. Chicago: University of Chicago Press, 1962.
Descriptions of the mythology and ritual of the Black Muslims.

NA
923
Estep, Glenn and William Dietchke. "A Study of Certain Aspects of Spiritualism and Powwow in Regard to the Folklore of Lancaster County," *Pennsylvania Folklife*, 5 (March, 1954), 10-11.
Contains an account of a visit to a Negro *powwower* (healer) in Lancaster, Pa.

NA
924
Estes, Phoebe Beckner. "The Reverend Peter Vinegar," *SFQ*, 23 (1959), 239-252.
Life and legendary tales about a well-known black preacher in Kentucky.

NA   Eustis, Celestine. *Cooking in Old Creole Days*. New York: Russell, 1903.
925   Cookbook with 8 Creole songs, street cries, proverbs, etc.

NA   Evans, David. "Africa and the Blues," *Living Blues*, No. 10 (Autumn, 1972),
926   27-29.
            A response to Richard Waterman's discussion on African retentions in
            the blues (see Nos. NA 3116, 2272).

NA   Evans, David. "Afro-American One-Stringed Instruments," *WF*, 29 (1970),
927   229-246.
            Describes 13 one-stringed instruments from Mississippi of African
            origin; illustrations.

NA   Evans, David. "Babe Stovall," in *Back Woods Blues*. Oxford: Blues Unlimited,
928   1968, 50-55.
            Biography of a bluesman.

NA   Evans, David. "Black Fife and Drum Music in Mississippi," *MFR*, 6 (1972),
929   94-107.
            History and description of rural bands; discography, illustrations.

NA   Evans, David. "Blues on Dockery's Plantation," *BU*, 1968, 14-15.
930

NA   Evans, David. "Bubba Brown: Folk Poet," *MFR*, 7 (1973), 15-31.
931   8 songs and a praise song from a songster.

NA   Evans, David. "Charles Patton's Life and Music," *Blues World*, 23 (1969),
932   3-7.

NA   Evans, David. "Record Reviews: Black Religious Music," *JAF*, 84 (1971),
933   472-480.
            A review essay of religious song and sermons on record.

NA   Evans, David. "Record Reviews: Black Religious Music," *JAF*, 86 (1973),
934   82-86.
            Reviews of contemporary recordings.

NA   Evans, David. "Techniques of Blues Composition among Black Folksingers,"
935   *JAF*, 87 (1974), 240-249.
            Techniques of learning and composing blues songs contrasted with white
            folksong techniques; includes 5 blues texts.

NA
936
Evans, David. *Tommy Johnson*. London: Studio Vista, 1971.
    Life of a Mississippi bluesman with a study of his musical style;
    bibliography.

NA
937
Evans, David, Don Stephen Rice, and Joanne Kline Partin. "Parallels in
    West African, West Indian and North Carolina Folklore," *NCF*, 17, No.
    2 (1969), 77-84.
    Parallels in beliefs in spirits, charms, etc.

NA
938
Evans, J.H. "Superstitions about Animals" and "Weather-Lore," *SW*, 25
    (1896), 15-16.
    Children's chants to "periwinkle," "doodle bug," and "daddy-long legs";
    snakes as sources for Southern black folk-traditions; weather signs.

NA
939
Ewen, David. "American Song from the Negro," *Common Ground*, 5, No. 2
    (1945), 76-83.
    Traces African rhythms in Negro "sorrow songs," "orgiastic shouts,"
    and "crucifixion songs"; bibliography.

NA
940
"Extracts from the Diary of Mrs. Ann Warder," *The Pennsylvania Magazine
    of History and Biography*, 17 (1893), 444-461.
    Includes a description of a black funeral in Philadelphia in the 1700's.

NA
941
Exum, Helen Cousins. "Legends From Lima, Oklahoma," *SFQ*, 23 (1959), 113-
    116.
    Contains 5 legends representative of two groups of blacks who were
    the early settlers of the village of Lima.

NA
942
"Ezekiel Saw de Wheel," *SW*, 36 (1907), 207.
    A spiritual with music.

NA
943
"Ezekiel Saw de Wheel," *SW*, 55 (1926), 432.
    A spiritual with music.

NA
944
F.A.S. "Voodooism: Is It a Myth?" *AA*, 1 (1888), 288-289.
    Discussion of the French influences in voodoo.

NA
945
Faber, A. Dilworth. "Negro-American Vocabulary," *Writer*, 50 (1937), 239.
    Glossary of urban slang.

NA
946
Fahey, John. *Charley Patton*. London: Studio Vista, 1970.
   Biography of a Mississippi blues musician with a musicological analysis
   of his recorded work.

NA
947
Fairbairn, Ann. *Call Him George*. New York: Crown, 1969. (Originally published as Jay Allison Stuart, *Call Him George*. London: Peter Davies,
   1961.)
   Biography of New Orleans jazz musician George Lewis; life in New Orleans in the early 1900's.

NA
948
Fairclough, G. Thomas. "New Light on Old Zion," *Names*, 8 (1960), 75-86.
   Study of the names of white and Negro Baptist churches in New Orleans.

NA
949
Fancher, Betsy. *The Lost Legacy of Georgia's Golden Isles*. Garden City,
   N.Y.: Doubleday, 1971.
   Historical and general information on the Sea Islands: Gullah speech,
   songs, interviews, etc. (Largely reprinted from *Southern Living*, *Atlantic* and *Holiday* magazines.) Bibliography, illustrations.

NA
950
Fasold, Ralph W. "Tense and the Form *Be* in Black English," *Language*, 45,
   No. 4 (1969), 763-776.

NA
951
Faulkner, W.J. "The Influence of Folklore upon the Religious Experience
   of the Ante-Bellum Negro," *Journal of Religious Thought*, 24, No. 2
   (1967-1968), 26-28.
   Religious implications of the Brer Rabbit tales.

NA
952
Fauset, Arthur Huff. "American Negro Folk Literature," in *The New Negro*,
   Alain Locke, ed. New York: Boni, 1925, 238-249.
   A plea for better ethnological and folkloric research in Afro-American
   folklore; the African background of the lore; includes 2 tale texts,
   1 of which was collected from an ex-slave who had learned it in Africa.

NA
953
Fauset, Arthur Huff. "Black Gods of the Metropolis," *Wayne State University Graduate Comment*, 7, No. 4 (1964), 100-108.
   An updating of Fauset's earlier book of the same title.

NA
954
Fauset, Arthur Huff. *Black Gods of the Metropolis: Negro Religious Cults
   in the Urban North*. Philadelphia: Philadelphia Anthropological Society,
   1944. (Reprinted, Philadelphia: University of Pennsylvania Press, 1971,
   with new introduction by John F. Szwed.)
   Ethnographic account of 5 urban cults and their functions.

NA   Fauset, Arthur Huff. "Folklore from the Half-Breeds in Nova Scotia," *JAF*,
955   38 (1925), 300-315.
            16 tales from Indians with possible black influences.

NA   Fauset, Arthur Huff. *Folklore From Nova Scotia*. Memoirs of the American
956   Folk-Lore Society, Vol. 24. New York: American Folk-Lore Society, 1931.
            172 tales, 20 songs; game songs, rhymes, riddles, beliefs, folk-medi-
            cine, magic, domestic practices, holiday practices, etc., "the majori-
            ty . . . told by Negroes" (informants are identified).

NA   Fauset, Arthur Huff. "Negro Folk Tales from the South (Alabama, Missis-
957   sippi, Louisiana)," *JAF*, 40 (1927), 213-303.
            81 tales, 186 riddles, 12 toasts, 31 spirituals and 2 play songs.

NA   Fauset, Arthur Huff. "Tales and Riddles Collected in Philadelphia," *JAF*,
958   41 (1928), 529-557.
            55 tales, 50 riddles, 1 joke.

NA   Federal Writers' Project. *Washington: City and Capital*. Washington, D.C.:
959   United States Government Printing Office, 1937.

NA   Federal Writers' Project, Louisiana. *New Orleans City Guide*. Boston: Hough-
960   ton Mifflin, 1938. (Revised edition published in 1952).
            Contains section on folkways of Negroes, including voodoo, etc.

NA   Feldstein, Stanley. *Once a Slave: The Slaves' View of Slavery*. New York:
961   W. Morrow, 1971.
            A portrait of slavery drawn from the slave narratives. Includes food,
            music, religion, beliefs, etc.; bibliography of slave narratives.

NA   Felton, David. "Richard Pryor: This Can't be Happening to Me," *Rolling
962   Stone*, October 10, 1974, 40-46, 69-72.
            The training, career and routines of a black comic.

NA   Felton, Ralph A. *These My Brethren: A Study of 570 Negro Churches and 542
963   Negro Homes in the Rural South*. Madison, N.J.: Department of the Rural
            Church, Drew Theological Seminary, 1950.

NA   Fenner, Thomas P. *Cabin and Plantation Songs as Sung by the Hampton Stu-
964   dents*. Hampton, Va., 1854. (Later enlarged editions are credited to
            T.P. Fenner and F.G. Rathburn and published in New York by Putnam,

1892 and 1901; retitled in a new edition as Thomas Fenner, *Religious Folk Songs of the Negro As Sung on the Plantations*. Hampton, Va.: Institute Press, 1909.)
145 songs with music.

NA   Ferguson, Otis. "Breakfast Dance in Harlem," *New Republic*, 86 (February 12,
965   1936), 15-16.
           A description of a Harlem night club.

NA   Ferm, Vergilius. *A Brief Dictionary of American Superstitions*. New York:
966   Philosophical Library, 1959.
           Includes Negro superstitions.

NA   Ferrero, Felice. "La Musica dei Negri Americani," *Rivista Musicale Itali-*
967   *ana* (Torino), 13 (1906), 393-436.
           General discussion of U.S. Negro folk music.

NA   Ferris, William R., Jr. "Black Folktales from Rose Hill," *MFR*, 7 (1973),
968   70-85.
           13 animal tales from the Vicksburg area; illustrations.

NA   Ferris, William R., Jr. "Black Prose Narrative in the Mississippi Delta:
969   An Overview," *JAF*, 85 (1972), 140-151.
           The content of narrative sessions among members of various age groups.

NA   Ferris, William R., Jr. "The Blues: Africa to America," *Close-up* (Jackson,
970   Miss.), 6, No. 10 (1971), 14-15, 23, 25.

NA   Ferris, William R., Jr. *Blues From the Delta*. London: Studio Vista, 1971.
971   A detailed treatment of the Mississippi Delta blues tradition recorded
           and collected by the author in the field. The poetry of the blues,
           means of improvising, etc.

NA   Ferris, William R., Jr. "Blues in the Mississippi Delta," *Druid* (Knoxville,
972   Tenn.), Spring 1970, 10-15.

NA   Ferris, William R., Jr. "Blues Roots and Development," *BPM*, 2 (1974), 112-
973   127.

NA 974   Ferris, William R, Jr. "The Collection of Racial Lore: Approaches and Problems," *NYFQ*, 27 (1971), 261-279.
Discussion of problems in collecting folklore from Mississippi blacks and whites, with evaluations of personal experiences by the author.

NA 975   Ferris, William R., Jr. "Creativity and the Blues," *BU*, No. 71 (April, 1970), 13-14.

NA 976   Ferris, William R., Jr. "Folklore and Racism," *Journal of the Folklore Society of Greater Washington* (D.C.), 4 (Spring, 1973), 1-6.
Differences between black and white stories of "racial conflict," includes 1 black text.

NA 977   Ferris, William R., Jr. "'From the Root and Branch': Composition and Competition in Delta Blues," *Jazz and Blues*, No. 1 (1971), 16-18.
Characteristic composition techniques among Mississippi Delta blues singers. (An extract from the author's *Blues From the Delta*.)

NA 978   Ferris, William R., Jr. "'If You Ain't Got It in Your Head, You Can't Do It in Your Hand': James Thomas, Mississippi Delta Folk Sculptor," *Studies in the Literary Imagination*, 3, No. 1 (1970), 89-107.
A discussion of the aesthetic values which guide an artist in his creation of material folklore and the role of this lore within a folk community.

NA 979   Ferris, William, R., Jr. "Lee Kizart Recalls the Delta Blues," *BU*, No. 72 (May, 1970), 9-10.

NA 980   Ferris, William R., Jr. "Mississippi Folk Architecture: Two Examples," *MFR*, 7 (1973), 91-114.
Description of a house, barn and smokehouse; illustrations.

NA 981   Ferris, William R., Jr. "The Negro Conversion Experience," *KFQ*, 15 (1970), 35-51.
A review-of-scholarship article, demonstrating a constant thread of American social science interest in Negro folk religious styles.

NA 982   Ferris, William R., Jr. "Prison Lore: A Neglected Tradition," *MFR*, 5 (1971), 114-120. (Also in *MFR*, 7 (1973), 41-46.)
Prisoners' poems and a letter.

NA   Ferris, William R., Jr. "Racial Repertoires among Blues Performers," *EM*,
983   14 (1970), 439-448.
           Repertoires variably used for white and black audiences; concealment
           of protest and obscenity.

NA   Ferris, William R., Jr. "Railroad Chants, Form and Function," *MFR*, 4
984   (1970), 1-14.
           Discussion of railroad chants, with an interview with a chanter on a
           bridge gang; illustrations.

NA   Ferris, William R., Jr. "Records and the Delta Blues Tradition," *KFQ*,
985   14 (1969), 158-165.
           Comments by Mississippi blues musicians on blues; the influence of
           recordings on musical style.

NA   Ferris, William R., Jr. "The Rose Hill Service," *MFR*, 6 (1972), 37-56.
986   Services, sermons, and songs of a Mississippi church; includes texts,
           illustrations.

NA   Fickling, Susan M. "Slave Conversion in South Carolina 1830-1860," *Bul-
987   letin of the University of South Carolina*, No. 146 (1924), 1-59.
           Includes description of singing, white preaching style adapted to
           blacks, dress, etc.

NA   Figh, Margaret Gillis. "Folklore in Bill Arp's Works," *SFQ*, 12 (1948),
988   169-174.
           Discussion of Arp's acquaintance with Negro lore and customs in 19th
           century Georgia and his use of it in his writings.

NA   Figh, Margaret Gillis. "Jumping Jeremiah," *JAF*, 63 (1950), 240.
989   1 rhyme from Alabama.

NA   Figh, Margaret Gillis. "Nineteenth Century Outlaws in Alabama Folklore,"
990   *SFQ*, 25 (1961), 126-135.
           Contains an account of Railroad Bill, legendary Negro bandit.

NA   Filmer, Vic. *Jive and Swing Dictionary*. Penzance, Cornwall: privately
991   printed, 1947.

NA   Finch, I. *Travels in the United States of America and Canada*. London: 1833.
992   Chapter 32 includes a description of musical instruments, preparation
           of cornmeal, manners, etc.

NA
993

Finch, Julia Neeley. "Mammy Song: A Negro Melody As Taken Down by Mrs.
Julian Neely Finch," *Music*, 13 (1897-1898), 604-605.
Text and music of a lullaby, with discussion.

NA
994

Fine, Elsa Honig. *The Afro-American Artist: A Search for Identity*. New
York: Holt, Rinehart & Winston, 1973.
A history of Afro-American art organized largely around the artists'
biographies; includes discussion of folk arts and crafts; illustrations, bibliography.

NA
995

Finestone, Harold. "Cats, Kicks, and Color," *Social Problems*, 5 (1957),
3-13.
The "cat," a male street figure, as an urban social type.

NA
996

Finkelstein, Sidney. *Jazz: A People's Music*. New York: Citadel, 1948.
A social history of Afro-American folk music, blues and jazz.

NA
997

Finkelstein, Sidney. "What Jazz Means to Me," *Studies in Ethnomusicology*,
Vol. 1, M. Kolinski, ed. New York: Folkways Records, 1961, 23-28.
The African, Afro-American, and Euro-American elements of jazz; jazz
as a product of the socio-economics of the United States.

NA
998

Firmin, Gloria. "Some Magical Practices among New Orleans Blacks," *LFM*,
3, No. 4 ("1975 for 1973"), 42-46.
Root work, candle practices, etc. and their relationship to Christianity and Biblical texts.

NA
999

"Fish Stories," *SW*, 26 (1897), 229-230.
2 variants of a tale.

NA
1000

Fishburne, Ann Sinkler. *Belvidere: A Plantation Memory*. Columbia, S.C.:
University of South Carolina Press, 1949.
South Carolina plantation memoirs include description of Christmas
festivities, a wake, dress, and whites learning African songs and
numerals from a slave.

NA
1001

Fisher, Miles Mark. *Negro Slave Songs in the U.S.* Ithaca: Cornell University, 1953.
A study using slave songs as a history of the black people in the U.S.
The use of slave songs as appraisals and records of past and contemporary events is discussed; bibliography.

NA
1002
Fisher, Miles Mark. "Organized Religion and the Cults," *Crisis*, 44
(1937), 8-10, 29-30.
A survey of cults, arguing that they lead in serving the political,
social, and religious needs of urban blacks.

NA
1003
Fisher, Rudolph. *The Conjure Man Dies: A Mystery Tale of Dark Harlem*.
New York: Covici, Friede, 1932.
Mystery novel with folkloric content.

NA
1004
Fisher, Ralph. "The South Lingers On," *Survey*, 53 (1925), 644-647.
Account of store-front preachers with a song text (possibly fictional).

NA
1005
Fisher, Rudolph. *The Walls of Jericho*. New York: Knopf, 1928.
Novel of Harlem with folkloric content.

NA
1006
Fisher, William Arms. *Seventy Negro Spirituals*. Boston: Oliver Ditson,
1926.
70 arranged spirituals.

NA
1007
Fishwick, Marshall, ed. *Remus, Rastus, Revolution*. Bowling Green, Ohio:
Bowling Green University Popular Press, n.d.
Essays on black culture, largely reprinted from other sources.

NA
1008
Fishwick, Marshall. "Uncle Remus Versus John Henry: Folk Tension," *WF*
(1961), 77-85.
Discussion of Uncle Remus and John Henry as products of folk and
racial tension. Contains part of a text of John Henry.

NA
1009
Fitchett, E. Horace. "Superstitions in South Carolina," *Crisis*, 43
(1936), 360-361, 370.

NA
1010
Fitchett, E. Horace. "The Traditions of the Free Negro in Charleston,
South Carolina," *JNH*, 25 (1925), 139-152.

NA
1011
Flanders, Ralph P. "Two Plantations and a County of Antebellum Georgia,"
GHQ, 12 (1928), 1-37.
Slave clothing, crafts, preparation of slave food, weekend activities,
marriages, July 4th celebrations.

NA 1012   Fletcher, Tom. *100 Years of the Negro in Show Business*. New York: Burdge, 1954.
Includes background and biographies of early minstrel and vaudeville men with chapters on the cakewalk, ragtime, etc.

NA 1013   Flint, Timothy. *Recollections of the Last Ten Years in the Valley of the Mississippi*. Boston: Cumings, Hilliard, 1826.
Description of the "King of the Wake" ceremonies and dancing in New Orleans.

NA 1014   Flouritt, Dave. "Ragtime in Retrospect," *Storyville*, No. 36 (1971), 203-206.
An examination of the factors in the emergence of the popularity of ragtime and jazz.

NA 1015   Flowers, Paul. "Picturesque Speech," *TFSB*, 10 (1944), 9-10.
Explanation and possible origin of the term "bo-dollar" used by blacks in the Mid-South.

NA 1016   Floyd, Marmaduke and Raven I. McDavid, Jr. "A Note on the Origin of Juke," *Studies in Linguistics*, 6 (June, 1948), 36-38.

NA 1017   Folb, Edith A. *A Comparative Study of Urban Black Argot*. UCLA Occasional Papers in Linguistics, No. 1. Los Angeles, 1972.
A study of argot among black youths in Los Angeles; glossary.

NA 1018   *Folk Blues*. New York: Arc Music, 1965.
Words and music to 103 blues and rhythm-and-blues songs by Muddy Waters, Chuck Berry, Willie Dixon, Sonny Boy Williamson, *et al*.

NA 1019   "Folk-Lore and Ethnology," *SW*, 22 (1893), 180-181.
Notes on the organization of material on Negro folklore and ethnology for the Hampton Institute's collection.

NA 1020   "Folk-Lore and Ethnology," *SW*, 23 (1894), 15-16.
Report of the first monthly meeting of the Hampton Folklore Society, December 11, 1893. Discussion of popular signs and "superstitions" among Southern blacks.

NA 1021   "Folk-Lore and Ethnology," *SW*, 23 (1894), 46-47.
"Superstitions" and riddles from Bradley, S.C.

NA   "Folk-Lore and Ethnology," *SW*, 23 (1894), 65-66.
1022   Mrs. Chloe Cabot Thomas' (Phyllis Wheatley's sister) memoirs of
             black folk medicine and practices.

NA   "Folk-Lore and Ethnology," *SW*, 23 (1894), 84-86.
1023   Folk beliefs about dreams and plants; children's games.

NA   "Folk-Lore and Ethnology," *SW*, 23 (1894), 209-210.
1024   Riddles, cures, precautions, signs, and proverbs of Southern blacks,
             collected by black and white correspondents.

NA   "Folk-Lore and Ethnology," *SW*, 24 (1895), 49-50.
1025   Medical techniques, nurses' signs, tests for criminals, hag lore, cat
             tales, "superstitions," and cures.

NA   "Folk-Lore and Ethnology," *SW*, 24 (1895), 78-79.
1026   Courtship dialogue; also includes an account of black symbols, signs
             and "superstitions," and several riddles.

NA   "Folk-Lore and Ethnology," *SW*, 24 (1895), 154-156. (Reprinted in No.
1027   NA 1568.)
             A plea for the collection of black folklore, with a sample of beliefs,
             folk medicine, "superstitions," etc.; suggestions for studying African-
             New World culture and genealogical continuities.

NA   "Folk-Lore and Ethnology," *SW*, 25 (1896), 38-39.
1028   Two short dialogues: "Courtship in Old Virginia" (describing Southern
             dating practices), and "The Rhode Island Vampire," (mentions hag-
             riding).

NA   "Folk-Lore and Ethnology," *SW*, 26 (1897), 122-123.
1029   2 ghost stories about Virginia hauntings.

NA   "Folk-Lore and Ethnology," *SW*, 26 (1897), 163.
1030   Extracts from student compositions: "Slave Marriages," "Wednesday
             Night, Wife Night," "How the Slaves Cooked and Ate," and "How They
             Were Dressed."

NA   "Folk-Lore and Ethnology," *SW*, 28 (1899), 32-33.
1031   5 explanatory tales and a collection of sayings.

NA   "Folk-Lore and Ethnology," *SW*, 28 (1899), 112-113.
1032   Includes a discussion of the trick bone of a cat; how to conjure;
            conjuration remedies; courtship; why the wren does not fly high; and
            how Brer Rabbit beats Brer Fox.

NA   "Folk-Lore and Ethnology," *SW*, 28 (1899), 314-315.
1033   3 tales describing conjure cures.

NA   "Folklore from St. Helena, South Carolina," *JAF*, 38 (1925), 217-238.
1034   21 tales, 8 riddles, 11 proverbs, and 16 texts of spirituals obtained
            from school children.

NA   "Folk-Lore Scrapbook," *JAF*, 10 (1897), 240-241.
1035   2 ghost stories from the *Southern Workman and Hampton School Record*,
            June, 1897.

NA   "Folk-Lore Scrapbook: A Correspondent," *JAF*, 3 (1890), 67.
1036   Tells of a voodoo festival held in the suburbs of New Orleans which
            included both black and white participants.

NA   "Folk Songs in the Making," *Literary Digest*, 101 (April 13, 1929), 27.
1037   A typhoon which destroyed areas of Puerto Rico and Florida is the
            subject of a Negro spiritual; with text.

NA   "Folktales from Students in the Georgia State College," *JAF*, 32 (1919),
1038   402-405.
            6 Brer Rabbit tales.

NA   "Folk-Tales from Students in Tuskegee Institute, Alabama," *JAF*, 32 (1919),
1039   397-401.
            6 tales with annotations.

NA   "Folk-Vocabulary," *The Folklorist* (Chicago), 1 (1892), 76.
1040   Definition of the expression "chewing the rag."

NA   Follin, Maynard D. "Two Notes," *AS*, 8 (1933), 78.
1041   The African origin of "goober."

NA   "The Fool Hunter," *SW*, 28 (1899), 230-232.
1042   Alabama "hard-times" tale.

NA
1043
Ford, Ira W. *Traditional Music of America*. New York: Dutton, 1940.
Music and texts of songs, a number having Negro influence.

NA
1044
Ford, Theodore P. *God Wills the Negro; An Anthropological and Geographical Restoration of the Lost History of the American Negro People, Being in Part a Theological Interpretation of Egyptian and Ethiopian Backgrounds. Compiled from Ancient and Modern Sources, with a Special Chapter of Eight Negro Spirituals.* Chicago: The Geographical Institute, 1939.
Attempts to prove Egyptian origins of the American Negro, culturally and physically; deals with "superstitions," religion, music.

NA
1045
Foreman, Ronald Clifford, Jr. "Jazz and Race Records, 1920-1932: Their Origins and Their Significance for the Record Industry and Society," *John Edwards Memorial Foundation Newsletter*, 4, No. 3 (1968), 97-99.
Abstract of a dissertation on race records.

NA
1046
Forten, C.L. "Life on the Sea Islands," *Atlantic Monthly*, 13 (1864), 587-596, 666-676.
Descriptions of boatmen singing hymns, the shout, dress, houses, manners.

NA
1047
Fortier, Alcée. "Bits of Louisiana Folk-Lore," *Transactions and Proceedings of the Modern Language Association of America*, Vol. 3, 1887. Baltimore, (1888), 100-168.
Includes "Tar-Baby" and other animal tales, proverbs, and song texts from Lower Louisiana.

NA
1048
Fortier, Alcée. "Contes Louisianais en Patois Créole," *CRAL*, 17 (September, 1900), 142.
4 animal tales in Louisiana Creole.

NA
1049
Fortier, Alcée. "Customs and Superstitions in Louisiana," *JAF*, 1 (1888), 136-140.
Customs and "superstitions" of Louisiana slaves.

NA
1050
Fortier, Alcée. *A Few Words about the Creoles of Louisiana*. Baton Rouge: Louisiana Department of Education, Circular 9, Series 1, 1892.

NA
1051
Fortier, Alcée. "Four Louisiana Folktales," *JAF*, 19 (1906), 123-126.
4 Creole texts translated into English.

NA
1052
    Fortier, Alcée. "The French in Louisiana and the Negro-French Dialect,"
        Modern Language Association Proceedings, 1885. Baltimore, (1886),
        96-111.
        Phonetics of Louisiana Creole.

NA
1053
    Fortier, Alcée. *Louisiana Folk Tales, in French Dialect and English*
        Translation. Memoirs of the American Folklore Society, Vol. 2.
        Boston: Houghton Mifflin, 1895.
        Includes 42 tales in Creole with English translation.

NA
1054
    Fortier, Alcée. "Louisiana Nursery Tales," *JAF*, 1 (1888), 140-145.
        2 tales in French Creole with English translations.

NA
1055
    Fortier, Alcée. "Louisiana Nursery Tales, II," *JAF*, 2 (1889), 36-40.
        2 tales in French Creole with English translations.

NA
1056
    Fortier, Alcée. *Louisiana Studies: Literature, Customs, Dialects, History*
        and Education. New Orleans: F.F. Hansell, 1894.
        Discussion of Creole English; includes descriptions of music and dance;
        lists a number of "superstitions."

NA
1057
    Foster, Barry. "Mississippi Fred McDowell," *Journal of Popular Culture*,
        5 (1971), 446-451.
        An interview with a bluesman.

NA
1058
    Foster, George G. *New York by Gas Light*. New York, 1850.
        Includes accounts of black dance and music in New York City in 1842.

NA
1059
    Foster, Herbert L. *Ribbin', Jivin', and Playin' the Dozens: The Unrecog-*
        nized Dilemma of Inner City Schools. Cambridge, Mass.: Ballinger, 1974.

NA
1060
    Foster, Laurence. *Negro-Indian Relationships in the Southeast*. Philadel-
        phia: published by the author, 1935.

NA
1061
    "Four Traditional Stories," in *American Stuff*. New York: Viking, 1937,
        229-231.
        4 texts from Arkansas.

NA
1062
    Fowke, Gerard. "Brer Rabbit and Brer Fox: How Brer Rabbit Was Allowed to
        Choose His Death," *JAF*, 1 (1888), 148-149.
        1 text.

NA 1063   Fowler, William C. "The Historical Status of the Negro in Connecticut," *The Historical Magazine* (3rd series), 3 (January, 1874), 2-18; (February, 1874), 81-85.
Describes the election of kings by blacks, the crown and sword worn, fife and drum players accompanying king, feasting, etc.; also discussion of black churches and religion.

NA 1064   Francis, Bettie G. "The 'Ruminatin' of Aunt Phoebe," *SW*, 35 (1906), 150-152.
Narrative prayer of a free Negro mother grieving over her son who was taken away from her, overheard by white boys; in dialect.

NA 1065   Frank, Stanley. "Now I Stash Me Down To Nod," *Esquire*, 21 (June, 1944), 53, 168-170.
Analysis of jive talk, music, etc., set in a biographical account of Dan Burley.

NA 1066   Franklin, John Hope. "James Boon, Free Negro Artisan," *JNH*, 30 (1945), 150-180.
Study of the life-style of a free Negro living in North Carolina between 1808 and 1857; bibliography.

NA 1067   Frazier, E. Franklin. *Black Bourgeoisie: The Rise of a New Middle Class in the United States*. New York: Crowell-Collier, 1962. (Originally published as *Bourgeoisie Noire*. Paris: Librarie Plen, 1955.)
Argues that Negroes in the South developed a new folk culture after having lost their African culture during slavery, and that urbanization destroyed the new folk culture in turn; includes a description of middle-class black life-styles.

NA 1068   Frazier, E. Franklin. *The Negro Church in America*. New York: Schocken, 1964.
Survey of Afro-American religion in the U.S.; changes in sacred music as indicators of changes in the social order; bibliographical footnotes.

NA 1069   Frazier, E. Franklin. "Psychological Factors in Negro Health," *Social Forces*, 3 (1925), 488-490.

NA 1070   Frazier, E. Franklin. "Racial Self-Expression," in *Ebony and Topaz*, Charles S. Johnson, ed. New York: National Urban League, 1927, 119-121.
Argues that the black man should develop an independent culture, but not one divorced from the balance of America.

NA   Frazier, George. "A Sense of Style," *Esquire*, 68, No. 5 (1967), 70-78.
1071   The Afro-American style in sports, dress, dance, and speech.

NA   "The Freedmen at Port Royal," *North American Review*, 101 (1865), 1-28.
1072

NA   Frey, Hugo. *Celebrated American Negro Spirituals*. New York: Robbins-
1073   Engel, 1926.

NA   Friedland, William H. and Dorothy Nelkin. *Migrant: Agricultural Workers*
1074   *in America's Northeast*. New York: Holt, Rinehart and Winston, 1971.
            An ethnographic study of migrant Florida Negroes; includes discussion
            of cuisine, dress, child training, material culture, religious be-
            liefs, folktales, humor, games, music and dance; lists jukebox selec-
            tions; illustrations.

NA   Friends, Society of, Mount Holly, N.J. *Anecdotes and Memoirs of William*
1075   *Boen, A Coloured Man*. Philadelphia: John Richards, 1834.
            Includes detailed account of a slave's religious experiences and be-
            liefs.

NA   "From Jim Crow to Jazz," *British Musician and Musical News*, 10 (October,
1076   1934), 223-225; 10 (November, 1934), 252-254. (The second section is
            titled "'The Spiritual,' Its Public Debut.")

NA   Fruit, J.P. "Uncle Remus in Phonetic Spelling," *Dialect Notes*, 1 (1896),
1077   196-198.

NA   Fry, Gladys Marie. "The System of Psychological Control," *Negro American*
1078   *Literature Forum*, 3, No. 3 (1969), 72-82.
            Examples from oral tradition and historical sources show the white
            psychological control of the Negro to have been based on his fear of
            the supernatural.

NA   Frye, Ellen. "Children's Rhythm Game from New York City," *WF*, 32 (1973),
1079   54-56.
            Texts and directions for playing 5 games from Harlem.

NA   Fullinwider, S.P. *The Mind and Mood of Black America*. Homewood, Ill.:
1080   Dorsey, 1969.
            A study of black American ideology, with some attention to humor,
            folktales, the "Sambo" theme, urban street figures, etc.

NA   Funk, Charles Earle. "Bill Robinson's 'Copesetic,'" *AS*, 28 (1953), 231.
1081   A note on a slang word.

NA   Furness, Clifton J. "Communal Music Among Arabians and Negroes," *MQ*,
1082   16 (1930), 38-51.
            Uses accounts of Arabian and South Carolina Negro religious music to
            demonstrate the communal process.

NA   G.W.S. "Negro Sermons," *Good Words* (London), 8 (March 1, 1867), 186-189.
1083   Excerpts from sermons from the South in modified dialect, with dis-
            cussion.

NA   Gagnon, Ernest. "Les Sauvages de l'Amérique et l'Art Musical," *Proceed-
1084   ings of the 15th International Congress of Americanists*. Vol. 1.
            Quebec: 1906, 179-189.
            The influence of the Christian Mission on Negro song and text.

NA   Gaines, Francis Pendleton. *The Southern Plantation: A Study in the De-
1085   velopment and the Accuracy of a Tradition*. New York: Columbia Uni-
            versity, 1924.
            Images of the plantation as shown by fiction, art, minstrelsy, and
            music, compared with those expressed by travellers, slaveholders,
            and historians; bibliography.

NA   Gaither, Frances. "Fanciful Are Negro Names," *New York Times Magazine*,
1086   February 10, 1929, 19.
            A list of names for people, places and animals with discussion.

NA   Galoob, Debra. "'Back in '32 When the Times Was Hard': Negro Toasts
1087   from East Texas," *Riata* (University of Texas), 1963, 24-33.
            Narrative poems of males featuring badman heroes: "The Monkey and
            the Baboon" and "Stackolee."

NA   Gammond, Peter, and Peter Clayton. *Dictionary of Popular Music*. New
1088   York: Philosophical Library, 1961.
            Contains entries on a variety of black musical topics.

NA   Garbett, A.S. "Blues!," *Etude*, 45 (1927), 434.
1089   Brief discussion of blues characteristics: themes of love, self-pity,
            rationalization. (Condensed from *Negro Workaday Songs*, by Howard
            Odum and Guy Johnson.)

NA
1090

Garnett, L.A. "Spirituals," *Outlook*, 130 (1922), 583.
3 songs.

NA
1091

Garon, Paul. "Blues and the Church: Revolt and Resignation," *Living Blues*,
1, No. 1 (Spring, 1970), 18-23.
Argues that a philosphical polarity between blues and the church is
evidenced in song lyrics.

NA
1092

Garon, Paul. "Blues and the Poetry of Revolt," *Arsenal* (Chicago), 1
(Autumn, 1970), 24-30.
Discussion of blues lyrics as poetry which expresses the view of the
artist on sexual pleasure and defiance.

NA
1093

Garon, Paul. *The Devil's Son in Law: The Story of Peetie Wheatstraw*.
London: Studio Vista, 1971.
Life of bluesman Wheatstraw, with an analysis of his music and song
texts; bibliography and discography.

NA
1094

Garon, Paul. "If Blues Was Reefers . . .," *Living Blues*, 1, No. 3 (1970),
13-18.
Discussion of blues lyrics having references to drugs.

NA
1095

Garon, Paul. "Texas Alexander," *Back Woods Blues*, Oxford: Blues Unlimited,
1968, 22-24.
Biography of a bluesman with emphasis on his records.

NA
1096

Garrett, Romeo B. "African Survivals in American Culture," *JNH*, 51 (1966),
239-245.
Survivals in language, customs, music and foods.

NA
1097

Garvin, Richard M. and Edmond G. Addeo. *The Midnight Special: The Legend
of Leadbelly*. New York: Bernard Geis, 1971.
Biography of a songster.

NA
1098

Garwood, Donald. *Masters of Instrumental Blues Guitar*. New York: Oak,
1968.
27 blues and ballads by Mance Lipscomb, Bo Carter, Mississippi John
Hurt, *et al.*, with notes.

NA
1099

Gaskins, Ruth L. *Every Good Negro Cook Starts Out With Two Basic Ingredi-
ents: A Good Heart and A Light Hand*. New York: Simon and Schuster,
1968.
Traditional recipes and notes on festive occasions.

NA   Gaul, Harvey. "Negro Spirituals," *Church Music Review*, 17 (1918), 147-
1100   151.
              Comments on spirituals, shouts, songs, love songs, "freedom songs";
              scores to 8 spirituals.

NA   Gaul, Harvey. *Nine Negro Spirituals*. New York: H.W. Gray, 1918.
1101   9 songs.

NA   Gay, Geneva and Roger D. Abrahams. "Black Culture in the Classroom," in
1102   *Language and Cultural Diversity in American Education*, Roger D.
              Abrahams and Rudolph C. Troike, eds. Englewood Cliffs: Prentice-Hall,
              1972, 67-84.
              Cultural differences between whites and blacks, and their importance
              for teaching.

NA   Gear, Robert F. "The National Guitar," *Living Blues*, No. 14 (Autumn 1973),
1103   9-10.
              Description and history of the "Dobro" guitar.

NA   Gehring, Carl E. "The Western Dance of Death," *Modern Quarterly*, 5
1104   (1930), 492-503.
              Jazz as black folk music.

NA   Gehrke, William Herman. "Negro Slavery among the Germans in North Caro-
1105   lina," *North Carolina Historical Review*, 14, No. 4 (1937), 307-324.
              Examples of the treatment of slaves, the use and retention of Penn-
              sylvania German expressions by blacks, a song, etc.

NA   Gellert, Lawrence. *Me and My Captain*. New York: Hours Press, 1931.
1106   24 chain gang songs with arrangements.

NA   Gellert, Lawrence. "Negro Songs of Protest," in *Negro Anthology*, Nancy
1107   Cunard, ed. London: Wishart, 1934, 366-377.
              An examination of plantation and chain gang songs and spirituals,
              among others, for elements of protest.

NA   Gellert, Lawrence. "Two Songs about Nat Turner," *The Worker Magazine*,
1108   (June 12, 1949), 8.

NA   Gellert, Lawrence, and Elie Seigmeister. *Negro Songs of Protest*. New
1109   York: American Music League, 1936.
              24 songs.

NA
1110
Genovese, Eugene D. "Black Plantation Preachers in the Slave South,"
Louisiana Studies, 11 (1972), 188-214.
The role of the preacher; sermons, songs, etc.

NA
1111
Genovese, Eugene D. *In Red and Black: Marxian Explorations in Southern and Afro-American History*. New York: Pantheon Books, 1971.
Essays on slavery and the nature of Afro-American culture.

NA
1112
Genovese, Eugene D. *Roll, Jordan, Roll: The World Slaves Made*. New York: Pantheon, 1974.
An account of slave life and influence in the South. Includes work, folklore, music, religion, celebrations, etc.

NA
1113
George, Zelma. "Negro Music in American Life," in *The American Negro Reference Book*, John P. Davis, ed. Englewood Cliffs, N.J.: Prentice-Hall, 1966, 731-758.
Brief overview of the history of black music, with emphasis on folk music.

NA
1114
Gerber, A. "Uncle Remus Traced to the Old World," *JAF*, 6 (1893), 245-257.
African and European parallels for Uncle Remus stories; stories learned from white masters.

NA
1115
Gerlach, Luther P., and Virginia H. Hine. *People, Power, Change: Movements of Social Transformation*. Indianapolis: Bobbs-Merrill, 1970.
Includes a study of beliefs and processes of change among black Pentecostal church groups; comparisons with other Afro-American religious groups; bibliography.

NA
1116
"'A Ghost Story' and 'Story of A Fox and A Pig,'" *SW*, 27 (1898), 124-125.
2 animal tales.

NA
1117
Gibbs, Samuel, Jr. "Voodoo Practices in Modern New Orleans," *LFM*, 3, No. 2 (1971), 12-14.
Malign magical practices.

NA
1118
Gibson, H.E. "Folk Medicine Among the Gullahs: African Legacy," *Negro Digest*, 11 (August, 1962), 77-80. (Reprinted from the Charleston, S.C. *News and Courier*.)

NA
1119
Gielow, Martha S. *Old Plantation Days*. New York: Russell, 1902.
Negro "dialect stories" by an Alabama slaveholder's daughter.

NA   Gilbert, Anne Kennedy. "Aunt Sukey's Apocalypse," *Literary Digest*, 96
1120   (March 31, 1928), 32.
            Negro spiritual describing "after-death."

NA   Gilbert, Will G. and C. Poustochkine. *Jazzmuziek, inleiding tot de*
1121   *Volksmuziek der Noord-Amerikaanse Negers*, 2nd edition. 's Gravenhage:
            Kruseman, 1948. (Originally published as Will G. Gilbert, *Jazzmuziek*.
            's Gravenhage: Kruseman, 1939.)

NA   Gillis, Frank. "Hot Rhythm in Piano Ragtime," in *Music in the Americas*,
1122   George List and Juan Orrego-Salas, ed. Bloomington: Indiana Univer-
            sity, 1967, 91-104.
            The presence of African rhythm in the ragtime compositions of Scott
            Joplin, James Scott, Joseph Lamb and others.

NA   Gillum, Ruth H. "The Negro Folksong in the American Culture," *JNH*, 12
1123   (1943), 173-180.
            Negro music as expression and its impact on American white music.

NA   Gilman, Caroline. "The Country Visit, Chapter 6: The Little Negroes," *The*
1124   *Southern Rose Bud*, 2 (1834), 183.
            Slave-master economic transactions; list of slave names.

NA   Gilman, Caroline. "The Country Visit, Chapter 10: Singing Hymns," *The*
1125   *Southern Rose Bud*, 2 (1834), 199.
            On spirituals, with 2 texts.

NA   Gilman, Caroline. *Recollections of A Southern Matron*. New York: Harper,
1126   1838.
            Account of everyday life in the slave South, including Negro dialect,
            descriptions of turbans, white speech to blacks, a Negro funeral,
            singing, whites' terms for blacks, celebration of a wedding, beliefs,
            etc.

NA   Gittings, Victoria. "What William Saw," *JAF*, 58 (1945), 135-137.
1127   Ghost appearances witnessed in Frederick County, Maryland.

NA   Glass, Julia Daingerfield. *Aunt Celey Talks*. n.p.: Published by the Author,
1128   1948.
            A black woman's memories and talk recollected from 1921-1922 by a
            white woman; in Louisiana dialect.

NA   Glass, Paul. *Songs and Stories of Afro-Americans*. New York: Grosset & Dun-
1129   lap, 1971.

NA   Glassie, Henry. *Pattern in the Material Culture of the Eastern United
1130   States*. Philadelphia: University of Pennsylvania, 1968.
            Includes Afro-American house styles, basketry, sling-shots and dolls.

NA   Glenn, Viola. "The Eating Habits of Harlem," *Opportunity*, 13 (March,
1131   1935), 82-85.

NA   Glover, Tony I. "Little Sun." *Blues Harp: An Instruction Method For Play-
1132   ing the Blues Harmonica*. New York: Oak, 1965.
            Includes a history of blues mouth harp playing, with a discussion of
            the styles of Sonny Terry, Sonny Boy Williamson I and II, Little Wal-
            ter, and Jimmy Reed. Illustrations, discography and bibliography.

NA   Godchaux, Elma. *Stubborn Roots*. New York: Macmillan, 1936.
1133   Novel of Louisiana life with folkloric content.

NA   Godrich, John. "'Ma' Rainey," *Storyville*, No. 35 (1971), 173-175.
1134   The career of blues singer Ma Rainey, emphasizing her minstrel years.

NA   Goffin, Robert. *Au Frontières du Jazz*. Paris: Sagittaire, 1932.
1135

NA   Goffin, Robert. "Big Eye Louis Nelson," *The Jazz Record*, (June, 1946),
1136   7-9.
            Narratives told by Nelson of New Orleans around 1900; information on
            Buddy Bolden and Scott Joplin.

NA   Goffin, Robert. "Hot Jazz," in *Negro Anthology*, Nancy Cunard, ed. London:
1137   Wishart, 1934, 378-379.
            A brief discussion of the history and evolution of "hot" or "impro-
            vised" jazz and its influence on European art.

NA   Goffin, Robert. *Jazz, from the Congo to the Metropolitan*. Garden City,
1138   New York: Doubleday, Doran, 1944.
            History of jazz: includes discussion of African influences, work
            songs, blues, spirituals, etc.

NA
1139
Goffin, Robert. *La Nouvelle-Orléans, Capitale du Jazz.* New York: Maison Francaise, 1946.

NA
1140
Goffman, Kimbal. "Black Pride," *Atlantic Monthly*, 163 (1939), 235-241.
Observations about originality of black culture expression in music and dance; descriptions of the Charleston, Susie Q., and Big Apple dances; deplores Negro shame in the uniqueness of black folklore and heritage.

NA
1141
Goines, Leonard. "Afro-American Music: The Spiritual," *Allegro*, August, 1971, 4, 15.
The features of religious song type in the United States, with discussion of the white-black origins controversy.

NA
1142
Goines, Leonard. "The Blues," *Allegro*, October, 1971, 4.
History and structure of blues form, and a list of common subjects.

NA
1143
Goines, Leonard. "The Blues as Black Therapy," *Black World*, November, 1973, 28-40.
Blues as a personalization of communal field holler, and as open statement of black condition and values. Gives a breakdown of blues by topic. Compares black realism with white sentimentalism.

NA
1144
Goines, Leonard. "The Classic Blues," *Allegro*, December, 1971, 7.
A discussion of the growth of blues in travelling shows and subsequent recordings, with short biographies of "Ma" Rainey and Bessie Smith.

NA
1145
Goines, Leonard. "The Country Blues," *Allegro*, November, 1971, 4.
Brief histories of some American country blues singers.

NA
1146
Goines, Leonard. "Early Afro-American Music in the United States--Sacred and Secular," *Allegro*, July, 1971, 11, 15.
Surveys American black song forms: worksongs, field hollers and cries, the song sermon, the ring or shuffle shout, and the spiritual.

NA
1147
Goines, Leonard. "Gospel Music," *Allegro*, September, 1971, 4.
Growth of gospel song-type out of spirituals and Southern churches.

NA
1148
Goines, Leonard. "Minstrelsy," *Allegro*, February, 1972, 7, 26.
Importance of black songs and performers in the development of the popular American theatrical form.

NA 1149   Goines, Leonard. "Ragtime," *Allegro*, March, 1972, 7.
Discussion of the history of black piano (and later orchestra) style, with emphasis on composer Scott Joplin.

NA 1150   Goines, Leonard. "Rhythm 'n' Blues," *Allegro*, January, 1972, 14.
Development of modern city blues tradition in the 1930-1950 era.

NA 1151   Goines, Leonard. "Traditional Jazz," *Allegro*, July, 1972, 4, 12.
Sketches of jazz pioneers Jelly Roll Morton and Louis Armstrong.

NA 1152   Gold, Robert S. *A Jazz Lexicon*. New York: Knopf, 1964.
A lexicon of the jazz, Negro and underworld communities, with literary references.

NA 1153   Gold, Robert S. "The Vernacular of the Jazz World," *AS*, 32 (1957), 271-282.
The nature and origin of jazz terminology.

NA 1154   "The Golden Age of Blues-Recordings," *RR*, 11 (1957), 3-4.
The beginnings of blues on record plus an account of a blues contest in 1922.

NA 1155   Goldsborough, Edmund K. *Ole Mars an' Ole Miss*. Washington, D.C.: National Publishing, 1900.
Tales of Eastern Shore Maryland blacks in dialect, with photographs; includes verses, sermons, songs and hymns.

NA 1156   Goldstein, Kenneth S., and Dan Ben-Amos, eds. *Thrice Told Tales*. Lock Haven, Pa.: Hammerhill Paper Co., 1970.
Includes 1 Tar Baby text from New Orleans (151-154), with notes on the literature of the tale type.

NA 1157   Goldstein, Richard. "The Graffiti Hit Parade," and "This Thing Has Gotten Completely Out of Hand," *New York*, 6, No. 13 (1973), 32-39.
Wall art and naming (African day-names and Puerto Rican Spanglish) in New York City; illustrations.

NA 1158   Goldstein, Walter. "The Natural Harmonic and Rhythmic Sense of the Negro," *Music Teachers' National Association Proceedings*, Series 12 (1917), 29-39.
Use of harmony and rhythm by blacks; with musical analysis.

NA 1159   Golightly, Cornelius L., and Israel Scheffler. "Playing the Dozens," *Journal of Abnormal and Social Psychology*, 43 (1948), 104-105.
Review of 3 earlier discussions of the dozens, a game of verbal dueling.

NA 1160   Gombosi, Otto. "The Pedigree of the Blues," *Volume of Proceedings of the Music Teachers National Association, Fortieth Series*, Theodore M. Finney, ed. Pittsburgh, Pa., 1956, 382-389.
Musical structure of the blues: rhythm, melody, and harmony.

NA 1161   Gonzales, Ambrose E. *The Black Border: Gullah Stories of the Carolina Coast*. Columbia, S.C.: The State Company, 1922.
Foreword on speech, and 42 Gullah stories written in Standard English with Gullah dialect in quotations; glossary.

NA 1162   Gonzales, Ambrose E. *The Captain, Stories of the Black Border*. Columbia, S.C.: The State Company, 1924.
22 stories in dialect; depicts plantation life after the Civil War in South Carolina and Georgia. Describes house-building, mining, farming, etc.

NA 1163   Gonzales, Ambrose E. *Laguerre, a Gascon of the Black Border*. Columbia, S.C.: The State Company, 1924.
Stories of Judge Laguerre and the "phases of Negro life" which he observed during his years on the bench.

NA 1164   Gonzales, Ambrose E. *Two Gullah Tales: The Turkey Hunter and At the Cross Roads Store*. New York: Purdy Press, 1926.

NA 1165   Gonzales, Ambrose E. *With Aesop Along the Black Border*. Columbia, S.C.: The State Company, 1924.
60 tales (mostly animal) from the Gullah of the South Carolina coast.

NA 1166   Gonzalez, Charles. "Runmo Riddles," *NCF*, 10, No. 1 (1962), 40-41.
Riddles from North Carolina children.

NA 1167   Gonzalez-Wippler, Migene. *Santeria: African Magic in Latin America*. New York: Anchor Press/Doubleday, 1975. (Originally published by the Julian Press, 1973.)
Includes materials on *Santeria* activities in New York City.

NA 1168   Goodell, Walter. *Forty-Two Popular Spirituals*. Chicago: Hall and McCreary Co., 1939.
 42 arranged spirituals.

NA 1169   Goodwin, W.T. and Peter Gold. "From 'Easter Sunrise Sermon,'" *Alcheringa* (New York), No. 4 (1972), 1-14.
 A transcription of a sermon (and the congregation's responses) by a John's Island, S.C. preacher; includes notes on the transcription and a disc recording.

NA 1170   Gordon, Robert W. *Folk Songs of America*. Washington, D.C.: National Service Bureau Publication 73-S, 1938.
 Original version of the articles that appeared in the *New York Times* between January 2, 1927 and January 22, 1928.

NA 1171   Gordon, Robert W. "Folk Songs of America: Negro Chants," *New York Times Magazine*, May 8, 1927, 11, 21.
 Traces the development of the black spiritual; sees no white influence other than text; includes examples.

NA 1172   Gordon, Robert W. "Folk Songs of America: Negro 'Shouts,'" *New York Times Magazine*, April 24, 1927, 4, 22.
 Discussion of 'shouts' (dance and music) in religious and secular life; discussion of field research with rural Negroes.

NA 1173   Gordon, Robert W. "Folk Songs of America: The Spirituals," *New York Times Magazine*, February 20, 1927, 7, 21.

NA 1174   Gordon, Robert W. "Folk Songs of America: Work Chanteys," *New York Times Magazine*, January 16, 1927, 7, 19.
 A collection of work songs, from the coast of south Georgia; discusses the musical and social aspects of the songs.

NA 1175   Gordon, Robert W. "The Negro Spiritual," in *The Carolina Low Country*, Augustine Smythe, ed. New York: Macmillan, 1931, 191-222.
 A treatment of the spiritual in the low-country, South Carolina, with emphasis on text, meaning, origin and function.

NA 1176   Gracy, David B., and Roger D. Abrahams. "Some Plantation Remedies and Recipes," *TFSB*, 29 (1963), 29-34.
 Descriptions of medical practices used with slaves from the manuscripts of white overseers.

NA
1177
Graham, Alice. "Original Plantation Melodies as One Rarely Hears Them,"
Etude, 40 (1922), 744.
An account of Negro singing at Columbus, Mississippi.

NA
1178
Graham, Effie. *Aunt Liza's "Praisin' Gate"*. Chicago: McClurg, 1916.
Sketches of Kansas life in dialect.

NA
1179
Graham, Effie. *The "Passin'-On" Party*. Chicago: McClurg, 1912.
Sketch of a Kansas wake, in dialect.

NA
1180
Graham, Katheryn Campbell. *Under the Cottonwood: A Saga of Negro Life in
Which the History, Traditions and Folklore of the Negro of the Last
Century Are Vividly Portrayed*. New York: Malliet, 1941.
Autobiography of a black woman, with details of post-Civil War life
and culture.

NA
1181
Graham, Roger. "Jazz Origin Again Discovered," *Music Trade Review*, 68,
No 24 (1919), 32-33.
Origin of the word jazz and the source of the music.

NA
1182
Graham, Rubye. "The Ancient Art of Cornrowing is Revived," *The Philadelphia Inquirer*, March 6, 1973, 1-B.
Hair-braiding patterns: their African background, how to do them; illustrations.

NA
1183
Grainger, Percy. "Percy Grainger's Tribute to the Music of the American
Negro," *Current Opinion*, 59 (1915), 100-101.
Argues for the universal influence of Negro music on the English-
speaking world.

NA
1184
Granberry, Edwin. "Black Jupiter: A Voodoo King in Florida's Jungle . . .,"
Travel, 58, No. 6 (1932), 32-35, 54.
Cult activities and conjure in the Florida pines.

NA
1185
"Grand-Daddy of the Blues," *SO*, 5, No. 2 (1955), 18-20.
Discussion of the structure and nature of blues and the tune "Joe
Turner."

NA
1186
Grandy, Moses. *Narrative of the Life of Moses Grandy, Late a Slave in the
United States of America*. Boston: O. Johnson, 1844.
Detailed story of life and condition; mentions herbs used for healing,
work conditions, treatment of slaves, religious instruction, reading,
etc.

NA 1187   Grant, Anne. *Memoirs of an American Lady*, 2 vols. London: Longman, Hurst, Rees, and Orme, 1808.

NA 1188   Grant, Faye W., and Gale Groom. "A Dietary Study among a Group of Southern Negroes," *Journal of the American Dietetic Association*, 35 (1959), 910-918.
A detailed study of the foods eaten by 59 Charleston families.

NA 1189   Grant, Frances R. "Negro Patriotism and Negro Music," *Outlook*, 121 (February 26, 1919), 343-347.
How the spirituals used at Penn School, Hampton and Tuskeegee led to "Americanization"; familiar expressions and lyrics from spirituals, with music and illustrations.

NA 1190   Grant, George C. "The Negro in Dramatic Art," *JNH*, 17 (1932), 19-29.
The origins and development of minstrelsy, musical comedy and drama among New World Negroes.

NA 1191   Grauer, Bill Jr., Orrin Keepnews, and Charles Edward Smith. "History of Classic Jazz," booklet included with Riverside LP record set SOP-11.
Brief history of early jazz, with emphasis on the social structure of New Orleans at the turn of the century; jazz slang.

NA 1192   Graydon, Nell S. *Tales of Edisto*. Columbia, S.C.: R.L. Bryan, 1955.
Description of a Sea Island sanctified church using drums; 6 hymn texts; recipes, samples of dialect, beliefs, folk medicine, witchcraft, "African" elements.

NA 1193   *Great Auction Sale of Slaves at Savannah, Georgia*. New York: American Anti-Slavery Society, (1859?).
The sale of Pierce Butler's slaves; describes the condition and occupations of the slaves; the nature of black families from the planters' and the slaves' viewpoint; dress (including "turbans"), etc.

NA 1194   Green, Alan W.C. "'Jim Crow,' 'Zip Coon': The Northern Origins of Negro Minstrelsy," *Massachusetts Review*, 11 (1970), 385-397.
Early history and origins of minstrelsy.

NA 1195   Green, Archie. *Only a Miner: Studies in Recorded Coal-Mining Songs*. Urbana, Ill.: University of Illinois Press, 1972.
Includes a chapter (10) on mining blues plus scattered Negro material, with a discussion of race and hillbilly records (Chapter 2) as research tools.

NA   Green, Bennet Wood. *Word-Book of Virginia Folk-Speech*. Richmond: W.E. Jones,
1196   1899.
            6000-7000 words, names, and similes drawn from Virginia speech; no in-
            formation on informants.

NA   Green, Elizabeth L. *The Negro in Contemporary American Literature*. Chapel
1197   Hill, N.C.: University of North Carolina Extension Bulletin, 7, 1928.

NA   Green, Gordan C. "Negro Dialect: The Last Barrier to Integration," *JNH*,
1198   32 (1963), 81-83.
            Folk idioms of Negro speech.

NA   Green, Paul. *Home to My Valley*. Chapel Hill, N.C.: University of North
1199   Carolina Press, 1970.
            Includes folk tales, legends, and prose sketches of Negroes in North
            Carolina.

NA   Green, Paul. "In Abraham's Bosom," in *Plays of Negro Life*, Alain Locke,
1200   ed. New York: Harper, 1924, 139-194.
            Drama with folkloric content.

NA   Green, Paul. *Lonesome Road*. New York: McBride, 1926.
1201   Drama with folkloric content.

NA   Green, Paul. "On the Road One Day, Lord," in *Ebony and Topaz*, Charles S.
1202   Johnson, ed. New York: National Urban League, 1927, 23-26.
            Short drama of chain gang life.

NA   Green, Paul. *Roll Sweet Chariot*. New York: French, 1935.
1203   Drama with folkloric content.

NA   Green, Paul. "Words and Ways: Stories and Incidents From My Cape Fear
1204   Valley Folklore Collection," *NCF*, 16, No. 4 (1968), 1-148.
            Includes several accounts of black life and beliefs.

NA   Green, Samuel Abbott. *Slavery at Groton, Massachusetts in Provincial
1205   Times*. Cambridge, Mass.: J. Wilson, 1909.

NA   Greene, Charles Richard. "Three Florida Negro Tunes And Words," *SFQ*, 9
1206   (1945), 103-105.
            Brief statements about each tune.

NA 1207   Greene, Maude. "The Background of the Beale Street Blues," *TFSB*, 7 (1941), 1-11.
    A study of Beale Street blacks.

NA 1208   Greenway, John. *American Folk Songs of Protest*. Philadelphia: University of Pennsylvania Press, 1953.
    Chapter 2, "Negro Songs of Protest," discusses the historical and social background of sacred and secular songs during slavery, abolition, segregation and racial discrimination.

NA 1209   Gregg, J. Chandler. *Life in the Army* . . . Philadelphia: Perkinpine and Higgins, 1868.
    Description of Congo Square celebrations in New Orleans--a parade, music, preaching (pp. 188, 207-208)--and in Lafayette Square (pp. 222-223); "unusual" names (p. 219).

NA 1210   Grew, Sidney. "Random Notes on the Spirituals," *Music and Letters*, 16 (April, 1935), 96-109.

NA 1211   Grier, William H., and Price M. Cobbs. *Black Rage*. New York: 1968.
    Chapter 6, "Character Traits," deals with Black English as pathology.

NA 1212   Grier, William H., and Price M. Cobbs. *The Jesus Bag*. New York: McGraw-Hill, 1971.
    Includes discussion of the dozens, toasts and slang as products of pathology.

NA 1213   Grierson, Francis. *The Valley of the Shadows*. Boston and New York: Houghton Mifflin, 1909.
    Includes a description of a Negro and white camp meeting.

NA 1214   Griffin, George H. "The Slave Music of the South," *American Missionary*, 36 (1882), 70-72.

NA 1215   Griffin, Junius. "Last Word from Soul City," *New York Times Magazine*, August 23, 1964, 62, 64.
    The vocabulary and use of slang terms from Harlem.

NA 1216   Griffin, Rev. William Elliot. "The Original of Uncle Remus' Tar Baby in Japan," *The Folklorist* (Chicago), 1 (1893), 146-149.
    Discussion of Japanese versions of the Tar Baby story with text.

NA   Griffith, Benjamin W. "A Longer Version of 'Guinea Negro Song': From a
1217   Georgia Frontier Songster," *SFQ*, 28 (1964), 116-118.
            Two versions of an original slave song.

NA   Grimes, Anne. "Possible Relationships Between 'Jump Jim Crow' and Shaker
1218   Songs," *MF*, 3 (1953), 47-57.
            The minstrel Jim Crow's connection with Shaker ritual.

NA   Grissom, Mary Alice. *The Negro Sings a New Heaven*. Chapel Hill: University
1219   of North Carolina Press, 1930.
            Forty-six melodies (with texts) from Kentucky: songs of death and of
            heaven, Bible stories in song; exhortations, shouting songs, and
            songs of personal experience and triumph.

NA   Groia, Philip. *They All Sang on the Corner: New York City's Rhythm-and-
1220   Blues Vocal Groups of the 1950's*. Setauket, N.Y., 1973.

NA   Groom, Bob, ed. *Blind Lemon Jefferson*. Blues World Booklet, No. 3, Knuts-
1221   ford, England, 1970.
            The texts of most of Jefferson's blues with a biography and discography.

NA   Groom, Bob. *The Blues Revival*. London: Studio Vista, 1971.
1222   Survey of recording activity of skiffle, r & b, rediscovered blues
            singers, etc. of recent times; includes a chapter on blues bibli-
            ography.

NA   Grossman, Stefan. *The Country Blues Guitar*. New York: Oak, 1968.
1223   23 blues by Mississippi John Hurt, Furry Lewis, *et al.*, with notes.

NA   Grossman, Stefan. *Delta Blues Guitar*. New York: Oak, 1969.
1224   26 blues, with notes, from the Mississippi Delta region.

NA   Grossman, Stefan. *Ragtime Blues Guitarists*. New York: Oak, 1970.
1225   Instruction book with transcribed guitar solos by Blind Lemon Jeffer-
            son, Rev. Gary Davis, Blind Blake, *et al.*

NA   Grossman, Stefan. *Reverend Gary Davis: The Holy Blues*. New York: Robbins
1226   and Chandos Music, 1970.
            80 songs, with music of religious folksongs, from the repertoire of
            1 singer.

NA 1227   Grossman, William L., and Jack W. Farrell. *The Heart of Jazz*. New York: New York University Press, 1956.
    Chapters 4 and 5, "The Christian Element in New Orleans Jazz"; Chapters 6 and 7, "Secular Elements in New Orleans Jazz." Overall, the African element in jazz is minimized. (See *JM*, 3, No. 5 (1957), 28-30, for critical comments.)

NA 1228   Grover, Carrie B. *A Heritage of Songs*. (Bethel, Maine): n.p., n.d. (Reprinted Norwood, Pa.: Norwood Editions, 1973.)
    A white Nova Scotian's song repertoire; includes 3 songs and 2 shanties from slaves in the U.S.; a description of juba dancing (pp. 147-151).

NA 1229   Gruver, Rod. "The Blues as Dramatic Monologues," *John Edwards Memorial Foundation Quarterly*, 6, No. 17 (1970), 28-31.
    Argues that the blues are best understood as dramatic monologues rather than as autobiographies. (See Jeff Titon, "Autobiography and Blues Texts," *JEMFQ*, 6, No. 18 (1970), 79-82; and Rod Gruver, "The Autobiographical Theory Re-examined," *JEMFQ*, 6, No. 19 (1970), 129-131 for an exchange on the subject.)

NA 1230   Gruver, Rod. "The Blues as Poetry," in *Down Beat's Music '69*. Chicago: Maher, 1969, 38-43.
    Application of literary criticism to blues.

NA 1231   Gruver, Rod. "The Blues as Secular Religion," *Down Beat's Music '70*. Chicago: Maher, 1970, 24-29.
    The antipuritan and life-affirming aspects of the blues.

NA 1232   Gruver, Rod. "Blues, Poets, Interviewers and Literary Critics," *Coda* (Toronto), 11, No. 8 (1974), 12-14.
    Contrasts interviews with blues singers with literary critiques of blues performances in order to argue for the priority of the latter.

NA 1233   Gruver, Rod. "A Closer Look at the Blues," in *Down Beat's Music '67*. Chicago: Maher, 1967, 50-53. (Reprinted in *Blues World*, 26 (January, 1970), 4-10).
    A literary approach to the blues--dramatic structure, poetic devices, etc.

NA 1234   Gruver, Rod. "The Funny Blues," in *Down Beat's Music '68*. Chicago: Maher, 1968, 52-55.
    The blues of humor; includes excerpts of texts.

NA 1235   Gruver, Rod. "The Origin of Blues," in *Down Beat's Music '71*, Chicago: Maher, 1971, 16-21.
    The origin of the blues is said to lie in instrumental dance music in the South--the evidence is in the stanza form, rhyme, rhythm, etc.

NA 1236   Gruver, Rod. "Sex, Sound, Cows and the Blues," *John Edwards Memorial Foundation Quarterly*, 7, No. 21 (1971), 37-39.
    Discussion of the origin of the term "Sukey Jump."

NA 1237   Gruver, Rod. "Towards a Criticism of the Blues," *JM*, No. 155 (1968), 2-5.
    Essay arguing that principles of literary criticism should be applied to the blues; includes the texts of 7 blues. (See Paul Oliver, "Blues Ramblers," *JM*, No. 156 (February, 1968), 11, for reply to Gruver.)

NA 1238   Guial, E.L. "Among the Sable Singers," *Lakeside Monthly* (Chicago), 2 (1869), 421-426.
    Description of religious services and hymns in "one of the large cities on the Ohio River."

NA 1239   Guion, David. *Darkey Spirituals*. New York: Witmark, 1918.
    12 songs.

NA 1240   "A Gullah Story: De Flagg Storm," in *American Stuff*. New York: Viking, 1937, 65-69.
    1 text from South Carolina.

NA 1241   Gunn, Larry. "Three Negro Folk Songs from the Northern Mississippi Delta," *MFR*, 3, No. 3 (1969), 89-94.
    3 spirituals with music and short analysis.

NA 1242   Gunter, Carolyn Pell. "Tom Day--Craftsman," *Antiquarian*, 10 (September, 1928), 60-62.

NA 1243   Guralnick, Peter. "Blues as History," *Blues World*, 22 (December, 1968), 5-13.

NA 1244   Guralnick, Peter. *Feel Like Going Home: Portraits in Blues and Rock 'n' Roll*. New York: Outerbridge and Diensterey, 1971.
    Biographical interviews and essays on Muddy Waters, Johnny Shines, Skip James, Robert Pete Williams, Howlin' Wolf; the performers on

Chess and Sun records; brief history of blues and rock 'n' roll; discography, bibliography, illustrations.

NA
1245
Gushee, Larry. "A Reconsideration: A Review of Marshall Stearns, *The Story of Jazz*," *Jazz: A Quarterly of American Music* (Berkeley), No. 5 (1960), 57-66.
A critical review, with emphasis on the question of African origins.

NA
1246
H.B.L. "The Negro's Art Lives in his Wrought Iron," *New York Times Magazine*, August 8, 1926, 14-15.
Discussion of New Orleans iron work (grills, balconies, etc.); argues that since it was not done under white supervision, then it must have African origins; illustrations.

NA
1247
H.J.W. "The Negro in South Carolina," *New York Times*, July 19, 1862, 2.
Description of Hilton Head Sunday school dress; a parade of Negro soldiers; a soldier's formal speech.

NA
1248
"Hags and Their Ways," *SW*, 23 (1894), 26-27.
Discussion of hags' activities; story of a woman who captured the skin of a hag; variations of the game "Hully Gully."

NA
1249
Hair, P.E.H. "Sierra Leone Items in the Gullah Dialect of American English," *Sierra Leone Language Review*, 4 (1965), 79-84.

NA
1250
Haley, Alex. "My Furthest-Back Person--'The African,'" *New York Times Magazine*, July 16, 1972, 12-16.
Account of how an American black traced an African ancestor to Gambia by means of oral history (legends, African name for the banjo, etc.)

NA
1251
Hall, Ella R. "A Comparison of Selected Mississippi and North Carolina Remedies," *MFR*, 5 (1971), 94-113.
Remedies known by both blacks and whites.

NA
1252
Hall, Frederick. "The Negro Spiritual," *Literary Digest*, 98, No. 12 (1928), 34.
Discussion of the origin and nature of the spiritual.

NA
1253
Hall, Julien A. "Negro Conjuring and Tricking," *JAF*, 10 (1897), 241-243.
Cites methods used to conjure or trick.

NA 1254   Hall, L.A. "Some Early Black-Face Performers and the First Minstrel Troop," *Harvard Library Notes*, 1, No. 2 (1920), 39-45.

NA 1255   Hall, Robert A. "The African Substratum in Negro English," *AS*, 25 (1950), 51-54.
Review and discussion of Lorenzo D. Turner's book, *Africanisms in the Gullah Dialect*.

NA 1256   Hall, Wade. "Humor and Folklore in Vinnie Williams' *Walk Egypt*," *SFQ*, 26 (1962), 225-231.
Use of black speech, jokes, religion, etc. in Williams' novel.

NA 1257   Hallock, Ted. "Bop Jargon Indicative of Intellectual Thought," *Down Beat*, 15, No. 15 (1948), 4.
5 terms used by jazz musicians with their definitions.

NA 1258   Hallowell, A. Irving. "American Indians, White and Black: The Phenomenon of Transculturization," *Current Anthropology*, 4 (1963), 519-531.
On Negroes who became Indians in the United States.

NA 1259   Hallowell, Emily. *Calhoun Plantation Songs*. Boston: C.W. Thompson, 1901 (2nd revised edition Boston: C.W. Thompson, 1907).
69 religious songs collected from students at the Calhoun Colored School in Alabama.

NA 1260   Halpert, Herbert. "The Cante Fable in Decay," *SFQ*, 5 (1941), 191-200.
Discussion of the *cante fable*, its origins and content. Includes Negro verses.

NA 1261   Halpert, Herbert. "Negro Riddles in New Jersey," *JAF*, 56 (1943), 200-203.
19 riddles with sources.

NA 1262   Halpert, Herbert. "An Ohio Tale," *HFB*, 1 (1942), 103.
1 anecdote from Canton.

NA 1263   Halpert, Herbert, C. Bradford Mitchell, and David H. Dickason. "Folktales from Indiana University Students," *HFB*, 1 (1942), 85-97.
1 legend (p. 87) and 1 folktale (pp. 86-87).

NA 1264   Hame, Olli. *Rytmin Voittokulu-Kirja Tanssimusiikista*. Helsinki: Fazer's Music Store, 1949.

NA
1265
Hamilton, Charles V. *The Black Preacher in America*. New York: William
Morrow, 1972.
A history of preaching and preachers.

NA
1266
Hamilton, James. *An Account of the Late Intended Insurrection among the
Portions of the Blacks of this City*. Charleston, S.C.: A.E. Miller,
1822.
Testimony to "Gullah Jack's" or "Coter Jack's" conjuring powers;
charms used by him, etc.

NA
1267
Hamner, Laura V. *Somebody Might Come*. Dallas: American Guild, 1958.
Includes a chapter on cookery and conjure-doctors in Alabama.

NA
1268
Hampton, Bill R. "On Identification and Negro Tricksters," *SFQ*, 31 (1967),
55-65.
Examines the nature of black identification with various trickster
characters.

NA
1269
Hampton Institute. *Twenty-Two Years Work of the Hampton Normal and Agricultural Institute*. Hampton, Va.: Hampton Normal School Press, 1893.
Autobiographical sketches of the lives of educated blacks and Indians
in the South; includes songs gathered from students.

NA
1270
Handy, Sarah M. "Negro Superstitions," *Lippincott's Monthly Magazine*, 48
(1891), 735-739. (A fragment is reprinted in *JAF*, 5 (1892), 63.)
Accounts of voodoo and medical practices of Southern Negroes; cites
African parallels; includes a list of folk beliefs, 1 chant, etc.

NA
1271
Handy, William C. *Blues, An Anthology*. New York: Albert and Charles Boni,
1926. (Reprinted as *A Treasury of the Blues*. New York: Boni, 1949.)
A collection of mainly popular blues; introduction by Abbe Niles.

NA
1272
Handy, William C. *Collection of Blues*. New York: Robbins-Engle, 1925.
Words and music of 9 of Handy's compositions.

NA
1273
Handy, William C. *Father of the Blues*. New York: Macmillan, 1941.
Autobiography.

NA
1274
Handy, William C. "The Heart of the Blues," *Etude*, 58 (1940), 152, 193,
211.
Blues as a distinct expression of the Negro which can only be written
by a Negro. Handy discusses the elements of blues and jazz.

NA   Handy, William C. "Negro Roustabout Songs," *TFSB*, 13 (1947), 86-88.
1275   A collection of Negro work songs.

NA   Handy, William C., ed. *W.C. Handy's Collection of Negro Spirituals*. 2
1276   vols. New York: Handy Brothers Music, 1938.

        Handy, William C. See Lee, George W., No. NA 1811.

        Handy, William C. See Scarborough, Dorothy, No. NA 2652.

        Handy, William C. See Wilson, Edmund, No. NA 3245.

NA   Hannerz, Ulf. "Gossip, Networks and Culture in a Black American Ghetto,"
1277   *Ethnos*, 32 (1967), 35-60.
            A study of gossip as the medium of a social network in a Washington,
            D.C. neighborhood.

NA   Hannerz, Ulf. "The Notion of Ghetto Culture," in *Black America*, John F.
1278   Szwed, ed. New York: Basic Books, 1970, 99-109.
            Review of social science conceptions of culture and life in North
            American black ghettos.

NA   Hannerz, Ulf. "The Rhetoric of Soul: Identification in Negro Society,"
1279   *Race*, 9 (1968), 453-465.
            The various meanings of "soul" in the U.S. in the 1960's.

NA   Hannerz, Ulf. *Soulside: Inquiries into Ghetto Culture and Community*. New
1280   York: Columbia University Press, 1969.
            Ethnography of an Afro-American neighborhood in Washington, D.C. Dis-
            cussions of "soul," rapping, the dozens, music, folk tales, street
            behavior and styles, etc.

NA   Hannerz, Ulf. "The Study of Afro-American Cultural Dynamics," *SWJA*, 27
1281   (1971), 181-200.
            Argues for combining the ecological and cultural approaches to the
            study of black American communities.

NA   Hansen, Barry. "The Gospel Revival: Is God on Their Side?," *SO*, 14,
1282   No. 1 (1964), 25-27.
            Brief account of the origin and development of gospel music.

NA 1283   Hansen, Barry. "This Is How It All Began, vol. 1, The Roots of Rock and Roll As Recorded from 1945 to 1955 on Specialty Records," record notes to Specialty LP record SPS 2117.
Notes on gospel quartets and choirs, country and city blues.

NA 1284   Hansen, Chadwick. "Jenny's Toe: Negro Shaking Dances in America," *American Quarterly*, 19 (1967), 554-563.
Calls attention to a tradition of hip-shaking dances among American Negroes and relates it to the twist and other modern popular dances.

NA 1285   Hansen, Chadwick. "Social Influences on Jazz Style, Chicago 1920-1930," *American Quarterly*, 12 (1960), 493-507.
Effects of "acculturation" of the Southern Negro to white middle-class society as expressed by the jazz music of the 1930's.

NA 1286   Hantske, Madeline Horres. *The Song of the Cotton Picker*. Clinton, South Carolina: Jacobs, 1942.
Poems by a white author in Gullah dialect with folkloric content.

NA 1287   Haralambos, Michael. *Right On: From Blues to Soul in Black America*. London, 1974.

NA 1288   Haralambos, Michael. "Soul Music and Blues: Their Meaning and Relevance in Northern United States Black Ghettos," in *Afro-American Anthropology: Contemporary Perspectives*, Norman E. Whitten, Jr., and John F. Szwed, eds. New York: Free Press, 1970, 367-383.
An investigation of the concepts of "soul" and "soul music."

NA 1289   Harder, Kelsie B. "The Jake Leg," *TFSB*, 27, No. 3 (1961), 45-47.
Bootleg whiskey in the rural South (possibly black).

NA 1290   Harding, Vincent. "Religion and Resistance Among Antebellum Negroes, 1800-1860," in *The Making of Black America*, Vol. 1, August Meier and Elliot Rudwick, eds. New York: Atheneum, 1969, 179-197.
Christianity as a basis for protest among slaves.

NA 1291   Hare, Maud Cuney. "Folk Music of the Creoles," *Musical Observer*, 19, No. 9-10 (1920), 16-18; 19, No. 11 (1920), 12-14.

NA 1292   Hare, Maud Cuney. "Folk Music of the Creoles," in *Negro Anthology*, Nancy Cunard, ed. London: Wishart, 1934, 396-400.
Discusses the historical background and music of the Louisiana Creoles.

NA
1293
Hare, Maud Cuney. *Negro Musicians and Their Music*. Washington, D.C.:
Associated Publisher, 1936.
One chapter devoted to African sources of Afro-American folksong,
blues, ragtime, and jazz.

NA
1294
Hare, Maud Cuney. *Six Creole Folk Songs*. New York: Carl Fischer, 1921.
Louisiana French Creole Negro songs with English translations.

NA
1295
"Harlem Market Men Sing While They Sell," *New York Times*, June 16, 1935,
Section 8, 17.
Contends that street cries of the street vendors and chefs of Harlem
originate from the South and the West Indies; lists several tunes.

NA
1296
"Harlem's Streets Gay and Colorful," *New York Times*, September 6, 1931,
Section 12, 9.
Description of street life in Harlem.

NA
1297
Harlow, Alvin F. *Joel Chandler Harris (Uncle Remus), Plantation Story-
teller*. New York: Julian Meesner, 1941.
Includes "Miss Goose and Brer Rabbit" and a few other excerpts from
Harris' writings.

NA
1298
Harmon, Marion F. *Negro Wit and Humor, Also Containing Folk Lore, Folk
Songs, Race Peculiarities, Race History*. Louisville, Ky.: Harmon,
1914.
Chart of Negro synonyms; 58 proverbs, jokes and tales; 10 examples of
dialect verse; 4 spirituals; omens, sayings, conjurations; 1 Negro
ghost story included. Most of the material comes from *Southern Workman* articles. Illustrations.

NA
1299
Harn, Julia E. "Old Canoochee-Ogeechee Chronicles," in "Notes and Documents," *GHQ*, 15 (1931), 346-360; 16 (1932), 146-150, 232-240.
Description of a Negro cook (p. 349); the influence of old Negro
dances on modern dances (p. 359); Gullah shouts, hoodoo, tales told
to children, women's dress, singing, torchlight funerals, 1 song text
quoted, naming practices (pp. 146-150); Negro musicians at white
dances (pp. 149, 237).

NA
1300
Harper, Frances E.W. *Sketches of Southern Life*. Philadelphia, 1888.
(Third Edition; first published in Philadelphia, 1872.)
"Aunt Chloe" dialect poems by a black author.

NA   Harrell, David Edwin, Jr. *White Sects and Black Men in the Recent South*.
1301   Nashville: Vanderbilt University Press, 1971.
            Contains brief discussion and bibliography on black and white (inte-
            grated) fundamentalist cults in the South.

NA   Harris, Joel Chandler. *Aaron in the Wildwoods*. Boston: Houghton Mifflin,
1302   1897.
            14 tales set in "Middle Georgia."

NA   Harris, Joel Chandler. "An Accidental Author," *Lippincott Magazine*, 37
1303   (April, 1886), 417-420. (Reprinted in No. NA 1568.)
            The sources of "Uncle Remus" tales.

NA   Harris, Joel Chandler. *Balaam and His Master, and Other Sketches and
1304   Stories*. Boston: Houghton Mifflin, 1891.
            Includes 6 stories about Negroes.

NA   Harris, Joel Chandler. *The Bishop and the Boogerman*. New York: Doubleday,
1305   Page, 1909.
            A novelette with folkloric content.

NA   Harris, Joel Chandler. *The Chronicles of Aunt Minervy Ann*. New York:
1306   Scribner's, 1899.
            Includes 8 stories, the recollections of "Aunt Minervy Ann Perdue, a
            slave and servant in Georgia."

NA   Harris, Joel Chandler. *Daddy Jake the Runaway*. New York: Century, 1889.
1307   14 tales.

NA   Harris, Joel Chandler. *Free Joe and Other Georgian Sketches*. New York:
1308   Collier, 1887.

NA   Harris, Joel Chandler. *Little Mr. Thimblefinger and his Queer Country;
1309   What the Children Saw and Heard There*. Boston: Houghton Mifflin, 1894.
            19 stories; Harris says some are Negro, some English, some inventions.

NA   Harris, Joel Chandler. *The Making of a Statesman*. New York: McClure,
1310   Phillips, 1902.

NA   Harris, Joel Chandler. *Mingo, and Other Sketches in Black and White*.
1311   Boston and New York: Houghton Mifflin, 1884.
            Story of a Negro carriage driver, in dialect, plus a small amount of
            dialect in the other essays.

NA   Harris, Joel Chandler. *Mr. Rabbit At Home*. Boston and New York: Hough-
1312   ton Mifflin, 1895.
            27 tales.

NA   Harris, Joel Chandler. *Nights With Uncle Remus*. Boston: Houghton, Mifflin,
1313   1881.
            History and form of Negro folktales discussed in a 52-page introduc-
            tion; 34 animal tales.

NA   Harris, Joel Chandler. *On the Plantation*. New York: Appleton, 1892.
1314   14 tales of Georgia during the war; Harris says the reader must
            "sift the fiction from the fact."

NA   Harris, Joel Chandler. "Plantation Music," *The Critic*, 3 (1883), 505–
1315   506. (Reprinted in No. NA 1568.)
            An attempt to show that the banjo was not *the* instrument of Negro
            folk music and to illustrate white fantasies of black folklore (See
            the letters of objection to this article in *The Critic*, 3 (1883),
            523, 534-535.)

NA   Harris, Joel Chandler. *Plantation Pageants*. Boston: Houghton, Mifflin,
1316   1899.
            14 stories.

NA   Harris, Joel Chandler. "The Sea Island Hurricanes," *Scribner's*, 15 (1894),
1317   229-247; 267-284.
            Speech and beliefs of the Sea Islands (stresses the difference between
            the Negroes of coastal and central Georgia).

NA   Harris, Joel Chandler. *Seven Tales of Uncle Remus*. Thomas H. English, ed.
1318   Atlanta, Ga.: Emory University Sources and Reprints, 1948.
            7 animal tales.

NA   Harris, Joel Chandler. *Stories of Georgia*. New York: American, 1896.
1319

NA   Harris, Joel Chandler. *The Story of Aaron, So Named the Son of Ben Ali*.
1320   Boston: Houghton, Mifflin, 1896.
            Fictional account of a Georgia slave.

NA   Harris, Joel Chandler. *Tales from Uncle Remus*. New York: Houghton, Mif-
1321   flin, 1881.
            Introduction discussing history and form of the tales by Julia Col-
            lier Harris. 12 animal tales.

NA   Harris, Joel Chandler. *The Tar-Baby and Other Rhymes by Uncle Remus*. New
1322   York: Appleton, 1904.
            50 rhymes.

NA   Harris, Joel Chandler. *Told By Uncle Remus. New Stories of the Old Plan-
1323   tation*. New York: McClure, Phillips, 1905.
            17 tales.

NA   Harris, Joel Chandler. *Uncle Remus and Brer Rabbit*. New York: Frederick A.
1324   Stokes, 1907.
            6 animal tales.

NA   Harris, Joel Chandler. *Uncle Remus and His Friends: Old Plantation Stor-
1325   ies, Songs and Ballads, with Sketches of Negro Character*. Boston:
            Houghton Mifflin, 1892.
            24 legends and stories of animals, 21 Negro stories and 16 song and
            ballad texts.

NA   Harris, Joel Chandler. *Uncle Remus and the Little Boy*. Boston: Small,
1326   Maynard, 1910.
            13 tales and rhymes which first appeared in *Uncle Remus' Magazine*.

NA   Harris, Joel Chandler. *Uncle Remus, His Songs and His Sayings*. New York:
1327   Appleton, 1880.
            34 tales, 9 songs, 21 explanatory tales, animal tales and proverbs.

NA   Harris, Joel Chandler. *Uncle Remus Returns*. Boston: Houghton Mifflin,
1328   1918.
            11 tales and sketches, which first appeared in *Metropolitan Magazine*
            of the *Atlanta Constitution*.

NA   Harris, Joel Chandler. *The Witch Wolf; An Uncle Remus Story*. Cambridge,
1329   Mass.: Bacon & Brown, 1921.
            1 tale, with a corn shucking song and a description of singing.

        Harris, Joel Chandler. See Cousins, Paul M., No. NA 667.

        Harris, Joel Chandler. See Harlow, Alvin F., No. NA 1297.

        Harris, Joel Chandler. See Ives, Sumner, No. NA 1559.

Harris, Joel Chandler. See Russell, Irwin, No. NA 2625.

Harris, Joel Chandler. See *Southern Stories*, No. NA 2812.

Harris, Joel Chandler. See Stafford, John, No. NA 2840.

Harris, Joel Chandler. See Turner, Darwin, No. NA 3035.

Harris, Joel Chandler. See Walton, David, Nos. NA 3097 and NA 3098.

Harris, Joel Chandler. See Weeden, Howard, No. NA 3138.

Harris, Joel Chandler. See Wiggins, Robert Lemuel, No. NA 3195.

Harris, Joel Chandler. See Wolfe, Bernard, No. NA 3266.

NA
1330
Harris, Leon R. *I'm a Railroad Man*. n.p., 1948.
    8 songs, some with music.

NA
1331
Harris, Leon R. "The Steel-Drivin' Man," *Messenger*, 7 (1925), 386-387,
    402. (Reprinted in Dundes, No. NA 854; also, with minor changes, in
    Phylon, 18 (1957), 402-406.)
    John Henry text.

NA
1332
Harris, Middleton, *et al. The Black Book*. New York: Random House, 1974.
    A miscellany of voodoo recipes and chorus, shout and song texts, a
    source for the dozens, slave crafts (cabinetmaking, dolls, clothes,
    tools, ironwork, quilts, clothing, baskets), slang, escaped slave
    ads, game chants, street cries, recipes, rent party invitations,
    dream interpretations, number lore, etc., most from other unacknow-
    ledged sources; illustrations.

NA
1333
Harris, Sara. *Father Divine: Holy Husband*. Garden City: Doubleday, 1953.
    Biography of the founder of the Father Divine movement and a descrip-
    tion of the church, its ceremonies and beliefs.

NA
1334
Harris, Ira E. "The Storefront Church as a Revitalization Movement,"
    Review of Religious Research, 7 (1964), 160-163.
    Study of 16 storefront churches in Syracuse, N.Y.

NA   Harrison, J.A. "The Creole Patois of Louisiana," *American Journal of*
1335   *Philology*, 3 (1882), 285-296.
             An early study of Louisiana Creole.

NA   Harrison, J.A."Negro English," *Anglia*, 7 (1884), 232-279.
1336   Analysis of Negro speech in Virginia, South Carolina, Georgia, and
             other Mid-Southern states; includes rules, pronunciations, vocabulary,
             and local expressions.

NA   Harrison, Lowell H. "The Folklore of Some Kentucky Slaves," *KFR*, 17
1337   (1971), 25-30; 53-60.
             6 ex-slave narratives from the WPA collection containing folkloric
             material.

NA   Harrison, Max. "Around Paul Whiteman," *JM*, July, 1970, 7-12.
1338   A review of some early recordings by Paul Whiteman develops the thesis
             that European classical music had an important influence on the de-
             velopment of jazz. (For an earlier version of this argument with
             different evidence, see No. NA 1340.)

NA   Harrison, Max. "Boogie-Woogie," in *Jazz*, Nat Hentoff and Albert J. McCar-
1339   thy, eds. New York: Rinehart, 1959, 107-135, 360-362.
             The folk background and development of boogie-woogie piano playing;
             discography.

NA   Harrison, Max. "Record Reviews: Continental Jazz," *JM*, June, 1970, 24-28.
1340   A review of a number of early recordings of jazz in Europe argues for
             the important influences of European music on the development of jazz.
             (This argument is extended in No. NA 1338.)

NA   Harrison, R.C. "The Negro as Interpretor of his Own Folk Songs," *PTFS*,
1341   No. 5 (1926), 144-153.
             The evolution of Negro attitudes toward folk songs; bibliography.

NA   Harrison, W.S. *The Gospel among the Slaves; A Short Account of Mission-*
1342   *ary Operations Among the African Slaves of the Southern States*. Nash-
             ville: Publishing House of the Methodist Episcopal Church of the
             South, 1893.
             Accounts of black singing, sermons, "African" religion among slaves.

NA   Harrison, W.S. *Sam Williams: A Tale of the Old South*. Nashville: Publish-
1343   ing House of the Methodist Episcopal Church of the South, 1892.
             Fictionalized memoirs include cures, conjuring, speech, etc.; dis-

cussion of slaves' public conversations, "loudness," etc.

NA   Hart, James D. "Jazz Jargon," *AS*, 7 (1932), 241-254.
1344   The vernacular of "jazz" (pop) and blues song texts and titles.

NA   Harvey, Emily N. "A Br'er Rabbit Story," *JAF*, 32 (1919), 443-444.
1345   1 text from Alabama, including music.

NA   Haskell, Joseph A. "Sacrificial Offerings Among North Carolina Negroes,"
1346   *JAF*, 4 (1891), 267-269.
               Instances of "superstitions" held by a black overseer.

NA   Haskell, Marion Alexander. "Negro Spirituals," *Century Magazine*, (n.s.)
1347   36 (1899), 577-581. (Reprinted in No. NA 1698.)
               Argues that the educated Negro is fast abandoning his musical heri-
               tage--spirituals; also discusses the meaning, context and texts of
               10 spirituals.

NA   Hatch, Dave, and John Williams. "The Country Blues: A Musical Analysis,"
1348   *BU*, No. 21 (April, 1965), 8.
               Musicological analysis of several blues songs; the musical basis of
               regional song styles.

NA   Hatcher, William E. *John Jasper, The Unmatched Negro Philosopher and
1349   Preacher*. New York: F.H. Revell, 1908.
               Several of Jasper's sermons and various incidents of his life are
               included "in his own broken words."

NA   Hauptmann, O.H. "Spanish Folklore from Tampa, Florida: Superstitions,"
1350   *SFQ*, 2 (1938), 11-30.
               A collection of "superstitions" which includes Afro-Cuban material.

NA   Hauptmann, O.H. "Spanish Folklore from Tampa, Florida: Witchcraft,"
1351   *SFQ*, 3 (1939), 197-200.
               Afro-Cuban lore; notes on *Shango* and dialects; examples of folk
               medicine, etc.

NA   Haurigot, Georges. *Contes Nègres* (Negro Stories). Paris: Charavay, Man-
1352   tour, Martin, 1895.

NA
1353
Hawkins, Beverly. "Folklore of a Black Family," *Journal of the Ohio Folk-lore Society*, 2 (1973), 2-19.
Tales, proverbs, beliefs, rhymes and jokes of the members of a Dayton, Ohio family.

NA
1354
Hawkins, John. "An Old Mauma's Folk-Lore," *JAF*, 9 (1896), 129-131.
Brief description of a folk-figure; includes 1 short tale.

NA
1355
Hawkins, Walter Everette. "Debunking the Spirituals," *Challenge*, 1, No. 2 (September, 1934), 13-14.
(A reply to Harry T. Burleigh in *Challenge*, 1, No. 1 (March 1, 1934), 26-27.) Argues that spirituals are "hodge-podges of nonsense," moronic "imbecilities," etc., which are means of keeping the Negro "meek and lowly."

NA
1356
Haywood, Charles. "Negro Minstrelsy and Shakespearean Burlesque," in *Folklore and Society: Essays in Honor of Benjamin A. Botkin*, Bruce Jackson, ed. Hatboro, Pa.: Folklore Associates, 1966, 77-92.
The use of Shakespeare in the stump speeches, monologues and skits of minstrelsy.

NA
1357
Heaps, Willard A., and W. Porter. *The Singing Sixties*. Norman: University of Oklahoma Press, 1960.
"The Negro and the Contraband" (pp. 268-294) contains some published songs by blacks from the Civil War period, but most of the songs on blacks are by whites.

NA
1358
Hearn, Lafcadio. "Attention! Azim!," in *Creole Sketches*, Charles W. Hutson, ed. Boston: Houghton Mifflin, 1924, 102-105. (Reprinted from the *New Orleans Item*, July 8, 1880.)
Recipes for *gombo févi* and *gombo filé*; comments on African and West Indian origins of New Orleans food; notes the secrecy of cooks.

NA
1359
Hearn, Lafcadio. "Banjo Jim's Story," in *An American Miscellany*, Vol. 1, Albert Mordell, ed. New York: Dodd, Mead, 1924, 181-189. (Reprinted from the *Cincinnati Commercial*, October 1, 1876.)
Ghost stories from Cincinnati includes a description of a dance, voodoo, etc.

NA
1360
Hearn, Lafcadio. "Black Varieties: The Minstrels of the Row," in *Occidental Gleanings*, Vol. 1, Albert Mordell, ed. New York: Dodd, Mead, 1925, 119-125. (Reprinted from the *Cincinnati Commercial*, April 9, 1876.)
Describes a black minstrel performance in 19th century Cincinnati.

NA
1361

Hearn, Lafcadio. "Butler's," in *Children of the Levee*, O.W. Frost, ed.
Lexington, Kentucky: University of Kentucky Press, 1957, 91-94. (Reprinted from the *Cincinnati Enquirer*, November 22, 1874.)
Description of Cincinnati tavern life.

NA
1362

Hearn, Lafcadio. "Char-coal," in *Creole Sketches*, Charles W. Hutson, ed.
Boston: Houghton Mifflin, 1924, 70-71. (Reprinted from the New Orleans
Item, August 25, 1880.)
Street cries from New Orleans.

NA
1363

Hearn, Lafcadio. "A Child of the Levee," in *Children of the Levee*, O.W.
Frost, ed. Lexington, Kentucky: University of Kentucky Press, 1957,
9-12. (Reprinted from the *Cincinnati Commercial*, June 27, 1876.)
Account of a Cincinnati steamboat whistle imitator.

NA
1364

Hearn, Lafcadio. "The City of the South," in *Occidental Gleanings*, Vol.
1, Albert Mordell, ed. New York: Dodd, Mead, 1925, 179-194. (Reprinted from *Cincinnati Commercial*, December 10, 1877.)
Includes discussion of Louisiana French Creole, compared to West
Indian Creole.

NA
1365

Hearn, Lafcadio. "The Creole Doctor," in *Occidental Gleanings*, Vol. 2,
Albert Mordell, ed. New York: Dodd, Mead, 1925, 195-208. (Reprinted
from the *New York Tribune*, January 3, 1886.)
Includes brief discussion of New Orleans black folk cures.

NA
1366

Hearn, Lafcadio. "The Creole Patois," in *An American Miscellany*, Vol. 2,
Albert Mordell, ed. New York: Dodd, Mead, 1924, 144-153. (Reprinted
from *Harper's*, January 10, 17, 1885.)
The speech and folklore of blacks in Martinique and Louisiana and
their influence on whites.

NA
1367

Hearn, Lafcadio. "Creole Servant Girls," in *Creole Sketches*, Charles W.
Hutson, ed. Boston: Houghton Mifflin, 1924, 160-163. (Reprinted from
the New Orleans *Item*, December 20, 1880.)
Notes on the character of servants--their style, discretion, songs,
etc.

NA
1368

(Hearn, Lafcadio.) *La Cuisine Creole*. New York: Will H. Coleman, 1885.
Recipes from New Orleans.

NA
1369
Hearn, Lafcadio. "Dolly: An Idyl of the Levee," in *An American Miscellany*, Vol. 1, Albert Mordell, ed. New York: Dodd, Mead, 1924, 171-180. (Reprinted from the *Cincinnati Commercial*, August 27, 1876.)
Portrait of a Cincinnati black woman includes fragments of folklore--hoodoo, a spiritual, etc.

NA
1370
Hearn, Lafcadio. *Ghombo Zhèbes*. New York: W.H. Coleman, 1885.
A "dictionary of Creole proverbs selected from 6 Creole dialects," with French and English translations.

NA
1371
Hearn, Lafcadio. "The Grandissimes," in *Creole Sketches*, Charles W. Hutson, ed. Boston: Houghton Mifflin, 1924, 117-123. (Reprinted from the New Orleans *Item*, September 27, 1880.)
A review of George W. Cable's novel *The Grandissimes*, with notes on the "African chant" and examples of voodooism in it.

NA
1372
Hearn, Lafcadio. "Jot--the Haunt of the Obi-Man," in *Children of the Levee*, O.W. Frost, ed. Lexington, Kentucky: University of Kentucky Press, 1957, 49-53. (Reprinted from the *Cincinnati Commercial*, October 22, 1876.)
Account of a Cincinnati obeah man.

NA
1373
Hearn, Lafcadio. "The Last of the New Orleans Fencing Masters," in *An American Miscellany*, Vol. 2, Albert Mordell, ed. New York: Dodd, Mead, 1924, 185-200. (Reprinted from *Southern Bivouac*, November, 1886.)
Includes discussion of black fencing masters in New Orleans.

NA
1374
Hearn, Lafcadio. "The Last of the Voodoos," in *An American Miscellany*, Vol. 2, Albert Mordell, ed. New York: Dodd, Mead, 1924, 201-208. (Reprinted from *Harper's Weekly*, November 7, 1885.)
Career and beliefs of a New Orleans hoodoo doctor from Africa.

NA
1375
Hearn, Lafcadio. "Levee Life," in *An American Miscellany*, Vol. 1, Albert Mordell, ed. New York: Dodd, Mead, 1924, 147-170. (Reprinted from the *Cincinnati Commercial*, March 17, 1876.)
Roustabout songs in Cincinnati; descriptions of juba, black singers of Irish songs in Irish dialect, dancing, orchestras; includes 8 song texts.

NA
1376
Hearn, Lafcadio. *The Life and Letters of Lafcadio Hearn*, by Elizabeth Bisland. Vol. 1. Boston: Houghton Mifflin, 1906.
Hearn's letters to H.E. Krehbiel include discussion of New Orleans

and West Indian Negro music and its relation to West African music;
dialect; dance; instruments; includes 2 fragments of song texts.

NA   Hearn, Lafcadio. "Morning Calls--Very Early," in *Creole Sketches*,
1377   Charles W. Hutson, ed. Boston: Houghton Mifflin, 1924, 11-13. (Re-
            printed from the New Orleans *Item*, July 7, 1880.)
            1 song text.

NA   Hearn, Lafcadio. "New Orleans," in *Occidental Gleanings*, Vol. 1, Albert
1378   Mordell, ed. New York: Dodd, Mead, 1925, 223-234. (Reprinted from the
            Cincinnati Commercial, December 27, 1877.)
            Includes discussion of Louisiana French Creole and 1 song text.

NA   Hearn, Lafcadio. "New Orleans Superstitions," in *An American Miscellany*,
1379   Vol. 2, Albert Mordell, ed. New York: Dodd, Mead, 1924, 209-220. (Re-
            printed from *Harper's Weekly*, December 25, 1886.)
            Hoodoo practices, beliefs, etc., in New Orleans.

NA   Hearn, Lafcadio. "Old Man Pickett," in *Children of the Levee*, O.W. Frost,
1380   ed. Lexington, Kentucky: University of Kentucky Press, 1957, 54-60.
            (Reprinted from the *Cincinnati Enquirer*, February 21, 1875.)
            Account of a Cincinnati tavern and its owner.

NA   Hearn, Lafcadio. "Pariah People: Outcast Life by Night in the East End,"
1381   in *Occidental Gleanings*, Vol. 1, Albert Mordell, ed. New York: Dodd,
            Mead, 1925, 71-86. (Reprinted from the *Cincinnati Commercial*, August
            22, 1875.)
            Description of Negro-West Indian- Amerindian slum life in Cincinnati.

NA   Hearn, Lafcadio. "Des Perches," in *Creole Sketches*, Charles W. Hutson,
1382   ed. Boston: Houghton Mifflin, 1924, 85-87. (Reprinted from the New
            Orleans *Item*, August 30, 1880.
            Account of a clothes-pole vendor and his street cries.

NA   Hearn, Lafcadio. "The Poisoners--Curiosities of Criminal History," in
1383   *An American Miscellany*, Vol. 1, Albert Mordell, ed. New York: Dodd,
            Mead, 1924, 126-146. (Reprinted from the *Cincinnati Commercial*,
            December 12, 1875.)
            Includes discussion of hoodoo poisoners in Cincinnati and Africa.

NA   Hearn, Lafcadio. "The Scenes of Cable's Romances," in *An American Mis-
1384   cellany*, Vol. 2, Albert Mordell, ed. New York: Dodd, Mead, 1924,
            168-184. (Reprinted from *Century Magazine*, November, 1883.)
            Descriptions of New Orleans life; Congo Square music and dancing,

dock workers, etc.; includes 1 song text in Creole.

NA
1385

Hearn, Lafcadio. "The Scientific Value of Creole," in *An American Miscellany*, Vol. 2, Albert Mordell, ed. New York: Dodd, Mead, 1924, 159-163. (Reprinted from the *New Orleans Times Democrat*, June 14, 1886.)
A brief discussion of Louisiana French Creole language compared to other French Creoles in Africa and the Americas.

NA
1386

Hearn, Lafcadio. "A Sketch of the Creole Patois," in *An American Miscellany*, Vol. 2, Albert Mordell, ed. New York: Dodd, Mead, 1924, 164-167. (Reprinted from the *New Orleans Times Democrat*, October 17, 1886.)
Discusses early work in French Creole language and folklore.

NA
1387

Hearn, Lafcadio. "Some Notes on Creole Literature," in *An American Miscellany*, Vol. 2, Albert Mordell, ed. New York: Dodd, Mead, 1924, 154-158. (Reprinted from the *New Orleans Times Democrat*, June 13, 1886.)
A review of Gaidoz and Sebillot's *Bibliographie des Traditions et de la Litterature Populaire des Frances d'Outre-Mer*, which discusses early writings on French Creole language and folklore, and outlines early study of African-New World continuities.

NA
1388

Hearn, Lafcadio. "Some Pictures of Poverty," in *An American Miscellany*, Vol. 1, Albert Mordell, ed. New York: Dodd, Mead, 1924, 214-227. (Reprinted from the *Cincinnati Commercial*, January 7, 1877.)
Portrait of the black poor of Cincinnati includes a description of art on the walls of a home, and a fragment of a spiritual.

NA
1389

Hearn, Lafcadio. "Voices of Dawn," in *Creole Sketches*, Charles W. Hutson, ed. Boston: Houghton Mifflin, 1924, 197-201. (Reprinted from the New Orleans *Item*, July 22, 1881.)
Street cries.

NA
1390

Hearn, Lafcadio. "Wayside Notes," in *Lafcadio Hearn's American Days*, by Edward Laroque Tinker. New York: Dodd, Mead, 1924, 130-132. (Reprinted from the New Orleans *Item*, March 30, June 7, and November 8, 1879.)
Descriptions of voodoo charms and singing (with an early account of "blue notes"), and the text of a voodoo chant, all from New Orleans.

NA
1391

Hearn, Lafcadio. "Wayside Notes: Back of Town," in *Lafcadio Hearn's American Days*, by Edward Laroque Tinker. New York: Dodd, Mead, 1924, 83-84. (Reprinted in part from the New Orleans *Item*, May 20, 1879.)
An anecdote involving folk cure, in dialect.

NA
1392

Hearn, Lafcadio. "Why Crabs Are Boiled Alive," in *Creole Sketches*,
Charles W. Hutson, ed. Boston: Houghton Mifflin, 1924, 59. (Re-
printed from the New Orleans *Item*, October 5, 1879.)
Humor in "Gumbo" dialect.

Hearn, Lafcadio. See *Historical Sketch Book and Guide to New Orleans*,
No. NA 1449.

NA
1393

Heaton, C.P. "The 5-String Banjo in North Carolina," *SFQ*, 35 (1971), 62-
82.
Includes a brief discussion and description of early Negro banjos.

NA
1394

Heck, Jean Olive. "Folk Poetry and Folk Criticism," *JAF*, 40 (1927), 1-
77.
1 game song from Cincinnati (pp. 17-18).

NA
1395

Heckman, Don. "Black Music and White America," in *Black America*, John F.
Szwed, ed. New York: Basic Books, 1970, 158-170.
Brief review of the history of black popular music and jazz.

NA
1396

Heide, Karl Gert zur. *Deep South Piano: The Story of Little Brother Montgomery*. London: Studio Vista, 1970.
Autobiography of a Louisiana blues pianist and short biographies of
other blues musicians; discography, illustrations.

NA
1397

Heilbut, Tony. *The Gospel Sound: Good News and Bad Times*. New York: Simon
and Schuster, 1971.
The ritual and musical aspects of gospel singing; conversion and possession experiences; portraits of the most famous singers.

NA
1398

Helander, Olle. *Jazzens Väg*. Stockholm: Nordiska Musikforlaget, 1947.

NA
1399

Hemenway, Robert. "Zora Neale Hurston and the Eatonville Anthropology,"
in *The Harlem Renaissance Remembered*, Arna Bontemps, ed. New York:
Dodd, Mead, 1972, 190-214.
Discussion of Hurston's folkloric research and its critical reception; includes material from unpublished letters.

NA
1400

Henderson, George Wylie. *Ollie Miss*. New York: Stokes, 1935.
Novel of Alabama life with folkloric content.

NA
1401

Henderson, Stephen E. "Blues for the Young Blackman," *Negro Digest*, 16,
    No. 10 (1967), 10-17.

NA
1402

Henderson, Stephen E. "'Survival Motion': A Study of the Black Writer
    and the Black Revolution in America," in *The Militant Black Writer
    in Africa and the United States*, by Mercer Cook and Stephen E. Hen-
    derson. Madison: University of Wisconsin Press, 1969, 63-129.
    Includes the contribution of relevant folklore forms to black litera-
    ture and cultural consciousness.

NA
1403

Henderson, Stephen E. *Understanding the New Black Poetry: Black Speech
    and Black Music as Poetic References*. New York: William Morrow, 1972.
    An anthology of poetry with discussion of the influences of speech
    and music.

NA
1404

Hendricks, George D. "Voodoo Powder," *WF*, 17 (1958), 132. (AP dispatch
    from Conroe, Texas, to the Dallas *Morning News*, July 13, 1957.)
    An account of a Negro woman's use of "Voodoo powder" in opposition
    to the defendant in a court case.

NA
1405

Hendricks, W.C., ed. *Bundle of Troubles and Other Tarheel Tales*. Writers'
    Program of the Work Projects Administration in the State of North
    Carolina. Durham, N.C.: Duke University Press, 1943.
    Literary reshapings of traditional stories.

NA
1406

Hendrix, W.S. "The Hell Hounds," *PTFS*, No. 1 (1916), 75-77.
    Tale from Alabama of a hell hound chasing a man through heaven and
    hell.

NA
1407

Henry, Frances. *Forgotten Canadians: The Blacks of Nova Scotia*. Don Mills,
    Ontario: Longman Canada, 1973.
    An ethnography of several Nova Scotian black communities, arguing
    that there is an absence of a distinctive black culture in the vil-
    lages; includes discussion of music, dance, religion and speech.

NA
1408

Henry, Mellinger E. "More Songs from the Southern Highlands," *JAF*, 44
    (1931), 61-115.
    Includes Negro sacred and secular songs.

NA
1409

Henry, Mellinger E. "Negro Songs from Georgia," *JAF*, 44 (1931), 437-447.
    14 songs with comments.

NA 1410   Henry, Mellinger E. "Nursery Songs and Game-Songs from Georgia," *JAF*, 47 (1934), 334-340.
     A collection of rhymes.

NA 1411   Hensel, W.V. *The Christiana Riot and the Treason Trials of 1851*. Lancaster, Pa.: New Era Printing Co., 1911.
     Interviews with blacks in Lancaster, Pa.: accounts of gatherings, "kissing parties," apple-butter making parties, songs, etc.

NA 1412   Hentoff, Nat. "Elijah in the Wilderness," *Reporter*, 23 (August, 1960), 37-40.
     The message of Elijah Muhammad to black Americans; customs of Muslim leaders and converts.

NA 1413   Hentoff, Nat. "Filling Holes in the Soul; Negro Music," *Reporter*, 32 (March, 1965), 44.
     Influence of Southern bluesmen on black culture; the original intent of blues was to identify plantation laborers and aid communication between them.

NA 1414   Hentoff, Nat. "Mahalia Jackson," *JJ*, 11, No. 5 (1958), 16-17, 30.
     Discusses the development of gospel song.

NA 1415   Herndon, James. *The Way It Spozed to Be*. New York: Simon and Schuster, 1968.
     A white teacher's account of urban black students' speech, rhyming, interactions, etc.

NA 1416   Herriford, Merrill. "Idioms of the Present-day American Negro," *AS*, 13 (1938), 313-314.
     Distinguishing characteristics of 20 common expressions used by urban Negroes.

NA 1417   Herriford, Merrill. "Slang among Nebraska Negroes," *AS*, 13 (1938), 316-317.
     30 examples of slang terms with origins.

NA 1418   Herring, James V. "The American Negro as Craftsman and Artist," *Crisis*, 49 (1942), 116-118.
     Tom Day, cabinetmaker of the early 18th century in North Carolina; early 19th century Negro painters.

NA
1419

Herron, Miss, and A.M. Bacon. "Conjuring and Conjure-Doctors in the Southern United States," *JAF*, 9 (1896), 143-147; 224-226. (Reprinted from
SW, 24 (1895), 117-118.)
Describes some of the methods, charms and poisons used to conjure. The
continuing article describes the work of a "conjure doctor."

NA
1420

Herskovits, Melville J. "Acculturation and the American Negro," *Southwestern Political and Social Science Quarterly*, 8 (1927), 211-224.
Argues that American Negroes are largely acculturated to "American"
culture; denies the "African" nature of the spiritual.

NA
1421

Herskovits, Melville J. "The Ancestry of the American Negro," *American
Scholar*, 8 (1938-1939), 84-94.
Review of the West African cultural sources of slaves and the process
of slavery.

NA
1422

Herskovits, Melville J. "The Dilemma of Social Pattern," *Survey*, 53
(1925), 676-678.
Argues that Harlem is like any other American community and lacks any
African influences.

NA
1423

Herskovits, Melville J. "Letter to the Editor Concerning the Review of
Hurston's *Mules and Men* by J.J. Williams," *Folklore* (London), 48
(1937), 219-221.
Criticism of Williams' contention that (1) Hurston's informants were
liars, and (2) only animal tales are African; bibliography.

NA
1424

Herskovits, Melville J. *The Myth of the Negro Past*. New York: Harper,
1941. (Reprinted, with a new preface and bibliography, Boston: Beacon, 1958.)
The case for a distinctive Afro-American culture in the United States
and the survival of African traditions. Extensive material on religion,
language, style, domestic life, folklore, music, etc.; the nature of
Afro-American accultration; parallels to the other Afro-American cultures; critical treatment of the major writings on Afro-Americans in
the United States prior to 1941.

NA
1425

Herskovits, Melville J. "The Negro's Americanism," in *The New Negro*,
Alain Locke, ed. New York: Boni, 1925, 353-360.
Argues that Harlem is not culturally different from any other Ameri-
can community.

NA
1426
Herskovits, Melville J. "The Significance of West Africa for Negro Research," *JNH*, 21 (1936), 15-30.
Evidence of the West African sources of American Negroes; the need to
view Negroes in a cultural-historical context.

NA
1427
Herskovits, Melville J. "Some Comments by Professor Herskovits," (let-
ter to the editor re: Brearley's article, "Ba-ad Nigger"), *South
Atlantic Quarterly*, 39 (1940), 350-351.
Further remarks on the "Bad Nigger" in Africa and Afro-America. See
No. NA 335.

NA
1428
Herskovits, Melville J. "What Africa Gave to America," *New Republic*, 84,
No. 1083 (1935), 92-94. (Reprinted in No. GEN 120.)
Argues that much of Southern culture (etiquette, cuisine, music, dia-
lect, etc.) is of African origin.

NA
1429
Herzog, George. "African Influences in North American Indian Music," in
Papers of the International Congress of Musicology, New York, 1939.
New York, 1944, 130-143.

NA
1430
Herzog, George. "Music Tunes Held Not from Africa," *New York Times*,
September 14, 1939, 4.
Contends that Negro spirituals are versions of white folk song,
not African survivals.

NA
1431
Heuvelmans, Bernard. *De la Bamboula au Be-bop: De l'Evolution de la
Musique de Jazz*. Paris: Editions de la Main Jetée, 1951.
History of jazz; includes sections on African dancing in New Orleans,
work songs, blues.

NA
1432
Heyward, Dorothy. "'Porgy's' Native Tongue," *New York Times*, December 4,
1927, section 10, 2.
Gullah speech, its development and African origins; describes how it
had to be modified for use in *Porgy and Bess*.

NA
1433
Heyward, Du Bose. *The Half Pint Flask*. New York: Farrar and Rinehart,
1929.
Fictional account of plat-eye spirit beliefs, grave decorations, and
interracial etiquette on the South Carolina Sea Islands.

NA 1434   Heyward, Du. Bose. *Mamba's Daughters. A Novel of Charleston.* New York: Cowell, 1928.
Novel of South Carolina life with folkloric content.

NA 1435   Heyward, Du Bose. *Porgy.* New York: Grosset and Dunlap, George H. Doran, 1925.
Novel of South Carolina life with folkloric content.

NA 1436   Heyward, Mrs. (Jane Screven). *Brown Jackets.* Columbia, S.C.: The State Co., 1923.
Short sketches of black life in South Carolina, quoting both "urban" and "rural" Gullah speech.

NA 1437   Heywood, Duncan Clinch. *Seed from Madagascar.* Chapel Hill, N.C.: University of North Carolina Press, 1937.
Brief description of coastal Negroes in South Carolina, their dress, work teams; photos of dress and cabins.

NA 1438   Hibbard, Addison. "Aesop in Negro Dialect," *AS*, 1 (1926), 495-499.
The use of dialect in folkloric materials.

NA 1439   Hickerson, Daisy Faulkner. "My Black Mammy Cautions Me," *TFSB*, 15 (1949), 16-17.
A short study of "superstition" in dialect.

NA 1440   Higginson, Thomas Wentworth. *Army Life in a Black Regiment.* Boston: Fields, Osgood, 1870.
Memoirs of the commander of a black regiment in the Civil War. Discusses music, speech, religion, parade style, etc.

NA 1441   Higginson, Thomas Wentworth. *Letters and Journals of Thomas Wentworth Higginson, 1846-1906,* Mary Thacher Higginson, ed. Boston: Houghton Mifflin, 1921.
Descriptions of children's "shouting" (with 2 texts); dress, and dialect.

NA 1442   (Higginson, Thomas Wentworth.) "Negro Spirituals," *The Atlantic Monthly,* 19 (1867), 685-694. (Reprinted in No. NA 1698 and No. NA 1568.)
Texts of 36 spirituals and 1 secular song from South Carolina with annotations.

NA   Hill, Mozell C. "The All-Negro Communities of Oklahoma: The Natural His-
1443   tory of a Social Movement," *JNH*, 31 (1946), 254-268.
             Nineteenth and twentieth century establishment of all-Negro towns on
             the Oklahoma frontier.

NA   Hill, Olive. *Patsy's Easter*. n.p., n.d. (ca. 1880).
1444   Story (in dialect) of the South, with descriptions of dress, houses,
             music, religion, etc.

NA   Hilliard, Sam. "Hog Meat and Cornpone," *Proceedings of the American
1445   Philosophical Society*, 113 (February, 1969), 1-13.

NA   Himes, Joseph S. "Negro Teen-Age Culture," *Annals of the American Academy
1446   of Political and Social Science*, 338 (November, 1961), 91-101.
             Sociological report focusing on "low-prestige" Negro youths and their
             material and oral culture, against the background of the total Ameri-
             can culture.

NA   Hinton, Norman D. "The Language of Jazz Musicians," *Publications of the
1447   American Dialect Society*, No. 30 (1958), 38-48.
             A glossary of basic terms in the jazzman's vocabulary. Introduction
             treats jazz's influence on language.

NA   Hirschfield, Albert, and William Saroyan. *Harlem as Seen by Hirschfield*.
1448   New York: Hyperion Press, 1941.
             Drawings of Negro life in Harlem; music, dance, night clubs, etc.;
             text by William Saroyan.

NA   *Historical Sketch Book and Guide to New Orleans*. New York: Will H. Cole-
1449   man, 1885.
             Contains articles on New Orleans Negroes by Lafcadio Hearn, George W.
             Cable, and others.

NA   Hitchcock, Edward. *The Blind Slave in the Mine*. n.p.: American Tract
1450   Society, n.d.
             Describes a hymn sung by a blind mineworker.

NA   Hitchcock, H. Wiley. *Music in the United States: A Historical Introduc-
1451   tion*. Englewood Cliffs, N.J.: Prentice-Hall, 1969.
             Includes sections on minstrelsy, ragtime, blues, and jazz.

NA
1452
Hobart, George. *John Henry*. New York: G.W. Dillingham, 1901.

NA
1453
Hobson, Anne. *In Old Alabama, Being the Chronicles of Miss Mouse, the Little Black Merchant*. New York: Doubleday, Page, 1903.
10 explanatory tales, mostly non-traditional, of Alabama Negroes; 54 spirituals and songs.

NA
1454
Hobson, Charles. "Gospel," *Sounds and Fury*, No. 2 (1965), 10-11.
Includes discussion of the Five Blind Boys of Mississippi and the Jackson Harmoneers.

NA
1455
Hobson, Charles. "The Gospel Truth," *Down Beat*, 35, No. 11 (1968), 17-20.
Background and survey of gospel music and its best known performers.

NA
1456
Hodges, H. Eugene. "How to Lose the Hounds: Technology of the Gullah Coast Renegade," in *The Not So Solid South: Anthropological Studies in a Regional Subculture*. Southern Anthropological Society Proceedings No. 4, J. Kenneth Morland, ed. Athens, Georgia: University of Georgia Press, 1971, 66-73.
Escape techniques of Sea Island outlaws.

NA
1457
Hodgson, W.B. *The Gospels, Written in the Negro Patois of English, with Arabic Characters, by a Mandingo Slave in Georgia*. New York: Ethnological Society of New York, 1857.
Introduction to a manuscript written by a slave of Mohammedan background; discussion of slaves from Islamic areas of Africa, slaves of royal birth, etc.; samples of spoken and written pidgin English.

NA
1458
Hoefer, George. "History of the Drum in Jazz," *Jazz* (New York), No. 10 (1965), 11-15.
The origins and development of jazz drumming.

Hoetink, Harmannus. "Americans in Samana." See No. DR 11.

NA
1459
Hoffman, Daniel G. "The Folk Art of Jazz," *Antioch Review*, 5 (1945), 110-120.
Jazz as an art stemming from folk sources. The African background and its evidence in early New Orleans and Chicago jazz.

NA   Hoffman, Daniel G. "Jim's Magic: Black or White?," *American Literature*,
1460   32 (1960), 47-54.
            The use of "superstitions" in *The Adventures of Huckleberry Finn*.

NA   Hogen, Rochus. "Eine Entlegere Variante der Raumvorstellung. Meinhof's
1461   'Lokalvorstellung' und ihre Bedeutung fur die Textanalyse Afroameri-
            kanischer Folklore und Literatur," (A Distant Variant of Place-
            Representation; Meinhof's 'Local Representation' and its Meaning for
            the Text Analysis of Afro-American Folklore and Literature), *Sprache
            im Technischer Zeitalter*, 24 (1967), 324-334.

NA   Holliday, Carl. *A History of Southern Literature*. New York: Neale, 1906.
1462   Texts and discussion of "plantation melodies," pp. 187-192, without
            music.

NA   Holliday, Carl. *Three Centuries of Southern Poetry*. Nashville, Tenn.:
1463   Publishing House of the Methodist Episcopal Church, 1908.
            Texts of "plantation melodies," pp. 107-111.

NA   Holmes, Issac. *An Account of the United States of America, Derived from
1464   Actual Observation, During a Residence of Four Years in that Republic*.
            London: H. Fisher, 1823.
            Description of "Congo" dancing and instruments in rural Mississippi
            and Louisiana, p. 332.

NA   Holmes, Urban T. "A Study of Negro Onomastics," *AS*, 5 (1930), 463-467.
1465   First and middle names of 722 Negro school children in North Carolina.

NA   Holsey, Albon L. "Learning How to be Black," *American Mercury*, 16 (1929),
1466   421-425.
            Boyhood experiences of a Georgia Negro; games, marriage, and religious
            rituals, and the "struggle for dignity."

NA   Holt, Grace Sims. "'Inversion' in Black Communication," in *Rappin' and
1467   Stylin' Out*, Thomas Kochman, ed. Urbana, Ill.: University of Illinois
            Press, 1972, 152-159.
            The process of transvaluation of Standard English and white ethnocen-
            tric symbols by blacks.

NA   Holt, Grace Sims. "Stylin' Outta the Black Pulpit," in *Rappin' and Stylin'
1468   Out*, Thomas Kochman, ed. Urbana, Ill.: University of Illinois Press,
            1972, 189-208.
            Ritual and preaching style in black churches; secular use of religious

techniques; includes samples of sermons and speeches.

NA
1469
Holzknecht, K.J. "Some Negro Song Variants from Louisville," *JAF*, 41 (1928), 558-578.
30 religious and 15 secular songs and rhymes obtained from teachers in Kentucky.

NA
1470
Hopkins, Isabella T. "In the M.E. African," *Scribner's*, 20 (1880), 422-429.
Description of a church service with fragments of spirituals.

NA
1471
Hornbostel, Ernst Moritz von. "American Negro Songs," *International Review of Missions*, 15 (1926), 748-753.
An attempt to separate European and African elements; emphasizes the unity of dance and religious songs.

NA
1472
Hornbostel, Ernst Moritz von. "Ethnologisches zu Jazz," *Melos* (Berlin), 6 (1927), 510-512.
African influence on Negro music in the U.S.

NA
1473
Horne, Eliott. "For Cool Cats and Far-Out Chicks," *New York Times Magazine* (August 28, 1957), 26. (Reprinted in *The Jazz World*, Dom Cerulli, *et al.* New York: Ballantine, 1960, 155-159, as "The Argot of Jazz.")
Jazz slang in the mid-1950's.

NA
1474
Horosko, Marian. "Tap, Tapping, and Tappers," *Dance Magazine*, 45 (October, 1971), 32-37.
Brief history of tap dancing drawn from Marshall Stearns' *Jazz Dance* and interviews with choreographer-tappers Buddy Bradley and Bert Gibson.

NA
1475
Horton, George Moses. *Poems by a Slave*. Raleigh, N.C.: Gale and Son, 1829.
Poems by a 32 year-old slave who "cannot write."

NA
1476
Horton, John. "Time and Cool People," *Trans-Action* (April, 1967), 5-12. (Reprinted in *Soul*, Lee Rainwater, ed. Chicago: Aldine, 1970, 31-50.)
C.P.T. (Colored People's Time): the concept of time among people who carry out much of their activities on the streets.

NA
1477
Hoshor, John. *God in a Rolls Royce: The Rise of Father Divine, Madman, Menace, or Messiah*. New York: Hillman-Curl, Inc., 1936.

NA
1478
Hough, Walter. "Folk Medicine," *JAF*, 15 (1902), 191.
    1 cure.

NA
1479
House, Son. "I Can Make My Own Song," *SO*, 15, No. 3 (1965), 38-45.
    Autobiography of Son House, bluesman from Mississippi.

NA
1480
"How Brer Wolf Divide de Hog, How Brer Wolf Caught Brer Rabbit, etc.,"
    SW, 25 (1896), 205-206.
    2 tales.

NA
1481
Howard, John Tasker. *Our American Music*. New York: Thomas Crowell, 1931.
    Includes a discussion (pp. 415-427) of the structure, nature, and con-
    tent of Negro secular and religious songs.

NA
1482
Howard, John Tasker, and George Kent Bellows. *A Short History of Music in
    America*. New York: Thomas Crowell, 1957.
    Includes a section on ragtime, jazz, and Negro folk music.

NA
1483
Howe, M.A. De Wolfe. "The Song of Charleston," *Atlantic*, 146 (1930),
    108-111.
    Describes the Charleston, S.C. Society for the Preservation of Spirit-
    uals, a group consisting of plantation-bred whites which sings tradi-
    tional spirituals collected from Gullah Negroes.

NA
1484
Howe, R. Wilson. "The Negro and his Songs," *SW*, 51 (1922), 381-383.
    Excerpts from spirituals, freedom songs, labor songs, and dance and
    game songs exhibiting the "exhilaration and sorrow" evident in black
    music. Thematic analysis of Negro songs.

NA
1485
Howell, Elmo. "William Faulkner's 'Christmas Gift!'," *KFR*, 8 (1967), 37-
    40.
    The use of plantation Christmas customs in the novel *The Sound and the
    Fury*.

NA
1486
Howler, Casper. *Negro Spirituals en hun Beeldspraak* (Negro Spirituals and
    their Imagery). Bussum: W. De Haan, 1971.

NA
1487
Howse, Ruth Whitener. "Folkmusic of West Tennessee," *TFSB*, 13 (1947), 77-
    78.
    Includes Negro roustabout and work songs.

NA 1488   Hubbard, William L., ed. "Negro Music and Negro Minstrelsy," in *The American History and Encyclopedia of Music*, Vol. 4, Toledo: Irving Square, 1908, 49-70.

NA 1489   Hubbell, Jay. B. "Negro Boatmen's Songs," *SFQ*, 18 (1954), 244-245.
Various boatmen's songs, from *Chicora* (August 13 and 21, 1942) a Charleston, S.C., publication.

NA 1490   Hubbell, Jay B. "Note on 'Old Virginia Never Tire,'" *NCF*, 12, No. 2 (1964), 26. (Reprinted from *Southern Literary Gazette* (Charleston), 2 (new series 1), No. 77 (July 1, 1829).)
1 secular song text from Virginia.

NA 1491   Hucks, J. Jenkins. *Plantation Negro Sayings on the Coast of South Carolina in Their Own Vernacular*. Georgetown, S.C.: Charles W. Rouse, 1899.
"Humorous" examples of Gullah speech as recalled from a magistrate's court (pamphlet).

NA 1492   Hudson, Arthur Palmer. "Ballads and Songs from Mississippi," *JAF*, 39 (1926), 93-194.
Includes texts of Negro secular and religious songs.

NA 1493   Hudson, Arthur Palmer. *Humor of the Old Deep South*. New York: Macmillan, 1936.
Chapter 18, "Darkies," contains miscellaneous dialogues, beliefs, etc.; reprinted from newspapers and journals.

NA 1494   Hudson, Arthur Palmer. "Some Curious Negro Names," *SFQ*, 2 (1938), 179-193.
Names derived from the Bible, geography, ornaments, animals, etc., with a discussion.

NA 1495   Hudson, Arthur Palmer. "Some Folk Riddles From the South," *The South Atlantic Quarterly*, 42 (1943), 78-93.
43 riddles from Mississippi, North Carolina, Kentucky and Alabama.

NA 1496   Hudson, Arthur Palmer. *Specimens of Mississippi Folk-Lore*. Ann Arbor, Michigan: Edwards, 1928.
14 Negro songs, with notes on singers; beliefs, weather lore, games, etc.

NA   Hudson, Julius. "The Hustling Ethic," in *Rappin' and Stylin' Out*, Thomas
1497   Kochman, ed. Urbana, Ill.: University of Illinois Press, 1972, 410-
            424.
        The style, slang, values and "games" of a street hustler.

NA   Hudson, Wilson M. "I Want My Golden Arm," *PTFS*, No. 25 (1953), 183-194.
1498   Traces several versions of "The Golden Arm" to Negro origins.

NA   Huggins, Nathan Irvin. *Harlem Renaissance*. New York: Oxford University
1499   Press, 1971.
        Includes a discussion of the influence of folk culture on the black
        artistic renaissance in New York City in the 1920's and 1930's; blacks
        in minstrelsy, etc.

NA   Hughes, Langston, ed. *The Book of Negro Humor*. New York: Dodd, Mead, 1966.
1500   7 stories by contemporary Negro comics (Markham, Gregory, etc.); 30
        jokes; 8 preacher stories, 17 joke-rhymes, 5 downhome tales, etc.

NA   Hughes, Langston. "Jokes Negroes Tell on Themselves," *Negro Digest*, 9,
1501   No. 8 (1951), 21-25. (Reprinted in Dundes, No. NA 854.)
        "In-jokes," retold.

NA   Hughes, Langston. "Out of Work; Love Again Blues," *Poetry*, 56 (April, 1940),
1502   20-21.
        The blues emerge from life's troubles and lovers' heartaches.

NA   Hughes, Langston. *Simple Speaks His Mind*. New York: Simon and Schuster,
1503   1950.
        Short stories of Harlem life with folkloric content.

NA   Hughes, Langston. *Simple Takes a Wife*. New York: Simon and Schuster, 1953.
1504   Short stories of Harlem life with folkloric content.

NA   Hughes, Langston. *Simple's Uncle Sam*. New York: Hill and Wang, 1965.
1505   Short stories of Harlem life with folkloric content.

NA   Hughes, Langston. "Songs Called the Blues," *Phylon*, 2 (1941), 143-145.
1506   Definition and types of blues, mention of famous blues people.

NA   Hughes, Langston. *Tamborine to Glory*. New York: Day, 1958.
1507   A novel of a gospel's singer's life.

Hughes, Langston. See Mintz, Lawrence E., No. NA 2075.

Hughes, Langston. See Rosenblatt, Roger, No. NA 2612.

NA   Hughes, Langston, and Arna Bontemps, eds. *The Book of Negro Folklore*. New
1508   York: Dodd, Mead, 1958.
            Collection mainly from printed sources: animal tales, rhymes, recollec-
            tions of slavery; belief tales; tales of God, man and the devil; tales
            about preachers; ghost stories; sermons, prayers, testimonials; beliefs,
            "superstitions," and tales of black magic; 31 spirituals (words only),
            11 gospel songs, 12 ballads, 12 blues, 14 "workday" songs, 6 street
            cries, 20 playsongs and games; stories concerning racial issues.

NA   Hughes, Langston, and Milton Meltzer. *Black Magic: A Pictorial History of
1509   the Negro in American Entertainment*. Englewood Cliffs, N.J.: Prentice-
            Hall, 1967.
            Covers African background, plantation life, minstrelsy, dance, T.O.B.A.
            shows, circus , vaudeville, etc.

NA   Hugill, Stan. *Shanties from the Seven Seas*. London: Routledge, Kegan; New
1510   York: E.P. Dutton, 1961.
            Includes reports and texts of West Indians and American Negroes.

NA   Huguenin, Charles A. "The Legend of Martense's Love in Brooklyn," *NYFQ*,
1511   21 (1956), 112-118.

NA   Hundley, D.R. *Social Relations in Our Southern States*. New York: Henry B.
1512   Price, 1860.
            Conjuring, poisoning, witchcraft among slaves; cuisine, religious prac-
            tices, keeping Christmas; numerous other features of imputed behavior.
            In defense of slavery.

NA   Hungerford, James. *The Old Plantation*. New York: Harper, 1859.
1513   Observations on a plantation: tales, folk customs, music, etc., includes
            2 songs with texts and music.

NA   Hunter, Charlayne. "An Entrepreneur's Trucks Bring Southern Soul Food to
1514   Harlem," *New York Times*, December 20, 1971, 70.
            Account of Southern local foods' popularity in a Northern black commu-
            nity.

NA
1515
Hunter, Rosa. "Ghosts as Guardians of Hidden Treasure," *JAF*, 12 (1899),
64-65.
Two Negro ghost stories from *SW*, March, 1898.

NA
1516
Huntley, Fred H. *The National Collection of Spirituals*, Vol. 1. Chicago:
Franklin Earl Hathaway, 1935.
Includes 1 spiritual from Georgia and 1 from Louisiana.

NA
1517
Hurdle, Virginia Jo. "Folklore of a Negro Couple in Henry County," *TFSB*,
19 (1953), 71-78.
Plant and animal beliefs, folk medicines, customs, stories of the supernatural and some song fragments.

NA
1518
Hurll, Margaret M. "Studies of Art in American Life IV; In Negro Cabins,"
Brush and Pencil, 7 (January, 1901), 239-244.
An appreciation of artistry in rural Negro art, music, housing, etc.;
illustrations.

NA
1519
Hurston, Zora Neale. "Characteristics of Negro Expression," in *Negro Anthology*, Nancy Cunard, ed. London: Wishart, 1934, 39-46.
Includes short essays on Negro drama, speech, dancing, culture heroes
and the jook.

NA
1520
Hurston, Zora Neale. "Conversions and Visions," in *Negro Anthology*, Nancy
Cunard, ed. London: Wishart, 1934, 47-49.
3 visions are recounted and a background of conversions and visions in
religion is given.

NA
1521
Hurston, Zora Neale. "Cudjo's Own Story of the Last African Slaver," *JNH*,
12 (1927), 643-663.
Accounts of the voyage and arrival of the *Clotilde*, the last ship to
bring slaves to the U.S. (apparently drawn from Emma Langdon Roche,
Historic Sketches of the South, No. NA 2592).

NA
1522
Hurston, Zora Neale. *Dust Tracks on a Road*. Philadelphia: Lippincott,
1942.
An autobiography which discusses her field research in folklore: includes
song texts, folktales told by Negroes about Negroes, and a sermon.

NA
1523
Hurston, Zora Neale. "Dust Tracks on a Road," *Negro Digest*, 1 (January,
1943), 75-81.
A condensation of Hurston's views of Negro folklore from her autobiography of the same name.

NA
1524
    Hurston, Zora Neale. "The Gilded Six Bits," *Story*, 3, No. 14 (1933), 60-
        70.
        Short story with folkloric content.

NA
1525
    Hurston, Zora Neale. "High John De Conquer," *American Mercury*, 57 (1943),
        450-458.
        The development of the "John and Ole' Master" folktale; includes texts.

NA
1526
    Hurston, Zora Neale. "Hoodoo in America," *JAF*, 44 (1931), 317-417.
        Stories of hoodoo doctors with explanation of some of their spells,
        paraphernalia and prescriptions. Hoodoo doctors in New Orleans,
        Florida, Alabama, and the Bahamas.

NA
1527
    Hurston, Zora Neale. *Jonah's Gourd Vine*. Philadelphia: J.B. Lippincott,
        1934.
        Novel of Florida with folkloric content; includes a sermon.

NA
1528
    Hurston, Zora Neale. *Moses: Man of the Mountain*. Philadelphia: Lippincott,
        1939.
        Novel with folkloric content.

NA
1529
    Hurston, Zora Neale. "Mother Catherine," in *Negro Anthology*, Nancy Cunard,
        ed. London: Wishart, 1934, 54-57.
        Account of the activities of a religious leader.

NA
1530
    Hurston, Zora Neale. *Mules and Men*. Philadelphia and London: J.B. Lippin-
        cott, 1935.
        70 folk tales; descriptions and rituals of hoodoo; 9 folk songs with
        music, 23 hoodoo doctors' formulas, 38 items used in conjuring, and
        25 prescriptions of root doctors. (See also No. NA 1423.)

NA
1531
    Hurston, Zora Neale. "Possum or Pig?" *Forum*, 76 (1926), 465.
        1 folktale text.

NA
1532
    Hurston, Zora Neale. "The Sermon," in *Negro Anthology*, Nancy Cunard, ed.
        London: Wishart, 1934, 50-54.
        Transcription of a sermon in Florida in 1929.

NA
1533
    Hurston, Zora Neale. "Shouting," in *Negro Anthology*, Nancy Cunard, ed.
        London: Wishart, 1934, 49-50.
        A description of "shouting" (possession) during revival meetings.

NA
1534
Hurston, Zora Neale. "Spirituals and Neo-Spirituals," in *Negro Anthology*, Nancy Cunard, ed. London: Wishart, 1934, 359-361.
Discusses the elements which differentiate true spirituals from pseudo-spirituals.

NA
1535
Hurston, Zora Neale. "Spunk," *Opportunity*, 3 (June, 1925), 171-173.
Short story in dialect with folkloric content.

NA
1536
Hurston, Zora Neale. "Story in Harlem Slang," *The American Mercury*, 55, No. 223 (1942), 84-96.
A story of Harlem life, with a glossary.

NA
1537
Hurston, Zora Neale. *Their Eyes Were Watching God*. Philadelphia: Lippincott, 1937.
Novel with folkloric content.

NA
1538
Hurston, Zora Neale. "Uncle Monday," in *Negro Anthology*, Nancy Cunard, ed. London: Wishart, 1934, 57-61.
Concerns a conjurer, and his effect on a small village.

Hurston, Zora Neale. See Byrd, James W., No. NA 450.

Hurston, Zora Neale. See Hemenway, Robert, No. NA 1399.

Hurston, Zora Neale. See Jackson, Blyden, No. NA 1563.

Hurston, Zora Neale. See Lomax, Alan, No. NA 1893.

Hurston, Zora Neale. See Neal, Larry, No. NA 2160.

NA
1539
Huston, John. *Frankie and Johnny*. New York: Boni, 1930.
A play based on the incidents of the song "Frankie and Johnnie," 12 versions of the song and an account of its "underworld" history.

NA
1540
Hutson, Katherine C., Josephine Pinckney, and Caroline Rutledge. "Some Songs the Negro Sang," in *The Carolina Low County*, Augustine Smythe, ed. New York: Macmillan, 1931, 225-327.
49 tunes and texts, with a brief descriptive introduction.

NA 1541   Hyatt, Harry Middleton. *Hoodoo--Conjuration--Witchcraft--Rootwork*, 4 vols. Hannibal, Mo.: Western Publishing, 1970-
Compilation of texts about ghost lore and conjuring from the American South.

NA 1542   Hyman, Stanley Edgar. "American Negro Literature and the Folk Tradition," in *The Promised End: Essays and Reviews, 1942-1962*, by Stanley Edgar Hyman. Cleveland and New York: World, 1963, 295-315. (Originally published in *Partisan Review*, 25 (1958), 197-222.)
Afro-American fiction linked to the folk tale, the blues, and the sermon.

NA 1543   "I Know I Would Like to Read," *SW*, 36 (1907), 89.
Chorus of a plantation song.

NA 1544   Iglauer, Blues, Jim O'Neal, and Bea Van Geffen. "Lowell Fulsom," *Living Blues*, 2, No. 5 (1971), 19-25; No. 6 (1971), 10-20.
Life and views of a contemporary bluesman.

NA 1545   Illinois Writers' Program. *Cavalcade of the American Negro*. Chicago: Diamond Jubilee Exposition Authority, 1940.

NA 1546   Imes, G. Lake. "The Last Recruits of Slavery," *SW*, 46 (1917), 355-359.
Account of a visit to the ex-slaves of Plateau, Alabama, who arrived in the U.S. on the ship *Clotilde*; mentions scarification, trades, etc.

NA 1547   "In Egypt Lands," *Time*, 48 (December 30, 1946), 59-64.
Autobiographical account of the origin of spirituals by Marian Anderson; illustrations.

NA 1548   Ingersoll, Ernest. "Decoration of Negro Graves," *JAF*, 5 (1892), 68-69.
Comments on grave decorations in South Carolina.

NA 1549   Ingle, Edward. "The Negro in the District of Columbia," in *Labor, Slavery and Self-Government*, Vol. 2, Johns Hopkins University Studies in Historical and Political Science, Herbert B. Adam, ed. Baltimore: Johns Hopkins Press, 1893, 99-209.
Contains a description of street dancing and religion among free blacks.

NA 1550   Ingraham, Joseph Holt. *The Southwest*. Vol. 2. New York: Harper's, 1835.
Discussion of slave dress, markets, work, child care, burial, etc.

NA   Ingraham, Joseph Holt, ed. *The Sunny South; or, The Southerner at Home,*
1551   *Embracing Five Years Experience of a Northern Governess.* Philadelphia:
             G.G. Evans, 1860.
             Describes slave weddings, giving of baptismal names, differences of
             field and house servants, religious meetings, singing, dancing and
             drumming, teaching of African tunes to young blacks, dress, African
             speech, etc.

NA   "An Interview with a Hoodoo Curer," *LFM*, 3, No. 2 (1971), 44-47.
1552   Describes an interview and gives the New Orleans informant's biography.

NA   "Irishman Stories Told by Negroes," *JAF*, 12 (1899), 226-230.
1553   5 tales related by American Negroes concerning the stupidity of the
             Irishman and 5 selections dealing with conjuring. (Taken from *SW*,
             28 (1899), 192-194.)

NA   Irvis, K. Leroy. "Negro Tales from Eastern New York," *NYFQ*, 11 (1955),
1554   165-176.
             Narratives remembered from childhood about witches, ghosts, people who
             went to Heaven, the Negro race, etc.

NA   Issacs, Edith J.R. *The Negro in the American Theater.* New York: Theatre
1555   Arts, 1947.

NA   Isham, Caddie S. "Games of Danville, Va.," *JAF*, 34 (1921), 116-120.
1556   2 games, 4 songs with music.

NA   Italiaander, Rolf. *Tanz in Afrika; Ein Phänomen im Leben der Neger.* Ber-
1557   lin: Rembrandt, 1960.

NA   "Itinerant Observations in America," in *Collections of the Georgia Histori-*
1558   *cal Society*, Vol. 4 Savannah: J.H. Estill, 1878. (Reprinted from the
             London Magazine, 1745-1746.)
             Descriptions of the location of Negro huts on plantations; family life;
             refusal of new slaves "to learn" (pp. 37-38); white children imitating
             Negro manners, speech (p. 48).

NA   Ives, Sumner. "The Phonology of the Uncle Remus Stories," *Publications*
1559   *of the American Dialect Society*, No. 22 (November, 1954), 3-59.
             Description of the dialect of Joel Chandler Harris' Uncle Remus stories
             and its verification from dialect atlas records.

NA 1560   J.K., Jr. (J. Kinnard, Jr.). "Who Are Our National Poets?" *Knickerbocker Magazine* (New York), 26 (1845), 331-341. (Reprinted in No. NA 1568.)
Texts of minstrel songs; description of boat-rowing to music; comments on white commercialization of Negro music.

NA 1561   J.M. "The Dance: Negro Art Loses in Originality," *New York Times*, July 8, 1928, section 8, 6.
Negro dance style as a result of "laziness."

NA 1562   J.R.M. *Robert Johnson: King of the Delta Blues*. London: Immediate Music Ltd., 1969.
29 texts and music without annotation.

NA 1563   Jackson, Blyden. "Some Negroes in the Land of Goshen," *TFSB*, 19 (1953), 103-107.
Zora Neale Hurston's handling of Negro folklore in her novel, *Moses, Man of the Mountain*.

NA 1564   Jackson, Bruce. "Circus and Street: Psychosocial Aspects of the Black Toast," *JAF*, 85 (1972), 123-139.
Analysis of themes and characters in toasts; includes 7 texts.

NA 1565   Jackson, Bruce. "Genres in Negro Oral Poetry and Song," in *Festival of American Folklife*. Washington, D.C.: The Smithsonian Institution, 1968, 28.
Surveys the development of new styles and the preservation of old styles in black music.

NA 1566   Jackson, Bruce. *Get Your Ass in the Water and Swim Like Me: Narrative Poetry from Black Oral Tradition*. Cambridge, Mass.: Harvard University Press, 1974.

NA 1567   Jackson, Bruce. "The Glory Songs of the Lord," in *Our Living Traditions*, Tristram P. Coffin, ed. New York: Basic Books, 1968, 103-110.
Origins of Negro spirituals.

NA 1568   Jackson, Bruce, ed. *The Negro and his Folklore in Nineteenth-Century Periodicals*. Austin: University of Texas Press and the American Folklore Society, 1967.
Anthology of 35 articles, letters, reviews, and literature on Negro folklore. Summaries and versions of a few animal tales; articles present and discuss folksong, speech, belief, custom and story; bibliography.

NA 1569   Jackson, Bruce. "Negro Folklore from Texas State Prisons," booklet included with Elektra LP record EKS-7296.
Texts and discussion of work songs, spirituals, a *cante-fable*, toasts, and a sermon parody.

NA 1570   Jackson, Bruce. "The Personal Blues of Skip James," *SO*, 15, No. 6 (1966), 26-30.
Biographical notes on a Negro blues guitarist-pianist-singer from Mississippi.

NA 1571   Jackson, Bruce. "Prison Nicknames," *WF*, 26 (1967), 48-54.
Notes the prevalence of nicknames in prison, especially in the rural South and Southwest. Includes inmates' anecdotes.

NA 1572   Jackson, Bruce. "Prison Worksongs: The Composer in Negatives," *WF*, 16 (1967), 245-268.
The compositional techniques of a worksong singer-composer; includes texts and tunes.

NA 1573   Jackson, Bruce. "Stagolee Stories: A Badman Goes Gentle," *SFQ*, 29 (1965), 188-194. (Also appeared on pp. 228-233, with slight changes.)
3 tales and a ballad with discussion, from Mississippi John Hurt.

NA 1574   Jackson, Bruce. "Talkin' about My Time," booklet included with Folk Legacy LP record FSA-12.
Essay on a blues singer in the Indiana State Prison.

NA 1575   Jackson, Bruce. "The Titanic Toast," in *Veins of Humor*, Harvard English Studies 3, Harry Levin, ed. Cambridge, Mass.: Harvard University Press, 1972, 205-223.
An analysis of the meaning of a toast; includes 7 texts.

NA 1576   Jackson, Bruce. *Wake Up Dead Man: Afro-American Worksongs from Texas Prisons*. Cambridge, Mass.: Harvard University Press, 1972.
65 songs and their variants with music, annotation, and discography; 1 toast; notes on performance, setting, metrics, content, functions, pronunciation, responsorial patterns; comments on the songs and on prison life; notes on nicknames; glossary; bibliography; illustrations.

NA 1577   Jackson, Bruce. "What Happened to Jody," *JAF*, 80 (1967), 387-396.
The "Jody" songs sung by Negroes in the army and prisons. Background material and 3 variants, 2 with music.

NA   Jackson, Bruce. "White Dozens and Bad Sociology," *JAF*, 79 (1966), 374-377.
1578   Argues that the dozens are far more elaborate and pervasive among
            blacks than whites. (See Millicent Ayoub and Stephen A. Barnett, No.
            NA 98.)

        Jackson, Bruce. See White, Newman I., No. NA 3177.

NA   Jackson, Clyde Owen. *The Songs of Our Years: A Study of Negro Folk Music*.
1579   New York: Exposition Press, 1968.
            History of the spiritual, with emphasis on Antonin Dvorak's influence
            on public attitudes towards the spiritual.

NA   Jackson, George Pullen. "The Genesis of the Negro Spiritual," *American
1580   Mercury*, 26 (1932), 243-248.
            An argument for the origin of the Negro spiritual from Southern white
            singing style.

NA   Jackson, George Pullen. *White and Negro Spirituals*. New York: J.J. Augus-
1581   tin, 1943.
            Documents the case for the white-to-Negro theory of the development
            of spirituals.

NA   Jackson, George Pullen. *White Spirituals of the Southern Uplands*. Chapel
1582   Hill: University of North Carolina Press, 1933.
            Mostly white material, but chapters 19 and 20 attempt to show that
            black spirituals are European-derived.

NA   Jackson, Harriet. "American Dancer, Negro," *Dance Magazine*, 40 (September,
1583   1966), 35-42.
            Historical survey of black dance in America: minstrel dances of the
            ante-bellum South, tap and jazz dancing, etc.; short discussion of
            the work of two black dancers trained in anthropology, concerning
            origins of black dance.

NA   Jackson, J. *The Colored Sacred Harp*. Ozark, Alabama: J. Jackson, 1931.
1584   Songs with music for shape-note singing congregations.

NA   Jackson, Luther P. "Religious Development of the Negro in Virginia from
1585   1760 to 1860," *JNH*, 16 (1931), 168-239.
            Virginia movements to bring Negroes to Christianity: preachings, revi-
            val meetings, etc., particularly among black Methodists and Baptists;
            bibliography.

NA   Jackson, Luther P. "Religious Instruction of Negroes, 1830-1860, with
1586   Specific references to South Carolina," *JNH*, 15 (1930), 72-114.
              Includes descriptions of religious services.

NA   Jackson, Mahalia, with Wylie Evan McLeod. *Movin' On Up*. New York: Hawthorn,
1587   1966.
              A gospel singer's memoirs: life in New Orleans, Louisiana cuisine, etc.

NA   Jackson, Margaret. "Folklore in Slave Narratives Before the Civil War,"
1588   *NYFQ*, 11 (1955), 5-19.
              Texts of dreams and visions, fortune telling, devil and death lore,
              falling stars, witchcraft and magic, and songs.

NA   Jacobs-Bond, Carrie. *Old Melodies of the South*. Chicago: The Bond Shop,
1589   n.d.
              9 songs arranged for chorus.

NA   Jahn, Janheinz. *Negro Spirituals*. Frankfurt and Hamburg: Fisher Bucherei,
1590   1962.
              Anthology of spirituals with texts in both English and German; bibli-
              ography and discography.

NA   Jahn, Janheinz, and Alfons Michael Dauer. *Blues und Work Songs*. Frankfurt
1591   am Main: Fischer, 1964.

NA   Jahoda, Gloria. *The Other Florida*. New York: Scribner's, 1967.
1592   Includes a chapter on turpentine camps (Chapter 12), *Bolita* (a gambling
              game), and juke joints; and a chapter on a rural church (Chapter 17)
              with a description of a service and singing; with fragments of blues
              and gospel texts.

NA   James, U.P. *The Negro Melodist*. Cincinnati: Bulison, 1857.
1593

NA   James, Virginia E. *"La Creole" Cook Book*. Memphis: Van Fleet-Mansfield,
1594   1892.

NA   James, Willis Laurence. "The Romance of the Negro Folk-Cry in America,"
1595   *Phylon*, 16 (1955), 15-30.
              The folk cry as a distinctive art form and influence; 11 musical tran-
              scriptions and 5 excerpts from verse.

NA
1596
"James Cleveland, King of Gospel," *Ebony*, 24 (November, 1968), 74-76.
   Account of James Cleveland's 7-day gospel show at Harlem's Apollo
   Theater.

NA
1597
Jamison, Mrs. C.V. "A Louisiana Legend Concerning Will O' the Wisp," *JAF*,
   18 (1905), 250-251.
   1 tale.

NA
1598
Jansen, William Hugh. "Tales from a Steel Town (Part 2)," *HFB*, 1 (1942),
   78-81.
   1 ghost story (pp. 78-79) and 1 legend (pp. 79-80) from East Chicago,
   Indiana.

NA
1599
Jarmon, Charles. "The Sploe House: A Drinking Place of Lower Socio-Economic
   Status Negroes in a Southern City," *Bulletin of the Southern University
   and A & M College*, 55 (June, 1969), 53-61.

NA
1600
Jasen, David A. "Another Look at Ragtime," *The Rag Times*, 3, No. 3 (1969),
   6-7.
   Asserts 7 ragtime styles: folk, classic, Tin Pan Alley, advanced classic, New Orleans, stride and novelty.

NA
1601
Jaskoski, Helen. "Power Unequal to Man: The Significance of Conjure in
   Works by Five Afro-American Authors," *SFQ*, 38 (1974), 91-108.
   Literary uses of conjuration (in the writings of Ann Petry, Frederick
   Douglass, George Marion McClellan, Charles W. Chesnutt, and Ernest
   Gaines).

NA
1602
Jeanneret, Albert. "Le Negro et le Jazz," *Revue Musicale*, 8 (1927), 24-27.
   (Also published as "El Negro y el Jazz," *Advance* (Havana), 1, No. 12
   (1927), 314-315.
   Jazz derived from African arts; rhythm modeled on body movement.

NA
1603
Jeffreys, M.D.W. "Names of American Negro Slaves," *AA*, 50 (1948), 571-573.
   Comments on Newbell Niles Puckett's writings on West African day-name
   practices and their survival in the U.S.; African names and their
   anglicization (*Eyamba - Iron Bar; Orok - Duke; Okun - Hogan, et al.*).

NA
1604
Jeffreys, M.D.W. "The North Carolina Carvings," *International Anthropological and Linguistic Review* (Miami), 2, Nos. 3-4 (1955-1956), 103-111.
   Argues that 2,000 artifacts in North Carolina are the remains of a
   13th century African voyage.

NA   Jeltz, W.F. "The Relations of Negroes and Choctaw and Chickasaw Indians,"
1605   *JNH*, 33 (1948), 24-37.
             Negro enslavement among U.S. Indians.

NA   Jesseye, Eva A. *My Spirituals*. New York: Robbins-Engle, 1927.
1606   16 songs from Kansas with notes.

NA   "Jive Papa," *Ebony*, 1 (August, 1946), 19-24.
1607

NA   Johns, Altona Trent. *Play Songs of the Deep South*. Washington, D.C.:
1608   Associated Publishers, 1944.

NA   Johnson, Charles Albert. *The Frontier Camp Meeting: Religion's Harvest
1609   Time*. Dallas: Southern Methodist University Press, 1955.
             Slave participation in white camp meetings surveyed (pp. 113-118).

NA   Johnson, Charles S., ed. *Ebony and Topaz*. New York: National Urban League,
1610   1927.
             A collection of essays, poems and sketches on Negro life.

NA   Johnson, Charles S. *Growing Up In The Black Belt*. New York: American
1611   Council on Education, 1941.
             Contains some information on singing the dozens, the church, and
             racial attitudes.

NA   Johnson, Charles S. *Patterns of Negro Segregation*. New York: Harper, 1943.
1612   Chapter 6 describes interracial etiquette in the Deep South.

NA   Johnson, Charles S. *Shadow of The Plantation*. Chicago: University of
1613   Chicago Press, 1934.
             The influence of plantation life on rural Alabama Negroes in the 1930's;
             description of curing, religion, funerals, housing, etc.; texts of
             several sermons are included.

         Johnson, Charles S. See Johnson, Clifton H., No. NA 1614.

NA   Johnson, Clifton H., ed. *God Struck Me Dead: Religious Conversion Experi-
1614   ences and Autobiographies of Ex-Slaves*. Philadelphia: Pilgrim, 1969.
             (Originally published in fuller form as *God Struck Me Dead*, Charles

Johnson and Paul Radin, eds. Social Science Source Documents, No. 2;
Nashville: Fisk University, 1945.)
Accounts collected between 1927 and 1929. Introductory essays by Paul
Radin and Charles S. Johnson; essay on fundamentalist Baptist services
and sermons by Andrew P. Watson.

NA
1615

Johnson, Clifton H. *Highways and Byways of the South*. New York: Macmillan,
1904.
Memoirs which include Brer Rabbit tales, descriptions of work, etc.

NA
1616

Johnson, Clifton H. *What They Say in New England and Other American Folklore*, 2nd Edition, Carl Withers, ed. New York: Columbia University
Press, 1963.
Includes 3 South Carolina Brer Rabbit stories (pp. 240-245) and 5 folktales from Mississippi (pp. 246-252).

NA
1617

Johnson, Eldridge R., III. "Crescent City Blues," *LFM* 3, No. 2 (1971),
53-55.
Notes on 3 New Orleans blues singers.

NA
1618

Johnson, F. Roy. *The Fabled Doctor Jim Jordan: A Story of Conjure*. Murfreesboro, North Carolina: Johnson, 1963.
The biography of a conjure man. Includes folk tales, jokes, proverbs,
beliefs, songs, descriptions of slave instrument making, voodoo techniques, cures; description of a ghost story-telling session.

NA
1619

Johnson, F. Roy, ed. *How and Why Stories in Carolina Folklore*. Murfreesboro, North Carolina: Johnson, 1971.
Contains Negro folktales and legends, though only occasionally identified as such.

NA
1620

Johnson, F. Roy. *The Nat Turner Story*. Murfreesboro, North Carolina: Johnson, 1970.
A study of the folk hero, using historical and legendary materials.

NA
1621

Johnson, F. Roy, ed. *Tales from Old Carolina*. Murfreesboro, North Carolina:
Johnson, 1965.
North Carolina legends and historical sketches: slave lore, escapes in
Dismal Swamp, N.C., slave outlaws, etc.

NA
1622

Johnson, F. Roy. "Two John Stories," *NCF*, 20 (1972), 120-122.
2 texts.

NA   Johnson, F. Roy. *Witches and Demons in History and Folklore*. Murfreesboro,
1623   North Carolina: Johnson, 1969.
            Negro sorcery discussed in the context of a history of American witch-
            craft.

NA   Johnson, Georgia Douglas. *Plumes*. New York: French, 1927.
1624   Drama with folkloric content.

NA   Johnson, Guion Griffis. *A Social History of the Sea Islands*. Chapel Hill,
1625   North Carolina: University of North Carolina Press, 1930.
            Chapter 7, "The Slave Community," discusses slave entertainments, re-
            ligion, etc.

NA   Johnson, Guy B. "Double Meaning in the Popular Negro Blues," *Journal of
1626   Abnormal and Social Psychology*, 22 (1927), 12-20.
            Sexual meaning in blues texts and titles.

NA   Johnson, Guy B. *Folk Culture on St. Helena Island, South Carolina*. Chapel
1627   Hill, North Carolina: University of North Carolina Press, 1930. (Re-
            printed, Hatboro, Pa.: Folklore Associates, 1968.)
            Studies of Gullah dialect, Negro secular and religious songs (with
            particular reference to kinship of Negro spirituals with white spirit-
            uals) and other folklore. Includes 21 folktales, 47 riddles, 10 proverbs,
            toasts, rhymes, games and folk beliefs. (1968 reprint has a new fore-
            word by Don Yoder which includes 5 pages of new material by Guy B.
            Johnson arguing against M.J. Herskovits' and Lorenzo D. Turner's views
            of Gullah speech.)

NA   Johnson, Guy B. "Folk Values in Recent Literature on the Negro," *Folk-Say*,
1628   2 (1930), 359-372.
            Examines the use of Negro dialects, songs, "superstitions," beliefs,
            tales, etc., in works by E.C.L. Adams, Roark Bradford, DuBose Heyward,
            Howard W. Odum, Julia Peterkin, and John B. Sale.

NA   Johnson, Guy B. "John Henry," *SW*, 56 (1927), 158-160.
1629   Notes on a black ballad; includes texts.

NA   Johnson, Guy B. "John Henry," in *Negro Anthology*, Nancy Cunard, ed. Lon-
1630   don: Wishart, 1934, 363-365.
            3 versions of "John Henry," with music.

NA
1631
    Johnson, Guy B. "John Henry--A Negro Legend," in *Ebony and Topaz*, Charles S. Johnson, ed. New York: National Urban League, 1927, 47-51.
        Essay on John Henry, with text and music of a ballad and a work song.

NA
1632
    Johnson, Guy B. *John Henry: Tracking Down a Negro Legend*. Chapel Hill, North Carolina: University of North Carolina Press, 1929.
        Inquiry into the genesis of the ballad and the legend; numerous stories, 11 hammer songs (few with music), 30 John Henry ballads (half with music).

NA
1633
    Johnson, Guy B. "The Negro and Musical Talent," *SW*, 56 (1927), 439-444.
        Argues that there are no significant inborn differences in talent between black and white musicians; (only black vocal quality is superior, but reflects anatomical differences rather than superior musicality).

NA
1634
    Johnson, Guy B. "Negro Folk Songs in the South," in *Culture in the South*, W.T. Couch, ed. Chapel Hill, N.C.: University of North Carolina Press, 1934, 547-569.
        The development of Negro songs in the South; the relationship of white and Negro song tradition; characteristics of Negro songs; examples of typical song texts.

NA
1635
    Johnson, Guy B. "The Negro Spiritual: A Problem in Anthropology," *AA*, 33 (1931), 157-171.
        Argues that "on the whole . . . the religious music which the negro (*sic*) developed during slavery was borrowed from white music."

NA
1636
    Johnson, Guy B. "Newspaper Advertisements and Negro Culture," *Social Forces*, 3 (1924-1925), 706-709.
        Gives several examples of ads for skin lightener, hair straightener, good luck charms, etc. Suggests this indicates a belief in magic and voodoo.

NA
1637
    Johnson, Guy B. "Recent Contributions to the Study of American Negro Songs," *Social Forces*, 4 (1926), 788-792.
        Review of literature on Negro secular and spiritual songs.

NA
1638
    Johnson, Guy B. "The Speech of the Negro," *Folk-Say*, 2 (1930), 346-358.
        Discusses characteristics of the speech in Negro narrative--phonology, grammar, vocabulary. Argues for the English origin of most of Negro speech.

Johnson, Guy B. See Odum, Howard W., and Guy B. Johnson, Nos. NA 2253, NA 2254, NA 2255.

Johnson, Guy B. See Woofter, T.J., Jr., No. NA 3283.

NA
1639
Johnson, Hall. *The Green Pastures Spirituals*. New York: Farrar and Rinehart, 1930.
25 spirituals from Louisiana.

NA
1640
Johnson, Hall. *Thirty Negro Spirituals*. New York: G. Schirmer, 1949.
Spirituals arranged for choral singing.

NA
1641
Johnson, J.H., and Ben Burns, eds. *The Best of Negro Humor*. Chicago: Johnson, 1945.

NA
1642
Johnson, J. Hugh. "Documentary Evidence of the Relations of Negroes and Indians," *JNH*, 14 (1929), 21-43.
Documented accounts of social attitudes of U.S. Indians and Negroes regarding language, customs, and intermarriage during the slavery era.

NA
1643
Johnson, J. Rosamond. *Rolling Along in Song: A Chronological Survey of American Negro Music*. New York: Viking, 1937.
Arrangements of 80 work songs, street cries, spirituals, ragtime tunes, etc.

NA
1644
Johnson, J. Rosamond. *Utica Jubilee Singers Spirituals*. Boston: Ditson, 1930.
38 songs with music.

NA
1645
Johnson, James Weldon. *Black Manhattan*. New York: Knopf, 1930.
A history of Harlem which includes discussion of early drama and musical theatre, dance, sports, parades, night life, etc.

NA
1646
Johnson, James Weldon. *The Book of American Negro Poetry: Chosen and Edited with an Essay on the Negro's Creative Genius*. New York: Harcourt, Brace, 1922.
Preface gives a brief history of Negro dialect poetry; a few narrative poems in Negro dialect.

NA 1647   Johnson, James Weldon. *The Book of American Negro Spirituals*. New York: Viking, 1925.
      A collection of 62 spirituals with an introduction by James W. Johnson and musical arrangements by J. Rosamond Johnson.

NA 1648   Johnson, James Weldon. *God's Trombones*. New York: Viking, 1927.
      7 sermons in verse written by the author but having their basis in actual practice. Discussion of preachers and their style.

NA 1649   Johnson, James Weldon. "Negro Folk Songs and Spirituals," *Mentor*, 17 (February, 1929), 50-52.

NA 1650   Johnson, James Weldon. *The Second Book of Negro Spirituals*. New York: Viking, 1926.
      61 songs with musical arrangements by J. Roseamond Johnson; introduction by James W. Johnson.

Johnson, James Weldon. See No. NA 1911.

NA 1651   Johnson, Mrs. John L. "Brer Terrapin Learns to Fly," *NCF*, 2, No. 1 (1954), 14-15.
      1 tale from Mississippi.

NA 1652   Johnson, Mrs. John L. "The Old Blind Mule," *NCF*, 12, No. 2 (1964), 25-26.
      1 protest tale with notes on its setting.

NA 1653   Johnson, Kenneth R. "Black Kinesics--Some Non-Verbal Communication Patterns in the Black Culture," *Florida FL Reporter*, 9 (Spring-Fall, 1971), 17-21, 57.
      Eye-rolling, eye aversion, stance, walk, laughter, greeting postures, handshakes and audience responses described and compared with those of whites.

NA 1654   Johnson, Kenneth R. "The Vocabulary of Race," in *Rappin' and Stylin' Out*, Thomas Kochman, ed. Urbana, Ill.: University of Illinois Press, 1972, 140-151.
      Terms for whites and blacks among blacks.

NA 1655   Johnson, Ruth Rogers. "A Love Letter from de Lord," in *Eve's Stepchildren*, Lealon N. Jones, ed. Caldwell, Idaho: Caxton Printers, 1942, 103-111.
      A description of an Afro-American church services in Missouri.

NA
1656
Johnston, Richard Malcolm. "The Old Field School in Middle Georgia," *SW*, 26 (1897), 76–77.
 Education of black children on the Georgia plantation.

NA
1657
Johnston, Ruby F. *The Development of Negro Religion*. New York: Philosophical Library, 1954.

NA
1658
Johnston, Ruby F. *The Religion of Negro Protestants*. New York: Philosophical Library, 1956.
 Sociological treatment of Negro religion; 3 chapters on "The Status of Emotionalism in Rural and Urban Areas,"--sermons, ritual behavior, etc.

NA
1659
Johnston, Mrs. William Preston. "Negro Hymn of the Judgment Day," *JAF*, 9 (1896), 210.
 Text of a hymn from North Carolina.

NA
1660
Johnston, Mrs. William Preston. "Two Negro Tales," *JAF*, 9 (1896), 194–198.
 2 animal tales with note on sources.

NA
1661
Jolas, Eugene. *Le Nègre Qui Chante*. Paris: Cahiers Libres, 1928.
 Collection of secular songs of uncertain provenience in the United States with an introductory essay.

NA
1662
Jones, A.M. "Blue Notes and Hot Rhythm," *African Music*, 1, No. 4 (1951), 9–12.
 The African element in jazz and blues.

NA
1663
Jones, Bessie, and Bess Lomax Hawes. *Step It Down: Games, Plays, Songs, and Stories from the Afro-American Heritage*. New York: Harper and Row, 1972.
 Texts and music of baby games, clapping plays, jumps and skips, singing plays, ring plays, dances, house plays, outdoor games, songs, tales, and riddles; with comments, directions for performing, notes on child care, terms for dance steps, bibliography, discography.

NA
1664
Jones, Charles Colcock. *Negro Myths from the Georgia Coast, Told in the Vernacular*. Boston, New York: Houghton, Mifflin, 1888.
 61 tales from the swamp region of Georgia and the Carolinas, from "rice-field" and "Sea-Island" Negroes. Collected before 1888. 23 rabbit tales, the remainder on various animals; 1 spirit tale, 1 vision tale.

NA
1665
Jones, Dazzie Lee. "Some Folktales from Negro College Students," *TFSB*, 24 (1958), 102-111.
10 short tales from students from urban backgrounds.

NA
1666
Jones, F.A. "Some Medical Superstitions among the Southern Negroes," *Journal of the American Medical Association*, 50 (1908), 1207.
A short letter from a Memphis doctor giving 3 folk cures.

NA
1667
Jones, Harry L. "Black Humor and the American Way of Life," *Satire Newsletter* (Oneonta, N.Y.), 7, No. 1 (1969), 1-4.
Black humor and its relation to American racial realities; Langston Hughes' "Simple" stories and their use of urban black folklore and speech.

NA
1668
Jones, Harry L. "An Essay on the Blues," *CLA Journal*, 13, No. 1 (1969), 62-67.

NA
1669
Jones, J. Ralph. "Portraits of Georgia Slaves," *Georgia Review*, 21 (1967), 126-132, 268-273, 407-411, 521-525; 22 (1968), 125-127, 254-257.
Slave narratives include reference to religious meeting, song fragments, manners, domestic life, dress, etc.

NA
1670
Jones, LeRoi (Imamu Amiri Baraka). "Blues, Jazz and the Negro," in *The American Negro Reference Book*, John P. Davis, ed. Englewood Cliffs, N.J.: Prentice-Hall, 1966, 759-765.
Brief history of jazz and its folk music components.

NA
1671
Jones, LeRoi (Imamu Amiri Baraka). *Blues People*. New York: Morrow, 1963.
A social study of the black man's music--blues and jazz--and its influence on American life. Includes discussion of the African and slave backgrounds, as well as the emergence of the contemporary Negro middle class in the city and its effects.

NA
1672
Jones, LeRoi (Imamu Amiri Baraka). *Home: Social Essays*. New York: Morrow, 1966.
Essays on Afro-American cuisine, music, language.

NA
1673
Jones, LeRoi (Imamu Amiri Baraka). *Raise Race Rays Raze: Essays since 1965*. New York: Random House, 1971.
Essays on black poetry, art, music and dance.

NA   Jones, LeRoi (Imamu Amiri Baraka). *Tales*. New York: Grove, 1967.
1674   Short stories of Northern urban life with folkloric content.

NA   Jones, Max. "Balladeer for America," *Folk*, 1 (February, 1945), 27-32.
1675   Essay, with texts, on blues singer Josh White.

NA   Jones, Max, and Albert McCarthy. *A Tribute to Huddie Ledbetter*. London:
1676   Jazz Music Books, 1946.

NA   Jones, Ralph H. *The Pepperpot Man*. New York: Vantage, 1965.
1677   Novel of free Negro life in Philadelphia in the 18th and 19th centuries;
            contains recipes.

NA   Jones, Raymond Julius. *A Comparative Study of Religious Cult Behavior
1678   Among Negroes with Special Reference to Emotional Group Conditioning
            Factors*. Washington, D.C.: Howard University Studies in Social Science,
            Vol. 2, No. 2, 1939.
            13 cults in New York City and Washington, D.C. seen as originating in
            white Protestant services, and in the psychological needs of the oppres-
            sed, but not in Africa; includes detailed accounts of services and a
            taxonomy and directory of cults.

NA   Jones, William H. *Recreation and Amusement Among Negroes in Washington,
1679   D.C. A Sociological Analysis of the Negro In an Urban Environment*.
            Washington, D.C.: Howard University Press, 1927.
            Chapters on cabarets, pool rooms, excursion boats, dance halls, barber
            shops, gangs, clubs, gambling, etc.

NA   Jones, William M. "Name and Symbol in the Prose of Eudora Welty," *SFQ*,
1680   22 (1958), 173-185.

NA   Joplin, Scott. *Collected Piano Works*, Vera Brodsky Lawrence, ed. New York:
1681   New York Public Library, 1971.
            Texts and music of Joplin's ragtime compositions and a discussion of
            the artist's life and music by Rudi Blesh.

NA   Jordan, Weymouth T. "Plantation Medicine in the Old South," *Alabama Review*,
1682   3 (1950), 83-107.
            Whites' cures for black illnesses based on the belief that blacks were
            of a different species.

NA
1683

Joseph, Stephen M. "Etc.; Playing the Dozens," *Commonwealth*, 91 (October 24, 1969), 101-102.
　　Formalized verbal training in Harlem; text of one "game."

NA
1684

Joyner, Charles W. *Folk Song in South Carolina*. Columbia: University of South Carolina Press, 1971.
　　Includes 2 ballads and 11 religious songs previously published and 2 other secular songs with discussion; bibliography, discography.

NA
1685

Joyner, Charles W. "Soul Food and the Sambo Stereotype: Foodlore in the Slave Narrative Collection," *KFQ*, 16 (1971), 171-178.

NA
1686

Joyner, Charles W. "Southern Folklore as a Key to Southern Identity," *Southern Humanities Review*, 1 (1967), 211-222.
　　Discusses Southern oral tradition, both musical and non-musical; argues that "Brer Rabbit" and "John the Conqueror" are European in origin; bibliography and discography.

NA
1687

The Jubilee. n.p., 1882-1883.
　　6 page broadsheet giving testimonials and descriptions of the Fisk University Jubilee Singers.

NA
1688

Jubilee and Plantation Songs. Boston: Ditson, 1887.
　　104 songs.

NA
1689

Jung, Carl G. "Your Negroid and Indian Behavior," *Forum*, 83 (April, 1930), 193-199.
　　The African influence on white America's humor, style, kinesics, etc.

NA
1690

Kaiser, Inez Y. *Soul Food Cookery*. New York: Pitman, 1968.

NA
1691

Kalm, Peter. *Travels into North America*. New York: Dover, 1966. (Original English version, Warrington: William Eyres, 1770, Vols. 1 & 2.)
　　Discusses poisoning of blacks by blacks.

NA
1692

Kane, Elisha K. "The Negro Dialects Along the Savannah River," *Dialect Notes*, 5, Part 8 (1925), 354-367.
　　An early attempt to transcribe Negro dialect phonetically.

NA
1693

Kane, Harnett T. *The Southern Christmas Book*. New York: David McKay, 1958.
Includes John Canoe, recipes, gift exchanges, etc.

NA
1694

Kane, Helen P. "Reception by the Dead," *JAF*, 5 (1892), 148.
Note on funeral customs and practices.

NA
1695

Kantrowitz, Nathan. "The Vocabulary of Race Relations in a Prison," *Publications of the American Dialect Society*, 51 (April, 1969), 23-34.

NA
1696

Kantrowitz, Nathan and Joanne. "Meet 'Mr. Franklin': An Example of Usage,"
in *Mother Wit from the Laughing Barrel*, Alan Dundes, ed. Englewood
Cliffs, New Jersey: Prentice-Hall, 1973, 348-352.
Prison usage of "motherfucker."

NA
1697

Kardiner, Abraham, and Lionel Ovesey. *The Mark of Oppression: Explorations
in the Personality of the American Negro*. New York: World Publishing,
1951.
Argues that Afro-Americans have no true culture of their own; for example, dance is a product of rage; treats folktales.

NA
1698

Katz, Bernard, ed. *The Social Implications of Early Negro Music in the
United States*. New York: The New York Times-The Arno Press, 1969.
Reprints 19th century periodical articles concerning ring shouts,
spirituals, hymns, etc.

NA
1699

Kaufman, William I., and Mary Cooper. *The Art of Creole Cookery*. New York:
Doubleday, 1962.

NA
1700

Kay, George W. "An Interview with Roy Carew," *The Ragtime Society*, 5, No.
6 (1966), 67-69.
Discusses origins and styles of ragtime.

NA
1701

Kay, George W. "William Christopher Handy, Father of the Blues--A History
of Published Blues," *JJ*, 24, No. 3 (1971), 10-12.
Examination of blues and "blues-like" compositions copyrighted before
and during 1912 (the year that W.C. Handy published "Memphis Blues.")

NA
1702

Kayser, Erhard. *Mahalia Jackson*. Wetzlar: Pegasus, 1962.

NA 1703 Kearney, Belle. *A Slaveholder's Daughter*. New York: Abbey Press, 1900.
Contains a sermon, description of slave dress, religious services, etc.

NA 1704 Keber, Helen Phillips. "Higher on the Hog," in *The Not So Solid South: Anthropological Studies in a Regional Subculture*. Southern Anthropological Society Proceedings No. 4, J. Kenneth Morland, ed. Athens, Georgia: University of Georgia Press, 1971, 4-15.
An ethnographic account of a healing cult in North Carolina.

NA 1705 Keeler, Ralph. "Three Years as a Negro Minstrel," *Atlantic Monthly*, 24 (1869), 71-85.

NA 1706 Keil, Charles. "Motion and Feeling through Music," *Journal of Aesthetics and Art Criticism* (1965-1966). (Reprinted in Kochman, No. NA 1756.)
Physical elements in the playing of jazz bassists and drummers.

NA 1707 Keil, Charles. *Urban Blues*. Chicago: University of Chicago Press, 1966.
A sociological study of the blues singer as a culture hero from the urban ghetto; includes a chart of blues styles and singers.

NA 1708 Keiser, R. Lincoln. *The Vice Lords: Warriors of the Streets*. New York: Holt, Rinehart and Winston, 1969.
An anthropological study of a Chicago gang: includes recreational activities, ideology, verbal routines, graffiti, the autobigraphy of a member, etc.

NA 1709 Keller, John E. "The Source of 'The Wolf, the Fox, and the Well,'" *NCF*, 7 (1959), 23-25.
Includes part of the tale, with discussion of its "oriental origin."

NA 1710 Kemble, Frances Anne. *Journal of a Residence on a Georgian Plantation in 1838-1839*. London: Longmans, 1863.
Descriptions of music, rowing songs, dress, cures, cuisine, manners, child training, etc.

NA 1711 Kempf, Paul, Jr. "Striking the Blue Note in Music," *Musician*, 34 (1929), 29.
A discussion of the blues, its content and musical form. Refers to W.C. Handy and his association with the blues.

NA   Kendall, John Smith. "New Orleans Negro Minstrels," *Louisiana Historical*
1712   *Quarterly*, 30 (1947), 128-148.
             Accounts of ante-bellum and reconstruction minstrels, mostly white;
             descriptions of parts, plays and props; society's reactions, etc.

NA   Kennedy, John Pendleton. *Swallow Barn, or A Sojourn in the Old Dominion*.
1713   Philadelphia: Carey and Lea, 1832.
             Novel include pen and ink sketches of black life and African houses in
             the U.S. South; the story is interwoven with anecdotes of blacks, music,
             dress, etc.

NA   Kennedy, Phillip Houston. "An Unusual Work-Song Found in North Carolina:
1714   'Ginnie's Gone to Ohio,'" *NCF*, 15, No. 1 (1967), 30-34.
             Origin of a work song.

NA   Kennedy, Rennick C. "Alas Poor Yorick," *Alabama Historical Quarterly*, 21
1715   (1940), 405-415.
             Includes black funeral customs.

NA   Kennedy, Robert Emmet. *Black Cameos*. New York: Boni, 1924.
1716   Stories and 17 songs with music from Southern Louisiana.

NA   Kennedy, Robert Emmet. *Gritny People*. New York: Dodd, Mead, 1927.
1717   Sketches of folklife in Louisiana.

NA   Kennedy, Robert Emmet. *Mellows: A Chronicle of Unknown Singers*. New York:
1718   Boni, 1925.
             Collection of work songs, street cries and spirituals from Louisiana
             with background of informants and introduction on the general history
             of spiritual literature.

NA   Kennedy, Robert Emmet. *More Mellows*. New York: Dodd, Mead, 1931.
1719   Collection of 7 spirituals, 16 "ballets," 12 arranged spirituals and
             2 folksongs from Louisiana. Discussion of texts and informants.

NA   Kennedy, Robert Emmet. *Red Bean Row*. New York: Dodd, Mead, 1929.
1720   Novel of Louisiana life with folkloric content.

NA   Kennedy, Stetson. "Cantantes Callejeros y la Cucaracha," *SFQ*, 6 (1942),
1721   149-151.
             A Cuban street song from Tampa and Key West (possibly black).

NA 1722   Kennedy, Stetson. "Nañigo In Florida," *SFQ*, 4 (1940), 153-156.
           An explanation and origin of the *Nañigo*, an Afro-Cuban cult.

NA 1723   Kennedy, Stetson. *Palmetto Country*. New York: Duell, Sloan, & Pearce,
           1942.
           Contains a chapter ("Black Magic") on voodoo and conjure practices in
           Florida.

NA 1724   Kent, Don. "An Interview with Rev. F.E. McGee," *American Folk Music Oc-
           casional, No. 2*, New York: Oak, 1970.
           Biography of an influential pentecostal preacher who recorded in the
           1920's.

NA 1725   Kent, George. *Blackness and the Adventure of Western Culture*. Chicago:
           Third World Press, 1972.
           Essays on black writers: includes the folk backgrounds for the writings
           of Claude McKay, Langston Hughes, Ralph Ellison and others.

NA 1726   Kent, George. "Ralph Ellison and Afro-American Folk and Cultural Tradition,"
           CLA Journal, 13 (1970), 265-276. (Reprinted in *Ralph Ellison: A Col-
           lection of Critical Essays*, John Hersey, ed. Englewood Cliffs, N.J.:
           Prentice-Hall, 1974, 160-170.
           Folk symbols and themes in Ellison's writings.

NA 1727   Kerby, Marion. "A Warning Against Over-Refinement of the Negro Spiritual,"
           The Musician, 33 (July, 1928), 9, 29-30.
           The "refinement" of black folk music may cause a loss of the special
           qualities which make the music form distinct.

NA 1728   Kerlin, Robert Thomas. "'Canticles of Love and Woe': Negro Spirituals,"
           SW, 50 (1921), 62-64.
           The emotional appeal of the Negro spiritual.

NA 1729   Kerlin, Robert Thomas. *Negro Poets and Their Poems*. Washington, D.C.:
           Associated Publishers, 1923.
           Chapter 1 includes samples of spirituals and secular songs.

NA 1730   Keyes, Frances Parkinson. *All This is Louisiana*. New York: Harper, 1950.
           An "illustrated story book" with miscellaneous material on Mardi Gras,
           baptisms, etc. Includes a photo of a slave-built African house in
           Louisiana (p. 112).

NA   Kibbins. "Negro Maxims," *New York Times*, September 15, 1889, 1.
1731   A list of sayings.

NA   Kidd, Jim. "Louis Hooper," *RR*, 77 (1966), 2-9.
1732   The background of a blues-jazz pianist from the early jazz years; dis-
            cography.

NA   Kilham, Elizabeth. "Sketches in Color: 4," *Putnam's Monthly*, 15 (March,
1733   1870), 304-311. (Reprinted in No. NA 1568.)
            Description of a church service; texts and style of hymns.

NA   Killion, Ronald, and Charles Waller, eds. *Slavery Time When I Was Chillun
1734   Down on Marster's Plantation*. Savannah, Georgia: Beehive Press, 1973.
            WPA interviews with ex-slaves in Georgia; illustrations.

NA   Killion, Ronald G., and Charles T. Waller, eds. *A Treasury of Georgia
1735   Folklore*. Atlanta: Cherokee, 1972.
            A collection of miscellaneous folklore material from the WPA collec-
            tion; contains black material scattered throughout.

NA   King, Bruce. "The Formative Years," *JM*, 13, No. 4 (1967), 5-7.
1736   A discussion of African influences in New Orleans Jazz, as evidenced
            in travelers' writings.

NA   King, Bruce. "The Gigantic Baby Dodds," *The Jazz Review*, 3, No. 7 (1960),
1737   12-15.
            Analysis of the playing of an early New Orleans drummer.

NA   King, Edward. *The Great South*. Hartford, Conn.: American Publishing Co.,
1738   1875.
            Discusses Negro songs and singing, housing, religion, speech making,
            diet, vocabulary, and "military" drilling.

NA   King, Henry T. *Sketches of Pitt County, 1804-1910*. Raleigh, N.C.: Brough-
1739   ton & Co., 1911.

NA   King, Woodie, Jr. "The Game," *Liberator* (New York City), 5 (1965), 20-25.
1740   (Reprinted in No. NA 1756.)
            Description of urban street life, "gaming," and verbal art.

NA   "King Emanuel," *SW*, 36 (1907), 394.
1741   A spiritual with music.

NA   "King of the Gospel Writers," *Ebony*, 18 (November, 1962), 122-127.
1742

NA   Kingsley, Walter. "Enigmatic Folksongs of the Southern Underworld," *Current Opinion*, 17 (1919), 165-166.
1743   Evidence of white performers' early use of the blues; the public view of blues as outlaw music.

NA   Kingsley, Z. *A Treatise on the Patriarchal, or Co-operative, System of Society as It Exists in Some Governments, and Colonies in America, and in the United States, Under the Name of Slavery, with its Necessity and Advantages.* 2nd edition. n.p., 1829.
1744

NA   Kirby, Percival R. "A Study of Negro Harmony," *MQ*, 16 (1900), 404-414.
1745   Demonstrates that Negro spirituals have a basic African musical structure, influenced by European harmony.

NA   Kirke, Edmund. *Among the Pines*. New York: Carleton, 1863.
1746   Contains descriptions of slave life: bands, parades, singing (song texts, pp. 42-43), dialect, "superstitions," beliefs in omens; descriptions of cabins, furniture, etc.

NA   Kirke, Edmund. *My Southern Friends*. New York: Carleton, 1863.
1747   Contains descriptions of slave meetings for worship, with a fiddle orchestra accompanying Watts' hymns; an African woman's clairvoyance and possession; conjurer's bags called "waiters;" a plantation Christmas; dress, speeches and dancing at a wedding, etc.

NA   Klatzko, Bernard. "In the Spirit, No. 1 and No. 2," record notes to Origin Jazz Library LP records 12 and 13.
1748   History and music of the Negro church with an interview with Rev. F.W. McGee and sketches of a number of artists; emphasis on the Church of God in Christ in Mississippi; discography.

NA   Kloe, Donald R. "Buddy Quow: An Anonymous Poem in Gullah-Jamaican Dialect Written circa 1800," *SFQ*, 38 (1974), 81-90.
1749   An early Creole poem of race consciousness and protest.

NA   Kmen, Henry A. *Music in New Orleans: The Formative Years 1791-1841*. Baton
1750   Rouge: Louisiana State University Press, 1966.
           Chapter 12, "Negro Music," covers folklore and social dancing.

NA   Kmen, Henry A. "Old Corn Meal: A Forgotten Urban Negro Folksinger," *JAF*,
1751   75 (1962), 29-34.
           Description of the style of performance of a New Orleans folksinger of
           the 1830's and 1840's.

NA   Kmen, Henry A. "The Roots of Jazz and the Dance in Place Congo: A Reap-
1752   praisal," in *Yearbook for Interamerican Musical Research* (Austin, Texas),
           8 (1972), 5-16.
           An assessment and interpretation of the various writings on Place Congo
           dancing and music.

NA   Knight, Henry C. *Letters from the South and West*. Boston, 1824.
1753   Account of Congo Square dancing in New Orleans (pp. 127), slave funer-
           als and the spirits' return to Africa (pp. 77, 352), etc.

NA   Kochman, Thomas. "Black American Speech Events and a Language Program for
1754   the Classroom," in *Functions of Language in the Classroom*, Courtney B.
           Cazden, Vera P. John, and Dell Hymes, eds. New York: Teachers College
           Press, 1972, 211-261.
           A brief ethnography of types of Afro-American speech events and oral
           genres; includes texts.

NA   Kochman, Thomas. "The Kinetic Element in Black Idiom," in *Rappin' and
1755   Stylin' Out*, Thomas Kochman, ed. Urbana, Ill.: University of Illinois
           Press, 1972, 160-169.
           Connotations of motion and stasis in black vocabulary.

NA   Kochman, Thomas, ed. *Rappin' and Stylin' Out: Communication in Urban Black
1756   America*. Urbana, Ill.: University of Illinois Press, 1972.
           Essays on nonverbal communication, vocabulary, expressive roles and
           verbal art.

NA   Kochman, Thomas. "'Rappin' in the Black Ghetto," *Trans-action*, 6 (May,
1757   1969), 26-34. (Abbreviated version of No. NA 1758.)

NA   Kochman, Thomas. "Toward an Ethnography of Black American Speech Behavior,"
1758   in *Afro-American Anthropology: Contemporary Perspectives*, Norman E.
           Whitten, Jr. and John F. Szwed, eds. New York: Free Press, 1970, 145-
           162.
           Techniques and varieties of speaking in a northern U.S. city.

NA 1759   Kohl, Herbert. "Names, Graffiti, and Culture," *The Urban Review*, 3, No. 5 (1969), 24-38.
Wall graffiti explained; illustrations.

NA 1760   Kohl, Herbert, and James Hinton. *Golden Boy as Anthony Cool: A Photo Essay on Naming and Graffiti*. New York: Dial Press, 1972.
The meaning and functions of graffiti and wall paintings in American black and Puerto-Rican communities; naming practices; book, notebook and jacket names; insults and slogans.

NA 1761   Krapp, George P. "The English of the Negro," *American Mercury*, 2 (1924), 190-195.
Argues that the speech of the American Negro is Old English and that he has retained little if any African patterns or words.

NA 1762   Krapp, George P. "Notes and Queries, No. 155," *American Mercury*, 8 (1926), 240.
Suggests an origin for "coon."

NA 1763   Krehbiel, Henry Edward. *Afro-American Folksongs*. New York: G. Schirmer, 1914.
A study of the musical elements of Afro-American songs with emphasis on comparative analysis to discover distinctive idioms and origins of the musical style. Language and songs of the black Creoles also included.

NA 1764   Krehbiel, Henry Edward. "Folk Music Studies: Slave Songs in America," *New York Tribune*, September 10, 1899, 1-11.

NA 1765   Krehbiel, Henry Edward. "Lafcadio Hearn and Congo Music," *The Musician*, 11 (1906), 544-545.

NA 1766   Kriss, Eric. *Six Blues-Root Pianists*. New York: Oak, 1973.
The styles of Jimmy Yancey, Speckled Red, Roosevelt Sykes, *et al.*, with transcriptions, discography, bibliography.

NA 1767   Krueger, E.T. "Negro Religious Expression," *American Journal of Sociology*, 38 (1932), 22-31.
Cultural explanation of Negro religious expression; the revival, rhythm, interest in magic, etc.

NA
1768
Kunkel, Peter, and Sara Sue Kennard. *Spout Spring: A Black Community*. New York: Holt, Rinehart and Winston, 1971.
An ethnographic study of a black Arkansas community; includes discussion of cultural themes, material culture, domestic life, dress, recreation, music and dance, sports, religious activities, etc.; illustrations.

NA
1769
Kunstadt, Len. "The Lucille Hegamin Story," *RR*, 39 (November, 1961), 3-7; 40 (January, 1962), 3, 19; 41 (February, 1962), 4-5; 43 (May, 1962), 6.
Biography of a "city" blues singer of the 1920's and 1930's.

NA
1770
Kunstadt, Len. "Mamie Smith--The First Lady of the Blues," *RR*, No. 57 (1964), 3-12.
Background of a blues singer with other information by Victoria Spivy. Illustrations, discography.

NA
1771
Kups of Kauphy: A Georgia Book, in Warp and Woof, Containing Tales, Incidents, etc., of the "Empire State of the South," with a Slight Sketch of the Well-Known and Eccentric "Colored Gemman," Old Jack C . . . By "K of K." Athens, Georgia: Christie and Kelsea, 1853.

NA
1772
Kurath, Gertrude P. "Afro-Wesleyan Liturgical Structures," *MF*, 13 (1963), 29-32.
The structure of ritual events in Methodist and Baptist Afro-American churches compared to those of West Africa, Brazil, and Trinidad.

NA
1773
Kurath, Gertrude P. "Rhapsodies of Salvation: Negro Responsory Hymns," *SFQ*, 20 (1956), 178-182.
The musical structure of such hymns and certain elements related to blues and jazz found in them.

NA
1774
Kurath, Gertrude P. "Stylistic Blends in Afro-American Dance Cults of Catholic Origin," *Papers of the Michigan Academy of Science, Arts and Letters*, 48 (1963), 577-584.

NA
1775
Kurath, Gertrude P. "Syncopated Therapy," *MF*, 1 (1951), 179-186.
Hymn singing in an Ann Arbor, Michigan church; includes 2 texts with music.

NA
1776
Kurath, Gertrude P., and Nadia Chilkovsky. "Jazz Choreology," in *Man and Culture: Proceedings of the Fifth International Congress of Anthropological and Ethnological Sciences*, Anthony Wallace, ed. Philadelphia:

University of Pennsylvania Press, 1960, 152-159.
The folk sources of a variety of popular songs and jazz dances: Big
Apple, Truckin', Jitterbugging, Lindy Hop, etc.; the common character-
istics of dances; Afro-American analogues elsewhere in the Americas.

NA
1777
Labov, William. "The Logic of Non-Standard English," in *Georgetown University Monograph in Language and Linguistics*, No. 22, J. Alatis, ed.,
1969, 1-44. (Published in condensed form as "Academic Ignorance and
Black Intelligence," *Atlantic Monthly*, 229, No. 6 (1972), 59-67.)

NA
1778
Labov, William. "Rules for Ritual Insults," in *Rappin' and Stylin' Out,*
Thomas Kochman, ed. Urbana, Ill.: University of Illinois Press, 1972,
265-314.
Rules for sounding, playing the dozens and signifying among blacks
and whites; includes texts.

NA
1779
Labov, William, Paul Cohen, Clarence Robins, and John Lewis. *A Study of
the Non-Standard English of Negro and Puerto Rican Speakers in New
York City*, 2 vols. (mimeo) New York: Columbia University, 1968.
Vol. 1 contains phonological and grammatical analysis. Vol. 2 contains
narrative analysis, discussion, and examples of toasts and ritual insults.

NA
1780
Ladner, Robert, Jr. "Folk Music, Pholk Music, and the Angry Children of
Malcolm X," *SFQ*, 34 (1970), 131-145.
Discussion of the use of modern folk music in racial pride.

NA
1781
Lagarde, Marie-Louise. "A South Louisiana Negro 'Baptizing,'" *LFM*, 2,
No. 4 (1968), 45-55.
Baptismal ceremonies; white-black interaction at the rituals, etc.

NA
1782
Lake, Mary Daggett. "Pioneer Christmas Customs of Tarrant County," *PTFS*,
No. 5 (1926), 107-111.
Includes a brief description of the Christmas celebration for the
slaves (p. 111).

NA
1783
Lake, Mary Daggett. "Superstitions about Cotton," *PTFS*, No. 9 (1931),
145-152.
Collections of "superstitions" written by Negro pupils.

NA
1784
La Mer, Nathaniel. "Creole Love Song," *Atlantic Monthly*, 195, No. 6 (June,
1955), 39-45.
Short story of New Orleans life with folk medicine content.

NA   Lamkin, Marjorie, and Wendell Hall. *Southern Songs and Spirituals*. Chicago:
1785   Forster Music, 1926.
            Includes 4 spirituals from Mississippi.

NA   Landes, Ruth. "Negro Slavery and Female Status," in *Les Afro-Américains*,
1786   Mémoir 27, Institut Français d'Afrique Noir, Dakar, 1953, 265-268.
            African cultural precedents combined with slavery practices to elevate
            the status of black women vis-a-vis black men.

NA   Lane, Ann J., ed. *The Debate Over Slavery: Stanley Elkins and His Critics*.
1787   Urbana, Ill.: University of Illinois, 1971.
            Collection of critical essays on Elkins' *Slavery* with a rejoinder by
            Elkins.

NA   Lane, George S. "The Negro-French Dialect," *Language*, 11 (1935), 5-16.
1788   Linguistic study of Creole in St. Martinville, Louisiana.

NA   Lang, Iain. *Jazz in Perspective; the Background of the Blues*. London:
1789   Hutchinson, 1947. (Incorporates earlier versions: "The Background of
            the Blues," in *The Saturday Book 1941-42*, Leonard Russell, ed. London:
            Hutchinson, 1941, 330-357; *Background of the Blues*. London: Workers'
            Music Association, 1943.)
            A discussion of the history and development of jazz from New Orleans
            into the 1920's; African and European influences; one section is devoted
            to themes and poetry in blues; includes 60 blues texts.

NA   Langhor, Mrs. O. "Street Scene in a Virginia Village," *SW*, 23 (1894), 158-
1790   159.
            Sketches of Southern black children's street play; games and riddles.

NA   Lanier, Sidney. *The Science of English Verse*. New York: Scribner's, 1880.
1791   Brief discussion of the metrics of Juba dancing, pp. 186-187.

NA   Lanusse, Armand, *et al. Les Cenelles. Choix de Poésies Indigènes*. New Or-
1792   leans: H. Lauve, 1845. (Reprinted as *Creole Voices*, Edward M. Coleman,
            ed. Washington, D.C., 1945.)
            An anthology of poetry in Creole and Standard French by 17 free "mu-
            latto" poets from New Orleans. Also see Edward L. Tinker, No. NA 2999.

NA   Latrobe, Benjamin Henry. *Impressions Respecting New Orleans*. New York:
1793   Columbia University Press, 1951. (Originally published New York, 1905).
            Describes Congo square dancing, a funeral, musical instruments; illus-
            trations.

NA 1794   Laubenstein, Paul F. "Race Values in Afro-American Music," *MQ*, 16 (1930), 378-403.
    The "religious nature" of the Negro as the source of the spirituals.

NA 1795   Law, Robert Adger. "A Note on Four Negro Words," *PTFS*, No. 6 (1927), 119-120.
    Origins traced of "buckra," "pinder," "Niam," and "broadus."

NA 1796   Lawless, Ray M. *Folksingers and Folksongs in America*, 2nd revised edition. New York: Duell, Sloan, 1965. (First published, New York: Duell, Sloan, 1960.)
    Research guide includes bibliography, discography, biographies of Negro folksingers.

NA 1797   Laws, G. Malcolm, Jr. *Native American Balladry: A Descriptive Study and a Bibliographical Syllabus*. Philadelphia: The American Folklore Society, 1964.
    Discussion of themes, subjects, and patterns of Negro ballads with portions of over 20 ballads as examples.

NA 1798   Lawton, Samuel Miller. *The Religious Life of South Carolina Coastal and Sea Island Negroes*. Abstract of Contribution to Education No. 242, George Peabody College for Teachers, Nashville, Tennessee, 1939.
    A 6-page abstract of a dissertation, an ethnographic study of church organization, "Pray's House," singing, theology, possession, grave decorations, African backgrounds, etc.

NA 1799   Leach, MacEdward, and Horace P. Beck. "Songs from Rappahannock County, Va.," *JAF*, 63 (1950), 257-284.
    Includes 8 songs with music.

NA 1800   Leach, Maria. *The Rainbow Book of American Folk Tales and Legends*. Cleveland: World, 1958.
    Includes Negro folk tales republished from other collections.

NA 1801   Leadbitter, Mike. *Crowley, Louisiana Blues*. Oxford, U.K.: Blues Unlimited, 1968.
    Story of J.D. Miller, blues recording entrepreneur of Louisiana, and background of the artists he recorded: Slim Harpo, Cleve White, Henry Clement, Jimmy Anderson, Silas Hogan, Joe Johnson, Moses Smith, Jim Dotson, Katie Webster, and Charlier Morris. Illustrations.

NA 1802   Leadbitter, Mike. *Delta Country Blues*. Oxford, U.K.: Blues Unlimited, 1968.
   Biographies of bluesmen Howlin' Wolf, Sonny Boy Williamson, Elmore
   James, Doctor Ross, Ike Turner, Robert Nighthawk, B.B. King, Willie
   Nix, Sharkey Hortar, Junior Parker, James Cotton, Woodrow Adams, Elwar
   'Slim' Mickle. Uses lyrics in an attempt to trace them back to their
   original source. Illustrations.

NA 1803   Leadbitter, Mike, ed. *Nothing But the Blues*. London: Hanover, 1971.
   A tour of blues "regions" of the U.S.; anthology of blues articles
   from the magazine *Blues Unlimited*; illustrations.

NA 1804   Leadbitter, Mike, and Eddie Shuler. *From the Bayou*. Oxford, U.K.: Blues
   Unlimited, 1967.
   Story of Goldband Records in Lake Charles, Louisiana which recorded
   many Cajun bands and bluesmen; with background of musicians. Illustrations.

NA 1805   Lear, Martha Weinman. "New York's Haitians: Working, Waiting, Watching,
   Watching Bé Bé Doc," *New York Times Magazine*, October 10, 1971, 22-23,
   25, 27, 30, 32, 34, 36, 39, 41.
   Includes discussion of Haitian culture in New York City; attitudes
   towards voodoo, etc.

NA 1806   LeConte, Joseph. *The Autobiography of Joseph LeConte*. New York: Appleton,
   1903.
   A coastal Georgia slaveholder's memoirs; includes discussion of having
   learned to count in Fulani (African) from a slave.

NA 1807   LeDoux, David. "Tales and Superstitions," *TFSB*, 32 (1966), 55-56.
   An "old folk story" told in Cajun dialect.

NA 1808   Lee, Collins. "Some Negro Lore from Baltimore," *JAF*, 5 (1892), 110-112.
   A list of "superstitions."

NA 1809   Lee, F.H., ed. *Folk Tales of All Nations*. New York: Tudor, 1946.
   Negro tales, pp. 112-119.

NA 1810   Lee, Florence Whiting. "An Old-Time Virginia Party," *SW*, 36 (1907), 624-
   627.
   Includes a description of Negro musicians at a white party and the
   music played.

NA   Lee, George W. *Beale Street: Where the Blues Began*. New York: R.O. Bal-
1811   lou, 1934.
            Comments on street life, music, etc.; introduction by W.C. Handy.

NA   Lee, Hector. "Leadbelly's 'Frankie and Albert,'" *JAF*, 64 (1951), 314-317.
1812   An example of Leadbelly's use of spoken narration and exposition in a
            song.

NA   Lee, Hector. "Some Notes on Leadbelly," *JAF*, 76 (1963), 135-140.
1813   Description of several days spent with Leadbelly in 1946. Includes song
            texts of "We're in the Same Boat Brother" and an improvised song about
            Salt Lake City.

NA   Lee, Robert Charles. "The Afro-American Foundations of the Jazz Idiom,"
1814   *Jazz Forum* (Warsaw), No. 11 (1971), 68-79; No. 12 (1971), 68-81; No.
            13-14 (1971), 86-93; No. 15 (1972), 84-86; No. 16 (1972), 74-77.
            A survey of the African backgrounds of jazz, Afro-American folk music,
            minstrelsy, etc.; includes examples, bibliography.

NA   Lee, Robert Charles. "The American Negro Work Songs," *Jazz Forum* (Warsaw),
1815   No. 6 (1969), 63-64.

NA   Lee, Robert Charles. "Semantic Phenomena in Early Jazz Popularization and
1816   its Social Opposition," *Jazz Forum* (Warsaw), No. 5 (1969), 52.

NA   Lee, Robert, and Ralph L. Roy. "The Negro Church," *Christian Century*,
1817   74 (1957), 1285-1287.
            Organization of Negro churches; beliefs, possession, etc.

NA   Lee, Rosa Fairfax. "How the Clock Saved 'Ole Mis', A Colonial Tale of
1818   Jamestown Island," *SW*, 40 (1911), 46-51.
            1 tale.

NA   Lee, Rosa Fairfax. "Sis Ho'net's Ne's," *SW*, 35 (1906), 42-45.
1819   1 tale.

NA   Lee, Rosa Fairfax. "Unc' Hardy's Witch," *SW*, 34 (1905), 150-153.
1820   1 tale.

NA   Lee, Rosa Fairfax. "Uncle Jim and Aunt Meg," *SW*, 36 (1907), 97-104.
1821   Story of an ex-slave's recollections of "Massa" and plantation life.

NA
1822
"Legitimizing the Music of the Negro," *Current Opinion*, 54 (1913), 384-385.
    Accounts of awakened interest in Negro folksongs and folklore; Negro music as a source of interracial harmony; illustrations.

NA
1823
Legman, G. "Poontang," *AS*, 25 (1950), 234-235.
    Origin and usage of term.

NA
1824
Lehmann, Theo. "Die Bedeutung der Negro Spirituals für Unseren Kirchenge-sang," *Die Zeichen der Zeit*, 15 (1961), 28-30.

NA
1825
Lehmann, Theo. *Blues and Trouble*. Berlin: Henschelverlag, 1966.

NA
1826
Lehmann, Theo. *Negro Spirituals: Geshichte und Theologie*. East Germany: Eckart, 1965.
    Negro social and religious history and its relation to the spiritual and gospel song; spirituals as poetry, theology and eschatology; the relation of the spiritual to the blues and jazz; symbolism; bibliography; discographical references in footnotes.

NA
1827
Leiding, Harriette K. *Street Cries of an Old Southern City*. Charleston, S.C.: Dagget Printing, 1910.
    8 texts with melodies.

NA
1828
Leigh, James Wentworth. *Other Days*. London: Unwin, 1921.
    Description of plantation life on the Sea Islands of South Carolina and Georgia.

NA
1829
Leiser, Willie. *I'm a Road Runner Baby*. Oxford, U.K.: Blues Unlimited, 1969.
    Itinerary of Leiser's visit to the U.S. and an account of the blues and gospel musicians he met.

NA
1830
Leiser, Willie. *Touch Me, Lord Jesus*. Oxford, U.K.: Blues Unlimited, Collectors Classics 11, 1966.
    Report of a "field trip" into the gospel music of the Eastern and Mid-Western United States.

NA
1831
LeJeune, Emilie. "Creole Folk Songs," *Louisiana Historical Quarterly*, 2 (1919), 454-462.
    Contains the texts of a number of songs.

NA   LeJeune, Emilie. "Creole Songs," *Music Teachers National Association,*
1832   *Proceedings*, Series 12 (1917), 23-28.
            2 songs with a short discussion of expression and content.

NA   Lemmerman, Karl. "Improvised Negro Songs," *New Republic*, 13 (December 22,
1833   1917), 214-215.
            Texts of 6 spirituals sung by black dam workers ca. 1907.

NA   Leonard, Neil. *Jazz and the White Americans*. Chicago: University of Chicago
1834   Press, 1962.
            An account of resistance to the diffusion of jazz in the United States.

NA   Lester, Julius. *Black Folktales*. New York: Richard W. Baron, 1969.
1835   12 rewritten folk tales, with notes to original sources.

NA   Lester, Julius. "Country Blues Come to Town: The View from the Other
1836   Side of the Tracks," *SO*, 14 (1964), 37-39.

NA   Lester, Julius. "Gospel," *SO*, 16, No. 6 (1967), 23.
1837   Description of a gospel meeting and its implications.

NA   Lester, Julius. "High John the Conqueror," *SO*, 14, No. 6 (1964), 18-22.
1838   Several "John" tale texts with discussion.

NA   Lester, Julius. *The Knee-High Man and Other Tales*. New York: Dial, 1972.
1839   6 retold tales.

NA   Lester, Julius. "'Mister White, Take a Break' An Interview with Booker
1840   (Bukka) White," *SO*, 18, No. 4 (1968), 4-15, 18-19, 23, 67.
            An interview covering Southern music traditions, the blues revival,
            etc.

NA   Lester, Julius, and Pete Seeger. *The Folksinger's Guide to the 12-String
1841   Guitar as Played by Leadbelly*. New York: Oak, 1965.
            An instruction manual with songs by Leadbelly; bibliography and dis-
            cography.

NA   "Let De Heaven Light Shine on Me," *SW*, 37 (1908), 272.
1842   A plantation song with music.

NA   "Let Us Cheer the Weary Traveler," *SW*, 54 (1925), 368.
1843   1 spiritual text.

NA   Lett, Anna. "Some West Tennessee Superstitions about Conjurers, Witches,
1844   Ghosts and the Devil," *TFSB*, 36, No. 2 (1970), 37-45.
             A fortune-teller and sorceress in Jackson, Tennessee relates "supersti-
             tions" and magical practices.

NA   Levine, Lawrence W. "The Concept of the New Negro and the Realities of
1845   Black Culture," in *Key Issues in the Afro-American Experience*, Vol. 2,
             Nathan I. Huggins, Martin Kilson, and Daniel M. Fox, eds. New York:
             Harcourt, Brace, Jovanovich, 1971, 125-147.
             Black folk music as protest.

NA   Levine, Lawrence W. "Slave Songs and Slave Consciousness," in *Anonymous
1846   Americans: Explorations in Nineteenth Century Social History*, Tamara K.
             Hareven, ed. Englewood Cliffs, New Jersey: Prentice-Hall, 1971, 99-
             130.
             An analysis of political consciousness, world view and theology as re-
             flected in slave songs.

NA   Levinson, Andre. "The Negro Dance under European Eyes," *Theatre Arts
1847   Monthly*, 11 (1927), 282-293. (Reprinted in *The Negro in American
             Theatre*, Edith J.R. Isaacs, ed. New York: Theatre Arts, Inc., 1947.)
             Analysis of Josephine Baker's dancing, compared to "classic" dance,
             with commentary on its "savage" implications.

NA   Lewis, George. *Impressions of America and the American Churches*. Edin-
1848   burgh: W.P. Kennedy, 1845.
             Description of slave house furnishings and dress in Washington, D.C.;
             funeral parties in Augusta, Georgia; "shouting."

NA   Lewis, Hylan. *Blackways of Kent*. Chapel Hill: University of North Carolina
1849   Press, 1955.
             A community study in the South with mention of music and religion.

NA   Lewis, Julian H. "In Defense of Chittlins," *Negro Digest*, 8 (April, 1950),
1850   74-78.

NA   Light, Kathleen. "Uncle Remus and the Folklorists," *The Southern Literary
1851   Journal*, 7 (1975), 88-104.
             Joel Chandler Harris' knowledge of folklore studies during his time and
             its effect on his publications.

NA 1852   Lightfoot, William E. "Charlie Parker: A Contemporary Folk Hero," *KFQ*, 17 (1972), 51-62.
Legends of a jazz musician.

NA 1853   Lilje, Hanns, Kurt Heinrich Hansen, and Siegfried Schmidt-Joos. *Das Buch den Spirituals und Gospel Songs*. Hamburg: Furche Verlag, 1961.
Discusses the history and form of gospel music.

NA 1854   Lindemann, Bill. "Black Gospel Music," *Living Blues*, No. 6 (Autumn, 1971), 21-22.
Discussion of the background and style of gospel music.

NA 1855   Linton, William J., ed. *Poetry of America*, London: George Bell, 1878, 379-387.
Includes texts of 5 spirituals, 3 work songs; 1 lyric, 4 spirituals with music reprinted from other sources.

NA 1856   Lipskin, Mike, and Len Kundstadt. "This is William D. Gant," *RR*, No. 60, (1960), 3-4, 16.
Story of Gant, a blues-jazz pianist in New York during the early 1900's.

NA 1857   "Literature of the Day: *Slave Songs of the United States* (review)," *Lippincott's Magazine*, 1 (March, 1868), 341-343. (Reprinted in No. NA 1568.)
The slaves's songs seen as inferior music.

NA 1858   Livermore, Mary. A. *The Story of My Life or The Sunshine and Shadows of Seventy Years*. Hartford, Conn.: A.D. Worthington, 1899.
Describes a sermon, beliefs, broom-jumping ceremonies, corn-shucking, etc.; includes a shucking song.

NA 1859   Lloyd, John U. "The Language of the Kentucky Negro," *Dialect Notes*, 2 (1901), 179-184.

NA 1860   Lloyd, John U. *Springtime on the Pike*. New York: Dodd, Mead, 1900.
Novel of life in Kentucky during the Civil War contains "superstitions" and 2 folktale texts.

NA 1861   Locke, Alain Le Roy. *The Negro and His Music*. Washington, D.C.: Associates in Negro Folk Education, 1936.
The folk, popular and classical contribution of the Negro to American

music, including discussions of spirituals, blues, work songs, minstrelsy, ragtime, etc.

NA   Locke, Alain Le Roy. "The Negro Spirituals," in *The New Negro*, Alain Locke,
1862   ed. New York: Boni, 1925, 199-213.
           Review of early literature on spirituals and a plea for their develop-
           ment into art music.

NA   Locke, Alain Le Roy. "Spirituals," in *75 Years of Freedom. Commemoration
1863   of the 75th Anniversary of the 13th Amendment to the Constitution of
           the U.S.* Washington, D.C.: Library of Congress, 1943, 7-15.
           An essay on symbolic meanings in the spiritual.

NA   Locke, Alain Le Roy, and Sterling A. Brown. "Folk Values in a New Medium,"
1864   *Folk-Say*, 2 (1930), 340-345.
           Reviews of two movies dealing with Negroes: "Hearts in Dixie," and
           "Hallelujah."

NA   Locke, Don. "The Importance of Jelly Roll Morton," *JJ*, 12, No. 6 (1959),
1865   2-4.
           The role of early jazzman Morton in American music.

NA   Locke, Don. "Jelly Roll Morton--the Library of Congress Recordings," *JJ*,
1866   13, No. 1 (1960), 15-18.
           Discussion of Morton's recorded musical biography.

NA   Lockwood, J. Palmer. *Darkey Sermons from Charleston County.* Columbia, S.C.:
1867   The State Co., 1925.
           3 "sermons" by a white in Gullah dialect.

NA   Logan, Rayford W., ed. *The New Negro: Thrity Years Afterward.* Washington,
1868   D.C.: Howard University Press, 1955.
           Articles on black culture, literature, art, etc., by Logan, E. Franklin
           Frazier, Charles S. Johnson, *et al.*

NA   Logan, William A. "Song Gleaning among the Cabins," *The Musician*, 44
1869   (July, 1939), 122, 127.
           Memoirs of a search for spirituals.

NA   Logan, William A., and Allen M. Garrett. *Road to Heaven.* University, Ala-
1870   bama: University of Alabama Press, 1955.
           28 spirituals (with music) from Alabama, Arkansas, Georgia, Kentucky,
           Mississippi, North Carolina, South Carolina, and Virginia.

NA 1871   Loman, Bengt, ed. *Conversations in a Negro American Dialect*. Washington, D.C.: Center for Applied Linguistics, 1967.
Transcribed conversations of Washington, D.C. children; includes several folktales.

NA 1872   Lomax, Alan. "Afro-American Blues and Game Songs," booklet included with Library of Congress Music Division LP record AFS 14.
Texts and discussion of 24 songs.

NA 1873   Lomax, Alan. "Afro-American Spirituals, Work Songs and Ballads," booklet included with Library of Congress Music Division LP record AAFS L3.
Texts and discussion of 17 songs.

NA 1874   Lomax, Alan. "American Folksongs for Children," booklet included with Atlantic LP record 1350.
Discussion of 7 children's game songs, lullabies, and banjo tunes from the Deep South.

NA 1875   Lomax, Alan. "The Blues Roll On," booklet included with Atlantic LP record record 1352.
Notes on contemporary Southern country blues.

NA 1876   Lomax, Alan. "Deep South, Sacred and Sinful," booklet included with Prestige LP record Int 35005.
Notes on quartet singing, blues, etc., with texts.

NA 1877   Lomax, Alan. "The Eastern Shores," booklet included with Prestige LP record Int 25008.
Notes on sacred singing in the Carolinas and Georgia, with texts.

NA 1878   Lomax, Alan. "Honor the Land: The Belleville A Capella Choir of the Church of God and Saints of Christ," booklet included with Prestige LP record Int 25012.
Notes on 19 spirituals from Belleville, Virginia.

NA 1879   Lomax, Alan. "I Got the Blues," *Common Ground*, 8, No. 4 (1948), 38-52. (Reprinted in "Blues in the Mississippi Night," booklet included with United Artists LP record UAL 4027.)
Transcription of a discussion between bluesmen Memphis Slim, Big Bill Broonzy and Sonny Boy Williamson I, recorded in 1943; includes the origins of the blues, protest in the blues, life in the South, in Southern prisons, etc.

NA
1880
Lomax, Alan. *Mister Jelly Roll*. New York: Duell, Sloan and Pearse, 1950.
Biographical account of Jelly Roll Morton with Morton's own autobiographical monologue making up the bulk of the text.

NA
1881
Lomax, Alan. *The Folk Songs of North America in the English Language*. Garden City, N.Y.: Doubleday, 1960.
Includes 22 spirituals, 17 reels, 23 work songs, 9 ballads, and 11 blues, with music and notes; notes on playing banjo and guitar, discography, map of folk song styles; introductions, essay on the relation of singing style to culture.

NA
1882
Lomax, Alan. "Georgia Sea Islands, Vols. 1, 2," booklet included with Prestige LP records Int 25001, 25002.
Notes on a variety of songs, with texts.

NA
1883
Lomax, Alan. "Negro Church Music," booklet included with Atlantic LP record 1351.
Discussion of 14 sacred songs from the Deep South.

NA
1884
Lomax, Alan. "Negro Prison Songs from the Mississippi State Penitentiary," booklet included with Tradition LP record TLP 1020.
Texts and discussion of 15 prison work songs, field hollers, and blues: includes texts of 2 interviews.

NA
1885
Lomax, Alan. "Negro Sinful Songs Sung by Leadbelly," booklet included with Musicraft 78 r.p.m. record album no. 31.
Texts of 9 songs, with notes.

NA
1886
Lomax, Alan. "The Passing of a Great Singer--Vera Hall," *SO*, 14, No. 3 (1964), 30-31.
Obituary of an Alabama singer.

NA
1887
Lomax, Alan. *The Rainbow Sign: A Southern Documentary*. New York: Duell, Sloan and Pearce, 1959.
Sketches (developed from tape recorded narratives) of a Southern black woman and a Louisiana preacher. Includes song texts and miscellaneous folkloric material, including 1 sermon text. Introduction discusses religion in Haiti and the Southern United States.

NA
1889
Lomax, Alan. "Reels and Work Songs," in *75 Years of Freedom: Commemoration of the 75th Anniversary of the 13th Amendment to the Constitution of the United States*. Washington, D.C.: Library of Congress, 1943, 27-36.
Discussion of songs used in various work situations.

NA
1890
Lomax, Alan. "Roots of the Blues," booklet included with Atlantic LP record 1348.
Discussion of older blues forms, field hollers, and work songs from the Deep South.

NA
1891
Lomax, Alan. "Sounds of the South," booklet included with Atlantic LP record 1346.
Includes discussion of field hollers, fife and drum music, etc., from the Deep South.

NA
1892
Lomax, Alan. "Yazoo Delta Blues and Spirituals," booklet included with Prestige LP record Int 25010.
Texts and discussion of 16 blues, game songs, work songs, and spirituals from the Mississippi Delta.

NA
1893
Lomax, Alan. "Zora Neale Hurston--A Life of Negro Folklore," *SO*, 10, No. 3 (1960), 12-13.
Life and work of folklorist Hurston.

NA
1894
Lomax, Alan, and Raoul Abdul, eds. *3000 Years of Black Poetry*. New York: Dodd, Mead, 1970.
Anthology includes texts of a sermon, a spiritual, a blues, a work song, a ballad, a slave song, and 2 folk poems, with an introduction (pp. 191-203).

NA
1895
Lomax, John A. "Adventures of a Ballad Hunter," *PTFS*, No. 19 (1944), 9-20.
Stories of preachers.

NA
1896
Lomax, John A. *Adventures of a Ballad Hunter*. New York: Macmillan, 1947.
Includes lengthy descriptions of collecting from Negro informants and touring with Leadbelly; song texts from Alabama, Texas, *et al.*

NA
1897
Lomax, John A. "Self Pity in Negro Folk Songs," *Nation*, 105 (1917), 141-145.
Discussion of evidence of "self pity" in songs and parts of song texts, religious and secular.

NA
1898
Lomax, John A. "Sinful Songs of the Southern Negro," *MQ*, 20 (1934), 177-187.
Ballads and work songs collected by Lomax at a Texas penitentiary with a number of verses.

NA   Lomax, John A. "Sin-Killer's Sermon," *PTFS*, No. 26 (1954), 175-182.
1899   A sermon by the Reverend Sin-Killer Griffin, employed by the State as
            Chaplain to the Negro convicts of the Texas Penitentiary System; with
            discussion.

NA   Lomax, John A. "Some Types of American Folk-Songs," *JAF*, 28 (1915), 1-17.
1900   Mostly white material, but contains texts of "John Henry" and "Boll
            Weevil."

        Lomax, John A. See "Seven Negro Convict Songs," No. NA 2692.

NA   Lomax, John A., and Alan Lomax. *American Ballads and Folk Songs*. New York:
1901   MacMillan, 1934.
            Folk songs from Georgia, Mississippi, South Carolina, Texas; Creole
            songs from Louisiana.

NA   Lomax, John A., and Alan Lomax. *Folk Song U.S.A.* New York: Duell, Sloan
1902   and Pearce, 1947.
            Texts, music and historical background of 111 tunes, a number of which
            are of Negro origin.

NA   Lomax, John A., and Alan Lomax, eds. *The Leadbelly Legend: A Collection of
1903   World-Famous Songs by Huddie Ledbetter*. New York: Folkways, 1959.

NA   Lomax, John A., and Alan Lomax. *Negro Folk Songs as Sung by Leadbelly*.
1904   New York: Macmillan, 1936.
            A study of a Negro guitar player and singer of the Southwest with many
            examples of recitative ballads.

NA   Lomax, John A., and Alan Lomax. *Our Singing Country*. New York: Macmillan,
1905   1949.
            Chapters on the spirituals, game songs, work songs, and the blues from
            the U.S. and the Bahamas; texts with discussion; illustrations.

NA   Lomax, Ruby Terrill. "Negro Baptizings," *PTFS*, No. 19 (1944), 1-8.
1906   Eyewitness account of baptismal ceremonies.

NA   Lomax, Ruby Terrill. "Negro Nicknames," *PTFS*, No. 18 (1943), 163-171.
1907   Name-giving, the coining of nicknames, their origins and significances;
            humorous and cruel nicknames.

NA
1908
> *The London Mathews*. Philadelphia: Morgan and Yeager, 1824.
>> Pamphlet containing perhaps the first American Negro folk song in print ("Oppossum Up a Gum Tree"); describes a visit to the African Theatre of New York City and the black audience's responses.

NA
1909
> Long, Margaret. "Strictly Subjective," *New South*, 16, No. 10 (1961), 2-3, 11.
>> A defense of the use of Negro dialect in novels by white authors.

NA
1910
> Long, Richard A. "'Man' and 'Evil' in American Negro Speech," *AS*, 34 (1959), 305-306.
>> Two words in jazz slang.

NA
1911
> Long, Richard A. "A Weapon of My Song: The Poetry of James Weldon Johnson," *Phylon*, 32 (1971), 374-382.

NA
1912
> Longini, Muriel Davis. "Folk Songs of Chicago Negroes," *JAF*, 52 (1939), 96-111.
>> 34 texts of blues, ballads, children's songs, etc., with an introduction.

NA
1913
> Longstreet, Augustus B. *Georgia Scenes*. New York: Harper, 1855. (Original edition published in 1835, as "by a Native Georgian.")
>> Includes the use of "aunt" in the up-country, "Mauma" in the lowlands of Georgia, for female house servants (p. 103); description of dances and musicians (pp. 110, 124).

NA
1914
> "Looking for Three Fools," in *American Stuff*. New York: Viking, 1937, 287-292.
>> 1 tale text from Alabama.

NA
1915
> Lord, Donald C. "The Slave Song as a Historical Source," *Social Education* (Washington, D.C.), 35 (1971), 736-767, 821.

NA
1916
> "Louisiana Loup-Garou," *Frontier and Midland* (Missoula), 19 (1938), 100-104.
>> WPA interviews on werewolves.

NA
1917
> Lovell, John, Jr. *Black Song: The Forge and the Flame. The Story of How the Afro-American Spiritual Was Hammered Out*. New York: Macmillan, 1972.
>> A study of the development of the black spiritual: includes the Afri-

can and Euro-American influences, characteristics, meaning and functions, social history, the spread of spirituals through the world,
influences on other musical forms and styles, and other religions;
discography, bibliography, illustrations, index of spiritual titles.

NA
1918
Lovell, John, Jr. "Reflections on the Origins of the Negro Spiritual,"
Negro American Literature Forum, 3, No. 3 (1969), 91-97.
The spiritual as literature; sources, themes, and influence of black
religious songs.

NA
1919
Lovell, John, Jr. "The Social Implications of the Negro Spritual," *JNE*,
8 (1939), 634-643. (Reprinted in No. NA 1698.)
Discussion of the spiritual as mirroring the slave's opinion of his
surroundings.

NA
1920
Lowe, Berenice. "Michigan Days of Sojourner Truth," *NYFQ*, 12 (1956), 127-
135.
Concerns legendary religious speaker born in New York State ca. 1797,
and died in Michigan in 1883.

NA
1921
Lowery, Rev. I.E. *Life on the Old Plantation in Ante-Bellum Days*. Columbia, S.C.: The State Co., 1911.
Descriptions of voodoo, funerals, corn-shucking, log-rolling, speech,
naming, hymns, etc., in Mayesville, S.C., by a black clergyman; includes the text of a sermon.

NA
1922
Lucchese, John A. *Pachanga*. New York: Avon, 1961.

NA
1923
Lucke, J.R. "A Dozen with a Black Cat, a Pair of Hobos, and a Fin (Cotton Trucker Number Language)," *AS*, 35 (1960), 237-238.
New Orleans truckers' use of a secret language to record figures.

NA
1924
Ludlow, Helen W. "Georgia's Investment," *SW*, 36 (1907), 219-235.
Discussion of Georgia plantation life, prayer missions, and spirituals.

NA
1925
Ludlow, Helen W. *Tuskegee Normal and Industrial School for Training Colored
Teachers at Tuskegee, Alabama: Its Story and Its Songs*. Hampton, Virginia:
Normal School Press, 1884.
Includes 17 songs with music.

NA   Lueg, Maurita Russell. "Russell Tales," *PTFS*, No. 28 (1958), 160-166.
1926   Superstition, ghosts, etc.

NA   Lumiansky, R.M. "New Orleans Slang in the 1880's," *AS*, 25 (1950), 28-40.
1927   Listing of 325 slang terms, a number of which are of Negro derivation,
             from the *Lantern*, a New Orleans magazine.

NA   Lumpkin, Ben Gray. "The Hawk and the Buzzard: How Tellers Vary the Story,"
1928   *NCF*, 18 (1970), 114-147.
             Notes on variations in an Uncle Remus story.

NA   Lumpkin, Ben Gray, and Jere Fryett. "A Negro Spiritual from Holly Springs,"
1929   *MFR*, 4 (1970), 39-40.
             Text (with music) of "Swing Low, Sweet Chariot."

NA   Luschan, Felix von. "Zusammenhange und Konnergenz," *Mitteilungen der*
1930   *Anthropologischen Gessellschaft in Wien*, 48 (1919).

NA   Lyell, Charles. *A Second Visit to the United States of North America.*
1931   2 vols. New York, 1849.
             Description of slave Christmas festivities, dirt-eating, sermons, music.

NA   McBryde, John McLaren, Jr. "Brer Rabbit in the Folk-Tales of the Negro and
1932   Other Races," *Sewanee Review*, 19 (1911), 185-206.
             Brer Rabbit tales as the embodiment of the cultural heritage of Ameri-
             can Negroes.

NA   McCall, George J. "Symbiosis: The Case of Hoodoo and the Numbers Racket,"
1933   *Social Problems*, 10 (1963), 361-371.
             The use of hoodoo (dream books, charms, etc.) in playing the numbers
             game.

NA   McCarthy, Albert J. *Louis Armstrong.* New York: A.S. Barnes, 1959.
1934   Account of the trumpeter's life; discography.

NA   McCarty, Mary Wylie. *Flags of Five Nations.* Sea Island, Georgia: Cloister
1935   Hotel, n.d.
             Booklet includes discussion of spirituals, shouts, work songs and row-
             ing songs on the Sea Islands of Georgia; description of dugout canoe
             races (pp. 66-71).

NA
1936
McCloud, Velma. *Laughter in Chains*. New York: Lenox, 1901.

NA
1937
McCormick, Mack. "A Conversation with Lightnin' Hopkins," *JJ*, 14, No. 1
(1961), 16-18; No. 2, 18-19.
Memoirs of an early blues singer; responses to records played by the
interviewer.

NA
1938
McCormick, Mack. "Mance Lipscomb: Texas Sharecropper and Songster," booklet included with Arhoolie LP record F 1001.
Notes on 14 song texts.

NA
1939
McCormick, Mack. "The Midnight Special," *Jazz Review*, 3, No. 5 (1960),
11-14. (Reprinted from *Caravan*, No. 19 (1960), 10-21.)
The stories behind the jail ballads of Texas.

NA
1940
McCormick, Mack. "Robert Shaw: Texas Barrelhouse Piano," booklet included
with Almanac LP record 10.
Notes on 10 Texas blues and the Texas blues piano tradition; illustrations.

NA
1941
McCormick, Mack. "Sam 'Lightnin' Hopkins--A Description," *SO*, 10, No. 3
(1960), 4-8.
Biography and account of the repertoire of a Texas bluesman (Reprinted
from *JM*.)

NA
1942
McCormick, Mack. "Tradition Rediscovered," *Rhythm and Blues Magazine*, 4
(1964), 15-16.

NA
1943
McCormick, Mack. "A Treasury of Field Recordings, Vol. 2: Regional and
Personalized Song," booklet included with 77 LP record LA 12/3.
Texts and notes on a Texas work song, a blues, a hymn parody, and a
gospel quartet song.

NA
1944
McCutcheon, Lynn Ellis. *Rhythm and Blues*. Arlington, Va.: Beatty, 1971.
History of R'n'B with discography.

NA
1945
McDaniel, Paul, and Nicholas Babchuk. "Negro Conceptions of White People
in a Northeastern City," *Phylon*, 21 (1960), 7-19.
A study of Negro attitudes and beliefs about white people.

NA
1946
McDavid, Raven I., and Virginia Glenn McDavid. "The Relationship of the Speech of American Negroes to the Speech of Whites," *AS*, 26 (1951), 3-17.
The survival of African and English words in American Negro and white speech.

NA
1947
Macdonald, Clare I. *Recollections of Juliana: A Sketch in Ebony*. Columbia, S.C.: The State Co., 1924.
Memoirs concerning a "mammy," largely written in Gullah dialect.

NA
1948
McDowell, Fred. "Fred McDowell Talks to Pete Welding," in *Back Woods Blues*. Oxford, U.K.: Blues Unlimited, 1968, 8-9.
Autobiography of a bluesman.

NA
1949
McDowell, John H. "Performance and the Folkloric Text: A Rhetorical Approach to 'The Christ of the Bible,'" *Folklore Forum*, 6 (1973), 139-148.
The analysis of a sermon text.

NA
1950
McDowell, Tremaine. "Notes on Negro Dialect in the American Novel to 1821," *AS*, 5 (1930), 291-296.
A survey of uses in fiction.

NA
1951
McDowell, Tremaine. "Use of Negro Dialect by H.B. Stowe," *AS*, 6 (1931), 322-326.
On the inconsistency of Stowe's use of Negro speech, with examples from *Uncle Tom's Cabin*.

NA
1952
McGhee, Brownie, and Happy Traum. *Guitar Styles of Brownie McGhee*. New York: Oak, 1971.
The guitar style of a Tennessee bluesman.

NA
1953
McGhee, Nancy B. "The Folk Sermon: A Facet of the Black Literary Heritage," *CLA Journal*, 13 (1969), 51-61.

NA
1954
McGhee, Z. "A Study in the Play Life of Some South Carolina Children," *Pedagogical Seminary* (Worcester, Mass.), 7 (1900), 415-478.

NA
1955
MacGirnsey, Robert. "Sleeping in a Manger," *Woman's Home Companion*, 68 (January, 1941), 15.
1 spiritual with music.

NA   McIlhenny, Edward A. *Befo' De War Spirituals*. Boston: Christopher Publish-
1956   ing, 1933.
            120 pre-Civil War spirituals from Louisiana with music for most.

NA   McIlhenny, Edward A. "Trubble, Brudder Alligator, Trubble," *PTFS*, 14
1957   (1938), 135-144.
            1 tale from Louisiana.

NA   McIlwaine, Shields. *Memphis: Down in Dixie*. New York: Dutton, 1948.
1958   History of the city of Memphis. Chapter 12, "What Negroes Mean to
            Memphis," discusses the black community, Beale Street, W.C. Handy,
            etc.

NA   McIntire, Carl. "Slave Made Markers," *Jackson Clarion Ledger and Jackson
1959   Daily News* (Mississippi), May 4, 1969.
            Pictorial essay of grave markers made by 18th century slaves.

NA   McKay, Claude. *Gingertown*. New York: Harper, 1932.
1960   Short stories of Harlem and Jamaica with folkloric content.

NA   McKay, Claude. *Harlem, Negro Metropolis*. New York: E.P. Dutton, 1940.
1961   Includes material on religion, occult practices, the numbers game, etc.

NA   McKay, Claude. *Home to Harlem*. New York: Harper, 1928.
1962   Novel with folkloric content.

NA   McKay, Claude. *A Long Way from Home*. New York: Furman, 1936.
1963   Autobiography with folkloric content.

NA   McKayle, Donald. "The Negro Dancer in Our Time," in *The Dance Has Many
1964   Faces*, 2nd edition, Walter Sorrell, ed. New York: Columbia University
            Press, 1966.

NA   McKim, J. Miller. *An Address Delivered by J. Miller McKim: The Freedmen
1965   of South Carolina*. Philadelphia: Willis P. Hazard, 1862.
            Describes the economic conditions of Sea Island blacks; quotes several
            songs and hymns, gives examples of folk medicine.

NA   McKim, J. Miller. "Negro Songs," *Dwight's Journal of Music*, 19 (1862),
1966   148-149. (Reprinted in No. NA 1568 and No. NA 1698.)
            Description of the singing of several hymns on the Sea Islands of
            South Carolina.

NA 1967   McKim, Lucy. "Songs of the Port Royal Contrabands," *Dwight's Journal of Music*, 22 (1862), 254-255. (Reprinted in No. NA 1568 and No. NA 1698.)
Discusses musical qualities of Negro folksong.

NA 1968   McKinney, Harold. "Negro Music: A Definitive American Expression," *NHB*, 27, No. 5 (1964), 120-121, 126-127.
Blues and jazz are described as combinations of European and African music that have become influential expressions of American music on the international scene. (Based on secondary accounts.)

NA 1969   McKinnow, William. "Neighbors: A Route of the Underground Railroad, Pennsylvania and New York," *NYFQ*, 8 (1952), 227-229.
Description of escape and hiding places of slaves in the underground railroad of Central Pennsylvania.

NA 1970   McLaughlin, Wayman B. "Symbolism and Mysticism in the Spirituals," *Phylon*, 24 (1963), 69-77.
An attempt to explore some basic aspects of symbolism and mysticism in spirituals and to argue that the spirituals are highly artistic and spiritually motivated.

NA 1971   McLennan, Marcia. "Origin of the Cat: Negro Tale," *JAF*, 9 (1896), 71.
1 tale.

NA 1972   MacLeod, W.C. "The Chewing of Tobacco in Southeastern North America," *AA*, 32 (1930), 574-575.
A note on snuff using, blowguns (as toys) and the chewing of lime with herbs (for health, teeth whitening and pleasure) among the Negroes of Tidewater, Virginia.

NA 1973   McLin, Lena. "Black Music in Church and School," in *Black Music in Our Culture: Curricular Ideas on the Subjects, Materials and Problems*, Dominique-Réné de Lerma, ed. Kent, Ohio: Kent State University Press, 1970, 35-41.
Includes a definition of gospel song.

NA 1974   MacMillan, Dougald. "John Kuners," *JAF*, 39 (1926), 53-57.
A Christmas masking ritual in North Carolina and the Bahamas.

NA 1975   McNeil, W.K. "Syncopated Slander: The 'Coon Song,' 1890-1900," *KFQ*, 17 (1972), 63-82.
Content and stereotypes in songs, some of which were written by blacks.

NA   McTeer, J.E. *High Sheriff of the Low Country*. Beaufort, S.C.: Beaufort
1976   Book Co., 1970.
            A white sheriff's memoirs of Sea Island magic and witchcraft and his
            own practice of "root work"; notes on African and Afro-American paral-
            lels; comments on Sea Island speech and manners.

NA   McWhiney, H. Grady, and Francis B. Simkins. "The Ghostly Legend of the
1977   Ku-Klux Klan," *NHB*, 14 (1951), 109-112.
            Argues that Southern Negroes were not frightened by the disguises and
            ploys of the KKK because they were superstitious, but rather because
            of the physical threat posed by the Klan.

NA   Mackie, John Milton. *From Cape Cod to Dixie and the Tropics*. New York:
1978   Putnam, 1864.
            Discussion of slave dress, street behavior, banjo playing, trances,
            etc.

NA   Macon, J.A. *Uncle Gabe Tucker; Or Reflection, Song, and Sentiment in the
1979   Quarters*. Philadelphia: Lippincott, 1883.
            Songs, tales, and proverbs of uncertain provenience; appendix on the
            nature of Negro speech.

NA   Macy, James C. *Jubilee and Plantation Songs*. Boston: Ditson, 1887.
1980   Songs from Hampton Institute students.

NA   Mae, Verta. *Vibration Cooking; or, The Travel Notes of a Geechee Girl*.
1981   Garden City, New York: Doubleday, 1970.
            Recipes, cooking techniques, poems, memorabilia, etc., of a South
            Carolinian.

NA   Mahammitt, Sarah H.T. *Recipes and Domestic Service: the Mahammitt School
1982   of Cookery*. Omaha, 1939.

NA   Mailer, Norman. *Advertisements for Myself*. New York: Putnam's, 1959.
1983   Essays on black "hip" culture and its meaning to whites (pp. 306-356).

NA   Mailer, Norman. *Existential Errands*. Boston: Little, Brown, 1972.
1984   Includes essays on black boxing and body idiom and communication style
            (pp. 3-36, 305-316).

NA   Mailer, Norman. *The Presidential Papers*. New York: Putnam's, 1963.
1985   Notes on black culture and the problems of its maintenance in Ameri-
            can society (pp. 187-190, 199-212); essay on black style, boxing, etc.
            (pp. 213-267).

NA   Mailer, Norman, Mervyn Kurlansky, and Jon Noar. *The Faith of Graffiti*.
1986   New York: Praeger, 1974.

NA   Major, Clarence. *Dictionary of Afro-American Slang*. New York: International
1987   Publishers, 1970.
            A lexicon of street argot of uncertain provenience.

NA   "Making a Hamper of White Oak Splits," *Foxfire* (Rabun Gap, Georgia), 4
1989   (1970), 210-213.
            Basket-making methods in Georgia; illustrations.

NA   Malet, William W. *An Errand to the South in the Summer of 1862*. London:
1990   Richard Bentley, 1863.
            Descriptions of religious and secular songs of blacks; church services;
            plantation slave wedding; religious beliefs; crops in slaves' gardens,
            etc.

NA   Mallard, John P. "Liberty County, Georgia," *GHQ*, 2 (1918), 1-21.
1991   Description of three slave preachers and their techniques.

NA   Mallard, R.Q. *Plantation Life Before Emancipation*. Richmond: Whittet and
1992   Shepperson, 1892.
            Memoirs of plantation life in Georgia: 2 Br'er Rabbit stories, religious
            anecdotes, etc.

NA   Malone, Bill C. *Country Music U.S.A*. Austin: University of Texas Press,
1993   1968.
            Includes discussion of black performers of white country music style.

NA   Malone, Kemp. "Negro Proverbs from Maryland," *AS*, 4 (1928-1929), 285.
1994   3 proverbs with notes on the informant.

NA   Manago, Carol. "Old Ways in a New Place," *Encore*, February, 1974, 40-42.
1995   An account of an Afro-American group's attempt to establish a Yoruba
            (Africa) lifestyle in South Carolina.

NA
1996
Mangurian, David. "Big Joe Williams," *JJ*, 16, No. 6 (1963), 14-17.
   The life of the Mississippi blues singer.

NA
1997
Mann, Mary, and Page Newton. "Aunt Deborah Goes Visiting: A Sketch from
   Virginian Life," *JAF*, 4 (1891), 354-356.
   Sample of dialogue.

NA
1998
Mann, Woody. *Six Black Blues Guitarists*. New York: Oak, 1973.
   Styles and songs of Blind Blake, Blind Willie McTell, Rev. Robert
   Wilkins, *et al.*, with transcriptions; discography.

NA
1999
"Manner of Living of the Inhabitants of Virginia," *American Museum*, 1
   (March, 1787), 214-216.
   Daily work routines of slaves in Virginia, their diet, etc.; comments
   on dancing, a 3-stringed banjo, a drum (*qua-qua*), and clothing.

NA
2000
Maquet, J. "Africanité et Américanité," *Présence Africaine*, 31, 59 (1966),
   8-16.
   Review of the work of M.J. Herskovits (especially *The Myth of the Negro
   Past*) which suggests it is equally useful for understanding U.S. Negro
   and African culture change; differences between change in Africa and
   in the U.S.

NA
2001
Marcel (W.F. Allen). "The Negro Dialect," *Nation*, 1 (1865), 744-745. (Reprinted in No. NA 1568.)
   Description of South Carolina Sea Island dialect; texts of hymns;
   description of "shouting" procedures.

NA
2002
Markham, "Pigmeat," with Bill Levinson. *Here Come the Judge!* New York:
   Popular Library, 1969.
   The biography of a black comic; includes discussion of black minstrel
   shows, vaudeville, comedy, dance, etc.

NA
2003
Marsh, J.B.T. *The Story of the Jubilee Singers with Their Songs*. Boston:
   Houghton and Co., 1880.
   The history of the Jubilee Singers and 112 Jubilee songs (contains the
   same songs as those in G.D. Pike, *The Jubilee Singers . . .*).

NA
2004
Martin, John. "Inquiry into Boogie Woogie," *New York Times Magazine*
   (July 16, 1944), 18, 45-46.
   The history and rise of boogie woogie.

NA   Martin, Malcolm J. "Zombies and Ghost Dogs on the Harvey Canal," *LFM*, 2,
2005   No. 4 (1968), 103-104.
            Spirit beliefs in Louisiana.

NA   Martin, Margaret Rhett. *Charleston Ghosts*. Columbia, S.C.: University of
2006   South Carolina Press, 1963.

NA   Martin, S.R., Jr. "Four Undescribed Verb Forms in American Negro English,"
2007   *AS*, 35 (1960), 238-239.
            4 verbs, "josh," "toch," "jonah," and "slow around," defined.

NA   Martin, Sallie. *Twelve Gospel Song 'Hits' and Their Stories by Kenneth
2008   Morris*. Chicago: Martin & Morris Music Studio, 1941.

NA   Martinez, Raymond J. *Marie Laveau, Voodoo Queen, and Folk Tales along the
2009   Mississippi*. New Orleans: Hope, 1956.
            Tales and newspaper reports of Marie Laveau's work; miscellaneous black
            tales and legends of uncertain provenience; bibliography, discography.

NA   Martinez, Raymond J. *Portraits of New Orleans Jazz*. New Orleans: Hope,
2010   1971.
            Descriptions of black Mardi Gras clubs and their call-and-response
            singing; early jazzmen, etc.; illustrations.

NA   Marx, Gary T. "The White Negro and the Negro White," *Phylon*, 28 (1967),
2011   168-177.
            Cultural and racial identity in the beatnik-hipster movement of the
            1950's.

NA   Maryland, James. "Shoe-Shine on 63rd," in *Rappin' and Stylin' Out*, Thomas
2012   Kochman, ed. Urbana, Ill.: University of Illinois Press, 1972, 209-
            214.
            An example of signifying and rapping.

NA   Mason, Daniel Gregory. "Folk-Song and American Music," *MQ*, 4 (1918), 323-
2013   332.
            Argues that Negro spirituals, rather than ragtime, represent the only
            outstanding American music.

NA   Mason, Julian. "The Etymology of 'Buckaroo,'" *AS*, 35 (1960), 51-55.
2014   A discussion demonstrating that the term "buckaroo" was derived from
            "buckra" and not the Spanish *vaquero*.

NA   Mather, R.C. *The Storm Swept Coasts of South Carolina*. Woonsockett, R.I.:
2015   Charles E. Cook, 1894.
            Gives details of storm and destruction, actions of black during and
            after storm, relief efforts, etc.

NA   (Matthews, Brander.) "Banjo and Bones," *Saturday Review of Politics, Liter-
2016   ature, Science and Art* (London), 57 (1884), 739-740. Reprinted in No.
            NA 1568.)
            The development and influence of minstrelsy in Europe.

NA   Matthews, Brander. "The Rise and Fall of Negro-Minstrelsy," *Scribner's
2017   Magazine*, 57 (1915), 754-759.
            An historical background of the beginnings of minstrelsy and the rea-
            sons for its decline.

NA   Matthews, Elmora. *Neighbor and Kin: Life in a Tennessee Ridge Community*.
2018   Nashville, Tenn.: Vanderbilt University Press, 1965.
            Attitudes of whites toward Negroes; discussion of naming practices.

NA   Matthews, Essie Collins. *Aunt Phebe, Uncle Tom and Others: Character
2019   Sketches Among the Old Slaves of the South, Fifty Years After*. Colum-
            bus, Ohio: Champlin Press, 1915.
            Several hymn texts; samples of dialect, beliefs; descriptions of
            Christmas festivities, dancing, courtship and marriage; photographs
            of slaves; largely from North Carolina.

NA   Matthews, M.M. *A Dictionary of Americanisms on Historical Principles*.
2020   2 vols. Chicago: University of Chicago Press, 1951.
            Contains numerous words attributed to Africa.

NA   Matthews, M.M. *Some Sources of Southernisms*. University, Alabama: Univer-
2021   sity of Alabama Press, 1948.
            Chapter 3, "Africanisms in the Plantation Vocabulary," treats the Afri-
            can contribution to Southern U.S. speech; glossary of African words in
            English.

NA   Maultsby, Portia K. "Music of Northern Independent Black Churches During
2022   the Ante-Bellum Period," *EM*, 19 (1975), 401-420.

NA   May, Earl Chaplin. "Where Jazz Comes From," *Popular Mechanics*, 44 (Janu-
2023   ary, 1926), 97-102.

NA   Mays, Benjamin E. *The Negro's God as Reflected in His Literature*. Boston:
2024   Chapman and Grimes, 1938.
            The concept of God as expressed in the spirituals.

NA   Mays, Benjamin E., and J.W. Nicholson. *The Negro's Church*. New York: Insti-
2025   tute of Social and Religious Research, 1933.
            Includes a chapter on types of sermons with examples.

NA   Mees, Arthur. *Six Authentic Negro Melodies*. Mendelssohn Glee Club, 1899.
2026   6 choral arrangements.

NA   Meid, John. "Son House," in *Back Woods Blues*. Oxford, U.K.: Blues Unlimited,
2027   1968, 39.
            Eyewitness account of House at a concert.

NA   Meikleham, Randolph. "A Negro Ballad," *JAF*, 6 (1893), 300-301.
2028   1 song.

NA   Meine, Franklin J. *Tall Tales of the Southwest*. New York: Knopf, 1930.
2029   Contains several tales.

NA   Mellers, Wilfrid H. *Music in a New Found Land: Themes and Developments
2030   in the History of American Music*.
            Chapters on folk blues, ragtime, New Orleans jazz, etc. Includes an
            analysis of Gershwin's *Porgy and Bess* (pp. 392-413).

NA   Melnick, Mimi Clar. "I Can Peep through Muddy Water and Spy Dry Land:
2031   Boasts in the Blues," in *Folklore International*, D.K. Wilgus, ed.
            Hatboro, Pa.: Folklore Associates, 1967.
            Examines themes expressed in the "tall talk" of Negro blues songs.

NA   Mencken, H.L. *The American Language*, 4th Edition. New York: Alfred A.
2032   Knopf, 1936.
            Includes (p. 523 ff.) an account of Negro naming practices, with numer-
            ous examples and suggestions as to their origins, as well as proper
            names in general.

NA   Mencken, H.L. *The American Language: Supplement II*. New York: Alfred A.
2033   Knopf, 1948.
            Includes (pp. 509-515) a section on given names of Negroes, as well as
            proper names in general.

NA 2034   Mencken, H.L. "Designations for Colored Folk," *AS*, 19 (1944), 161-174.
    Use and origins of words for black people.

NA 2035   Mencken, H.L. "Songs of the American Negroes," *World Review*, 1 (1926),
    279.
    Argues that the main contribution of the Negro to spirituals is rhythm
    and harmony.

NA 2036   Mendes, Guy. "Found People: Some Figures on My Urn," *Place Rogues Gallery*
    (San Jose), 2, No. 2 (1973), 44-52.
    Notes on an Afro-American folk artist and his "found-art" architecture
    near Louisville, Kentucky; illustrations.

NA 2037   Mendl, Robert W.S. *The Appeal of Jazz*. London: P. Allan, 1927.

NA 2038   Mercier, Alfred. "Étude sur la Langue Créole en Louisiane," *CRAL*, July,
    1880, 378.
    The first article on Louisiana Creole grammar printed in Louisiana;
    contains 1 animal tale.

NA 2039   Mercier, Alfred. *L'Habitation Saint-Ybars, ou Maitres et Esclaves en
    Louisiane*. New Orleans: Franco-Americaine, 1881.
    Novel of life on a Louisiana plantation during the Civil War; contains
    Creole dialogue.

NA 2040   Meredith, Mamie. "Negro Patois and Its Humor," *AS*, 6 (1931), 317-321.
    Analysis of Negro speech and humor illustrated by the conversations
    of a Southern California railroad worker.

NA 2041   Merriam, Alan P. "Jazz and African Studies," *Down Beat's Music 1961*.
    Chicago: Maher, 1961, 42.
    Parallels between African music and musicians and jazz and jazzmen.

NA 2042   Merriam, Alan P. "Jelly Roll Morton: A Review Article," *MF*, 8 (1958),
    217-221.
    Review of the Library of Congress recordings of Jelly Roll Morton made
    by Alan Lomax.

NA 2043   Merriam, Alan P. "Music in American Culture," *AA*, 57 (1955), 1173, 1181.
    A review of literature on Negro music, stressing the use of music as a
    means of studying culture change.

NA 2044   Merriam, Alan P., and Fradley H. Garner. "Jazz--the Word," *EM*, 12 (1968), 373-396. Originally published in *Jazz Review*, 3, No. 3 (March-April, 1960), 39-40; 3, No. 4 (May, 1960), 40-42; 3, No. 5 (June, 1960), 40; 3, No. 6 (July, 1960), 40-41; 3, No. 7 (August, 1960), 36.
Origin of the word "jazz" attributed to a folktale printed in a 1919 issue of *Music Trade Review*; and to African, Arabic and French languages, as well as to American sources.

NA 2045   Merrick, George Byron. *Old Times on the Upper Mississippi*. Cleveland: Arthur H. Clark, 1909.
Stories of steamboats on the Mississippi in the 18th century, with an account of Negro firemen and their songs (pp. 157-160).

NA 2046   Meryman, Richard. *Louis Armstrong--A Self Portrait*. Millerton, New York: Eakins, 1971 (First published in abbreviated form in *Life* Magazine, April 15, 1966).
Interview in which Armstrong discusses wakes, funerals, parades, dancing, street hollers, etc. in New Orleans in the early 1900's. Illustrations.

NA 2047   Metfessel, Milton. *Phonophotography in Folk Music*. Chapel Hill: University of North Carolina, 1928.
A comparison of the styles of Negro folk singers and those of Euro-American art song singers using an audio-visual device designed by the author.

NA 2048   Mezzrow, Milton, and Bernard Wolfe. *Really the Blues*. New York: Random House, 1946.
The autobiography of Mezzrow, a white jazz musician involved with Afro-American culture in the 1920's and 1930's; includes a glossary of slang terms.

NA 2049   Michael, Dorothy Jean. "Grave Decoration," *PTFS*, No. 18 (1943), 129-136.
Meaning and symbolism of grave adornment (covered with bleached seashells, colored glass, doll heads, etc.) in burials of Negroes, Indians, Mexicans and Europeans in Texas.

NA 2050   Middleton, Richard. *Pop Music and the Blues*. London: Gollancz, 1972.
A study of the development of the blues, with emphasis on its synthesis with "white" song forms.

NA 2051   Middleton, Russell, and John Moland. "Humor in the Negro and White Sub-Cultures: A Study of Jokes among University Students," *American Socio-*

logical Review, 24 (1959), 61-69.
Study which seeks to realize the context and traditional stereotypes
within black and white jokes.

NA   Mikell, I. Jenkins. *Rumbling of the Chariot Wheels*. Columbia, S.C.: The
2052   State Co., 1923.
           A Sea Island slaveholder's memoirs: revival services, speech, dress,
           domestic life, description of a 12-man dugout canoe, rowing songs,
           etc.

NA   Milhaud, Darius. *Études*. Paris: C. Aveline, 1927.
2053   Contains a chapter on the evolution of the jazz band and music of the
           North American Negro.

NA   Milhaud, Darius. "Jazz Band and Negro Music," *Living Age*, 323 (1924), 169-
2054   173.
           Discussion of jazz elements: structure, instrumentation, orchestration
           and black origins.

NA   Millar, Bill. *The Drifters: The Rise and Fall of the Black Vocal Group*.
2055   New York: Macmillan, 1972.
           Includes discussion of gospel quartets and their influence on popular
           music; discography; illustrations.

NA   Miller, Daisy. "Negro Dialect in American Literature," *Opportunity*, 2
2056   (1924), 327-329.
           Traces the history of Negro dialect on the stage and in literature;
           attributes white difficulties in transcribing it to tribal differences
           in African languages; list of authors who wrote in Negro dialect.

NA   Miller, George A. "Sounding the New Note of Freedom in Negro Music," *Musi-
2057   cal America*, 36, No. 8 (1922), 9.
           Nature, content, and meaning of spirituals, with 4 texts and a discus-
           sion.

NA   Miller, Harry. "Cotton Fields," in *Negro Anthology*, Nancy Cunard, ed. Lon-
2058   don: Wishart, 1934, 362.
           Text and music of a spiritual.

NA   Miller, Heather R. "The Candlewalk: A Midwinter Fire-Festival," *NCF*, 19
2059   (1971), 153-156.
           Christmas and New Year's religious rites in Bladen County and Elizabeth-

town, North Carolina; chants are sung "in Swahili, or a kind of pidgin English understandable only to the congregation."

NA 2060
Miller, James W. *Sing with Africa: Negro Spirituals Taken from Plantation Melodies*. Chicago: Rodeheaven Co., 1906.

NA 2061
Miller, Kelly. "The Artistic Gifts of the Negro," in *Radicals and Conservatives and Other Essays on the Negro in America*, Kelly Miller, ed. New York: Schocken, 1968, 246-257. (First published in *The Voice of the Negro*, 3, April, 1906.)
Argues that black music is evidence of the genius of the Afro-American spirit.

NA 2062
Miller, Linda. "'Playing the Dozens' among Black High School Students," *Journal of the Ohio Folklore Society*, 2 (1973), 20-29.
Transcription of a performance of insults in front of a high school class.

NA 2063
Miller, Lloyd, and James K. Skipper, Jr. "Sounds of Protest: Jazz and the Avant-Garde," in *Approaches to Deviance: Theories, Concepts and Research Findings*, Mark Lefton, James K. Skipper, Jr. and Charles H. McCaghy, eds. New York: Appleton Century Crofts, 1968, 129-140.
After a short discussion of slavery and the church, the authors discuss the social expressions of jazz using Louis Wirth's four minority types: 1) pluralistic, 2) assimilationist, 3) secessionist, 4) militant.

NA 2064
Miller, Paul Eduard. "Fifty Years of New Orleans Jazz," in *Esquire's 1945 Jazz Book*, Paul Eduard Miller, ed. New York: A.S. Barnes, 1945, 1-14.
Includes a map of Storyville with a discussion of musical opportunities for blacks and the personnel of marching bands.

NA 2065
Milling, Chapman J. "Delia Holmes--A Neglected Negro Ballad," *SFQ*, 1 (1937), 3-8.
3 variants.

NA 2066
Milling, Chapman J. "A Passel uh Snakes," *Folk-Say*, 3 (1931), 103-112.
A tale containing snake beliefs.

NA 2067
Millstein, Gilbert. "A Negro Says It with Jokes," *New York Times Magazine*, April 30, 1961, 34-35.

NA
2068
Milner, Christina, and Richard B. Milner. *Black Players: The Secret World of Black Pimps*. Boston: Little, Brown, 1972.
An ethnography of pimps: slang, style, rituals, cultural exchange between hippies and pimps, interracial sex as a theme, the pimp as hero and trickster, legend and toast texts, graffiti; glossary, bibliography.

NA
2069
Milner, Richard B. "The Trickster, the Bad Nigga, and the New Urban Ethnography," *Urban Life and Culture* (Beverly Hills, Calif.), 1, No. 1 (1972), 109-117.
The pimp as a social type, based on traditional heroic figures.

NA
2070
Mims, A. Grace. "Soul: The Black Man and His Music," *NHB*, 33 (1970), 141-146.
Origins of black American music and the development of popular song.

NA
2071
Minelli, Maria Gioia. *Canto Popolare Negro-Americano* (Black American Popular Song). Ivrea: Cardinale, 1971.

NA
2072
Miner, Leigh Richmond. "Two Negro Lullabies," *Outlook*, 123 (September 17, 1919), 84.
2 songs in dialect.

NA
2073
Minne, Pierre. "Une Resurgence de la Mentalité Africaine aux U.S.A.: La Musique de Jazz de la Nouvelle-Orleans" (A Resurgence of African Mentality in the U.S.A.: New Orleans Jazz), *Présence Africaine*, 77 (1971), 109-130.

NA
2074
Minor, Mary Willis. "How to Keep Off Witches," *JAF*, 11 (1898), 76.
3 methods of warding off witches.

NA
2075
Mintz, Lawrence E. "Langston Hughes's Jesse B. Simple: The Urban Negro as Wise Fool," *Satire Newsletter* (Oneonta, N.Y.), 7, No. 1 (1969), 11-21.
Hughes' use of folklore, dialect, the tall tale, etc., in the "Simple" stories.

NA
2076
Mintz, Sidney W. "Une Culture à Retrouver ou à Créer?" *L'Homme* (Paris), 11, No. 3 (1971), 112-117.
A review-essay of Roger D. Abraham's *Deep Down in the Jungle* and *Positively Black*.

NA
2077
Mitcham, Mildred Barnett. "A Tale in The Making: The Face in The Window," *SFQ*, 12 (1948), 241-257.
Gives an explanation of the face-in-the-window motif and contains numerous tales which center on blacks.

NA
2078
Mitchell, George. *Blow My Blues Away*. Baton Rouge: Louisiana State University Press, 1971.
Autobiographies and interviews with Mississippi Delta blues singers, church singers and members of a fife and drum band; includes song texts and preachers' sermons. Illustrations.

NA
2079
Mitchell, Henry H. *Black Belief: Folk Beliefs of Blacks in America and West Africa*. New York, 1975.

NA
2080
Mitchell, Henry H. *Black Preaching*. Philadelphia: Lippincott, 1970.
Contains a history of prominent preachers in the larger black churches, a discussion of Black English, features of preaching style, samples of sermons, etc.

NA
2081
Mitchell, Joseph. *The Bottom of the Harbor*. Boston: Little, Brown, 1959.
Includes a description of grave decorations in a black community in Rhode Island ca. 1952 (p. 124).

NA
2082
Mitchell, Joseph. *McSorley's Wonderful Saloon*. New York: Duell, Sloan and Pearce, 1943.
"Houdini's Picnic" (pp. 155-168) describes a performance of a calypsonian in New York City; gives his biography; includes several texts.

NA
2083
Mitchell, Loften. *Black Drama: The Story of the American Negro in the Theatre*. New York: Hawthorn, 1967.
Includes discussion of minstrelsy, early black theatre, etc.

NA
2084
Mitchell, Minnie Belle. *Gray Moon Tales*. Indianapolis: Bobbs-Merrill, 1926.
13 dialect tales of uncertain provenience; includes several Brer Rabbit tales.

NA
2085
Mitchell-Kernan, Claudia. *Language Behavior in a Black Urban Community*, Monographs of the Language Behavior Laboratory, No. 2, University of California, Berkeley, 1971. (Excerpts reprinted in Dundes, No. NA 854.)

NA   Mitchell-Kernan, Claudia. "On the Status of Black English for Native
2086   Speakers: An Assessment of Attitudes and Values," in *Functions of
            Language in the Classroom*, Courtney B. Cazden, Vera P. John, and Dell
            Hymes, eds. New York: Teachers College Press, 1972, 195-210.
            Black views of Black English and its uses.

NA   Mitchell-Kernan, Claudia. "Signifying and Marking: Two Afro-American Speech
2087   Acts," in *Directions in Sociolinguistics*, John Gumperz and Dell Hymes,
            eds. New York: Holt, Rinehart and Winston, 1972, 161-179.
            Analysis of 2 speech acts in their linguistic and social setting.

        Mitra, Sarat Chandra. "Indian Ophiolatry and the Snake Worship of the
            Negroes of the West Indies," See No. HA 242.

NA   "Modern Conjuring in Washington," *JAF*, 12 (1899), 289-290.
2088   In a case tried in the police court, the accused is charged with
            larceny by trickery on six different occasions (from the *Washington
            Post*, March 7, 1899).

NA   Moderwell, Hiram Kelly. "The Epic of the Black Man," *New Republic*, 12
2089   (1917), 154-155.
            Brief survey of the development of black folk music.

NA   Moe, Albert F. "'Man' as a Form of Direct Address," *AS*, 36 (1961), 136-
2090   137.
            Notes use before the "jazz era."

NA   Molette, Carlton W., III. "Afro-American Ritual Drama," *Black World*, 22,
2091   No. 6 (1973), 4-12.
            Notes toward a definition of Afro-American religious ritual and its
            possibilities as a basis for drama.

NA   Mongeau, Beatrice, *et al*. "The 'Granny' Midwife: Changing Roles and Func-
2092   tions of a Folk Practitioner," *American Journal of Sociology*, 66
            (1961), 497-505.
            The conflict between "granny" midwives and clinic-trained midwives
            over traditional folk practices.

NA   Monroe, Harriet. "Negro Sermon Poetry," *Phylon*, 30 (1923), 291-293.
2093

NA   Monroe, Mina. *Bayou Ballads*. New York: G. Shirmer, 1921.
2094   12 songs with music in Louisiana French Creole translated into English
             and French.

NA   Montell, William L. *The Saga of Coe Ridge*. Knoxville: University of Tennes-
2095   see Press, 1970.
             Oral histories added to written materials to form an account of a
             black community in Southern Kentucky which was also populated with
             white females.

NA   Montgomery, Charles J. (with a Note by Frederick Starr). "Survivors from
2096   the Cargo of the Negro Slave Yacht *Wanderer*," *AA*, 10 (1908), 611-623.
             An account of Congolese slaves brought to the U.S. in 1858: descrip-
             tions of their dress, housing, vocabulary, customs, etc.; their ac-
             counts of African life; illustrations.

NA   Moody, Minnie Hite. *Death Is a Little Man*. New York: Julian Messner, 1936.
2097   Novel of Georgia life with folkloric content.

NA   Moody, William Vaughn. *The Faith Healer*. New York: Macmillan, 1910.
2098   Drama with folkloric content.

NA   Moon, Henry Lee. "Thank You Father So Sweet," *New Republic*, 88 (1936),
2099   147-150.
             Critical history of the rise of Father Divine and his church.

NA   Mooney, James. "Myths of the Cherokee," *Bureau of American Ethnology 19th
2100   Annual Report, 1897-1898*, Part 1. Washington, D.C., 1900, 3-576.
             Includes discussion of the relationship of Negro folktales to those of
             the Cherokee of North Carolina.

NA   Mooney, James. "The Negro Genesis," *AA*, 1 (1888), 230.
2101   The "earth diver" myth among Negroes; its similarity to American Indian
             and African myths.

NA   Moore, Arthur K. "Jouk," *AS*, 16 (1941), 319-320.
2102   Meaning and origin of a term.

NA   Moore, Carman. *Somebody's Angel Child: The Story of Bessie Smith*. New
2103   York: Crowell, 1970.
             Biography of blues singer Bessie Smith, intended for children.

NA   Moore, Frank. *The Civil War in Song and Story, 1860-1865*. New York:
2104   P.F. Collier, 1889.
           Examples of Negro speech, prayer; description of worship, etc., taken
           from contemporary sources.

NA   Moore, John Hammond. "A Hymn of Freedom--South Carolina, 1813," *JNH*, 50
2105   (1965), 50-53.
           Text of a hymn possibly used in the planning of a slave insurrection
           during the War of 1812.

NA   Moore, Leroy, Jr. "The Spiritual: Soul of Black Religion," *Church History*,
2106   40 (March, 1971), 79-81.
           Music as the core of black religion.

NA   Moore, Merrill. "Hair Into Snake," *TFSB*, 22 (1956), 61-63.
2107   2 short tales.

NA   Moore, Ruby Andrews. "Superstitions from Georgia," *JAF*, 7 (1894), 305-306.
2108   List of sayings, beliefs, traditions and "superstitions."

NA   Moore, Ruby Andrews. "Superstitions in Georgia," *JAF*, 6 (1893), 230-231.
2109   Accounts of "superstitions."

NA   Moore, Ruby Andrews. "Superstitions of Georgia, No. 2," *JAF*, 9 (1896),
2110   226-228.
           Describes a number of "superstitions" held by Southern blacks.

NA   Morais, Herbert M. *The History of the Negro in Medicine*. New York: Pub-
2111   lishers Co., 1967.
           Brief description of plantation medicine and slave doctors (pp. 11-20).

NA   "Morality and Religion in Slavery Days," *SW*, 26 (1897), 210.
2112   Brief humorous tales.

NA   "Morals and Manners among Negro Americans," *Atlanta University Publica-
2113   tions*, No. 18 (1914), 1-136.

NA   Morath, Max. *Guide to Ragtime*. New York: Hollis Music, 1964.
2114   Texts and music to pre-ragtime songs, rags, and contemporary songs in-
           fluenced by ragtime, with commentary.

NA 2115   Morath, Max. *100 Ragtime Classics*. Denver: Donn Printing, 1963.
       Facsimile copies of rags, cakewalks and waltzes.

NA 2116   Moreland, John Richard. "De Promise Lan'," *Catholic World*, 133 (1931), 435.
       1 hymn text in dialect.

NA 2117   Moreland, John Richard. "Doomsday: A Negro Spiritual," *Catholic World*, 130 (1930), 438.
       1 hymn text in dialect.

NA 2118   Morgan, Edmund S. *Virginians at Home: Family Life in the Eighteenth Century*. Williamsburg, Va.: Colonial Williamsburg, Inc., 1952.
       Brief sketch of slave life: recreations, work, housing, marriage, etc.

NA 2119   Morgan, Harry. "Music--A Lifeforce in the Black Community," *Music Educators Journal*, 58, No. 3 (1971), 34-37.

NA 2120   Morgan, Kathryn L. "Caddy Buffers: Legends of a Middle Class Negro Family in Philadelphia," *KFQ*, 11 (1966), 67-88.
       Personal narratives telling how a slave and her descendants found dignity in dealing with the white world.

NA 2121   Morgan, Kathryn L. "Jokes among Urban Blacks in the North: Revelation of Conflict," *Blackfolk*, 1, No. 1 (1973-1974), 23-29.
       An analysis of jokes in terms of blacks' self-image and their image of others.

NA 2122   Morgan, Raleigh. "The Lexicon of St. Martin Creole," *Anthropological Linguistics*, 2, (January, 1960), 7-29.
       Dictionary of over 600 terms of St. Martin Creole (Louisiana); entries in alphabetical order, showing examples of common words, words of unusual derivation, or of unusual semantic range.

NA 2123   Morgan, Raleigh. "Structural Sketch of St. Martin Creole," *Anthropological Linguistics*, 1, No. 8 (1959), 20-24.

NA 2124   Morris, J. Allen. "Gullah in the Stories and Novels of William Gilmore Simms," *AS*, 22 (1947), 46-53.
       The use and discussion of Gullah dialect in stories by Simms (ca. 1833), who himself had an extensive Gullah vocabulary.

NA
2125
Morton, A.L. *The Language of Men*. London: Cobbett Press, 1945.
Includes "Promise of Victory: A Note on the Negro Spiritual."

NA
2126
Morton, Jelly-Roll. "A Fragment of an Autobiography," *RC*, (March, 1944),
15-16; (April, 1944), 27-28.
A manuscript written by jazzman Morton in 1938, discussing his early
life in New Orleans.

NA
2127
"Mortuary Customs and Beliefs of South Carolina Negroes," *JAF*, 7 (1894),
318-319.
Newspaper article by Mary A. Waring including examples of burial customs and belief in the "spirit" of the deceased.

NA
2128
The Most Popular Plantation Songs. New York: Hinds, Nobel and Eldredge,
1911.
110 minstrel and slave songs and spirituals.

NA
2129
Moton, R.R. "Sickness in Slavery Days," *SW*, 28 (1899), 74-75.
Means of warding off diseases.

NA
2130
Moton, R.R. "Universal Language," *SW*, 56 (1927), 349-351.
Argues that Negro folk songs are the only American folk music; examines
spirituals by the Fisk singers.

NA
2131
Moton, R.R. *et al.* "Folklore and Ethnology," *SW*, 25 (1896), 185-186.
3 tales; John "talks at the big gate," the Marsh Light (Will o' the
Wisp) legend, and a Brer Rabbit tale.

NA
2132
Mott, Ed. *The Black Homer of Jimtown*. New York: Grosset and Dunlap, 1900.
18 dialect stories from the Cape Fear, N.C. area: beliefs, charms, hoodoo, witches, etc.

NA
2133
Mullen, Patrick. "The Function of Folk Belief Among Negro Fishermen of
the Texas Coast," *SFQ*, 33 (1969), 80-91.
Discussion of the role "superstitions" play in the lives of fishermen;
with texts.

NA
2134
Mullen, Patrick. "A Negro Street Performer: Tradition and Innovation,"
WF, 29 (1970), 91-103.
The songs and routines of a Texas drummer-comedian-singer.

NA 2135   Mullin, Gerald W. *Flight and Rebellion: Slave Resistance in Eighteenth-Century Virginia*. New York: Oxford University Press, 1972.
Africans in Virginia, their nations, dress, culture, etc.

NA 2136   Muro, Eleanor C. (E.C.M.). "Carved and Wrought in America, 1750-1850," *Art News*, 52, No. 6 (1953), 33.
Photo of an iron figure from Virginia.

NA 2137   Murphey, Charles. "The Protest Motif in Children's Folklore," *LFM*, 3, No. 2 (1971), 48-50.
2 song-games from urban children.

NA 2138   Murphey, Edward F. "Black Music," *Catholic World*, 130 (March, 1930), 687-692.
Spirituals as black emotion outpourings; 5 texts of "African origin."

NA 2139   Murphey, Edward F. "The Negro Spiritual," *Literary Digest*, 98, No. 12 (1928), 34.
Origins and uses of spirituals described; the jubilees as expressions of the religious fervor of black labors.

NA 2140   Murphy, Jeannette Robinson. "Gawd Bless Them Yankees," *Century*, n.s., 34 (1898), 797-798.

NA 2141   Murphy, Jeannette Robinson. *Southern Thoughts for Northern Thinkers*. New York: The Bandanna Publishing Co., 1904.
Includes reprints of "The Survival of African Music in America," (originally published in *Appleton's Popular Science Monthly*, 55, No. 5 (1899), 660-672); "The True Negro Music and Its Decline," (originally published in *The Independent*, 55, No. 2851 (1903), 1723-1730). ("The Survival of African Music in America" is reprinted in No. NA 1568.)

NA 2142   Murray, Albert. *The Omni-Americans: New Perspectives on Black Experience and American Culture*. New York: Outerbridge and Dienstfrey, 1970.
Essays on the blues, jazz, style, dance, and literature. Afro-Americans as an inextricable part of "mainstream" U.S. culture and history.

NA 2143   Murray, Albert. *South to a Very Old Place*. New York: McGraw-Hill, 1971.
Discussion of black culture and life style, especially in the South.

NA   Murray, Chalmers S. *Here Comes Joe Mungin*. New York: Putnam's, 1924.
2144   Novel of Sea Island people with folkloric content.

NA   "Music Tunes Held Not from Africa," *New York Times*, September 14, 1939, 4.
2145   George Herzog contends that Negro spirituals are versions of white
            folk song, not African survivals.

NA   "Musikers Unabridged Dictionary of Jazz Terms," *Metronome*, 62 (February,
2146   1936), 21, 61.

NA   "My Soul Wants Something That's New," *SW*, 37 (1908), 400.
2147   1 spiritual with music.

NA   Myrdal, Gunnar. *An American Dilemma: The Negro Problem and Modern Democra-
2148   cy*. 2 vols. New York: Harper and Row, 1944.
            Includes scattered discussions of folk music, religion, recreation,
            style, speech, etc., all seen as variations of Euro-American proto-
            types.

NA   Myron, H.B. "Another Negro Name," *AS*, 5 (1929), 177-178.
2149   Origin of a name in Atlanta, Georgia.

NA   *Narrative of Sojourner Truth, a Northern Slave*. New York: published for
2150   the author, 1853.
            Describes family and religious life of New York slaves, names, etc.

NA   Nathan, Hans. "Charles Mathews, Comedian, and the American Negro," *SFQ*,
2151   10 (1946), 191-197.
            Deals with the development of the American style of Negro impersona-
            tion.

NA   Nathan, Hans. *Dan Emmett and the Rise of Early Negro Minstrelsy*. Norman,
2152   Okla.: University of Oklahoma Press, 1962.
            Negro impersonations and Negro performers in England and early America.

NA   Nathan, Hans. "Early Banjo Tunes and American Syncopation," *MQ*, 42 (1956),
2153   455-472.
            Discussion of types of banjo tunes, including their relationship to
            ragtime and early jazz.

NA
2154
Nathan, Hans. "The First Negro Minstrel Band and Its Origin," *SFQ*, 16 (1952), 132-144.
An account of the origin of the Virginia Minstrels, the first black minstrel band.

NA
2155
Nathanson, Y.S. "Negro Melodies and National Music," *Music Review*, 2 (1893), 514-516.

NA
2156
Nathanson, Y.S. "Negro Minstrelsy, Ancient and Modern," *Putnam's Monthly*, (1855), 72-79. (Reprinted in No. NA 1568.)
Memories of life in the South, with notes on comic presentations of "Jim Crow," "Hard Times in Old Virginny," *et al.*

NA
2157
National Council of Negro Women. *The Historical Cookbook of the American Negro*. Washington, D.C.: Corporate Press, 1958.

NA
2158
National Jubilee Melodies. Nashville, Tenn.: National Baptist Publishing Board, n.d.
161 songs.

NA
2159
National Portrait Gallery. *"A Glimmer of Their Own Beauty": Black Sounds of the Twenties*. Washington, D.C.: Smithsonian Institution, 1971.
Photos of black musical performers and night life of the 1920's.

NA
2160
Neal, Larry. "Eatonville's Zora Neale Hurston: A Profile," in *Black Review No. 2*, Mel Watkins, ed. New York: William Morrow, 1972, 11-24.
An account of life and work of the black folklorist-writer.

NA
2161
Neal, Larry. "Ellison's Zoot Suit," *Black World*, 20, No. 2 (1970), 31-50. (Reprinted in *Ralph Ellison: A Collection of Critical Essays*, John Hersey, ed. Englewood Cliffs, N.J.: Prentice-Hall, 1974, 58-79.)
Comments on Ralph Ellison's conception of black folk culture.

NA
2162
Neal, Larry. "My Lord, He Calls Me by the Thunder," *Essence* (New York), 1 (December, 1970), 38-39, 76.
The "Africanization" of Christianity by slaves in North America.

NA
2163
"The Negro Cesar's Cure for Poison," *The Massachusetts Magazine*, 4 (1792), 103-104.
A plantation slave-doctor's remedies.

NA
2164
Negro Culinary Art Club of Los Angeles. *Eliza's Cook Book*. Los Angeles:
    Wetzel, 1936.

NA
2165
"Negro Dances in Arkansas," *JAF*, 1 (1888), 83.
    The use of conjuring to return the dead (taken from the *Boston Herald*,
    May 7, 1887).

NA
2166
"A Negro Explains Jazz," *Literary Digest*, 61, No. 4 (1919), 28-29.
    James Reese Europe discusses the origins of the term "jazz" and Negro
    music in general.

NA
2167
"Negro Fables," *Riverside Magazine*, 2 (1868), 505-507; 3 (1869), 116-118.
    Animal tales from South Carolina rewritten in a childrens' magazine.

NA
2168
"Negro Folk Songs," *SW*, 34 (1895), 30-32.
    Deals with "Run, Nigger, Run," and "Juba" in a paper given and performed
    by several Hampton students at the 1894 American Folklore Society Meet-
    ing.

NA
2169
"A Negro Ghost Story," *SW*, 28 (1899), 449-450.
    1 tale.

NA
2170
"Negro Hymn of the Judgment Day," *JAF*, 9 (1896), 210.
    Text of a spiritual from North Carolina.

NA
2171
"The Negro in the Nation's Press," *Opportunity*, 10 (1932), 392.
    Discusses a North Carolina carpenter and his famous chairs.

NA
2172
"Negro Minstrels," *Saturday Review* (London), (June 7, 1884), 739-740.
    Origin of minstrel music; includes slave songs and discussion of instru-
    ments used by black performers.

NA
2173
"Negro Music in America," *Playground*, 23 (1929), 4-5.
    A speech by Thomas A. Long, discussing spirituals and work songs and
    their influence on America.

NA
2174
"Negro Music of the United States," *Grove's Dictionary of Music and Mu-
    sicians*, Vol. 3. London: Macmillan, 1921, 359-362.
    Discusses slave and minstrel music, with transcribed examples.

NA   "Negro Poisoners," *Harper's Weekly*, 57 (January 25, 1913), 30.
2175   Descriptions of African poisons and their use by Afro-Americans.

NA   "Negro Policeman 'Hoodooed'," *New York Times*, March 18, 1903, 2.
2176   A Washington, D.C. policeman shoots two other officers, claiming hoo-
             doo influence over him.

NA   "Negro Proverbs," *New York Times*, November 26, 1882, 11.
2177   A list of proverbs.

NA   *The Negro Singer's Own Book*. Philadelphia: Turner and Fisher, 1846.
2178

NA   "Negro Spiritual Contest in Columbus," *SW*, 55 (1926), 372-373.
2179   Account of a children's song contest.

NA   "A Negro Spiritual Contest in Columbus," *Playground*, 20 (1926), 90-92;
2180   20 (1927), 605-606.
             Describes a Georgia children's song contest; list of songs sung; il-
             lustrations.

NA   "Negro Spirituals," *Living Age*, 309 (1912), 38-41.
2181   Origin and nature of spirituals, with 2 texts.

NA   "Negro Superstitions," *Atlantic Monthly*, 75 (1895), 136-139.
2182   Legends and "superstitions" about the "hell hounds," a spectral pack
             of large dogs whose baying assures anyone who hears them death within
             the year.

NA   "Negro Superstitions Concerning the Violin," *JAF*, 5 (1892), 392-330.
2183   It was felt by slaves that the devil is a violinist; consequently
             there were few Negro violinists (taken from the Boston *Transcript*,
             October, 1892).

NA   "Negro Superstitions in South Carolina," *JAF*, 8 (1895), 251-252.
2184   List of "superstitions" taken from an article by Mary A. Waring in the
             Atlanta Constitution.

NA   "Negro Wakes in Los Angeles," *California Folklore Quarterly*, 3 (1944),
2185   326-328.
             California W.P.A. writers' description of 4 West Indian Negro wakes
             witnessed in 1939.

NA   "The Negro's Contribution to American Art," *Literary Digest*, 55, No. 16
2186   (1917), 26-27.
            Discussion of the folkloric importance of Uncle Remus stories, spirit-
            ual and slave songs, the clog and the jug, ragtime and blues as Negro
            artistic creations.

NA   Nelson, Mildred M. "Folk Etymology of Alabama Place Names," *SFQ*, 14 (1950),
2187   193-214.
            Includes a black place-name origin.

NA   Nelson, Mildred M. "A Folk Motif: The Face in the Window," *SFQ*, 15 (1951),
2188   255, 261.
            2 Negro tales.

NA   Nelson, Paul. "Jug Band! Jug Band!" *SO*, 13, No. 5 (1963-1964), 8-14.
2189   Discusses the rise of Southern Negro jug bands in the 1920's and
            their adaptation by white musical groups.

NA   Nelson, Randy F. "George Black: A New Folk Hero," *NCF*, 20 (1972), 30-35.
2190   Biography and craft of a clay brick-maker; illustrations.

NA   Nelson, W. "Superstition Concerning Drowning," *JAF*, 2 (1889), 308.
2191   A ritual from Patterson, New Jersey.

NA   Neuffer, Claude Henry. "The Bottle Alley Song," *SFQ*, 29 (1965), 234-238.
2192   A Gullah song concerning a second-hand clothing store on the corner of
            King Street and Bottle Alley in Charleston, South Carolina.

NA   Neuffer, Claude Henry, ed. *Names in South Carolina*, Vol. 12. Columbia,
2193   S.C.: Department of English, University of South Carolina, 1967.

NA   "New Orleans Voodoo," *WF*, 16 (1957), 60-61.
2194   Description of voodoo vendors and their wares.

NA   "New York City School Strike," *Folklore Forum*, 1, No. 4 (1968), 45-46.
2195   Poems (similar to toasts), used as propaganda in the New York City
            school strike of 1968.

NA   "New York's Negro Types Observed by Our Artist Covarrubias," *Vanity Fair*,
2196   29, October, 1927, 60.
            Caricatures by a Mexican artist.

NA 2197   Newell, W.W. "Folk-Lore and Ethnology," *SW*, 23 (1894), 131-133.
  Address on the importance and utility of the collection of Negro folk-lore.

NA 2198   Newell, W.W. "The Ignis Fatuus, Its Character and Legendary Origin," *JAF*, 17 (1904), 36-60.
  A tale of Maryland Negroes and its history.

NA 2199   W.W.N. "Negro Superstitions of European Origin," *JAF*, 12 (1889), 294-295.
  The author discusses how Negro "superstitions" and tales are thematically connected with an ancient heroic saga.

NA 2200   W.W.N. "Plantation Courtship," *JAF*, 8 (1895), 106.
  Comments on riddling in courtship.

NA 2201   Newell, W.W. "Record of Folklore and Mythology," *JAF*, 4 (1891), 180-182.
  Two notes, the first unsigned but probably by W.W. Newell, commenting on Mary Pamela Milne-Holmes' *Mama's Black Nurse Stories*; the second, signed by Newell, concerning voodoo and hoodoo, and a confluence of practice and a confusion of terms.

NA 2202   Newell, W.W. "Reports of Voodoo Worship in Hayti and Louisiana," *JAF*, 2 (1889), 41-47.
  Review of early accounts of voodoo in Haiti and Louisiana.

NA 2203   Newman, Dora Lee. "The Rabbit That Wouldn't Help Dig a Well," in *Marion County in the Making*, Fairmont, West Virginia: n.p., 1918.
  1 tale.

NA 2204   Newman, Lucile F. "Folklore of Pregnancy: Wives' Tales in Contra Coasta County, California," *WF*, 28 (1969), 112-135.
  Discussion of psychological and social motivation involved in "superstitions" of pregnancy, with 136 black beliefs.

NA 2205   Newton, Francis (E.J. Hobsbawn). *The Jazz Scene*. London: MacGibbon and Kee, 1959.
  Chapters on jazz and blues as protest and on the social and political setting of blues and jazz; mentions the "Creole bias" of jazz history.

NA 2206   Newton, Mary Mann-Page. "Aunt Deborah Goes Visiting: A Sketch from Virginia Life," *JAF*, 4 (1891), 354-356.
  A conversation in dialect with description of an old woman's dress.

NA   Nicholas, A.X. *Wake Up the Morning: The Poetry of the Blues*. New York:
2207   Bantam, 1973.
           Blues lyrics from recordings, with an introduction.

NA   Nichols, Charles H., Jr. *Many Thousand Gone, the Ex-Slaves' Account of*
2208   *their Bondage and Freedom*. Leiden: E.J. Brill, 1963.
           A survey of the contents of the slave autobiographies, with a section
           on slave songs of freedom (99-104), and "superstition" and the occult
           (121-122).

NA   Nichols, Charles H., Jr. "Slave Narratives," *NHB*, 15 (1952), 107-114.
2209   A review of the history of the narratives; comments on their contents;
           bibliography.

NA   Nichols, Charles H., Jr. "Who Read the Slave Narratives?" *Phylon*, 20
2210   (June, 1959), 149-162.
           Overview of publications based on the slave narratives; bibliography.

NA   Nichols, E.J., and W.L. Werner. "Hot Jazz Jargon," *Vanity Fair*, 45, No. 3
2211   (1935), 38, 71.
           Discussion of expressions used by jazz musicians.

NA   Nikolov, Wesselin. "Faktura Instrumentalna Muzyki Jazzowej po II Wojnie
2212   Swiatowej: Wybrane Zagadnienia," *Muzyka* (Breslau), 14, No. 2 (1969),
           68-92.
           Musical elements shared by traditional music and jazz.

NA   Niles, Abbe. "Ballads, Songs and Snatches," *The Bookman*, 66 (1928), 653-
2213   655; 67 (1928), 67-69, 168-170, 290-292, 422-424, 565-567, 687-689;
           68 (1928), 75-77, 213-215, 327-329, 457-459, 570-572.
           A series of reviews of jazz and blues records; includes popular song
           material and texts of lyrics.

NA   Niles, Abbe. "Blues Notes," *New Republic*, 45 (1926), 292-293. (Reprinted
2214   as "The Blues," in *Frontiers of Jazz*, Ralph de Toledano, ed. New
           York: Durrell, 1947, 32-57; and as "The Story of the Blues," in *A
           Treasury of the Blues*, W.C. Handy, ed. New York: Boni, 1949, 9-32.)
           Speculates about the origin of the blues form; says that blues lyrics
           are conceived from a common stock of traditional themes; points out
           the relationship of the blue note in blues to the music of popular
           composers such as Gershwin.

NA 2215 Niles, Abbe. "Rediscovering the Spirituals," *Nation*, 123 (1926), 598-600.
Review of current thinking and literature on spirituals.

NA 2216 Niles, John J. *Impressions of a Negro Camp Meeting*. New York: Carl Fischer, 1925.
8 songs.

NA 2217 Niles, John J. "In Defense of Backwoods," *Scribner's*, 83 (1928), 738-745.
Texts and discussion of Negro secular and religious songs from Kentucky.

NA 2218 Niles, John J. *Seven Negro Exaltations*. New York: Schirmer, 1929.
7 songs.

NA 2219 Niles, John J. "Shout, Coon, Shout!," *MQ*, 16 (1930), 516-530.
A discussion of the shout with comparisons drawn between international idioms which resemble the American expression.

NA 2220 Niles, John J. "Singing Soldiers," *Scribner's*, 80 (1926), 662-670; 81 (1927), 90-95.
A collection of 29 songs from Negroes in U.S. army regiments, presented in a narrative describing their collection.

NA 2221 Niles, John J. "White Pioneers and Black," *MQ*, 18 (1932), 60-75.
Characteristics of black folk music.

NA 2222 Nixon, Nell Marie. *Gullah and Backwoods Dialect in Selected Works by William Gilmore Simms*. Chapel Hill: University of North Carolina Press, 1971.

NA 2223 Noble, Gilbert Clifford. *The Most Popular Plantation Songs*. New York: Hinds, Hayden & Eldridge, 1911.

NA 2224 Noble, Hollister. "Negro Songs Lay a Spell on America," *New York Times*, February 28, 1926, Section 4, 4.
The rising popularity of Negro spirituals and folk songs; the portrait of life they offer.

NA 2225 Noble, Hollister. "Sad, Raucous Blues Charm World Anew," *New York Times*, September 28, 1926, Section 2, 1, 16.
Origins of the blues and a discussion of how it has filtered into white

society and Tin Pan Alley; considers that it has degenerated into
sentimentality within white society.

NA   Noblett, R.A. "Stavin' Chain," *Blues World*, 31 (June, 1970), 20-21.
2226

NA   Noblett, R.A. *Stavin' Chain: A Study in a Folk-Hero*. London: published by
2227   the author, 1969.
            A study of the published and recorded versions of a song concerning a
            "sexual" hero; includes texts, bibliography, discography.

NA   Nordhoff, Charles. *Nine Years a Sailor*. Cincinnati, 1857.
2228   Describes shantying in Mobile Bay in the late 1840's.

NA   Noreen, Robert G. "Ghetto Worship: A Study of the Names of Chicago Store-
2229   front Churches," *Names*, 13 (1965), 19-38.
            A list and analysis of church names.

NA   Norman, Henderson Daingerfield. "Native Wood Notes," *Atlantic Monthly*,
2230   138 (1926), 771-775.
            Discussion of content and expression in ballads, spirituals, etc.

NA   Norris, Thaddeus, "Negro Superstitions," *Lippincott's Magazine*, 6 (July,
2231   1870), 90-95. (Reprinted in No. NA 1568.)
            Includes beliefs, hoodoo, cures; a text of the Tar Baby story.

NA   Northrup, A. Judd. *Slavery in New York*. State Library Bulletin of History
2232   No. 4. Albany: University of the State of New York, 1900.
            Describes various conditions of blacks, songs, a lineage rivalry, mar-
            riage practices, etc.

NA   Northrup, Solomon. *Twelve Years a Slave*. Cincinnati, 1853.
2233   Autobiography of an ex-slave musician; description of music, dance,
            festivals; includes song texts, and a transcription of a fiddle tune.

NA   Norton, Arthur A. "Linguistic Persistence," *AS*, 6 (1921),
2234   Argues that Gullah speech was derived from French Canadian dialects.

NA 2235   Nuves, Mary L. "The Phonologies of Cape Verdean Dialects of Portuguese," *Boletim de Filologia* (Lisbon), 7 (1963), 1-56.
The Cape Verdean-Portuguese spoken by Afro-Americans (called "Bravas") living near New Bedford, Mass.

NA 2236   Nye, Russel B. "Musician's Word List," *AS*, 12 (1937), 45-58.
A glossary of jazz musician's terms.

NA 2237   "Objecting to the Negro Dialect," *Literary Digest*, 53 (1916), 1253.
Argues that folk and dialect songs are inspired by intense spiritual feelings and need to be expressed in dialect.

NA 2238   O'Connell, P. "Negro Ministry," *SW*, 57 (1928), 200-204.
Examines the position of black ministers as loan company owners.

NA 2239   O'Connor, Kate. "How Mr. Polecat Got His Scent," *PTFS*, No. 7 (1928), 137-138.
1 tale.

NA 2240   O'Donnell, E.P. "Fragments from Alluvia," *Scribner's*, 90 (1931), 401.
Negro memoirs of life, traditions and "superstitions" along the lower Mississippi.

NA 2241   O'Donnell, E.P. *Green Margins*. Boston: Houghton, Mifflin, 1936.
Novel of Louisiana life with folkloric content.

NA 2242   Odum, Anna Kranz. "Some Negro Folk-Songs From Tennessee," *JAF*, 27 (1914), 255-265.
25 texts of songs collected from children in Sumner County, Tennessee, with discussion.

NA 2243   Odum, Howard W. "Black Ulyssees Goes to War," *American Mercury*, 17 (1929), 385-400.
Short story in dialect having folkloric content and interspersed with song texts.

NA 2244   Odum, Howard W. "Black Ulysses in Camp," *American Mercury*, 18 (1929), 47-59. (Reprinted in Dundes, No. NA 854.)
A quasi-fictional account of a black soldier in World War I; includes excerpts of song texts.

NA
2245
Odum, Howard W. *Cold Blue Moon: Black Ulysses Afar Off*. Indianapolis:
    Bobbs-Merrill, 1931.
    Folkloric novel based on collected material; third volume of the trilogy,
    with Nos. NA 2249, NA 2252.

NA
2246
Odum, Howard W. "Down that Lonesome Road," *Country Gentleman*, 91 (May,
    1926), 18-19, 79.
    A brief discussion of secular songs with examples; source of the blues;
    illustrations.

NA
2247
Odum, Howard W. "Folk-Song and Folk-Poetry as Found in the Secular Songs of
    the Southern Negroes," *JAF*, 24 (1911), 255-294, 351-396.
    115 texts of Negro social and work songs, with discussion.

NA
2248
Odum, Howard W. "Negro Hymn," *JAF*, 26 (1913), 374-376.
    Text of a Negro hymn collected by Mrs. Emma M. Backus in Georgia.

NA
2249
Odum, Howard W. *Rainbow Round My Shoulder: The Blue Trail of Black Ulysses*.
    Indianapolis: Bobbs-Merrill, 1928.
    Folkloric novel based on collected material; first volume of the
    trilogy, with Nos. NA 2245, NA 2252.

NA
2250
Odum, Howard W. "Religious Folk Songs of the Southern Negro," *American
    Journal of Religious Psychology and Education*, 3 (1908-1909), 265-
    365.
    100 songs included in a discussion of the "psychological needs" of
    the Negro.

NA
2251
Odum, Howard W. "Swing Low, Sweet Chariot," *Country Gentleman*, 91 (March,
    1926), 18-19, 49-50.
    A discussion of spirituals, with examples, illustrations.

NA
2252
Odum, Howard W. *Wings on My Feet*. Indianapolis: Bobbs-Merrill, 1929.
    Folkloric novel based on collected materials; second volume of the
    trilogy, with Nos. NA 2245, NA 2249.

NA
2253
Odum, Howard W., and Guy B. Johnson. *The Negro and his Songs*. Chapel Hill:
    University of North Carolina Press, 1925. (Reprinted, Hatboro, Pa.:
    Folklore Associates, 1964, with a new foreword by Roger D. Abrahams.)
    Discussion of religious and secular Negro songs in their social set-
    ting, with 205 illustrative song texts.

NA
2254
Odum, Howard W., and Guy B. Johnson. *Negro Workaday Songs*. Chapel Hill: University of North Carolina Press, 1926.
    Compilation of Negro songs and discussion of their social background with a chapter on commercial phonograph recordings of the blues.

NA
2255
Odum, Howard W., and Guy B. Johnson. "Songs of Labor," *Scholastic*, 32 (March 5, 1938), 20.
    3 work songs.

NA
2256
Oertel, Hanns. "Notes on Six Negro Myths from the Georgia Coast," *JAF*, 2 (1889), 309.
    List of tales, from Charles Jones' collection, which have a resemblance to traditions current in Europe at the time.

NA
2257
"Old Slave Names," *Atlantic Monthly*, 66 (1890), 428.
    A list of "peculiar" slave names.

NA
2258
"Old-Time Burials," *Foxfire* (Rabun Gap, Georgia), 6, No. 1 (1972), 9-25.
    Description of black funeral preparations in rural Georgia (pp. 20-22).

NA
2259
Oliphant, Laurence. *Patriots and Filibusters*. London: Blackwood, 1860.
    Descriptive accounts of blacks in the Southern U.S., New Orleans, Panama, Nicaragua, Costa Rica, etc.; includes descriptions of sing-ing, with texts.

NA
2260
Oliver, Paul. "African Influence and the Blues," *Living Blues*, No. 8 (1972), 13-17.
    A reply to Richard Waterman in *Living Blues*, No. 6.

NA
2261
Oliver, Paul. *Aspects of the Blues Tradition*. New York: Oak, 1970. (Origi-nally published as *Screening the Blues: Aspects of the Blues Tradition*. London: Cassell, 1968.)
    Analysis of the subjects and genres of blues: preaching blues, "44's," policy blues, etc.; discusses obscenity in the blues, symbolism, cen-sorship, sung "dozens"; includes texts; bibliography and discography.

NA
2262
Oliver, Paul. *Bessie Smith*. New York: Barnes, 1959.
    An account of the singer's early career, influences and works; dis-cography.

NA   Oliver, Paul. "Big Maceo," *JM*, 3, No. 6 (1957), 7-10.
2263   Biographical notes and a review of the recordings of a Detroit blues-
            man; includes texts.

NA   Oliver, Paul. "Bill Wiliams," *Jazz and Blues*, 1 (August-September, 1971),
2264   10-11.
            Discussion of a Kentucky songster and the question of songster tradi-
            tions vs. blues singer traditions.

NA   Oliver, Paul. "Blind Lemon Jefferson," *The Jazz Review*, 2, No. 7 (1959),
2265   9-12.
            A tribute to the Texas guitarist-singer comes in an interview with a
            friend; an analysis of his music and some commemorative words from a
            minister.

NA   Oliver, Paul. "Blues as an Art Form," *Blues World*, 22 (October, 1968),
2266   1-7.

NA   Oliver, Paul. *Blues Fell this Morning: The Meaning of the Blues*. London:
2267   Cassell, 1960; New York: Horizon, 1961. (Published as *The Meaning of
            the Blues*. New York: Collier, 1963.)
            Analysis of 350 text fragments of the blues used for themes; also a
            presentation of historical and sociological background.

NA   Oliver, Paul. "Blues to Drive the Blues Away," in *Jazz*, Nat Hentoff and
2268   Albert J. McCarthy, eds. New York: Rinehart, 1959, 85-103, 357-359.
            An historical and definitional essay on the blues, its origin and
            spread; discography.

NA   Oliver, Paul. "Bull City Red," in *Back Woods Blues*, Oxford: Blues Un-
2269   limited, 1968, 10-12.
            3 page biography with lyrics from his blues.

NA   Oliver, Paul. *Conversation with the Blues*. New York: Horizon, 1965.
2270   Conversations with bluesmen recorded on a research tour of the U.S.;
            illustrations.

NA   Oliver, Paul. "Creoles, Cajuns and Confusion," in *Back Woods Blues*,
2271   Oxford: Blues Unlimited, 1968, 45-47.
            Identification of Creoles and Cajuns; historical background.

NA   Oliver, Paul. "Echoes of the Jungle," *Living Blues*, No. 13 (Summer, 1973),
2272   29-32.
            African retentions in the blues: a reply to David Evans' comments,
            No. NA 926.

NA   Oliver, Paul. "Georgia Tom: A Biographical Note," *JM*, 7, No. 9 (1961),
2273   6-8.
            The blues background of gospel composer Thomas A. Dorsey.

NA   Oliver, Paul. "Gutter Man Blues--Champion Jack Dupree," *JM*, 5 (January,
2274   1960), 4-8.
            The life of a New Orleans pianist-singer; memoirs of Negro music, enter-
            tainment and theatre in the early 1900's.

NA   Oliver, Paul. "Key to the Highway," *JM*, 4, No. 6 (1958), 2-5, 31.
2275   The biography of Tennessee bluesman Brownie McGhee.

NA   Oliver, Paul. "Kokomo Arnold," *JM*, 8, No. 3 (1962), 10-15.
2276   Life and music of a Mississippi blues singer-musician; includes song
            texts; illustrations, discography.

NA   Oliver, Paul. "Muddy Waters--1960," in *Back Woods Blues*, Oxford, U.K.:
2277   Blues Unlimited, 1968, 13-19.
            Biography with a bibliography of Waters.

NA   Oliver, Paul. "Policy Blues," *SO*, 16, No. 3 (1966), 16-19. (Reprint from
2278   *Jazz*.)
            An interpretation of the symbols associated with numbers gambling as
            they appear in many popular songs.

NA   Oliver, Paul. "Railroad Bill," *Jazz and Blues*, 1, No. 2 (1971), 12-14.
2279   The sources of a black ballad.

NA   Oliver, Paul. "Remembering Sonny Boy," *American Folk Music Occasional*,
2280   No. 2. New York: Oak, 1970, 39-44.
            The story of blues singer and mouth harpist Sonny Boy Williamson.

NA   Oliver, Paul. *Savannah Syncopators: African Retentions in the Blues*.
2281   New York: Stein and Day, 1970.
            Anthropologists' and jazz scholars' findings on musical links between
            Africa and the New World; discography.

NA
2282
Oliver, Paul. "Shoutin' Home to Glory," *JJ*, 9, No. 2 (1956), 1-2.
   Brief account of the Fisk Singers.

NA
2283
Oliver, Paul. "Special Agents," *Jazz Review*, 2, No. 2 (1959), 20-25.
   A discussion of how human, physical and commercial elements dictated
   which blues singers were recorded in the 1920's.

NA
2284
Oliver, Paul. *The Story of the Blues*. Philadelphia: Chilton, 1969.
   An illustrated history of the blues with discussion of work songs,
   spirituals, minstrelsy, vaudeville, medicine shows, boogie-woogie,
   jug bands, radio and the recording industry. Includes musical examples, bibliography and discography.

NA
2285
Oliver, Paul. "String Ticklers and Skillet Lickers," *JM*, 8, No. 12 (1963),
   8-10.
   The relation between white and black folk music; illustrations.

NA
2286
Oliver, Paul. "Too Tight: Bill Williams in Person," *Jazz and Blues*, 1,
   No. 8 (1971), 37-38.
   Interview with a Virginian-Kentuckian songster; notes on track-lining
   and calls.

NA
2287
Oliver, Paul, and Mike Leadbitter. *Muddy Waters*. Collectors Classic 1.
   Oxford, U.K.: Blues Unlimited, 1964.
   Brief bibliography and extensive discography of a Mississippi blues
   singer-guitarist.

NA
2288
Olmstead, Charles H. "Savannah in the '40's," *GHQ*, 1 (1917), 243-253.
   Description of black fire companies singing on the way to and from
   fires.

NA
2289
Olmsted, Frederick Law. *The Cotton Kingdom: A Traveller's Observations
   on Cotton and Slavery in the American Slave States*, 2 vols. New York:
   Mason, 1861.
   Accounts of a Negro funeral, Sunday dress, talk (Vol. 1, pp. 43-47);
   Christmas (Vol. 1, p. 97); use of fires (Vol. 1, p. 215); role of
   preachers (Vol. 1, pp. 259-261); singing, dancing (Vol. 2, pp. 72-73);
   religion (Vol. 2, pp. 221-228).

NA
2290
Olmsted, Frederick Law. *A Journey in the Back Country*. New York: Mason,
   1860.
   Accounts of slave religion, speech, dance, musical instruments, etc.

NA
2291
Olmsted, Frederick Law. *A Journey in the Seaboard Slave States*. New York: Dix and Edwards, 1856.
Accounts of a Negro funeral (pp. 24-29), singing at work (p. 394), burial practices (pp. 405-407), housing (pp. 421-425), marriages (p. 448), entertainments (p. 551), boating chanties (pp. 607-610).

NA
2292
Olmsted, Frederick Law. *A Journey through Texas*. New York: Dix and Edwards, 1857.
Southern speech (p. 728); black attitudes toward divinity.

NA
2293
Olsen, Douglas. "Legends and Tales From Alabama," *TFSB*, 28 (1962), 31-36.
7 stories.

NA
2294
Olsen, Louis P. "You Never Can Tell Where You'll Find a Tall Tale!" *MF*, 1 (1951), 105-108.
3 tall tales in "fancy" folk speech, told by a Negro from Boston, Mass.

NA
2295
Olsson, Bengt. *Memphis Blues and Jug Bands*. London: Studio Vista, 1970.
The blues musicians of Memphis; medicine shows, jug bands, etc. 16 song texts, bibliography and discography.

NA
2296
O'Neal, Jim, and Bill Greensmith. "Living Blues Interview: Jimmy Rogers," *Living Blues*, No. 14 (Autumn, 1973), 11-20.
Musical activities and background of a Chicago bluesman.

NA
2297
Ortiz Oderigo, Néstor R. "Una Expresión Genuina del Folklore Negro: Los Blues" (A Genuine Expression of Negro Folklore: The Blues), *Vea y Lea*, 4 (March 17, 1949), 41-43, 60.

NA
2298
Ortiz Oderigo, Néstor R. *Historia del Jazz*. Buenos Aires: Ricordi Americana, 1952.
Includes a chapter on the blues (pp. 80-95).

NA
2299
Ortiz Oderigo, Néstor R. "El Negro Norteamericano y sus Cantos de Labor," *Sustancia* (Tucuman, Argentina), 2 (1941), 552-560.
Discussion of U.S. Negro work songs with texts, in Spanish.

NA
2300
Ortiz Oderigo, Néstor R. *Panorama de la Musica Afroamericana* (Panorama of Afro-American Music). Buenos Aires, 1944.

NA   Ortiz Oderigo, Néstor R. *Rostros de Bronce: Musicos Negros de Ayer y de
2301   Hoy*. Buenos Aires: Mirasol, 1964.
            Essays on Negro musicians and composers, including Leadbelly.

NA   Oserjeman, Ofuntola. *Orisha: A First Glimpse of the African Religion of
2302   Brazil, Cuba, Haiti, Trinidad, and Now U.S.A.* See No. GEN 192.

NA   Osgood, Henry Osborne. "The Anatomy of Jazz," *American Mercury*, 7 (1926),
2303   385-395.
            The evolution of jazz orchestras.

NA   Osgood, Henry Osborne. "The Blooey Blues," *Musical Courier*, 93 (1926), 7,
2304   33.
            Asserts that blues owes its origins to W.C. Handy; includes lyrics to
            "St. Louis Blues" and "Gulf Coast Blues."

NA   Osgood, Henry Osborne. "The Blues," *Modern Music*, 4 (1926), 25-28.
2305   Opinions about blues by "serious" musicians of the time and their feel-
            ings that it offers nothing to "art."

NA   Osgood, Henry Osborne. "Jazz," *AS*, 1 (1926), 513-518.
2306   Discussion of the origin of the term "jazz."

NA   Osgood, Henry Osborne. *So This is Jazz*. Boston: Little, Brown, 1926.
2307   Early consideration of the origin, history and development of jazz.
            Discusses the origin of the word "jazz," etc. Also discusses spirituals
            and the blues.

NA   Osgood, Henry Osborne. "Sperichils," *Musical Courier*, 93 (August 12, 1926),
2308   8.
            Characteristics and origin of spirituals (reprinted in *So This
                is Jazz*, No. NA 2307).

NA   O'Sheel, Shaemas. "Two Spirituals," *Commonwealth*, 9 (1929), 480.
2309   2 texts.

NA   Osofsky, Gilbert, ed. *Puttin' on Ole Massa*. New York: Harper and Row,
2310   1969.
            3 slave narratives and 2 essays by Osofsky: "The Significance of Slave
            Narratives," (an introduction to their meaning and use) and "A Note on
            the Usefulness of Folklore" (understanding the folkloric elements in the
            slave narratives).

NA 2311 Oster, Harry. "The Afro-American Folktale in Memphis: Theme and Function," *Negro American Literature Forum*, 3, No. 3 (1969), 83-87.
5 tales provide examples of the various functions and themes of Afro-American folktales in contemporary society.

NA 2312 Oster, Harry. "Angola Prison Spirituals Recorded at Louisiana State Penitentiary in Angola," record notes to Folk-Lyric LP record LFS A6.
Discussion of 13 songs; includes 4 texts.

NA 2313 Oster, Harry. "Angola Prison Worksongs," booklet included with Folk-Lyric LP record LFS A5.
Notes on group and solo work songs in Louisiana.

NA 2314 Oster, Harry. "Background of the Blues," in *Black America*, John F. Szwed, ed. New York: Basic Books, 1970, 143-157.
Brief review of the history and variety of blues songs; includes several texts and excerpts.

NA 2315 Oster, Harry. "The Blues as a Genre," *Genre* (Chicago), 2 (1969), 259-274.
Discusses stanza variation, stylistic features, and functions of blues as a means of defining the blues genre.

NA 2316 Oster, Harry. "Country Negro Jam Sessions," booklet included with Folk-Lyric LP record FL 111.
Notes on 14 country blues and dance songs and the country instrumental tradition in the Deep South.

NA 2317 Oster, Harry. "Easter Rock Revisited: A Study in Acculturation," *LFM*, 1, No. 3 (1958), 21-43.
Description of a Louisiana religious ceremony; African sources.

NA 2318 Oster, Harry. *Living Country Blues*. Hatboro, Pa.: Folklore Associates, 1969.
Blues texts with discussion of origins, themes, functions: blues as poetry.

NA 2319 Oster, Harry. "Negro French Spirituals of Louisiana," *JIFMC*, 14 (1962), 153-167.
Catholic "spirituals" sung in Standard French rather than Creole French.

NA   Oster, Harry. "Negro Humor: John and Old Marster," *JFI*, 5 (1968), 42-57.
2320   5 tales and notes on informants, with some discussion.

NA   Oster, Harry. "A Sampler of Louisiana Folksongs," booklet included with
2321   Folk-Lyric LP record AFS Al.
             Notes on a ring shout, spirituals in French and English, blues, etc.

NA   Ott, Eleanor. *Plantation Cookery of Old Louisiana*. New Orleans: Harmand-
2322   son, 1938.

NA   Ottenberg, Simon. "Leadership and Change in a Coastal Georgia Negro Com-
2323   munity," *Phylon*, 20 (1959), 7-18.
             Religious institutions and their role in community organization and
             activities.

NA   Ottley, Roi. *Black Odyssey: The Story of the Negro in America*. London:
2324   John Murray, 1949.
             Social and cultural history of American Negroes from WPA writings,
             slave narratives, etc.; material on music, urban religious cults,
             slave life; index contains a lengthy entry entitled "slang terms and
             nicknames."

NA   Ottley, Roi, and William J. Weatherby. *The Negro in New York: An Informal
2325   Social History*. New York: New York Public Library; Dobbs Ferry, N.Y.:
             Oceana Publications, 1967.
             Edited manuscripts from the Federal Writers Project. Miscellaneous
             material on Afro-American life and entertainment in New York City.

NA   Otto, John Solomon, and Augustus M. Burns. "The Use of Race and Hillbilly
2326   Recordings as Sources for Historical Research: The Problems of Color
             Hierarchy among Afro-Americans in the Early Twentieth Century," *JAF*,
             85 (1972), 344-355.
             The complexities of color preference and symbolism as exemplified by
             commercial recordings.

NA   Overstreet, Harry A. "Images and the Negro," *Saturday Review* (New York),
2327   27 (August 26, 1944), 5-6.

NA   Owen, Guy. "Playing the Dozens," *NCF*, 21 (1973), 53-54.
2328   6 examples from North Carolina.

NA 2329   Owen, Mary Alicia. "Ole Rabbit an' de Dawg He Stole," *JAF*, 3 (1890), 135-138.
1 tale.

NA 2330   Owen, Mary Alicia. "Pig-Tail Charley," *JAF*, 16 (1903), 58-60.
1 text.

NA 2331   Owen, Mary Alicia. "True Stories," *The Folklorist* (Chicago), 1 (1893), 101-106.
3 tales and a song.

NA 2332   Owen, Mary Alicia. *Voodoo Tales, as Told among the Negroes of the Southwest*. New York: G.P. Putnam's, 1893. (Published in England as *Old Rabbit, the Voodoo and Other Sorcerers*. London: Knickerbocker, 1893.)
19 animal and bird tales written from recollections of the author who was born and brought up among a group of people of Negro and Indian descent in Missouri.

NA 2333   Owen, May West. "Negro Spirituals: Their Origin, Development and Place in American Folksong," *Musical Observer*, 19, No. 12 (1920), 12-13.

NA 2334   Owens, Guy. "Three Negro Folk Tales," *TFSB*, 34 (1968), 34-35.
Texts of 3 jests and their use in novels.

NA 2335   Owens, J. Garfield. *All God's Children*. Nashville, Tenn. and New York: Abingdon, 1971.
Essays on the theological influences on spirituals.

NA 2336   Owens, Tary. "Poetry from Texas Prisons," *Riata* (University of Texas), Spring, 1966, 22-33.
"Willy, the Weeper," a fantasy concerning opium smokers, in long-line verse form; a sample of the dozens; text of the toast "The Titanic."

NA 2337   Owens, William A. "The Blue-Tailed Fly," *PTFS*, No. 23 (1950), 212-214.
Text and music of 1 folk song that originated as a minstrel song.

NA 2338   Owens, William A. "Folklore of the Southern Negroes," *Lippincott's Magazine*, 20 (1877), 748-755. (Reprinted in No. NA 1568.)
"Superstitions," beliefs; 9 folktales.

NA   Owens, William A. "Go To Sleepy," *PTFS*, No. 23 (1950), 267-268.
2339   Text and music of a lullaby.

NA   Owens, William A. "The Roving Gambler," *PTFS*, No. 23 (1950), 183-185.
2340   Text and music of 1 song.

NA   Owens, William A. "Seer of Corsicana," *PTFS*, No. 29 (1959), 14-31.
2341   Interview with a fortuneteller in Corsicana, Texas.

NA   P.S.M. "Voodooism in Tennessee," *Atlantic*, 64 (1889), 376-380; 75 (1895),
2342   136-144, 714-720.
            Accounts of beliefs, "jay-bird witches," voodoo, etc.

NA   Packwood, Mrs. L.H.C. "Care for an Aching Tooth," *JAF*, 13 (1900), 66-67.
2343   1 remedy.

NA   Paddleford, Clementine. "What's Cooking in Harlem?" *Negro Digest*, 1 (Octo-
2344   ber, 1943), 11-12.

NA   Paine, Lewis W. *Six Years in a Georgia Prison*. New York: published by the
2345   author, 1851.
            Discussion of speech, corn shucking, Christmas, log-rolling, etc.

NA   Paneth, Donald. "Bergman's Queenie," *Commentary*, 12 (1951), 260-268.
2346   Descriptions of dress, customs, and religious beliefs of a young Harlem
            woman.

NA   Parker, Robert Allerton. *The Incredible Messiah: The Deification of Father
2347   Divine*. Boston: Little, Brown, 1937.

NA   Parkhurst, Jessie W. "The Role of the Black Mammy in the Plantation House-
2348   hold," *JNH*, 23 (1938), 349-369.
            Differences in the role of the "mammy" in plantation households, with
            an account of her real (and legendary) physical, emotional and intel-
            lectual attributes; relationship of mammy to the children and to the
            mistress in Southern plantations.

NA   Parkinson, Tom. "Circus Chanteys of Yesteryear Raised the Big Top to Song,"
2349   *SO*, 8, No. 2 (1958), 29-31. (Reprinted from *The Billboard*.)
            Description of Negro circus crews, with song texts.

NA 2350   Parks, Etta. "Big Sam and De Golden Chariot," *PTFS*, No. 19 (1944), 29-35.
          1 tale.

NA 2351   Parks, H.B. "Follow the Drinking Gourd," *PTFS*, No. 7 (1928), 81-84.
          Traces the origin and symbolic meaning of a song.

NA 2352   Parks, Lillian V. "Black Jests from Virginia," *Journal of the Folklore Society of Greater Washington* (D.C.), 4 (Spring, 1973), 18-20.
          8 tale texts.

NA 2353   Parler, Mary Celestia. "The Forty-Mile Jumper," *JAF*, 64 (1951), 422-423.
          1 witch tale from South Carolina.

NA 2354   Parrish, Charles H. "Color Names and Color Notions," *JNE*, 15 (1946), 13-20.
          The connotations of 25 terms for skin color among blacks.

NA 2355   Parrish, Lydia. "The Plantation Songs of Our Old Negro Slaves," *Country Life*, 69 (December, 1935), 50-54, 62-64, 75-76.

NA 2356   Parrish, Lydia. *Slave Songs of the Georgia Sea Islands*. New York: Creative Age Press, 1942. (Reprinted, with new Foreword by Bruce Jackson. Hatboro, Pa.: Folklore Associates, 1965.)
          Introduction includes information on the preservation of slave songs and African survivals, beliefs, language, etc., on the Georgia coast; a collection of 12 shout songs, 19 ring plays, dance, fiddle songs, 33 religious songs, and 27 work songs; includes bibliography and photos of singers, carvings, houses, etc.

NA 2357   Parsons, Elsie Clews. "Accumulative Tales Told by Cape Verde Islanders in New England," *JAF*, 33 (1920), 34-42.
          3 folktale texts.

NA 2358   Parsons, Elsie Clews. "Die Flucht auf den Baum," *Zeitschrift für Ethnologie*, 54 (1922), 1-29.
          Tales collected from Cape Verde Negroes in Massachusetts and Rhode Island; included are 4 texts in English.

NA 2359   Parsons, Elsie Clews. "Folklore from Aiken, South Carolina," *JAF*, 34 (1921), 1-39.
          36 tales, 92 riddles, 2 songs' verses and 4 ring-games collected from school children.

NA
2360

Parsons, Elsie Clews. *Folk-Lore from the Cape Verde Islands*. Memoirs of the American Folk-Lore Society, Vol. 15 (Parts 1 and 2). New York: The American Folklore Society, 1923.
A collection from Cape Verdean immigrants in New England. Part 1 contains an introduction and 133 tales in English translation; Part 2 includes linguistic notes, 133 tales in Portuguese (with music), 182 proverbs, and 292 riddles with English translations.

NA
2361

Parsons, Elsie Clews. "Folklore from Georgia," *JAF*, 47 (1934), 386-389.
Contains 13 riddles, 4 play rhymes and 6 tales collected in Georgia and Florida.

NA
2362

Parsons, Elsie Clews. "Folklore of the Cape Verde Islanders," *JAF*, 34 (1921), 89-118.
Superstitions, beliefs, and practices from Massachusetts and Rhode Island, with 2 songs.

NA
2363

Parsons, Elsie Clews. "Folklore of the Cherokee of Robeson County, North Carolina," *JAF*, 32 (1919), 384-393.
Indian-Negro riddles, tales, and quilting.

NA
2364

Parsons, Elsie Clews. *Folklore of the Sea Islands, South Carolina*. Memoirs of the American Folk-Lore Society, Vol. 16. Cambridge, Mass. and New York: The American Folklore Society, 1923.
178 tales, 187 riddles, 3 proverbs, 12 toasts and rhymes, 18 songs; beliefs, folklife data, the majority of which were collected on St. Helena Island in 1919. Some tales heard from sailors from the Iberian Peninsula; others of African provenience; others brought from the North, since the Islanders visited or lived there periodically.

NA
2365

Parsons, Elsie Clews. "Folktales Collected at Miami, Florida," *JAF*, 30 (1917), 222-227.
16 tales in dialect.

NA
2366

Parsons, Elsie Clews. "From 'Spiritual' to Vaudeville," *JAF*, 35 (1922), 331.
Brief background of a spiritual and its inclusion in popular culture.

NA
2367

Parsons, Elsie Clews. "Games of the Cape Verde Islands," *JAF*, 33 (1920), 80-81.
3 games of residents of Massachusetts and Rhode Island, with discussion.

NA
2368
Parsons, Elsie Clews. "Joel Chandler Harris and Negro Folklore," *Dial*, 66 (1919), 491-493.
Harris' influence on the collection of Southern Negro folk-tales.

NA
2369
Parsons, Elsie Clews. "Notes on Folklore of Guilford Gounty, North Carolina," *JAF*, 30 (1917), 201-208.
55 riddles, 2 counting-out games, and a tale.

NA
2370
Parsons, Elsie Clews. "The Provenience of Certain Negro Folktales, V," *Folklore*, 34 (1923), 363-370.
Discussion of variants of "The House-Keepers" tale in Europe, Cape Verde (in New England), Africa, and the U.S. Includes a number of fragments of texts.

NA
2371
Parsons, Elsie Clews. "Spirituals from the 'American' Colony of Samana Bay, Santo Domingo." See No. DR 17.

NA
2372
Parsons, Elsie Clews. "Tale and Song from Virginia," *JAF*, 34 (1921), 125.
Text of a tale and a song collected from a black soldier returning from France.

NA
2373
Parsons, Elsie Clews. "Tales from Guilford County, North Carolina," *JAF*, 30 (1917), 168-200.
62 tales.

NA
2374
Parsons, Elsie Clews. "Tales from Maryland and Pennsylvania," *JAF*, 30 (1917), 209-217.
11 tales.

NA
2375
Parsons, Elsie Clews. "Tar-Baby," *JAF*, 35 (1922), 330.
Discussion of the origin of the "Tar-Baby" tale.

NA
2376
Parsons, Elsie Clews. "Ten Folktales from the Cape Verde Islands," *JAF*, 30 (1917), 230-238.
10 tales collected from immigrants resident in Rhode Island and Massachusetts.

NA
2377
Parsons, Elsie Clews. "War Verses," *JAF*, 47 (1934), 395.
Verses from a sergeant in a Negro regiment in France.

NA
2378
Parsons, Elsie Clews. "A West Indian Tale," *JAF*, 32 (1919), 442-443.
1 tale from a Trinidadian in New York City.

NA
2379
Parsons, Mildred. "Negro Folklore from Fayette County," *TFSB*, 19 (1953),
67-70.
Legends, beliefs and customs.

NA
2380
Paskman, Dailey, and Sigmund Spaeth. *"Gentlemen Be Seated": A Parade of
the Old-Time Minstrels*. New York: Doubleday, Doran, 1928.
Descriptions of minstrel shows, with sample songs, jokes and routines;
includes some Negro material and references.

NA
2381
Patterson, Cecil L. "A Different Drum": The Image of the Negro in the Nineteenth Century Songster," *CLA Journal*, 8 (1964), 44-50.
The changing role of the Negro as portrayed in American songbooks.

NA
2382
Patterson, Dan. "A Sheaf of North Carolina Folksongs," *NCF*, 4, No. 1 (1956),
23-31.
Includes 1 black ballad, "Uncle Ananias' Funeral Song," with music.

NA
2383
Patterson, Pernet. *The Road to Canaan*. New York: Minton, Balch, 1931.
Short stories of Richmond, Virginia life with folkloric content.

NA
2384
Paulding, James K. *Letters from the South Written During an Excursion in
the Summer of 1816*. New York, 1817.
Description of slave songs (pp. 126-127), musical instruments (p. 118),
dances (p. 119), etc.

NA
2385
Paulson, Frank M. "A Hair of the Dog and Some Other Hang-Over Cures from
Popular Tradition," *JAF*, 74 (1961), 152-168.
Includes Negro material.

NA
2386
Pavie, Théodore. *Souvenirs Atlantiques*, 2 vols. Paris, 1833.
Description of dancing and music in the South, Vol. 2, 319-320.

NA
2387
Payne, Bishop Daniel. *Recollections of Seventy Years*. Nashville, Tenn.,
1888.
Description of a ring shout in Philadelphia in the 1870's.

NA
2388

Payne, L.W. "A Word List from East Alabama," *Dialect Notes*, 3 (1903), 279-328, 343-391.
Argues that Negro speech has had the largest influence on white Alabama speech.

NA
2389

Peabody, Charles. "Notes on Negro Music," *JAF*, 16 (1903), 148-152. (Reprinted in *SW*, 33 (1904), 305-309.)
A description of Negro music in Mississippi; 1 musical example and notes on collecting.

NA
2390

Pearce, J.E. "Folklore and Its Influence in Determining Institutions," *PTFS*, No. 1 (1916), 65.
Statement about the prevalence of "superstition, immorality, and general unreason" among Southern Negroes' professions of faith in Christianity.

NA
2391

Pearson, Elizabeth Ware, ed. *Letters from Port Royal*. Boston: W.B. Clarke, 1906.
Description of Sea Island life, including religion, work, dress, naming, language, etc.

NA
2392

Pearson, W.D. "Going Down to the Crossroads: The Bluesmen and Religion," *Jazz and Blues*, 2, No. 1 (1972), 13-15.
Religious imagery and themes in the blues; discography.

NA
2393

Pebworth, Ted. "Graveyard Working: The Passing of a Custom," *LFM*, 2 (1961), 44-49.

NA
2394

Pederson, Lee A. "Negro Speech in *The Adventures of Huckleberry Finn*," *Mark Twain Journal*, 13, No. 1 (1966), 1-4.

NA
2395

Pederson, Lee A. "Non-Standard Negro Speech in Chicago," in *Non-Standard Speech and the Teaching of English*, William A. Stewart, ed. Washington, D.C.: Center for Applied Linguistics, 1964, 16-23.
Notes differences between white and Negro speech in Chicago, and between the speech of native-born Chicago Negroes and Southern-born immigrant Negroes.

NA
2396

Pederson, Lee A. "Terms of Abuse for Some Chicago Social Groups," *Publications of the American Dialect Society*, 42 (1964), 26-48.
Over 100 abusive terms of Negroes for Negroes; discusses origin and significance of pejoratives in Chicago.

NA
2397

Peebles, Edwin A. *Swing Low*. Boston: Houghton Mifflin, 1945.
Novel with folkloric content.

NA
2398

Pendleton, Lewis. "Notes on Negro Folklore and Witchcraft in the South," *JAF*, 3 (1890), 201-207.
Witchcraft, animal myth, the "Tar-Baby" story and voodooism in the South.

NA
2399

Pennington, Patience (Elizabeth W. Allston Pringle). *A Woman Rice Planter*.
New York: Macmillan, 1913.
Gullah customs and traditions.

NA
2400

Penrod, James H. "The Folk Hero as Prankster in the Old Southwestern Yarns," *KFR*, 2 (1956), 5-12.
White punishments and jokes against Negroes in Alabama derived from literary sources.

NA
2401

Penrod, James H. "Folk Motif in Old Southwestern Humor," *SFQ*, 19 (1955), 117-124.
Contains a section on the "origin of the colored race."

NA
2402

Penrod, James H. "Minority Groups in Old Southwestern Humor," *SFQ*, 22 (1958), 121-128.
A consideration of the treatment of two racial groups by nine writers, with the contention that they generally presented the folk concept of the Negro and the Indian.

NA
2403

Perdue, Chuck. "I Swear to God It's the Truth if I Ever Told It!," *KFQ*, 14 (1969), 1-54.
63 texts from one husband and wife team of tale-tellers, with background data, commentary, tale-type and motif numbers.

NA
2404

Perdue, Chuck. "John Jackson: Blues and Country Dance Tunes from Virginia," record notes to Arhoolie LP record F 1025.
A Virginia singer and guitarist who performs in both white and black traditions.

NA
2405

Perdue, Robert E., Jr., "'African' Baskets in South Carolina," *Economic Botany*, 22 (1968), 289-292.
The techniques and raw materials used in basket-weaving near Charleston; African sources of the tradition; differences from American Indian basketry. Illustrations.

NA 2406   Pereda Valdés, Ildefonso. "A Note on Blues," in *Negro Anthology*, Nancy
Cunard, ed. London: Wishart, 1934, 377.
The "mood" projected by the blues.

NA 2407   Perkins, A.E. "Negro Spirituals From the Far South," *JAF*, 35 (1922), 223-
249.
Texts of 48 spirituals with comments.

NA 2408   Perkins, A.E. "Riddles from Negro School-Children in New Orleans, Louisiana," *JAF*, 35 (1922), 105-115.
64 folk riddles and 57 "modern" conundrums.

NA 2409   Perrow, E.C. "Songs and Rhymes from the South," *JAF*, 25 (1912), 137-155.
Includes 2 Negro song texts (p. 155).

NA 2410   Perrow, E.C. "Songs and Rhymes from the South," *JAF*, 26 (1913), 123-173.
Texts collected from white and black Southerners with some musical
notation: animal songs (27 texts), religious songs and parodies (30
texts), and railroad songs (10 texts), pp. 125-136, 149, 153-172.

NA 2411   Perrow, E.C. "Songs and Rhymes from the South," *JAF*, 28 (1915), 129-190.
Texts collected from white and black Southerners with some musical
notation: drinking and gambling songs (8 texts), songs of the plantation (27 texts), love songs (23 texts), pp. 129-144, 176, 180, 186-190.

NA 2412   Pesquinne, Blaise. "Le Blues, La Musique Negre des Villes; Naissance et
Avenir du Jazz," *La Revue Musicale*, 15, No. 150 (1934), 273-282.
Essay on the nature and essence of jazz and blues.

NA 2413   Peterkin, Julia. *Black April*. New York: Bobbs-Merrill, 1927.
20 stories of Sea Island life which include "superstitions," tales,
beliefs, and folkways of the South Carolina low-country Negroes.

NA 2414   Peterkin, Julia. *Bright Skin*. Indianapolis: Bobbs-Merrill, 1932.
A novel of Sea Island Negro life, including conversations, beliefs,
stories written in modified Negro dialect.

NA 2415   Peterkin, Julia. *The Collected Short Stories of Julia Peterkin*. Frank
Durham, ed. Columbia, S.C.: University of South Carolina Press, 1970.
Short stories with folkloric content from the Sea Island culture.

NA
2416
Peterkin, Julia. *Green Thursday*. New York. Knopf, 1924. (Reprinted in No. NA 2415).
Short stories of Gullah life with folkloric content.

NA
2417
Peterkin, Julia. "Gullah," in *Ebony and Topaz*, Charles S. Johnson, ed. New York: National Urban League, 1927, 35.
Discusses what "Gullah" means in terms of language, region, and people.

NA
2418
Peterkin, Julia. *A Plantation Christmas*. Boston: Houghton, Mifflin, 1934.
Sea Island Christmas memoir.

NA
2419
Peterkin, Julia. *Scarlet Sister Mary*. Indianapolis: Bobbs-Merrill, 1928.
Novel which includes slave recollections and plantation life of Gullahs.

NA
2420
Peterkin, Julia. "Seeing Things," *American Magazine*, 105 (January, 1928), 26-27, 115-116.

NA
2421
Peterkin, Julia. "Venner's Sayings," *Poetry*, 23 (1923), 59-67, 114.
10 poems based on traditional South Carolina sayings.

NA
2422
Peterkin, Julia. "Vinner's Sayings," *Poetry*, 25 (1925), 240-243.
A poem based on traditional South Carolina sayings.

NA
2423
Peterkin, Julia, and Doris Ulmann. *Roll, Jordan, Roll*. New York: Robert O. Ballou, 1933.
Description of Negro life in the old South which includes tales, sermons, beliefs, grave decorations, dress, samples of dialect, etc.; 70 photos by Doris Ulmann.

NA
2424
Peters, Paul. "Dockwallopers," *American Mercury*, 20 (1930), 319-326.
Myths, prejudices and cultural climate of life along the wharf in Arkansas, Missouri and Illinois; includes 3 work songs with texts.

NA
2425
Peterson, Mrs. Clara Gottschalk. *Creole Songs from New Orleans in the Negro Dialects*. New Orleans: Grunewald, 1902.
Creole dialect texts with English translation and music.

NA
2426
Peterson, Owen. "Celery Stalks Along the Highway," *JM*, 16 (August, 1970), 17-19.
    The meanings of arcane titles of jazz recordings and compositions.

NA
2427
Peterson, Tracey. "The Witch of Franklin," *SFQ*, 32 (1969), 297-312.
    Biography and background of a witch (possibly black).

NA
2428
Pharr, Robert Deane. *The Book of Numbers*. Garden City: Doubleday, 1969.
    Novel of Southeastern urban life with folkloric content; the black numbers racket; Gullah speech, etc.

NA
2429
Phillips, R.E. *Plantation Melodies Old and New*. New York: G. Schirmer, 1901.
    Several songs and a sermon.

NA
2430
Phillips, Romeo Eldridge. "White Racism in Black Church Music," *NHB*, 36 (1973), 17-20.

NA
2431
Phillips, Waldo B. "Negro Spirituals in Retrospect," *NHB*, 22 (1958), 51-53.
    Comments on the protest element of the spirituals.

NA
2432
"Phrases of the People," in *American Stuff*. New York: Viking, 1937, 149-152.
    Proverbs, verses and folktales from Vicksburg, Mississippi.

NA
2433
"Phrases of the People," in *American Stuff*. New York: Viking, 1937, 258.
    Proverbs from Arkansas.

NA
2434
Pickens, William. *American Aesop: Negro and Other Humor*. Boston: Jordan and Moore, 1926.
    Contains a number of Negro stories (pp. 3-107).

NA
2435
Piersen, William D. "An African Background for American Negro Folktales?" *JAF*, 84 (1971), 204-214.
    Review of the literature of the controversy over the source of U.S. Negro folktales, which cautions against rejecting Africa as a source.

NA
2436
Pierson, Hamilton W. *In the Brush, or, Old-Time Social, Political and Religious Life in the Southwest*. New York: Appleton, 1881.
    Includes description of an "old-time midnight slave funeral," music, preachers, sermons, etc.

NA   Pike, G.D. *The Jubilee Singers and their Campaign for Twenty Thousand Dol-*
2437   *lars*. Boston: Lee and Shephard; New York: Lee, Shephard and Dillingham,
           1873.
           Anecdotes of travel through the North and South; biographical sketches
           of each of the singers; music and texts of songs; brief essay on the
           music by Theo F. Seward. (Basically the same work as J.B.T. Marsh, *The
           Story of the Jubilee Singers*. Boston: Houghton, Osgood, 1880.)

NA   Pinchbeck, Raymond B. *The Virginia Negro Artisan and Tradesman*. Publica-
2438   tion of the University of Virginia Phelps-Stokes Fellowship Papers,
           No. 7, Richmond, Va.: William Byrd, 1926.
           The trades of Negroes in Virginia from 1619 to 1926.

NA   Pinkney, Alphonso. *Black Americans*. Englewood Cliffs, N.J.: Prentice-Hall,
2439   1969.
           Chapter 7, "Contributions to American Life," draws attention to Afro-
           American music, dance and social values.

NA   Pinkowski, Edward. "Philadelphia Street Cries," *KFQ*, 5 (1959), 10-12.
2440   Traditional street cries, 2 from Negroes.

NA   Pipes, James. *Ziba*. Norman, Okla.: University of Oklahoma Press, 1944.
2441   Poetry based on folk speech, beliefs, etc. from rural Louisiana.

NA   Pipes, William H. *Say Amen, Brothers: Old-Time Negro Preaching*. New York:
2442   William Frederick, 1951.
           Sermons and ritual in Macon County, Georgia; 7 sermon texts.

NA   Pitkin, Helen. *An Angel by Brevet*. Philadelphia: Lippincott, 1904.
2443   Novel contains texts and music of 5 Creole songs.

NA   "Plantation Singing," in *Negro Anthology*, Nancy Cunard, ed. London: Wis-
2444   hart, 1934, 363.
           Description of singing in Georgia.

NA   "Plantation Song," *SW*, 29 (1900), 481.
2445   1 spiritual.

NA   "Plantation Songs," *SW*, 29 (1900), 41, 114, 150, 206, 288, 352, 436, 464.
2446   12 spirituals.

NA   "Plantation Songs," *SW*, 30 (1901), 88, 196, 294, 406, 510, 558, 590.
2447   7 spirituals.

NA   "Plantation Songs," *SW*, 31 (1902), 122, 339, 617, 678.
2448   4 spirituals.

NA   "Plantation Songs," *SW*, 32 (1903), 35, 102, 228a, 410, 461, 592.
2449   7 spirituals.

NA   "Plantation Song," *SW*, 32 (1904), 161.
2450   1 spiritual.

NA   "Plantation Songs," *SW*, 35 (1906), 163, 528, 655.
2451   3 spirituals.

NA   "Plantation Songs," *SW*, 36 (1907), 144, 207, 394b, 689.
2452   4 spirituals.

NA   "Plantation Songs," *SW*, 37 (1908), 272, 400.
2453   2 spirituals.

NA   "Plantation Song," *SW*, 41 (1912), 208.
2454   1 spiritual.

NA   "Plantation Songs," *SW*, 42 (1913), 48, 704.
2455   2 spirituals.

NA   "Plantation Songs," *SW*, 45 (1916), 88, 336, 413, 646.
2456   4 spirituals.

NA   "Plantation Song," *SW*, 46 (1917), 126.
2457   1 spiritual.

NA   "Plantation Songs," *SW*, 49 (1920), 388, 340, 435.
2458   3 spirituals.

NA   "Plantation Song," *SW*, 50 (1921), 560.
2459   1 spiritual.

NA   "Plantation Songs," *SW*, 53 (1924), 48, 144, 230.
2460   3 spirituals.

NA   "Plantation Songs," *SW*, 54 (1925), 368, 432.
2461   2 spirituals.

NA   Platt, James, Jr. "The Negro Element in English," *Athenaeum*, 2 (1900),
2462   283.
            Short article on Negro dialect and terms with references to the place
            of origin and meaning.

NA   Platt, Orville H. "Negro Governors," *Papers of the New Haven Colony His-*
2463   *torical Society*, 6 (1900), 315-335.
            Election of Negro governors and kings in the New England states in the
            eighteenth and nineteenth centuries; descriptions of parades, dances,
            music, and costumes.

NA   Pleat, Geraldine R., and Agnes N. Underwood. "Pinkster Ode, Albany, 1803,"
2464   *NYFQ*, 8 (1952), 31-45.
            Poem describing the celebration of the Pinkster (Pentecost) festival by
            Negro slaves in Albany, New York in 1803.

NA   Poe, William Baxter. "Negro Life in Two Generations. Observations of a
2465   Southern Farmer," *Outlook* (New York), 75 (1903), 493.
            The author describes the diversity of slaves in the old South, citing
            example of varying African backgrounds, "superstitions," etc.

NA   Polk, William T. *Southern Accent: From Uncle Remus to Oak Ridge*. New
2466   York: William Morrow, 1953.
            Chapter 4: "Uncle Remus Spake Queen's English" argues that Afro-Ameri-
            cans speak English dialects of several centuries' vintage; Chapter 9:
            "Take Two and Butter 'Em While They're Hot" concerns Southern cuisine.

NA   Pollard, Edward Alfred. *Black Diamonds Gathered in the Darkey Homes of the*
2467   *South*. New York: Pudney and Russell, 1860.
            Accounts of hymns and preaching rhymes (pp. 23, 34, 36, 76, 128), hair
            style (p. 22), funerals (pp. 38, 89), influence of slave culture on
            whites (pp. 49-50, 74-75, 88, 91-98, 115-122), a "Guinea-speaking"
            conjurer (p. 58), tales and songs (pp. 76, 129), and slave fantasies
            (pp. 98-106).

NA 2468   Polsky, Ned. *Hustlers, Beats and Others*. Chicago: Aldine, 1967 (Revised edition, Garden City: Doubleday, 1969).
Includes discussion of the influence of Afro-American culture on hustlers, beatniks, hippies and other American subcultural types.

NA 2469   Porter, Grace Cleveland. *Negro Folk Singing Games and Folk Games of the Habitants*. London: Curwin, 1914.
16 traditional games with directions, of which 13 are from Negroes in the South.

NA 2470   Porter, James A. "The Trans-Cultural Affinities of African Negro Art," in *Africa Seen by American Negroes*, John A. Davis, ed. Paris: Présence Africaine, 1958, 119-130.
Review of African influences in Afro-American art.

NA 2471   Porter, James A. "Versatile Interests of the Early Negro Artist: A Neglected Chapter of American Art History," *Art in America* (New York), 24 (1936), 116-127.
Brief survey of Negro painters from Colonial times to the beginning of the 20th century.

NA 2472   Porter, Kenneth W. "Children's Songs and Rhymes of the Porter Family: Robert Porter, 1828-1910; Ellis K. Porter, 1860-1936," *JAF*, 54 (1941), 167-175.
2 songs from Iowa.

NA 2473   Porter, Kenneth W. "A Legend of the Biloxi," *JAF*, 59 (1946), 168-173.
The legend of the Biloxi Indians drowning themselves *en masse* in defiance of the whites is unified with similar legends of the Ibo in South Carolina in the lore of the Seminole Negroes of Brackettville, Texas.

NA 2474   Porter, Kenneth W. "Notes on Negroes in Early Hawaii," *JNH*, 19 (1934), 193-197.
The prevalence of interracial marriage between American Negroes, Portuguese blacks, "African natives," and Hawaiians, and its effect on the cultural mores and traditions of Hawaii; bibliography.

NA 2475   Porter, Kenneth W. "Racism in Children's Rhymes and Sayings, Central Kansas, 1910-1918," *WF*, 24 (1965), 191-196.
Use of "nigger" in counting-out rhymes, sayings and toys and their racial implications.

NA   Porter, Kenneth W. "Willie Kelley of the Lost Nigger Mine," *WF*, 13 (1954),
2476   13-26.
         Information about the background and identity of the Negro who supposed-
         ly found the "Lost Nigger Mine."

NA   Porter, Leroy. "Tale 1," *Blackfolk* (Los Angeles), 1, No. 1 (1972), 23.
2477   An anecdote concerning a "bad nigger."

NA   Porter, Mrs. M.E. *Mrs. Porter's New Southern Cookery Book* . . . Philadel-
2478   phia: J.E. Potter, 1871.

NA   Post, Lauren C. "A Recollection of the Bleeding of Our Sick Mare by a
2479   'Voodoo Doctor'," *LFM*, 3, No. 5 (1975), 6-8.
         Account of a cure in 1913.

NA   Postell, William Dosite. *The Health of Slaves on Southern Plantations*.
2480   Baton Rouge: Louisiana State University Press, 1951.
         Descriptions of daily plantation activities, slave clothing, food,
         housing, diseases and medical practices; illustrations, bibliography.

NA   Pound, Louise. "The Ancestry of a 'Negro Spiritual'," *Modern Language
2481   Notes*, 33 (1918), 442-444.
         Traces the Negro Spiritual "Weeping Mary" to a Methodist revival hymn.

NA   Powdermaker, Hortense. *After Freedom: A Cultural Study in the Deep South*.
2482   New York: Viking, 1939.
         A study of race relations and acculturation in Indianola, Mississippi;
         discusses religion and magic; includes the text of a written sermon.

NA   Powe, Marilyn. "Black 'Isms'," *MFR*, 6 (1972), 76-82.
2483   194 dream interpretations, predictions, signs, cures, etc., from Missi-
         ssippi.

NA   Prange, Arthur J., Jr., and M.M. Vitols. "Jokes among Southern Negroes:
2484   The Revelation of Conflict," *Journal of Nervous and Mental Diseases*,
         136 (1963), 162-167.
         Jokes collected by blacks, from blacks, with analysis.

NA   "The Preacher's Song," in *American Stuff*. New York: Viking, 1937, 214-215.
2485   1 song text from Arkansas.

NA 2486   Pred, Allen. "Business Thoroughfares as Expressions of Urban Negro Culture,"
           Economic Geography, 39 (1963), 217-233.
           A survey of business types.

NA 2487   Preece, Harold. "The Negro Folk Cult," *Crisis*, 43 (1936), 364, 374.
           (Reprinted in Dundes, No. NA 854.)
           A political critique of the folkloristic writings of collectors of
           black folklore.

NA 2488   Preece, Harold, and Celia Kraft. *Dew on Jordan*. New York: Dutton, 1926.
           Includes a spiritual from Arkansas.

           Pressoir, Charles Fernand. See No. HA 288.

NA 2489   Preston, Denis, and Albert McCarthy. "Poetry of Afro-American Folk-Song.
           The Impact of Christianity," *Folk*, February, 1945, 22-26.
           Style of preaching and singing in American black churches. Songs and
           sermon texts from printed sources.

NA 2490   "Pretty Pa-Tree," *JAF*, 11 (1898), 272.
           A song of uncertain provenience.

           Price, Richard, and Sally Price. "Saramaka Onomastics: An Afro-American
           Naming System." See No. FGS 143.

NA 2491   Price, Sadie F. "Kentucky Folklore," *JAF*, 14 (1901), 30-38.
           Includes a section on Negro "superstitions" (pp. 33 ff).

NA 2492   Pride, Armistead Scott. "The Names of Negro Newspapers," *AS*, 29 (1954),
           114-118.
           Newspaper names listed with commentary.

NA 2493   Primus, Pearl. "Primitive African Dance (and its Influence on the Churches
           of the South)," in *The Dance Encyclopedia*, Anatole Chujoy, ed. New
           York: A.S. Barnes, 1949.

NA 2494   Proctor, H.H. "The Theology of the Songs of the Southern Slave," *SW*, 36
           (1907), 584-592; 652-656.
           The moral values of the Negro as expressed through the texts of spir-
           ituals.

NA
2495
*Protestant-Episcopal Freedmen's Commission Narrative of a Visit to the
Schools of the P.E. Freedmen's Commission in Norfolk and Petersburg.*
n.p. (1867?).
Accounts of singing, verses of songs, types of songs; mentions body
movements and emotional fervor.

NA
2496
Puckett, Newbell. N. "American Negro Names," *JNH*, 23 (1938), 35-48.
"Unusual" names among Afro-Americans and their apparent increase in
frequency.

NA
2497
Puckett, Newbell N. *Folk Beliefs of the Southern Negro.* Chapel Hill, N.C.:
University of North Carolina Press, 1926. (Reprinted as *Magic and Folk
Beliefs of the Southern Negro.* New York: Dover, n.d.)
Southern Negro speech, music, dance, games, riddles, proverbs, and
folktales discussed. Chapter-length treatments of 1) burial customs,
ghosts and witches; 2) voodooism and conjuration; 3) charms and cures;
4) taboos; 5) signs and omens; 6) the relation to Christianity; bibliography, illustrations.

NA
2498
Puckett, Newbell N. "Names of American Negro Slaves," in *Studies in the
Science of Society*, George P. Murdock, ed. New Haven: Yale University
Press, 1937, 471-494.
Names and name sources during slavery.

NA
2499
Puckett, Newbell N. "Negro Character as Revealed in Folklore," in *Racial
Contacts and Social Research*, Publications of the American Sociological
Society, 28, No. 2, Chicago, 1934, 12-23.
A content analysis of Southern Negro beliefs.

NA
2500
Puckett, Newbell N. "The Negro Church in the U.S.," *Social Forces*, 4
(1926), 581-587.
A brief history of the development of black religion up to the Civil
War.

NA
2501
Puckett, Newbell N. "Race Pride and Folklore," *Opportunity*, 4, No. 39
(1926), 82-84. (Reprinted in Dundes, No. NA 854.)
An essay on the importance of black folklore.

NA
2502
Puckett, Newbell N. "Religious Folk Beliefs of Whites and Negroes," *JNH*,
16 (1931), 9-35.
Discusses similarities and differences of white and Negro beliefs, songs
and visions, the devil, Christmas, taboos, camp meetings, etc.

NA 2503 Puckette, Clara Childs. *Old Mitt Laughs Last*. Boston: Bobbs-Merrill, 1944.
Novel portraying the folk characteristics and speech of the Gullah.

NA 2504 Pugh, Griffith T. "George W. Cable's Theory and Use of Folk Speech," *SFQ*, 24 (1969), 287-293.
Includes analysis of Cable's use of Creole dialect in his writings.

NA 2505 Purcell, J.M. "Mrs. Stowe's Vocabulary," *AS*, 13 (1938), 230-231.
Notes on words not listed in dictionaries.

NA 2506 Purvis, Robert. *Remarks on the Life and Character of James Forten*. Philadelphia: Merrihew and Thompson, 1842.
Life of free black sailmaker and merchant James Forten; tells of his childhood, service under Decatur, beliefs and religious life, etc.

NA 2507 Pyrnelle, Louisa-Clark. *Diddie, Dumps, and Tot; or, Plantation Child-Life*. New York: Harper, 1898.
Memoirs of Mississippi plantation games, songs, folktales, religious services and sermons, weddings, Christmas, cures, etc.

NA 2508 Quad, M. *Brother Gardner's Lime-Kiln Club*. Chicago: Belford, Clarke, 1883.

NA 2509 Quitt, Michael. "Some Traditional Negro Tales in the City," *Journal of the Folklore Society of Greater Washington*, 2, No. 1 (1970-1971), 16-18.
2 Brer Rabbit tales from Baltimore, with notes on the teller.

NA 2510 "Rabbits'-Foot Lore," *The Folklorist* (Chicago), 1 (1893), 169.
4 versions of getting a rabbit's foot charm.

NA 2511 "A Race for a Wife," *SW*, 26 (1897), 78-79.
2 tales.

NA 2512 Radcliffe, Charles. "Blues Walking Like a Man," *Anarchy*, 5, No. 5 (1965), 140-158.

NA 2513 Radcliffe, Charles, and Mike Rowe. "Chicago Blues, the Post-War Scene," *JM*, 11 (September, 1965), 20-23; (November, 1965), 19-23.
Social and musical aspects of urban blues; the black Chicago audience for blues; includes portions of texts of 10 songs.

Radin, Paul. See Johnson, Clifton H., No. NA 1614.

NA
2514
Raichelson, Richard. "Lil McClintock's 'Don't You Think I'm Santa Claus',"
John Edwards Memorial Foundation Quarterly, 6 (1970), 132-134.
Discussion of the origins of a song.

NA
2515
Raim, Walter, ed. *The Josh White Song Book*. Chicago: Quadrangle Books,
1967.
A songster's songs with notes and biography by Robert Shelton.

NA
2516
Rainwater, Lee, ed. *Soul*. Chicago: Aldine, 1970.
Articles on black life and culture reprinted from *Trans-action* magazine.

NA
2517
Ramos, Artur. "O Negro nos Estados Unidos" (The Negro in the United States),
in *Brasil-Estados*. Rio de Janeiro: Diariode Noticias, 1939, 323-326.

NA
2518
Ramsey, Frederic, Jr. "Baby Dodds: Talking and Drum Solos," booklet included with Folkways LP record FJ 2290.
Notes to a recorded interview and examples of early New Orleans jazz
drumming.

NA
2519
Ramsey, Frederic, Jr. *Been Here and Gone*. New Brunswick, New Jersey:
Rutgers University Press, 1960.
Photographic essay on the life and audience of country musicians.

NA
2520
Ramsey, Frederic, Jr. "Elder Songsters," *JM*, 3, No. 12 (1958), 6-8, 31.
Older Negro folk music and its influence on jazz.

NA
2521
Ramsey, Frederic, Jr. "Leadbelly: A Great Long Time," *SO*, 15, No. 1 (1965),
7-11, 13-24.
The life and music of a Louisiana songster; includes 2 transcribed
songs; illustrations.

NA
2522
Ramsey, Frederic, Jr. "Lines from Buckner's Alley," *Saturday Review*, 40
(September 14, 1957), 61, 63-64. (Reprinted in *JM*, 3, No. 9 (1957),
2-4).
Profile of "Cat-Iron," a Mississippi bluesman; includes blues texts.

NA
2523
Ramsey, Frederic, Jr. "Music from the South, Vol. 1: Country Brass Bands,"
booklet included with Folkways LP record 650.
The nature and sources of black brass bands in town and country; tran-
script of a conversation among a group of musicians; illustrations.

NA 2524 Ramsey, Frederic, Jr. "Music from the South, Vols. 2, 3, 4: Horace Sprott," booklet included with Folkways LP records 651, 652, 653.
Notes and texts of an Alabama singer: blues, church songs, work songs, buck dances, etc.

NA 2525 Ramsey, Frederic, Jr. "Music from the South, Vol. 5: Songs, Play and Dance," booklet included with Folkways LP record 654.
Notes and texts of game songs, buck dances, blues guitar, etc. from Alabama and Mississippi; illustrations.

NA 2526 Ramsey, Frederic, Jr. "Music from the South, Vols. 6, 7: Elder Songster," booklet included with Folkways LP records 655, 656.
Notes and texts of spirituals, hollers and work songs of elderly singers from Alabama, Mississippi and Louisiana; texts of interviews; includes a selection of excerpts from 18th and 19th century sources on Negro music in the United States; illustrations.

NA 2527 Ramsey, Frederic, Jr. "Music from the South, Vols. 8, 9: Young Songsters; Song and Worship," booklet included with Folkways LP records 657, 658.
Notes and texts of gospel songs, prayers, and church services in Alabama and Louisiana; illustrations.

NA 2528 Ramsey, Frederic, Jr. "A Photographic Documentary of Jazz and Folk Backgounds," *RC*, 12, No. 7-8 (July-August, 1953), 23-47.
Photos from Deep South locales.

NA 2529 Ramsey, Frederic, Jr. *Where the Music Started: A Photographic Essay*. New Brunswick, N.J.: The Institute of Jazz, Rutgers University, 1970.
Photographs and notes on Southern music and life.

NA 2530 Ramsey, Frederic, Jr., and Charles Smith, eds. *Jazzmen*. New York: Harcourt, Brace, 1939.
A series of articles portraying the story of blues and jazz and their origins.

NA 2531 Randel, W. "Edward Eggleston on Dialects," *AS*, 30 (1955), 111-114.
Discussion of Eggleston's manuscripts describing dialects, especially "The Dialect of the Negro," in which he catalogues vowels, citing passages from Southern Negro dialects.

NA   Randolph, A. Philip. "Dialogue of the Old and the New Porter," *Messenger*,
2532   9 (1927), 94, 131-132. (Reprinted in Dundes, No. NA 854.)
            Dialogue containing proverbs and dialect.

NA   Randolph A. Philip. "The Human Hand Threat," *Messenger*, 4 (1922), 499-
2533   500. (Reprinted in Dundes, No. NA 854.)
            Account of the Ku Klux Klan's use of black folklore for intimidation.

NA   Randolph, Laura. "Uncle Si'ah and the Ghosts," *SW*, 32 (1903), 506.
2534   1 tale.

NA   Randolph, Peter. *From Slave Cabin to Pulpit*. Boston, 1893.
2535   Includes accounts of slave escapes, religion, dress, work, hunting,
            speech, etc.

NA   Randolph, Peter. *Sketches of Slave Life*. . ., 2nd edition, enlarged. Bos-
2536   ton: published by the author, 1855.
            Describes clothing, food, work, hunting and trapping, making of traps,
            house vs. field slaves; city and town slaves, religion (citing hymns)
            of the free blacks and of slaves, funeral customs, family ties, etc.

NA   Randolph, Vance. *Ozark Folksongs*, Vol. 2. Columbia, Mo.: The State Histori-
2537   cal Society of Missouri, 1948.
            Chapter 7, "Negro and Pseudo-Negro Folksongs," (pp. 322-390) has 53
            songs, with notes.

NA   Randolph, Vance, and George P. Wilson. *Down in the Holler: A Gallery of
2538   Ozark Folk Speech*. Norman, Okla.: University of Oklahoma Press, 1953.
            Negro vocabulary items listed but not identified as such.

NA   Raper, Arthur F. *Preface to Peasantry: A Tale of Two Black Belt Counties*.
2539   Chapel Hill: University of North Carolina Press, 1936.
            A study of Green and Macon Counties, Georgia, between 1927 and 1936.
            Contains the section "Leisure Time and Recreational Activities."

NA   Rapp, Marvin A. "'Nigger' in the Woodpile," *NYFQ*, 14 (1958), 16-25.
2540   Claims that the origin of this saying, which expressed deep suspicion,
            was from the Putneyville slave escape route to Canada.

NA   Rasky, Frank. "Harlem's Religious Zealots," *Tomorrow*, 9 (November, 1949),
2541   11-17.
            Discusses religious cult leaders Elder Lightfoot, Solomon Michaux and
            Mother Rose Artimus Horne.

NA   Rathburn, F.G. "The Negro Music of the South," *SW*, 22 (1893), 174.
2542   Comments on plantation slaves' music and the difficulties of discover-
            ing origins and sustaining purity.

NA   Raum, Green. *The Existing Conflict*. Washington, 1884.
2543   Describes rise of KKK, black reactions, etc. One account (pp. 273-274)
            of Negro fife and drum clubs in Mississippi tapping drums to show
            applause, and white opposition to the practice.

NA   Ravenel, H.W. "Recollections of Southern Plantation Life," *Yale Review*, 25
2544   (1936), 748-787.
            Written in 1876, contains descriptions of South Carolina customs, "super-
            stitions," and vocabulary.

NA   Ravenel, Rose Pringle. *Piazza Tales: A Charleston Memory*, Anthony Harrigan,
2545   ed. Charleston, S.C.: Shaftesbury, 1952.
            A white woman's memoirs of Charleston Negro slave life: naming, beliefs,
            Christmas festivities, dancing, music, etc.

NA   Ravitz, Abe C. "John Pierpont and the Slaves' Christmas," *Phylon*, 21 (1960),
2546   383-386.
            Describes a plantation Chirstmas: dancing, foods, etc.

NA   Rawick, George P., ed. *The American Slave: A Composite Autobiography*.
2547   Westport, Connecticut: Greenwood, 1972.
            19 volumes of ex-slave autobiographies and accounts, compiled by the
            WPA and Fisk University in the 1920's and 1930's. (Vol. 1, George P.
            Rawick, *From Sundown to Sunup: The Making of the Black Community*, is
            an introduction and appraisal of the collection.)

NA   Rawick, George P. *From Sundown to Sunup: The Making of the Black Communi-
2548   ty*, (Vol. 1 of *The American Slave: A Composite Autobiography*.) West-
            port, Connecticut: Greenwood, 1972.
            The WPA and Fisk collections of ex-slave accounts assessed; the making
            of black communities in America; includes folklore, religion, domestic
            life, etc.

NA   Rawick, George P. "West African Culture and North American Slavery: A
2549   Study of Culture Change among American Slaves in the Ante-Bellum
            South with Focus upon Slave Religion," in *Migration and Anthropology*.
            Proceedings of the 1970 Annual Spring Meeting of the American Ethno-
            logical Society, Robert F. Spencer, ed. Seattle: American Ethnological
            Society, 1970, 149-164.
            Discussion of cultural survivals and adaptation under slavery, with

special emphasis on the use of pots in slave religious services. (See Sidney W. Mintz and A. Norman Klein, "Some Aspects of Involuntary Migration and Slavery: Comments on the Papers by Rawick and Cohen," same volume, 181-189, for discussion and additional evidence in support and in opposition to this paper.)

NA
2550   Read, Allen Walker. "The Speech of Negroes in Colonial America," *JNH*, 24 (1939), 247-258.
        Records of 18th century Negro dialect speech; vocabulary included, with comparisons of linguistic variations between blacks of Jamaica, Barbados, Bermuda and the U.S. when speaking English.

NA
2551   Read, William A. *Louisiana-French*. Baton Rouge: Louisiana State University Press, 1931.
        Study of the varieties of French spoken in Louisiana contains 15 words (pp. 116-128) of African origin; contains a Creole song text with translation (p. 148).

NA
2552   Reaver, J. Russell. "Folk History from North Florida," *SFQ*, 32 (1968), 7-16.
        Contains 3 Negro stories around which the author discusses the importance of the informant in collecting folk history.

NA
2553   "Recording the Indian's Music," *Literary Digest*, 46 (1913), 951.
        Argues that Negroes may have borrowed syncopation from the Indians.

NA
2554   Reddihough, John. "Country Brass Bands and New Orleans Jazz," *JM*, 2, No. 6 (1956), 7-8.
        Discussion of Southern black country brass bands as prototypes of New Orleans jazz bands.

NA
2555   Redfearn, Susan Fort. "Songs from Georgia," *JAF*, 34 (1921), 121-124.
        4 song texts.

NA
2556   Reeves, Dick. "Gullah: Some Say the Carolina Low-Country Patois is Disappearing," *Sandlapper*, (Columbia, S.C.), May, 1970, 8-11.

NA
2557   Reger, Muriel. "Scat Singing," *News Graphic*, (Mexico City), 1949.
        The use of language sounds (not words) in jazz tunes, Brazilian singing, etc.

NA 2558   Reid, Ira De A. "The John Canoe Festival," *Phylon*, 3 (1942), 349-370.
A study of the John Canoe festival that occurred in the U.S. along the coastal region of eastern North Carolina, reaching its peak during the period 1880-1890; contains 3 rhythmic chants and a brief description of the performance.

NA 2559   Reid, Ira De A. "Let Us Prey!" *Opportunity*, 4 (1926), 274-278.
Storefront churches and spiritualists.

NA 2560   Reid, Ira De A. "Mrs. Bailey Pays the Rent," in *Ebony and Topaz*, Charles S. Johnson, ed. New York: National Urban League, 1927, 144-148.
Description of rent parties in Atlanta and Harlem, their organizational structure, music, food, slang, etc.

NA 2561   Reid, Ira De A. *The Negro Immigrant: His Background, Characteristics, and Social Adjustment, 1899-1937*. New York: Columbia University Press, 1939.
Study of Antillean, Haitian, Puerto Rican, and the Cape Verdean immigrants in the U.S.: includes discussion of language, social clubs, religion, beliefs, magic, celebrations, national stereotypes, foods, funerals, and wakes, 4 song texts; life histories of immigrants (pp. 171-214); contains references to novels of West Indian culture in the U.S. (p. 138).

NA 2562   Reinders, Robert C. "Sound of the Mournful Dirge," *Jazz: A Quarterly of American Music* (Albany, California), No. 4 (1959), 296-298.
Argues that the *form* (but not the *style*) of black New Orleans funeral parades, bands and organizations were derived from whites in the nineteenth century.

NA 2563   Reisner, Robert G. *The Jazz Titans*. Garden City, New York: Doubleday, 1960.
Includes "The Parlance of Hip," a slang glossary.

NA 2564   Render, Sylvia Lyons. "North Carolina Dialect: Chestnutt Style," *NCF*, 15, No. 2 (1967), 67-70.
Negro dialect and vocabulary in the novels of Charles W. Chestnutt.

NA 2565   Render, Sylvia Lyons. "Tar Heelia in Chestnutt," *CLA Journal*, 9 (1965), 39-50.

NA 2566   Reynolds, Harry. *Minstrel Memories*. London: A. Rivers, 1928.
Minstrelsy in England from 1836 to 1927.

NA   Reynolds, Horace. "Old Virginny Neber Tire," *Christian Science Monitor*
2567   *Magazine*, July 5, 1947, 5.
            Discusses Negro proverbs.

NA   Rhame, John M. "Flaming Youth," *AS*, 8 (1933), 39-43.
2568   Story in Gullah dialect with a short analysis.

NA   Rhone, George E. "Curing a Haunted Fiddle," *KFQ*, 8 (1963), 81-83.
2569   A ghost story told by Pennsylvania boatmen circa 1910; describes a black
            circle dance.

NA   Rhone, George E. "The Swamp Angel," *KFQ*, 10 (1965), 86-91.
2570   Story of conjuration.

NA   Rice, Edward LeRoy. *Monarchs of Minstrelsy from "Daddy" Rice to Date.*
2571   New York: Kensey, 1911.
            Contains biographical sketches of early minstrels and notes on their
            impersonations.

NA   Rice, James Henry. *Glories of the Carolina Coast.* Columbia, S.C.: R.L.
2572   Bryan, 1936.
            Life, traditions and folklore of the Gullah.

NA   Rice, John. "Storytelling in West Philadelphia," *KFQ*, 18, Nos. 1-2 (1973),
2573   59-64.
            5 tale texts.

NA   Richard, Mrs. M.B. "Easter Day on the Plantation," *The Plantation Mission-
2574   ary* (Beloit, Alabama), 3, No. 2 (1892), 12-14.
            Describes decorations of homes of blacks, dress, sermons, distribution
            of rations; religious ceremonies.

NA   Richardson, Clement. "Some Slave Superstitions," *SW*, 41 (1912), 246-248.
2575   Sign "superstitions," conjures, child-birth lore, etc.

NA   Rickels, Patricia K. "The Folklore of Sacraments and Sacramentals in South
2576   Louisiana," *LFM*, 2, No. 2 (1965), 27-44.
            Includes Negro folk-Catholic beliefs and rituals.

NA
2577
Rickels, Patricia K. "Some Accounts of Witch Riding," *LFM*, 2, No. 1 (1961), 1-17.
Tales of witches from students at the University of Southwestern Louisiana.

NA
2578
Riley, Edward Miles, ed. *The Journal of John Harrower, An Indentured Servant in the Colony of Virginia, 1773-1776*. Williamsburg, Virginia: Colonial Williamsburg, 1963.
Mentions the *barrafou*, an African xylophone played by a slave near Fredericksburg.

NA
2579
Rinder, Irwin D. "A Note on Humor as an Index of Minority Group Morale," *Phylon*, 26 (1965), 117-121.
Review of research on minority humor and an interpretation of its meaning.

NA
2580
Rinzler, Ralph. "Traditional Music at Newport, Part I," booklet included with Vanguard LP record VRS 9182.
Discussion of 3 blues (Alabama and Mississippi), 2 sacred songs (South Carolina), and 3 songs on panpipes (Alabama).

NA
2581
Roach, Hildred. *Black American Music: Past and Present*. Boston: Crescendo, 1973.

NA
2582
Robb, Bernard. *Welcum Hinges*. New York: Dutton, 1942.
Plantation tales and sayings in dialect from Virginia.

NA
2583
Roberts, Hermese, compiler. "Glossary," in the *Living Webster Encyclopedic Dictionary of the English Language*, 1971.

NA
2584
Roberts, Hermese E. *The Third Ear: A Black Glossary*. Chicago: The English Language Institute of America, 1971.
Glossary of Afro-American slang in the United States.

NA
2585
Roberts, Hilda. "Louisiana Superstitions," *JAF*, 40 (1927), 144-208.
Discussion of "superstitions" among the blacks, whites and Indians of Louisiana with 1,585 "superstitions" collected.

NA
2586
Roberts, Leonard E. *The Negro Chef Cookbook*. East Falmouth, Mass.: published by the author, 1969.
Recipes; notes on the importance of some Negro chefs in the United States.

NA   Roberts, William F. *Dixie Darkies: Negro Stories--Mule Tales--Race Rela-*
2587   *tionships.* Boston: Humphries, 1942.
            Traditional stories of whites about blacks in the South, includes black-
            white interaction, "superstitions," various black speech occasions (in
            dialect).

NA   Robin, C.C. *Voyages dans l'Intérieur de la Louisiane.* Paris: F. Buisson,
2588   1807.
            Volume 3 (pp. 185-189) contains an early discussion of Creole speech
            and grammar in Louisiana.

NA   Robinson, F.L. "The Coloured People of the United States," *Leisure Hour,*
2589   38 (1889), 54-59, 697-700.
            Discusses Negro character in the South and North and includes descrip-
            tions of a cakewalk, clapboard supper, camp-meeting, funeral.

NA   Robinson, John Bell. *Pictures of Slavery and Anti-Slavery.* Philadelphia,
2590   1863.
            Contains a detailed description of a slave's construction of his own
            home upon being given his freedom (pp. 142-144).

NA   Robinson, Norborne T.N., Jr. "Blind Tom, Musical Prodigy," *GHQ,* 51 (1967),
2591   336-358.
            Account of a piano prodigy's musical skills, compositions, his stage
            behavior, his "idiosyncrasies" of naming, conversation, fantasies, etc.,
            his influence on the speech of whites.

NA   Roche, Emma Langdon. *Historic Sketches of the South.* New York: Knicker-
2592   bocker, 1914.
            Includes an account of the voyage of the Clotilde (the last ship to
            bring slaves to the U.S.) and the history of her human cargo. (See
            Fauset, No. NA 952, for folk tales collected from one of the Clotilde's
            "passengers"; also see Hurston, No. NA 1521.)

NA   Rock, John. *Africa Sings and the Psychology of Jazz.* Colombo, Ceylon:
2593   General, 1946.

NA   Rockmore, Noel. *Preservation Hall Portraits.* Baton Rouge: Louisiana State
2594   University Press, 1968.
            History of New Orleans as an early jazz center and photographs of jazz
            musicians with biographical sketches.

NA
2595
Rodeheaver, Homer A. *Plantation Melodies*. Chicago: Rodeheaver, 1918.
47 songs with music.

NA
2596
Rodeheaver, Homer A. *Rodeheaver's Negro Spirituals*. Chicago: Rodeheaver, 1923.
51 spirituals.

NA
2597
Rodenbough, Jean. "The Magic Sinder Seed and Other Matters," *NCF*, 19 (1971), 180-184.
A singing game, with a description of how it was sung by a slave.

NA
2598
Rodgers, Carolyn. "Black Poetry--Where It's At," *Negro Digest*, 18, No. 11 (1969), 7-16. (Reprinted in Kochman, No. NA 1756.)
The influence of vernacular speech on black poetry. Includes a typology of black linguistic expressions.

NA
2599
Rodman, Lyda T. "The Black Baby and the Bear," *NCF*, 7, No. 2 (1959), 28-30.
1 tale.

NA
2600
Roffeni, Alessandro, ed. *Il Blues: Saggio Critico e Antologia*. Milano: Edizioni Academia, 1973.
An anthology of transcribed texts of blues records (in English, with Italian translations); includes an essay on the blues and the poetics of the blues; biographical notes on performers, discography.

NA
2601
Rogers, Charles Payne. "Delta Jazzmen," *Jazz Forum*, No. 1 (1946), 11-12.
Reminiscence by George Lewis of old New Orleans musicians and bands: Chris Kelly, Buddy Petit and others.

NA
2602
Rogers, J.A. "Jazz at Home," *Survey*, 53 (1925), 665-667.
Brief essay on jazz, its background, and purpose.

NA
2603
Rogge, Heinz. "Das Erbe Afrikas in Sprache und Kultur de Nordamerikanischen Gullahs" (The African Heritage of the Language and Culture of the North American Gullahs), *Zeitschrift für Volkskunde*, 61 (1965), 30-37.

NA
2604
Rohrer, John, and Munro Edmonson. *The Eighth Generation: Cultures and Personalities of New Orleans Negroes*. New York: Harper, 1960. (Reprinted as *The Eighth Generation Grows Up*. New York: Harper, 1964.)
A study of the culture and personalities of New Orleans Negroes; includes sections on the psychological content of Creole folksongs, pop songs, and on dialect and social class.

NA   Rollins, Charlemae, ed. *Christmas Gif': An Anthology of Christmas Poems,*
2605   *Songs and Stories, Written by and about Negroes.* Chicago: Follett,
             1963.
             Contains recipes, descriptions of Christmas customs, etc., up until
             the 1930's.

NA   Rookmaker, H.R. *Jazz, Blues, Spirituals.* Leiden: Zomer and Keunings,
2606   1960.

NA   Rooney, James. *Bossmen: Bill Monroe and Muddy Waters.* New York: Dial,
2607   1971.
             Interview-biographies of a Kentucky bluegrass musician and a Mississippi
             blues musician; illustrations.

NA   Rose, Al, and Edmond Souchon. *New Orleans Jazz: A Family Album.* Baton
2608   Rouge: Louisiana State University Press, 1967.
             Biographies and photos of jazzmen, bands, cabarets, dance halls, steam-
             boats and graveyards in New Orleans from the late 1800's to recent
             times.

NA   Rosenberg, Bruce A. *The Art of the American Folk Preacher.* New York:
2609   Oxford University Press, 1970.
             A stylistic analysis of contemporary Afro-American sermons, with many
             texts. (See Samarin, William J., No. NA 2637.)

NA   Rosenberg, Bruce A. "The Formulaic Quality of Spontaneous Sermons," *JAF,*
2610   83 (1970), 3-20.
             A discussion of American black sermon style.

NA   Rosenberger, Homer. "The Witch of Pine Station," *KFQ,* 4 (1959), 121-126.
2611

NA   Rosenblatt, Roger. "The 'Negro Everyman' and His Humor," in *Veins of*
2612   *Humor,* Harvard English Studies 3, Harry Levin, ed. Cambridge, Mass.:
             Harvard University Press, 1972, 225-241.
             The humor of Langston Hughes' fictional character Jesse B. Simple.

NA   Rossac, Guy. "El Negro Spiritual," *Boletín de Programas* (Bogota), 20, No.
2613   209 (1961-1962), 24-28.

NA   Rossi, Nick. "Father of the Blues," *Music Journal* (New York), 29, No. 5
2614   (1971), 24-26, 58-59.

NA
2615
Rourke, Constance. *American Humor: A Study of the National Character*. New York: Harcourt, Brace, 1931.
Chapter 3, on minstrelsy, discusses its role in American fantasy and humor.

NA
2616
Rourke, Constance. *The Roots of American Culture*. New York: Harcourt, Brace and World, 1942.
Chapter titled "Traditions for a Negro Literature" argues that all aspects of white minstrelsy were derived from Negro folk culture.

NA
2617
Roussere, Charles B. *The Negro in Louisiana: Aspects of His History and His Literature*. New Orleans: Xavier University Press, 1927.

NA
2618
Rowe, G.S. "The Negroes of the Sea Islands," *SW*, 29 (1900), 709-715.
A description of South Carolina plantation life, music and dialect.

NA
2619
Royal, Aylett. "I'se Sho' Nuff Lucky," *PTFS*, No. 13 (1937), 137-145.
Revelations of luck and charms.

NA
2620
Rublowsky, John. *Black Music in America*. New York: Basic Books, 1971.
Popular version of the history of black music from Africa to "soul."

NA
2621
"Rufus' Funeral," *Blackfolk* (Los Angeles), 1, No. 1 (1972), 31.
1 tale.

NA
2622
Rugbean (Mr. Dixon). *Transatlantic Rambles*. London: George Bell, 1851.
Includes descriptions of a New York minister's sermon and dress (pp. 42-43), Virginia Negro songs (p. 54), Sea Island laughter (p. 57), dancing to fiddle music (p. 59), Sunday dress in Charleston (p. 62), a Negro funeral and train car (pp. 62-63); brief notes on Brazilian Negroes.

NA
2623
Ruspoli, Mario, ed. *Blues: Poésie de l'Amérique Noire* (Blues: Poetry of Black Americans). Paris: Les Publications Techniques et Artistiques, 1947.

NA
2624
Russell, Gordon W. *"Up Neck" in 1825*. Hartford: Cage, Lockwood, and Brainerd, 1890.
Additional detail on the material on Negro governors found in I.W. Stuart, *Hartford in the Olden Time*; also on "Nigger Lane" in Hartford, and some black residents.

NA
2625
Russell, Irwin. *Christmas Night in the Quarters*. Kansas City, Mo.: W.O.
Graham, 1913. (Reissued, with an introduction by Joel Chandler Harris.
New York: Century, 1917.)
Dialect verse by a white man, with a few beliefs and domestic prac-
tices.

NA
2626
Russell, Ross. *Bird Lives! The High Life and Hard Times of Charlie (Yard-
bird) Parker*. New York: Charterhouse, 1973.
Music, musicians and hipsters of Kansas City in the 1930's and New
York of the 1940's and 1950's; includes slang terms.

NA
2627
Russell, Ross. *Jazz Style in Kansas City and the Southwest*. Los Angeles:
University of California Press, 1971.
Includes chapters on blues, folksong and ragtime music in the South-
western states.

NA
2628
Russell, Tony. *Blacks, Whites and Blues*. New York: Stein and Day, 1970.
The relationship of Negro and white blues and folk music before the
late 1930's; discography, illustrations.

NA
2629
Russell, Tony. "Clarkside Piccolo Blues: Jukebox Hits in Black Taverns
Thirty Years Ago," *Jazz and Blues*, 1, No. 7 (1971), 30.
List of records in 5 Clarksdale, Mississippi black jukeboxes in 1941.

NA
2630
Russell, William Howard. *My Diary North and South*. New York: Harpers,
1863.
Description of South Carolina Sea Island dugout canoes; boaters' songs,
fishing techniques, slave houses, poultry-marking by owners, etc.

NA
2631
Rutledge, Archibald. *God's Children*. Indianapolis: Bobbs-Merrill, 1947.
Stories of coastal South Carolina craftsmen and hunters, with examples
of beliefs, cures, woods-lore, etc.; illustrations.

NA
2632
Rutledge, Archibald. "Insight (of Negroes)," *Atlantic Monthly*, 162 (1938),
366-373.
Conversation with plantation slaves reveals the "psychic power" of the
Negro, and his religious attitude toward life and death, as exhibited
in rituals and songs.

NA
2633
Ryder, C.J. "The Theology of the Plantation Songs," *American Missionary*,
46 (1892), 9-16.

NA
2634
S.M.P. "Voodooism in Tennessee," *Atlantic Monthly*, 64 (1889), 376-380.
Memoirs recalling a young black girl's belief in a spirit about to
claim her life after touching a vial. Recounts prevalent "superstitions" in Tennessee.

NA
2635
Sackheim, Eric. *The Blues Line: A Collection of Blues Lyrics*. New York:
Grossman, 1969.
270 blues texts transcribed from records with some singers' autobiographical comments.

NA
2636
Sale, John B. *The Tree Named John*. Chapel Hill: The University of North
Carolina Press, 1929.
25 explanatory, spirit, witch, and animal tales from the author's boy-
hood recollections of life on a plantation near Columbus, Mississippi.

NA
2637
Samarin, William J. "An Analytical Review of Bruce A. Rosenberg's *The
Art of the American Folk Preacher*," *Folklore Forum*, 5 (1972), 106-
111.
A critique which reinterprets some material and suggests further research possibilities.

NA
2638
Samarin, William J. *Tongues of Men and Angels: The Religious Language of
Pentecostalism*. New York: Macmillan, 1972.
Includes black material from the U.S. with comparisons to West Indian
groups; brief notes on scat singing and jive talk.

NA
2639
Sampson, Emma Speed. *Miss Minerva's Cook Book*. Chicago: Reilly and Lee,
1931.
Written in dialect. Each recipe is threaded with anecdotes.

NA
2640
Sandburg, Carl. *The American Song Bag*. New York: Harcourt, Brace, 1927.
280 texts with music, including a number of blues, spirituals, ballads,
and work songs.

NA
2641
Sandburg, Carl. "Imports from Africa," *Poetry*, 20 (1922), 56-57.
Argues against Negro origins of jazz.

NA
2642
Sargant, Norman, and Tom Sargant. "Negro American Music or the Origin of
Jazz," *Musical Times*, 72 (1931), 653-655; 751-772; 847-848.
Development of jazz from its origin to its present position in society.

NA
2643
Sargeant, Winthrop. *Jazz: A History*. New York: McGraw-Hill, 1964. (Originally published as *Jazz: Hot and Hybrid*. New York: Arrow, 1938.)
Musical analysis of jazz, gospel music, ragtime, blues, and discussion of African derivations--jazz treated in the context of "comparative musicology."

NA
2644
Sargent, Charles J., Jr. "Statements of Concern; Negro Spirituals," *Christian Century*, 76 (1959), 1090.
Protests reinterpretation and use of Negro spirituals out of religious contexts.

NA
2645
Saucier, Corinne L. *Folk Tales from French Louisiana*. New York: Exposition Press, 1962.
Folktales from French tellers; includes black material though not identified as such.

NA
2646
Saunders, William. "Sailor Songs and Songs of the Sea," *MQ*, 14 (1928), 339-357.
Mention of the Negro origin of a number of sea chanties with texts.

NA
2647
Sawyer, J.J. *Jubilee Songs and Plantation Melodies*. Nashville, Tenn.: Colored Concert Co., 1884.

NA
2648
Saxon, Lyle. *Children of Strangers*. Boston: Houghton, Mifflin, 1937.
Novel of Louisiana with folkloric content.

NA
2649
Saxon, Lyle. *Old Louisiana*. New Orleans: Robert L. Crager, 1950.
Chapters on Afro-American "superstitions" (pp. 345-352) with 121 texts, and proverbs, with 60 texts.

NA
2650
Saxon, Lyle. "Voodoo," *New Republic*, 50 (1927), 135-139.
Account of a conjurer's rituals for a white client.

NA
2651
Saxon, Lyle, Robert Tallant, and Edward Dreyer. *Gumbo Ya-Ya, A Collection of Louisiana Folktales*. Boston: Houghton Mifflin, 1945.
Chapters on Mardi Gras lore, jazz, gambling and gambling songs, Creoles, ghosts, buried treasure legends, "superstitions," funerals and wakes, river front lore, church services, customs, folk speech, songs; includes texts.

NA
2652
Scarborough, Dorothy. "The 'Blues' as Folksongs," *PTFS*, No. 2 (1923),
52-66.
An interview with W.C. Handy, who attributes his composed blues to
folk sources. General discussion of other blues texts.

NA
2653
Scarborough, Dorothy. *From a Southern Porch*. New York: G.P. Putnam, 1919.
In the midst of local color description, texts of songs (including
"The Titanic" and "Bachelor's Hall"), rhymes, beliefs, customs, and
a wedding.

NA
2654
Scarborough, Dorothy. "New Lights on an Old Song," in *Ebony and Topaz*,
Charles S. Johnson, ed. New York National Urban League, 1927, 59.
African source of the melody of "Swing Low, Sweet Chariot."

NA
2655
Scarborough, Dorothy. *On the Trail of Negro Folk Songs*. Cambridge, Mass.:
Harvard University Press, 1925. (Reprinted, Hatboro, Pa.: Folklore
Associates, 1963, with a new Foreword by Roger D. Abrahams.)
140 songs with music and numerous other texts including sections on
dance songs, game songs, Creole songs, lullabies, animal songs, work
songs, railroad songs and blues and a chapter on the Negro's part in
transmitting the traditional British songs and ballads.

NA
2656
Scarborough, Dorothy. *The Wind*. New York: Harper, 1925.
Novel, set in Texas, includes 2 spirituals from Virginia.

NA
2657
Scarborough, W.H. "Creole Folk Tale-- 'Compair Beuki and Compair Lapin',"
SW, 25 (1896), 186.
1 tale.

NA
2658
Scarborough, W.H. "Negro Folklore and Dialect," *Arena*, 17 (1897), 186-
192.
Illustrations of how Negro folk-lore is enhanced by Negro speech;
problems of defining Negro dialect.

NA
2659
Scarborough, W.H. "Negro Speech and Folklore," *SW*, 25 (1896), 144-147.
Argues that omens, tales and fables give insights into ancient cultural
practices; speech and dialect examined through proverbs, humor, beliefs
and charms.

NA
2660
Schaeffner, André. "La Musique Noire d'un Continent à un Autre," *La
Musique dans la Vie* (Paris), 2 (1969), 7-23.
Argues that U.S. Negroes gave up African modes of music and adopted

European forms, unlike Negroes in the other areas of the Americas who produced African instruments.

NA 2661   Schafer, William J., and Johannes Riedel. *The Art of Ragtime: Form and Meaning of an Original Black Art*. Baton Rouge: Louisiana State University Press, 1973.
Analysis and history of rag music; comparisons to other white and and black musical forms; bibliography, discography.

NA 2662   Schecter, William. *The History of Negro Humor in America*. New York: Fleet, 1971.
Negro humor in folktales, minstrel shows, lyrics, nightclubs, etc.

NA 2663   Scherpf, John C. *African Quadrilles*. New York: E. Riley, 1844.
5 dance songs.

NA 2664   Schiffman, Jack. *Uptown: The Story of Harlem's Apollo Theatre*. New York: Cowles, 1971.
The entertainers and audiences of a Harlem theatre. Illustrations.

NA 2665   Schlesinger, Marilyn Ruth. "Riddling Questions from Los Angeles High School Students," *WF*, 19 (1960), 191-195.
A collection of riddles.

NA 2666   Schoepf, Johann David. *Travels in the Confederation* (1783-1784), 2 vols. Alfred J. Morrison, trans. & ed. Philadelphia, 1911. (Originally published Erlanger: J.J. Palm, 1788.)
Describes music aboard slave ships (Vol. 2, pp. 410-412).

NA 2667   Schonemann, A.C.E. "Jazzing Up Our Musical Terms," *AS*, 1 (1926), 500-501.
Short discussion of musical terms arising from jazz music.

NA 2668   Schoolcraft, Mrs. Henry R. *The Black Gauntlet: A Tale of Plantation Life in South Carolina*. Philadelphia: Lippincott, 1860.
Includes references to musical instruments (p. 31), footman dress (p. 26), a funeral (p. 161), slave housing (p. 36), etc. (pp. 42, 110, 167, 201, 212, 236).

NA 2669   Schrodt, Helen, and Bailey Wilkinson. "Sam Lindsey and Milton Roby: Memphis Blues Musicians," *TFSB*, 30 (1964), 52-56.
Contains information about two of the men who were active in the Memphis bands during a period of Negro blues and skiffle music.

NA
2670

Schuller, Gunther. *Early Jazz: Its Roots and Musical Development*. New York: Oxford University Press, 1968.
Schuller discusses the elements of Jazz: rhythm, form, harmony, melody, and improvisation and its early beginnings with an emphasis on the most important innovators. The African elements of blues and jazz are discussed.

NA
2671

Schultz, Christian. *Travels on an Inland Voyage* . . . 2 vols. New York, 1810.
Descriptions of dancing, instruments and costumes in New Orleans, Vol. 2, p. 197.

NA
2672

Schulz, David A. *Coming Up Black: Patterns of Ghetto Socialization*. Englewood Cliffs, N.J.: Prentice-Hall, 1969.
Contains a short discussion of the function of the dozens and commentary on singing.

NA
2673

Schuyler, George S. "Craftsman in the Blue Grass," *Crisis*, 47 (1940), 143-157.
Negro cabinet maker in Kentucky noted for his skill in reproducing antiques.

NA
2674

Schuyler, Jack. "Hipped to the Tip," *Current History and Forum*, 52-53 (November 7, 1940), 21-22.
The invention, development and use of slang in prison, with special reference to the predominantly Negro penitentiary.

NA
2675

Schwartz, Jack. "Men's Clothing and the Negro," *Phylon*, 24 (1963), 224-231.
A brief survey of Negro clothing styles under slavery and since; sees their origins in status deprivation.

Schwartz, William Leonard. "American Speech and Haitian Creole." See No. HA 325.

NA
2676

Scott, F. *That Passing Laughter: Stories of the Southland*. Birmingham, Alabama: Southern University Press, 1968.

NA
2677

Scroggins, Elizabeth McRae. "Gullah Baskets," *ETV Guide* (Columbia, S.C.), 4, No. 14 (1971), 2-5.
Notes on the making of baskets on the South Carolina coast; illustrations.

NA
2678
"The Sea Islands," *Harper's,* 57 (1878), 839-861.
   Includes illustrations of a children's band, slave cabins, field workers, and a 3-string violin-like instrument.

NA
2679
Seale, Lea Marianna. "Easter Rock: A Louisiana Negro Ceremony," *JAF*, 55
   (1942), 212-218.
   Easter festival in Corcordia Parish, Louisiana. Texts of songs.

NA
2680
Seashore, C.E. "Three New Approaches to the Study of Negro Music," *Annals*
   of the American Academy of Political and Social Science, 140 (1928),
   191-192.
   The use of phonophotography to help differentiate and understand
   Negroes' music; with special concern with tonal, temporal, and dynamic
   talents.

NA
2681
Seaworthy, Captain Gregory (George Higby Throop). *Bertie: or Life in the*
   Old Field. Philadelphia, 1851.
   Includes a description of "John Kooner" festivities and calypso-like
   singing in North Carolina (pp. 217-219).

NA
2682
Sebastian, Hugh. "Negro Slang in Lincoln University," *AS*, 9 (1934), 287-
   290.
   Glossary of slang at an all-black school.

NA
2683
Seeger, Peter. "Negro Prison Camp Work Songs," booklet included with
   Folkways LP record 475.
   Notes and texts of 10 prison work songs from Texas.

NA
2684
Seeger, Ruth Crawford. *American Folk Songs for Children*. Garden City,
   N.Y.: Doubleday, 1948.
   Songs transcribed from Library of Congress field recordings or repub-
   lished from other sources.

NA
2685
Seeger, Ruth Crawford. *American Folk Songs for Christmas*. Garden City,
   N.Y.: Doubleday, 1953.
   Includes songs transcribed from Library of Congress field recordings
   or reprinted from other sources.

NA
2686
Seeger, Ruth Crawford. *Animal Folk Songs for Children*. Garden City, N.Y.:
   Doubleday, 1950.
   Songs transcribed from Library of Congress field recordings or repub-
   lished from other sources.

NA
2687

Seidleman, Morton. "Survivals in Negro Vocabulary," *AS*, 12 (1937), 231-
232.
"Old English survivals" in New Jersey Negro speech.

NA
2688

"Seize Price Lists of Voodoo Doctor," *New York Times*, August 14, 1925, 3.
Atlantic City, N.J. Police seizure of voodoo circulars from New York
City.

NA
2689

Seldes, Gilbert. "Shake Your Feet," *New Republic*, 44 (1925), 283-284.

NA
2690

"Sermons and Prayers of the Negroes," *SW*, 24 (1895), 59-61.
Religious customs and prayers as recorded in spirituals.

NA
2691

Sessions, Gene A. "Camp Meeting at Willowtree, 1881," *JAF*, 87 (1974),
361-364.
A Mormon's account of a camp meeting in North Carolina: includes descriptions of housing, singing and possession.

NA
2692

"Seven Negro Convict Songs," in *American Stuff*. New York: Viking, 1937,
186-192.
7 texts with brief notes; recorded by John A. Lomax.

NA
2693

Sevilli-Capponi, James B. *Ham and Dixie*. St. Augustine, 1895.
Discussion of the "Negro Problem" by a black Floridian; includes anti-
Negro proverbs used by blacks; a 53-page play in dialect.

NA
2694

Seward, Theodore F., and George L. White. *Jubilee Songs as Sung by the
Jubilee Singers*. New York: Bigelow and Main, 1872.
24 songs.

NA
2695

Shaler, N.S. "African Element in America," *Arena*, 2 (1890), 660-673.
Acclimatization of the American Negro: climatic similarity between
Africa and Southern Tennessee, Mississippi, Georgia, and its effect
on Afro-American culture.

NA
2696

Shapiro, Nat, and Nat Hentoff, eds. *Hear Me Talkin' to Ya*. New York:
Rinehart, 1955.
The story of jazz through interviews with musicians. Life in early
20th Century New Orleans.

NA
2697
    Sharf, J. Thomas, and Thompson Westcott. *History of Philadelphia*. 2 vols.
        Philadelphia: L.H. Everts, 1884.
          Includes accounts of street cries (Vol. 2, 929-932), black mummers
          (Vol. 2, 934-935; 1090-1092), musicians (Vol. 2, 1092), etc.

NA
2698
    Sharma, Mohan Lal. "Afro-American Music and Dance," in *The Negro Impact
        on Western Civilization*, Joseph S. Roucek and Thomas Kiernan, eds.
        New York: Philosophical Library, 1970, 139-157.
        Brief outline-history of Afro-American music.

NA
2699
    Sharp, Cecil. *English Folk Chanteys*. London: Simpkin Marshall, 1911.
        Discusses influence of Negroes on sea shanty tunes.

NA
2700
    Shaw, Arnold. *The World of Soul*. New York: Cowles, 1970.
        Includes chapters surveying blues and gospel music.

NA
2701
    Shea, Tom. "Bart Howard," *The Ragtimer*, 6, No. 3 (1967), 4-5.
        Account of a Detroit ragtime pianist prominent in the early 1900's.

NA
2702
    Sheivers, Susie B. "Alabama Folk-Lore," *SW*, 29 (1900), 179-180, 443-444.

NA
2703
    Shelby, Gertrude Mathews, and Samuel Gaillard Stoney. *Po' Buckra*. New
        York: Macmillan, 1930.
        Novel of South Carolina life with folkloric content.

NA
2704
    Sheldon, George A. *Negro Slavery in Old Deerfield*. Boston, 1893.
        Account of Lucy Terry, African storyteller.

NA
2705
    Shelly, Lou. *Hepcats Jive Talk Dictionary*. Derby, Conn.: T.W.O. Charles,
        1945.

NA
2706
    Shelton, Jane de Forest. "The New England Negro," *Harper's*, 88 (1894),
        533-538.
        Discusses slavery in New England, especially the election of black
        governors and kings.

NA
2707
    Shepard, Eli. "Superstitions of the Negro," *Cosmopolitan*, 5 (March, 1888),
        47-50. (Reprinted in No. NA 1568.)
        Contains more than 80 signs, beliefs, and "superstitions."

NA
2708
Sheppard, E. (Martha Young). *Plantation Songs for My Lady's Banjo and Other Negro Lyrics and Monologues*. New York: R.H. Russell, 1901.
25 hymns and songs in dialect; of uncertain provenience.

NA
2709
Sherlock, Charles. "From Breakdown to Rag-Time," *Cosmopolitan*, 31 (1901), 631-639.

NA
2710
Sherman, Joan R. *Invisible Poets: Afro-Americans of the Nineteenth Century*. Urbana, Illinois: University of Illinois Press, 1974.
A survey of little-known black poets, many of whom used folk themes and wrote in dialect; includes examples, bibliography.

NA
2711
Sherman, Mandel, and Thomas R. Henry. *Hollow Folk*. New York: Thomas Y. Crowell, 1933.
Contains material on social life, "superstitions," religion, etc., of people in Rappahannock County, Virginia.

NA
2712
Sherrard, Virginia B. "Recollections of My Mammy," *SW*, 30 (1901), 86-87.
Memoirs; records that "mammy" sang the ballad "Lord Lovell" to the children.

NA
2713
Sherwood, John. "The A-rabbers," *The Evening Star* (Washington, D.C.), Monday, June 5, 1972, C-1, C-4.
Street cries and street vendors' names in Baltimore.

NA
2714
Shine and the Titanic, The Signifying Monkey, Stackolee and Other Stories from Down Home. Atlanta: More, n.d.
Texts of 12 rhymed narratives from black tradition (taken from Abrahams, *Deep Down in the Jungle*, and Hughes and Bontemps, *Book of Negro Folklore*).

NA
2715
Shines, Johnny. "The Robert Johnson I Knew." *American Folk Music Occasional*, No. 2, New York: Oak, 1970.
A blues musician's memoirs on an important Mississippi bluesman.

NA
2716
Shirley, Kay, ed. *Book of the Blues*. New York: Leeds Music Corporation and Crown Publishing, 1963.
100 blues, texts and music, as published; includes discography and annotation.

NA
2717   Showers, Susan. "Alabama Folk-Lore," *SW*, 29 (1900), 179-180; 443-444.
        Proverbs, "superstitions," dreams, curing practices, ring game texts.

NA
2718   Showers, Susan. "'How the Jays Saved Their Souls' and 'The Jay and the
        Martin'," *SW*, 27 (1898), 17-18. (Also in *JAF*, 11 (1898), 74-75.)
        2 tales describing "superstitions" about the blue-jay's visits to
        hell.

NA
2719   Showers, Susan. "How the Rabbit and the Frog Caught a Deer," *SW*, 27
        (1898), 230.
        1 animal tale from Alabama with conjure material.

NA
2720   Showers, Susan. "Snakes and Conjure Doctors," *SW*, 27 (1898), 37.

NA
2721   Showers, Susan. "A Weddin' and a Buryin' in the Black Belt," *New England
        Magazine*, 18 (1898), 478-483. (Reprinted in No. NA 1568.)
        Marriage and funeral ceremonies; witch-lore, games, etc.

NA
2722   Sidran, Ben. *Black Talk*. New York: Holt, Rinehart and Winston, 1971.
        Blues and jazz in a "culture history" setting; politics and music.

NA
2723   Silber, Irwin. *Soldier Songs and Home-Front Ballads of the Civil War*.
        New York: Oak, 1964.
        1 marching song from a Negro regiment (pp. 38-39).

NA
2724   Silber, Irwin. *Songs of the Civil War*. New York: Columbia University
        Press, 1960.
        Includes spirituals, minstrel songs, etc., with annotations and music.

NA
2725   Silverman, Jerry. *The Art of the Folk-Blues Guitar*. New York: Oak, 1964.
        An instruction book for blues with sample tunes; illustrations.

NA
2726   Silverman, Jerry, ed. *Folk Blues*. New York: Macmillan, 1958.
        110 blues, arranged with an essay on blues playing and blues singers;
        bibliography, discography.

NA
2727   Simmons, Donald C. "Possible West African Sources for the American Negro
        'Dozens'," *JAF*, 70 (1963), 339-340.
        Points to 3 possible sources for the American "dozens": (1) tone

riddles, (2) curses, (3) sarcasm among the Efik of Nigeria.

NA
2728
Simmons, Donald C. "Protest Humor: Folkloristic Reaction to Prejudice," *American Journal of Psychiatry*, 120 (1963), 567-570.
Examples of Negro and Jewish protest tales and songs emerging from the grievances of minority groups.

NA
2729
Simmons, Gloria M., Helene D. Hutchinson, and Henry E. Simmons, eds. *Black Culture: Reading and Writing Black*. New York: Holt, Rinehart and Winston, 1972.
Reprints a number of articles on black speech and slang, including portions of writings by Dan Burley.

NA
2730
Simms, David McD. "The Negro Spiritual: Origins and Themes," *JNE*, 35 (1966), 35-41.
A thematic analysis of American spirituals, surveying the recent literature.

NA
2731
Simms, William Gilmore. *The Wigwam and the Cabin*. 2 vols. New York: Wiley and Putnam, 1845.
Contains a number of Gullah tales.

NA
2732
Sims, Mamie Hunt. *Negro Mystic Lore*. Chicago: To-Morrow Press, 1907.
18 tales (including a ghost story, a dream story, animal tales and others) from a Southern slave as gleaned from the recollections of a white woman.

NA
2733
Singleton, Calvin. "Negro Folk Beliefs Collected in Los Angeles," *WF*, 17 (1958), 277-279.
55 superstitions collected from informants in Los Angeles having Louisiana, Chicago and Tennessee backgrounds.

NA
2734
Sisk, Glenn. "Churches in the Alabama Black Belt, 1875-1917," *Church History*, 23 (1954), 153-174.
Black religious attitudes in 10 Southern counties during the antebellum period; description of rural camp meetings and revivals during the 1870's.

NA
2735
Sisk, Glenn. "Funeral Customs in the Alabama Black Belt, 1870-1910," *SFQ*, 23 (1959), 169-171.
Includes descriptions of Negro practices of keeping the bodies of the

dead "sitting up" at home, turning the body over to the "watchers," and the extensive preparations of the burial societies.

NA
2736
Sister Esther Mary. "Spirituals in the Church," *SW*, 63 (1934), 308-314.
Argues for the preservation of original spirituals and chants at church services and meetings.

NA
2737
Sister Mary Collista. "Negro Folk Songs," *Catholic World*, 164 (March, 1947), 537-540.
Negro lullabies, with descriptions of "black mammy," Br'er Rabbit Tales, old-time fiddlers, and banjo pickers.

NA
2738
Sister Mary Hilarian. "Negro Spiritual," *Catholic World*, 143 (April, 1939), 80-84.
Origin of spirituals; Afro-American adaptation of Bible stories ("Noah," "Niger-Demus," etc.); includes texts.

NA
2739
Sithole, Elkin T. "Black Folk Music," in *Rappin' and Stylin' Out*, Thomas Kochman, ed. Urbana, Ill.: University of Illinois Press, 1972, 65-82.
African backgrounds to black music, dance, and preachers' sermons; includes fragments of music and texts.

NA
2740
"Six Negro Market Songs of Harlem," in *American Stuff*. New York: Viking, 1937, 158-160.
6 texts, one of West Indian origin.

NA
2741
Sketches of Old Virginia Family Servants. Philadelphia: Isaac Ashmead, 1847.
Accounts of 12 individuals and a church: an African slave, tatooed, dancing and telling tales of the Congo (pp. 12-23); the use of Watt's Hymns in church (pp. 60-70); attendance of white children at black churches with their "mammies" (pp. 77-83).

NA
2742
"Slim Gaillard et le Vout-o-Reeney," *Hot Club Magazine* (Paris), 19, August 15, 1947, 9.

NA
2743
Slotkin, J.S. "Jazz and Its Forerunners as an Example of Acculturation," *American Sociological Review*, 8 (1943), 570-575.
Characteristics of Negro music adopted by whites. Discussion of "coon" songs, ragtime, blues and early jazz.

NA
2744
Smedes, Susan Dabney. *Memorials of A Southern Planter*. Baltimore: Cushing and Bailey, 1887. (Reprinted, with a new introduction and notes by Fletcher M. Green, ed., New York: Knopf, 1965.)
Memoirs of plantation life in Virginia and Mississippi: includes comments on the etiquette of slaves' "titles of respect" (p. 71).

NA
2745
Smiley, Portia. "Courtship Customs," *SW*, 25 (1896), 15-16.
Courtship proposals from Alabama.

NA
2746
Smiley, Portia. "Folk-Lore from Virginia, South Carolina, Georgia, Alabama, and Florida," *JAF*, 32 (1919), 357-383.
Tales, riddles, proverbs, toasts, etc.

NA
2747
Smiley, Portia. "The Foot Wash in Alabama," *SW*, 25 (1896), 101-102.
Practices of the "Foot-Wash Baptists" in North Carolina, Georgia and Alabama; discussion of the roles of preacher, deacon and congregation in the Christian shout.

NA
2748
Smith, A.L. "Socio-Historical Perspectives of Black Oratory," *Quarterly Journal of Speech*, 56 (1970), 264-269.
The common features of African and Afro-American oratory.

NA
2749
Smith, C. Alphonso. "Ballads Surviving in the United States," *MQ*, 2 (1916), 109-129.
Includes some examples collected from Negroes.

NA
2750
Smith, C. Alphonso. "The Negro and the Ballad," *Alumni Bulletin of the University of Virginia*, Series 3, 1 (1913), 88.
Negro revival and camp meeting songs seen as prototypes of the ballad; evidences of communal composition.

NA
2751
Smith, Charles Edward. "The Blues Jumped a Mechanical Rabbit," *SO*, 16, No. 2 (1966), 10-12.
The juke box's influence in changing tastes in blues and folk music.

NA
2752
Smith, Charles Edward. "Blues Stanzas," *New Republic*, 96 (1938), 184.
2 stanzas, including "John Henry."

NA
2753
Smith, Charles Edward. "The Blues Was the Mother," *Jazz: A Quarterly of American Music*, No. 5 (Winter, 1960), 23-29.
A highly critical review of Samuel B. Charters' *The Country Blues*.

NA
2754

Smith, Charles Edward. "Can Jazz Be Defined?." *Metronome*, 78, No. 7 (1961), 12-13.
     Discussion of the folk music roots of jazz.

NA
2755

Smith, Charles Edward. "Down Home: A Portrait of a People," booklet included with Folkways LP record set 2691.
     Essay and notes on a variety of Deep South Negro folk songs.

NA
2756

Smith, Charles Edward. "Folk Music, the Roots of Jazz," *Saturday Review of Literature*, 33 (July 29, 1950), 35-36, 48.
     A discussion of Harold Courlander's research in Alabama.

NA
2757

Smith, Charles Edward. "Folk Music, U.S.A.," booklet included with Folkways LP record set, FE 4530.
     Includes discussion of a jug band song, a work song, a train song, a blues, a spiritual, a game song, and an example of early jazz drumming.

NA
2758

Smith, Charles Edward. "Jazz Begins: Sounds of New Orleans Streets--Funeral and Parade Music by the Young Tuxedo Brass Band," record notes to Atlantic LP record 1297.
     Notes on New Orleans funeral traditions.

NA
2759

Smith, Charles Edward. "Ma Rainey and the Minstrels," *RC*, 14 (1955), 5-6.
     Ma Rainey, a blues singer, and her early years in tent and minstrel shows.

NA
2760

Smith, Charles Edward. "New Orleans and Traditions in Jazz," in *Jazz*, Nat Hentoff and Albert J. McCarthy, eds. New York: Rinehart, 1959, 21-41, 352-356.
     The social and musical setting of New Orleans jazz; discography.

NA
2761

Smith, Charles Edward. "The Origin of a Term, or, Jass Me for a Donkey," *Down Beat*, 33, No. 3 (1966), 24-25.
     A humorous review of the literature on the origin of the word "jazz."

NA
2762

Smith, Charles Edward. "Rock and Roll: A Historical Perspective," in *Down Beat's Music 1960*. Chicago: Maher, 1960, 48-52.
     The sacred and secular roots of rock and roll.

NA 2763   Smith, Charles Edward, and William Russell. "New Orleans Style," *Modern Music*, 18 (1941), 235-241.
Includes background of jazz in New Orleans together with a description of its style.

NA 2764   Smith, Grace Partridge. "Folklore from 'Egypt'," *JAF*, 54 (1941), 48-59.
12 folktales showing influence of Negro belief in Southern Illinois; informants given; annotation of texts; also jokes and anecdotes, folk medicine and superstitions.

NA 2765   Smith, Grace Partridge. "Folklore from 'Egypt'," *HF*, 5 (1946), 45-82.
1 legend (pp. 76-77) from Southern Illinois.

NA 2766   Smith, Grace Partridge. "Negro Lore in Southern Illinois," *MF*, 2 (1952), 159-162.
28 beliefs.

NA 2767   Smith, Grace Partridge. "Scraps of Southern Lore," *SFQ*, 9 (1945), 169-173.
Fragments of "superstitions," tales, and songs with annotation and background of informants.

NA 2768   Smith, Harry. "American Folk Music, Vol. 1 (Ballads), Vol. 2 (Social Music), Vol. 3 (Songs)," booklet included with Folkways LP records FA 2951, 2952, 2953.
Discussion and "condensations of texts" of a number of Afro-American folk songs and instrumentals; bibliography and discography.

NA 2769   Smith, Hope. "A Description of a Black Party," *Journal of the Ohio Folklore Society*, 2 (1973), 30-37.
Examples of rapping and the dozens; description of a college party.

NA 2770   Smith, Hugh L. "George W. Cable and Two Sources of Jazz," *African Music*, 2, No. 3 (1961), 59-62.
Cable's use of Afro-American song in his novels *The Grandissimes* and *Bonaventure*.

NA 2771   Smith, Joseph H. "Folksongs of the American Negro," *Sewanee Review*, 32 (1924), 206-224.
Discussion of African origins and the development of Negro hymns, shouts, dances, rhymes, etc. with examples.

NA   Smith, L.H. "Negro Musicians and their Music," *JNH*, 20 (1935), 428-432.
2772   Discussion of origins of Negro music, with several texts included;
            black ballads and spirituals.

NA   Smith, Myrtle E. *A Civil War Cook Book*. Harrogate, Tenn.: n.p., 1961.
2773

NA   Smith, N. Clark. *Favorite Folk-Melodies as Sung by Tuskegee Students*.
2774   Wichita, Kansas: published by the author, 1914.

NA   Smith, N. Clark. *New Plantation Melodies as Sung by the Tuskegee Students*.
2775   Tuskegee, Alabama: Tuskegee Press, 1909.

NA   Smith, Nicholas J.H. "Six New Negro Folksongs with Music," *PTFS*, No. 7
2776   (1928), 113-118.
            Songs from Virginia and North Carolina.

NA   Smith, Reed. *Gullah*. Columbia, S.C.: University of South Carolina Bulletin
2777   190, 1926.
            A study of Negro dialect from the Sea Islands and coastal area with a
            number of spirituals.

NA   Smith, Reed. *South Carolina Ballads*. Cambridge: Harvard University, 1928.
2778   Communal composition among Negroes; dialect poetry; texts of several
            black ballads.

NA   Smith, Reed. *The Traditional Ballad and Its South Carolina Survival*. Bul-
2779   letin of the University of South Carolina, May 1, 1925.
            Communal composition among Negroes. (Also included in No. NA 2778.)

NA   Smith, Richard. "Richard's Tales," *PTFS*, No. 25 (1953), 220-253.
2780   Includes several Negro tales.

NA   Smith, Robert A. "A Note on the Folktales of Charles W. Chesnutt," *CLA
2781   Journal*, 5 (1962), 229-232.

NA   Smith, William B. "The Persimmon Tree and the Beer Dance," *Farmer's Regis-
2782   ter*, 6 (April, 1838), 58-61. (Reprinted in No. NA 1568.)
            Descriptions of music, banjo, a ritual dance, juba, and costumes on a
            Virginia plantation.

NA 2783   Smith, Willie the Lion, with George Hoefer. *Music on My Mind: The Memoirs of an American Pianist*. London: MacGibbon and Kee, 1965.
Autobiography of a ragtime pianist; Negro life and entertainment in New Jersey and Harlem in the early 1900's.

NA 2784   Smythe, Augustine T., *et al*. *The Carolina Low Country*. New York: Macmillan, 1932.
Contains 49 Negro songs, and a number of essays, including a chapter on "The Negro Spiritual" by Robert W. Gordon.

NA 2785   Snethen, Worthington G. *The Black Code of the District of Columbia. In Force September 1st, 1848*. New York: Published for the A. & F. Anti-Slavery Society by William Harned, 1848.
Laws proscribe colored persons from fighting cocks, damaging public pumps, lying on market benches, setting off firecrackers, etc.

NA 2786   Snow, Loudell F. "'I Was Born Just Exactly with the Gift': An Interview with a Voodoo Practitioner," *JAF*, 86 (1973), 272-281.
Background, patients, witchcraft and techniques of a folk healer in Tucson, Arizona.

NA 2787   Snyder, Howard. *Earth Born: A Novel of the Plantation*. New York: Century, 1929.
Novel of plantation life in Georgia with folkloric content.

NA 2788   Snyder, Howard. "Paradise Negro School," *Yale Review*, 11 (1921), 158-169.
Account of a Negro plantation school includes samples of folk beliefs, folk medicine and dialect.

NA 2789   Snyder, Howard. "Plantation Pictures: The Ordination of Charles," *Atlantic Monthly*, 127 (1921), 338-342.
Account of a revival service in Mississippi.

NA 2790   Snyder, Howard. "A Plantation Revival Service," *Yale Review*, 10 (1920), 169-180.
Description of a church service and a baptism in rural Mississippi in 1919.

NA 2791   Snyder, Howard. "Traits of My Plantation Negroes," *Century Magazine*, 80 (1921), 367-376.
Disucssion of plantation Negroes: customs of 'bedding', attitudes, etc.

NA   "Soldier-Man Blues from Somewhere in France," *Literary Digest*, 93, No. 12
2792   (1927), 50, 52.
            A review of some song texts from John J. Niles' "Singing Soldiers."

NA   "Some Conjure Doctors We Have Heard Of," *SW*, 26 (1897), 37-38.
2793   Transcriptions of student essays on magic.

NA   "Some Negro Slang," in *Negro Anthology*, Nancy Cunard, ed. London: Wishart,
2794   1934, 75-78.
            A glossary of slang.

NA   "Some Negro Superstitions," *Atlantic Monthly*, 75 (1895), 136-139.
2795   "Superstitions" and their function as a "warning" for impeding events.

NA   Somers, Dale A. *The Rise of Sports in New Orleans 1850-1900*. Baton Rouge,
2796   La.: Louisiana State University Press, 1972.
            Accounts of black cockfighting, boxing, racing, etc.

NA   "Songs of the Blacks," *Dwight's Journal of Music*, 9 (November 15, 1856),
2797   51-52. (Reprinted in No. NA 1568.)
            The "artistic nature" of blacks contrasted with the "joyless nature"
            of whites.

NA   Soper, Michael. "Voodoo Flourishes on Sea Islands," *The News and Courier*
2798   (Charleston, South Carolina), April 9, 1961, 1-C.
            Notes on hoodoo and conjuration; the psychology of conjure; illustra-
            tions of a blue painted house (to keep off spells) and a "root."

NA   "Sorcery among Negroes," *New York Times*, 6 (December 20, 1874), 4.
2799

NA   Sorenson, E. Richard. "Street and Gangland Rhythms," booklet included with
2800   Folkways record FD 5589.
            Notes to a set of monologues of some children's street adventures in
            New York City; chants, songs, bongo drums, rhythms, etc.

NA   Souchon, Edmond, M.D. "King Oliver, A Very Personal Memoir," *Jazz Review*,
2801   3, No. 4 (1960), 6-11.
            An admirer recalls the effects of the trumpet player on his own life.

NA
2802
(Souder, Caspar, Jr.) "A Sketch of the Condition of the Lowest Classes,"
in *The Mysteries and Miseries of Philadelphia* . . . Philadelphia,
1853, 11-20. (Reprinted from the *Evening Bulletin*.)
Description of the apartment of and jobs performed by "Crazy Nancy," a
Negro astrologer; mixing of poor blacks and whites in groggeries and
flop houses, etc.

NA
2803
South Carolina Folk Tales: Stories of Animals and Supernatural Beings.
Compiled by Workers of the Writers' Program of the Works Project Administration in the State of South Carolina. Columbia, S.C., 1941.
32 animal stories including Tar-Baby, Brer Rabbit stories and many
others; 32 stories of ghosts, devils, witch doctors, hags, conjures,
etc.

NA
2804
"South Carolina Gullahs Hold Ethiopian Traits," *New York Times*, January 5,
1936, Section 4, 6.
Argues for a relationship between Gullah Negroes and people of Southern
Ethiopia; with a comment on linguistic factors which differentiate
Gullahs from other American Negroes.

NA
2805
Southall, E.P. "The Attitudes of the Methodist Episcopal Church, South,
toward the Negro from 1844 to 1870," *JNH*, 16 (1931), 359-370.
Chronological survey of prevalent religious customs and attitudes of
Southern Negroes; bibliography.

NA
2806
Southall, Geneva. "Blind Tom: A Misrepresented and Neglected Pianist-
Composer," *BPM*, 3 (1975), 141-159.

NA
2807
Southern, Eileen. "Afro-American Musical Materials," *BPM*, 1 (1973), 24-32.
General discussion of black music which argues that the spiritual
originated in Northern urban churches.

NA
2808
Southern, Eileen. *The Music of Black Americans: A History*. New York:
Norton, 1971.
A comprehensive history of Afro-American music and dance with a dis-
cussion of the African background; bibliography and discography.

NA
2809
Southern, Eileen. *Readings in Black American Music*. New York: Norton,
1971.
Anthology of articles on early music; collection of escaped slave advertisements with music mentioned, letters from clergymen on early
church singing, etc.

NA   Southern, Eileen. "Some Guidelines: Music Research and the Black Aesthetic,"
2810   *Black World*, November, 1973, 4-13.
             Black awareness through an understanding of past work by blacks in their
             folk music.

NA   "A Southern Barbecue," *Harper's Weekly*, 31 (1887), 487.
2811   Origins of barbecue pig roasts with description of cooking styles.

NA   *Southern Stories Retold from St. Nicholas*. New York: Century, 1907.
2812   Includes several stories in dialect, including 1 by J.C. Harris.

NA   *Southland Spirituals*. Chicago: Rodeheaver, 1936.
2813   64 spirituals with music.

NA   Spaeth, Sigmund. "Dixie, Harlem and Tin Pan Alley: Who Writes Negro Music
2814   and How?" *Scribner's*, 99 (1936), 23-26.
             Rhythm, melody and harmony in blues, spirituals, work songs, slave
             songs, and dance forms: the influence of black musicians on popular
             culture.

NA   Spalding, Henry D., ed. *Encyclopedia of Black Folklore and Humor*. Middle
2815   Village, N.Y.: Jonathan David, 1972.
             A collection of tales, anecdotes, songs, recipes, etc., from other
             collections; with brief notes on Black English, dance, etc.

NA   Spaulding, Henry George. "Under the Palmetto," *Continental Monthly*, 4
2816   (1863), 188-203. (Reprinted in Nos. NA 1568 and NA 1698.)
             Contains a section on Negro "shouts" and shout songs from South Carolina
             which includes a description of the shout, 3 texts with music, and a
             description of a Negro minstrel band.

NA   "Speaking of Pictures," *Life*, 26, No. 2 (1949), 24-26.
2817   Pageantry of a Negro baptismal rally with evangelist Elder Lightfoot
             Solomon Michaux; illustrations.

NA   Spears, James E. "Favorite Southern Negro Folk Recipes," *KFR*, 16 (1970),
2818   1-5.
             22 recipes from Arkansas and Tennessee.

NA   Spears, James E. "Five Original Negro Folk Vignettes," *TFSB*, 36 (1971),
2819   40-45.
             5 texts from Arkansas.

NA
2820
Spears, James E. "Negro Folk Maternal-Natal Care, Practices and Remedies: A Glossary," *MFR*, 5 (1971), 19-22.

NA
2821
Spears, James E. "Notes on Negro Folk Speech," *NCF*, 18, No. 3 (1970), 154-157.
Comments on syntax, morphology, phonology, and vocabulary.

NA
2822
Spears, James E. "Playing the Dozen *(sic)*," *MFR*, 3 (1969), 127-129.
A brief description of the verbal game of insulting repartee.

NA
2823
Spears, James E. "Some Negro Folk Pregnancy Euphemisms and Birth Superstitions," *MFR*, 4 (1970), 24-27.
Terms and beliefs of uncertain provenience.

NA
2824
Specht, Will. "Has the Creole a Music of his Own?" *Musical America*, 48, No. 15 (1928), 5, 22, 25.
Essay on the origin and nature of Creole music; 5 songs with music. Includes a description of a voodoo ritual.

NA
2825
Speck, F.G. "Negroes and the Creek Nation," *SW*, 37 (1908), 106-110.
Examines the Creek Indians' language, harvest ceremonies and mythology in light of cultural changes in both the Indian and Negro cultures brought about by the influence of Negro slaves.

NA
2826
Speck, F.G. "Notes on Creek Mythology," *SW*, 38 (1909), 9-11.
African influence on Amerindian tales discussed.

NA
2827
Speers, Mary Walker Finley. "Maryland and Virginia Folk-Lore," *JAF*, 25 (1912), 284-286.
5 tales, "superstitions," and folk remedies in dialect.

NA
2828
Speers, Mary Walker Finley. "Maryland and Virginia Folklore," *JAF*, 26 (1913), 190-191.
A camp meeting hymn with music, 10 beliefs in dialect, and remedies for chills.

NA
2829
Speers, Mary Walker Finley. "Negro Songs and Folk-lore," *JAF*, 23 (1910), 435-439.
2 songs and an animal tale collected from Chesapeake blacks with a description of the dance performed to the songs.

NA
2830   Speers, Mary Walker Finley. "The Spirituals and Race Relations," *Christian Century*, 48 (1931), 230-231.
   Origin and use of spirituals; Negro religion as outgrowth of work and weariness.

NA
2831   Spencer, Onah. "First Blues Disc was Made by Mamie Smith," *Down Beat*, 8, No. 12 (1941), 8.
   Article about the first blues recording, its impact and the singer.

NA
2832   Spenney, Susan Dix. "Riddles and Ring-games from Raleigh, North Carolina," *JAF*, 34 (1921), 110-115.
   7 riddles and 7 ring-games with music.

NA
2833   Sperling, Samuel J. "On The Psychodynamics of Teasing," *Journal of the American Psychoanalytic Association*, 1 (1953), 458-483.
   Discussion of teasing in several cultures, with reference to the dozens.

NA
2834   Sperry, Margaret. *Portrait of Eden*. New York: Liveright, 1934.
   Novel of Florida life with folkloric content.

NA
2835   Spillers, Hortense J. "Martin Luther King and the Style of the Black Sermon," *The Black Scholar*, 3 (September, 1971), 14-27.
   Analysis of the content and style of King's sermons.

NA
2836   *Spirituelles, (Unwritten Songs of South Carolina), Sung by the Carolina Singers, During Their Campaigns in The North, in 1872-73, Written for the First Time, from Memory, by Christine Rutledge, (One of the Singers).* Philadelphia: Henry L. Acker, n.d.
   36 texts.

NA
2837   Spivak, John L. "Flashes from Georgia Chain Gangs," in *Negro Anthology*, Nancy Cunard, ed. London: Wishart, 1934, 210-216.
   An account of a chain gang--songs, punishments, etc.

NA
2838   Spratling, William. "Cane River Portraits," *Scribner's*, 83 (1928), 411-418.
   Description of dress and houses of mulattoes living north of New Orleans; illustrations.

NA
2839
Spruill, Julia Cherry. "Southern Housewives before the Revolution," *North Carolina Historical Review*, 13, No. 1 (1936), 25-46.
Describes the behavior of table servants and their dress.

NA
2840
Stafford, John. "Patterns of Meaning in *Nights with Uncle Remus*," *American Literature*, 18 (1946), 89-108.
Examination of Joel Chandler Harris and the psychology behind Uncle Remus.

NA
2841
"'Stale Bread's' Sadness Gave 'Jazz' to the World," *Literary Digest*, 61, No. 4 (1919), 47-48.
Discussion of the origin of the word "jazz" developed around Stale Bread's Spasm Band from New Orleans, as the first to play jazz; Joseph K. Gorham as being the first to introduce the music to Chicago; and Bert Kelly as the first to use the phrase "jazz band."

NA
2842
Standish, Tony. "Joseph Robichaux--Those Early Days," *JJ*, 12, No. 4 (1959), 10-12.
A jazz musician's reminiscenses of New Orleans music in the early 1900's.

NA
2843
Standish, Tony. "Robert Johnson and the Mississippi Blues," *JJ*, 15, No. 10 (1962), 9-10, 40.
An assessment of the style and influence of Johnson on other Delta blues singers and the blues in general. (For a reply, see John Berrie. "Standards in Blues Criticism: A Change in Emphasis," *JJ*, 17, No. 7 (1964), 6-7.)

NA
2844
Stanley, Oma. "Negro Speech of East Texas," *AS*, 16 (1941), 3-16.
Discussion with 3 transcriptions.

NA
2845
Stansberry, Freddye Belle. "Folklore and Its Effects Upon Black History," *MFR*, 7 (1973), 115-122.
General comments on various forms of folklore as providing models of survival.

NA
2846
Stavisky, Leonard Price. "Negro Craftsmanship in Early America," *American Historical Review*, 54 (1948-1949), 315-325.
Origin and extent of skilled craftsmanship among slaves in colonial America; slave carpenters, coopers, sawyers, blacksmiths, tanners, curriers, shoemakers, spinners, weavers, knitters, silversmiths, cabinetmakers, jewelers, clockmakers, etc.; bibliography.

NA
2847
Steagall, Archie. "The Voodoo Man of the Brazos," *PTFS*, No. 17 (1941), 113-114.
　　Folklore of a man from Wharton, Texas, who sold his soul to the devil by practicing voodoo (which gave him powers of invisibility).

NA
2849
Stearns, Charles. *The Black Man of the South, and the Rebels*. Boston: N.E. News, 1872.
　　Descriptions of Georgia houses and their contents, slave theology, preaching, and music.

NA
2850
Stearns, Marshall. "If You Want to go to Heaven, Shout," *High Fidelity*, 9 (August, 1959), 36-38, 92-93.
　　Gospel song, its evolution and development.

NA
2851
Stearns, Marshall. "Negro Blues and Hollers," booklet included with Library of Congress LP record AAFS L59.
　　Notes on 8 blues, 2 spirituals, and 2 hollers from Mississippi and Arkansas.

NA
2852
Stearns, Marshall. *The Story of Jazz*. New York: Oxford University Press, 1956. (3rd edition, 1958, has corrections and new bibliography.)
　　Historical presentation of jazz, including its African roots, blues, church and work song background, and jazz styles up to the mid-fifties; also considers the musical elements in jazz, and Latin American influences; bibliography, discography. (For a critical review see Larry Gushee, *Jazz: A Quarterly of American Music*, No. 5 (1960), 57-66.)

NA
2853
Stearns, Marshall, and Jean Stearns. "Frontiers of Humor; American Vernacular Dance," *SFQ*, 30 (1966), 227-235.
　　A brief history of black humor and dance.

NA
2854
Stearns, Marshall, and Jean Stearns. *Jazz Dance: The Story of American Vernacular Dance*. New York: Macmillan, 1968.
　　History of jazz dance, told through material from interviews. Analysis of basic Afro-American dance movements. List of popular dances, films and kinescopes; bibliography; illustrations.

NA
2855
Stearns, Marshall, and Jean Stearns. "Vernacular Dance in Musical Comedy. Harlem Takes the Lead," *NYFQ*, 9 (1966), 251-261.
　　Records the importance of the Darktown Follies (opened in 1913 in N.Y.) in the history of the Negro theatre in the U.S.

NA 2856   Stearns, Marshall, and Jean Stearns. "Williams and Walker and the Beginnings of Vernacular Dance of Broadway," *KFQ*, 11 (1966), 3-11.
A history of Negro acts and the Cakewalk in the North American theatre around the turn of the century.

NA 2857   Steele, Wilbur Daniel. *The Man Who Saw Through Heaven and Other Stories*. New York: Harper, 1927.
Short stories with folkloric content.

NA 2858   Steiner, Bernard Christian. *History of Slavery in Connecticut*. Baltimore: Johns Hopkins Press, 1893.
Includes material on Negro Governors.

NA 2859   Steiner, Roland. "Braziel Robinson Possessed of Two Spirits," *JAF*, 13 (1900), 226-228. (Reprinted in Dundes, No. NA 854.)
A story of a root doctor and conjurer.

NA 2860   Steiner, Roland. "Negro Conjuring," *Current Literature*, 32 (1902), 568-569.
12 conjuring beliefs.

NA 2861   Steiner, Roland. "Observations on the Practice of Conjuring in Georgia," *JAF*, 14 (1901), 173-180.
Beliefs relating to witchcraft or conjuring.

NA 2862   Steiner, Roland. "Seeking Jesus," *JAF*, 14 (1901), 172.
A religious rite in Georgia.

NA 2863   Steiner, Roland. "Sol Lockheart's Call," *JAF*, 13 (1900), 67-70.
A man's call to preach; a story about transferring chills and fever to a persimmon tree.

NA 2864   Steiner, Roland. "Superstitions and Beliefs from Central Georgia," *JAF*, 12 (1899), 261-271.
139 Negro and white "superstitions," under the following headings: spirits and witches, cross marks, luck, signs, weather, seasons, members of the body.

NA 2865   Stephens, Nan Bagby. *Glory*. New York: John Day, 1932.
Novel of Georgia life with folkloric content.

NA   Stephens, Nan Bagby. "Negro Spirituals," *New York Times*, January 27, 1924,
2866   section 7, 4.
            A brief musical analysis of spirituals; the diversity of rhythms and
            styles in the South.

NA   Stephenson, Richard M. "Conflict and Control Functions of Humor," *Ameri-*
2867   *can Journal of Sociology*, 56 (1951), 569-574.
            Black humor as a mechanism to minimize status conflict and conscious-
            ness.

NA   Sterling, Philip, ed. *Laughing on the Outside: The Intelligent White*
2868   *Reader's Guide to Negro Tales and Humor*. New York: Grosset and Dunlap,
            1965.
            Stories and tales collected from oral and printed sources include 12
            animal tales, 16 descriptive tales, and 10 religious tales from slavery
            days; 56 tales of the war years; 58 stories from Reconstruction days;
            57 tales of preachers, sermons, and religion; 55 race and color stories;
            and others; illustrations; bibliography.

NA   Stevenson, Robert Murrell. "Negro Spirituals: Origins and Present Day
2869   Significance," in *Protestant Church Music in America: A Short Survey*
            of Men and Movements from 1564 to the Present. New York: Norton, 1966,
            92-105.
            Discussion of the background and style of spirituals with reference to
            early publications and social meaning.

NA   Steward, T.G. "Negro Imagery," *New Republic*, 12 (1918), 248.
2870   1 religious song discussed.

NA   Stewart, Horace. "Kindling of Hope in the Disadvantaged: A Study of the
2871   Afro-American Healer," *Mental Hygiene*, 55, No. 1 (1971), 96-100.
            A study of folk healers (possibly in Georgia); the African sources of
            the cures.

NA   Stewart, Sadie E. "Seven Folk-Tales from the Sea Islands, South Carolina,"
2872   *JAF*, 32 (1919), 394-396.
            Tales in dialect.

NA 2873   Stewart, William A. "Acculturative Processes and the Language of the American Negro," in *Language and its Social Setting*, William A. Gage, ed. Washington, D.C.: Anthropological Society of Washington, 1975. A critique of social scientists' views of the acculturation of American Negroes, largely argued on the basis of linguistic evidence.

NA 2874   Stewart, William A. "Continuity and Change in American Negro Dialects," *Florida FL Reporter*, 6, No. 2 (1968), 3-14. Literary and comparative U.S. white non-standard dialect evidence for the existence of distinct Negro dialects in contemporary America.

NA 2875   Stewart, William A. "Sociolinguistic Factors in the History of American Negro Dialects," *Florida FL Reporter*, 5, No. 2 (1967), 11-29. Literary and comparative linguistic evidence for determining the early stages of U.S. Negro dialects and their relation to modern forms.

NA 2876   Stewart, William A. "Understanding Black Language," in *Black America*, John F. Szwed, ed. New York: Basic Books, 1970, 121-131. An introduction to Black English as spoken in the U.S., with suggestions for reading instruction.

NA 2877   Stewart, William A. "Urban Negro Speech: Sociolinguistic Factors Affecting English Teaching," in *Social Dialects and Language Learning*, Roger W. Shuy, ed. Champaign, Ill.: National Council of Teachers of English, 1965, 10-19.

NA 2878   Stewart-Baxter, Derrick. "Blues and Views," *JJ*, 27, No. 4 (1974), 24-25. Brief comments on Southern medicine shows and their musical influence; illustrations.

NA 2879   Stewart-Baxter, Derrick. *Ma Rainey and the Classic Blues Singers*. New York: Stein and Day, 1970. Critical discussion of Ma Rainey, Bessie Smith and women blues singers of the 1920's; discography, illustrations.

NA 2880   Still, James. *Early Recollections and Life of Dr. James Still*. Philadelphia: Lippincott, 1877. The autobiography of a New Jersey folk doctor: includes medicinal recipes and cures.

NA
2881
Stillman, C.A. "The Freedman in the United States," *Catholic Presbyterian*, 1 (1879), 119-127.

NA
2882
Stoddard, Albert H. *Buh Partridge Outhides Buh Rabbit*. Savannah: Published by the Author, 1939.
1 tale in pamphlet form, with a preface discussing Gullah speech from the Sea Islands.

NA
2883
Stoddard, Albert H. *Gullah Tales and Anecdotes of the South Carolina Sea Islands*. Savannah: Published by the Author, 1940.
18 tales in dialect with notes on pronounciation.

NA
2884
Stoddard, Albert H. *How Buh Wasp Got his Small Waist*. Savannah: Published by the Author, 1941.
1 Sea Island tale in pamphlet form; Gullah text with translation.

NA
2885
Stoddard, Albert H. "Origins, Dialect, Beliefs and Characteristics of the Negroes of the South Carolina and Georgia Coast," *GHQ*, 28 (1944), 186-196.
Discusses the origin of Negro dialect compared to other immigrants'; examples of multiple meanings for the same word, gives creation story in dialect, discusses spirits and creatures of the night.

NA
2886
Stoddard, Tom. "Blind Tom--Slave Genius," *Storyville*, No. 28 (1970), 134-138.
Early background and career of Blind Tom, a pianist and composer.

NA
2887
Stoeltje, Beverly. "Bow-Legged Bastard: A Manner of Speaking (Speech Behavior of a Black Woman)," in *Folklore Annual of the Univeristy Folklore Association*, Tom Ireland, Joanne Krauss and Beverly Stoeltje, eds., No. 4 and 5 (1972 and 1973), 152-178.
Discussion of black female categories of speech; with transcribed interviews.

NA
2888
Stone, Chuck. *Tell It Like It Is*. New York: Trident, 1968.
Includes essays on black aesthetics, popular tastes, dress, etc.

NA
2889
Stoney, Samuel Gaillard, and Gertrude Mathews Shelby. *Black Genesis, A Chronicle*. New York: Macmillan, 1930.
Introductory notes on the background of Gullah folk speech and folk tales, as well as 5 retold myths on creation, 4 on "Adam An' Ebe,"

15 more on Cain, Abel, and "De Secon' Sin;" 6 animal tales--all in Gullah dialect; African sources of Gullah words.

NA 2890   Stowe, Harriet Beecher. *Men of Our Time*. Hartford: Hartford Publishing Company, 1868.
Includes a chapter on Frederick Douglass and slave songs.

NA 2891   Strachwitz, Chris. "Cajun Music on LP--A Survey," in *American Folk Music Occasional*, No. 2. New York: Oak, 1970, 25-29.
Contents of and annotations to Zydeco recordings.

NA 2892   Strachwitz, Chris. "Negro Religious Music: Singing Preachers and Their Congregations," record notes to America's Music Series LP record BC 19.
Discussion of fundamentalist preachers, especially those of the Church of God in Christ.

NA 2893   Strachwitz, Chris. "Zydeco Music--i.e., French Blues," *American Folk Music Occasional*, No. 2. New York: Oak, 1970, 22-24.
The music of the black Cajuns of Louisiana.

NA 2894   Strecker, John Kern. *Common English and Folk Names for Texas Amphibians and Reptiles*. Waco, Texas, n.p., 1928.

NA 2895   Strecker, John Kern. *Folk-lore Relating to Texas Birds*. Austin, Texas, n.p., 1928.

NA 2896   Street, James H. *Look Away! A Dixie Notebook*. New York: Viking, 1936.
Memoirs and legends from Mississippi, some retold from a slave woman's stories; essays on John Henry, etc.

NA 2897   Street, Julian. *American Adventures*. New York: Century Co., 1917.
Includes discussion of Gullah beliefs, conjure, street cries, and speech (pp. 242-247).

NA 2898   "Street Calls of the South," *New York Times*, December 18, 1927, Section 9, 24.
Several examples of cries and calls.

NA   Stribling, T.S. *The Forge*. Garden City, N.Y.: Doubleday, Doran, 1931.
2899   Novel of plantation life with folkloric content.

NA   Strong, Samuel M. "Negro-White Relations as Reflected in Social Types,"
2900   *American Journal of Sociology*, 52 (1946), 23-30.
             Urban black conceptions of the variety of roles played in race rela-
             tions ("white man's nigger," "bad nigger," "race leader," "mammy,"
             etc.).

NA   Strong, Samuel M. "Social Types in a Minority Group; Formulation of a
2901   Method," *American Journal of Sociology*, 48 (1943), 563-573.
             Social types ("jack-leg preacher," "hoodoo man," "jive-cat," the
             "dicty," *et al.*) as recognized by the Negroes of Chicago.

NA   Stronks, James B. "Chicago Store-Front Churches: 1964," *Names*, 12 (1964),
2902   127-128.
             A list of storefront churches to be seen in Chicago in June, 1964,
             principally along West Roosevelt Road.

NA   Stronks, James B. "Names of Store-Front Churches in Chicago," *Names*,
2903   10 (1962), 203-204.

NA   Stronks, James B. "New Store-Front Churches in Chicago," *Names*, 11 (1963),
2904   136.

NA   Stroyer, Jacob. *My Life in the South*. Salem, Mass., 1885.
2905   An ex-slave's accounts include Christmas celebrations, music, dance,
             etc.

NA   Stuart, Issac William. *Hartford in the Olden Time*. Hartford, Conn.: F.A.
2906   Brown, 1853.
             Includes a chapter on Negro slave governors, election parades, slave
             justices of the peace.

NA   Stuart, Ruth McEnery. *Napoleon Jackson: The Gentleman of the Plush Rock-
2907   er*. New York: Century, 1902.
             A novel of a Negro family in Louisiana with folkloric content.

NA   Stuart, Ruth McEnery. *Plantation Songs*. New York: Appleton, 1916.
2908

NA   Stuart, Ruth McEnery. "A Pulpit Orator," *Harper's*, 88 (1894), 643-645.
2909   A sketch concerning "fancy talk" and sermon language.

NA 2910   Stuart, Ruth McEnery. "Uncle Riah's Christmas Eve," *Century Magazine*, 35 (1898), 220-231.
    Short story with folkloric content.

NA 2911   Stuart, Ruth McEnery. "Uncle Still's Famous Weather Prediction," *Century Magazine*, 35 (1898), 345-353.
    Short story with descriptions of Christmas preparations on a plantation.

NA 2912   Stuckey, Sterling. "African and Afro-American Relationships: Research Possibilities," in *Expanding Horizons in African Studies*, Gwendolen M. Carter and Ann Paden, eds. Evanston, Ill.: Northwestern University Press, 1969.
    Calls for various kinds of research, including folkloric studies.

NA 2913   Stuckey, Sterling. "Through the Prism of Folklore: The Black Ethics in Slavery," *Massachusetts Review*, 9, No. 3 (1968), 417-437. (Reprinted in *Black and White in American Culture: An Anthology from the Massachusetts Review*, Jules Chametzky and Sidney Kaplan, eds. Amherst, Mass.: University of Massachusetts Press, 1969, 172-191.)
    Discussion of black life style under slavery.

NA 2914   Stuckey, Sterling. "Twilight of Our Past: Reflection on the Origins of Black History," in *Amistad 2*, John A. Williams and Charles F. Harris, eds. New York: Vintage, 1971, 261-295.
    A critique of the writing of Afro-American history which calls for the use of folklore materials.

NA 2915   Subor, Charles. "Jazz and the New Orleans' Press," *Downbeat*, 36, No. 12 (1969), 18-19.
    A brief history of the treatment of jazz in New Orleans' newspapers. Includes a reprint of a 1918 article on jazz.

NA 2916   Sullivan, Ronald. "Putting a Hex on Voodoo," *New York Times Magazine*, November 11, 1962, 136-137.
    Discusses "voodoo" shops in New York City, with descriptions.

NA 2917   Sullivan, T.P. *Plantation and Up-to-Date Humorous Negro Stories*. Chicago: M.A. Donahue & Co., 1905.

NA 2918   "Superstitions of Negroes in New Orleans," *JAF*, 5 (1892), 330-332.
    "Superstitions" held by Negroes in Louisiana and in New Orleans, taken from the *St. Louis Republic*, June 6, 1891.

NA
2919
Surge, Frank. *Singers of the Blues*. Minneapolis: Lerner, 1969.

NA
2920
Suthern, Orrin Clayton, II. "Minstrelsy and Popular Culture," in *Remus, Rastus, Revolution*, Marshall Fishwick, ed. Bowling Green, Ohio: Bowling Green University Popular Press, n.d., 57-72.
An overview of black musical theatre.

NA
2921
Sutter, Alan. "Playing a Cold Game: Phases of a Ghetto Career," *Urban Life and Culture* (Beverly Hills, California), 1, No. 1 (1972), 77-91.
Study of ghetto street life and drug dealing in San Francisco includes slang terms.

NA
2922
Suttles, Gerald D. *The Social Order of the Slum: Ethnicity and Territory in the Inner City*. Chicago: University of Chicago Press, 1968.
Chapter 4, "Communicative Devices," and Chapter 5, "Communicative Channels," discuss dress, speech, recreational behavior among Chicago blacks, Puerto Ricans, Italians, and Mexicans, and their conflicts.

NA
2923
Suttles, William C., Jr. "African Religious Survivals as Factors in American Slave Revolts," *JNH*, 56 (1971), 97-104.
Voodoo and other "African" religious practices as used in slave revolts.

NA
2924
Swados, Felice. "Negro Health on the Ante-Bellum Plantations," *Bulletin of the History of Medicine*, 10 (1941), 460-472.
The diseases and influences of slaves; geophagy and indigestion of foreign bodies.

NA
2925
Swan, Alfred Julius, ed. *Eight Negro Songs from Bedford County, Virginia*, collected by Francis H. Abbot. London: Enoch, 1923.
8 songs in dialect.

NA
2926
Sweeney, Margaret. "Tales and Legends Collected by Jeffersonville Students," *HFB*, 3 (1944), 39-48.
1 tale (p. 44) from Indiana.

NA
2927
"Swing Notes," *AS*, 13 (1938), 158.
News about the word "swing" in 1937.

NA 2928   Swint, Henry L., ed. *Dear Ones at Home: Letters from Contraband Camps.*
Nashville, Tenn.: Vanderbilt University Press, 1966.
Account of two Quaker spinsters in the South in the 1860's, including some material relating to Negro health and medicine (pp. 50, 102,
143, 199, 204, 214), dialect, songs and hymns (pp. 35, 90-91, 125-
126, 246), description of a turpentine still (p. 150), etc.

NA 2929   Synadinos, Th. N. *Pos Eida Ten Ameraken.* Athens: Aetos A.E., 1948.
Chapter on "Blacks and Whites" (pp. 165-173), discusses Negro folk
music in the United States, its meaning, its commercialization, and
its potential for use in classical music.

NA 2930   Szwed, John F. "Africa Lies Just Off Georgia," *Africa Report*, 15, No.
7 (1970), 29-31.
The history and culture of the Gullah people of the Sea Islands of
South Carolina and Georgia; their meaning for understanding Afro-
American culture history in general.

NA 2931   Szwed, John F. "An American Anthropological Dilemma: The Politics of
Afro-American Culture," in *Reinventing Anthropology*, Dell Hymes,
ed. New York: Pantheon, 1972, 153-181.
A critique of anthropological studies of Afro-Americans; the need
to rebalance social structural studies with those of culture.

NA 2932   Szwed, John F., ed. *Black America.* New York: Basic Books, 1970.
Collection of essays on Afro-American life, music, language style,
folktales, religion, etc. in North America.

NA 2933   Szwed, John F. "Discovering Afro-America," in *Black America*, John F.
Szwed, ed. New York: Basic Books, 1970, 286-296.
The need to view North American blacks in the larger social and
cultural framework of the blacks of the other Americas.

NA 2934   Szwed, John F. "Musical Adaptation among Afro-Americans," *JAF*, 82 (1969),
112-121. (Reprinted in *Afro-American Anthropology*, Norman E. Whitten,
Jr. and John F. Szwed, eds. New York: Free Press, 1970, 219-227; and
in *Man in Adaptation*, Vol. 3, Yehudi Cohen, ed. Chicago: Aldine,
1971, 463-469.)
The importance of music in adapting to social and economic change; the
implications of the blues and spirituals for other aspects of social
life; parallel Caribbean and South American musical adaptations.

NA
2935
Szwed, John F. "Musical Style and Racial Conflict," *Phylon*, 27 (1966),
358-366.
The "soul" movement in jazz--the use of folk music in the establishment of black hegemony.

NA
2936
Szwed, John F. "Negro Music: Urban Renewal," in *Our Living Traditions*,
Tristram P. Coffin, ed. New York: Basic Books, 1968, 305-315. (Reprinted in the John Edwards Memorial Foundation Reprint Series, UCLA,
1970.)
The movement of the Negro to the city and its relationship to blues,
gospel and jazz. The importance of phonograph record dissemination
and the limitation of recording time is discussed.

NA
2937
Szwed, John F. "Some Insights into the Blues: What Are Its Functions?"
Festival of American Folklife. Washington, D.C.: Smithsonian Insti-
tution, 1972, 47.
The social and psychological functions of the blues.

Szwed, John F. See Fauset, Arthur H., No. NA 954.

NA
2938
T. D. "Folk Heroes and Protest," *The Appalacian South*, 1, No. 3 (1966),
26-27.
5 protest songs.

NA
2939
Tackett, Santa Maria. *Some Mississippi Negro Oddities*. Nashville, Tennessee: n.p., 1930.

NA
2940
Talbot, Edith Armstrong. "True Religion in Negro Hymns," *SW*, 51 (1922),
213-216; 260-264; 334-339.
A discussion of religious elements in Negro hymns; fragments of texts.

NA
2941
"Tales of the Rabbit from Georgia Negroes," *JAF* (1899), 108-115.
6 stories.

NA
2942
Talese, Gay. "Harlem for Fun," *Esquire*, 58 (September, 1962), 135-142.
Revival of white interest in Harlem nightlife; focus on: the Twist,
a dance.

NA
2943
Tallant, Robert. *Mardi Gras*. Garden City, N.Y.: Doubleday, 1948.
The organization and content of the Mardi Gras celebrations in New

Orleans, with comparisons to those in Mobile, Alabama and elsewhere in Louisiana; includes song texts from the Zulu band; illustrations.

NA 2944 Tallant, Robert. *Voodoo in New Orlenas*. New York: Macmillan, 1946.
Accounts of Marie Laveau and other practitioners of voodoo; current customs; "brand-name" voodoo; the "street literature" of magic.

NA 2945 Talley, Thomas W. "De Wull er de Wust (The Will o' the Wisp)," *TFSB*, 21 (1955), 57-78.
A mother's explanation to her small son of the nature and origins of "African cannibals" or "'em Outlandish Folks-eaters.'"

NA 2946 Talley, Thomas W. *Negro Folk Rhymes: Wise and Otherwise*. New York: Macmillan, 1922.
Hundreds of songs and game and dance rhymes collected at Fisk University, and a few rhymes from Jamaica, Venezuela and Africa; includes an essay, "A Study in Negro Folk Rhymes," on songs, poetry, musical instruments, juba, dance, etc.

NA 2947 Talley, Thomas W. "The Origins of Negro Tradition," *Phylon*, 3 (1942), 371-376; 4 (1943), 30-38.
An examination of Negro tales as bearers of traditional knowledge and exploration rather than as a mere source of amusement.

NA 2948 Tallmadge, William H. "Afro-American Music," *Music Educators' Journal*, 44 (September-October, 1957), 37-39. (Reprinted in revised form as *Afro-American Music*. Buffalo: State University College, College Bookstore, 1969.)
Brief history of Afro-American folk music and jazz with a chronology of recordings and events.

NA 2949 Tallmadge, William H. "Dr. Watts and Mahalia Jackson--The Development, Decline and Survival of a Folk Style in America," *EM*, 5 (1961), 95-99.
The origin, development and continued use of the "lining out" style of congregational singing by white and Negro religious groups and its influence on gospel solo singing, secular blues and a form of the Negro prison work song.

NA 2950 Tallmadge, William H. "The Responsorial and Antiphonal Practice in Gospel Song," *EM*, 12 (1968), 219-238.
Discussion of possible sources for response and antiphony includes

madrigals, motifs, anthems, marching bands and hymns; brief discussion of jubilee groups and modern gospel and rock singers.

NA 2951 Tamony, Peter. "Bessie: Vocumentary," *Jazz: A Quarterly of American Music*, No. 4 (1959), 280-285.
Analysis of meaning of lyrics in Bessie Smith's recording of "Gimme a Pigfoot."

NA 2952 Tartt, Ruby Pickens. "Carrie Dykes--Midwife," *PTFS*, No. 19 (1944), 21-28.
A midwife relates her experiences with voodoo; description of various practices and beliefs of witchcraft, midwifery, etc.

NA 2953 Tartt, Ruby Pickens. "Richard the Tall-Hearted, Alabama Sketches," *Southwest Review*, 29 (1944), 234-244.
Literary sketch, in dialect, of Negro life.

NA 2954 Tate, Paul. "The Cajuns of Louisiana," *The American Folk Music Occasional*, No. 2. New York: Oak, 1970, 8-12.
A definitional essay on the white Acadians of Louisiana; includes sample texts of a possible "dozens" tradition among Cajuns.

NA 2955 Tate, Thad W., Jr. *The Negro in Eighteenth-Century Williamsburg*. Charlottesville, Va.: University of Virginia Press, 1965.
Descriptions of social activities, language, religions and religious revivals, education, etc.

NA 2956 Taylor, Clyde. "Black Folk Spirit and the Shape of Black Literature," *Blackfolk* (Los Angeles), 1, No. 1 (1972), 11-17.
The social and political functions of Afro-American folklore; the links between Afro-American folklore and literature.

NA 2957 Taylor, Helen Louise, and Rebecca Wolcott. "Items from New Castle, Delaware," *JAF*, 51 (1938), 92-94.
Beliefs and legends (the origin of the Moors, a Delaware group of mixed ancestry).

NA 2958 Taylor, Jo Gray. *Negro Slavery in Louisiana*. Baton Rouge: Louisiana Historical Association, 1963.
Includes religion, music, drums used on plantations, tribal music, cult groups, work practices, slave escapes, etc.

NA 2959   Taylor, John E. "Somethin' on My Mind: A Cultural and Historical Interpretation of Spiritual Texts," *EM*, 19 (1975), 387-399.

NA 2960   Taylor, Marshall W. *A Collection of Revival Hymns and Plantation Melodies*. Cincinnati: Taylor and Echals, 1883.
Includes 170 songs, most with music.

NA 2961   Taylor, Nicholas G. "Jazz Music and Its Relation to African Music," *Musical Courier*, 84 (June 1, 1922), 7.
Argues that African rhythms are retained in jazz; with musical examples.

NA 2962   Taylor, Nicholas G. "The Language of the Jitterbug," *Better English*, 2, No. 5 (1938), 51.

NA 2963   Taylor, Orville W. *Negro Slavery in Arkansas*. Durham, N.C.: Duke University Press, 1958.
Sections on the material culture and domestic life of slaves.

NA 2964   Taylor, Rosser Howard. *Carolina Crossroads: A Study of Rural Life at the End of the Horse-and-Buggy Era*. Murfreesboro, N.C.: Johnson, 1966.
The etiquette of race relations in the Carolinas circa 1900; customs; fragments of texts and interviews.

NA 2965   Ten-Eyck, Martha. "Washington Folklore," *The Folklorist* (Chicago), 1 (1893), 159-162.
Recollections of Negro herb vendors and the story of the Night Doctor, a malign conjuror.

NA 2966   Terrel, Clemmie S. "Spirituals from Alabama," *JAF*, 43 (1930), 322-324.
Texts of 5 spirituals.

NA 2967   Terry, Richard. *Voodooism in Music and Other Essays*. London: Burns, Oates & Washburne, 1934.
Argues against the Negro origins of jazz.

Testut, Charles. See No. FWI 124.

NA
2968
Thacker, Eric. "Gottschalk and a Prelude to Jazz," *Jazz and Blues*, 2, No. 12 (1973), 10-12, 17.
The folk music elements in Louis Moreau Gottschalk's (1829-1869) compositions; comments on Negro folk music influences on pre-1900 classical composers; discography; bibliography.

NA
2970
Thacker, Eric. "Ragtime Roots," *Jazz and Blues*, 3, No. 8 (1973), 6-7; 3, No. 9 (1973), 4-6.
Classical, African and minstrel influences on ragtime music.

NA
2971
Thacker, Page. *Plantation Reminiscences*. n.p.: published by the author, 1878.
Accounts of Virginia slave "Africanisms," a funeral shout, corn shuckings, etc.

NA
2972
Thanet, Octave. "Folklore in Arkansas," *JAF*, 5 (1892), 121-125.
Dialect traits which reflect "the pioneer's rude and toilmarked philosophy."

NA
2973
Theriot, Marie, and Marie Haye. "The Legend of Foolish John," *SFQ*, 7 (1943), 153-156.
1 text.

NA
2974
These Are Our Lives. Chapel Hill, North Carolina: University of North Carolina Press, 1939.
WPA collection includes 10 life histories from black Southerners, with information on religion, plantation life, etc.

NA
2975
Thomas, Daniel Lindsey, and Lucy Blayney Thomas. *Kentucky Superstitions*. Princeton: Princeton University Press, 1920.
4000 "superstitions," "the majority" of which are shared by Negroes and whites in Kentucky.

NA
2976
Thomas, Gates. "Six Negro Songs from the Colorado Valley," *PTFS*, No. 26 (1954), 162-166.
Collection of songs from the Colorado River area in the period from 1886 to 1906.

NA
2977
Thomas, Gates. "South Texas Negro Work Songs," *PTFS*, No. 5 (1926), 154-180.
A collection of 30 songs.

NA
2978
Thomas, Will H. "The Decline and Decadence of Folk Metaphor," *PTFS*, No. 2 (1923), 16-17.
Contains passages about the use of folk metaphors by blacks.

NA
2979
Thomas, Will H. *Some Current Folk-Songs of the Negro*. Austin, Texas: Texas Folk-Lore Society, 1912. (Reprinted in *PTFS*, No. 5 (1926); reprint edition, Hatboro, Pa.: Folklore Associates, 1965, separately numbered, following p. 190.)
12 songs, with discussion.

NA
2980
Thompson, Kay C. "The Western Heritage of Jazz," *RC*, 9, No. 4 (1950), 8, 17.
Western classical music, rather than the blues and Negro folk music, is seen to be the source of jazz; the piano as the basis for collective improvisation.

NA
2981
Thompson, Lawrence S. "More Buzzard Lore," *KFR*, 4 (1958), 155-162.
Includes Negro beliefs about buzzards.

NA
2982
Thompson, Robert Farris. "African Influence on the Art of the United States," in *Black Studies in the University: A Symposium*, Armstead L. Robinson, *et al.*, eds. New Haven: Yale University Press, 1969, 122-170.
The carving, pottery, and basket-making traditions of Missouri, South Carolina, Georgia, and New York.

NA
2983
Thompson, Robert Farris. "Dance Music in the Fifties," *Saturday Review*, 44 (March 11, 1961), 92-93, 97.
Brief summary of trends in Afro-Cuban dance music in the U.S. in the 1950's.

NA
2984
Thompson, Robert Farris. "Enter Cuban Pete and Millie," *Ballroom Dance Magazine*, January, 1961, 16-26.
Biographical details on a stylistically influential pair of New York City mambo dancers.

NA
2985
Thompson, Robert Farris. "New Voice from the Barrios," *Saturday Review*, 50 (October 28, 1967), 53-55.
Historical sketch of a leading New York Afro-Cuban band of the late 1960's.

NA   Thompson, Robert Farris. "Palladium Mambo--1: Ballroom U.S.A.," *Dance*
2986   *Magazine*, 33, No. 9 (1959), 73-75.
            Mambo experts described and analyzed.

NA   Thompson, Robert Farris. "Portrait of the Pachanga," *Saturday Review*, 44
2987   (October 28, 1961), 42-43, 54.
            Brief impressions of an Afro-Cuban dance of the early 1960's, its
            Yoruba sources, etc.

NA   Thomson, Virgil. "Jazz," *American Mercury*, 2 (1924), 465-467.
2988   The components of jazz: fox-trot rhythm and syncopated melody; the
            evolution of syncopation from music of the Indians, Negroes and
            Mexicans.

NA   Thurman, Howard. *Deep River: An Interpretation of Negro Spirituals*. Oak-
2989   land, Calif.: Mills College, Eucalyptus Press, 1946. (Revised edition,
            *Deep River: Reflections on the Religious Insight of Certain of the
            Negro Spirituals*. New York: Harper, 1955.)

NA   Thurman, Howard. *The Negro Spiritual Speaks of Life and Death*. New York:
2990   Harper, 1947.

NA   Thurman, Sue Bailey, ed. *The Historical Cookbook of the American Negro*.
2991   Washington, D.C.: Corporate Press, 1958.

NA   Thurman, Wallace. *Negro Life in New York's Harlem*. Girard, Kansas: Halde-
2992   man-Julius, n.d.
            Brief account of Harlem's churches, night clubs, rent parties, gambling
            activities, etc.

NA   Tidewell, James Nathan. "Mark Twain's Representation of Negro Speech,"
2993   *AS*, 17 (1942), 174-176.
            Examples of Missouri Negro speech as expressed in Mark Twain's *Adven-
            tures of Huckleberry Finn* through the dialogues of Jim.

NA   Tidewell, James Nathan, ed. *A Treasury of American Folk Humor*. New York:
2994   Crown, 1956.
            Includes a number of texts reprinted from other sources, some tradi-
            tional, some rewritten.

NA
2995
    Tiersot, Julien. *Chansons Nègres d'Amérique*. Paris: Heugel, 1933.

NA
2996
    Tiersot, Julien. *La Musique chez les Peuples Indigènes de l'Amérique du Nord (États-Unis et Canada)*, Notes d'Ethnographie Musicale, Series 2, Paris: Libraries Fischbacher, 1910.
A commentary on Negro music largely derived from existing publications on French Creole songs from Louisiana; argues that Negro music is almost entirely derived from European sources.

NA
2997
    Tinker, Edward Larocque. "Bibliography of the French Newspapers and Periodicals of Louisiana," *Proceedings of the American Antiquarian Society*, 42 (1932), 247-370.
Contains the history of the *Carillon* and the *Meschacebe*, two newspapers which published Negro folktales, songs, dialect verse, proverbs, etc., between 1858 and 1879.

NA
2998
    Tinker, Edward Larocque. "Cable and the Creoles," *American Literature*, 5 (1934), 311-326.

NA
2999
    Tinker, Edward Larocque, ed. *Les Cernelles: Afro-French Poetry in Louisiana*. New York: Spiral, 1930. (Reprinted from *The Colophon*, Part 3, September, 1930.)
"Mulatto" poets in New Orleans in the mid-19th century who published in French. (See Armand Lanusse, No. NA 1792.)

NA
3000
    Tinker, Edward Larocque. *Creole City*. New York: Longmans, Green, 1953.
Includes discussion of Negro "superstitions," healers, the Mardi Gras, Creole speech, proverbs, folktales, music, dance, improvised taunts, street cries, etc., in New Orleans.

    Tinker, Edward Larocque. *Les Écrits de Langue Française en Louisiane* . . . See No. BIB 62.

NA
3001
    Tinker, Edward Larocque. "Gumbo, the Creole Dialect of Louisiana; with a Bibliography," *Proceedings of the American Antiquarian Society,* 45 (1935), Part 1, 101-142. (Also reprinted by the author, Worcester, Mass., 1935.)
Louisiana Creole grammar, African influences; fables, proverbs, songs and street cries; voodoo; "lyrical lampooning" as an "African trait"; bibliography.

NA
3002
Tinker, Edward Larocque. "Louisiana Gumbo," *Yale Review*, 21 (1932), 566-579.
Discussion, with examples, of black Louisiana Creole speech--called "Gumbo" by whites and "Congo" by younger blacks; includes songs texts.

NA
3003
Tinker, Edward Larocque. *Toucoutou*. New York: Dodd, Mead, 1928.
Novel of slave life in New Orleans with folkloric content; includes description of *bamboula*, *calinda*, and *counjaille* dancing in Place Congo, voodoo rituals, tribal groupings, Creole speech, folksongs, etc.; glossary.

Tinker, Edward Larocque. See No. HA 353.

NA
3004
Tinling, David C. "Voodoo, Root Work, and Medicine," *Psychosomatic Medicine*, 29 (1969), 483-490.
Brief history of root work; the beliefs of 7 patients in the northern United States.

NA
3005
Tirindelli, Pier Adolfo. *Slave Song*. Milano: Ricordi, 1907.

NA
3006
Todd, Arthur. "Four Centuries of American Dance: Dance before the American Revolution--1734-1775," *Dance Magazine*, 34 (March, 1950), 20-21, 35.

NA
3007
Todd, Arthur. "Four Centuries of American Dance. Negro American Theatre Dance, 1840-1900," *Dance Magazine*, 34 (November, 1950), 20-21, 33-34.

NA
3008
Todd, Arthur. "Four Centuries of American Dance: Part 3: The Negro Folk Dance in America," *Dance Magazine*, 34 (January, 1950), 14-15, 41.

NA
3009
Todd, Arthur. "Two Way Passage for Dance," *Dance Magazine*, 36 (July, 1962), 39-41.

NA
3010
Todd, T.W. "Anthropology and Negro Slavery," *Medical Life*, 36 (1929), 157-167.

NA
3011
Toll, Robert C. *Blacking Up: The Minstrel Show in Nineteenth-Century America*. New York: Oxford University Press, 1974.
A history of the blackface minstrel show in America, covering

music, dance, costumes, political issues satirized, leading figures, etc.; illustrations, bibliography.

NA 3012   Toll, Robert C. "From Folktale to Stereotype: Images of Slaves in Ante-bellum Minstrelsy," *JFI*, 8 (1971), 38-47.
Discusses white minstrel songs and skits which used black folklore materials.

NA 3013   Tonsor, Johann. "Negro Music," *Music* (Chicago), 3 (1892-1893), 119-122.
Musical characteristics of Negro songs with an account of a praise meeting.

NA 3014   Torian, Sarah, ed. "Ante-Bellum and War Memories of Mrs. Telfair Hodg-son," *GHQ*, 27 (1943), 350-356.
Account of slave language, grave decorations, quilts, carving, boat songs, etc.

NA 3015   Torrence, Frederic Ridgely. *Granny Maumee, The Rider of Dreams, Simon the Cyrenian: Plays for a Negro Theatre*. New York: Macmillan, 1917.
1-act plays with folkloric content.

NA 3016   Torres, Jose. . . . *Sting like a Bee: The Muhammad Ali Story*. New York: Abelard-Schuman, 1971.
Includes discussion of black style in the context of an account of the Joe Frazier-Muhammad Ali fight.

NA 3017   Torrey, Jane W. "Illiteracy in the Ghetto," *Harvard Educational Review*, 40, No. 2 (1970), 253-259.

NA 3018   Touchstone, Blake. "Voodoo in New Orleans," *Louisiana History*, 13 (1972), 371-386.
An attempt to separate voodoo "folklore" from "fact" by the comparison of newspaper accounts to those of the more popular books.

NA 3019   Towne, Laura M. *Letters and Diary of Laura M. Towne written from the Sea Islands of South Carolina 1862-1884*. Rupert S. Holland, ed. Cambridge: The Riverside Press, 1912.
Northern School teacher's letters describe black life and customs: shouts and praise meetings, naming, singing, etc.

NA   "Traces Negro Spirituals," *New York Times*, June 1, 1930, Section 2, 8.
3020   N.G.J. Ballanta on the origins of spirituals (African rhythms plus
            Christianity).

NA   "Track-Lining Chantey," *Atlantic Monthly*, 146 (1930), 281.
3021   Text and music.

NA   Tragle, Henry Irving. *The Southampton Slave Revolt of 1831: A Compila-
3022   tion of Source Material*. Amherst, Mass.: University of Massachusetts
            Press, 1971.
            Documents of the Nat Turner revolt; includes material on the ritual
            aspects and some oral accounts of the revolt.

NA   "Transplanted Negroes Get Supply of Red 'Chewin' Cane'," *New York
3023   Times*, December 8, 1929, Section 3, 1.
            Northern Negroes' taste for red sugar cane from Southern Georgia.

NA   Traum, Happy. *The Blues Bag*. New York: Consolidated Music, 1968.
3024   29 songs with music from a variety of blues guitarists.

NA   Traum, Happy. *Finger-Picking Styles for Guitar*. New York: Oak, 1966.
3025   Includes transcriptions of recorded guitar solos by Mississippi John
            Hurt, Etta Baker, Elizabeth Cotton, Blind Lemon Jefferson and Joseph
            Spence. With texts and photos.

NA   Trent-Johns, Altona. *Play Songs of the Deep South*. Washington, D.C.:
3026   Associated Publications, 1945.
            12 children's game songs with directions for playing: includes 1
            lullaby.

NA   Trotter, James Monroe. *Music and Some Highly Musical People*. Boston:
3027   Lee and Shepard, 1878.
            Biographies and historical accounts of black musicians, the Jubilee
            Singers, *et al*.

NA   Troubridge, Sir St. Vincent. "Notes on the DAE: VII. Negroes and Slavery,"
3028   *AS*, 26 (1951), 27-28.
            15 lexical items.

NA 3029   Trux, H.J. "Negro Minstrelsy Ancient and Modern," *Putnam's*, 5 (1855), 73-79.
           Parallels minstrel and Elizabethan songs; includes examples of texts; a footnote discusses Negro names.

NA 3030   Tucker, George. *Letters from Virginia*. Baltimore, 1816.
           Describes slave dancing and night celebrations "with legendary ballads, narratives of alternate dialogue and singing."

NA 3031   (Tucker, George). *The Valley of Shenandoah*, 2 vols. New York, 1824.
           Novel contains an account of a corn dance.

NA 3032   Tucker, H. Clay. "The Language of Jazz," *TFSB*, 20 (1954), 77-81.
           Three categories of jazz lingo: 1) terms descriptive of the music itself; 2) terms descriptive of personal conduct; and 3) names of objects and people.

NA 3033   Tudor, Dean. "The Real Blues," *Library Journal*, 97 (1972), 633-649.
           Discussion of blues origins, styles, etc., with discography, bibliography.

NA 3034   Turner, Arlin. *George W. Cable: A Biography*. Baton Rouge: Louisiana State University Press, 1966.
           Contains information on the sources of Cable's folkloric work in New Orleans.

NA 3035   Turner, Darwin T. "Daddy Joel Harris and His Old-Time Darkies," *Southern Literary Journal*, 1, No. 1 (1968), 20-41.
           An assessment of the Negro characters in Joel Chandler Harris' fiction.

NA 3036   Turner, Fred W. "Black Jazz Artists: The Dark Side of Horatio Alger," *The Massachusetts Review*, 10, No. 2 (1969), 341-353.
           The value of black jazz autobiographies for the understanding of black life in the U.S.

NA 3037   Turner, Harriet. *Folksongs of the American Negro*. Boston: The Boston Music Co., 1925.

NA 3038   Turner, James K. "Slavery in Edgecomb County," *Trinity College Historical Papers*, Series 12 (1966), 5-36.

NA
3039

Turner, Joseph Addison. *The Old Plantation: A Poem by Joseph Addison Turner, 1862*, Henry Prentice Miller, ed. Atlanta: Emory University, 1945.
Includes a section on Negroes, their dances, songs, houses, religion, etc.

NA
3040

Turner, Lorenzo Dow. *Africanisms in the Gullah Dialect*. Chicago: University of Chicago Press, 1949.
A study of the phonology, morphology and syntax of the Gullah speech of the South Carolina and Georgia coast; West African names and words in Gullah; intonation; song and tale texts; bibliography.

NA
3041

Turner, Lorenzo Dow. "Linguistic Research and African Survivals," *American Council of Learned Societies, Bulletin No. 32* (1941), 68-69.

NA
3042

Turner, Lorenzo Dow. "Notes on the Sounds and Vocabulary of Gullah," *Publications of the American Dialect Society*, No. 3 (1945), 13-28.
Phonology, personal names from Africa, phrases heard only in folktales and songs, etc.

NA
3043

Turner, Lorenzo Dow. "Problems Confronting the Investigation of Gullah," *Publications of the American Dialect Society*, No. 9, 1948, 74-84.
Study of African linguistic survivals in Gullah speech; contributions of Wolof, Ewe, and Congo languages to the spoken language of slaves in Charleston, South Carolina; includes over 100 examples.

NA
3044

Turner, Lucile Price. "Negro Spirituals in the Making," *MQ*, 17 (1931), 480-485.
Account of a Holiness service in Arkansas with mention of the use of broadside spirituals at a conference; 5 spirituals, texts and music.

NA
3045

Tuttle, Joseph F. "The Morristown Ghost," *The Historical Magazine*, 3rd series, 1 (January, 1872), 2-10.
Discusses the influence of blacks on "superstition" in the Morristown, New Jersey area, mostly in antebellum times.

NA
3046

"Twenty-One Negro Spirituals" in *American Stuff*. New York: Viking, 1937, 96-106.
21 texts from South Carolina.

NA
3047

Twining, Mary Arnold. "An Anthropological Look at Afro-American Folk Narrative," *CLA Journal*, 14, No. 1 (1970), 57-61.
A survey article on sources for the study of black American folktales.

NA
3048

Twining, Mary Arnold, and William C. Saunders. "'One of these Days': The Function of Two Singers in the Sea Island Community," *Studies in the Literary Imagination*, 3, No. 1 (1970), 65-71.
Discussion of the social setting of songs; includes 4 song texts.

NA
3049

Two Months in the Confederate States, by an English Merchant. London: Richard Bentley, 1863.
Descriptions of slaves' life, food, dress, etc.

NA
3050

"Two Negro Witch-Stories," *JAF*, 12 (1899), 145-146.
2 witch stories involving black cats.

NA
3051

Tyree, Marion Cabell, ed. *Housekeeping in Old Virginia*. Louisville, Ky.: Morton, 1879.
Recipes collected from 250 Virginia housewives, probably Afro-American.

NA
3052

Ulanov, Barry. *A History of Jazz in America*. New York: The Viking Press, 1950.
Includes discussion of the folk sources of the blues and jazz; argues against a significant African contribution.

NA
3053

Uldall, Elizabeth T. "(m?m), ETC," *AS*, 29 (1964), 232.
Note on the black "grunt of negation" in speech.

NA
3054

Unbelievable Beliefs. Beaufort, South Carolina: n.p., n.d. (1971?)
A collection of beliefs, hag lore, root work, folk cures, etc., by a Beaufort high school class; illustrations.

NA
3055

"Uncle Sam's Peculiarities. American Niggers--Hudson River Steam-Boat Dialogues," *Bentley's Miscellany* (London), 6 (1839), 262-271. (Reprinted in No. NA 1568.)
Accounts of a sermon in New York, a baptism in Philadelphia; a black-white dialogue; a text of a sea shanty; mention of blacks celebrating the Declaration of Independence on July 5th, etc.; presented in justification of slavery.

NA   United States Congress. *Report on Joint Committee to Inquire into the*
3056   *Condition of Affairs in the Late Insurrectionary States*, 42nd Con-
             gress, 2nd Session, 13 vols., Washington, D.C., 1872.
             Includes the testimonies of 167 Negroes on their reactions to the Ku-
             Klux Klan's efforts to frighten and control.

NA   Updike, Wilkins. *A History of the Episcopal Church in Narragansett, Rhode*
3057   *Island*, 3 vols., 2nd edition. Boston: D.B. Updike, 1907.
             Material on election of slave governors.

NA   Utley, Francis Lee. "Review of 'Gullah: A Breath of the Low Country,' by
3058   Dick Reeves," *SFQ*, 34 (1970), 365-368.
             Discusses phonograph recordings of Gullah dialect and folklore; in-
             cludes samples of Gullah jokes and tales.

NA   Uyldert, Herman. *Vorstin van de Gospel: Mahalia Jackson*. Tielt and Den
3059   Haag: Lanroo, 1962.

NA   Van Blarcom, Carolyn Corant. "Rat Pie among the Black Midwives of the
3060   South," *Harper's*, 160 (1930), 322-332.
             Beliefs and practices of midwives with accounts of how they learned
             their trade.

NA   Vance, Joel. "The Latin Connection," *Stereo Review* (New York), 30, No. 5
3061   (1973), 78-81.
             Overview of Latin music in New York City, its connection to *santeria*,
             etc.; illustrations, discography.

NA   Vance, L.J. "Folk-Lore Studies," and "Plantation Folk-Lore," *The Open*
3062   *Court*, 1 (1887), 612-615, 662-664; 2 (1888), 1029-1032, 1074-1076,
             1092-1095.
             Folklore traditions of Indians, Negroes and Canadians; the develop-
             ment of animal tales.

NA   Van Gogh, Rupert. "The Evolution of Jazz," *West African Review* (Liver-
3063   pool), 6 (March, 1935), 15-17.
             The Negro contribution to jazz.

NA   Vann, William H. "Two Negro Folk Tales," *PTFS*, No. 18 (1943), 172-180.
3064   2 folktales bearing resemblance to Uncle Remus tales.

NA
3065
Van Patten, N. "Vocabulary of the American Negro as Set Forth in Contemporary Literature," *AS*, 7 (1931), 24-31.
Discusses misrepresentations of Negro dialect, with over 200 illustrations in inauthentic vocabulary.

NA
3066
Vanstory, Burnette. *Georgia's Land of the Golden Isles*. Athens, Ga.: University of Georgia Press, 1956.
Brief mentions (pp. 49, 94) of "Mohamadan" slaves and their speech,
writing and character, and a slave chef, skilled in French cuisine
(p. 46).

NA
3067
Vanstory, Burnette. *Ghost Stories and Superstitions of Old Saint Simons*.
n.p., n.d.
Sea Island folklore pamphlet: 8 rewritten stories and a number of
"superstition" texts.

NA
3068
Van Vechten, Carl. "The Black Blues," *Vanity Fair*, 24 (August, 1925), 57,
86, 92.
The blues as poetry.

NA
3069
Van Vechten, Carl. "The Folk Songs of the American Negro," *Vanity Fair*,
24 (July, 1925), 52, 92.
Brief history of Negro folk spirituals; description of Southern plantation life and the impact of work songs, convict songs, and ragtime
and blues on popular music.

NA
3070
Van Vechten, Carl. "Negro 'Blues' Singers," *Vanity Fair*, 26, No. 1 (1926),
67, 106, 108.
The styles of Bessie Smith, Ethel Waters, and Clara Smith compared.

NA
3071
Van Vechten, Carl. *Nigger Heaven*. New York: Knopf, 1926.
Novel of life in Harlem in the 1920's; includes a slang glossary.

NA
3072
Vaughn-Cooke, Anna Fay. "The Black Preaching Style: Historical Development and Characteristics," in *Language and Linguistics: Working
Papers, No. 5: Sociolinguistics*, William K. Riley and David M. Smith,
eds. Washington, D.S.: Georgetown University Press, 1972. 28-39.

NA
3073
Vauthier, Simone. "Une Brèche Sudiste dans l'Image Traditionelle de l'Es-
clave: Life in the South, 1849," *Journal de la Société des American-
istes*, 58 (1969), 235-258.
Sociological analysis of plantation life as derived from Lyle A.
Wright's *Life in the South*.

NA
3074
Verdier, Eva L. *"When Gun Shoot": Some Experiences While Taking the Census Among the Low Country Negroes of South Carolina*. n.p., 1932.
A pamphlet with remarks on Sea Island customs: time-reckoning, grave decoration, naming practices, and tactics of verbal evasion.

NA
3075
Victor, Metta Victoria Fuller. *Maum Guinea and Her Plantation "Children," A Story of Christmas Week with the American Slaves*. London and New York: Beadle, 1861.
Maum Guinea's appearance, character and position of respect (p. 11), Christmas Eve storytelling rituals (pp. 25-35), ghosts and alligator hunting stories (p. 48, 106-116), Maum Guinea's life and an account of the Nat Turner revolt (pp. 82-100, 139-187); also accounts of slave dances, music, beliefs, etc.; illustrations.

NA
3076
Villere, Sidney, Roy Alciatore, and George Reinecke. "A Nineteenth Century Creole Menu and Its Proverbs," *LFM*, 2 (1968), 105-110.
Proverbs used to introduce each course at an 1898 banquet.

NA
3077
Virginia Writers' Program. *The Negro in Virginia*. New Hastings, N.Y.: Virginia State Writers' Program, Works Progress Administration, 1940.

NA
3078
"Visit to a Negro Cabin in Virginia," *The Family Magazine*, 3 (1836), 242-245.
Description of the daily activities of some plantation slaves, including a corn-shucking.

NA
3079
Vlach, John M. "The Fabrication of a Traditional Fire Tool," *JAF*, 86 (1973), 54-57.
Description of the making of a fire poker by a Charleston blacksmith.

NA
3080
Vlach, John M. "Folktale Diffusion Across the Sahara and Afro-American Folklore: A Note," *Folklore Forum*, 3 (1970), 128-134.
Argues that rather than being from European sources, parallel African and Afro-American folktales were either of African origin, or diffused to Africa by way of Muslim contact before European contact.

NA
3081
Vlach, John M. *Phillip Simmons: Afro-American Blacksmith,* Folklore Students Association Preprint Series (Indiana), 1, No. 2 (August, 1973).
Simmons' background; history, techniques and procedures of Negro blacksmithing; illustrations.

NA 3082   Von Kolnitz, A.H. *Crying in de Wilderness*. Charleston, S.C.: Walker, Evans and Cogswell, 1935.
A white man's poems in dialect, drawn from Gullah (South Carolina) sermons; with introductory notes and settings.

NA 3083   "A Voodoo Festival near New Orleans," *JAF*, 10 (1897), 76.
Account of an expedition in search of a voodoo "orgy," taken from the New Orleans *Times-Democrat*, June 24, 1896.

NA 3084   Wade, Richard C. *Slavery in the Cities: The South 1820-1860*. London: Oxford University Press, 1964.
Chapter Six ("Beyond the Master's Eye") gives accounts of urban slave social events, drinking, dress, gambling, preachers and preaching, bible classes, funerals and cemeteries, and general "free-time" activities.

NA 3085   Wagner, Jean. *Les Poètes Nègres des Etats-Unis*. Paris: Istra, 1963. (Also published as *Black Poets of the United States*. Urbana, Ill.: University of Illinois Press, 1973.)
A study of the writers of the Negro Renaissance of the 1920's and 1930's develops a critical base with which to condemn the poetry of the writers influenced by folklore.

NA 3086   Wake, C.S. "The Philosophy of Folk Tales," *Lippincott's Magazine*, 46 (1890), 415-418.
Argues that folk tales are designed to enforce a lesson in wordly experience on religious truth; includes examples of black tales.

NA 3087   Wakefield, Edward. "Wisdom of Gombo," *Nineteenth Century*, 30 (1891), 575-582.
Proverbs from Louisiana.

NA 3088   Walker, Sheila. "Black English: Expression of the Afro-American Experience," *Black World*, 20, No. 8 (1971), 4-16.
Argues for bi-dialectal education.

NA 3089   Wallace, Anthony F.C., and Raymond D. Fogelson. "The Identity Struggle," in *Intensive Family Therapy: Theoretical and Practical Aspects*, Ivan Boszormenyi-Nagy and James L. Framo, eds. New York: Hoeber, 1965, 365-406.
Interprets "playing the dozens" in terms of identity struggles; includes a list of synonyms for dozens (pp. 394-396).

NA   Wallaschek, Richard. *Primitive Music: an Inquiry into the Origin and*
3090   *Development of the Music, Songs, Instruments, Dances, and Pantomimes*
              of Savage Races. London: Longmans, 1893.
              Negro folk music as described in travel accounts; sees spirituals as
              derived from Europe.

NA   Waller, Tom, and Gene Killian. "Georgia Folk Medicine," *SFQ*, 36 (1972),
3091   71-92.
              Medicinal cures compiled by the WPA Georgia Writer's Project between
              1935 and 1941.

NA   Walrond, Eric. "Charleston, Hey! Hey!," *Vanity Fair*, 26, No. 2 (1926),
3092   73, 116.
              An attempt to trace the origin of the dance.

NA   Walrond, Eric. *Tropic Death*. New York: Boni and Liveright, 1926.
3093   Short stories of West Indies in New York City and the West Indies.
              (See pp. 35-58, 237-283 for folkloric content.)

NA   Walser, Richard. "His Worship the John Kuner," *NCF*, 19 (1971), 160-172.
3094   The John Canoe ritual in the West Indies and in North Carolina; indi-
              cates that it occured in a wide area on the East Coast.

NA   Walser, Richard. "Negro Dialect in 18th Century American Drama," *AS*, 30
3095   (1955), 269-276.
              Examples from 10 plays emphasize the dramatic and comic character
              of Negro vernacular.

NA   Walsh, William S. *Curiosities of Popular Customs and of Ceremonies,*
3096   *Observances, and Miscellaneous Antiquities*. Philadelphia: J.B. Lippin-
              cott, 1898.
              Account of the "Toto Dance" of Pinkster Day celebrations in Albany,
              N.Y. in the 18th and 19th centuries.

NA   Walton, David A. "Folklore as Compensation: A Content Analysis of the
3097   Negro Animal Tale," *Ohio Folklore*, 1, No. 1 (1966), unnumbered.
              A content analysis of Uncle Remus tales.

NA   Walton, David A. "Joel Chandler Harris as Folklorist: A Reassessment,"
3098   *KFQ*, 11 (1966), 21-26.
              Argues that although Harris was not a folklore scholar, his work is a
              reliable source of information about the Negro tale during slavery.

NA
3099

Walton, Ortiz M. *Music: Black, White and Blue*. New York: William Morrow, 1972.
   Includes survey chapters on folk music, ragtime, etc.

NA
3100

"Wandering Negro Minstrels," *Leisure Hour*, 20 (1871), 600-602.
   Blackface minstrelsy in England.

NA
3101

Ward, Jerry W. "Folklore and the Study of Black Literature," *MFR*, 6 (1972), 83-90.
   An essay on the importance of studying folklore in black literature.

NA
3102

Ward, Martha Coonfield. *Them Children: A Study in Language Learning*. New York: Holt, Rinehart and Winston, 1971.
   Child training and language learning among rural Louisiana Negroes; includes child-care, domestic life, toys, verbal games.

NA
3103

Wardlow, Gayle Dean. "Rev. D.C. Rice--Gospel Singer," *Storyville*, No. 23 (1969), 164-167, 183.
   Early beginnings of the Sanctified Church and Rice's recording career in the 1920's.

NA
3104

Waring, Martha Gallaudet, ed. "Charles Seton Henry Hardee's Recollections of Old Savannah," in "Notes and Documents," *GHQ*, 12 (1928), 353-389; 13 (1929), 13-48.
   Beliefs on ensuring good crops (p. 360); recollections of an African nurse (pp. 382, 385), etc.

NA
3105

Waring, Martha Gallaudet, and Mary Alston Waring. "Impressions of the Eighties upon a Child of Georgia," in "Notes and Documents," *GHQ*, 17 (1933), 40-53.
   Discusses songs of the '80's ("Bye Bye Brer Rabbit," spirituals, etc., p. 44); description of a Negro wedding and baptism (p. 45).

NA
3106

Warner, Charles Dudley. *Studies in the South and West with Comments on Canada*. New York: Harper, 1889.
   Description of voodoo ceremonies and dancing.

NA
3107

Warren, Edward. *A Doctor's Experiences in Three Continents*. Baltimore: Cushings and Bailey, 1885.
   Includes black beliefs, customs, dances, music, etc. Description of "John Koonering" rituals with parallels from Africa.

NA
3108
Warren, Robert Penn. *Who Speaks for the Negro?* New York: Random House, 1965.
Warren's interview with Ralph Ellison (pp. 325-354) stresses the nature and importance of Afro-American folk culture for the South and the U.S.

NA
3109
Washington, Booker T. "Interesting People: Bert Williams," *American Magazine*, 70 (1910), 600-604.

NA
3110
Washington, Joseph R. *Black Religion*. Boston: Beacon, 1964.
The relationship between black religion, folk tradition, Protestant paternalism, white religion and current protest movements; music (pp. 51-52, 96-102).

NA
3111
Washington, Joseph R. *Black Sects and Cults: The Power Axis in an Ethnic Elite*. Garden City, N.Y.: Doubleday, 1972.
An account of sects and cults as responses to deprivation and injustice.

NA
3112
"Watch Meeting," *SW*, 28 (1899), 151-154.
Description of a New Year's ceremony, prayers; 3 hymns.

NA
3113
"A Watch-Night Meeting," *American Missionary*, 44 (1890), 82-84.

NA
3114
Waterman, Guy. "Joplin's Late Rags: An Analysis," *RC*, 14 (1956), 5-8.
Analysis of Scott Joplin's ragtime compositions.

NA
3115
Waterman, Guy. "A Survey of Ragtime," *RC*, 14 (1956), 7-9.
Description of composition, form and structure of ragtime.

NA
3116
Waterman, Richard A. (as told to Lynn S. Summers). "African Influence and the Blues," *Living Blues*, No. 6 (Autumn, 1971), 30-36.
Discussion of the relationship between blues and African music.

NA
3117
Waterman, Richard A. "Gospel Hymns of a Negro Church in Chicago," *JIFMC*, 8 (1951), 87-93.
Description of the music of a Pentecostal church; its similarities to jazz; the social functions of gospel music.

NA
3118
Waters, Ethel, and Charles Samuels. *His Eye Is on the Sparrow*. Garden City, N.Y.: Doubleday, 1951.
Memoirs which include descriptions of tent shows, vaudeville, and medicine shows.

NA
3119
Watkins, Floyd C. "De Dry Bones in the Valley," *SFQ*, 20 (1956), 136-149.
Text of a sermon with background notes.

NA
3120
Watkins, Floyd C., and Charles Hubert Watkins. *Yesterday in the Hills*. Chicago: Quadrangle Books, 1963.
Chapter on a Negro family, including folk life and beliefs in the Georgia Hills.

NA
3121
Watkins, Mel. "The Lyrics of James Brown: Ain't it Funky Now, or Money Won't Change Your Licking Stick," in *Amistad 2*, John A. Williams and Charles F. Harris, eds. New York: Vintage, 1971, 20-42.
Pop singer James Brown as an extension of the Afro-American folk tradition.

NA
3122
Watson, Annah Robinson. "How the Dog's Mouth Came to be Ragged," *The Folklorist* (Chicago), 1 (1893), 107-108.
1 tale in dialect.

NA
3123
Watson, John F. *Annals of Philadelphia, and Pennsylvania, in the Olden Time*. Philadelphia: Edwin S. Stuart, 1857.
Vol. 2 (for 1830, p. 261) says that "many can still remember when the slaves were allowed the last days of the fairs for their jubilees, which they employed . . . in dancing for the whole afternoon in the present Washington Square, then a general burying ground. . . . In that field could be seen at once more than a thousand of both sexes, divided into numerous squads, dancing and singing 'each in their own tongue,' after the customs of their several nations in Africa."

NA
3124
Watson, John F. *Methodist Error*. Trenton, N.J., 1819.
Contains an early description of the singing of spirituals and shouts among members of the Rev. Richard Allen's church in Philadelphia.

NA
3125
Waugh, Butler H. "Negro Tales of John Kendry from Indianapolis," *MF*, 8 (1958), 125-141.
Texts of 13 tales with comparative notes.

NA   Waugh, Elizabeth. "All God's Children: A Sunday on the Sea Island," *Travel*,
3126   77 (May, 1941), 26-29, 45-46.
              Accounts of church services noting in one the use of musical instru-
              ments and in another, a quartet.

NA   Wax, Donald D. "Negro Resistance to the Early American Slave Trade," *JNH*,
3127   51 (1956), 1-15.
              An account of Negro rebellions and mutinies during slaving voyages
              from Africa to the American market; subsequent resistance strategies
              of landed slaves; bibliography.

NA   Weatherford, W.D. *The Negro from Africa to America*. New York: George H.
3128   Doran, 1924.
              "The Negro and Self-Expression" (pp. 390-423) deals with folklore in
              Africa and America.

NA   Weatherly, Tom. "Black Oral Poetry in America: An Open Letter," *Alcheringa*
3129   (New York), No. 3 (1971), 94-95.
              Argues that the roots of black American poetry are in oral traditions
              such as the blues, sermons, etc.

NA   Weaver, Gordon. "Two Negro Folk-Poems," *MFR*, 4 (1970), 98-104.
3130   2 toasts concerning "The Signifying Monkey" described, but no texts
              given. (See D. K. Wilgus, "A Note on Two Negro Folk-Poems," *MFR*, 5
              (1971), 26-27.)

NA   Webb, H. Brook. "The Slang of Jazz," *AS*, 12 (1937), 179-184.
3131   Discussion of the term "jazz," and a listing of musician's terms with
              definitions.

NA   Webb, James Wilson. "Irwin Russell & Folk Literature," *SFQ*, 12 (1948),
3132   137-149.
              Negro character, dialect and folk material as seen in the work of
              Russell, a Southern dialect poet.

NA   Webb, Julie Yvonne. "Louisiana Voodoo and Superstitions Related to
3133   Health," *Health Services and Mental Health Administration Health
              Reports*, 86, No. 4 (1971), 291-301.
              A survey of cases of belief in various voodoo medical practices in
              two parishes in Louisiana. Illustrations of charms, amulets, etc.

NA
3134

Webb, W. Prescott. "Miscellany of Texas Folklore: Negro Songs and Stories," *PTFS*, No. 2 (1923), 45-49.
2 stories and the texts of 7 songs.

NA
3135

Webb, W. Prescott. "Notes on Folk-Lore of Texas," *JAF*, 28 (1915), 290-299.
Includes an 80 stanza blues collected from a black singer and 4 other texts.

NA
3136

Webb, William. *The History of William Webb*. Detroit, 1873.
An ex-slave's autobiography; includes an account of his becoming a conjurer.

NA
3137

Weeden, Howard. "At East," *SW*, 38 (1909), 704.
3 stanzas without music.

NA
3138

Weeden, Howard. *Bandanna Ballads*. New York: Doubleday, 1899.
23 texts without music; introduction by Joel Chandler Harris; Illustrations.

NA
3139

Weil, Dorothy. "Folklore Motifs in Arna Bontemps' *Black Thunder*," *SFQ*, 35 (1971), 1-14.
Folklore material used in a novel on slavery.

NA
3140

Weileman, W.E. "Southern Plantation Terms," *AS*, 25 (1950), 230.
Expressions used by tenants and landowners in Mississippi.

NA
3141

Weinstein, Allen, and Frank Otto Gatell. *American Negro Slavery: A Modern Reader*. New York: Oxford, 1968.
Collection of basic papers on slave life and personality; bibliography.

NA
3142

Weinstein, Robert V. "Black 'n Blues," *NHB*, 32, No. 5 (1969), 13-15.
In praise of the blues.

NA
3143

Welch, Charles E. "The 'Blackface' Controversy in the Philadelphia Mummer's Parade," *KFQ*, 9 (1964), 154-165.
Mentions use of blackface in 18th and 19th century parades.

NA
3144
Welch, Charles E. *Oh! Dem Golden Slippers*. New York and Camden, N.J.:
    Thomas Nelson, 1970.
    The story of the Philadelphia Mummers Parade. Contains evidence of
    Afro-American influence, though the author only occasionally draws
    attention to it.

NA
3145
Welding, Pete. "The Blues of Clarence Clay and William Scott: The New
    Gospel Keys," record notes to Prestige Bluesville LP record 1066.
    Notes on two gospel street-singers from Philadelphia.

NA
3146
Welding, Pete. "Hell Hound on his Trial: Robert Johnson," in *Down Beats'*
    Music '66, Don DeMichael, ed. Chicago: Maher, 1966, 73-74, 76, 103.
    The life and blues of a Mississippi bluesman; includes several texts.

NA
3147
Welding, Pete. "I Sing for the People," *Down Beat*, 34, No. 25 (1967), 20-
    23.
    Story of Howlin' Wolf, blues singer from Mississippi.

NA
3148
Welding, Pete. "Long Steel Rail: Blues by Maryland Songster Bill Jackson,"
    record notes to Testament LP record T-201.
    Notes to 13 blues and blues-ballads by an East Coast singer.

NA
3149
Welding, Pete. "Negro Religious Music: Sanctified Singers, Parts I and
    II," record notes to America's Music Series LP records BC 17-18.
    Discussion of 28 sacred songs from old, country forms to gospel and
    storefront church songs.

NA
3150
Welding, Pete. "The Rise of the Folk-Blues," *Down Beat*, 28, No. 19 (1961),
    15-17.
    Sources of the blues revival in the late 1950's and early 1960's.

NA
3151
Welding, Pete. "The Robert Johnson I Knew: An Interview with Henry Town-
    send," *Down Beat*, 35, No. 22 (1968), 18, 32.
    Additional information on an influential bluesman; discography.

NA
3152
Welding, Pete. "Sleepy John: The Story of a Bluesman," in *Down Beat's*
    Music '63, Don DeMichael, ed. Chicago: Maher, 1962, 68-70.
    The life and blues of Tennessee musician Sleepy John Estes; includes
    2 blues texts.

NA 3153   Welding, Pete. "The Spread of the Gospel," in *Down Beat's Music '62*, Don
           DeMichael, ed. Chicago: Maher, 1961, 32-35.
           Brief historical and descriptive review of gospel music; discography.

NA 3154   Welding, Pete. "Stringin' the Blues!," *Down Beat*, 32, No. 19 (1965), 22-
           24, 56.
           Classification of blues into styles: Mississippi Delta, Texas, East
           Coast and postwar. Includes discography.

NA 3155   Weldon, Fred O., Jr. "Negro Folktale Heroes," *PTFS*, No. 29 (1959), 170-
           189.
           Studies the development of Negro folklore, the "Quest Hero," the "Feat
           Hero," the "Contest Hero," and the "Clever Hero" (trickster).

NA 3156   Wells, Dicky. *The Night People: Reminiscences of a Jazzman*. Boston:
           Crescendo, 1971.
           Includes a slang glossary.

NA 3157   Wepman, Dennis, Ronald B. Newman, and Murray B. Binderman. "Toasts: The
           Black Urban Folk Poetry," *JAF*, 87 (1974), 208-224.
           36 toasts from New York State prisons; classifications and definition
           of the genre; comments on the culture of its performers.

NA 3158   Werner, A. "The Tar-Baby Story," *Folklore*, 10 (1899), 282-293.
           On the African origin of the tale.

NA 3159   Wertheim, James F. "Barrelhouse, Boogie-Woogie and the Blues," *Sound
           and Fury* (Ithaca, N.Y.), July-August, 1965, 53-55.
           The reasons for the continuity of interest in the blues.

NA 3160   Wesley, Charles H. "The Folk Song from the Historical Point of View,"
           Howard University Record, 13 (1919), 226-231.

NA 3161   West, Harry C. "Negro Folklore in Pierce's Novels," *NCF*, 19, No. 2 (March,
           1971), 66-72.
           Discussion of the use of black speech, conjuration, etc. in Ovid Wil-
           liam Pierce's novels.

NA 3162   West, Hollie I. "The Man Who Started the Gospel Business," *The Washington
           Post*, December 7, 1969, H-10.
           Interview with gospel writer Thomas A. Dorsey.

NA   West, Hollie I. "Singing About Holiness and the Salvation of Man," *The*
3163   *Washington Post*, December 7, 1969, H-1.
            Discussion of gospel music, white and black.

NA   Whaley, Marcellus S. *The Old Types Pass. Gullah Sketches of the Carolina*
3164   *Sea Islands*. Boston: Christopher, 1925.
            Includes sermons, prayers, legendary fables, "superstitions" and be-
            liefs in sketches drawn from incidents and happenings on the Sea Is-
            lands; glossary, illustrations.

NA   Whaley, W.P. "An Extreme Case of Negro Superstition," *Current Literature*,
3165   35 (1903), 227-229.
            Account of a black exodus from Pine Bluff, Arkansas, after a doomsday
            prophecy.

NA   "What Kind of Shoes You Gwine to Wear," *SW*, 38 (1909), 329.
3166   A spiritual with music.

NA   "What Yo' Gwine to Do When de Lamp Burn Down?," *SW*, 35 (1906), 528.
3167   A Georgia spiritual with music. Also in *SW*, 40 (1911), 272.)

NA   Wheeler, Mary. *Roustabout Songs: A Collection of Ohio River Valley Songs*.
3168   New York: Remick Music, 1939.
            9 songs with texts and music.

NA   Wheeler, Mary. *Steamboatin' Days: Folk Songs of the River Packet Era*.
3169   Baton Rouge: Louisiana University Press, 1944.
            Songs and lore of Negro riverboat workers, largely from Louisiana.

NA   "Where the Word 'Jazz' Started," *Music Trade Review*, 68, No. 18 (1919),
3170   50.
            Attributes the origin of the word to a black trio named the 'Jassacks'
            band, the term being a variant of 'Jackson.'

NA   Whipple, Henry Benjamin. *Bishop Whipple's Southern Diary, 1843-1844*.
3171   Lester B. Shipee, ed. Minneapolis: University of Minnesota Press,
            1937.
            Includes an account of boatmen's songs (pp. 33-34), instruments and
            Christmas festivities (pp. 48-52), and speech (p. 112).

NA 3172   White, Clarence C. *Forty Negro Spirituals*. Philadelphia: Theodore Presser, 1927.
           Arranged songs.

NA 3173   White, Clarence C. "The Labor Motif in Negro Music," *Modern Quarterly*, 4 (1927-1928), 79-81.
           The importance of work in the origin of Negro music.

NA 3174   White, Clarence C. "Negro Music a Contribution to the National Music of America," *Musical Observer*, 18, No. 11 (1919), 18-19; 19, No. 1 (1920), 16-17; No. 2, 50-51; No. 3, 13.

NA 3175   White, Clarence C. "The Story of the Negro Spiritual, 'Nobody Knows the Trouble I've Seen'," *Musical Observer*, 23, No. 6 (1924), 29.

NA 3176   White, J.E. "Topography of Savannah and its Vicinity; A Report to the Georgia Medical Society, May 3, 1806," *GHQ*, 1 (1917), 236-242.
           Includes a description of the burial of free Negroes and slaves (p. 238).

NA 3177   White, Newman Ivey. *American Negro Folk Songs*. Cambridge: Harvard University Press, 1928. (Reprinted Hatsboro, Pa.: Folklore Associates, 1965, with a new foreword by Bruce Jackson.)
           About 800 fragmentary texts, 15 tunes in a study of the history of Negro folk song. Includes material on minstrels.

NA 3178   White, Newman Ivey. "Racial Traits in Negro Song," *Sewanee Review*, 28 (1920), 396-404.
           Argues that the character of the Negro can be found in his songs; with song texts.

NA 3179   White, Newman Ivey. "The White Man in the Woodpile: Some Influences on Negro Secular Folk Songs," *AS*, 4 (1929), 207-215.
           Influence of white minstrel and dance songs on Negro secular songs in the mid-19th Century using "Taint Gwina Rain no Mo'," "De Original Ole Jim Crow," "What's de Matter, Susey," and others as examples of Negro borrowings.

NA 3180   White, Walter. *The Negro's Contribution to American Culture*. Girard, Kansas: Haldeman-Julius, 1928.
           Brief review of the literature of the Negro Renaissance in N.Y.C. in the 1920's, including books on folk literature and music.

NA   Whitefield, Irene Therese. *Louisiana Folksongs*. Baton Rouge: Louisiana
3181   State University Press, 1939.
            Includes 24 Creole songs, with discussion.

NA   Whitehead, Henry S. "Negro Dialect of the Virgin Islands," *AS*, 7 (1932),
3182   175-179.

NA   Whiting, Bartlett Jere. "William Johnson of Natchez: Free Negro," *SFQ*,
3183   16 (1952), 145-153.
            Excerpts of Johnson's diary of 1835-1851 with a number of proverbial
            sayings, names, and samples of language.

NA   Whitney, Annie Weston. "De Los' Ell an' Yard," *JAF*, 10 (1897), 293-298.
3184   English provenience of a Negro expression.

NA   Whitney, Annie Weston. "Items of Maryland Belief and Custom," *JAF*, 12
3185   (1899), 263-264.
            A charm and a text of a devil tale.

NA   Whitney, Annie Weston. "Negro American Dialects," *Independent*, 53 (1901),
3186   1979-1981, 2039-2042.
            The variety of Negro dialects and their differences.

NA   Whitney, Annie Weston, and Caroline Canfield Bullock. *Folklore from Mary-*
3187   *land*. Memoirs of the American Folklore Society, Vol. 18. New York:
            American Folklore Society, 1925.
            Includes Negro beliefs, love divinations, tales and notes on dialect.

NA   Whitten, Norman E., Jr. "Contemporary Patterns of Malign Occultism Among
3188   Negroes in North Carolina," *JAF*, 75 (1962), 311-325.
            Beliefs in occult practices among Piedmont Negroes; argues that these
            practices were originally European.

NA   Whitten, Norman E., Jr. "Notes on Negro Folk Medicine," *Folk Healthways*
3189   (Pittsburgh, Pa.), 1, No. 2 (1960), 5-8.
            A list of folk medicines used in Central North Carolina; the world view
            within which conjuration and healing are seen to contrast and co-exist.

NA
3190

"Why the Fox's Mouth is Sharp, Why the Possum Has No Hair on His Tail, and Why the Rabbit Has a Short Tail and White Spot on His Forehead," *SW*, 25 (1896), 101-102.
   3 tales.

NA
3191

"'Why the Terrapin Has Red Eyes,' 'Why the Mole Has No Eyes,' 'Where de Owl Fus' Come From,'" *SW*, 26 (1897), 58.
   3 tales.

NA
3192

"Why the Tiger is Striped," *SW*, 25 (1896), 82.
   1 Brer Rabbit tale.

NA
3193

Wickiser, Ralph, Caroline Durieux, and John McCrady. *Mardi Gras Day*. New York: Holt, 1948.

NA
3194

Wier, Albert E., ed. *Songs of the Sunny South*. New York: Appleton, 1929.
   Collection of spirituals, plantation and minstrel songs, etc.

NA
3195

Wiggins, Robert Lemuel. *The Life of Joel Chandler Harris*. Nashville: M.E. Church Publishing House, 1918.
   Includes previously unpublished Uncle Remus tales.

NA
3196

Wiggins, William H., Jr. "Black Folk Tales in the Novels of John O. Killens," *Black Scholar* (Atlanta), 3, No. 3 (1971), 50-58.
   Folkloric elements in Killens' novels.

NA
3197

Wiggins, William H., Jr. "'I Am the Greatest': The Folklore of Muhammad Ali," *Black Lines*, 2, No. 1 (1971), 56-68.

NA
3198

Wiggins, William H., Jr. "Jack Johnson as Bad Nigger: The Folklore of His Life," *Black Scholar*, 2, No. 5 (1971), 34-46.
   The "bad nigger" folk motif and boxer Jack Johnson's life.

NA
3199

Wiggins, William H., Jr. "'Lift Every Voice': A Study of Afro-American Emancipation Celebrations," in *Discovering Afro-America*, Roger D. Abrahams and John F. Szwed, eds. Leiden: E.J. Brill, 1975.
   Includes dancing to drums, sports, speech-making, etc.

NA
3200

Wiggins, William H., Jr. "The Structure and Dynamics of Folklore in the Novel Form: The Case of John L. Killens," *KFQ*, 3 (1972), 92-118.
Folkloric elements in Killens' novels.

NA
3201

Wightman, Francis P., ed. *Little Leather Breeches and Other Southern Rhymes*. New York: Taylor, 1899.
Street cries, songs, rhymes, etc.

NA
3202

Wightman, Orrin Sage, and Margaret Davis Cate. *Early Days of Coastal Georgia*. St. Simon Island, Ga.: Fort Frederika Association, 1955.
Photos and commentaries on building techniques, baskets, stone cabins, and grave decorations on the Georgia Sea Islands. 2 song texts, notes on beliefs, conjure, and cures.

NA
3203

Wilgus, D.K. "Afro-American Tradition," *JAF*, 85 (1972), 99-107.
A review-essay on a number of recordings of Afro-American music and humor.

NA
3204

Wilgus, D.K. *Anglo-American Folksong Scholarship since 1898*. New Brunswick, N.J.: Rutgers University Press, 1959.
Afro-American folksongs and their collectors discussed throughout as part of the development of folksong scholarship; an appendix (pp. 345-364) treats the controversy over the sources of the spiritual; discography and bibliography.

NA
3205

Wilgus, D.K. "Arch and Gordon," *KFR*, 6 (1969), 51-56.
Text and music of a Negro ballad with background notes.

NA
3206

Wilgus, D.K. "Folksongs of Kentucky, East and West," *KFR*, 3 (1957), 89-118.
Includes texts and music of 2 Negro ballads (pp. 104-107).

NA
3207

Wilgus, D.K. "From the Record Review Editor: Negro Music," *JAF*, 80 (1967), 104-109; 81 (1968), 89-94; 276-280; 84 (1971), 265-271.
Reviews, with analyses, of hundreds of LP recordings.

NA
3208

Wilgus, D.K. "A Note on Two Folk-Poems," *MFR*, 5 (1971), 26-27.
A note on toasts. (See Gordon Weaver, "Two Negro Folk-Poems," *MFR*, 4 (1970), 98-104.)

NA 3209   Wilgus, D.K., and Lynwood Montell. "Clure and Joe Williams: Legend and Blues Ballad," *JAF*, 81 (1968), 295-315.
Investigation of a ballad in South-Central Kentucky and North-Central Tennessee for its historical background. Variations of the text are presented along with music and detail of the history of the Williams family. Ballad seems to have a white and Negro tradition.

NA 3210   Wilkenson, Andrew. *Plantation Stories of Old Louisiana*. Boston: Page, 1914.

NA 3211   Wilkinson, Lupton A. "Gullah vs. Grammar," *North American Review*, 236 (1933), 539-542.
Gullah dialect as lacking "grammar."

NA 3212   *William Johnson's Natchez: The Ante-Bellum Diary of a Free Negro*. William R. Hogan and Edwin A. Davis, eds. Baton Rouge: Louisiana State University, 1951.

NA 3213   Williams, Alberta. "A Race History Told in Song," *World Review*, 4 (February 14, 1927), 30.
The content and appeal of secular and religious songs with 2 texts.

NA 3214   Williams, Annette Powell. "Dynamics of a Black Audience," in *Rappin' and Stylin' Out*, Thomas Kochman, ed. Urbana, Ill.: University of Illinois Press, 1972, 101-106.
Black audience reactions and expressions; illustrations.

NA 3215   Williams, Chancellor. *Have You Been to the River?* New York: Exposition Press, 1952.
"Novelistic" study of religious cults in New York City.

NA 3216   Williams, Charles A. *"Cotton Needs Pickin'," Characteristic Negro Folk Dances*. Norfolk, Va.: Guide Publishing Co., 1928.

NA 3217   Williams, George Walton. "Slave Names in Ante-Bellum South Carolina," *AS*, 33 (1958), 294-295.
600 African name survivals mentioned in South Carolina church registers.

NA 3218   Williams, Girlene Marie. "Negro Stories from the Colorado Valley," *PTFS*, No. 29 (1959), 161-169.
14 tales collected from people born and raised in the Colorado River Valley.

NA   Williams, John G. *De Ole Plantation: Elder Cotenay's Sermons*. Charleston,
3219   S.C.: Walker, Evans and Cogswell, 1895.
            Gullah dialect "sermons" by a white man.

NA   Williams, Lance A. "Cognition and the Interactive Process of the Afro-
3220   American Folk Culture," *Blackfolk* (Los Angeles), 1, No. 2 (1973-1974),
            38-45.

NA   Williams, Martin. "The Bystander," *Down Beat*, 30, No. 14 (1963), 36.
3221   The nature of "blue notes" and their adoption by piano players and
            jazz bands.

NA   Williams, Martin. "The Bystander," *Down Beat*, 30, No. 17 (1963), 38.
3222   Discussion of the sources and nature of 8, 12, 16 and 32 bar blues
            and those of other lengths.

NA   Williams, Martin. "The Bystander," *Down Beat*, 30, No. 24 (1963), 33.
3223   Challenges the view that jazz was born in New Orleans brothels.

NA   Williams, Martin. "The Bystander," *Down Beat*, 31, No. 29 (1964), 33-34.
3224   Discussion of blues poetry.

NA   Williams, Martin. "The Bystander," *Down Beat*, 32, No. 3 (1965), 39.
3225   Problems of jazz lexicography, including a derivation of "ofay."

NA   Williams, Martin. "Free Flow--Secular and Sacred Negro Music," in *Down
3226   Beat's Music '64*, Don DeMichael, ed. Chicago: Maher, 1964, 80-83.
            An historical survey of the mutual influences of blues, gospel, jazz,
            and spirituals.

NA   Williams, Martin. *Jazz Masters of New Orleans*. New York: Macmillan, 1967.
3227   Discussion of New Orleans music in the late 1800's and early 1900's.

NA   Williams, Martin. *Jelly Roll Morton*. London: Cassell, 1962.
3228   A biography of an early jazzman; discography.

NA   Williams, Martin. "Jelly Roll Morton and the Library of Congress Records,"
3229   *JM*, 6 (May, 1960), 8, 9, 31.
            Notes on ragtime and the use of Latin American rhythms in jazz.

NA
3230

Williams, Martin. "Recording Limits and Blues Form," in *The Art of Jazz*, Martin Williams, ed. New York: Oxford University Press, 1959, 91-93.
An analysis of a blues song in terms of poetry and "superstition."

NA
3231

Williams, Martin. "A Rock Cast in the Sea: Some Notes on Blues Lyrics," *Metronome*, 78, No. 9 (1961), 18-19.
Brief comments on the poetics and themes of blues; with examples, discography.

NA
3232

Williams, Melvin D. *Community in a Black Pentecostal Church: An Antropological Study*. Pittsburgh: University of Pittsburgh Press, 1974.
An ethnography of a Pittsburgh church which includes material on beliefs, symbolism, ritual, sermons, the social structure of the church, and North-South continuities.

NA
3233

Williams, Melvin D. "Food and Animals: Behavioral Metaphors in a Black Pentacostal Church in Pittsburgh," *Urban Anthropology*, 2 (1973), 74-79.
Symbols used for establishing identity among church members.

Williams, N.W. "The Treatment of Negro Slaves in the Brazilian Empire: A Comparison with the United States of America." See No. BR 524.

NA
3234

Williams, Nancy Middleton. *Melody in Ebony: Little Stories in Verse and Folk Ballads from Tales of the Old Southern Plantation Negro*. Hot Springs National Park, Arkansas, 1944.

NA
3235

Williams, Roy. "De Gullah Man," *The News and Courier* (Charleston, South Carolina), November 25, 1962, 1-C.
Notes on Gullah speech and on Dick Reeves, a white performer of Gullah.

NA
3236

Williams, Timothy Shaler. "The Sports of Negro Children," *Saint Nicholas*, 30 (1903), 1004-1007.
Includes descriptions and texts of ring games and Christmas activities.

NA
3237

Williams-Jones, Pearl. "Afro-American Gospel Music: A Brief Historical and Analytical Survey (1930-1970)," in *Development of Material for a One Year Course in African Music for the General Undergraduate Student*, Vada E. Butcher, *et al.*, eds. Washington, D.C.: U.S. Department of Health, Education and Welfare, 1970, pp. 199-219.
Compares spirituals and gospel songs; includes transcribed examples; stylistic and historical materials; protest themes in gospel songs.

NA   Williams-Jones, Pearl. "Afro-American Gospel Music: A Crystallization of
3238   the Black Aesthetic," *EM*, 19 (1975), 373-385.

NA   Williamson, George. "Superstitions From Louisiana," *JAF*, 18 (1905), 229-
3239   230.
            35 "superstitions."

        Willis, N. Parker. See No. FWI 132.

NA   Willoughby, William. "Storefront Churches: Social Stabilizers," *Christian-
3240   ity Today*, 13 (May 9, 1969), 44-45.

NA   Wills, Garry. "Martin Luther King is *Still on the Case*," in *The New
3241   Journalism*, Tom Wolfe and E.W. Johnson, eds. New York: Harper & Row,
            1973, 356-376. (Originally published in *Esquire*, August, 1968.)
            Includes an account of oratory at King's funeral.

NA   Wilmer, Valerie. "Jessie Fuller," *JJ*, 12, No. 5 (1959), 4-6.
3242   Life and music of a one-man band.

NA   Wilson, Al. *Son House*. Blues Unlimited, Collectors Classics, 14, 1966.
3243   Biography and discography of a Mississippi blues singer and guitarist.

NA   Wilson, Calvin D. "Negroes Who Owned Slaves," *Popular Science Monthly*,
3244   81 (1912), 483-494.
            Practice traced to African slave-holding and tribal differences;
            accounts of blacks who owned, sold and bought slaves in the U.S.

NA   Wilson, Edmund. "Shanty-Boy Ballads and Blues," *New Republic*, 47 (1926),
3245   227-229.
            A description and review of *Blues, An Anthology* by W.C. Handy.

NA   Wilson, Ellen Dickson. "The Aunt Hannah Stories," *SW*, 41 (1912), 40-43;
3246   101-104; 162-165; 237-238; 436-440.
            A Maryland ex-slave's monologues; beliefs, life-history, religion, etc.

NA   Wilson, Gold Refined. "The Religion of the American Slave: His Attitude
3247   Toward Life and Death," *JNH*, 8 (1923); 41-71.
            Argues that African religious ideas disappeared during slavery and
            were replaced by Christianity with a focus on afterlife; uses spirituals
            as examples.

NA
3248
Wilson, H.J. "The Negro and Music," *Outlook*, 84 (1906), 823-826.
    Negro harmony explored as a "racial characteristic"; music and text
    of "Let My People Go."

NA
3249
Wiltse, Henry M. "A Hoodoo Charm," *JAF*, 13 (1900), 212.
    A recipe for making a charm.

NA
3250
Wingfield, Roland. "New Orleans Marching Bands: Choreographer's Delight,"
    Dance Magazine, 33, No. 1 (1959), 34-35.
    Description of street dancers following a New Orleans marching band.

NA
3251
Winkleman, Donald M. "Three American Authors as Semi-Folk Artists," *JAF*,
    68 (1968), 130-135.
    Discusses the folklore in Charles W. Chesnutt's writings; includes a
    short interview with a blues singer on methods of composition.

NA
3252
Winslow, David J. "Bishop E.F. Everett and Some Aspects of Occultism in
    Negro Philadelphia," *KFQ*, 14 (1969), 59-80.
    Discussion of a store selling charms, amulets, etc.; illustrations.

NA
3253
Winslow, David J. "A Negro Corn-Shucking," *JAF*, 86 (1973), 61-62.
    Reprints an 1852 description of a South Carolina ritualized work
    event.

NA
3254
Winslow, David J. "Occupational Superstitions of Negro Prostitutes in an
    Upstate New York City," *NYFQ*, 24 (1968), 294-301.
    15 "superstitions" with discussion.

NA
3255
Winslow, Thyra Samter. "The Charleston--30 Years After," *Dance Magazine*,
    29, No. 1 (1955), 26-33.

NA
3256
Winston, Celia M. "Genuine Negro Melodies," *New York Times*, August 8,
    1887, 6.
    Several spirituals collected in eastern Virginia; description of a
    church's services.

NA
3257
Wintemberg, W.J. "Some Items of Negro Canadian Folklore," *JAF*, 38 (1925),
    621.
    13 beliefs and cures from Ontario.

NA 3258   Winter, Marian Hannah. "Juba and American Minstrelsy," in *Chronicles of the American Dance*, Paul D. Magriel, ed. New York: Henry Holt, 1948, 38-63. (Also published in *Dance Index*, 6, No. 2 (1947), 28-49.)
Life of William Henry Lane ("Juba") as a focal point in discussing minstrel dances, their sources, and the Negro position in minstrelsy; the importance of the black minstrel men to jazz, tap dance, and European painters and clowns; Africa and the sources of minstrel stereotyping; Jim Crow in the theatre.

NA 3259   Wise, C.M. "Negro Dialect," *Quarterly Journal of Speech*, 19 (1933), 522-528.
Argues (against G. Krapp) that Negro dialect is distinct from that of the British and white Americans.

NA 3260   "A Wise Woman of Color," *New York Times*, August 23, 1896, 16.
Includes a few Negro proverbs.

NA 3261   Wittke, Carle. *Tambo and Bones: A History of the American Minstrel Stage*. Durham, N.C.: Duke University Press, 1930.
A history of Negro (mostly white imitative) minstrelsy: its origin, rise and fall and stage techniques.

NA 3262   Wolf, John Quincy. "Aunt Caroline Dye: The Gypsy in the 'St. Louis Blues'," *SFQ*, 33 (1969), 339-346.
Background of a conjurer.

NA 3263   Wolf, John Quincy. "Tales and Superstitions," *TFSB*, 32 (1966), 56-57.
2 beliefs pertaining to death.

NA 3264   Wolfe, Bernard. "Ecstatic in Blackface: The Negro as Song-and-Dance Man," in *The Scene before You: A New Approach to American Culture*, Chandler Brossard, ed. New York: Rinehart, 1955, 51-70.
Argues that black culture developed as a reaction to white prejudice; discusses the ties between "Bohemia" and the "Ghetto."

NA 3265   Wolfe, Bernard. *The Magic of Their Singing*. New York: Scribner's, 1961.
Novel with a description of urban black-white "hip" interaction, speech, music, style, etc.; includes a note on black hipsters' speech.

NA 3266   Wolfe, Bernard. "Uncle Remus and the Malevolent Rabbit," *Commentary*, 8 (1949), 31-41. (Reprinted in Dundes, No. NA 854.)
Uncle Remus' folktales as protest literature; Joel Chandler Harris'

attitude towards blacks as archetypal of white American race feelings.

NA
3267
Wolfe, Charles K. "Where the Blues Is At: A Survey of Recent Research," *Popular Music and Society*, 1 (1972), 152-166.

NA
3268
Wolfe, Tom. *Radical Chic and Mau-Mauing the Flak Catchers*. New York: Farrar, Straus and Giroux, 1970.
Notes differences between white and black interactional and dress styles.

NA
3269
Wolfram, Walter A. "Black-White Speech Differences Revisited," *Viewpoints: Bulletin of the School of Education, Indiana University*, 47, No. 2 (1971), 27-50.

NA
3270
Wolfram, Walter A. *A Sociolinguistic Description of Detroit Negro Speech*. Washington, D.C.: Center for Applied Linguistics, 1969.
Structural characteristics of the speech of Detroit Negroes; correlations with age, sex, and economic status; comparisons with white usage in Detroit and Negro usage in other cities.

NA
3271
Wolfram, Walter A., and Nora H. Clarke, eds. *Black-White Speech Relationships*. Washington, D.C.: Center for Applied Linguistics, 1971.
Collection of papers on Black English.

NA
3272
Wood, Clement. *The Earth Turns South*. New York: Dutton, 1919.
Dialect poetry on Southern life with folkloric content.

NA
3273
Wood, Clement. *Nigger*. New York: Dutton, 1922.
Novel of life in Birmingham, Alabama, with folkloric content.

NA
3274
Wood, Gordon R. "Heard In the South," *TFSB*, 21 (1955), 111-116.
Discussion of Southern Negro speech with numerous references to the will-o'-the wisp story.

NA
3275
Wood, Henry Cleveland. "Negro Camp-Meeting Melodies," *New England Magazine*, n.s., 6 (March, 1892), 61-64. (Reprinted in No. NA 1698.)
7 texts with music and a discussion of the background of the camp-meeting and a description of such meetings.

NA
3276
Wood, M.T. "Community Preservation of Negro Music," *SW*, 53 (1924), 60-62.
Description of Negro music festivals in Indiana, Kansas, and Georgia; influence of black music on American folk music.

NA
3277
Wood, Peter H. *Black Majority: Negroes in Colonial South Carolina, 1670 to the Stono Rebellion*. New York: Knopf, 1974.
African material and ideological culture and its influence on the whites of South Carolina.

NA
3278
Wood, Samuel. *The Cries of New York*. New York, 1822.

NA
3279
Woodall, N.F. "Old Signs in Alabama," *JAF*, 43 (1930), 325-326.
A list of signs and "superstitions."

NA
3280
Woods, Frances Jerome. *Marginality and Identity: A Colored Creole Family through Ten Generations*. Baton Rouge, La.: Louisiana State University Press, 1972.
Includes notes on naming practices, hoodoo, cuisine, speech, etc., in rural Louisiana.

NA
3281
Woodson, Carter G. *The African Background Outlined: or, Handbook for the Study of the Negro*. Washington, D.C.: Association for the Study of Negro Life and History, 1936.
An early treatment of African cultural survivals in the United States.

NA
3282
Woodson, Carter G. *The History of the Negro Church*. Washington: Associated Publishers, 1921.

NA
3283
Woofter, T.J., Jr. *Black Yeomanry: Life on St. Helena Island*. New York: Henry Holt, 1930.
Chapter on folklore by Guy Johnson. Includes short descriptions of folk stories of St. Helena with no texts; 21 spirituals with musical illustrations. Other chapters discuss religious services, children's games, etc.

NA
3284
Woolridge, Nancy Bullock. "The Slave Preacher--Portrait of a Leader," *JNH*, 14 (1945), 28-37.
The Negro preacher, his functions as a leader and as a slave.

NA 3285   "Word Shadows," *Atlantic Monthly*, 67 (1891), 143-144. (Reprinted in No. NA 1568.)
Examples of black speech at the turn of the 20th Century; interpreted as faulty white speech.

NA 3286   "The Words," *American Folklore Occasional No. 2*. New York: Oak, 1970, 53-57.
Discussion of the texts of blues recordings on the Mississippi River Floods of 1927.

NA 3287   Work, Frederick J. *New Jubilee Songs, as Sung by the Fisk Jubilee Singers of Fisk University*. Nashville, Tenn.: Fisk University, 1902.
47 arrangements for chorus.

NA 3288   Work, Frederick J. *Some American Negro Folk Songs*. Boston: Schmidt, 1909.

NA 3289   Work, John Wesley. *American Negro Songs*. New York: Howell, Soskin, 1940.
A collection of 230 religious and secular songs: evolution and history with classification.

NA 3290   Work, John Wesley. "Changing Patterns in Negro Folk Songs," *JAF*, 62 (1949), 136-144.
Changes in Southern fundamentalist church music; includes 3 texts with music.

NA 3291   Work, John Wesley. "The Development of the Music of the Negro from the Folk Song to the Art Song and the Art Chorus," *Music Supervisors' National Conference*, 12th Meeting, 1919, 42-46.
Discusses the structure and nature of Negro music with references to African music.

NA 3292   Work, John Wesley. *Folk Song of the American Negro*. Nashville: Fisk University Press, 1915. (Originally published, Nashville, Tenn.: Work Brothers, 1907.)
Makes comparisons between African and Afro-American song texts and discusses the evolution and the nature of the spirituals. Includes over 100 texts of spirituals, a few with music.

NA 3293   Work, John Wesley. *I, John, Saw the Holy Number*. Galaxy Music Corp., 1962.

NA   Work, John Wesley. "Negro Folk Song," *Opportunity*, 1 (1923), 292-294.
3294   Argues for the originality of Negro folk songs, their African sources,
           etc.

NA   Work, John Wesley. "Plantation Meistersinger; Alabama State Sacred Harp
3295   Shape-Note Singing Convention," *MQ*, 27 (1941), 97-106.
           Discusses the work of the compiler of the *Colored Sacred Harp*, Judge
           Jackson.

NA   Work, Monroe N. "Folk-Tales From Students in the Georgia State College,"
3296   *JAF*, 32 (1919), 402-405.
           6 tales and 1 variant.

NA   Work, Monroe N. "Geechee and Other Proverbs," *JAF*, 32 (1919), 441-442.
3297   25 proverbs.

NA   Work, Monroe N., ed. *The Negro Year Book, 1937-38*. Tuskegee Institute,
3298   Alabama: Negro Year Book Publishing Co., 1938.
           Contains information on religious sects (Chapter 11) and music (Chapter
           33): includes discussion of ragtime, jazz, the tango, the rumba, folk
           songs and their origins.

NA   Work, Monroe N. "Some Geechee Folk-Lore," *SW*, 34 (1905), 633-635; 696-
3299   697.
           Proverbs and folk beliefs from the Georgia tidewater section.

NA   Work, Monroe N. "The Spirit of Negro Poetry," *SW*, 37 (1908), 73-77.
3300   A comparison of spirituals and slave poetry with later dialect
           poetry.

NA   Wright, Albert Hazen. *Our Georgia-Florida Frontier: The Okefinokee Swamp,
3301   Its History and Cartography*. Ithaca, N.Y.: A.H. Wright, 1945.
           Part VI, "The Seminoles," describes slave-Indian and maroon-Indian
           contacts, mentions black towns and kings, etc.

NA   Wright, Richard. *Black Boy*. New York: Harper, 1945.
3302   Autobiography with folkloric content.

NA   Wright, Richard. *Twelve Million Black Voices: A Folk History of the Negro
3303   in the United States*. New York: Viking, 1941.
           Argues that African culture was destroyed by slavery; Negro religion as
           a phenomenon of oppression, etc.

NA
3304
Wright, Richard. *White Man, Listen!* Garden City, N.Y.: Doubleday, 1957.
Chapter 3 ("The Literature of the Negro in the United States") includes
a discussion of blues, spirituals, dozens, and contains a fragment of
a toast.

NA
3305
Wright, Richardson. *Hawkers and Walkers in Early America*. Philadelphia:
Lippincott, 1927.
Chapter 15, "Local Vendors and Street Cries," includes Afro-American
cries from Philadelphia, Charleston, New Orleans, *et al.*

NA
3306
Wyeth, John Allan. *With Sabre and Scalpel*. New York: Harper, 1914.
Descriptions of juba, banjo playing, etc., on an Alabama plantation.

NA
3307
Yancy, Henrietta Miller. "The Contribution of the American Negro to the
Music Culture of the Country," *School Musician* (Joliet, Ill.), 41, No.
5 (1970), 55-57; No. 6, 60-62; No. 7. 60-61, 73; No. 8, 62-63.

NA
3308
Yancey, William, and Boone Hammond. *Glossary of Negro Jive*. Social
Science Institute, Washington University, St. Louis, Missouri, 1965.

NA
3309
Yarmolinsky, Avraham. *Picturesque United States of America 1811, 1812,
1813*. New York: Edwin Rudge, 1930.
Includes a description of a church service in Philadelphia (pp. 20-
21).

NA
3310
Yates, Irene. "A Collection of Proverbs and Proverbial Sayings from
South Carolina Literature," *SFQ*, 11 (1947), 187-199.
A collection of proverbs and proverbial sayings about black folklife
which appear in South Carolina fiction (1922-1932).

NA
3311
Yates, Irene. "Conjures And Cures In The Novels of Julia Peterkin," *SFQ*,
10 (1946), 137-149.
The use of the conjure figure in four of Julia Peterkin's novels.

NA
3312
Yates, Norris W. "Folksongs in the Spirit of The Times," *SFQ*, 26 (1962),
326-334.
Contains one fragment of a folksong sung by Negro firemen on a river-
boat and an article describing the funeral of a Negro huntsman.

NA
3313
Yates, Norris W. "Four Plantation Songs Noted by William Cullen Bryant,"
SFQ, 15 (1951), 251-253.
Songs from the Barnwell District, South Carolina, including "Johnny
Come Down de Hollow," "Jimmy Crack Corn," and "John, John Crow."

NA
3314
Yates, Thelma. "Unwritten Negro Folksongs," *Michigan History* (Lansing),
37 (1953), 183-196.
Words and music of 24 religious and other folksongs.

NA
3315
Yetman, Norman R. "The Background of the Slave Narratives Collection,"
American Quarterly, 19 (1967), 534-553.
The collectors and means used to collect the narratives of ex-slaves.

NA
3316
Yetman, Norman R. *Life Under the "Peculiar Institution": Selections from
the Slave Narrative Collection*. New York: Holt, Rinehart and Winston,
1970.
Over 100 complete narratives from the WPA ex-slave narrative collection; includes some essays on the background of the collection and a
photo essay.

NA
3317
Yoder, Don. *Pennsylvania Spirituals*. Lancaster, Pa.: Pennsylvania Folklife Society, 1961.
A book which largely covers white traditions but refers to Negro
camp-meetings and discusses the origin of Negro spirituals.

Yoder, Don. See Johnson, Guy B., No. NA 1627.

NA
3318
Yoffie. Leah Rachel Clara. "Three Generations of Children's Singing Games
in St. Louis," *JAF*, 60 (1947), 1-51.
Includes Negro material.

NA
3319
York, Dorothea. *Mud and Stars: An Anthology of World War Songs and
Poetry*. New York: Henry Holt, 1931.
Includes some black material.

NA
3320
Young, Aurelia. "Black Folk Music," *MFR*, 6 (1972), 1-4.
Stresses the continuity between sacred and secular black folk music,
and between African and Afro-American.

NA
3321
Young, Martha. "Aunt Cinthy's Valuntine," *Century Magazine*, 35 (1898),
477.
Story with song.

NA
3322
Young, Martha. *Behind the Dark Pines*. New York and London: D. Appleton,
1912.

NA 3323   Young, Martha. *Plantation Bird Legends*. New York: R.H. Russell, 1902.
             Dialect verse.

NA 3324   Young, Nathan Ben. "Eighteenth Street: An Anthology in Color," in *Ebony and Topaz*, Charles S. Johnson, ed. New York: National Urban League, 1927, 37-46.
             Description of Birmingham street people: musicians, priests, tramps, etc.

NA 3325   Young, Stark. "Slightly Ghosts," *New Republic*, 93 (1937), 131.

NA 3326   Young, Virginia Heyer. "Family and Childhood in a Southern Negro Community," *AA*, 72 (1970), 269-288.
             Family interaction and domestic life in a rural Georgia town; details on interpersonal style in children's play.

NA 3327   Yourcenar, Marguerite. "Chants Noirs," *Mercure de France*, 315 (1952), 251-261.
             French translations of several spirituals and shouts.

NA 3328   Yourcenar, Marguerite. *Fleuve Profond, Sombre Rivière: Les "Negro Spirituals," Commentaires et Traductions*. Paris: Gallimard, 1964.
             Anthology of spirituals with an introductory essay.

NA 3329   Zenetti, Lothar. *Peitsche und Psalm*. Munich: J. Pfeiffer, 1967.
             Black religious music discussed in the context of religious and racial history in the U.S. and Africa; characteristics of Negro folksong, the history of spirituals and gospel songs, black religious ritual, religious songs, and the Civil Rights movement; includes a section of brief abstracts from the accounts of modern European travellers' visits to black religious services; discography, bibliography.

NA 3330   Zimmerman, Dick. "An Evening with Shelton Brooks," *The Rag Times*, 3, No. 3 (1969), 2-3, 7.
             Discusses Brooks' life, some of his songs, and other ragtime pianists.

NA 3331   "Zoot Lore," *New Yorker*, 19 (June 19, 1943), 14-15.
             The naming of "zoot suits," "reet pleats," etc., as an outgrowth of Harlem slang rhymes.

INDEXES

[Part II, pages 407 to 750, is bound in a separate
volume. The following indexes apply to both Part I
and Part II.
    Entries are listed by their item designations--
the letters and numbers that appear in the left-
hand margin throughout the bibliography. The
Locale Index does not include those areas that
are itemized in the table of contents for Part I
or Part II.]

Africa: questions of antecedents and influences
GEN 2, 3, 4, 8, 14, 15, 16, 21, 22, 28, 34, 36, 47, 48, 50, 51, 53, 59, 68,
    70, 71, 77, 78, 80, 81, 82, 83, 88, 95, 96, 97, 99, 103, 104, 105, 106,
    107, 108, 109, 110, 111, 112, 114, 115, 116, 117, 118, 119, 120, 121, 122,
    123, 124, 125, 126, 127, 128, 129, 132, 134, 137, 138, 139, 141, 142, 148,
    149, 150, 155, 156, 157, 158, 161, 163, 164, 165, 166, 168, 170, 173, 175,
    182, 183, 184, 185, 186, 187, 188, 189, 190, 191, 192, 197, 198, 199, 205,
    206, 208, 209, 210, 211, 214, 215, 216, 218, 219, 220, 221, 222, 223, 230,
    231, 234, 236, 237, 240, 241, 242, 243, 244, 245, 248, 262, 263, 264, 265,
    266, 267, 268, 269, 270, 274, 275, 276, 277, 278, 282, 285, 287, 288, 289,
    290, 294, 295, 296, 299
NA 37, 54, 55, 73, 79, 87, 113, 124, 166, 174, 199, 223, 248, 269, 271, 272,
    273, 274, 275, 330, 335, 388, 389, 411, 426, 442, 489, 514, 515, 585, 603,
    605, 614, 637, 659, 660, 662, 686, 707, 708, 709, 721, 725, 741, 759, 775,
    776, 777, 778, 779, 781, 783, 784, 796, 841, 844, 853, 882, 891, 902, 909,
    913, 914, 915, 926, 927, 939, 952, 956, 961, 996, 997, 1000, 1001, 1027,
    1041, 1043, 1096, 1112, 1122, 1137, 1138, 1141, 1157, 1182, 1192, 1227,
    1245, 1246, 1249, 1250, 1255, 1270, 1293, 1338, 1340, 1342, 1358, 1371,
    1374, 1376, 1383, 1385, 1387, 1420, 1421, 1422, 1423, 1424, 1425, 1426,
    1427, 1428, 1429, 1431, 1432, 1457, 1464, 1471, 1472, 1509, 1521, 1546,
    1551, 1557, 1580, 1581, 1582, 1602, 1603, 1604, 1627, 1662, 1663, 1671,
    1678, 1689, 1722, 1730, 1736, 1737, 1745, 1747, 1753, 1761, 1763, 1765,
    1786, 1789, 1793, 1798, 1806, 1814, 1917, 1946, 1968, 1976, 1995, 2000,
    2020, 2021, 2032, 2033, 2041, 2044, 2047, 2056, 2059, 2073, 2096, 2101,
    2122, 2135, 2138, 2141, 2142, 2145, 2148, 2162, 2175, 2235, 2260, 2268,
    2272, 2281, 2307, 2308, 2312, 2317, 2355, 2356, 2358, 2362, 2364, 2367,
    2370, 2376, 2399, 2405, 2435, 2465, 2466, 2467, 2470, 2471, 2473, 2474,
    2482, 2493, 2551, 2553, 2562, 2578, 2593, 2603, 2640, 2643, 2654, 2660,
    2670, 2687, 2695, 2704, 2727, 2737, 2741, 2743, 2748, 2771, 2804, 2808,
    2852, 2854, 2871, 2873, 2874, 2875, 2876, 2889, 2912, 2923, 2945, 2958,
    2961, 2967, 2970, 2971, 2980, 2982, 2983, 2985, 2987, 2996, 3000, 3001,
    3020, 3040, 3041, 3043, 3052, 3063, 3080, 3090, 3104, 3107, 3116, 3123,
    3158, 3188, 3217, 3244, 3247, 3258, 3277, 3280, 3281, 3291, 3292, 3294,
    3303, 3320, 3329

Africa: questions of antecedents and influences *(continued)*

African "nations." *See also* Churches, sects and cults; Clubs, associations
   and societies
   GEN 50, 57, 58, 72, 80, 97, 168, 192, 240, 267, 270
    NA 143, 389, 1457, 1793, 2096, 2135, 2958, 3003, 3123, 3244
   EWI 24, 141, 241, 388, 539, 654
    HA 2, 3, 11, 74, 305
    CU 9, 24, 25, 28, 35, 37, 47, 48, 49, 57, 65, 66, 67, 73, 84, 85, 92, 93,
       103, 108, 110, 130, 139, 161, 162, 163, 164, 166, 167, 173, 174, 181,
       191, 192, 194, 196, 216, 220, 221, 246, 256, 259, 260, 261, 263, 264,
       265, 274, 276, 281, 282, 295, 301, 302, 323, 329, 334, 335, 346, 347,
       351
    PR 1
    CR 5
    MX 7, 8
   PAN 21, 29, 32, 36
    BR 47, 119, 141, 170, 193, 218, 243, 247, 255, 265, 269, 281, 295, 297,
       309, 332, 350, 406, 443, 454, 455, 457, 472, 488, 490, 491, 492, 493,
       500, 501, 502, 508
    CO 34
    UR 5
    VE 6

Afro-American contacts with American Indians. *See also* Black Caribs
   GEN 5, 8, 11, 99, 168, 206, 226, 229, 296, 297, 298, 299
    NA 42, 223, 254, 518, 520, 853, 955, 1060, 1258, 1269, 1381, 1429, 1605,
       1642, 2100, 2101 2332, 2363, 2473, 2553, 2825, 2826, 2988, 3301
   EWI 108, 176, 352, 381, 389, 467, 556, 620, 621, 704, 744
   FWI 3, 14
    HA 5, 9, 104, 189
    CU 337
    PR 41
   FGS 41, 69, 83, 96, 97, 102, 141
    MX 16
   NIC 1
   PAN 16, 20, 34
    BR 102, 164, 200, 215, 245, 327, 359, 384, 402
    CO 7
   PER 1, 4, 9
    VE 7, 11, 42, 43, 65, 67, 68, 70, 87, 91

Afro-American contacts with Asians
   GEN 99, 116, 297
    CU 74
    BR 215

Afro-American influences on Africa
   GEN 140, 170, 222, 243, 269
    NA 22, 407, 786, 1917
    BR 104, 207, 352, 485, 488, 500, 502, 503, 504, 505

Alphabet. *See* "Jamaican alphabet"

Anancy (*Anansi, Nanzi,* Aunt Nancy). *See* Tales and tale telling: animal tales

Architecture and housing
    GEN 174, 185, 250
     NA 56, 97, 222, 324, 480, 620, 645, 704, 737, 751, 831, 846, 980, 1046, 1129,
         1246, 1437, 1444, 1518, 1558, 1613, 1713, 1730, 1738, 1746, 2036, 2096,
         2118, 2290, 2356, 2480, 2591, 2630, 2668, 2678, 2691, 2838, 2849, 3039,
         3202
    EWI 24, 82, 103, 126, 238, 239, 240, 423
    FWI 14, 25, 88
     HA 229, 230
     CU 107, 138
    FGS 61, 82, 160
     MX 4, 6
    PAN 28
     BR 139, 207, 245, 360, 502, 503, 504
     VE 12, 13

Argot. *See* Slang, argot and jargon; Slang, jazz

Art. *See* Visual arts

Autobiography and biography
     NA 443, 492, 510, 619, 806, 994, 1180, 1229, 1269, 1399, 1523, 1527, 1619,
         1677, 1708, 1751, 1886, 1887, 1963, 2078, 2082, 2160, 2506, 2561, 2591,
         2806, 2880, 2974, 2985, 3307
     HA 117
     BR 280

         blues singers and musicians [*see also* Blues and blues performers]:
     NA 314, 360, 363, 512, 537, 538, 539, 544, 897, 928, 932, 936, 946, 1093,
         1094, 1095, 1097, 1134, 1136, 1144, 1145, 1221, 1273, 1396, 1479, 1570,
         1701, 1732, 1769, 1770, 1796, 1856, 1937, 1941, 1948, 1996, 2078, 2103,
         2262, 2263, 2269, 2270, 2284, 2286, 2287, 2296, 2521, 2522, 2607, 2635,
         2759, 2879, 3146, 3147, 3151, 3152, 3243

         jazz musicians:
     NA 54, 77, 94, 95, 541, 720, 728, 729, 796, 947, 1151, 1852, 1856, 1866,
         1880, 1934, 2042, 2046, 2048, 2126, 2594, 2783, 3036, 3156, 3228, 3330

         minstrel and vaudeville performers:
     NA 533, 542, 712, 713, 727, 729, 752, 1012, 1134, 1796, 2002, 2569, 3118,
         3242, 3258

         religious leaders and singers:
     NA 443, 1333, 1397, 1414, 1477, 1529, 1702, 1724, 1742, 1748, 1796, 1887,
         1920, 1921, 2078, 2150, 2347, 3059, 3103, 3118, 3162
    EWI 654
     BR 54, 232

         slaves, ex-slaves and free Negroes:
    GEN 57

Autobiography and biography *(continued)*

      slaves, ex-slaves and free Negroes *(continued)*
  NA 94, 95, 283, 289, 342, 443, 459, 740, 828, 884, 901, 961, 1337, 1508,
     1521, 1614, 1619, 1734, 1821, 2150, 2208, 2209, 2210, 2233, 2310, 2324,
     2325, 2548, 2549, 2741, 2890, 2905, 3136, 3246, 3315, 3316
  CU 21, 22, 294

Ballads. *See also* Railroad songs; Songs, secular
  NA 290, 302, 342, 368, 371, 382, 385, 410, 417, 438, 615, 618, 640, 661,
     671, 672, 674, 717, 1098, 1325, 1573, 1629, 1630, 1631, 1632, 1684, 1719,
     1797, 1812, 1873, 1881, 1894, 1896, 1898, 1900, 1901, 1902, 1903, 1904,
     1912, 1939, 2028, 2065, 2094, 2230, 2340, 2382, 2404, 2640, 2655, 2712,
     2749, 2750, 2772, 2778, 2779, 3030, 3138, 3148, 3205, 3206, 3209, 3234
  EWI 65, 100, 408, 409, 440, 523
  BR 374

Bands and orchestras
  NA 675, 1375, 1746, 1810, 2678, 2680

      brass and marching:
  NA 552, 2064, 2523, 2554, 2562, 2608, 2696, 2758, 3250
  EWI 667

      fife and drum:
  NA 312, 1063, 1891, 2078, 2543

      jazz:
  NA 77, 185, 248, 267, 271, 272, 273, 274, 412, 473, 493, 494, 541, 547, 721,
     840, 996, 997, 1138, 1139, 1431, 1671, 1736, 1934, 2010, 2046, 2048, 2053,
     2064, 2159, 2205, 2303, 2530, 2554, 2594, 2601, 2608, 2626, 2627, 2670,
     2696, 2763, 2842, 2852, 3223

      jug and skiffle:
  NA 231, 536, 546, 1222, 2186, 2189, 2284, 2295, 2669, 2757, 2841

      Latin:
  CU 12, 42, 45, 111
  BR 225, 267

      minstrel:
  NA 2154, 2816

      steel:
  EWI 93, 108, 127, 134, 275, 277, 307, 324, 468, 488, 607, 608, 631, 678, 697,
     711, 715
  DWI 14

      string:
  NA 1747, 2316
  VE 54

Banjo. *See also* Musical instruments
    NA 33, 252, 296, 913, 914, 915, 1250, 1315, 1393, 1874, 1881, 1978, 1999,
        2153, 2737, 2782, 3306
    EWI 690

Batuque (Brazil). *See* Dance, dance music and songs

Beliefs. *See* Religion; Supernatural beliefs and practices; *also see* Birth,
    beliefs and practices concerning; Death, beliefs and practices concerning;
    Domestic life; Food and cooking

Biography. *See* Autobiography and biography

Birth, beliefs and practices concerning. *See also* Children; Medicine
    NA 478, 956, 2092, 2204, 2575, 2823, 2952, 3060
    EWI 238, 537, 598
    HA 42, 65

Black Caribs. *See also* Afro-American contacts with American Indians
    GEN 5, 296
    EWI 61, 176, 238, 239, 268, 704, 744
    FWI 2, 5, 14, 18, 59, 89, 109, 110, 111, 112, 113, 114, 115, 116, 117, 118,
        122, 131
      B 1, 2, 3, 7, 9, 11, 12, 14, 15
     AR 4

Black English. *See* Dialect: Afro-English

Black Jews. *See also* Churches, sects and cults
    GEN 28
    NA 361, 953, 954, 1068, 2324

Black Muslims. *See* Islam, influence of; Politics and nationalism

Black nationalism. *See* Politics and nationalism

Black-white social interaction. *See also* Africa; Etiquette; Stereotypes
    GEN 15, 19, 47, 77, 95, 116, 162, 166, 180, 191, 204, 207, 211, 212, 225, 226,
        229, 235, 297
    NA 98, 139, 148, 158, 183, 208, 223, 241, 309, 375, 382, 388, 398, 401, 430,
        443, 480, 491, 504, 507, 547, 612, 621, 632, 640, 680, 684, 690, 770, 800,
        814, 835, 836, 842, 847, 852, 976, 983, 1000, 1036, 1059, 1102, 1114, 1123,
        1126, 1193, 1213, 1218, 1258, 1299, 1301, 1366, 1375, 1415, 1428, 1433,
        1460, 1522, 1558, 1560, 1578, 1580, 1581, 1582, 1609, 1611, 1612, 1627,
        1634, 1635, 1638, 1671, 1678, 1682, 1686, 1689, 1695, 1743, 1781, 1806,
        1810, 1822, 1834, 1867, 1881, 1909, 1927, 1946, 1947, 1975, 1976, 1977,
        1983, 1985, 1993, 2009, 2011, 2018, 2021, 2048, 2050, 2068, 2095, 2120,
        2121, 2124, 2142, 2143, 2148, 2189, 2195, 2225, 2285, 2326, 2348, 2381,
        2388, 2399, 2400, 2401, 2402, 2404, 2420, 2430, 2467, 2468, 2474, 2482,
        2543, 2562, 2587, 2591, 2607, 2628, 2650, 2651, 2655, 2712, 2732, 2741,
        2743, 2764, 2867, 2868, 2900, 2922, 2942, 2949, 2968, 2970, 2997, 3055,
        3056, 3074, 3108, 3179, 3235, 3265, 3266, 3267, 3277, 3280

Black-white social interaction *(continued)*
EWI 102, 139, 199, 208, 358, 366, 537, 572, 601
FWI 50, 52, 70, 84, 98
HA 289
CU 107, 268, 303, 333
PAN 7
AR 7, 16, 17
BR 64, 69, 93, 211, 214, 242, 243, 244, 245, 246, 341, 396, 402, 410, 437, 524, 525

Blues and blues performers. *See also* Autobiography and biography: blues singers and musicians
GEN 28, 137, 138, 143, 184
NA 32, 39, 61, 70, 89, 120, 133, 152, 177, 180, 204, 207, 210, 211, 226, 231, 232, 244, 248, 251, 252, 257, 258, 266, 268, 269, 271, 272, 276, 279, 313, 314, 336, 342, 360, 363, 375, 376, 377, 385, 409, 472, 512, 525, 536, 537, 538, 539, 542, 543, 544, 545, 546, 547, 549, 570, 618, 619, 633, 640, 647, 660, 661, 669, 717, 761, 859, 900, 926, 928, 929, 930, 931, 932, 935, 936, 946, 970, 971, 972, 973, 975, 977, 979, 983, 985, 996, 1018, 1057, 1089, 1091, 1092, 1093, 1094, 1097, 1098, 1132, 1138, 1142, 1143, 1144, 1145, 1150, 1154, 1160, 1185, 1195, 1207, 1221, 1222, 1223, 1224, 1225, 1226, 1229, 1230, 1231, 1232, 1233, 1234, 1235, 1236, 1237, 1243, 1244, 1271, 1272, 1273, 1274, 1276, 1283, 1287, 1293, 1343, 1344, 1348, 1390, 1401, 1413, 1431, 1451, 1502, 1506, 1508, 1542, 1562, 1574, 1591, 1592, 1617, 1626, 1668, 1670, 1671, 1675, 1676, 1701, 1711, 1732, 1743, 1766, 1773, 1789, 1796, 1801, 1802, 1803, 1804, 1811, 1812, 1825, 1830, 1834, 1836, 1840, 1841, 1856, 1861, 1872, 1875, 1876, 1879, 1880, 1881, 1882, 1885, 1890, 1891, 1892, 1893, 1894, 1897, 1901, 1902, 1903, 1904, 1905, 1912, 1937, 1938, 1940, 1941, 1942, 1943, 1952, 1968, 1998, 2027, 2030, 2031, 2047, 2048, 2050, 2078, 2142, 2186, 2205, 2207, 2213, 2214, 2225, 2226, 2227, 2245, 2246, 2247, 2249, 2252, 2253, 2254, 2260, 2261, 2262, 2263, 2264, 2265, 2266, 2267, 2268, 2269, 2270, 2271, 2272, 2273, 2274, 2275, 2276, 2277, 2278, 2279, 2280, 2281, 2283, 2284, 2285, 2286, 2287, 2295, 2296, 2297, 2298, 2300, 2301, 2304, 2305, 2307, 2314, 2315, 2316, 2318, 2321, 2392, 2404, 2406, 2412, 2513, 2514, 2515, 2519, 2520, 2521, 2522, 2524, 2525, 2528, 2529, 2530, 2580, 2600, 2606, 2607, 2614, 2623, 2627, 2628, 2629, 2635, 2640, 2643, 2652, 2655, 2669, 2670, 2696, 2700, 2715, 2716, 2722, 2725, 2726, 2743, 2751, 2752, 2753, 2757, 2759, 2814, 2831, 2843, 2851, 2852, 2878, 2879, 2891, 2893, 2919, 2934, 2936, 2937, 2949, 2951, 3024, 3025, 3033, 3052, 3068, 3069, 3070, 3099, 3116, 3129, 3135, 3142, 3146, 3147, 3148, 3150, 3151, 3152, 3154, 3159, 3209, 3221, 3222, 3224, 3226, 3227, 3228, 3230, 3231, 3245, 3251, 3267, 3286, 3304
EWI 116

Boating songs. *See* Chanties

Body decoration and modification (cicatrization, tattooing, tooth mutilation)
GEN 188, 248
NA 842, 1546, 2741
EWI 102, 103, 111, 238, 239

Churches, sects and cults   *(continued)*
    PR 13, 22, 29
    FGS 62, 136, 167, 168, 173, 174
    BR 26, 27, 28, 31, 34, 35, 40, 54, 60, 61, 62, 67, 68, 69, 70, 71, 72, 73,
        74, 76, 77, 78, 80, 81, 82, 83, 89, 90, 91, 98, 99, 101, 103, 104, 106,
        107, 108, 109, 110, 113, 115, 116, 117, 118, 119, 120, 121, 122, 125,
        128, 129, 138, 139, 140, 141, 145, 146, 149, 152, 161, 165, 169, 171,
        178, 186, 190, 191, 194, 195, 196, 198, 200, 201, 202, 213, 214, 215,
        216, 217, 222, 223, 224, 226, 227, 228, 232, 233, 234, 235, 236, 237,
        238, 239, 242, 243, 252, 261, 262, 263, 265, 267, 268, 269, 270, 271,
        272, 273, 274, 275, 276, 282, 286, 290, 291, 292, 294, 295, 300, 301,
        302, 303, 306, 308, 309, 310, 311, 315, 316, 317, 319, 320, 321, 331,
        336, 337, 346, 349, 350, 354, 355, 358, 360, 361, 363, 367, 370, 373,
        376, 377, 378, 379, 380, 381, 382, 384, 386, 387, 388, 392, 395, 396,
        398, 400, 404, 405, 407, 419, 420, 421, 422, 423, 430, 431, 432, 434,
        435, 436, 439, 444, 446, 450, 451, 452, 453, 456, 457, 458, 462, 463,
        464, 466, 468, 469, 470, 471, 475, 476, 482, 483, 489, 490, 491, 492,
        493, 500, 501, 502, 503, 504, 505, 506, 507, 519, 520, 521, 523, 526
    VE 5, 19, 22, 26, 42, 43, 44, 61, 62, 65, 67, 70, 71, 72, 73, 74, 75, 77,
        87, 88, 91

Cicatrization. *See* Body decoration and modification

Cimarróns. *See* Escaped slaves

Circus chanties. *See* Work songs

City life
    NA 5, 7, 145, 146, 191, 267, 312, 358, 400, 433, 473, 493, 494, 508, 567,
        581, 624, 656, 668, 738, 769, 814, 837, 859, 878, 893, 894, 945, 947,
        953, 954, 959, 960, 965, 995, 1002, 1003, 1004, 1005, 1036, 1058, 1067,
        1080, 1136, 1152, 1153, 1191, 1209, 1215, 1277, 1278, 1280, 1281, 1287,
        1288, 1295, 1296, 1361, 1362, 1380, 1381, 1384, 1422, 1425, 1448, 1449,
        1476, 1514, 1536, 1549, 1587, 1599, 1645, 1665, 1671, 1674, 1679, 1707,
        1721, 1740, 1750, 1751, 1757, 1758, 1811, 1880, 1958, 1961, 1978, 1983,
        1985, 1986, 2011, 2046, 2064, 2068, 2076, 2085, 2120, 2121, 2126, 2137,
        2176, 2195, 2196, 2428, 2513, 2561, 2594, 2604, 2608, 2624, 2626, 2671,
        2696, 2697, 2713, 2760, 2763, 2783, 2800, 2802, 2807, 2916, 2921, 2936,
        2944, 3000, 3003, 3071, 3084, 3093, 3096, 3180, 3223, 3227, 3250, 3254,
        3265, 3273, 3324
    EWI 100, 129, 130, 276, 347, 352, 517, 518, 541, 558, 684, 714
    DWI 34
    HA 51
    CU 23
    AR 1
    BR 103, 180, 242, 280, 306, 338, 357, 368, 373, 415, 460, 487, 512

Clothing. *See* Dress

Clubs, associations and societies. *See also* Carnival; Churches, sects and
    cults; Festivals; Funerals, burials and wakes; Gangs; Parades
    GEN 85, 161, 272
     NA 166, 243, 389, 657, 769, 1679, 2238, 2323, 2561, 2562, 2696, 2735
    EWI 196, 244, 416, 451, 548, 732
    FWI 18, 25, 27, 31
     HA 51, 69, 139, 235, 239, 272, 305, 318, 334
     CU 99, 104, 197, 232, 295, 297
     MX 4
     BR 338, 413, 474, 480, 523
     CO 22
    PER 2
     VE 5, 44, 85

Cock-fighting. *See* Sports

Combites (Haiti). *See* Clubs, associations and societies; Work practices;
    Work songs

Congo Square *(Place Congo)*, New Orleans
     NA 44, 65, 456, 509, 915, 1209, 1384, 1431, 1750, 1752, 1753, 1793, 3003

Conjuring. *See also* Witchcraft and magic
     NA 31, 79, 96, 112, 170, 225, 282, 330, 357, 501, 506, 553, 554, 556, 600,
        634, 658, 660, 695, 699, 733, 748, 769, 810, 814, 816, 820, 822, 841,
        867, 882, 956, 998, 1003, 1032, 1033, 1253, 1266, 1267, 1298, 1343,
        1374, 1404, 1419, 1512, 1526, 1530, 1538, 1541, 1553, 1601, 1618, 1723,
        1747, 1961, 1976, 2009, 2088, 2165, 2208, 2467, 2482, 2497, 2569, 2570,
        2575, 2650, 2720, 2793, 2798, 2799, 2803, 2859, 2860, 2861, 2897, 2965,
        3000, 3054, 3136, 3161, 3187, 3188, 3189, 3202, 3252, 3262, 3311
     CU 263
     BR 279, 321

Conversion experiences
     NA 229, 342, 510, 517, 981, 987, 1397, 1520, 1614

Cookbooks. *See* Food and cooking

Corn-shucking activities
     NA 97, 157, 405, 625, 675, 687, 915, 1329, 1858, 1921, 2345, 2971, 3078,
        3253

Costume. *See* Dress

Counting-out rhymes. *See* Games; Singing games; Speech play

Courtship. *See* Marriage, courtship and weddings

Credit societies *(susu)*. *See* Clubs, associations and societies

Creole. *See* Dialect

Cries (calls, hollers, shouts)
   GEN 143
   NA 102, 178, 285, 291, 336, 391, 395, 481, 567, 738, 925, 1143, 1146,
      1295, 1332, 1362, 1382, 1388, 1389, 1413, 1508, 1595, 1643, 1718, 1721,
      1827, 1884, 1891, 2046, 2440, 2526, 2697, 2713, 2740, 2851, 2852, 2897,
      2898, 3000, 3001, 3202, 3278, 3305
   CU 107
   PR 26
   UR 6

Cults. *See* Churches, sects and cults

Curing. *See* Medicine

Curses. *See* Speaking, ways of; Verbal and musical dueling

Dance, dance music and songs. *See also* Games, Singing games; Songs, sacred;
   Songs, secular; Stick-fighting
   GEN 6, 7, 11, 30, 33, 40, 62, 68, 78, 79, 85, 86, 87, 89, 90, 103, 137, 140,
      142, 145, 147, 148, 149, 150, 151, 157, 163, 164, 168, 170, 203, 222,
      230, 232, 243, 250, 263, 264, 265, 266, 269
   NA 40, 79, 87, 134, 141, 173, 234, 254, 272, 327, 411, 440, 441, 455, 456,
      461, 473, 475, 481, 509, 515, 549, 565, 625, 632, 641, 651, 668, 675,
      711, 729, 739, 741, 752, 753, 754, 769, 798, 855, 856, 882, 902, 965,
      1012, 1013, 1056, 1058, 1071, 1074, 1112, 1140, 1146, 1228, 1235, 1284,
      1299, 1359, 1375, 1376, 1384, 1407, 1464, 1471, 1474, 1484, 1509, 1519,
      1549, 1551, 1557, 1561, 1583, 1602, 1645, 1663, 1671, 1673, 1679, 1706
      1747, 1750, 1752, 1768, 1774, 1776, 1793, 1847, 1881, 1889, 1913, 1922,
      1964, 2002, 2019, 2046, 2115, 2142, 2186, 2233, 2289, 2290, 2316, 2356,
      2384, 2386, 2404, 2439, 2463, 2493, 2497, 2519, 2524, 2525, 2545, 2546,
      2560, 2569, 2589, 2608, 2655, 2662, 2671, 2689, 2698, 2771, 2808, 2814,
      2829, 2852, 2853, 2854, 2855, 2856, 2905, 2942, 2946, 2983, 2984, 2985,
      2986, 2987, 3000, 3003, 3006, 3007, 3008, 3009, 3011, 3030, 3031, 3039,
      3061, 3075, 3092, 3094, 3096, 3106, 3107, 3109, 3123, 3216, 3250, 3255,
      3258
   EWI 20, 25, 59, 60, 64, 67, 74, 103, 108, 110, 114, 128, 139, 143, 148,
      177, 192, 197, 203, 215, 237, 241, 247, 249, 252, 273, 284, 286, 307,
      317, 323, 347, 356, 366, 377, 388, 390, 418, 419, 422, 428, 429, 434,
      437, 438, 439, 451, 452, 453, 467, 474, 476, 491, 496, 506, 513, 537,
      539, 547, 557, 593, 599, 615, 619, 628, 629, 657, 685.
   DWI 11
   FWI 25, 31, 37, 42, 51, 67, 74, 79, 85, 88, 98, 123
   HA 2, 40, 42, 68, 69, 102, 104, 107, 109, 116, 117, 146, 147, 152, 157,
      162, 171, 193, 213, 215, 218, 219, 225, 230, 245, 246, 247, 255, 272,
      278, 292, 334, 380, 381
   DR 3, 16
   CU 12, 13, 20, 23, 39, 42, 43, 72, 86, 90, 150, 156, 173, 174, 175, 178,
      182, 183, 184, 219, 230, 249, 256, 259, 260, 280, 307, 324, 329, 334
   PR 1, 2, 4, 5, 14, 23, 25, 37, 38, 41
   FGS 6, 14, 61, 82, 88, 122, 162, 167, 169
     B 2, 3, 11

Dialect *(continued)*

    Louisiana French Creole:
  NA 222, 585, 591, 777, 1047, 1048, 1049, 1050, 1051, 1052, 1053, 1054,
     1055, 1056, 1335, 1364, 1366, 1376, 1378, 1385, 1386, 1387, 1763,
     1788, 2038, 2122, 2123, 2504, 2551, 2588, 2651, 3000, 3001, 3002, 3003

    Surinam Creole *(Sranan):*
  FGS 28, 32, 47, 49, 62, 82, 93, 132, 146, 148, 163, 164, 165, 167, 171

Dictionaries, vocabulary lists and glossaries. *See also* Dialect; Etymology;
  Motif, tale-type and song indices
  GEN 26, 59, 143, 159, 195, 228, 252, 262, 273, 274, 297, 298
  NA 26, 35, 99, 140, 367, 422, 423, 434, 467, 468, 639, 650, 698, 708, 709,
     736, 749, 774, 785, 830, 883, 945, 991, 1017, 1161, 1196, 1215, 1298,
     1336, 1447, 1473, 1536, 1576, 1654, 1927, 1987, 2021, 2048, 2068, 2096,
     2122, 2236, 2324, 2354, 2396, 2462, 2505, 2538, 2544, 2550, 2584, 2682,
     2794, 2820, 3003, 3028, 3065, 3071, 3164, 3308
  DWI 30
  EWI 20, 32, 35, 50, 78, 80, 138, 148, 156, 185, 186, 187, 195, 274, 300,
     369, 383, 395, 447, 522, 606, 617, 666
  HA 54, 66, 69, 80, 104, 123, 184, 238, 257, 279, 310, 355, 373
  CU 48, 49, 63, 75, 103, 109, 126, 139, 140, 145, 146, 185, 251
  PR 4, 22, 32, 42
  FGS 30, 175
  PAN 25
  AR 2, 15
  BO 1
  BR 1, 16, 101, 128, 129, 138, 143, 156, 165, 192, 193, 198, 238, 251, 270
     283, 286, 319, 334, 336, 343, 356, 386, 423, 450, 463, 466
  CO 8, 30, 36, 38
  EC 8
  UR 8, 15

Dirt-eating
  NA 772, 1931, 2924
  FGS 95

Divination. *See also* Witchcraft and Magic
  NA 956, 2341, 2483
  EWI 111, 354
  HA 10, 224
  CU 35
  FGS 55
  BR 157, 388, 422, 432, 436, 514

Domestic life. *See also* Material culture; Slavery, slave life and the Ante
  Bellum
  GEN 96, 174
  NA 47, 135, 136, 166, 173, 179, 195, 305, 322, 324, 327, 416, 459, 475,
     478, 480, 492, 559, 561, 625, 637, 644, 645, 661, 692, 702, 737, 743,
     748, 841, 956, 1049, 1126, 1162, 1163, 1178, 1180, 1186, 1193, 1199,

Fairies. *See* Supernatural figures

Festivals. *See also* Carnival; Christmas; Easter; Epiphany; John Canoe;
  July 4th and Juneteenth; New Year's; Pinkster; Religious rites and services
  GEN 171, 203
  NA 486, 491, 769, 2561
  EWI 92, 203, 206, 208, 537, 568, 657, 707, 738
  FWI 18, 25, 27, 37, 103, 107
  HA 2, 3, 46, 195
  DR 13
  CU 28, 190, 229, 249, 250, 292, 308, 313, 351, 352
  PR 1, 2, 9, 15, 19, 21, 24
  GU 1
  ES 1
  BR 26, 43, 46, 47, 48, 56, 106, 107, 181, 192, 206, 210, 217, 257, 259,
    287, 303, 309, 340, 367, 406, 426, 442, 493, 502, 503, 505
  CO 7, 19, 33
  VE 12, 15, 16, 17, 18, 21, 33, 34, 37, 38, 39, 44, 47, 48, 50, 52, 53,
    61, 63, 64, 65, 69, 71, 72, 73, 74, 75, 77, 82, 83

Folklore scholars and the study of Afro-American folklore
  GEN 6, 20, 28, 47, 67, 107, 113, 114, 115, 121, 122, 125, 126, 127, 128,
    136, 143, 161, 173, 175, 202, 213, 239, 241, 244, 245, 279, 290, 294,
    295
  NA 5, 99, 113, 115, 126, 142, 152, 153, 159, 165, 186, 220, 221, 245, 252,
    282, 313, 333, 335, 340, 341, 357, 374, 386, 387, 426, 441, 444, 449,
    471, 576, 598, 648, 667, 678, 680, 691, 710, 807, 811, 813, 814, 823,
    824, 890, 897, 898, 908, 909, 910, 911, 916, 917, 918, 919, 944, 952,
    981, 1019, 1020, 1027, 1065, 1067, 1068, 1070, 1104, 1114, 1141, 1159,
    1170, 1171, 1172, 1183, 1121, 1212, 1216, 1227, 1229, 1230, 1231, 1232,
    1233, 1234, 1235, 1237, 1245, 1274, 1278, 1303, 1313, 1315, 1321, 1355,
    1407, 1420, 1422, 1423, 1424, 1425, 1426, 1427, 1428, 1461, 1484, 1486,
    1506, 1522, 1523, 1534, 1542, 1580, 1581, 1582, 1626, 1627, 1632, 1633,
    1634, 1635, 1671, 1678, 1686, 1697, 1727, 1745, 1761, 1763, 1765, 1787,
    1814, 1816, 1822, 1851, 1862, 1869, 1881, 1893, 1896, 1897, 1915, 1917,
    2000, 2041, 2043, 2044, 2047, 2076, 2142, 2143, 2145, 2160, 2161, 2197,
    2199, 2201, 2205, 2368, 2375, 2389, 2435, 2487, 2549, 2652, 2653, 2655,
    2680, 2750, 2778, 2779, 2873, 2874, 2875, 2912, 2914, 2931, 2933, 3034,
    3035, 3080, 3098, 3108, 3138, 3177, 3178, 3179, 3195, 3204, 3264, 3266
  EWI 345, 347, 407, 408, 470, 538, 570, 647, 655, 677, 737
  HA 4, 5, 12, 16, 17, 19, 23, 24, 32, 81, 82, 110, 187, 188, 194, 220, 254,
    264, 266, 277, 289, 291, 293, 299, 302, 315, 341, 364
  CU 133, 134, 215, 285, 357
  FGS 5, 31, 108
  BR 68, 70, 72, 73, 173, 174, 175, 176, 438, 465
  UR 11
  VE 77

Food and cooking. *See also* Dirt-eating; Domestic life
  GEN 13, 37, 206, 281, 297
  NA 56, 77, 79, 97, 184, 222, 233, 300, 408, 459, 465, 475, 480, 483, 631,

Graphic arts. *See* Visual arts

Graves. *See* Cemeteries and graves

Gullah and Sea Island culture (Georgia and South Carolina). *See also*
    Dialect: Gullah; South Carolina (Locale Index)
        NA 71, 117, 184, 197, 198, 199, 200, 201, 202, 203, 295, 327, 477, 486,
            487, 489, 491, 492, 564, 565, 607, 608, 609, 610, 614, 621, 626, 637,
            644, 645, 646, 692, 703, 704, 762, 776, 850, 907, 949, 1009, 1010,
            1034, 1046, 1072, 1082, 1118, 1124, 1125, 1126, 1161, 1162, 1163,
            1164, 1165, 1166, 1169, 1174, 1175, 1188, 1192, 1193, 1240, 1247,
            1249, 1286, 1299, 1317, 1424, 1432, 1433, 1434, 1435, 1436, 1437,
            1456, 1483, 1489, 1491, 1540, 1625, 1627, 1628, 1663, 1664, 1686,
            1749, 1798, 1867, 1882, 1935, 1947, 1965, 1966, 1967, 1976, 1981,
            2001, 2006, 2015, 2052, 2124, 2144, 2192, 2222, 2234, 2355, 2356,
            2359, 2364, 2391, 2399, 2405, 2413, 2414, 2415, 2416, 2417, 2418,
            2419, 2420, 2421, 2422, 2423, 2428, 2503, 2544, 2545, 2568, 2572,
            2603, 2618, 2622, 2630, 2631, 2668, 2677, 2678, 2731, 2777, 2778,
            2779, 2784, 2798, 2803, 2804, 2816, 2872, 2874, 2875, 2876, 2882,
            2883, 2884, 2885, 2889, 2897, 2930, 2982, 3019, 3040, 3041, 3042,
            3043, 3048, 3054, 3058, 3066, 3067, 3074, 3079, 3081, 3082, 3104,
            3105, 3126, 3164, 3202, 3211, 3219, 3235, 3283, 3297, 3299, 3310,
            3311

Haglore. *See also* Supernatural figures; Witchcraft and magic
    NA 190, 492, 1025, 1028, 1248, 2577, 2803, 3054

Hair-styling. *See* Dress

Heroes
    NA 4, 5, 7, 12, 16, 125, 410, 417, 863, 990, 1087, 1427, 1519, 1707,
        2068, 2069, 2226, 2227, 2477, 2938, 3155, 3197, 3198, 3241

Hollers. *See* Cries

Hoodoo. *See* Witchcraft and magic

Houses. *See* Architecture and housing

Humor. *See* Joking

Indices. *See* Motif, tale-type and song indices

Initiation. *See* Clubs, associations and societies; Religious rites and
    services; Supernatural beliefs and practices

Insults. *See* Speech play; Verbal and musical dueling

Islam, influence of. *See also* Churches, sects and cults
    NA 57, 74, 637, 771, 922, 1412, 1457, 3066, 3080
    FGS 7
    BR 78, 113, 194, 417, 440, 490, 491

Joking   *(continued)*
   FWI 55
    HA 221
    CU 5
    BR 301

Juba.   *See also* Dance, dance music and songs
   NA 915, 1228, 1375, 1791, 2168, 2946, 3258, 3306

July 4th and Juneteenth
   NA 43, 348, 1011, 3055, 3199

Jumbies.   *See* Supernatural figures

Kalinda.   *See* Stick-fighting

Kinesic behavior.   *See* Non-verbal communication

Kinship, ritual
   NA 63, 79
   BR 178

Language.   *See* Dialect; Dictionaries, vocabulary lists and glossaries;
  Etymology; Slang, argot and jargon

Legends.   *See also* Tales and tale telling
   NA 200, 253, 292, 368, 623, 661, 751, 793, 941, 1199, 1250, 1263, 1511,
     1597, 1619, 1620, 1621, 1632, 1852, 2006, 2009, 2068, 2182, 2293,
     2379, 2473, 2476, 2569, 2651, 2765, 2896, 2957, 2973
   EWI 20, 27, 87, 108, 294, 364, 509, 510, 512, 539, 542, 568, 583, 696
   FWI 44, 91, 122
    HA 283, 340
    CU 60, 63, 117, 145, 154, 210
    PR 41
   FGS 11, 43, 103
     B 4
    AR 4, 16
    BR 48, 56, 95, 141, 153, 162, 172, 235, 241, 283, 318, 369, 449, 450,
     514
    CO 7, 36
    VE 40, 42, 43

Lent.   *See* Carnival; Easter; Festivals

Literature (novels, drama, poetry) with folkloric content
   GEN 10, 27, 34, 47, 55, 61, 133, 138, 161, 163, 167, 195, 203, 205
   NA 62, 63, 93, 99, 126, 127, 172, 175, 181, 188, 192, 200, 206, 230, 251,
     252, 279, 307, 308, 310, 311, 315, 316, 317, 318, 319, 320, 322, 323,
     358, 366, 374, 378, 379, 380, 383, 384, 388, 396, 415, 416, 432, 435,
     441, 450, 455, 457, 475, 476, 528, 553, 554, 559, 560, 561, 562, 621,
     626, 629, 650, 651, 654, 659, 660, 697, 736, 744, 768, 773, 848, 849,
     850, 861, 880, 882, 896, 988, 1003, 1004, 1005, 1085, 1133, 1152,
     1197, 1200, 1201, 1202, 1203, 1256, 1286, 1300, 1302, 1304, 1305,

Medicine *(continued)*
    DR 4, 10
    CU 31, 60, 62, 89, 263, 291, 295, 298
    FGS 92, 95, 124
    CR 7
    MX 10
    PAN 1, 34
    AR 5, 13
    BR 80, 89, 116, 212, 243, 279, 315, 388, 450, 466, 479, 523
    CO 10, 37
    EC 3, 8
    UR 14
    VE 5, 22, 28, 40, 88, 89

Migration. *See* Escaped slaves; West Indian and Latin American peoples in
    North America

Minstrelsy (black and white)
    GEN 138, 159, 185, 225
    NA 40, 146, 272, 299, 394, 533, 547, 712, 747, 799, 852, 869, 1012,
        1081, 1085, 1144, 1148, 1190, 1194, 1254, 1356, 1360, 1451, 1488,
        1499, 1509, 1560, 1583, 1705, 1712, 1771, 1814, 1861, 1975, 2002,
        2016, 2017, 2083, 2128, 2151, 2152, 2153, 2154, 2155, 2156, 2171,
        2172, 2174, 2284, 2337, 2380, 2381, 2566, 2571, 2615, 2616, 2662,
        2724, 2743, 2759, 2917, 2920, 2970, 3011, 3012, 3029, 3100, 3143,
        3144, 3177, 3179, 3194, 3258, 3261

Motif, tale-type and song indices
    GEN 65, 102, 109
    NA 1796

Mumming. *See also* Drama
    EWI 3, 4, 5, 12, 68, 72, 73

Music. *See also* Dance, dance music and songs; Singers and singing; Songs,
    general; Songs, sacred; Songs, secular
    GEN 11, 15, 25, 28, 37, 40, 41, 47, 52, 70, 78, 79, 82, 83, 86, 87,
        89, 90, 94, 95, 103, 112, 124, 132, 140, 146, 157, 158, 163, 164,
        170, 182, 183, 184, 187, 189, 191, 203, 206, 220, 222, 227, 234, 242,
        243, 246, 247, 250, 269, 280, 288, 289, 290
    NA 41, 44, 79, 87, 97, 118, 124, 126, 134, 145, 146, 153, 166, 192, 234,
        243, 247, 248, 295, 368, 389, 427, 428, 432, 441, 575, 589, 592, 612,
        617, 651, 662, 668, 680, 700, 710, 721, 723, 740, 741, 746, 747, 770,
        798, 834, 843, 865, 882, 890, 908, 909, 913, 938, 961, 967, 996, 1044,
        1056, 1058, 1065, 1074, 1085, 1088, 1096, 1100, 1104, 1112, 1113,
        1121, 1140, 1158, 1183, 1235, 1280, 1291, 1292, 1376, 1384, 1403,
        1407, 1424, 1428, 1429, 1440, 1444, 1448, 1451, 1472, 1482, 1488,
        1499, 1513, 1518, 1551, 1565, 1593, 1671, 1672, 1673, 1686, 1706,
        1710, 1713, 1716, 1750, 1751, 1763, 1767, 1768, 1780, 1793, 1810,
        1811, 1814, 1822, 1840, 1849, 1861, 1913, 1917, 1931, 1993, 2013,
        2043, 2053, 2054, 2070, 2089, 2119, 2130, 2148, 2155, 2166, 2212,

Proverbs and proverbial expression. *See also* Riddles; Speaking, ways of;
   Speech play
   GEN 109, 195, 291
     NA 38, 113, 139, 140, 158, 327, 342, 368, 376, 390, 414, 451, 523, 526,
        579, 599, 654, 675, 670, 683, 727, 739, 792, 814, 904, 925, 1024,
        1031, 1034, 1040, 1047, 1196, 1198, 1298, 1327, 1353, 1370, 1416,
        1491, 1519, 1618, 1627, 1731, 1760, 1979, 1994, 2108, 2177, 2360,
        2364, 2421, 2422, 2423, 2432, 2433, 2475, 2497, 2532, 2540, 2567,
        2582, 2598, 2649, 2659, 2693, 2702, 2717, 2746, 2823, 2978, 2997,
        3000, 3001, 3076, 3087, 3140, 3183, 3184, 3260, 3297, 3299, 3310
    EWI 17, 20, 35, 41, 52, 57, 64, 68, 69, 88, 107, 122, 137, 140, 162, 173,
        195, 214, 228, 229, 230, 252, 268, 293, 304, 311, 337, 346, 352, 369,
        379, 391, 463, 511, 513, 514, 515, 516, 521, 522, 524, 525, 543, 557,
        564, 569, 574, 595, 609, 666, 672, 712
    DWI 5, 9, 10, 26, 27, 28
    FWI 11, 33, 34, 41, 49, 57, 105, 134
     HA 13, 31, 48, 123, 135, 137, 150, 165, 257, 270, 343, 378
     DR 2
     CU 64, 204
     PR 10
    FGS 9, 61, 62, 151, 167
      B 5, 10, 13
     BR 116, 211, 270, 314, 375, 450
     CO 31, 37, 38

Quilombo (Brazil). *See* Dance, dance music and songs; Escaped slaves

Ragtime
     NA 180, 272, 276, 493, 494, 495, 496, 532, 534, 535, 547, 701, 720, 728,
        729, 1012, 1013, 1014, 1122, 1136, 1149, 1225, 1293, 1451, 1482,
        1600, 1643, 1681, 1700, 1861, 2013, 2030, 2114, 2115, 2153, 2186,
        2627, 2643, 2661, 2701, 2709, 2743, 2783, 2970, 3069, 3099, 3114,
        3115, 3229, 3330

Railroad songs. *See also* Chanties; Work songs
     NA 208, 293, 327, 615, 616, 661, 984, 1330, 2279, 2286, 2410, 2655, 2757

Rara (Haiti). *See* Churches, sects and cults

Rastafarianism (Jamaica). *See also* Churches, sects and cults
    EWI 55, 96, 97, 369, 396, 400, 534, 535, 588, 639, 642, 643, 648, 660,
        684

Recipes. *See* Food and cooking

Recordings
     NA 32, 684, 790, 840, 985, 1045, 1144, 1154, 1195, 1338, 1340, 1801,
        1804, 2213, 2267, 2283, 2284, 2326, 2629, 2831, 2936, 3203, 3207,
        3230
    EWI 18, 198, 438
     CU 43
     BR 17, 484

Reels. *See* Dance, dance music and songs

Reggae (English-speaking West Indies). *See* Music: popular

Religion. *See also* Religious rites and services
    GEN 12, 14, 16, 21, 22, 23, 26, 31, 32, 37, 68, 82, 83, 92, 97, 103, 108,
        142, 148, 149, 161, 185, 193, 194, 208, 214, 218, 237, 240, 287, 298
     NA 1, 23, 29, 30, 94, 172, 204, 243, 402, 475, 580, 583, 617, 633, 658,
        724, 737, 771, 784, 814, 835, 837, 843, 844, 845, 846, 902, 951, 953,
        954, 961, 963, 981, 1044, 1063, 1068, 1075, 1091, 1112, 1115, 1186, 1192,
        1227, 1231, 1256, 1290, 1342, 1407, 1424, 1440, 1444, 1499, 1549, 1586,
        1611, 1613, 1625, 1657, 1658, 1738, 1794, 1798, 1817, 1826, 1845,
        1846, 1849, 1887, 1917, 1924, 1961, 1990, 1992, 2024, 2025, 2063,
        2080, 2106, 2148, 2150, 2162, 2229, 2289, 2290, 2292, 2323, 2335,
        2345, 2387, 2390, 2391, 2392, 2482, 2497, 2500, 2502, 2506, 2519,
        2535, 2536, 2548, 2549, 2561, 2632, 2633, 2734, 2741, 2830, 2849,
        2892, 2940, 2955, 2974, 2992, 3039, 3084, 3110, 3247, 3282, 3303
    EWI 23, 64, 82, 90, 102, 103, 110, 115, 204, 208, 238, 285, 301, 347, 353,
        452, 501, 537, 560, 567, 570, 588, 599, 604, 605, 610, 657, 708, 710,
        721, 732, 733, 734
    DWI 21
    FWI 10, 25, 46, 60, 67, 99, 104, 123
     HA 51, 66, 98, 134, 259, 273
     CU 21, 22, 30, 36, 83, 148, 329, 334, 345, 352
    FGS 62, 65, 68, 74, 75, 82, 86, 93, 99, 118, 159, 168
     MX 4, 9, 10
    PAN 8, 28, 35
     AR 15
     BR 2, 14, 34, 40, 64, 69, 81, 82, 83, 87, 89, 113, 120, 137, 140, 191,
        192, 201, 213, 214, 219, 226, 236, 242, 243, 246, 248, 270, 273,
        275, 282, 283, 295, 315, 319, 373, 386, 387, 388, 396, 404, 406,
        407, 418, 431, 437, 445, 446, 468, 469, 476, 479, 490, 516, 519,
        520, 523
     CO 10, 11, 24
     UR 18
     VE 88

Religious leaders (preachers, priests, priestesses *et al.*). *See* Autobiography and biography: religious leaders and singers; Sermons and preaching

Religious rites and services. *See also* Camp meetings and revivals; Churches,
   sects and cults; Festivals; Initiation; Marriage, courtship and weddings;
   Possession, spiritual
    GEN 12, 108, 174, 185, 208, 237, 250
     NA 1, 23, 43, 46, 47, 51, 82, 202, 312, 321, 338, 364, 389, 406, 452,
        484, 501, 516, 565, 583, 613, 646, 668, 675, 686, 715, 716, 724,
        725, 800, 844, 845, 846, 852, 878, 895, 915, 922, 986, 998, 1172,
        1192, 1218, 1238, 1299, 1333, 1334, 1412, 1466, 1468, 1470, 1512,
        1551, 1586, 1592, 1614, 1655, 1658, 1669, 1678, 1703, 1730, 1733,
        1747, 1767, 1768, 1772, 1773, 1774, 1775, 1781, 1798, 1837, 1906,
        1990, 2022, 2059, 2091, 2104, 2317, 2387, 2442, 2482, 2495, 2507,

Religious rites and services *(continued)*

    NA 2527, 2574, 2576, 2632, 2651, 2679, 2690, 2711, 2736, 2747, 2782,
        2789, 2790, 2805, 2817, 2862, 3013, 3019, 3044, 3055, 3105, 3112,
        3113, 3117, 3124, 3126, 3232, 3233, 3256, 3283, 3309, 3329

   EWI 53, 55, 64, 102, 103, 115, 124, 129, 137, 141, 176, 192, 238, 265,
        285, 340, 342, 347, 353, 471, 472, 476, 506, 537, 539, 562, 563,
        570, 604, 605, 632, 633, 634, 636, 637, 639, 640, 641, 642, 643,
        644, 645, 646, 647, 648

   DWI 22

   FWI 31, 37, 95, 108

    HA 2, 3, 7, 10, 11, 14, 15, 16, 19, 24, 25, 26, 27, 28, 29, 39, 40,
        42, 44, 45, 46, 51, 65, 66, 68, 69, 70, 71, 72, 74, 90, 93, 99,
        100, 101, 102, 103, 104, 105, 106, 110, 111, 112, 113, 116, 117,
        119, 131, 136, 138, 146, 147, 149, 152, 154, 155, 162, 164, 169,
        170, 171, 172, 173, 174, 175, 178, 181, 183, 184, 185, 186, 188,
        189, 193, 194, 196, 197, 199, 200, 201, 202, 203, 204, 205, 207,
        208, 211, 212, 213, 215, 216, 217, 218, 219, 221, 222, 223, 225,
        226, 227, 230, 232, 233, 234, 236, 237, 238, 240, 241, 242, 243,
        244, 245, 246, 247, 249, 250, 252, 253, 256, 257, 258, 272, 274,
        278, 279, 280, 281, 282, 284, 287, 300, 307, 308, 309, 310, 311,
        315, 319, 320, 321, 325, 326, 327, 328, 329, 330, 331, 337, 338,
        339, 342, 366, 367, 370, 371, 373, 374, 375, 376, 377, 378, 379,
        380, 381

    CU 47, 48, 54, 57, 59, 65, 67, 71, 73, 75, 77, 78, 82, 83, 99, 103,
        108, 110, 112, 130, 136, 138, 139, 140, 147, 161, 162, 166, 211,
        212, 238, 249, 259, 260, 261, 263, 264, 266, 267, 274, 276, 281,
        282, 292, 329, 334, 335, 346, 347, 351, 352, 355

    PR 1, 2, 4

   FGS 61, 62, 65, 68, 88, 136

     B 9

    CR 1, 5, 7

    AR 2, 4, 15

    BR 26, 27, 28, 31, 44, 46, 66, 89, 94, 98, 99, 104, 115, 117, 118,
        119, 121, 122, 128, 129, 132, 133, 136, 138, 139, 140, 141, 145,
        146, 149, 152, 165, 169, 171, 186, 190, 192, 198, 200, 201, 202,
        206, 215, 216, 218, 222, 224, 226, 227, 228, 232, 233, 234, 235,
        236, 237, 238, 239, 242, 243, 252, 261, 262, 263, 265, 266, 267,
        268, 269, 270, 271, 272, 273, 274, 276, 282, 286, 290, 291, 292,
        294, 295, 300, 301, 302, 303, 306, 308, 309, 310, 311, 315, 316,
        317, 320, 321, 331, 336, 337, 349, 350, 354, 355, 358, 360, 361,
        363, 367, 370, 373, 376, 377, 378, 379, 380, 381, 382, 386, 387,
        388, 398, 400, 404, 405, 407, 419, 420, 421, 422, 423, 430, 431,
        432, 435, 436, 439, 446, 450, 452, 453, 456, 457, 458, 462, 463,
        464, 466, 468, 469, 470, 471, 475, 476, 482, 489, 490, 491, 492,
        493, 494, 500, 501, 502, 503, 504, 505, 506, 507, 519, 520, 521,
        523, 526

    EC 7, 8, 9, 10

    VE 5, 19, 21, 31, 33, 42, 43, 44, 53, 54, 61, 62, 63, 64, 65, 66, 67,
        68, 69, 70, 71, 72, 73, 74, 82, 84, 87, 88, 89

Rent parties. *See also* Clubs, associations and societies

    NA 1332, 2560, 2992

Revivals. *See* Camp meetings and revivals

Rhymes. *See* Speech play

Rhythm and blues. *See* Blues and blues performers; Music: popular; "Soul"

Riddles
    GEN 109, 195, 291
    NA 11, 17, 115, 137, 259, 342, 368, 404, 661, 734, 820, 956, 957, 958,
        1021, 1024, 1026, 1034, 1166, 1261, 1495, 1627, 1663, 1790, 2200,
        2359, 2360, 2361, 2363, 2364, 2369, 2408, 2497, 2665, 2746, 2832
    EWI 35, 67, 293, 379, 520, 521, 522, 525, 526, 528
    FWI 55
    HA 257
    DR 2
    CU 5, 38
    PR 33
    FGS 62, 135
    B 10
    AR 9, 10
    BR 116, 209
    CO 29
    VE 57

Ring plays. *See* Games; Singing games

Rock and roll. *See* Music: popular

Roles. *See* Social roles

Root work and root doctors. *See* Conjuring

Samba. *See* Carnival; Clubs, associations and societies; Dance, dance
    music and songs

Santaria. *See* Churches, sects and cults

Sacrification. *See* Body decoration and modification

Sea and boating songs. *See* Chanties

Sea Island culture. *See* Gullah and Sea Island culture

Secret societies. *See* Clubs, associations and societies

Sects. *See* Churches, sects and cults; Religious rites and services

Sermons and preaching. *See also* Religious rites and services
    NA 25, 27, 29, 79, 182, 284, 321, 342, 364, 385, 411, 479, 492, 500,
        661, 686, 748, 786, 800, 832, 833, 846, 900, 933, 986, 1083, 1110,
        1146, 1155, 1169, 1209, 1342, 1349, 1468, 1508, 1522, 1527, 1532,
        1542, 1569, 1613, 1614, 1648, 1658, 1703, 1858, 1867, 1887, 1899,
        1921, 1931, 1949, 1953, 1991, 2025, 2078, 2080, 2093, 2261, 2423,

Songs, sacred *(continued)*

     texts and music *(continued):*
  NA 766, 767, 786, 787, 789, 803, 825, 834, 860, 879, 882, 900, 901, 912,
     942, 943, 956, 957, 964, 986, 1001, 1004, 1006, 1034, 1037, 1043,
     1073, 1090, 1101, 1105, 1106, 1107, 1109, 1120, 1125, 1129, 1155,
     1168, 1170, 1171, 1172, 1173, 1175, 1189, 1192, 1208, 1219, 1226,
     1239, 1241, 1259, 1269, 1270, 1271, 1276, 1298, 1332, 1347, 1369,
     1388, 1390, 1397, 1408, 1409, 1440, 1441, 1442, 1450, 1453, 1462,
     1463, 1469, 1470, 1484, 1492, 1496, 1508, 1516, 1540, 1543, 1569,
     1580, 1581, 1582, 1584, 1588, 1590, 1592, 1606, 1627, 1628, 1639,
     1640, 1643, 1644, 1647, 1650, 1659, 1661, 1663, 1669, 1684, 1688,
     1718, 1719, 1729, 1733, 1741, 1775, 1785, 1826, 2833, 1842, 1843,
     1853, 1855, 1870, 1873, 1876, 1877, 1881, 1882, 1883, 1887, 1892,
     1894, 1896, 1897, 1925, 1929, 1938, 1955, 1956, 1979, 1980, 2001,
     2003, 2008, 2019, 2026, 2057, 2058, 2060, 2078, 2105, 2116, 2117,
     2138, 2141, 2147, 2158, 2170, 2178, 2180, 2181, 2216, 2217, 2218,
     2214, 2223, 2233, 2242, 2248, 2250, 2251, 2253, 2312, 2317, 2319,
     2321, 2355, 2356, 2364, 2366, 2407, 2410, 2429, 2437, 2445, 2446,
     2447, 2448, 2449, 2450, 2451, 2452, 2453, 2454, 2455, 2456, 2457,
     2458, 2459, 2460, 2461, 2488, 2489, 2495, 2507, 2524, 2526, 2527,
     2537, 2580, 2595, 2596, 2605, 2606, 2640, 2647, 2656, 2679, 2685,
     2692, 2694, 2708, 2724, 2738, 2755, 2757, 2772, 2777, 2784, 2813,
     2816, 2824, 2828, 2836, 2946, 2960, 2966, 3044, 3046, 3166, 3167,
     3172, 3177, 3194, 3213, 3237, 3248, 3256, 3275, 3283, 3287, 3288,
     3289, 3290, 3292, 3293, 3314, 3328
  EWI 20, 60, 67, 94, 106, 137, 164, 189, 231, 269, 377, 440, 460, 479, 498,
     528, 537, 642, 703
   HA 18, 47, 69, 154, 167, 180, 256, 339
   CU 162, 168, 205
  FGS 62, 136, 167
    B 12, 53, 54
   BR 70, 92, 101, 110, 122, 129, 138, 165, 200, 223, 228, 235, 238, 239, 274,
     276, 282, 317, 421, 463, 466, 475, 505, 526
   CO 16, 32, 42
   UR 21
   VE 61, 63, 81

Songs, secular. *See also* Ballads; Chanties, Motif, tale-type and song
   indices; Music: popular; Railroad songs; Recordings "Soul"; Work songs

     discussion:
  GEN 1, 39, 71, 137, 138, 141, 157, 163, 178, 204, 222, 232, 282, 289, 291
  NA 30, 48, 49, 51, 58, 60, 61, 79, 89, 231, 260, 263, 266, 272, 275, 306,
     327, 336, 385, 469, 486, 489, 492, 497, 498, 628, 661, 662, 675, 692,
     739, 710, 846, 860, 882, 911, 915, 1043, 1106, 1107, 1109, 1112, 1123,
     1170, 1208, 1228, 1341, 1367, 1375, 1408, 1409, 1451, 1481, 1496,
     1539, 1540, 1577, 1627, 1628, 1637, 1661, 1684, 1719, 1721, 1813,
     1881, 1882, 1885, 1887, 1891, 1894, 1896, 1897, 1912, 1931, 1938,
     1965, 1975, 1990, 1993, 2010, 2045, 2047, 2078, 2114, 2134, 2168,
     2174, 2217, 2224, 2226, 2227, 2242, 2246, 2247, 2254, 2351, 2355,
     2356, 2380, 2381, 2404, 2472, 2507, 2519, 2521, 2529, 2537, 2580,

Supernatural beliefs and practices *(continued)*
    HA 7, 54, 64, 145, 146, 153, 154, 156, 191, 250, 252, 257, 271, 317, 335,
        338
    DR 2
    CU 16, 18, 21, 62, 119, 238, 295, 304, 345
    PR 24
    FGS 42, 62, 89, 129, 136, 139, 173, 174
     B 4
    MX 4, 5
    AR 2, 4, 5
    BR 56, 95, 102, 116, 142, 163, 212, 227, 254, 259, 271, 369, 386, 400,
        401, 403, 404, 432, 450, 466, 491, 514, 520
    CO 10, 21
    UR 15
    VE 5, 32, 40, 50, 56, 57, 58, 59, 62

Supernatural Figures. *See also* Deities
    GEN 180
    NA 1433, 1916, 2005, 2497, 2885
    EWI 64, 74, 90, 99, 124, 137, 180, 182, 290, 300, 325, 363, 364, 395, 462,
        537, 568, 600, 601, 623, 673, 676, 681, 699, 727, 728
    DWI 22
    FWI 32, 51, 89, 127, 167
    HA 39, 99, 222, 223, 224, 226, 230, 236, 238
    CU 16, 249
    PR 9, 10
     B 4
    PAN 37
    BR 458
    VE 58

"Superstitions." *See* Supernatural beliefs and practices

Susu. *See* Clubs, associations and societies

Tales and tale telling. *See also* Joking; Legends; Myth
    GEN 50, 53, 61, 65, 74, 90, 109, 133, 195, 196, 197, 199, 270, 277, 278,
        283, 291
    NA 25, 26, 29, 68, 92, 105, 111, 115, 132, 135, 136, 149, 197, 198, 216,
        234, 240, 254, 280, 281, 283, 290, 291, 292, 334, 341, 343, 345, 348,
        368, 381, 385, 403, 404, 414, 435, 439, 444, 455, 492, 501, 564, 585,
        586, 587, 590, 591, 596, 637, 643, 653, 654, 655, 664, 673, 714, 734,
        739, 795, 807, 808, 809, 810, 813, 815, 816, 817, 818, 819, 820, 821,
        823, 824, 841, 850, 853, 872, 873, 874, 891, 952, 955, 956, 957, 958,
        969, 999, 1034, 1039, 1042, 1051, 1053, 1054, 1055, 1061, 1074, 1080,
        1119, 1129, 1155, 1161, 1162, 1164, 1165, 1199, 1240, 1256, 1262,
        1280, 1298, 1299, 1302, 1307, 1309, 1331, 1353, 1354, 1405, 1500,
        1513, 1522, 1530, 1542, 1553, 1554, 1569, 1571, 1573, 1616, 1618,
        1619, 1627, 1628, 1663, 1665, 1686, 1716, 1771, 1800, 1807, 1809,
        1818, 1835, 1839, 1860, 1871, 1914, 1979, 2009, 2029, 2044, 2066,
        2075, 2077, 2084, 2100, 2101, 2107, 2112, 2120, 2121, 2188, 2198,
        2256, 2293, 2294, 2311, 2330, 2331, 2334, 2336, 2338, 2352, 2357,

Tales and tale telling *(continued)*

        animal tales *(continued)*:
    FWI 12, 47
     HA 63, 80, 168, 350, 351, 352, 359, 360
     CU 5, 49, 51, 63, 68, 241
    FGS 8, 31, 38, 62, 134, 167
     CR 2
     BR 154, 199, 514
     CH 1
     VE 24

        explanatory tales:
     NA 151, 292, 331, 357, 517, 521, 603, 722, 795, 1031, 1453, 1971, 2101,
        2239, 2636, 2884, 2885, 2889, 2945, 3122, 3190, 3191, 3192
    EWI 205, 269, 390, 513
     HA 168
     CU 63

        ghost and supernatural tales:
    GEN 180
     NA 25, 26, 52, 106, 183, 194, 198, 215, 216, 218, 219, 262, 280, 292, 309,
        344, 357, 492, 501, 606, 638, 742, 794, 816, 820, 822, 904, 1029, 1035,
        1116, 1161, 1298, 1359, 1406, 1498, 1508, 1515, 1517, 1530, 1554, 1598,
        1618, 1664, 1820, 1926, 2131, 2169, 2353, 2534, 2569, 2636, 2651, 2732,
        2803, 3050, 3067
    EWI 74, 205, 318, 325, 405, 462, 546, 559, 673
     HA 153, 331
      B 4

        John Henry and John Hardy tales:
     NA 88, 315, 316, 417, 529, 530, 811, 1008, 1452, 1530, 1630, 1631, 1632,
        2896
    EWI 406

        Master and John, John the Conqueror tales:
     NA 66, 283, 346, 347, 816, 820, 1525, 1622, 1838, 2131, 2320, 2868

        preacher and religious tales:
     NA 5, 283, 319, 320, 342, 344, 346, 392, 816, 820, 924, 1500, 1508,
        1554, 1895, 2350, 2868, 2885, 2889, 3086, 3185
    EWI 64
     HA 308
     BR 235, 282

        Uncle Remus tales [*see also* Folklore scholars and the study of Afro-
        American folklore; Tales and tale telling: animal tales]:
     NA 220, 240, 595, 891, 1008, 1077, 1114, 1216, 1297, 1303, 1312, 1313,
        1318, 1321, 1323, 1324, 1325, 1326, 1327, 1328, 1329, 1559, 1851,
        1928, 1932, 2186, 2368, 2840, 3064, 3097, 3098, 3158, 3195, 3266

Verbal and musical dueling *(continued)*
      CO 32
      EC 5
      UR 2, 6, 7, 10

Visual arts. *See also* Architecture and housing; Domestic life; Material
      culture; Pottery
      GEN 54, 55, 90, 103, 110, 111, 165, 263, 264, 265, 267, 268, 270, 299
      NA 551, 784, 831, 841, 843, 882, 926, 978, 994, 1085, 1388, 1418, 1499,
            1518, 1604, 1760, 2036, 2136, 2356, 2470, 2471, 2982, 3014
      EWI 178, 204, 359
      HA 129, 183, 190, 209, 274, 279, 295, 309, 310, 313, 324, 342, 346, 347,
            348, 373, 375
      CU 60, 77, 112, 161, 162, 164, 180, 201, 335, 337, 339, 340
      FGS 20, 24, 25, 34, 54, 60, 61, 65, 79, 81, 82, 107, 108 112, 116, 121,
            123, 141
      BR 1, 12, 13, 35, 52, 76, 206, 207, 283, 397, 445, 447, 457, 471, 494,
            495, 502, 504
      VE 34
Vodû. *See also* Witchcraft and magic
      GEN 60, 137, 138, 233, 284
      NA 65, 161, 183, 282, 309, 330, 389, 411, 431, 445, 446, 454, 462, 506,
            509, 556, 601, 617, 645, 695, 696, 784, 810, 814, 820, 847, 864, 892,
            944, 960, 1036, 1117, 1184, 1270, 1299, 1332, 1359, 1369, 1371, 1375,
            1383, 1390, 1526, 1552, 1637, 1723, 1921, 1933, 2132, 2176, 2194,
            2201, 2202, 2231, 2342, 2398, 2479, 2497, 2634, 2650, 2687, 2786,
            2798, 2824, 2847, 2916, 2923, 2944, 2952, 2958, 3000, 3001, 3003,
            3004, 3018, 3083, 3106, 3133, 3280
      EWI 118, 292, 402, 614, 728
      DWI 25
      FWI 77
      HA 10, 14, 15, 16, 17, 19, 24, 25, 26, 27, 28, 29, 30, 35, 36, 37, 38,
            39, 40, 42, 43, 44, 46, 57, 66, 68, 69, 70, 71, 72, 74, 75, 76, 77,
            81, 82, 89, 90, 93, 95, 100, 101, 102, 103, 104, 105, 106, 110, 111,
            112, 113, 116, 117, 119, 129, 130, 131, 134, 136, 138, 146, 147, 149,
            152, 154, 155, 159, 162, 164, 167, 169, 170, 171, 172, 173, 174, 175,
            178, 181, 182, 183, 184, 185, 186, 188, 189, 193, 194, 196, 197, 198,
            199, 200, 201, 202, 203, 204, 205, 206, 207, 208, 210, 211, 212, 213,
            215, 216, 217, 218, 219, 221, 222, 223, 225, 226, 227, 230, 232, 233,
            234, 237, 238, 241, 242, 243, 244, 249, 250, 252, 254, 256, 258, 262,
            272, 274, 275, 279, 280, 281, 282, 284, 291, 297, 298, 301, 306, 307,
            308, 309, 310, 311, 313, 315, 317, 319, 320, 321, 324, 325, 326, 327,
            328, 329, 330, 331, 337, 338, 339, 341, 342, 347, 354, 363, 366, 367,
            370, 371, 372, 373, 374, 375, 376, 377, 378, 379, 380, 381

Voodoo. *See Vodû*

Wakes. *See* Funerals, burials and wakes

Water spirits. *See* Supernatural figures

Weddings. *See* Marriage, courtship and weddings

LOCALE INDEX

ENGLISH-SPEAKING WEST INDIES *(continued)*

Nevis
    EWI 1, 2, 3, 4, 5, 6, 7, 8, 9, 10, 12, 15, 316, 522, 653

Providencia
    EWI 732, 733, 734

St. Kitts
    GEN 130
    EWI 2, 12, 301, 527, 653, 700, 723

St. Lucia
    GEN 130, 195
    EWI 202, 209, 268, 522, 713

St. Vincent
    GEN 33, 92, 195, 208
    EWI 6, 11, 16, 17, 19, 25, 61, 138, 139, 238, 299, 340, 341, 342, 384, 425,
        480, 481, 522, 552, 621, 658, 713

Tobago
    EWI 6, 8, 10, 13, 14, 15, 25, 26, 39, 44, 46, 99, 126, 214, 238, 276, 280,
        282, 283, 368, 416, 462, 463, 508, 509, 510, 511, 512, 513, 514, 515,
        516, 517, 559, 713

Trinidad
    GEN 31, 33, 52, 87, 92, 124, 143, 146, 159, 168, 181, 195, 208, 282, 289
    EWI 13, 18, 21, 24, 25, 26, 27, 44, 45, 46, 54, 91, 93, 116, 117, 118, 126,
        127, 128, 131, 132, 134, 139, 140, 141, 142, 144, 156, 157, 174, 177,
        179, 188, 189, 197, 198, 199, 206, 207, 208, 209, 213, 224, 233, 238,
        241, 274, 275, 277, 278, 279, 280, 281, 282, 283, 284, 285, 286, 287,
        288, 291, 297, 302, 303, 306, 307, 308, 313, 324, 344, 346, 347, 349,
        350, 351, 352, 358, 363, 365, 368, 375, 382, 383, 391, 399, 400, 403,
        414, 416, 438, 439, 447, 450, 456, 459, 460, 464, 468, 471, 472, 473,
        475, 477, 488, 489, 503, 504, 508, 509, 510, 511, 514, 515, 516, 517,
        522, 530, 538, 541, 542, 552, 553, 554, 561, 568, 575, 576, 589, 590,
        607, 608, 629, 631, 633, 634, 636, 638, 644, 645, 646, 654, 661, 678,
        683, 688, 689, 702, 703, 707, 711, 715, 716, 722, 724

Virgin Islands (British and U.S.)
    GEN 63, 150, 282
    EWI 23, 38, 100, 118, 119, 135, 165, 301, 326, 357, 366, 423, 461, 496,
        499, 522, 555, 558, 563, 597, 606, 615, 709, 710, 717

UNITED STATES

Alabama
    NA 36, 38, 81, 82, 137, 232, 284, 305, 332, 359, 391, 392, 393, 395, 452,
        488, 501, 538, 598, 599, 600, 661, 663, 664, 665, 743, 786, 957, 989,
        990, 1042, 1119, 1259, 1267, 1345, 1400, 1406, 1453, 1495, 1526, 1546,

1 2 3 4 5   82 81 80 79 78